Captured Germans

Captured Germans

British PoW Camps in the First World War

Compiled by Norman Nicol

First published in Great Britain in 2017 by
PEN & SWORD MILITARY
An imprint of
Pen & Sword Books Ltd
47 Church Street
Barnsley
South Yorkshire
S70 2AS

ISBN 978-1-78346-348-0

A CIP catalogue record for this book is available from the British Library.

Typeset by Concept, Huddersfield, West Yorkshire HD4 5JL.
Printed and bound in Malta by Gutenberg Press Ltd.

Pen & Sword Books Ltd incorporates the imprints of Pen & Sword Archaeology, Atlas, Aviation, Battleground, Discovery, Family History, History, Maritime, Military, Naval, Politics, Railways, Select, Social History, Transport, True Crime, and Claymore Press, Frontline Books, Leo Cooper, Praetorian Press, Remember When, Seaforth Publishing and Wharncliffe.

For a complete list of Pen & Sword titles please contact
PEN & SWORD BOOKS LIMITED
47 Church Street, Barnsley, South Yorkshire, S70 2AS, England
E-mail: enquiries@pen-and-sword.co.uk
Website: www.pen-and-sword.co.uk

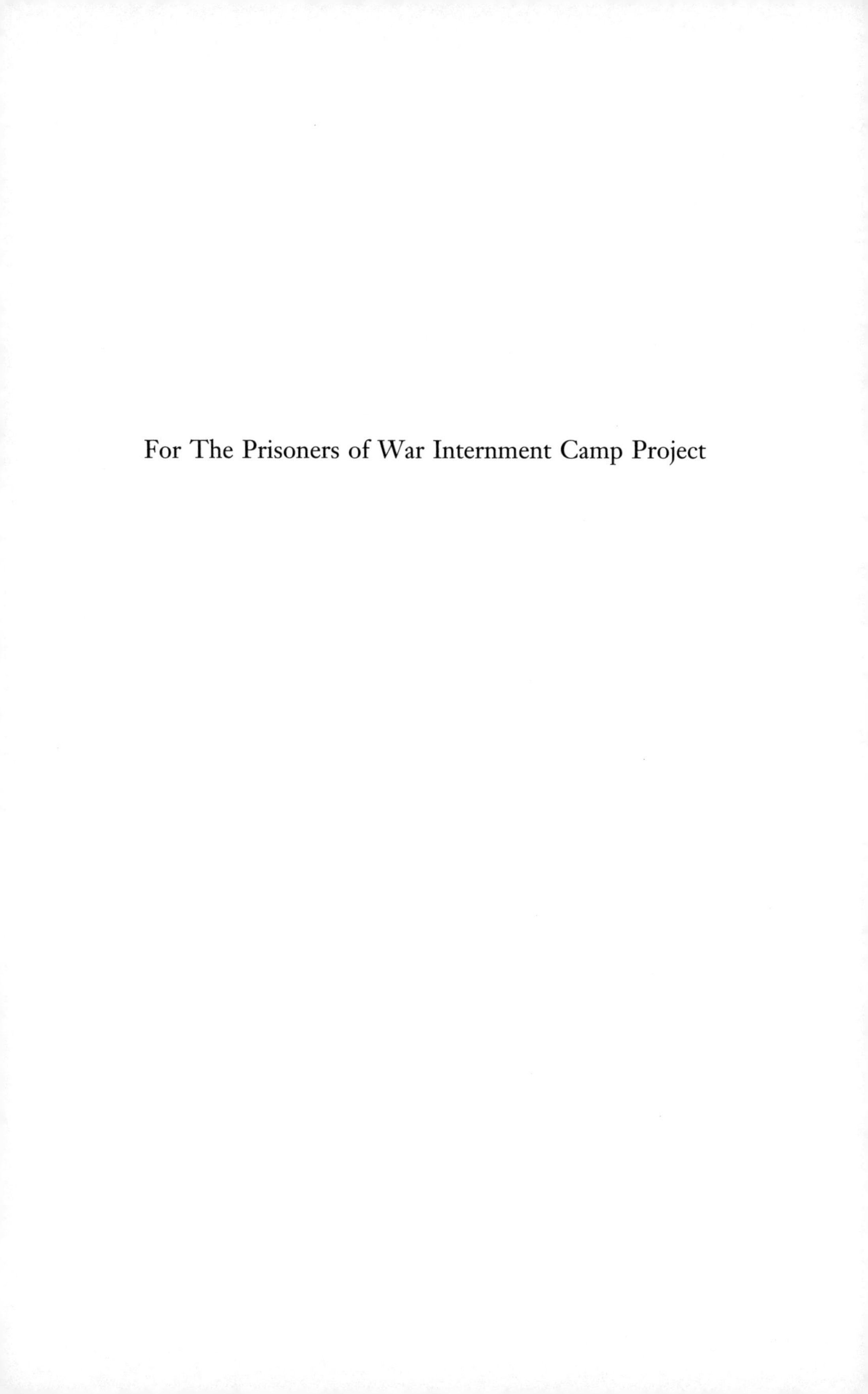

For The Prisoners of War Internment Camp Project

Contents

List of Plates

Preface

How I got involved
When, as a mature student, my group was asked to find aspects of the First World War that affected Derby and its environs, I did not realise then where this would take me. Topics quickly snapped up by my peers were: the role of women; damage caused by aerial attack; propaganda and media interest; and the regiments raised locally. Trying to find something different, a photograph published in a book by W.W. Winter of Derby caught my eye, showing three men wearing the uniforms of German officers from the First World War. These men were standing in the doorway of a building for which the caption informed its readers that the men were being interned at Donington Hall, which is just a few miles outside the city limits of Derby. I got the feeling the caption of the photograph did not match the picture somehow and it raised the hairs on the back of my neck as I had recently been to the area and had seen Donington Hall, an edifice created out of sandstone. These officers were standing in front of a doorway belonging to a building made of red brick, a bit too ornate to be that of just an outhouse; but perhaps it was one pulled down when the place was refurbished and extended some years ago as the headquarters of British Midland Airways. With some light research it became apparent that this – German prisoners of war camps – was an area of social history that has generally been ignored; and some in-depth investigation could be the basis of my study.

I arranged to meet the local historian, Bruce Townsend. When I told him about my reservations, he too doubted the authenticity of the caption, nor did he recognise the doorway in question. Mr Townsend showed me a book that contained pictures at Donington Hall as a PoW Camp, and of other camps. My interest in the topic soared.

The record offices of Derbyshire, Nottinghamshire and Leicestershire are all within easy travelling distances, and visits to each proved fruitful.

From the information I collected I was able to prove, with the assistance of Stan Cramer, a retired assistant librarian at the Sutton Bonington Campus of Nottingham University, that the photograph in the book was taken a few miles away from where the caption said. The doorway was not at Donington Hall, but at what I had discovered was another camp, at Kegworth, or to be more precise, at Sutton Bonington. Stan took the time to take me to that elusive doorway. He also told me about an audacious escape plan that failed from the camp. In my search for more details I also found out a PoW had died in the hospital wing of the old barracks in Derby, now demolished, and I was able to get a copy of his death certificate.

It later transpired that the present owner of the photographer's shop, who commissioned the book, was the grandson of the man who took the photograph. His grandfather had taken photographs at both camps and with the passage of time the glass plate negatives had been mixed together, and then catalogued erroneously. With Stan's help we were able to identify many taken at Sutton Bonington from those taken at Donington Hall.

Putting these facts together, the remit for my assignment was complete; I had evidence to back up my essay. But I did not stop there because I had found evidence of camps outwith the remit of my assignment. With my assignment completed I decided to carry on looking for more evidence of these, and possibly more camps. Visits to London and other county archives produced evidence of even more camps than I had anticipated. My list of places grew considerably when Dr Bob Moore, a professor at Manchester Metropolitan University, sent me a document that had emanated from the National Archives at Kew, listing PoW camps from the First World War. Because my list was growing, I needed to take stock of what I had.

So, what is internment? I had to find exactly what internment meant. The *Cambridge Dictionary* states it is to put someone in prison for political or military reasons, especially during a war. *Longman's Dictionary* expands on this by stating it is the practice of keeping people in prison during a war, or for political reasons, without charging them with a crime. I also found there were Laws of War; conventions to which Britain had become a signatory.

What was life really like for those interned during war? When I began, the first war in Iran was then at its height. Hostage John McCarthy had recently been released from his ordeal, and I remembered him saying that not knowing his fate, nor how long he was to endure being estranged from his family and friends, was his biggest fear. Terry Waite, too, another hostage, released after a long captivity, also commented on the uncertainty of his fate. I began to see parallels with those interned in the First World War.

It is a dark side of history and, for reasons that have never been fully resolved, many of the locations used to intern civilians and combatants during the First World War have been lost in time. Many may never be found again. Does our belief that we British could not incarcerate anyone without a trial blinker us? History shows us differently. Until recently people in Northern Ireland were being held in secure units without trial for their beliefs that Ireland should (or should not) be a unified state. I began to see the 'troubles' in Northern Ireland under a different light.

There is no one document that records every location that was used in the First World War. The intention of this project was to record where these camps were by researching contemporary newspapers, official documents, and other publications. It was never the intention to make comparisons between how each country apportioned its benevolence, as in theory most of the protagonists in the First World War were party to the same protocols and conventions of the day. Nor was there any intention on my part to judge how Britain treated those in internment, but one can never compile a document such as this without emotive issues being touched on. Without this, I was informed by an academic, my work would have no intrinsic value, as it would not contribute to the great historical debate. If my endeavours have not added anything to the 'academic argument', it will not cause me to have sleepless nights.

Useful documents have survived. Many of those that have not were apparently lost when London was bombed in the Second World War, although conspiracy theories abound about the way they were lost. Evidence of camps can be found in the National Archives, and in county archives. Amongst the documents that have survived are: a directory compiled by the Prisoner-of-war Information Bureau (POWIB), (London, *c.*1919); a document, issued in four parts by the Home Office, listing police authorities, camp locations and telegraphic addresses for camps in Scotland, England and Wales; minutes of County War Agricultiural Committee meetings; and a vast number of articles from contemporary newspapers.

It is said only the victor writes history, but fortunately German archives are able to contribute to this history. *Deutsche Kriegsgefangene in Feindesland – Amtliches Material – England* (Berlin, 1919) (DKF) provided some German perspective of how PoWs were treated in the UK. It also provided the names of some camps. National institutions in Austria and Hungary have also contributed useful material.

In 1932, F.J. Carter, a philatelist, created a *List of British Prison Camps.* But only fifty copies were produced for private distribution. In 1937, he published *The Post and Censor and Other Marks for Prisoners of war Letters, 1914–1919.* Part One contained his list of British prison camps, with over 570 entries. In 1971, Alan J. Brown re-created this list in a *Forces Postal History Newsletter*. In 1996, Neil Russell produced a 3rd edition of Carter's work. But each edition has variations; some of the places cited are unsafe, and not all their locations can be confirmed from other sources.

The purpose of this work was to record in one book all the places used for internment purposes in the UK during the First World War. Many camps have had their locations confirmed with physical evidence, but in some instances only word of mouth accounts remain as testimony to a camp's existence. Where the only evidence that a camp existed is an entry on a list, the Ordnance Survey references remain nominal. I have also included the political prisoners, brought from Ireland and held in mainland Britain at that time, because it would be disrespectful not to. Remember, the whole of Ireland was at this time still an integral part of the United Kingdom.

Finding that photograph kindled an interest in this topic that has remained inside me ever since. Nearly two decades have passed since I discovered that photograph, and today that ember burns still as fiercely. This is the fruit of my labour. In many ways it is delightful to see it in print, but something inside me says only the surface has been scratched and the task is well short of being complete. There are still so many questions unanswered, and too many avenues yet to explore. However, it is hoped this research has filled a void in our social history previously neglected.

Acknowledgements

To those individuals and organisations that made contributions I would like to thank them, for without their help this work would never have materialised. I am especially grateful for the contribution and support of Graham Mark, who produced *Prisoner of War in British Hands during WWI* in 2007. Without his input, this work would not be as comprehensive as it is. And to Martin Mace (*Britain at War Magazine*) for his indispensable help.

Introduction

In the beginning . . .

Do sanitised interpretations of conflict, made by the film and television industries, really reflect the harrowing experiences that internment brings? For no matter the historical period, the time spent in internment can never surely be described as pleasant. Internees and prisoners of war do not even have that luxury known to most common felons: knowing how long their incarceration will be. Unsure of their fate, some lost their sanity. Despairing, others took their own lives.

The term 'prisoner of war' (PoW) is associated with combatants taken in a time of conflict between two warring factions. But strictly speaking it refers to anyone from a belligerent state detained in a time of war that has not committed a criminal act. In the First World War, civilians were being detained in the interests of national security, along with captured combatants. At first there was little attempt to differentiate between them. The contemporary press often used the term concentration camp to describe their place of internment, a description that today has an even more sinister connation.

The terms 'prisoner of war' or 'internee' are often used for those put in internment without any attempt to draw some distinction between who were combatants and who were the civilians. In this work, wherever possible the term 'prisoner of war' (PoW) is used for those in the military, and that of internee, for those that were civilians. The term enemy alien was also used, and it is used in this work too.

There was a time when the question of what to do with prisoners of war would never have arisen. Those captured were simply tortured for information they may have held, and then put to death, or, at best, sold into slavery, when their captors had no more use for them. It is believed the term 'to give quarter' arose from the amount of bounty a wealthy PoW could fetch for his safe return.

Egyptians, Greeks, Romans, Persians, Aztecs, Mongols, Tartars, Vikings, Spanish Conquistadors, etc., all had their own way of dealing with the foot soldiers of those they conquered, as they first created their great empires, and then defended them. During the Middle Ages, noblemen received somewhat better treatment than their foot soldiers because they could be exchanged for ransom. By the eighteenth century, the situation for PoWs in general began to improve.

Throughout history Britain has been party to several accords with belligerent countries that relate to men being taken in battle, and to their exchange. Being an island, the welfare of any PoWs fell initially to the Admiralty. Their Commissioners of Sick and Wounded Seamen were responsible for exchanging PoWs.

For instance, in The Seven Years War (1756–63) conventions on the treatment of sick and wounded were agreed. But for reasons of personal greed, PoWs and deserters were ignored in these conventions.

During the American Revolutionary War, the British put captured Americans onto rotting hulks, kept in primitive conditions, a fact not lost by the Germans in their propaganda campaign of the First World War.

In what is thought to be a more enlightened and civilised society, those taken as prisoners of war today are protected by international law, and as a result now have rights. But the logistics of transporting, feeding and housing PoWs is, and always has been, problematic. Troops on the move are slowed down; vehicles have no space for additional passengers; and feeding and housing prisoners entails expenditure.

Niall Ferguson, in *The Pity of War*, 1998, cites his rationale of surrender in the First World War. To those in the trenches, there seemed to be no other option than to fight on until death, or victory. Their only alternatives were to be wounded and taken from the field, suicide or desertion. Self-inflicted wounds had to be severe enough to get you extracted from the war zone, and did not appeal too many as they could carry lifelong complications. Stories abounded of atrocities being committed as surrendering soldiers were allegedly shot. To those in the firing line, shooting captives was the easy option. Cases of entrapment were cited in the atrocities, too. But parading PoWs was a good moral booster for those not actually in the front line. It was the captor's dilemma when confronted with men surrendering: to kill or not to kill? Do those that fight on, knowing their position is precarious, fight on and die needlessly, in the belief that if they surrendered they would be ignominiously shot? Ferguson suggests this could prolong a war and cause unnecessary suffering.

The Treaty of Westphalia (1648) is a landmark document for PoWs. It effectively ended the principle of widespread enslavement of PoWs and was responsible for the release of those held in internment without a ransom having to be paid.

French philosopher, Montesquieu, in *L'Espirit des Lois* (1748), stated that the only right of the captor in war was to prevent a captive doing harm; no longer should prisoners be treated as property. Jean Jacques Rousseau argued in 1762 that prisoners of war were men who were endowed with natural rights and that no captor had the right to take their lives; instead, they should be treated humanely.

The first concrete steps towards the humane treatment of PoWs began shortly after the Italian War of Reunification. Jean-Henri Dunant viewed the suffering of the wounded at the Battle of Solferino and, in 1862, wrote *Souvenirs de Solferino*, describing the terrible conditions he observed in that battle. Dunant's efforts led to an international conference on PoWs in Geneva in 1864, when delegates took the first steps towards outlining a legal framework regarding the care and treatment of prisoners of war in *The Convention for the Amelioration of the Conditions of the Wounded in Armies of the Field.*

The American Civil War was raging at the time, and both the Confederate and Union armies amassed large numbers of prisoners, that they held in compounds. During the first part of the war, to relieve prison conditions, both sides exchanged PoWs. When the Union suspected the Confederate soldiers of breaking their parole, by taking up arms again, they ended the exchange system, and forced prisoners to wait out the war in crowded, and often unsanitary, conditions. Francis Lieber had studied the PoW problem and attempted to codify the treatment of war prisoners in 1863. He wrote a set of directives for the Union armies entitled *Instructions for the Government of Armies of the United States in the Field*, which regulated the treatment of Confederate prisoners. These instructions became the focus of an international attempt to codify his work into international law. In 1874, delegates met at a conference in Brussels to extend his ideas into global practice.

In 1870, in Basle, Gustave Moynierto and Dunant were influential in the setting up the International Committee of the Red Cross (ICRC). Their idea was to bring a stabilising factor to the treatment of the sick and wounded on the battlefield; now it also responds to the needs of displaced people in natural disasters. Their symbol was simple, they simply inverted the colours of the Swiss flag to have a red cross on a white background, to be worn by medical teams that should be recognised the world over on the battlefield. Muslim nations seeing the cross as symbolising a Christian ethic chose instead the crescent moon for their sister organisation, the International Red Crescent. In Israel, a Red Star of David is used. The ICRC has no formal authority over its sister bodies.

Dunant, with Frédéric Passy, would, in 1901, become the first recipients of the Nobel Peace Prize. Passy passionately believed that free trade would draw nations together as partners in a common enterprise that would result in disarmament, and lead to the abandonment of war forever. Dunant received the accolade for his work in establishing the Red Cross movement.

In July 1870, Lord Wantage of Lockinge wrote to *The Times* calling for a national society, for aiding sick and wounded soldiers in a time of war, to be formed in the UK, following the example of other European nations. On 4 August 1870, at a public meeting a resolution was passed that such a society should be formed, similar to those proposed by the Geneva Convention of 1864. Subsequently, The British National Society for Aid to the Sick and Wounded in War was established. In 1905, the society was re-constituted as The British Red Cross. It was then given its Royal Charter, in 1908, by King Edward VII and Queen Alexandra.

However not until a declaration was conceived in Brussels in 1874 laying down rules for the humane treatment of all prisoners of war, sick, wounded or healthy, did anything change for their welfare. They were still subjugated to the conditions that prevailed at the time between the belligerent nations. The articles were never materialised onto the statute books; but they were to be resurrected at The Hague Conference of 1899. In the intervening period, in Paris in 1889, a Concours International was proposed to set up mechanisms that would let belligerent nations exchange dialogue through Information Bureaux that they were expected to set up. These were to be organisations free of government control, set up in a time of conflict between belligerent states, to exchange information about the dead, and wounded, and to collect artefacts from the battlefield. In a time of war belligerent nation-states were expected to set up bureaux as quickly as possible.

The First Hague Peace Conference was convened at the request of Tsar Nicholas II of Russia in 1899. Its primary aim was the limiting of the type of armaments belligerent nations could use in a war. These talks lasted from 18 May to 29 July 1899 and failed to reach a consensus, but three conventions were adopted. These were: the peaceful settlement of disputes; the laws and customs of war on land; and of maritime warfare. This conference concluded with a wish that future dialogue would take place. Britain was a signatory to these conventions, but the Boers were not; therefore in the Second Boer War (1899–1903) Britain was not obliged to abide by The Hague's peace conference, and did not, resulting in 'concentration camps' being set up.

A Second Hague Peace Conference, initiated by Theodore Roosevelt of the USA, in 1904, was postponed because of the Russo-Japanese War. But the Second Geneva Convention on the Amelioration of the Sick and Wounded took place in 1906, and further strengthened the rights of the PoW.

Between 15 June and 18 October 1907, again at the request of Tsar Nicholas II, the Second Hague Peace Conference did take place. Again no arms limitation was agreed, but ten new conventions were formulated, along with those made at the Brussels Conference (1874), but with their content updated. In these new conventions, articles covering the plight of PoWs were addressed for the first time, including the status of interned civilians.

Requests for future debates never materialised before the world was plunged into the First World War.

Feeding and housing PoWs creates its own problems. Safe places have to be found to intern them which tie up men and resources. In the First World War the army specified a ratio of between one and two escorts for every ten prisoners taken.

Since the unification of Britain, its wars have been fought at sea or on foreign soil. Civilian communities in Britain, previously untouched, suddenly became embroiled. Those thought to be a risk to national security were arrested and detained under new legislation drawn up at the beginning of the First World War. Within days of Britain declaring war on Germany, the Defence of the Realm Act (DORA) was introduced. Many civilians from the belligerent countries (the Central Powers) were being put into internment camps. They were mostly men of military age that had been living and working in Britain when the war broke out. A few women were detained too. Most were subsequently set free but restrictions were put on where they could live and go. Areas, such as docks or military establishments were taboo.

An indication of the hysteria that was prevalent in the early stages of this war was played out in Norfolk. At Cromer, young Germans working at the Hotel de Paris were arrested and taken to Norwich, to be exhibited in the Market Place, as spies. Some of them had been working in Britain for a number of years. Their only 'crime' was that they were Germans living in Britain when war was declared. They wished to go home, but the ports had been closed to them leaving.

Around the turn of the century, it had been noted that large communities of eastern Europeans were settling in Britain. As most were poor, they tended to live in the cheapest accommodation, and so congregated into districts of cities that became virtually ghettos. They were often overcrowded, causing sanitation systems to fail, and disease was rife in these communities. Most of these immigrants were Jewish or of other faiths not found in mainstream Britain, and they became marginalised. They became known as aliens, which has never been an endearing term of anyone. With the war, these aliens became classed as either friendly or enemy and those of the latter group, of military age, were arrested and interned under the Alien Restriction Act of 1914.

Prior to the war many young Germans and Austrians worked in the hotel industry to help pay for their tuition fees. German technology, being to the forefront of engineering, meant there were also highly skilled Teutonic engineers working in this country. Many of those interned were permitted to return to their families, but restrictions were put on their movements; some had to re-locate. They also had to report frequently to a local police station.

In practice, different rules were applied to the different nationalities that were classed as enemy aliens. Some, such as the Czechs, did not wish to be associated with the Germans or the Austrians. In 1905, the British government had introduced the Alien Restriction Act, and for the first time, for immigration purposes, passports were needed to enter or exit this country. When the First World War began these aliens, depending on what country they originated from, were recognised as being friendly or enemy. Their politics were never a consideration in defining what group they belonged to. Enemy aliens fell into two main categories, those that wished to leave, but found they could not, and those that chose to stay for a number of reasons. In the second grouping were those that had settled in this country; many were married to British women. Those that did not concur with the Kaiser's ambitions for a Greater Germany could – or would – not go back, as they had no desire to be assimilated back home.

There were instances when aliens came under attack, and these incidents increased dramatically when the *Lusitania* was sunk. Many aliens, both enemy and friendly, had to seek protection and many of the former chose to go into voluntary internment. The majority of them were sent to the Isle of Man, to new camps at Douglas and Peel. Some aliens had changed their names, often by adopting their British born wives' surnames, many just anglicised their names. Others took Scottish or Welsh sounding names in an attempt to disguise their accents. The government, fearing subterfuge, stopped this practice, but not before the House of Saxe-Coburg-Gotha had changed its name to the House of Windsor on 26 June 1917.

The Establishment

For a country that boasted of an inter-departmental system that was the envy of the world and could adapt to any given situation, when German troops entered Belgium on 2 August 1914 its resolve was tested to the full – and it was found lacking.

Honour-bound by the Treaty of London of 1839, Britain was a party to the decision to recognise Belgium's neutrality in any future war. So when war was declared, this meant that the democratically elected government in Britain stayed in place and each ministry continued to perform the duties that it was created to perform. Each ministry also dealt with parts of the war that fell under its remit. Being an island, the role of the Admiralty was paramount in previous conflicts. But in what was predominately a land battle, the role of the War Office did become accentuated and posts were filled from other ministries that could spare the staff. New recruits then filled any vacancies that arose across the system. The total number of staff grew in the four years, from less than 2,000 to over 22,000. This expansion in personnel resulted in the scattering of many branches to annexes away from the main building.

The consensus of the layman was that this war would be a short one and it would never last six months; 'that it would all be over by Christmas', was an expression frequently used. However, this was never the opinion of the higher echelons of the British command, who were to be proved correct, as the conflict went on to became a war of attrition that lasted four years.

One of the first pieces of legislation of the war was the Defence of the Realm Act (DORA), created in August 1914. It gave the Home Office the power to arrest, and to detain, any foreign national it believed to be a threat to Britain's national security. The numbers put into internment quickly rose as Germans and Austrians living and working in the UK when the war started were arrested and interned. With no ready-made facility available to house them, a variety of places were used. Some were short-lived and others stayed in place for the duration of the war.

The obvious choice for the military-minded was to accommodate those interned into camps set out in a military fashion – wooden huts or tents in lines behind barbed-wire perimeter fences was their preference. But in reality all kinds of premises were quickly requisitioned: empty factories; old mills; school dormitories; stables; for a brief time, ocean-going passenger ships; and some large country houses and their estates.

In September 1914, a Directorate of PoWs was established by the War Office, headed by Lieutenant General Sir Herbert Eversley Belfield KGB KCMG KBE DSO. He was the colonel in chief of the Duke of Wellington's Regiment (1909–1938) and he worked in a section of the Adjutant General's Department (AGD) known as AG3.

J.C. Bird (*Control of Enemy Alien Civilians in Great Britain, 1914–1918*, 1986), states that in response to a request for alien enemies of military age to be interned, hundreds of men were arrested. Then, due to a lack of facilities to hold them, and men to guard them, this order was suspended. The order was re-instated again on 20 October 1914, only to be suspended again by 10 November 1914. Unhappy with the situation of large numbers being arrested and then released again back into their communities, Belfield sought, and got, Kitchener's approval to take the Home Office unit responsible for issuing internment notices under his wing on 20 November 1914. Under Belfield's remit, Maurice Waller, a former prison commissioner, headed the new office, which was known as the Home Office PoWs Division. As the system gradually settled down, those that could get a British subject to vouch for their character were given their freedom, if they agreed to stay out of areas restricted to them.

Many of those interned found themselves in segregated areas of army camps that were already overcrowded by the vast number of raw recruits undergoing training for the front. To accommodate Kitchener's New Army, family members were being moved out of army camps to maximise numbers. Those recruited who could not be housed under rigid roofing were put under canvas. All kinds of buildings were being requisitioned to accommodate troopers, not only from Britain, but also from Canada, Australia, New Zealand, India, South Africa, West Indies, and other parts of the Empire as they arrived. Civilian labour from Denmark and Canada was brought in to work the land and fell much-needed timber. They too required shelter from the elements. Refugees were appearing from Belgium and neighbouring countries; they too needed feeding and sheltering. At the same time places were being sought to intern civilians. The system just could not cope and this was why arrested internees were released on licence, to ease the strain. Many were able to return to their jobs and support their families. Those who could not find jobs became a burden on the state, and charitable institutions had to be set up to support them.

The Onus

When it comes to answering the simple question of who was responsible for the internment of the enemy in Great Britain during the First World War, the answer is not a straightforward one, as individual ministries of the day simply adapted their roles, as they had done in previous conflicts. Although each ministry had its role to perform, the dominant actor in the past had been the Admiralty, the Senior Service. From the onset of the First World War, personnel were moved around, as new departments within the War Office (WO), the Home Office (HO) and the Foreign Office (FO) sprang into action. This was how they had coped in past crises, but the magnitude of this conflict was greater than anyone could have visualised. The introduction of DORA gave powers to the military that it never had before. The principle ministry for the internment of foreign nationals deemed a threat to national security in Britain during the First World War was the HO. But as these men, and some women, were not British subjects, the Foreign Office, too, had its role to play. The latter was the instigator of interning enemy alien civilians considered to be a threat to national security. The Home Office, not having the facilities, released many of them again.

Although DORA gave the military its new powers it was still the British civilian police force that placed those to be interned under arrest, and it was they who controlled their movements, showing they were still under civil jurisdiction. Combatants brought into the country were the responsibility of the War Office. Armed guards controlled the movement of combatants, but they were escorted by police officers.

In the early stages a certain amount of duplication existed because of the inputs of the different ministries. Attempts were made to put all the internees under the control of one administration. In February 1915, there was an internal reshuffle of the Adjutant General's Department. It was divided into three, with Belfield remaining in overall charge of it. But, though the question was often broached, no one ministry was ever given full control for dealing with those interned.

Local Government Boards had their input, as it became their responsibility to find suitable accommodation for those placed in internment. A memorandum, held at the National Archives, that appears to have been edited by someone with the initials MLW, gives a brief general account of the process of interning civilians. Claims camps were set up at Olympia, Frimley, Hayward's Heath, Newbury, Stratford (London), Lancaster, Stobs, Oldcastle, Wakefield, York, Southampton, Douglas, Templemore, Queen's Ferry, Handforth, and several ships moored off Southend on Sea and the Isle of Wight. There seems to be no evidence to support a camp being at Hayward's Heath at this time, but instead it is known Christ's Hospital School near Horsham was briefly used. Additions to the list were Alexandra Palace, Islington, Knockaloe, Lancaster, Feltham, Hackney Wick, and Libury Hall.

A minute of the South Shields Council shows, in 1914, the Chief Constable of Durham sought recompense for expenses incurred by his police force in executing the provisions of the Alien Restriction Act. He wrote:

> As they [enemy aliens] were subsequently made PoWs, upon discharge from prison the Durham City Police having received and conveyed them, under the direction of the military authorities, to internment camps, the Chief Constable of the City of Durham has been in communication with the Home Office upon the subject of payment of the expenses incurred, and the Home Office reply that the Durham City Police Authority should be reimbursed by the Authority where prisoners were registered.

Prisons were briefly used, although this seems to flout the Articles of the Hague Convention. Another minute revealed the costs involved in dealing with 180 offences against the Alien Restriction Act. It was revealed that 699 prisoners had been conveyed to HM Prison, Durham in 1914: 'the cost of maintenance before committal or discharge was £51.11s.7d; this included the cost of subsistence, but another £127.17s.4d was required for conveyance charges.'

Allotments in Frimley, Fort George, dormitories of a school near Horsham, an army camp in Dorchester and the Olympia Exhibition Halls in London were amongst the first internment camps to be set up in the UK. Amongst the first to be interned were approximately 200 German and Austrian businessmen that lived in the Home Counties. Early in the war, a reporter from *The Times* cited seeing civilians in dinner jackets mixed in with Uhlans still in their distinctive cavalry uniforms at the Frith Hill allotments. Many internees found themselves forced to live in disused factories and warehouses. Many were put under canvas. Officers were sent to large country houses.

A number of ships were used, but these were soon rejected and land based accommodation was found to replace them because of the costs to hire them. In propaganda exercises the Germans reminded the then neutral Americans of the wooden hulks used by the British in their war for independence.

With few places ready to accept internees, the Board of Governors for Christ's Hospital School, near Horsham, was told to make its premises ready. A special meeting of the governors was convened on 12 August 1914 to discuss the matter. The War Office agreed to the governors' suggestion that the school could be used for one week, but it would have to be vacated by 1 September 1914, in time for the first term of the school to begin on time. The school's minutes show the War Office had apologised for the short notice to use the school, but they had to find suitable accommodation for internees within a matter of six to eight hours.

The care and welfare of prisoners of war became an important diplomatic issue not only between belligerents, but also for the neutral countries that accepted the responsibility of representing belligerent interests. Military mobilisation and the internment of thousands of enemy troops taxed the limited resources of small neutral European states; they were unable to meet the needs of PoWs detained behind the lines of the warring nations. After Italy entered the war in May 1915, the United States remained the only great neutral power capable of assisting PoWs. There was no League of Nations or United Nations Organisation then.

In Britain, by the end of September 1914 some 750,000 men had enlisted. The existing army camps in Britain could not accommodate all the volunteers coming forward. Many were billeted with families or put under canvas until new camps could be built. Within days of war being declared Robert McAlpine's firm won tenders to erect wooden huts at Shoreham, Halton, and Shorncliffe. That winter was an exceptionally wet one and caused problems on the sites, as fields turned into quagmires.

Before the war, a vast area of Wiltshire saw military camps springing up. Many of them still exist today. Crawford states in *Wiltshire and the Great War: Training the Empire's Soldiers* (1999), that the Military Manoeuvres Act of 1897 had permitted acres of land in Wiltshire to be bought by the War Office. A few had been augmented with wooden barracks huts, but the camps set up were generally tented sites, used mainly in the summer for training purposes, and until the outbreak of the First World War, had remained that way. Many of these military camps took on the name of the nearest railway station, which could be some miles off, rather than the name of its nearest village, a practice copied in the naming of some internment camps, too.

Within a few weeks of war being declared, a press bureau had been set up to regulate what could be printed in Britain's newspapers. Editors had to exercise discretion in what they printed. Restrictions were put in place that banned the naming of army camps and of manoeuvres taking place, but advertisements inviting tenders for goods and services to military establishments could often be found in the same newspapers. When reporting absconders, Scotland Yard always disclosed the name of the camp, which seemed to contravene the new regulations it should have policed.

Under the terms of the Geneva Convention (1906) and the Second Hague Peace Conference (1907), article 14 of the regulation respecting the Laws and Customs of War on Land, a body seen to be independent of governmental manipulation had to be set up. Created in August 1914, its aims were to deal with inquiries regarding those who had died behind enemy lines, those wounded or sick, and those taken prisoner. In Britain, this semi-quasi organisation was called the Prisoner-of-War Information Bureau (POWIB); its offices were in Wellington Street, London. Fifty men and women from the civil service, hand-picked for their linguistic skills, initially staffed it. Sir Paul Harvey headed it, and after a re-shuffle in 1915, Sir J.D. Rees, the Member of Parliament for Nottingham, replaced him. The POWIB had five primary functions to fulfil:

1. To keep records of those interned as PoWs.
2. To receive weekly reports from hospitals.
3. To forward lists of the enemy dead.
4. To receive from the battlefield personal effects found.
5. To answer all requests about PoWs and enemy dead.

Until February 1915, all combatants came under the control of Sir Herbert Belfield's AG3 (mentioned above). As its workload increased, it was split into three sections, but all remained under Belfield's remit. They were to become known as PW1, PW2, and PW3.

PW1 dealt with general policy and British PoWs; PW2 dealt with enemy prisoners of war; and PW3 looked after prisoner of war camps for both combatant and civilians according to a War Office List (1917).

Panayi (*The Enemy in Our Midst: Germans in Britain During the First World War*, 1991) cites Belfield as being responsible for the requisition of suitable locations and their subsequent administration. Belfield, in *Report on the Directorate of Prisoners of War*, 1920, cited the Directorate had two functions, 'the custody and control of all enemy PoWs wherever captured or interned, and care for the interests of British prisoners in enemy countries'. He qualified this by explaining each of these categories fell naturally into two sub-divisions: combatants (naval, military, and air personnel), and civilians.

So that they were easily recognised, combatant PoWs in British internment camps had to have a large circular hole cut into the backs of clothes not deemed to be their uniforms, and a smaller one in a trouser leg. These holes were subsequently replaced by a piece of blue cloth.

In a Whitehall Series of books, Hampden Gordon (1935) of the War Office, Troupe (1925) of the HO, and Tilley and Gaselee (1933) of the Foreign Office, each explained the functions of their respective ministries at the time. It was supposed to be a system that was flexible enough to incorporate change at a time of crisis. In theory, secondments taken from the less affected departments or ministries, and recruits, would fill any void in the affected areas. The First World War however stretched their resolve, resources, and initiatives to the full.

Belfield (1920) openly admits that at the outbreak of the war his remit of how PoWs should be treated was confined to a few 'text books'. These being the

Geneva Convention of 1906; Section I of the Annex to the 4th Hague Convention of 1907; Chapter II of the 5th Hague Convention of 1907; a few sections in Chapter XIV of the Field Service Regulations; and a Royal Warrant of 3 August 1914. His elaborate system of administration was developed over five years 'on the precepts and regulations contained in those publications and in some cases, in contravention of them'. He later questioned the involvement of so many departments, and he intimated that 'it complicated matters from the start'.

While the control of all aliens in the United Kingdom was the concern of the HO, who, in accordance with the policy of the government, took steps to arrest those enemy civilians who were to be interned, arrangements for their accommodation and custody rested with the War Office. For some six months of the winter and spring of 1914–1915 the PoWs Directorate was responsible for deciding whether an individual should be exempted from internment, interned, or released, a small staff being lent from the Home Office for this purpose; but this procedure was abandoned in May 1915 when it was decided that all such questions should be dealt with by the Home Secretary, who was assisted by an Advisory Committee specially set up to investigate each case. The Admiralty and Air Ministry were concerned in all questions of policy affecting naval and aerial operations, with all PoWs of the enemies' Naval and Air Services in their hands. The Foreign Office concerned itself with the care of civilians of British nationality in enemy countries.

So many relatives of British soldiers wrote to the POWIB seeking information of their nearest and dearest that a press release outlining their role was published in regional newspapers.

The Statistics

Belfield (1920), Machray (*Great Britain's Humane Treatment of German Prisoners-of-War*) in Wilson & Hammerton (eds) (*The Great War: The Standard History of the All-Europe Conflict*, Vol. 12, 1919), and Jackson (*The Prisoners 1914–1918*, 1989) provide some facts and figures as to the number of prisoners and their locations in the early phase of the war. A great deal of improvisation was required when the first combatant PoWs arrived in Britain. In April 1915, the number of interned men in Britain had risen to 26,000 (19,000 of whom were civilians). By the end of that year, the number of established camps was twenty-one in England and Wales, two on the Isle of Man, two in Scotland, one each in Ireland and Jersey. There were forty-two detention barracks; eight were military, six naval, and twenty-eight civilian. In that December the great majority of the internees, some 32,272 of them, were civilians; these were followed by the military, 12,349, and from the navy, 1,147 prisoners.

The Allied offensive of 1916 resulted in a marked increase in the number of combatants taken prisoner, but this increase was offset by the number of civilians and wounded that were repatriated. On the last day of 1916 there were 48,572 military, 1,316 naval, and approximately 31,000 civilians in internment. There were now thirty-eight camps in England and Wales, eight in Scotland, two on the Isle of Man, and one each in Ireland and Jersey. The number of detention barracks had increased too; there were twenty-four military, fourteen naval and twenty civilian establishments.

During 1917, the number of PoWs in the United Kingdom almost trebled. By the end of the year there were 118,864 German and Austrian military prisoners; 1,635 German, and one Turkish, naval prisoners; the interned civilians comprised of 25,120 Germans, 4,065 Austrians, 108 Turks, and 223 of other nationalities. There were now 142 internment camps in England and Wales; fourteen in Scotland; two on the Isle of Man, and one in Ireland. The number of military detention barracks had also been increased to thirty-three; the naval ones dropped to five; as had the civilian ones to nine.

War Office statistics (Ferguson, 1998) show a graph of German prisoners taken by the British army in France between July 1917 and December 1918 which reflects a dramatic rise in the numbers towards the end of the war.

Jackson (1989) suggested by October 1918 – after the collapse of the German Spring offensives, and the subsequent gains by the Allies – the number of PoWs held in Britain was in excess of 250,000 and 'to accommodate them the number of camps began to mushroom.' He cited there were no fewer than 492 internment camps in England and Wales, with another twenty-five in Scotland, two on the Isle of Man and one each in Ireland and Jersey. Each camp commandant was responsible to the General Officer Commanding in Chief of the area for the safe custody and transfer of all internees in their remit.

Bird (1986) cited that on his inspection of the camps in February 1915, John B. Jackson, a retired German speaking American diplomat, concluded in his report to the US Ambassador in Berlin:

> On the whole the present treatment (of those interned) seems to be as good as could be expected under the circumstances. The new camps are better than the old ones and everywhere there seemed to be an intention to improve on existing conditions. Lack of organisation and preparation would account for most of the hardships, which prevailed at first. Absolutely nowhere did there seem to be any wish to make conditions any harder or more disagreeable for the prisoners than was necessary, and I saw no instance and heard of none where any prisoner had been subjected either to intentional personal annoyance or undeserved discipline.

Jackson's inspection visits were taken after tours undertaken by Americans, Chandler S. Anderson and Chandler Hale, in September 1914.

In September 1916 a *Report of Visits of Inspection, made by Officials of the United States Embassy, to Various Internment Camps in the United Kingdom* was presented to the Houses of Parliament. Visits were also undertaken by delegations of the Swiss and the Swedish embassies, after America joined in the conflict. Belfield (1920) contends that there were very few guidelines at the beginning of the war on how to treat those interned. One such document was Article 6 of the 4th Hague Convention (1907).

Apart from a few internees that plied their skills within the camps – i.e. bakers, tailors, shoemakers, etc. – the British government refused to employ PoW labour from the onset of the war; unlike their counterparts. This was partly to alleviate the fears of the men at the front that their loved ones were safe and not being exposed to the kind of atrocities the 'Hun' had supposedly carried out in Belgium if they were allowed any latitude in how they were being incarcerated back home. But the main factor was to placate the trade unions as it was feared the use of cheap PoW labour would drive down the wage structures of skilled men left behind. The aforementioned convention stipulated that any work done by combatant PoWs had to be paid at rates commensurate with their opposite rank; and soldiers in the British army were not highly paid. Commissioned officers were exempt from working, as were any civilians interned. However, it transpired that many civilians deprived of their livelihoods took up an option to work to help support their families.

It has been mooted that the German High Command's attitude to putting lower rank prisoners to work was very different from that of the British from the onset of the war. Knowing the opposition by the British trade unions to the use of PoW labour, they put British internees to hard labour, knowing no reciprocal action or reprisals would be undertaken against their nationals.

In February 1916, the British government issued a new directive permitting the use of PoW labour outside of their camps. Belfield found it difficult to estimate how much money the state lost by what he described as 'enforced idleness' and believed this idleness was a source of much of the resentment formed amongst those interned as it was the prime cause in what became known as 'barbed-wired disease'. A compromise was agreed with the unions that PoW labour could be available to employers at rates of pay commensurate with local conditions. However the government kept the difference between what the employer paid and what the internee got.

That change in policy put the lower ranks to work. It also created the need for new camps to open in areas that previously had none. In what became a pyramid, many units opened that were satellites of others. These new satellite units fell into two broad categories: agricultural depots, and working camps; and they were administered from a parent camp.

Once the value of PoW labour had been recognised, and the unions placated, the demand for their services grew. Some internees were given clerical duties to perform within their camps. At parent camps, others, under adequate supervision, dealt with letters and parcels addressed to their colleagues billeted to satellite camps. A parent camp often had on their books ten to fifteen times the actual number of men on its site at any one time. At one point Dorchester, with accommodation for only 3,800 internees, had 42,000 names on its register, the remainder being distributed amongst its satellite camps.

Inundated by the demand, it became impossible for the Prisoner of war Directorate to assess the merits of schemes and still tend to their other duties; a new committee was formed to deal with these inquiries. This committee had limited experience of the many schemes put before it and was deemed ineffective, and was to be replaced soon after by the Prisoner of war Employment Committee. The

Committee had two civilians at its head, with representations from the appropriate government departments that were the main employers of interned labour filling the other chairs. Belfield stressed, 'It may be claimed that under this committee the labour of PoWs was distributed in the best interests of the countries.' This committee stayed under the remit of the War Office until February 1918, when it was put under the Ministry of National Service. Ramifications at the introduction of the Munitions of War Act (1915) and successive legislation at controlling the power of the unions and employers did the cause of the PoW working outside their places of internment no favours. But its 'corporate bias', seen as strengthening the power of employers over their work forces, was really an attempt by the government to control British industry. It sought to bring it into line with those of America and Germany, who had made advancements into world markets since the turn of the century at our expense.

At the end of 1915, some work was found for those interned in some British camps. This was primarily repairing and manufacturing mailbags, a task long associated with the incarcerated criminal. Civilians were never required to work but, for personal reasons, many choose to. Any work they did had to be paid for at rates commensurate with local conditions.

Belfield (1920) produced a list of work that was acceptable to be pursued by those interned. These included:

Construction and erection of huts
Railway construction and maintenance
Agriculture, forestry and timber felling
Construction of docks
Concrete block making
Portland cement production
Repair of motor transport
Road making and repairing
Laying telegraph and telephone lines
Quarrying limestone, ganister, iron-ore, etc.
Construction of aerodromes and landing places
Reclamation of land and extensive drainage schemes
Brick making
Navvying work
Brush making
Baling and pressing hay
Thermometer making
General Royal Engineer services
Mailbag making and repairs
Grooms for Remount Department
Carpentry, plumbing, glazing, etc.

Many of the civilians or combatants who were physically incapable of heavy labour carried out less onerous tasks such as the manufacture of brushes and mailbags. At a camp in Dorchester, some 300 thermometers were produced each week. The manufacture of blue glass eyes was discontinued when no market could be found for them. Some of the PoWs interned at Leigh caught the tram daily to a warehouse in Irlam, to pair up odd boots. If and when orders and instructions needed translating, many of the English-speaking internees were paid for their services.

In more remote places, for example where timber felling took place, accommodation was made from 'materials found on the spot'. Buildings erected under these conditions sometimes took the form of the wattle-and-daub Kaffir huts, well thatched, or simple huts with bunks in two tiers on either side of a central passage.

By April 1916, satellite camps began to flourish all over Britain and a pyramid system was created to administer the camps. Stobs, Leigh, Handforth, Brocton, Pattishall, Feltham, Frongoch, Dorchester, Blandford, and Shrewsbury were all camps that had been set up early in the war and became parent camps: the last two were replaced by Catterick and Oswestry respectively. Oldcastle fulfilled the role of a parent camp in Ireland. Camps set up on the Isle of Man and Jersey were subject to their respective island governments, but took their initiatives from the mainland.

A clue as to why two separate entities – working camps and agricultural depots – were set up is explained in Army Council Instruction (1918) 1324, as amended by Instruction (1919) 92. Under Arrangements for Employers (paragraph 22) it stated, 'The conditions on which prisoners are loaned to employers are different for agriculture employment and other employment.' Belfield (1920) suggested that the most expedient number of PoWs in a party, with guards, was seventy-five. His figure was to be reduced, mainly due to lack of accommodation for large groups.

A list of places used to intern combatants and civilians in the Empire, produced by the PoWs Information Bureau, c1919, has survived until today. Against each entry is a code that explains the camp's status. A typical code has two or three parts to it. The first part of this code denotes the parent camp, and the second part, shown in brackets, gives the unique code of the working camp or of the agricultural depot. Most agricultural depots had a third part, which was the camp's own code in a second set of brackets. A typical example of an agricultural group's coding would be similar to that of Abbess Roding. Its code was Pa (Ch O)(Ao). From this, one could deduce that it came under Chipping Ongar, which in turn was attached to Pattishall. Smaller units referred to as migratory gangs were set up later in the campaign; consisting initially of five men, they were often deployed to farmers as ploughing teams.

In 1923, Belfield was invited to give a paper to the Grotius Society in London. His paper was titled 'The Difficulties Experienced In Carrying Out The

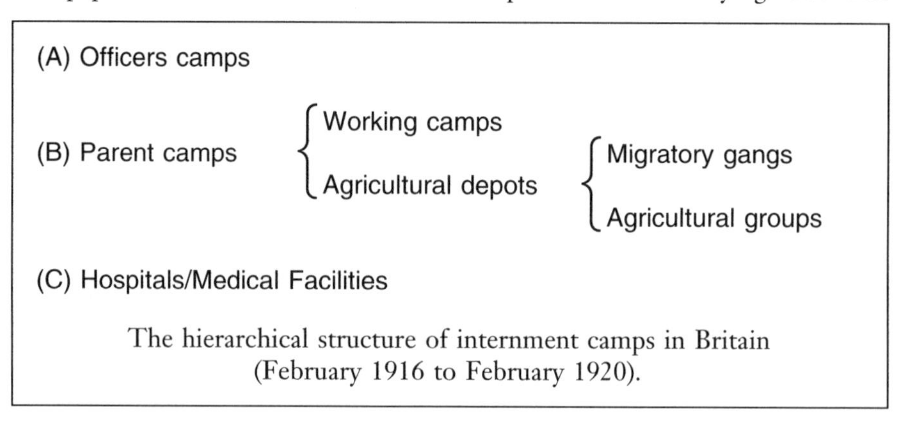

The hierarchical structure of internment camps in Britain (February 1916 to February 1920).

Provisions Of Some Of The Articles Of The Hague And Geneva Conventions Concerning Prisoners of war And Other Captive Enemy Personnel During The Recent War, With Some Comments on These Articles.' He had, in 1920, provided an account of the relationship between a satellite working camp and its parent. Each working camp or agricultural depot had been affiliated to a parent camp. The parent acted as the channel of communication and kept supervision over the camps affiliated to it. The larger working camps were self-contained, but the smaller, i.e. those with an establishment of less than 200 internees, looked to the parent camps for accounting, clothing, etc.

A working camp (or agricultural depot) was initially given a small advance from the canteen funds of its parent camp to set up a canteen of its own. When the satellite camp closed, any funds remaining were transferred back to the parent camp. What each canteen could sell was dependent on its availability. Certain items, such as strong liqueur could not be sold. Originally, the Army and Navy Co-operative Society ran these canteens, but in 1917, the Army Canteen Committee took on the role of provider, which then became the Army and Navy Board. Prisoners set to work were expected to work the same number of hours as a British worker when engaged in the same work. They were also required if necessary to march 3 miles to their place of work; calculated to take one hour. Any excess walking time was deducted from their working day. At some camps, they were marched back to their camps for lunch. It was universally agreed that Sunday was a day of rest, but those employed in agricultural pursuits could be called upon to tend livestock in their care for up to two hours on Sundays when required.

At the start of the releasing programme a man's word was taken as to what skills he had and work was issued appropriately. As this was open to abuse, the Board of Trade, the Ministry of National Service and the Air Ministry began carrying out trade tests of the PoWs, and alternative duties were set for any PoW that failed these tests. A register of their trades was set up showing their employment history. Those with trades in demand became nomadic within the camp system.

The work of PoWs in agriculture probably was the most productive according to Belfield (1920). The Board of Agriculture and the Prisoners of war Employment Committee drew up six schemes, which were introduced gradually.

Scheme 1: Published in January 1917, it provided for employment of groups of internees of not less than seventy-five men to be placed under the various County WACs. The Board and the area command inspected these centres to find if they were acceptable, and from those selected, men were sent out daily in small parties to work on farms in the neighbourhood. One stipulation was made: if the distance travelled was more than 3 miles, special arrangements had to be made for transporting them. Guards accompanied them.

Scheme 2: Small parties were sent out daily to work in the neighbourhood. The employer was responsible for their custody until handed back in the evening. He was obliged to inform the local police if any man escaped whilst in his charge.

Scheme 3: The above scheme was extended, in December 1917, to include agricultural groups.

Scheme 4: The scheme was modified to allow smaller groups, not exceeding fifty prisoners in number to be placed under a British non-commissioned officer with sufficient guards to guard the prisoners at night only. Workers from these small parties were dispatched daily to surrounding farms. This modification took place in December 1917.

Scheme 5: This permitted three PoWs to be handed over to an employer who was responsible for their maintenance, custody and housing. The WACs and local police carefully vetted potential employers. Again, this was introduced in December 1917.

Scheme 6: Migratory gangs, each consisting of ten PoWs, with a guard of two, were made available at harvest times. This scheme started in June 1918. Their accommodation and transport was made by the local representative of the Food Production Department of the Board of Trade in liaison with the area command from whom they drew their supplies and tents.

Belfield (1920) commented that there were few objections to the employment of such gangs (HO 45 / 11025 / 68577). By December 1918, there were over 370 such gangs engaged in agricultural tasks. This scheme in particular solved the difficulty in getting men quickly to any place labour was required.

Various arrangements were made for the inspection and disciplinary supervision of the small and widely scattered bodies employed in agriculture. These were all affiliated to a parent camp, but intermediate supervision was necessary. For instance, the parent camp at Pattishall had, at one time, 133 agricultural groups affiliated to it. Groups attached to Dorchester extended from Cornwall, through Dorset, Somerset, and Wiltshire to Worcestershire and Warwickshire, including Birmingham. Inspection of all these satellite units by the staff at the parent camps was impracticable. As a result the satellite units were attached to any parent or officers' camp or to any large working camp, which were within their reach. Others were grouped and controlled by an officer in a central position, and other expedients were employed as necessary. English speaking PoWs were employed as interpreters in these small camps.

Prisoners were selected carefully for migratory gangs as these men, engaged in agricultural work, had a modicum of freedom and generally worked hard, in fear of losing this privilege. The Board of Trade estimated that the output of the PoWs was around 55 to 60 per cent of the pre-war British worker. The Ministry of Munitions found that skilled men working under close supervision recorded figures of around 85 per cent.

In April 1919, The Prisoner of war Employment Committee investigated the pay-related performance of PoWs to make recommendations as to how the greatest output of work could be obtained. Their findings were overwhelming, that giving them more money by itself was not the answer. They realised money, to them, had no intrinsic value, as PoWs could not buy the things they coveted; and food was uppermost in their minds.

By August 1917 just over half of the combatant PoWs were being utilised outside of the camps. Of those not gainfully employed, most were exempt, through rank or medical condition.

Belfield (1920) provided a table showing the number of PoWs in work in 1917–1918:

Year	*Quarter*	*Combatants*	*Civilians*	*Total*
1917	March	–	–	7,029
	June	–	–	21,690
	September	–	–	25,147
	December	25,979	1,782	27,761
1918	March	31,730	2,159	33,889
	June	43,350	2,360	45,710
	September	59,533	2,573	62,106
	December	65,497	1,356	66,853

In this period many combatants taken prisoner of war in France were processed and retained there to do vital work rather than to be brought back to Britain. Hundreds of working companies were set up. Unhappy with this, the Germans sent their British PoWs to work camps in Poland.

Phases

The Hague Convention permitted the use of non-commissioned officers to do manual work of non-military importance alongside the lower ranks. From the onset of the war, the British did not do this, but the Germans did. In the early phase, many of the lower ranks brought to Britain were sent to France, behind the front line, helping to put in the infrastructure to get men and supplies to the war zone. Most work done by those interned took place in the confines of their camp. Then, with most of the non-combatants either released on licence, or interned on the Isle of Man, the second phase, more focused on the combatants, was able to release workers into the communities to do manual work deemed of a non-military nature. This change of direction coincided with the reduction of combatants being employed in France and being sent to the British mainland – this allowed camps to be put into two distinct phases: pre April 1916 and post March 1916.

The named places of internment cited in this work fall into these two distinct phases. The first phase contains mostly the civilians that had been detained under the newly created Defence of the Realm Act. Combatants were few in this phase. When Britain declared war, there were no places kept in readiness to detain large numbers of civilians put into internment. The Hague Convention did not condone the use of prisons and the only alternative was military bases which were being filled by recruits undergoing training. So a variety of places were quickly requisitioned to intern them. Disused buildings of all kinds were transformed into holding centres, as were the grounds of large country houses. In the early stages the crews of merchant shipping, classed as civilians, were detained, but gradually crews of naval vessels, along with men from the land army, were arriving at British ports to be put into internment too. At first, all were mixed in a random manner.

Gradually as new places came on line, segregation became possible in a system that allowed a few special sites to exist, such as those at Buckfast and Eastcote – set up to intern merchant seamen. As the number of lower ranking combatants grew some were sent to work for companies in France assisting in creating the infrastructure or put at the docks on the French west coast, loading and unloading ship manifests. The Germans protested that their men were being sent to France, but desisted when reassured they would remain under British control although on French soil.

When the majority of the infrastructure was in place in France, the methodology of internment changed. Those civilians not released on licence were shipped to the Isle of Man. The combatants held in the UK were put into work parties, to work outside the perimeters of their place of internment. Some civilian working parties were created, for those wishing to stay on the mainland.

The movement of the non-combatants to the Isle of Man coincided with the Irish Rising which again saw Irishman accused of civil unrest being put into prisons on mainland Britain. Many were quickly released, but around 100 were kept locked up, as the ringleaders were singled out to be executed.

The second phase of camps were created as fears were also being realised that the health of men kept confined with no worthwhile activity created its own problems. A.L. Visher, a Swiss psychologist, visited a number of camps to inspect them. He was later to diagnose the condition 'barbed-wire disease'. He pointed out that keeping men in an all-male environment for long periods had a detrimental effect on their physical and mental health. After the war he noted many had problems in later life developing relationships with women. Although he found it difficult to prove, he believed that many instances of suicide were related to being held in internment. He also suggested that where there were no women, men would adopt abnormal bonds with each other, though not necessarily engaging in homosexual acts. Homosexuality was then a crime, but apart from one case that occurred on the Isle of Man, no cases were tried in the courts, nor were any reports carried in the British press.

The original intention of this work was to list the places and provide the evidence of locations used for internment, for those arrested under the terms of the Defence of the Realm Act (civilian internees) or for those taken from the theatre of war (PoWs). In compiling this work a few anomalies arose, such as the Irishmen arrested and interned for their parts in the Easter Rising of 1916. Also included are British and foreign nationals convicted of treasonable offences and executed in the Tower of London or placed in prison.

Not all interned, especially those that came from the battlefield were healthy. Many could be treated within their place of internment by medical orderlies, supported by local doctors. But many had to be hospitalised; some had to be put into institutions for the insane. Whenever possible those declared unfit to fight again were exchanged by hospital ships that ferried these wretched souls from the docks at Boston to Holland.

There were many that died whilst in internment. Many simply succumbed to the wounds they sustained on the battlefield. But many died from illness and disease. Spanish flu swept Europe towards the end of the war, and was responsible for deaths of many thousands, including those interned. The internees that died were buried locally. In 1958, the then West German Government sought to have all the bodies of Germans who died in both wars moved to a centralised location. In 1962, those bodies not reclaimed by family members were exhumed and re-interred at Cannock Chase. A similar exercise took place in Ireland, where the dead were moved to Glencree.

List of Abbreviations

ADM	Admiralty
CO	Conscientious Objector
DKF	Deutsche Kriegsgefangene in Feindesland (Berlin, 1919)
FPHS	Forces Postal History Society
HO	Home Office
HMT	Hired Military Transport
IWM	Imperial War Museum
OS	Ordnance Survey
OSt	Osterreichisches Staatsarchiv (*Behandlung der Duetschen und Oesterreichischen Offiziere Kriegsgefangene im Vereinigten Koenigreiche*, June 1917)
Per. comm.	Personal communication
POWIB	Prisoners of war Information Bureau
TA	Telegraphic Address
WAC	War Agricultural Committee
WO	War Office

Places of Internment

Many camps were situated in rural locations, and like the army, many took their names from the nearest point of debarkation from the railway and not from the nearest settlement. The task of pinpointing many locations has been compounded as the different organisations involved labelled these camps to suit their purpose. Therefore, duplication by default is unavoidable.

Places used to intern civilians and combatants were varied. Disused factory buildings were utilised, as were under-utilised workhouses, large country houses, and their grounds, and farms. Tented encampments have left little or no evidence of their existence, nor have some small groups leased out for short periods of time to fulfil a project. Sometimes a concrete square that once was the floor of the latrine block, is all that remains. Some places of internment can be traced back to locations where an early airfield existed. Some of these airfields still exist today.

A

ABBESS RODING: The Old Rectory (OS: TL 583 2 098). According to the POWIB (1919), the camp was an agricultural group attached to the agricultural depot at Chipping Ongar and was based in the Old Rectory. Its code was Pa (Ch O) (Ao) (IWM: Facsimile K4655). The HO issued it with the TA, *Priswarian: Old Rectory, Abbess Roding, Leaden Roding* (ADM 1/8506/265–120667). Abbess Roding is cited by the FPHS (1973). The rectory which stands in School Lane, Abbess Beauchamp and Berners Roding, Essex has been a Grade II listed building since 1967.

ABBEY DORE: The Workhouse (OS: SO 385 326). *The Hereford Times* (25 May 1918) reports forty PoWs were being brought to Abbey Dore. It may be the workhouse was used to billet them.

Abbey Dore workhouse was designed by John Plowman. Standing to the north of Abbey Dore, at Upper Drew, to accommodate up to 100 inmates, it was built *c.*1838. The main building was built around two courtyard areas, one for males and the other for females. To the rear was the original infirmary block. A separate hospital block was later erected at the south east of the workhouse. In 1930 the workhouse became a council-run Public Assistance Institution. During the Second World War part of the site was used as a Chamber's tractor factory. The buildings were then sold to a Mr Woodhouse who converted the buildings into cottages. These were then refurbished by his grandson, and are now called Riverdale (www.ewyaslacy.org.uk).

The camp was visited by Dr A. de Sturler and Monsieur R. de Sturler during March and April 1919 (FO 383/506).

ABERGAVENNY: The Garage (OS: SO 305 135). A satellite of Leominster, it was an agricultural group, cited by the POWIB (1919) as being at 'The Garage', its code being Shrw (Lmr) (Aa) (IWM: Facsimile K4655). The Garage was a former bus depot. Its TA was Priswarian: Monmouth Road, Abergavenny (ADM 1/8506/265–120667).

Smith, in *The German Prisoner of war Camp at Leigh 1914–1919* (1968), cites on 3 November 1916 the first of two articles which appeared in *The Leigh Chronicle* regarding this camp. The first stated, 'About 250 German PoWs, most of whom left Leigh a few months ago to work at Abergavenny, were brought back to Leigh on Wednesday evening ...' The second report, dated Friday, 23 February 1917, states that 180 PoWs from the Leigh camp left on Saturday bound for Abergavenny.

The camp was visited Dr A. de Sturler and Monsieur R. de Sturler during March and April 1919 (FO 383/506). It is also cited by the FPHS (1973).

ABERGLASNEY (OS: SN 597 199). Situated near to Llangathen, this camp was a satellite of Brecon; with the POWIB (1919) code Fg (Bre) (Ag) (IWM: Facsimile K4655). It was also cited by FPHS (1973). It had the TA Priswarian: Broad Oak, Carmarthenshire (ADM 1/8506/265–120667). Sadly, the exact whereabouts of the camp and the number detained there have been lost in the passage of time. One possible location for this camp was Tylf Farm.

ADDLESTONE: New Haw (OS: TQ 044 646). Wey Manor was a large country estate near Addlestone with its own private cemetery, which was used until at least 1907. Described as a working camp, it had the POWIB (1919) code Fe (Adl) (IWM: Facsimile K4655). A HO list indicates the PoWs were billeted in what is now Wey Manor Golf Club House. The golf course stands on what was then Wey Manor Farm, which has also been known as New Haw Farm. The camp was operational between October 1918 and April 1919 and had the TA, Priswarian: Addlestone, Weybridge (ADM 1/8506/265–120667). The camp is also cited by the FPHS (1973)

ALDBOROUGH (OS: TG 186 339). There was a request for this camp to be set up recorded in the minutes of the Norfolk WAC meeting of 11 January 1918 (C/C10/17). These minutes state the men were to be engaged in river drainage work, but the camp's actual location was not noted. The camp may have been in the grounds of Aldborough Hall, built *c.*1750 for the Gay family.

There has been a mill at Aldborough since before the Domesday Book. Every few hundred years a new mill would be built, replacing the earlier one. The present mill stands on the joint parish boundaries of Aldborough, Alby and Thwaite and came into the ownership of the Cooke family in 1809; they were a family of millers. *c.*1910 a new water wheel, made by Thomas Cooke was installed. Made of elm, it was 15 feet in diameter; he was adamant his applewood cogwheel could outlast three cast iron ones. His waterwheel was finally taken out to make way for the first diesel engine in 1935. The mill was then producing flour and grist. At the end of the First World War, PoWs are known to have cleared out the mill's dam. Where they stayed is not noted, but they belonged to an agricultural group, with the POWIB (1919) code Pa (K L) (Alb) (IWM: Facsimile K4655). In the 1950s, the dam was back-filled and the Scarrow Beck diverted, leaving very little trace of the mill's watercourse. The machinery was buried in an old gravel pit, at the back of the mill.

A report on a visit of inspection to Aldborough was created by Dr A. de Sturler and Monsieur R. de Sturler, during the spring of 1919 and is held at the National Archives at Kew (FO 383/507).

ALDBURY (OS: SP 964 124). According to the Hertfordshire County Council WAC minutes, taken on 20 March 1918, a migratory gang suggested for Aldbury was abandoned as the site offered did not meet with the Board's approval. The Station Hotel at Tring was cited as an alternative.

ALTON (OS: SU 724 395). It is listed as being a working camp by the POWIB (1919), its code being Dor (Alt) (IWM: Facsimile K4655). It had the TA, Priswarian: Alton (ADM 1/8506/265–120667). It is also cited by FPHS (1973). Hawkins (*The Story of Alton*, 1973) revealed the location of the Alton internment camp when he wrote, 'German PoWs were employed on the farms and were billeted in the paper mills, which were otherwise unemployed . . .' The camp closed on 12 October 1918. This camp should not be confused with the abbey at Beech where German merchant seamen had been interned (see Alton Abbey).

ALTON ABBEY: nr Beech (OS: SU 675 378). After Charles Plomer Hopkins (1861–1922) was ordained into the priesthood, in 1884, his work took him to the Indian subcontinent where he established places where seamen could rest and be diverted from the baser forms of recreation. In 1894, he returned to Britain and joined a Benedictine community at Barry in South Wales. As Father Hopkins, he moved to Beech in 1894 and began cutting trees and clearing the land. From nothing, he created a wattle church that stood on 100 acres of land, in a peaceful part of the country. Then, under the guidance of the distinguished architect Sir Charles Nicholson, Hopkins and his fellow monks had erected the first permanent buildings by 1903. Sailors, and other travellers, moving between Southampton or Portsmouth and London were welcomed with food and shelter. The abbey stands 1 mile south west of Beech on the road to Medstead and is described in Pevsner's *Buildings of England*, 1967 as having been originally involved in looking after retired seafarers; it has twenty-three guestrooms and a separate guesthouse with cottages.

Father Hopkins was a Trustee of the National Sailors' and Firemen's Union and served as a member of the National Maritime Board. He also served on the local council at Alton, and was instrumental in settling the great seamen's strike of 1911–12. Made a CBE in 1920, he died in St Mawes, Cornwall, two years later. He is buried at the abbey. An obituary to him appeared in *The Times* (27 March 1922).

The Hampshire Herald (24 October 1914) reported that all German men in the district aged between 17 and 45 were being arrested under the Defence of the Realm Act. They were sent to Frith Hill for processing.

At the outbreak of war, there were hundreds of merchant seamen of foreign extraction left destitute as a result of not finding new employment when their ships were confiscated as prizes of war by the British government. As a result of their plight, around a hundred seamen, employed in the British Mercantile Marine, were found accommodation at the abbey. They were given free rail passes to allow them to travel to Alton by train. The first seven arrived in the evening of Monday, 10 August 1914. After registering at the local police station, they went to the abbey. More batches arrived in the following days. The fact that these men, and boys, had arrived without an escort alarmed and caused a lot of anger amongst the inhabitants of Beech and Alton. P. & L. Gillmann, *Collar the Lot: How Britain Interned and Expelled Its Wartime Refugees*, 1980, states, 'The National Sailors' and Firemans' Union of Great Britain asked the Abbot to take in a number of destitute German sailors stranded in Britain when the war began. The ships' officers were housed in the nave of the church, and the seamen slept in tents in the grounds. The boys were quartered in a corrugated iron building.'

Hampshire Herald & Alton Gazette (15 August 1914) cited there was much indignation being expressed in the area earlier that week when it became known that an internment camp for German seamen was being formed at the abbey, at Beech. The matter came before Alton UDC who decided to refer the matter to the Home Office and the War Office, before forming any opinion. The local press cited handbills had been distributed informing locals there were Germans at the abbey. It asked 'shall we have them – shall we be protected.' Sympathetic to the demonstrators' cause, the Chief Constable of Hampshire had several interned sailors locked up at the nearby army camp one night when they got drunk and became boisterous. The perimeter fence was being guarded by boy scouts. There was no report of any attempted escape from the abbey camp according to the *Hampshire Herald* (22 August 1914). Incensed at the latitude given to the seamen, the locals called a meeting, handing out leaflets about the Germans at the abbey. Locals were asked to attend a public meeting to protest. The paper stated the meeting was technically an offence against the Defence of the Realm Act. The meeting, organised by Councillor Frost was cancelled. Instead a letter was circulated, which the *Hampshire Herald* copied in full on 31 October 1914.

The cost of feeding and clothing the internees was borne by the British government, which infuriated Father Hopkins. He would have been happier if the shipping companies had offered to make a contribution to the welfare of the seamen. It is reported the government paid The National Sailors' and Firemen's Union 10 shillings (50p) a week per man, to cover food, clothing, medical and supervision.

The *Hampshire Herald* (29 August 1914) cited there were now around 200 seamen at the abbey. It also cited a party of officials visited the camp on the previous Sunday to see first-hand how the men were housed and cared for. Men from the War Office, the Admiralty and the Home Office were in this party to assess the situation. The paper also recorded another petition, signed by the locals, warning of the unguarded nature of the camp.

The *Hampshire Herald* (19 September 1914) cited two seamen had been removed from the abbey after a good deal of insubordination. It was thought they had been taken to Camberley under police escort.

The *Hampshire Herald* (10 October 1914) reported there had been more trouble at the abbey. This time several of the men became obstreperous. The trouble was not thought to be serious, but the boy scouts were having trouble with one man. With so many young men being congregated together, disagreements could easily escalate. To de-escalate the situation the four seamen believed to be the root cause were weeded out, and transferred to the Frith Hill camp.

The *Hampshire Herald* (20 March 1915) cited five German internees from the abbey were placed under arrest on Wednesday afternoon, for insubordination. They had been taken into custody to Alton Police Station awaiting transfer to a more secure camp. Concerns were still being expressed about the lack of a proper guard around the abbey's perimeter.

Two Germans died whilst being held at Alton Abbey. The first of the two was Ewald Stelter, aged 42. He died of heart failure on 30 December 1914. He had come to the camp on 19 August and appeared to be in good health when he arrived. Stelter collapsed, the nurse was called, and he died within five minutes. The second was Josef Wighard, who died on 23 September 1915. Diagnosed with consumption, he had become too ill to be transferred when the rest left in April. He was given dispensation to remain at the abbey. Both men were initially buried in the abbey's cemetery; their remains were moved to Cannock in 1966.

Without consultation, the sailors were moved out of the abbey on Thursday, 15 April 1915. On the previous evening a number of 11th Hussars came into the town and billeted for the night. They breakfasted and left early, under their officer, in the direction of the abbey. On their arrival they surrounded the place to prevent anyone from leaving. In a manoeuvre that must have been pre-planned, Superintendent Ruben then brought in a force of fifty police officers, assembled from surrounding towns. With the military in position around the perimeter, the police entered the grounds of the abbey, much to the consternation of the Germans, and Mr Morris, who represented Father Hopkins. The interned sailors were formally arrested and marched into the abbey chapel where the roll was called. They were handed over to the officer who had accompanied the Hussars. Orders were then given that each seaman was to pack his kit and be ready to march out of the abbey within a short time. Excuses and attempts to delay the process were met with the sternest of warnings. The baggage was packed onto two large military waggons and the men were marched to Medstead Station, under military escort, where a special train was waiting for them. The sailors, and their escort, left in the direction of London.

Contemporary reports state there were over eighty Germans in the camp that were taken away at the behest of the War Office. This was only half the number cited in the local press six months earlier. The discrepancy in figures may be accounted for by the fact that around fifty seamen were being housed at a 'daughter house' in Greenwich. Their fate is not recorded. Speculation as to why the seamen were moved out so quickly was reported in the local paper of 24 April 1915. It cited an Austrian national had covertly been in contact with the men at the abbey. The seamen had tried to get letters posted outside, instead of using the official box at the abbey.

Mr Jackson's inspection report of 27 February 1915 stated inter alia that he did not go to the camp at Alton.

ALTRINCHAM – SINDERLAND GREEN – DUNHAM MASSEY (OS: SJ 73-90-). The FPHS (1973) cites an internment camp at Altrincham. This is supported by an entry in *Deutsche Kriegsgefangene in Feindesland* (1919) that states those interned at Altrincham were involved in road and quarry work, and that the PoWs complained of not having adequate clothing or equipment to carry out these tasks in a safe manner. Local understanding is that they were constructing a road across a mossy area.

The Manchester Evening News (16 February 1917 and 21 March 1917) cites there was a camp under construction at Dunham Massey. PoWs were sent to Irlam from the parent camp at Leigh to sort out odd boots into pairs. As Irlam, Dunham Massey and Altrincham are close it is likely that this was one camp.

Trendath (Bowden Historical Society, 1998) believes the site became a bus depot for the Royal Air Force. Then it was taken over in the 1930s as a training centre for London's Metropolitan Police Force. Jamaican troops were stationed at the depot in the Second World War, as were liberated Italians, and then German PoWs. The base closed in the 1950s and the area was permitted to return to agriculture. All traces of the depot have now disappeared.

DKF: Den Straßen und Steinbrucharbeitern in Port Clarence fehlt genügendes Schuhwerk und in Altrinchan (sic) *ausreichende Kleider bzw Arbeitsanzüge.*

AMBERGATE (Crich) (OS: SK 350 541). A HO document cites a camp at Crich, giving its TA as Priswarian: Crich (ADM 1/8506/265–120667). The POWIB (1919) directory describes it as a working camp. It was a satellite of Brocton, with the code Bro (Am) (IWM: Facsimile K4655).

Flint and Judge (per. comm., 8 February 1998 & 15 March 1998) believed that a candle-making factory in Crich, now occupied by Allsopp's Bakery, was used to intern

PoWs. It is thought that they worked in a local quarry. Three PoWs were buried in St Mary's Church graveyard at Crich. They were Gehrhardt, O. (d. 4/12/1918); Kaminski, F. (d. 6/12/1918); and Kozab, F. (d. 7/12/1918). Their bodies were exhumed in the 1960s, and re-interred at Cannock Chase (D1372 API 65/75).

AMBERGATE (Bullbridge) (OS: SK 35- 52-). John Radford (per. comm., 12 February 1998), whose father was the landlord of the Canal Inn at that time, suggests PoWs were housed in an isolated lodging house at Bullbridge that stands near to the canal. A photograph exists showing PoWs working in a nearby quarry.

In his unpublished autobiography, *The Cry from the Soil*, Fredrick Fletcher states:

> ... as a youth, in 1918, one day when cycling he met some British soldiers looking for an escaped PoW near to the village of Ambergate. Later that day, at Riber Castle, near Matlock, he found the escapee hiding in bushes. Cold and hungry, and offering no resistance, the young absconder gave himself up. When asked his name, he replied it was Rolph ...

Fletcher persuaded Rolph to surrender to his uncle, the local constable, rather than be found by the soldiers that he had seen earlier in the day. On interrogation, Rolph stated he had travelled some 10 miles before being found. Known camps within a 10-mile radius of Matlock were: Bullbridge, Crich, Ashbourne, Duffield, Ilkeston, Denby, Kilburn and Wirksworth.

AMPLEFORTH – SPROXTON MOOR (OS: SE 598 788). There is no entry cited for Sproxton Moor or Ampleforth in the POWIB (1919) directory, but the same directory has an entry for Sinnington agricultural group that states it was attached to Sproxton Moor agricultural depot. As the Sinnington camp had the code Cat (Sp M) (Sin) it can be deduced that the Sproxton Moor camp's POWIB (1919) code would have been Cat (Sp M) (IWM: Facsimile K4655). The camp had the TA, Priswarian: Ampleforth College (ADM 1/8506/265–120667).

Details that PoWs were transferred from the camp at Leigh were given to the inspectorate of the US Embassy in London, when they visited the Lancashire camp on 8 September 1916.

The PoWs at Sproxton Moor were involved in forestry work. They complained of having nowhere to wash properly, or to relax and recuperate after working in the forest. Fresh, clean, drinking water was at a premium too.

An inspection report of Sproxton Moor (Yorkshire) is held at the National Archives at Kew (FO 383/432). The FPHS (1973) entry incorrectly cites that the Sproxton Moor camp was in Leicestershire.

AMPTHILL (OS: TL 035 374). The PoWs were interned at the Bird in Hand Public House. The camp had the TA, Priswarian, Ampthill (ADM 1/8506/265–120667). It was described as a working camp, and its POWIB (1919) code was Pa (Amp). This camp was also cited by Alan J. Brown and F.J. Carter of the FPHS (1973).

Twenty-eight names of PoWs that worked at Ampthill between 16 March 1918 and 22 February 1919, along with their guard, are recorded in an extract taken from the PoWs employment time sheets (WW1/AC/PW/1 & 2).

A 1927 map shows the Bird in the Hand stood next to the House of Correction in Park Hill. Today the pub is a private residence.

AMY DOWN (see St Mellion).

ANGMERING (see East Preston).

APPLETON (OS: SJ 638 839). Little is known of this camp. It appears in two lists produced by the HO. The first document states its TA as Priswarian, Appleton, Stretton, Cheshire. The later document list cites the camp had closed on 4 December 1918 (ADM 1/8506/265–120667).

ARRINGTON (OS: TL 324 505). A working camp, its POWIB (1919) code was Pa (Ar) (IWM: Facsimile K4655); its address is stated as being The Kardwick Arms (sic). Its TA is cited as Priswarian, Hardwick Arms, Arrington (ADM 1/8506/265–120667). Arrington is also cited by the FPHS (1973).

The Hardwick Arms stands on Ermine Street. In past times it was a coaching house. Set up in the second phase, the numbers interned have not been found, nor has the type of work they were engaged in.

ASHBOURNE: Ashbourne Hall (OS: SK 181 468). The town of Ashbourne has been no stranger to 'entertaining' PoWs. Prisoners from the Napoleonic Wars have been interned here, as have Italians and Germans during the Second World War.

Amongst the famous that have stayed in Ashbourne Hall, though not as a prisoner, was Charles Edward Stuart (a.k.a. Bonnie Prince Charlie), before, and after, making his monumental decision in 1745, at Derby's Exeter House, to return north, rather than continue on his epic march south to take London and capture the crown.

The *Derby Daily Telegraph* (14 March 1918) cites fifty-five PoWs were in Ashbourne engaged in hedging and ditching work and that more were expected. An article dated 10 July 1918 reinforces this. Former town councillor, Mr C.H. Birch, remembers seeing PoWs at Ashbourne's railway station in a year that was memorable to him, for it was at the time he started school, being five years old. He often saw the PoWs disembarking from the trains and being made to fall in, before being marched up the hill to the hall. He distinctly remembers their grey uniforms. In those days, Ashbourne Hall was much larger than it is now, having been partly demolished *c.*1930. A sketch by Mr Birch's shows clearly the location of the 'Old Hall'. Only part of the hall remains today, and it serves the community as its library. Mr Birch believes there may have been approximately 150 to 200 prisoners billeted at the hall, which had barbed wire added to its stone perimeter wall.

An agricultural depot, the camp's code was Bro (Ash) (IWM: Facsimile K4655). Ashbourne had two groups attached to it: one was based in a mill at Stone; the other was at Uttoxeter's racecourse. It is also cited by the FPHS (1973).

ASHBURY COURT (see North Lew).

ASHBY DE LA ZOUCH (OS: SK 357 168). Minutes dated 20 March 1918 record that a protest was made to Ashby Urban District Council that German PoWs were being allowed to use the public baths against the wishes of the local populace. How this matter was resolved was not stated (DE 1841/1–3).

The POWIB (1919) cites the address for the camp as being The Queen's Head Commercial Hotel and it was described as being an agricultural group attached to Loughborough agricultural depot. The code was Bro (Lo) (As) (IWM: Facsimile K4655) and its TA was Priswarian: Ashby de la Zouch (ADM 1/8506/265–120667). The premises stand on Market Street.

During March 1919, Dr A. de Sturler compiled a report, Ashby-de-la-Zouch, on his visit of inspection, which is held at the National Archives at Kew (FO 383/506).

Two PoWs were buried in Ashby's cemetery. The bodies were exhumed *c.*1961, and taken to Cannock Chase.

ASHCHURCH (OS: SO 925 335). On 10 March 1917, the *Evesham Journal* reported that eighty PoWs were being removed from Ashchurch, and were being taken to the new Drill Hall in Evesham. There are no other reports detailing where this camp actually was, or for how long it was in existence. It was also stated in the *Chelmsford Chronicle* (10 March 1917) and the *Midland Daily Telegraph* (9 March 1917) that eighty PoWs were destined for Evesham.

ASHWELL END: Fordham's Maltings (OS: TL 274 399). A minute dated 8 May 1918, belonging to the Hertfordshire WAC, states forty PoWs were expected to arrive at the Maltings on 26 April 1918. An original request of 13 February 1918 had sought fifty PoWs. A second minute, dated 19 June 1918, reported that fifty had arrived and were now working in the district.

A working camp, its POWIB (1919) code was Pa (Asw) (IWM: Facsimile K4655).

ASPATRIA. There were two camps in Aspatria, opened concurrently. One was in the agricultural college, and the other in the Noble Temple.

THE AGRICULTURAL COLLEGE (OS: NY 142 418). The college was established, in 1874, by John Twentyman, a founding member of the Aspatria Agricultural Co-operative Society and Sir Wilfred Lawson, a local MP. The early years were spent in Sir Wilfred's Temperance Hall before it moved to new premises in May 1886 when Dr Henry J. Webb became its owner and principal. Under his leadership the college gained some national notoriety. Webb was keen to develop a better butter manufacturing process, and, in 1889, opened the West Cumberland Dairy Company. The brands produced included 'Daisy' and 'Buttercup'. Webb died prematurely, and he was succeeded as Principal by John Smith Hill. On 3 November 1894, the Technical Education Committees of Cumberland, Westmorland and Northumberland met in Carlisle to consider establishing a fixed Dairy School and Farm for the three counties. Northumberland County Council withdrew but Cumberland and Westmorland County Councils decided to go ahead with the scheme. Newton Rigg Estate, near Penrith was bought with a seven-year lease that began on 2 February 1896. The new centre became known as the Newton Rigg Farm School (OS: NY 493 310). Aspatria continued as an annex to instruct pupils of both sexes in the science and practice of agriculture; especially dairy farming. Cheese and butter making and poultry husbandry were seen as specialities for women students and the 'Newton Rigg dairy maids' as they became known as, were prized on aristocratic estates. Some of the more able students progressed into higher education at the University of Durham, and by 1909 veterinary science and carpentry had been added to the curriculum.

The Cumberland WAC received a reply from the Chief Constable of the County saying, subject to approval from the military authority, he had no objections to PoWs being utilised in the county, provided an official guard accompanied all working parties. During the First World War, Newton Rigg ceased its residential courses temporarily as reconstruction took place between May 1914 and June 1915. The Aspatria campus was used to house fifty PoWs to clear out local watercourses in May 1919. A minute of the Cumberland WAC confirms it.

During the Second World War the college trained young women for The Land Army. By 1967 its name had changed to The Cumberland and Westmorland College of Agriculture and Forestry. In 1969 it was designated 'The National College of

Forestry Education at Supervisory Level.' Around this time the Aspatria site closed and Beacon Hill School was built on its site. The college continued to grow in the 1970s and 1980s. The Further and Higher Education Act (1992) allowed Newton Rigg to become an independent corporate body. Later in the same year, the college became part of the University of Central Lancashire. It was integrated fully, in 1998, to become its Cumbria Campus.

THE NOBLE TEMPLE (OS: NY 153 419). The Noble Temple is a Masonic Lodge that stands on Harriston Road, Aspatria. Apart from the minutes of the Cumberland WAC (CC1/39/1–2) there is no further evidence to show this camp existed.

ATHERSTONE (OS: SP 32- 97-). Cited in a HO document, its TA was Priswarian: Mancetter, Atherstone (ADM 1/8506/265–120667). Described as a working camp by the POWIB (1919), its code is Dor (At) (IWM: Facsimile K4655). Little is known about it. Atherstone is also cited by the FPHS (1973).

ATTLEBOROUGH: Rockland (OS: TL 993 970). The workhouse at Rockland All Saints was erected in 1836 to accommodate up to 250 inmates. Conditions became so bad that the matter was raised in the House of Commons (*Hansard*: 26 August 1907).

It was resolved to inform the Local Government Board that accommodation at the Wayland Union Workhouse, near Rockland All Saints, could be provided for PoWs to carry out drainage work on the River Wensum. On 6 July 1918 a minute of the Norfolk WAC intimated transport should be made available for conveying PoWs based at the Rockland camp to and from their places of work. One of these places was Mr Down's Farm in Rockland.

The camp's TA was Priswarian: Rockland, Norfolk (ADM 1/8506/265–120667). Both Rockland and Attleborough appear in the list produced for the FPHS (1973).

A hospital was built in 1912 at Attleborough, and for many years it was used by the National Health Service. The site is now used for residential housing.

AUCHTERARDER (OS: NN 945 125). Auchterarder is approximately 14 miles southwest of Perth. It was home to the agricultural depot for the area. The camp had the POWIB (1919) code, Stbs (Au) (IWM: Facsimile K4655). Very little is known about this Depot, or of its six satellites: Balgowan, Forteviot, Forgandenny, Kintillo, Tarrylaw Farm and Leystone Farm. The camp's TA was Priswarian: Auchterarder (ADM 1/8506/265–120667).

The Forfar Review and Strathmore Advertiser (30 August 1918) expressed its doubts about the calibre of the PoWs being brought onto their land, pointing to those working at Auchterarder as an example.

Bill Harding, in *On Flows The Tay* (2000), noted several escape attempts had taken place. One account published in the *Dundee Courier* (3 October 1917) cited two German sailors had been re-arrested near Dundee. An earlier paper (30 September 1917) gave an account of the Perthshire hills being searched for their recapture. Harding also stated there were approximately 700 PoWs in Perthshire.

This camp may have been located in the Upper Strathearn Combination Poorhouse, built in 1863. In the 1930s it became known as Strathearn Home, caring for the chronically sick and the elderly. In 1946, it had seventy-one beds. Today it is office accommodation.

The PoW camp closed on 18 February 1919.

There is also an entry for Auchterarder in the lists produced for the FPHS (1973) by Alan J. Brown and F.J. Carter.

AXBRIDGE: The Workhouse (OS: ST 429 545). Described as a satellite camp of Long Ashton, its POWIB (1919) code was Dor (L A) (Ax) (IWM: Facsimile K4655). It also had the TA Priswarian: Workhouse, Axbridge (ADM 1/8506/265–120667).

County WAC minutes for Somerset (15 April 1919) cite the PoW Horse Depots at Axbridge, Dulverton and Shepton Mallet had been closed, and arrangements were being made for the early closure of the depot at Hallatrow.

When Axbridge Poor Law Union was created, a new workhouse, designed by Samuel T. Welch to accommodate 250 inmates, was erected at the south side of West Street in 1837. A separate infirmary block was added in 1903 and the workhouse was still in use until the 1930s. After that it became St John's Hospital, which closed in 1993. After its closure the main building was adapted for residential use, whilst the workhouse's infirmary block was transformed to provide residential care for the elderly (www.rooksbridge.org.uk/workhouse).

AYLESBURY: HM Prison (OS: SP 815 135). The internment camp at Aylesbury differed significantly from other internment camps set up in Great Britain and Ireland during the First World War because it had been set up by the Home Office to detain women of various nationalities for whom internment orders had been granted under the Defence of the Realm Act.

The prison was built at Bierton Hill in 1847 to serve the county. It became an integral part of the national prison system through the introduction of The Penal Reform (1877) Act. Then, under the Inebriates Act of 1879, centres such as Aylesbury's Women's Inebriate Reformatory were established for the treatment and cure of habitual drunkards. Women were confined to 'E' wing.

In 1906, a government report concluded, upwards of 62 per cent of all the prison's inmates were found to be insane or defective in varying degrees. At the Aylesbury State Reformatory for Females, out of thirty-two admitted the previous year, eight were found to be insane. Most were over 60 years of age and had been bandied like shuttle-cocks between police courts and prisons because they had become drunkards. On average, they had all served between six and seven years in prison before being sent to reformatories.

On 2 July 1914, Miss Helena Fox MD was appointed to the post of Woman Superintendent and Deputy Medical Officer of Institutions at Aylesbury, comprising of the female convict prison, The Borstal Institution for Females, The State Inebriate Reformatory for Women, and The Preventive Detention Prison for Women.

Into this menagerie of criminals, drunks, and prostitutes, in 1914 were added women accused of treasonable offences, and in 1916, Irish women arrested for their roles in the Easter Rising.

One of those held for treason was Lizzie Luise Wertheim. She was sentenced to ten years imprisonment for aiding Georg Traugott Breeckow in acts of espionage. Wertheim had attempted to return to England from a failed marriage. When war was declared Lizzie had been trapped in Amsterdam. Short of money, she was recruited by German intelligence to act as a contact for agents sent to spy in England. In this capacity she met Breeckow several times. Unknown to Breeckow, his mail was being monitored by the British security services. When he was arrested, details of several Royal Navy vessels were found, written on rice paper, hidden inside his shaving brush. Wertheim was arrested on 9 June 1915; when her possessions were searched, a letter addressed to one of Breeckow's aliases was found. Because Wertheim was a British citizen, they were tried together at the Central Criminal Court in London, on

14–17 September 1915. Both pleaded not guilty to the charges, but the jury took just eight minutes to decide that they both were guilty. Breeckow was sentenced to death by shooting. Wertheim was sent to Aylesbury Prison. During 1918 she was certified as insane and transferred to Broadmoor Criminal Lunatic Asylum. Her behaviour and general medical condition worsened and she died there, of pulmonary tuberculosis, on 29 July 1920.

Seventy-three women were arrested for their parts in the Easter Rising of 1916. They were arrested under Section 14b of the Defence of the Realm Act. All but twelve of these were to be released by 8 May 1916. Six were detained at Aylesbury, but not all at the same time.

The first to be interned in Aylesbury for their parts in the struggle were Maire Perolz and Brigid Foley. Like the others that were to come to Aylesbury, they were members of *Cumann na mBan* (The Women's Council). Perolz and Foley were committed to Ireland's struggle for independence from British rule. Perolz was an advocate for the rights of working women.

Nell Ryan, Winifred Carney and Helena Maloney arrived at Mountjoy Prison, after Perolz and Foley had departed. Ryan, another trade union activist, was released in September 1916.

Carney was a suffragist, and an advocate of a strong trade union movement. As the secretary of the Irish Textile Workers' Union she became active in fund-raising and relief efforts for the Dublin workers during the 1913 lockout. Drawn into the republican movement, she was present at the founding of *Cumann na mBan* in Wynn's Hotel, Dublin on 2 April 1914. A close friend of James Connelly, she joined the Irish Citizen Army and was reputed to be a crack shot with a rifle. On 14 April 1916 she was to assist in the final preparations for the Easter Rising, and for the next week she typed dispatches and mobilisation orders. Despite being ordered to leave the General Post Office by Pearse at noon on Friday, 28 April 1916 she remained at her post, and was the only woman in the column that seized the GPO on Easter Monday. After the insurrection was quelled many of the leading figures in *Cumann na mBan* were arrested. Carney had stayed to tend the wounds of Connelly and others. After the surrender she was interned, first in Mountjoy and from July in Aylesbury prison, and was released 23 December 1916. In 1918 she was briefly imprisoned in Armagh and Lewes prisons. She stood for *Sinn Féin* in the general election of 1918, but polled badly.

Moloney was another political activist. She had joined *Inghinidhe na hÉireann* (Daughters of Ireland) in 1903. In 1908 *Inghinidhe na hÉireann* had launched a monthly magazine, *Bean na hÉireann*, which was edited by Moloney. Arrested for her part in the attack on Dublin Castle on 24 April 1916, she was taken to Ship Street Barracks before being sent to Kilmainham Jail. She was then taken to Aylesbury. She was also reputed to be an excellent markswoman, and proficient with explosives. She was released on 12 December 1916.

Of those sent to Aylesbury for their roles in the Easter Rising, possibly the better known one was Countess Constance de Markievicz. She had been sentenced to hang, but her sentence was commuted to life in prison and she was transferred to Aylesbury in June 1916. Hindsight suggests that the British government only approved the commuting of her sentence because of the furore caused by the execution, in Brussels, of Nurse Edith Cavell on 12 October 1915. She was kept on a separate wing from the others. During the General Amnesty, Markievicz was released on 18 June 1917.

According to Markievicz, Aylesbury was an antiquated rambling building that was damp and gloomy, and surrounded by a thick high wall, where silence was obligatory. In her opinion the food was inadequate; and all it did was to teach her how to steal.

In February 1918, five German women were being held there; one was Millie, the wife of Rupert Rocker, who wrote an account of being an internee at Olympia. She had been sent to Aylesbury in September 1916. At her hearing, she claimed she was being detained there against her will, amongst criminals and prostitutes, 'many of which were suffering from disease, with whom she had to share toilets, baths and crockery.'

AYLSHAM (OS: TG 19- 27-). The Norfolk WAC (C/C10/15–19) informed the Local Government Board that the farmhouse belonging to G. Durrell, at Aylsham, should be utilised to facilitate the PoWs designated for drainage work on the River Bures.

B

BACTON (OS: TG 34- 33-). Norfolk WAC minutes cite, that on his visit of 16 February 1917, Colonel Dawson put a proposed scheme of work for Bacton on hold, as the accommodation at Colling's Farm for the PoWs was found to be unsuitable (C/C10/15–19). A farm, under that name, does not appear on contemporary maps.

BADSEY MANOR (OS: SP 070 434). Badsey Manor stands at the northern end of High Street, on the site of a former retreat for sick monks from Evesham Abbey, Seyne House. After the dissolution of the monasteries in 1545, the house was re-built in the Tudor style, for the Hoby family. Then for many years it served the Wilson family. Prior to the First World War, the building was used as a boy's home. Although subjected to a number of alterations, Sparrow (*A Brief History of Badsey and Aldington*, 1983) states it had a passageway through its middle, wide enough for a horse and cart to pass through, when it housed German PoWs in the First World War. When the PoWs were billeted there the buildings were surrounded by a high fence, and the soldiers that guarded them stayed in the Old School (now the British Legion); their commandant, Lieutenant Stubbs, stayed with the Sparrow family, on Willersey Road. Most of the PoWs worked in the market gardens, some of them being adept basket makers – an important skill, required for getting produce to market, and also for carrying ammunition. Initially employers paid 4d per hour for the labour, of which the prisoner retained 1d. Correspondence in the *Evesham Journal* expressed concern that this was less than the going rate of pay and it was increased to 5d (2p) per hour to avoid a dispute about rate cutting.

The Evesham Journal (February 1918) cited there were 420 PoWs in the district, some of which had just moved into Badsey Manor. It also reported (23 November 1918) that three German PoWs were recaptured at Witney. Billeted at the Badsey Camp they had escaped from a working party at Broadway the previous Thursday.

Cited as being a working camp, its POWIB (1919) code was Dor (Bad) (IWM: Facsimile K4655). It is also cited by the FPHS (1973). It had the TA, Priswarian: Badsey, Evesham (ADM 1/8506/265–120667).

The *Badsey Parish Magazine* (December 1918) reported that the vicar was present at the funeral of Johann Rosskopf, a German soldier. Monsignor Patten officiated at the burial on 16 November 1918, the deceased being a Roman Catholic. German soldiers from the Manor House Camp attended and, at the close of the ceremony, filed past the grave, each casting a handful of earth upon the coffin, according to custom. There were some beautiful wreaths on display, too. Rosskopf's remains were exhumed on 21 February 1963 and moved to the German War Cemetery at Cannock Chase.

After the Second World War, the house was divided into two. According to Phillips (per. comm., 2003), the right hand side of the building was occupied by Dr Dennis Dickenson. It had stained-glass windows, several of which had a 'German theme'.

BAKEWELL (OS: SK 215 686). A report carried by *The Derby Daily Telegraph* (10 July 1918) is the only known evidence that suggests there was an internment camp at Bakewell. One possible location of this camp may have been the local workhouse.

The workhouse was built on 4 acres of land, at Newholme. It was commissioned to accommodate 220 inmates. Built in a Jacobean style, it originally had a central turret above the clock which contained a bell. Completed early in 1841, the workhouse had its own water supply, sourced from a spring. The north wing was converted into a hospital. Infirmary buildings were added, and the property was to be known as The Bakewell Public Assistance Institution in 1930. Since 1948, it has been Newholme Hospital and run by the National Health Service (www.letsgo-bakewell.co.uk).

BALBEGGIE: Tarrylaw Farm (OS: NO 184 293). The POWIB (1919) cites Tarrylaw Farm as the address of this satellite of Auchterarder. Situated near to Balbeggie, its code was Stbs (Au) (Tr) (IWM: Facsimile K4655). Balbeggie is approximately 22 miles to the north of Auchterarder. Balbeggie, not Tarrylaw, is cited by the FPHS (1973).

Now part of a larger concern, Brian Kaye (per. comm., 28 March 2004), the manager of Tarrylaw Farm, is unaware of PoWs being on the farm during the First World War. They would have been there in the second phase when PoWs were utilised outside of their camps.

BALDERSBY PARK (OS: SE 379 763). Based at Home Farm, Baldersby Park, this camp had the POWIB (1919) code Cat (Th) (Bd). Its TA was Priswarian: Home Farm, Baldersby Park, Skipton (ADM 1/8506/265–120667).

According to Page (*A History of the County of York North Riding*, 1923) Baldersby Park was originally called Newby Park and is near to Rainton with Newby. Its name was changed when George Hudson, the Victorian railway magnate, purchased it. He was the Member of Parliament for Sunderland and a Justice of the Peace, who over-extended himself financially before falling from grace. Declared bankrupt, he sold Baldersby Park in 1854.

BALDOCK: The Maltings (OS: TL 251 343). There was a proposal to send seventy-five PoWs to Bygrave in the minutes of the Hertfordshire County Council WAC of 3 October 1917. By 13 November 1917, thirty-five had arrived and a similar number was expected. This later minute also noted 150 PoWs were presently engaged in agricultural work in the county.

A connection to the camp at Bygrave cannot be dismissed, as the minutes of the WAC reported that seventy PoWs were billeted at Baldock by 2 January 1918. A month later another twenty internees had been applied for. By October the number of PoWs had risen to 100, before it dropped to just thirty a year later. Around 100 German PoWs were housed at The Maltings on Royston Road, Baldock; working under supervision, they were allotted to local farmers, to bring in the harvest, and plant spring crops.

The *Baldock News* (December 1976) related a story, told by retired greengrocer Ernie Piper, when he was 80 years old. He remembers being home on leave from the front, in 1917. As he passed by the internment camp one night, he remembers hearing the Germans singing to a piano. Piper reckoned there was not much real danger of the Germans trying to escape, as few of them wished to return to the German trenches.

Baldock was a working camp, with the POWIB (1919) code Pa (Bal) (IWM: Facsimile K4655) and had the TA, Priswarian: Baldock (ADM 1/8506/265–120667).

BALGOWAN (OS: NN 991 226). The POWIB (1919) cites the camp as near to Perth and attached to Auchterarder agricultural depot. It had the code, Stbs (Au) (Bw) (IWM: Facsimile K4655).

It was a custom of the military to name their camps after the nearest railway station, which was not always the name of the nearest place to the camp.

North of the station lay Balgowan House, which has since been demolished, and the land has been developed into an executive housing development. When Thomas Graham (1748–1843), Lord Lynedoch, owned the estates along the River Almond he carried out many experiments in new farming techniques and stock-breeding. A little further north stands Balgowan Home Farm, the most likely site of the camp.

The PoWs may have been involved in forestry work, as there was a sawmill at Balgowan in the latter half of the twentieth century run by Peter McAinsh who also had ties with Balgowan in South Africa. Very little trace of the sawmill remains today.

Balgowan is not recorded by FPHS (1973), but two unexplainable entries, for Balgewah and Balgowen, appear in its listings.

BALGEWAH (OS: n/a). Cited in lists produced for the FPHS (1973) by F.J. Carter and by Alan J. Brown, no location of this name can be found in British Gazetteers. This may be a mis-spelling of Balgowan which is thought to have been a location for PoWs.

BALGOWEN (OS: n/a). Cited in lists produced for the FPHS (1973) by F.J. Carter and by Alan J. Brown. No location of this name can be found in British Gazetteers. This may be a mis-spelling of Balgowan which is thought to have been a location for PoWs. No PoWs can be traced to alternatives, Balgown or Balgownie.

BANBURY: Union Workhouse (OS: SP 448 411). Described as a working camp with the POWIB (1919) code, Dor (Ba) (IWM: Facsimile K4655), it had a satellite at Deddington. It is also cited by the FPHS (1973). Its TA was Priswarian: Banbury (ADM 1/8506/265–120667).

The workhouse was built to a design by Sampson Kempthorne in 1835 to accommodate 300 inmates. The 6-acre site is on the north side of Warwick Road, at Neithrop.

During the First World War, the workhouse was home to some 200 PoWs. They were employed in building the bridge across the Warwick Road and also worked on the Ironstone Railway line.

From 1948 to 1958, the institution – now known as Neithrop Hospital – was part of the NHS. The National Assistance Board then ran it for a further three years. In 1961, the buildings were handed to the hospital's management committee to finance and run. In the mid-1990s, it was a geriatric unit. This was transferred to Horton General Hospital and the now obsolete workhouse was demolished. The site is now used for residential dwellings (www.oxfordshirehealtharchives.nhs.uk).

BANDEATH: Polmaise (OS: NS 850 914). In the directory produced by the POWIB (1919) the entry for Bandeath directs you to Polmaise, where, unfortunately, no entry exists. In keeping with other entries the code could have been, Stbs (Ban) or Stbs (Pol) (IWM: Facsimile K4655). Bandeath is listed by the FPHS (1973).

Today coal mining is no longer the industry it was. The Polmaise Colliery, owned by Archibald Russell Ltd, opened in 1904. It was still viable when a firedamp explosion killed three men in 1934. This resulted in shafts 3 and 4 being declared unsafe to work and they were closed. In 1950, when it was the property of the National Coal Board, a fifth shaft opened. This, along with shafts 1 & 2, closed in 1958. The railway line serving the pit closed in 1986. Around the time the PoWs were working in the area, miners were being laid off from the surrounding collieries. Many sought employment in the construction of a Royal Naval Armaments Depot at Thorsk. On completion, its purpose was to store the vast quantity of unused explosive shells from the returning fleet coming into Rosyth. Any PoWs sent to the area may have been engaged in its construction or worked on its infrastructure. Whatever the internees did, they ceased doing it by 14 December 1918, as the camp closed then.

BARDNEY: Tupholme Hall (OS: TF 174 688). Tupholme Hall, Bardney is cited by the POWIB (1919) as being the site of this agricultural group, a satellite of Bracebridge. The camp's POWIB (1919) code was, Bro (Bbe) (Bc) (IWM: Facsimile K4655). However its TA was Priswarian: Bucknall, Lincoln (ADM 1/8506/265–120667).

In 1536, with the dissolution of many of the monasteries by Henry VIII, the abbey, built for monks of the Premonstratensian Order, at Tupholme, *c.*1155, passed into the hands of Sir Thomas Heneage of Hainton. Heneage built the first hall on the site for his son-in-law, William Willoughby. In 1661, the Vyners of Gautby purchased it. *c.*1720, the hall was replaced by a large farmhouse, which over the next century was extended. In the 1970s the farmhouse lay derelict. *c.*1986, the farmhouse and its buildings were demolished. In 1988, the Heritage Trust of Lincolnshire acquired the land and began extensive restoration work on preserving the abbey's surviving wall.

The POWIB (1919) suggests the PoWs were used for agricultural work. The FPHS (1973) has entries for both Bucknell (sic) and Bardney.

BARKWAY: Newsells Bury (OS: TL 38- 37-). Minutes of the Hertfordshire County Council WAC for 13 February 1918 cite a camp as being formed at Newsells Bury to accommodate thirty-five PoWs. It was later reported that the location was deemed unsatisfactory and the proposed scheme was put into abeyance. On 19 June 1918, the scheme was abandoned in favour of one to be set up at Hare Street, Buntingford.

BARNET (OS: TQ 22- 95). A government directive stating migratory gangs could be established in areas not served by PoWs was issued on 22 June 1918. According to the Hertfordshire County Council WAC such a gang was formed at Barnet. No further evidence has been found to confirm that this camp existed.

BARNSTONE: Langar Hall (OS: SK 720 346). Langar Hall was built in 1837 on the site of a former great historic house, which dated back to *c.*1700, that was the home of

Admiral Lord Howe, hero of the naval victory the 'Glorious First of June', 1794. It stands in quiet seclusion, beside an early English church.

Wright's Trade Directory (1871) cites two halls at Langar. Mr Richard Marriott owned the first. The second, described as the Old Hall, was also reported as being lived in by Richard Marriott. The latter is described as a farmer. They may have been father and son.

Kelly's Trade Directory for 1900 states only one residence, which was not occupied. Later editions state:

1912: The Hall was owned by Harold Bayley, but occupied by Walter Wadsworth.
1925: Percy L. Huskinson occupied the Hall.

Today, Langar Hall is a hotel that specialises in private parties and exclusive bookings. The hall overlooks lovely gardens, ancient trees, and sheep graze in the park. Beyond its croquet lawn is a romantic network of medieval fishponds, stocked with carp.

The POWIB (1919) cite Langar Hall as an agricultural group attached to Plumtree; its code was Bro (Pl) (Bar) (IWM: Facsimile K4655). The camp's TA was, Priswarian: Langar Hall, Barnstone (ADM 1/8506/265–120667). It is also cited in the minutes of the Notts County WAC. According to the minutes of 1918, arrangements were almost complete for PoWs to work at Barnstone Blue Lias Lime Co. Ltd producing agricultural lime.

BARROW IN FURNESS: Biggar Bank (OS: SD 191 660). A working camp at Biggar Bank closed on 10 June 1919. As this is near Barrow in Furness it most probably was the derivation of the FPHS (1973) entry for that town. A report on their visits of inspection to Bigger Bank and North End by Dr A. de Sturler and Monsieur R. de Sturler during June 1919 is held at the National Archives at Kew (FO 383/508).

BARRY (OS: ST 141 678). Barry is perhaps better known for its World War Two camp than this earlier one that appears in *List of British Prison Camps*, produced for the FPHS (1973). It had the TA, Priswarian: Barry (ADM 1/8506/265–120667). It was described as a Civilian Camp; and was to close on 19 June 1918. The camp was situated near where the Old Windmill stood on the Hayes Road. This has succumbed to an industrial estate that now graces the site, on land once used by the chemical industry.

BARTON-LE-CLAY (OS: TL 08- 31-). The names of eleven PoWs that worked at Barton between October 1918 and October 1919, along with their guard, are recorded in an extract taken from the PoWs' employment time sheets held by the Bedfordshire Record Office (WW1/AC/PW/1 & 2).

BASINGSTOKE: Kempshott Park (OS: SU 605 505). Kempshott House was a former hunting lodge of the monarchy. It became a victim of the creation of the M3 motorway in 1965 (www.kempshottmanor.net).

Cited as an agricultural depot, near to Basingstoke, it had the POWIB (1919) code Dor (K P) (IWM: Facsimile K4655). No satellite camps are listed for it. It is also cited by the FPHS (1973), and had the TA, Priswarian: Kempshott House, Basingstoke (ADM 1/8506/265–120667).

Details of the PoWs are unknown, but the camp would have existed in the second phase of internment in Britain during the First World War.

BATH: Combe Down (OS: ST 741 621). Lying to the south of Bath, Combe Down was centred on quarrying for stone. The industry went into decline after 1840. The limestone quarried in this region was used in many of the buildings in Bath – as well as for other important buildings around the United Kingdom including Buckingham Palace.

De Montalt's Mill opened in 1805 and initially produced paper; it had also made cloth before being used by cabinetmakers until 1905 when it closed. The disused mill would have been an ideal base to intern PoWs working in the area. Described as having the TA, Priswarian: Combe Down (ADM 1/8506/265–120667), it was also cited by the FPHS (1973).

Details of the PoWs are unknown, but the camp would have existed in the second phase.

The Mill and its associated buildings were converted to residential use during 2007, with the main mill building being converted into four apartments. The quarries have been in-filled and landscaped.

BEACHLEY & CHEPSTOW: National Shipyards. In a desperate attempt to build more boats for the navy, the government created two national shipyards. The first was at Chepstow. The second was at Beachley. The siting of these yards was heavily criticized and plans to create other shipyards were shelved.

NATIONAL SHIPYARD No. 1: Chepstow (OS: ST 53- 93-). Concerned at the success rate of German *U-Boote* at sinking British ships in August 1917, a government led initiative – in accordance with the Defence of the Realm Act – resulted in the taking over of shipyards at Chepstow, to become National Shipyard No. 1. New slipways were created to increase the rate of British warships brought into service. Mr Noel Peck was appointed the yard's manager. E. Finch and Company was one of the companies taken over. Established as railway bridge builders, they had diversified into shipbuilding. The company can trace its origins back to 1849, with the construction of Brunel's Wye Railway Bridge. In 1925, Fairfield Shipbuilding and Engineering Ltd bought the shipyard and today trade as Fairfield-Mabey Ltd, specialising in steelwork structures (GB 0218 D2025).

The camp's TA was Priswarian: Chepstow (ADM 1/8506/265–120667).

NATIONAL SHIPYARD No. 2: Beachley (OS: ST 546 915). National Shipyard No. 2 was established at Beachley. As 6,000 Royal Engineers were employed laying new slipways, experienced shipyard workers were brought from Tyneside and Clydeside to build the new ships. Camps were built for the workers, along with workshops, a power station and hospital. Sceptical MPs cited the work would have been better allocated to already existing shipyards with proven histories, rather than re-locate hundreds of workers to South Wales. One of the reasons for siting these yards in the estuary of the Severn was that the unions had no control over them. Eight berths were planned, and many of the PoWs were helping to build the slipways as they augmented the construction workers. Thousands of passers-by witnessed them making concrete blocks for the scores of huts required for the incoming shipyard workers and the troops stationed in the area. The internment camp was at, what is now, Sudbury, at the junction of lanes, which was originally called Cingestune.

The internees made several complaints to the Swiss Delegates who visited the camp on 20 September 1918, with regard to the camp's poor water supply. They also expressed concerned about future food supplies. In March 1919, Dr A. de Sturler and

Monsieur R. de Sturler re-visited the camp on behalf of the Swiss Legation (FO 383/507). *The Dundee Evening Telegraph* (16 April 1919) cited there were around 4,000 PoWs working in the National Shipyard at Beachley.

As the war ended the two yards were taken over by the Admiralty, and new garden cities were created at Hardwick, Bulwark, and Pennsylvania. The yards became an emotive issue in the House of Commons (*Hansard*: 10 July 1918). An explanation as to why the yards were placed there initially and the futile attempts to continue with the scheme due to the costs and shortages of skilled men, and of their housing were debated. Servicemen were asked if they were prepared to stay on and work as civilians. After numerous disputes over the wage structure only thirty-six of their number agreed to the new terms. Some 7,000 officers and men were therefore demobilised unconditionally in 1919, and the yards were closed. A year later the local council purchased two of the wooden accommodation huts. They were taken and re-built at Gatehouse, as a public hall, capable of seating some 550 people. The hall was demolished in 1973 to make way for the inner relief road.

The War Office opened a Boys' Technical School, in 1924, which became the Army Technical School in 1929. As many of the instructors were civilians, Pennsylvania Garden City was sold to the local council. At Sedbury the last remaining buildings belonging to the PoW camp can be seen in Grahamstown Road and in Beachley's churchyard there are graves of German and Italian prisoners, presumably, from both World Wars. There were PoWs at Sedbury and Beachley during both World Wars.

It is also cited by the FPHS (1973). Standing outside the usual pyramid chain of administration, its POWIB (1919) code was simply Bch (IWM: Facsimile K4655).

DKF 21: In seinem Inspektion über das Lager Beachley vom 20 September 1918 berichtet der Vertreter der Schutzmacht über die Wasserversorgung: Eine beträchtliche Schwierigkeit ergibt sich indessen in bezug auf die Wasserversorgung. Das Wasser kommt von Chepstow, und die Einrichtung war ursprünglich nicht für den gegenwärtig beträchtlich erhöhten Bedarf gedacht. Die Lagerbehörden, welche den Mangel wohl eingesehen haben, haben alles Erdenkliche getan, um die Sache in Ordnung zu bringen, aber obgleich wiederholt eine vermehrte Versorgung versprochen wurde, ist die erforderliche Arbeit bis jetzt nicht ausgeführt worden. Betreffend die Verpflegung berichtet der Vertreter der Schutzmacht: Die Beschaffenheit der Räucherheringe und der Kartoffeln – neue Kartoffeln sind bisher an die Gefangenen nicht zur Ausgabe gelangt – ist gewiß zweifelhaft. Bei der englischen Regierung wurden Vorstellungen erhoben und insbesondere Einrichtung einer genügenden Wasserversorgung gefordert.

BEAMINSTER (OS: ST 47- 01-). A satellite of Gillingham, its POWIB (1919) code was Dor (Gil) (Bmr) (IWM: Facsimile K4655). The FPHS (1973) cite it too. The camp's TA was, Priswarian: Beominster (ADM 1/8506/265–120667).

Beaminster stands at the head of the Vale of the River Brit. It is cited as an area that has changed little since the advance of the industrial age, its tranquil beauty disturbed only by the turning of the mill wheels. It may that one of these mills, or a large house, may hold the key to the where these PoWs were accommodated.

BEAULY (Lentran & Kiltarlity) (OS: NH 637 439). J.M. MacLennan was a captain in the Highland Light Infantry. At the end of 1916, he was posted to the Prisoners of war Camp at Beauly. He described it as a small working camp with 200 internees engaged in woodcutting. The guard comprised of members of the Royal Defence

Corps, many of whom were 'of the Chelsea Pensioner type'. The camp buildings consisted of typical army huts, with the exception of the Mess.

> The prisoners had seven living huts, together with the usual camp offices, kitchen, hospital, and stores, the whole surrounded by a barbed wire fence 12 feet high. Sentry boxes were built at a height of 6 feet above the ground, and were reached by a wooden stairway in the rear. There was one in each corner of the compound and the main guardroom with two cells at the gate. The Guard buildings were practically identical with those of the prisoners, except that they had no hospital, men of the Guard being treated, when necessary, at the hospital in Inverness.

MacLennan ('A Prisoner of war Camp', *The Army Quarterly* 13, 1927) also cited there was an excellent water supply to the camp. Oil lamps provided lighting in the huts, and 'the compound was illuminated at night by half a dozen acetylene gas flares, which showed up everything almost as clearly as daylight.' As at other camps, the prisoners were responsible for the internal security of the camp. Breakfast was at 7.30am. The working parties paraded at 7.45 and at 8.00 they started work.

There were six men per gang, with one being in charge; their work consisted of cutting, peeling, snedding, and stacking. The work was hard. When MacLennan arrived the PoWs had no incentive to work harder, and as a result their output was poor. They only received a penny per hour, no matter how many trees they felled. When a better pay structure was put in place, the output increased. The scheme was criticised in many quarters for giving the PoWs too much money. In his time there, the record week's pay for one gang was nearly £6, almost £1 per man. Some gangs however were worse off under the new arrangement.

When another sawmill was established outside the camp, many of the big trees could be cut up on the spot. To transport the timber a light bogie railway was constructed that could take timber away from the farthest point of the wood, down to Bunchrew. A loading party at the station then transferred the timber onto awaiting trucks on the Inverness and Ross-shire Railway line (Crawford, www. railscot.co.uk).

McLennan wrote the relationship between the guard and the POWs was 'of the best'. With a few exceptions the internees were decent, kindly fellows, grateful for a kindness, and very willing to help. Once tested, they were allowed some latitude that was never abused. One day a working party returned from the saw mill, to the camp, with their guard, an elderly gentleman missing. One German, a large, fierce looking 'gentleman', had a rifle slung over his shoulder. Visions of the guard being murdered, and the camp being attacked, sprang to mind by the camp's perimeter guards. However, as it transpired, the 'Chelsea Pensioner' was asleep on the cart, and the German merely carrying his rifle. In the camp, there were no Prussian 'sabre-rattlers', the majority were convinced the war was the worst thing that happened to Germany. The Kaiser was not a popular figure with them; instead their idols were the Crown Prince and Hindenburg.

Several concerts were put on for the guard. There were several talented musicians and singers. A number of PoWs made toys in the evenings, which were bought by the camp's guard.

There were attempts to escape. *The Dundee Courier* (21 May 1917) cited three absconders had been re-captured and *The Times* (27 March 1918) reported Auguste Weigardt, who had escaped two days earlier, was also re-captured. MacLennan stated there were two escapes at the camp and was convinced these were to draw attention to disagreements inside the compound.

The entry by the POWIB (1919) cites Lentran and Kiltarlity in the address of the Beauly camp, citing its code as 'Stbs (Be)'. The FPHS (1973) suggest two camps: the first, being Kiltarlity, Beauly; and the other, Lentran. The camp's TA was, Priswarian: Lentran (ADM 1/8506/265–120667).

BEAUMARIS (OS: SH 605 784). By the early part of 1919 a lot of the troops in Britain were being demobbed or moved to other camps as German PoWs moved in. *The North Wales Chronicle* (20 June 1919) reported that fifty German PoWs were employed at Kingsbridge Camp, Llanfaes back-filling trenches, etc. On the Tuesday they had marched through the streets of Beaumaris for exercise, and their appearance created a lot of interest.

Kingsbridge Camp was established as a tented summer camp on Anglesey, in 1902, by the British Army as a training centre for the Royal Engineers, which included infantrymen. The engineers amongst them were taught 'smithy work, carpentry, bridge building and musketry'.

In 1911 the camp was used for training reservists as army engineers, all still housed under canvas.

With the outbreak of the First World War, the Kingsbridge Camp enlarged. Permanent huts began to be erected to accommodate 800 personnel instructed by the Engineers to build pontoon bridges, railways, stockades & wire entanglements. Hundreds of men arrived at the camp for training before going to France. Kingsbridge Camp closed at the end of the First World War.

A visit of inspection to Beaumaris was made by Dr A. de Sturler and Monsieur R. de Sturler during June 1919 (FO 383/508).

BECKENHAM (OS: TQ 379 680). A working camp, its POWIB (1919) code was Fe (Bek) (IWM: Facsimile K4655). It was also cited by the FPHS (1973). Local knowledge suggests there were officers interned at Langley Court, but this does not correlate to the POWIB (1919) description of the camp.

Langley Farm covered about 250 acres. The farm buildings were demolished in 1886, to be replaced by Langley Court. The architect was James Barnett, of Beckenham. Until 1910 the house was occupied by James Loyd Bucknall, and it was taken over in 1920 by the Wellcome Foundation Laboratories when they moved from Brockwell Park. Extensive premises for medical research had been added before the site was sold in the 1990s for re-development, when the gated Park Langley Estate was built.

BEE CRAIGS (Beecraigs) (OS: NS 996 759). Beecraigs Country Park, consisting of 913 acres, stands on the edge of the Bathgate Hills, near to the town of Linlithgow.

Long before the park was established, it was decided to build a reservoir at Beecraigs, to serve the local community, and it was estimated that the work would take two years to complete. Local limestone was to be used in its construction. The start of the work coincided with the start of the First World War and due to a lack of materials and manpower the work was put into abeyance. German PoWs were then directed to complete the project. However the work was not completed by the time they had to be repatriated. The *West Lothian Courier* (9 January 1920) reported that the work of constructing the reservoir was very slow, mainly due to a shortage of materials. It was suggested there was no hope of it being completed before the end of the year. In more recent times the reservoir has been used as a trout farm.

Local knowledge suggested Beecraigs was a tented encampment. It appears in the list produced for the FPHS (1973).

Horne (*The German Connection – The German Newspaper 1916–1919*, 1988) cited there were work camps at Grantham, Dalmellington, Kinlochleven, Glendevon, Crawford, Dawyck, Lentran, Nethy Bridge, Raasay, Hairmyres, Penstone (sic), Inverkeithing, Port Clarence, Catterick and Bee Craigs.

DKF 30: In den Lagern von Rosyth, Eastgate, Uppingham, Belton Park, Tern Hill, Bee Craigs, Hadnall, Sutton Veny, Larkhill, Fovant, Withley (sic) *und Radford sind die Kriegsgefangenen in Zelten untergebracht.*

BELAUGH PARK (Sedge Fen) (OS: TG 291 177). According to the minutes of the Norfolk WAC it was suggested 150 PoWs be divided amongst three new camps being established in Norfolk, in October 1917. The sites chosen were at Belaugh, Elmham Park and Neatherd Moor (C/C10/16).

In an area sometimes referred to as Sedge Fen stands *Hoveton Steam Mill*, which has also been known as Belaugh Mill. The 1891 Ordnance Survey Map refers to it as a flourmill. The FPHS (1973) list a camp at Sedge Fen.

BELTON PARK (see Grantham).

BERKHAMSTED (OS: SP 844 274). Described as a satellite of Hemel Hempstead; its POWIB (1919) code was Pa (Hem) (Bk). It was also cited by the FPHS (1973). The first time it was cited was in the minutes of the Hertfordshire County Council WAC, on 1 October 1918, when it was reported that thirty-five internees were *in situ*, but the camp's location is unknown.

BERKSWELL: Hampton in Arden (OS: SP 24- 79-). Berkswell is described as a working camp with the POWIB (1919) code, Dor (Ber). Berkswell is not cited by the FPHS (1973), but nearby Hampton in Arden is. It had the TA, Priswarian: Hampton in Arden (ADM 1/8506/265–120667). The Warwickshire WAC minutes record a PoW camp had been set up at Berkswell by 20 April 1918, but did not state the actual location.

BIDSTON (OS: SJ 28- 90-). Sargeaunt (*The Isle of Man and the Great War*, 1922) wrote, on 27 November 1915 the 2nd Manx Service Company was formed; 160 men left the island on 6 March 1915, to undergo rigorous training at Bidston Camp, near Birkenhead. Farrant (*Ellan Vannin*, 1928) explains, on arriving they were transferred to the 16th (King's) Liverpool Regiment, which on completion of their training was converted into the 2nd Company of the Cheshire Regiment, and left England on 2 January 1916 bound for Salonica.

It may be that this camp was later used to house the PoWs cited by the FPHS (1973) as being at Bidston, Cheshire. In March 1919, Dr A. de Sturler and Monsieur R. de Sturler visited the camp on behalf of the Swiss Legation (FO 383/507).

BIGGAR BANK (see Barrow in Furness).

BIGGLESWADE (see Old Warden).

BILLERICAY: Union Workhouse (OS: TQ 676 950). A working camp, its POWIB (1919) code was Pa (Bill) (IWM: Facsimile K4655). It was also cited by the FPHS

(1973). Located in the Union Workhouse, its TA was Priswarian: Billericay (ADM 1/8506/265–120667).

A new workhouse was built in Billericay in 1840 to the designs of George Gilbert Scott and William Bonython Moffatt. The main entrance was on Grey Lady Place. After 1930, the workhouse became Billericay Public Assistance Institution managed by Essex County Council. Under the National Service it became St Andrew's Hospital in 1948. In 1975 it was granted Grade II Listed building status. It closed in 1998 and underwent redevelopment for residential use.

Mary Needham was born 1908. Her father was the master of Billericay Workhouse and her mother was superintendent of the hospital. In a taped interview (16 July 1986), held by Essex Record Office, she talked about events at the workhouse in *c.*1914. A synopsis of the tape makes no reference to PoWs (SA 24/1595/1).

BILLINGFORD (OS: TM 167 786). The camp is reported to be at Maltings near to Diss. A prompt reply, to a request from the Norfolk WAC, to billet PoWs at Billingford Maltings, was sought on 7 September 1918. Its response was not noted.

Billingford is cited by the FPHS (1973), as was Scocles. This was probably meant to be Scole, near Diss. Its TA was Priswarian, Billingford, Scole (ADM 1/8506/265–120667). A report on their visit of inspection to Billingford by Dr A. de Sturler and Monsieur R. de Sturler, during April and May 1919 is held at the National Archives at Kew (FO 383/507).

BILLINGHAM (OS: NZ 454 241). In an attempt to replicate Germany's Haber-Bosch ammonia-making process, the Ministry of Munitions constructed a purpose-built plant in Billingham without being certain of what was required. This resulted in very little infrastructure being put into place, the original site only consisted of 'Tibbersley Grange', two stores, a collection of mixed wooden huts and a number of dumps of material. Brunner Mond Ltd acquired the plant after the war, and in 1926 it was to become a part of Imperial Chemical Industries group.

Parke (*Billingham: The First Ten Years*, 1957) provides an insight into the work done by PoWs sent to the area. Three roadways serving the plant were reputedly built with German PoW labour. The first was nothing more than an ash path; the second, recorded on plant drawings as Road No. 7, was for many years known by locals as 'The German Road'; and the third, again no more than a path, linked the other two. Presumably, the German internees were accommodated in some of the wooden huts that adorned the site. The work would have been done in the second phase of internment camps. JPHP Consultants of Billingham state that Victor E. Parke was an employee at the plant for a number of years, his station being that of Intelligence Officer.

What connection, if any, to the camp at Port Clarence has not been established.

BILSBY (OS: TF 46- 76-). The Society for Lincolnshire History and Archaeology suggests Bilsby had a military use it cannot fully explain. No visible remains of a camp exist but it was suggested that the site might have been the location of an internment camp. The society also suggested Brigg, Potterhanworth and Usselby Hall as other possible locations for internment camps, though not necessarily all from the First World War.

Any PoWs sent to Bilsby would have been in the second phase of camps.

BILSTON (see Ettingshall).

BINEGAR: Gurney Slade (OS: ST 61- 49-). A satellite of Shepton Mallet, Binegar had the POWIB (1919) code Dor (Sh M) (Bin) (IWM: Facsimile K4655). It is also cited by the FPHS (1973). It had the TA, Priswarian: Gurney Slade (ADM 1/8506/265–120667). Nothing is known of this camp, but the area has a history of stone quarrying, which may have utilised this pool of labour in the second phase of camps that were set up.

BINGLEY POLICE STATION (OS: SE 110 390). *The Yorkshire Herald* (9 August 1914) reported interned men were being held at the police station in Bingley. This was presumably a short-term measure, until new accommodation could be found for them.

BIRMINGHAM: HALLING (OS: SP 35- 82-). There is no Halling recorded in the Birmingham area, so the OS Grid Reference for Hall Green has been used. Cited only by the FPHS (1973), the most probable location for this camp is Halling, in Kent, where it is known PoWs worked at the Lee Cement Works.

BIRMINGHAM: NORTHFIELD – LONGBRIDGE PARK (OS: SP 003 784). Described as a working camp with the POWIB (1919) code, Dor (Nfd), it had an agricultural group attached to it: that of Clent. Northfield is also cited by the FPHS (1973). Cited by the HO as being at Longbridge Park, Northfield, its TA was Priswarian: Northfield (ADM 1/8506/265–120667).

Any connection to the 1st Southern General Hospital at Rubery Hill has not been established. But the hospital's administrators reminded Birmingham City Council of their obligation – as intimated by Army Council Instruction No. 1319 (1917) – to mark the grave of a German soldier interred at Lodge Hill Cemetery. It was resolved on 24 September 1917 (Minute 6305) that a memorial stone or cross, similar to that put on graves of our own countrymen, be put over his grave.

The camp closed on 22 January 1919.

BIRMINGHAM: MONKSPATH – SHIRLEY (OS: SP 14- 76-). *Derby Daily Telegraph* (13 July 1918) reported that a Birmingham Committee of the Workers' Union had forwarded a resolution to the Prime Minister protesting the actions of the Petrol Committee in allowing the use of petrol for conveying German PoWs about the city, when men returning from the front were obliged to wait at local railway centres from midnight until 5.00am without any means of transport to their homes. This article was in response to volunteer motorists having their petrol permits revoked, after undertaking to taxi men home as they arrived in the city. As to which camp (or camps) the PoWs were based was not stated in the newspaper article.

Although the Monkspath camp is recorded, its actual location has been lost in time. There was a racecourse at nearby Shirley, which may have been the site of the camp. A minute of the Warwickshire WAC records a camp at Shirley, which was operational by 20 April 1918. Its location was not cited.

Carter & Brown both cite Shirley and Monkspath in their FPHS (1973) listings. Monkspath had the POWIB (1919) code Dor (Mpa) (IWM: Facsimile K4655). Its TA was cited as *Priswarian: Monkspath* (ADM 1/8506/265–120667).

There was a camp at the Ice Rink, in Shirley, near Southampton, which should not be confused with this camp.

BIRMINGHAM: SOHO POOL (OS: SP 058 881). A working camp in Birmingham, it had the POWIB (1919) code Dor (Soh) (IWM: Facsimile K4655). It is also cited by the FPHS (1973). Its TA was Priswarian: Soho Pool, Hookley (sic), Birmingham (ADM 1/8506/265–120667).

It is thought the camp stood on railway sidings in the Hockley district of Birmingham, which was part of the Soho spur serving New Street Station. The sidings were built on what was formerly a pond, or pool, from which Matthew Boulton's engineering factory drew its water until *c.*1860. When open it was the largest factory of its kind in the world.

BISHOPS STORTFORD: Oak Hall (OS: TL 484 219). Hertfordshire's WAC minutes indicate accommodation for 120 PoWs had been sought for a scheme, based at Oak Hall. The War Office did not pass the plan, suggesting it would be too expensive to adopt, as the scheme only warranted forty men in their opinion. A second scheme, however, was approved for Oak Hall on 20 March 1918 that was awaiting a report from the Engineers Department before any other developments could take place. On 8 May 1918, the scheme was still in abeyance, but had opened by 1 October 1918, when a minute cited sixty PoWs had been allocated.

It is cited by the FPHS (1973). Its TA was Priswarian: Oak Hall, Bishops Stortford (ADM 1/8506/265–120667).

BLACKWELL (see Carlisle Racecourse).

BLAISDON (OS: SO 728 160). Although described by the POWIB (1919) as being an agricultural depot it had no satellite units attached to it; its code was Dor (Bla) (IWM: Facsimile K4655). The FPHS (1973) also cites this camp, which had the TA, Priswarian: Blaisdon. The camp closed on 5 February 1919.

The most likely location of this camp was near Northwood Green, at Grange Court where it is recorded German internees worked at a hay store. It was also cited that winter lodgings were required for a hundred internees and thirty-five guards. Gloucester Gaol was suggested. A later entry suggests the internees were no longer at the hay store as twenty-two girls were guarding the hay depot at Grange Court Station, Westbury (D37/1/182 & 199).

Nearby is Newnham, which is cited only by the FPHS (1973).

BLANDFORD CAMP (OS: ST 933 082). The PoW Camp at Blandford Camp was established adjacent to a wooded area called Cuckoo Clump on the eastern side of a naval camp. It is approximately 1 mile southwest of Tarrant Monkton. A 1902 map shows the area as Blandford Race Course (disused). A second camp was set up at Milldown, near to Blandford's town centre.

The navy opened the first camp on 27 November 1914. Timber, intended for construction of the camp, was used to improve the surface of the approach road from Blandford Station; traction engines bringing materials got bogged down in the lanes to the camp site. More troops arrived shortly after to find their lines were not ready so they had to be billeted out in the surrounding villages, whilst Major-General Paris and his staff occupied Stud House, at Pimperne. When operational, the camp had three main groups of huts, A1–A4, B1–B4 and C1–C4. Each section had twelve to sixteen barrack huts, plus ablution blocks and stores huts. Duckboard walkways were laid.

Harfield states (*Blandford and the Military*, 1984) the naval personnel were organised into two brigades. The Royal Marines left Blandford for Plymouth on 1 Feb 1915.

Then, on 28 February 1915, the majority of the men left by train, bound for Avonmouth. Blandford then became a depot

Blandford is listed by the POWIB (1919) as a working camp under Dorchester. A former parent camp, the downgrading occurred on 22 September 1918, according to a HO document (October 1918). The first visit to the camp, by neutral observers, took place on 30 March 1917. The Swiss visitors reported there were 1,378 men interned in thirty-four huts. These were all combatants. 680 of them were mostly employed in engineering activities, including motor repairs, electrical work, blacksmithing, plumbing, and working at the sawmill. Another 200 worked in agriculture. There had been twenty escape attempts in the previous twelve months. Before being downgraded, the camps at Yatesbury and Castle Bromwich were attached to it. Both subsequently came under Dorchester. Prisoners were employed on duties within the camps and also hired out to farmers. In 1917 the rates of pay were 4d per hour for labourers and 9d per day for the cook. In 1918 the rates for labourers had risen by one penny an hour.

During the influenza outbreaks of 1918 and 1919, four died at the Naval PoW camp. Their names were not recorded. They were buried at Tarrant Monkton. There were also deaths reported at the Milldown camp.

The Times (16 August 1918) reported two men, identified as Christopher and Heinz, had escaped on 8 August. They were re-captured.

The Times (13 February 1919) reported forged banknotes had been found at Bramley. The forgeries were thought to have emanated from Blandford.

In mid-1918 the RAF took over the camp. The PoWs were then moved out of their huts and put under canvas. In 1919 the RAF moved out. A railway branch line was laid in 1918, but was closed to traffic at the end of 1919. It re-opened in 1920 to remove material and stores. The camp was demolished in 1920 and the railway was removed in 1928.

On their visit of inspection to Blandford and Milldown in the spring of 1919, Dr A. de Sturler and Monsieur R. de Sturler created a report, held at the National Archives at Kew (FO 383/432).

When the Home Office created its first directory for 1918, Blandford Naval Camp was cited as a parent camp, which had the TA, Priswarian, Blandford Naval Camp (ADM 1/8506/265/120667). In a supplementary list issued later that year it stated the camp's status had changed to that of a working camp on 22 September 1918.

BLANDFORD: Mill Down (OS: ST 29- 78-). Also referred to as Milldown, it was a working camp, with the POWIB (1919) code, Dor (Mi) (IWM: Facsimile K4655). Its TA was Priswarian: Mill Down, Blandford (ADM 1/8506/265–120667). It is also cited by the FPHS (1973).

Those interned at Mill Down cited it as a tented camp. They complained that the water supply was insufficient for their needs as they were expected to wash at three troughs in the open. The kitchens too were cited as being unhygienic.

In a letter, written by Dr Beattie on 30 May 1917, there is a reference that 'nearly 500 Germans PoWs' were being kept in a camp near Blandford. He also noted an overheard dialogue between a guard and a PoW. When taunted as to how he liked being a prisoner, the internee replied that it was not he who was the prisoner, but him. Apparently, this reply had struck a poignant cord with Beattie, as he finished his quote by saying 'and after all it is quite true.'

On their visit of inspection to Blandford and Milldown during in the spring of 1919, Dr A. de Sturler and Monsieur R. de Sturler created a report, held at the National Archives at Kew (FO 383/432)

There were also camps at the nearby naval base and at Crichel.

DKF 33: In Upavon, Milldown, Corton (Dorset), und Hendon (Middlesex) waren die Gefangenen noch weiterhin in Zelten untergebracht. In Milldown und Hendon war die Beleuchtung mangelhaft, in Corton fehlte sie ganz. Für die in Bergwerken beschäftigten Gefangenen im Lager Corton sind die drei Wannen Gänzlich unzureichend, die Wannen stehen im Freien. In Milldown und Upavon war die Wasserzufuhr unzulänglich.

DKF 34: In Milldown und Upavon war die Wasserzufuhr unzulänglich. Die in den Lagern Upavon, Milldown und Corton als Küchen benutzten offenen Schuppen waren durchaus unhygienisch.

BLETCHLEY: Watling Street (OS: SP 865 349). Herbert Samuel Leon was a financier in the City of London who bought over 300 acres of land with two farms at Bletchley in 1883. He transformed one farmhouse and 60 acres into a country estate, Bletchley Park. In 1911, Leon had been awarded a baronetcy. On his death in 1926, Leon's widow, Lady Fanny, continued to live on the estate until she died in 1937.

During the First World War, an internment camp was established in Watling Street on part of the Bletchley Estate. A satellite of Leighton Buzzard's agricultural depot, it had the POWIB (1919) code Pa (L B) (By) (IWM: Facsimile K4655). Its TA was Priswarian: Bletchley (ADM 1/8506/265–120667). The FPHS (1973) cite this camp too.

Prior to the commencement of the Second World War, Captain Faulkner bought the estate with the intention of building houses on it. But before his vision materialised the Foreign Office acquired the site, and in 1938 created an annex to its Government Code and Cipher School. This happened because of political unrest on mainland Europe at that time.

The Bombe, a deciphering machine, was created at Bletchley Park. It greatly reduced the time required to break encrypted messages conveyed by Germany's Enigma machine, devised to send instructions to its predatory submarine fleet that threatened the British supply chain across the Atlantic in the Second World War. Colossus, the world's first working electronic computer, was also created in Bletchley Park.

This camp would probably have been active in the second phase of internment camps when PoWs labour was being utilised into work programmes.

BLETSOE (OS: TL 027 585). Private W. O'Hagan was cited as assisting the foreman at Bletsoe, in an extract taken from the PoWs' employment time sheets held by Bedfordshire Record Office (WW1/AC/PW/1 & 2).

This camp would probably have been active in the second phase of internment camps when PoWs labour was being utilised into work programmes.

BLICKLING MILL (OS: TG 163 303). The Norfolk WAC informed the Local Government Board that Blickling Mill could be utilised to facilitate PoWs designated to carry out drainage work on the River Bures. This camp would probably have been active in the second phase of internment camps when PoWs labour was being utilised into work programmes. The mill stands near to Itteringham, which is approximately 3 miles from Blickling Hall and dates back to *c.*1612 (C/C10/15–19).

BLOFIELD LODGE (OS: TG 335 104). It was thought by the Norfolk WAC that Blofield Lodge would make a suitable location to accommodate PoWs, and the Eastern Command approved its use (C/C10/18).

This camp would probably have been active in the second phase of internment camps when PoWs labour was being utilised into work programmes.

BLUNHAM (OS: TL 154 514). The POWIB (1919) cite the code for this camp as Pa (Bh) (IWM: Facsimile K4655). The FPHS (1973) cite this camp was at Blunham Sands (sic), Beds. Its TA was Priswarian: Blunham (ADM 1/8506/265–120667).

A farmer with local knowledge believes the camp was in a field, near to where Pound Close is today, just off the High Street.

Northampton Mercury (24 October 1919) cited PoWs, working on the River Ivel, in north Bedfordshire, went on strike on Sunday. Work was held up while they were confined to their barracks. Blunham stands on the River Ivel.

A wild flower not normally native to Britain grows at Blunham. Local legend says it came from Belgium, brought back in the hooves of the horses which came back from the front.

BLYTH (OS: SK 624 857). According to the minutes of the Notts County WAC there was a migratory gang at Blyth. Migratory gangs were small units leased to a group of farmers to mainly prepare the fields or gather in the harvests in the second phase of internment camps.

This camp is believed to have been near to Blyth Hall, which was built by Edward Melish *c.*1750. Like the camp that housed the PoWs, the hall in recent times has disappeared from the horizon.

BODDAM: nr Peterhead (OS: NK 132 424). The most likely candidature for work done by the PoWs in this area would have been the quarries of Longhaven or Bullers o' Buchan. Some may have been utilised at RNAS Longside's upkeep. When the station was being built, PoW labour was not being utilised in the UK, therefore when Jim Hughes (*A Steep Turn To See Stars*, 1991) makes no reference to PoWs being involved in its construction, it comes as no surprise. He wrote that the Aberdonian firm of Tawse undertook the task in 1915, constructing the base to house rigid framed airships. 'Thousands of Irish and Scottish navvies laboured night and day digging out the peat ...' The new station was named RNAD Lenabo, which in turn became RNAS Longside. The base was unlike most of the other wartime built military establishments – 'Longside was built to stand for eternity.' The powerhouse, gasworks, water works, steam generators, engineering workshops, canteens, cinema, church, messes and living quarters were all built of bricks made at Cruden Bay, a few miles to the south. The camp's perimeter was a steel spiked fence with a main entrance adorned with pseudo classical pillars. The largest buildings on the station were three airship sheds, which at 100 feet high would have dominated the Buchan skyline. The station was put there to protect Scapa Flow.

A branch line on the Formantine and Buchan Railway which was 3 miles long served the air station from 1915 until it was dismantled in 1919.

The first naval personnel arrived at Longside in the autumn of 1915, and it remained operational until the time of the Armistice. By the beginning of 1919 most of the airships had been deflated and sold, and the manpower rapidly dispersed. After the war, the station was taken over by the RAF on a care and maintenance basis, but as Longside could not be adapted for conventional aircraft, the camp was offered for redevelopment. As there were no takers the site was given to the Forestry Commission. They planted conifers over the whole area that have now enveloped the remains of the base. The only proof that a camp was at Boddam appears in the form of entries in the POWIB (1919) directory and the FPHS (1973) list. The former cites the camp's code as Stobs (Bdm) (IWM: Facsimile K4655). Listed as a working camp; its address is cited as Peterhead, Aberdeenshire. PoWs were used in other locations to help manoeuvre airships.

Nearby Stuartfield housed PoWs in the Second World War. Perhaps this camp could also have housed the internees sent to Boddam in the First World War. Vacated accommodation of the civilian workforce that built the Longside base in 1915 could have been used to house the internees sent to Boddam *c.*1917.

BODMIN: HM Prison (OS: SX 063 674). Archival documents record Captain Hans von Bauchhaupt, Naval-Leutnant Kurt Gebeschus, Major Ludwig Schrott and Major Rudolf Lorenz Bauer were being detained in Bodmin Prison as a retaliatory measure to Captain Bate, Major Bell, Major Higginson and Lt Lamble being held in Spandau Prison (FO 383/295).

Bodmin Prison was designed by Sir John Call. It was built in 1779 to hold the men that built it, French prisoners of war, and was operational for 150 years before closing in 1927.

When the Debtors Act of 1869 abolished imprisonment for debt, many prisons became under-utilized. The Admiralty then occupied an entire wing of the building for the incarceration of its naval prisoners until 1922.

During the First World War part of the prison was sealed off and was used to store the Domesday Book and the Crown Jewels.

BOLDER EAST (see East Boldre).

BOLSOVER CASTLE (OS: SK 471 707). *The Derbyshire Times* reported:

> The Chesterfield War Agricultural Executive met at the Hotel Portland on Saturday. The members present being Messrs ... It was reported that a scheme was to be arranged to organise the existing threshing sets in the district in order that the extra work by the upcrease in the area of arable land might be coped with. The Committee were informed that it was likely after all that camps of PoWs would be established at Bolsover Castle and Hasland Hall.

The need for labour in Derbyshire, in 1918, is described thus:

> General Chandos-Pole-Gell presided at a meeting of the Derbyshire War Agricultural Executive Committee on Wednesday, when the questions of labour and organisation were considered. With regard to labour, it was stated that the Government held firmly to the claim of over 550 men, who will be posted to the Colours by June 30. The committee keenly regretted this decision. It was felt that the result upon labour in this county would be disastrous, and it was resolved to set up a tribunal to consider agricultural cases, commencing on Monday next.

There were already camps for internees at Ashbourne, Bretby, and Burton, and, according to *The Derby Daily Telegraph* (8 June 1918), good reports had been received concerning these. Internees for camps in Willington, Denby, and Ilkeston were being sought. Danish labourers were also being brought to this country. The committee also considered, at length, horse and tractor schemes.

The POWIB (1919) directory has no entry for Sheffield agricultural depot, but the entry for Bolsover cites it as its satellite. The camp's TA was Priswarian: Bolsover, Chesterfield (IWM: Facsimile K4655).

The present castle dates back to 1616, being rebuilt by Sir Charles Cavendish. He died before the project was completed and it was his son, William, who completed it.

BOROUGHBRIDGE (OS: SE 39- 66-). Boroughbridge AG had the POWIB (1919) directory code Cat (Th) (Bor) (IWM: Facsimile K4655). Its code defines it as an agricultural group attached to Catterick through Thirsk. A HO document cites the camp's TA was Priswarian: Boroughbridge. Although the actual location of the camp is unknown, the timeframe that this camp would probably have been active was in the second phase of internment camps when PoW labour was being utilised into work programmes.

BOSMERE & CLAYDON (OS: TM 124 512). When the Bosmere and Claydon Poor Law Union was created in 1835 it adopted and refurbished the House of Industry buildings that had been built some sixty years before. Its isolation hospital stood at the end of Pesthouse Lane.

During the First World War PoWs were billeted in the workhouse. It was an agricultural group attached to Haughley AD with the code Pa (Hgy) (Cn) (IWM: Facsimile K4655). It is also cited by the FPHS (1973). It is believed the buildings lay dormant until the Second World War when Italian prisoners of war were interned in it. The buildings again lay empty until being demolished in 1963 partly to allow the widening of the A14.

BOSTON: Boston Dock (OS: TF 333 430). There are several references in the British press to Boston's port being used to ship out wounded PoWs, and in turn to receive British soldiers back from internment in Germany. Late in 1917 discussions began between Britain and Germany to exchange prisoners that would have no further involvement in the war, such as those who had been blinded or severely wounded. Holland, a neutral country, was chosen as the place to do the exchange. After much debate Boston was finally agreed upon as the English port of entry and departure for those to be exchanged. A bonus for Boston was that it received no more Zeppelin raids. The first exchange took place in January 1918, with 235 injured soldiers and 370 civilians being brought to the dock. A similar number of Germans were returned. More exchanges followed and everything proceeded smoothly until May 1918 when a Dutch ship was sunk on the return trip. This resulted in no further exchanges for three months as arguments ensued as to whether it was mined or had been torpedoed by a German *U-Boot*. Three more trips were made before the Armistice was called. In total over 5,000 civilians and wounded from both sides were exchanged.

Panayi (*The Enemy in Our Midst, Germans in Britain during the First World War*, 1991) also refers to civilians, of German or Austrian extraction, being deported from Boston.

The POWIB (1919) directory cites there was a camp for civilian internees at Boston Dock. That camp's code was Bro (Bos) (IWM: Facsimile K4655). Its TA was Priswarian: Boston (ADM 1/8506/265–120667). Reports on visits of inspection to PoW camps at Stainby, Boston Dock, and King's Lynn are held at the National Archives at Kew (FO 383/432). The FPHS (1973) cites both Boston, Lincs. and Boston Dock, Lincs. in its *List of British Prison Camps*.

BOUGH BEECH: Penshurst (OS: TQ 484 469). The camp's TA is cited as Priswarian: Penshurst (ADM 1/8506/265–120667). The same document gives its address as the White House, Bough Beech. A working camp, its POWIB (1919) code was Pa (Pst) (IWM: Facsimile K4655). This camp would probably have been active in the second phase of internment camps when PoWs labour was being utilised into work programmes. It was also cited by the FPHS (1973). Bough Beech lies approximately 3 miles to the north-east of Penshurst.

BOURN (OS: TL 325 565). A minute of the Cambridgeshire WAC (3 June 1918) cited that Mr Williams had undertaken to summer fallow land, on Barrance Farm, to the satisfaction of the Committee. It was further agreed that the ditches required attention, and that PoWs could be employed to do this work.

BOVINGTON CAMP (OS: SY 83- 89-). A working camp, it had the POWIB (1919) code Dor (Bv) (IWM: Facsimile K4655). Bovington is cited by the FPHS (1973), as is Lulworth, which also has strong military connections. It may be any internment camps would have been incorporated into the infrastructure of these army camps. Bovington had the TA Priswarian: Bovington, Poole (ADM 1/8506/265–120667).

Lea (per. comm., 2008) cites during the First World War Bovington Camp was developed as a tank-training centre. As a result a single-track branch line over 2 miles in length was constructed in 1918 by around 100 men from the Military Works Company of the Royal Engineers; German PoWs assisted them. The branch line from Wool to Bovington Camp lasted just ten years and was taken up in 1936.

BOWITHICK (OS: SX 18- 82-). Bowithick had the TA Priswarian: Bowithick, Altarnum, Launceston (ADM 1/8506/265–120667), and was also cited by the FPHS (1973).

Those interned at Bowithick claimed that lice infested the camp, and requests to have it disinfected were being ignored. The internees were also dissatisfied by the opportunity to hold church services, and believed that too much work was being demanded of them.

This camp would probably have been active in the second phase of internment camps when PoW labour was being utilised into work programmes.

DKF 31: In Bowithick muß gründliche Desinfizierung des gangen Lagers, zur Behebung der Läuseplage, Sofort gefordert werden.

DKF 31: Auch in Loch Doon, auf der Insel Raasay, in Newlandside, Ceal Aston (sic) *Sutton Veney* (sic), *Bowithick, Netheravon, Yatesbury, Rovrah* (sic), *Port Clarence und Hayrmyres* (sic) *werden die Leute zu sehr ausgenutzt.*

DKF 32: Die Katholiken in Wackerley (sic) *und Bowithick haben noch keine Gelegenheit zur Abhaltung Messen.*

BRACEBRIDGE (OS: SK 96- 68-). Referred to as Bracebridge Agricultural Depot by the POWIB (1919), it had six groups attached to it: Stow Park; Somerby Hall; Burton Hall; Glentham; Bucknall; and Coningsby. Its POWIB (1919) code was Bro (Bbe) (IWM: Facsimile K4655). It also had the TA Priswarian: Bracebridge (ADM 1/8506/265–120667). This camp would probably have been active in the second phase of internment camps when PoW labour was being utilised into work programmes. Bracebridge is also cited by the FPHS (1973).

The location of the camp is unknown. It was possibly connected to the army's flying establishment at Bracebridge Heath, which opened in 1916. RAF Waddington (OS: SK 982 630) was initially a flying training base belonging to the Royal Flying Corps. It was to close in 1920, but became operational again in 1926. Today, it fulfils two roles: it responds to early warning alerts, and it is used by NATO aircraft.

Another possible site for this camp may have been in the grounds of the mental hospital at Bracebridge Heath.

BRACKLEY (OS: SP 579 372). Brackley was a working camp; it had the POWIB (1919) code Pa (Br) (IWM: Facsimile K4655). This camp would probably have been active in the second phase of internment camps when PoW labour was being utilised into work programmes. It had the TA Priswarian: Brackley (ADM 1/8506/265–120667).

The probability that the camp was at the local cottage hospital is slight. A better solution would have been the town's workhouse, which stood off Banbury Road. It closed in the 1930s but is still shown on later maps. Today Westhill Housing Estate, built in the 1950s, graces the site.

BRADFORD ABBAS (OS: ST 584 145). An agricultural group that was a satellite of Gillingham, in Dorset, its POWIB (1919) code was Dor (Gil) (Brd) (IWM: Facsimile K4655). It is also cited by the FPHS (1973). It had the TA Priswarian: Bradford Abbas (ADM 1/8506/265–120667). This camp would probably have been active in the second phase of internment camps when PoW labour was being utilised into work programmes.

This camp should not be confused with Army barracks at Bradford Moor, Yorkshire, which may have held civilians at the start of the war.

BRADFORD MOOR CAVALRY & INFANTRY BARRACKS (OS: SE 185 336). Jackson (*The Prisoners 1914–1918*, 1989) cites Bradford Moor was a temporary camp at the start of the war. His claim may be supported by *The Yorkshire Herald* (9 August 1914) which states that men from Shipley who had been arrested under the Defence of the Realm Act were taken to an undisclosed location in Bradford.

A local directory, published in 1912, indicates No. 5 Depot, Royal Field Artillery was based at the Bradford Moor Barracks. A second directory, published in 1916, shows the Army Service Corps was based there.

At the onset of the hostilities there was no provision for accommodating internees. Instances of army camps having sections cordoned off, and used until other arrangements were made, are recorded. It may be that Bradford Moor Barracks was used in this way. As a temporary camp, it perhaps lasted only a short period of time until more appropriate accommodation was forthcoming. The site of the barracks, off Leeds Old Road, has long since been re-developed, and now forms part of a housing estate.

Later in the war, there was a camp at Bradford Abbas that had no connection to this camp.

BRAEMORE (see Loch Broom).

BRAILES: Springfield House (OS: SP 307 395). Described as a satellite of Chipping Norton, its POWIB (1919) code was Dor (C N) (Bri) (IWM: Facsimile K4655). The camp's address was stated as Springfield House. Its TA is Priswarian: Springfield House, Brailes (ADM 1/8506/265–120667). Brailes is also cited by the FPHS (1973).

The minutes of the Warwickshire WAC record the PoW camp had been set up at Brailes by 20 April 1918. Alfred Woodward (*Memories of Brailes*, n.d.) cites a photograph that exists, showing some PoWs standing outside Springfield House.

The Diocesan Registrar was able to show a Faculty granted on 22 November 1961 to the Commonwealth War Graves Commission to have the remains of W. Kilper (d. 10 May 1919) exhumed from the graveyard at Brailes, to be re-interred at the new German War Cemetery at Cannock Chase (Rotherham & Co., Coventry).

BRAMLEY (OS: SU 655 595). This camp had the POWIB (1919) code Brm (IWM: Facsimile K4655). The FPHS (1973) cite it too. The camp's TA was Priswarian: Bramley (ADM 1/8506/265–120667).

As a result of a meeting that took place between 'men in dark suits' on 14 May 1917, a ploughed field on the outskirts of Bramley was destined to become the Central Ammunition Depot. This meant over 1,000 acres of farmland in Bramley, Sherfield and Old Basing were requisitioned. With a civilian contractor chosen to complete the plant, construction work began a week later. Over 500 workers, including many Irishmen, were employed in the construction, and this was supplemented by PoW labour. The workmen and troops were housed in the North Camp. The PoWs, whose numbers swelled to around 3,500 by the end of that year, were detained in the South Camp, being guarded by the Royal Defence Force – men too old for military service and men invalided home from the front. Colonel Paine ran the camp. The first consignment of ammunition arrived at the arsenal on 1 January 1918, when only a few sheds had been built. The Reverend Toogood (*A History of Bramley*, 1990) described how Miss Chute, of the Vyne, enlisted local female labour to move the shells inside the depot. With the advent of the Armistice in November 1918, discipline within the internment camp became more relaxed. However, repatriation for those interned at Bramley did not begin until almost a year later.

The Glasgow Herald (4 September 1917) at the conclusion of its report, stated that thirteen PoWs had been taken back into custody. It cited Otto Hoake, aged 22, had escaped from Bramley. *The Coventry Evening Telegraph* (15 March 1918) reported three absconders from Bramley had been apprehended again.

Earmarked for closure in 1967, the decision was deferred until 1 September 1978. The site was then given over to the American forces that used the base until February 1987. Abandoned to the elements for a number of years, a section of the site has now been turned over to property developers.

DKF 32: In Yatesbury wurde seit September 1916 erst zweimal protestantischer Gottesdienst gehalten. In Bramley, hat seit dem 2 Juni 1917 erst einmal Gottesdienst stattgefunden.

BRAMPTON PARK (OS: TL 204 704). An agricultural group attached to Huntingdon, its POWIB (1919) code was Pa (Hu) (Brp) (IWM: Facsimile K4655). Brampton is cited by the FPHS (1973). It had the TA Priswarian: Brampton Park, Huntingdon (ADM 1/8506/265–120667).

The village of Brampton is a long and rather straggling one. The northern part, where the Church of St Mary the Virgin stands, is called the Bell End, and dates back to the Domesday Survey of 1086. The southern part of the town is known as the Bridge End. It is newer and takes its name from the bridge that crosses the brook. In 1901, the population of Brampton was recorded as being 1,020.

This camp would probably have been active in the second phase of internment camps when PoW labour was being utilised into work programmes.

BRANDON (OS: TL 785 865). A working camp, its POWIB (1919) code was Pa (Dw) (IWM: Facsimile K4655); its suffix clearly indicating Downham. Brandon, Suffolk is cited by the FPHS (1973). It had the TA Priswarian: Brandon (ADM 1/8506/265–120667).

Downham Hall was demolished *c.*1926; it stood near to Brandon, Suffolk. Probably built for the Paulet family *c.*1750, it was altered, in 1836, by Lord William Paulet and at some stage in-between, the Mackenzie family had owned it.

This camp would probably have been active in the second phase of internment camps when PoW labour was being utilised into work programmes.

BRAUGHING: The Mount (OS: TL 393 251). A minute of 26 February 1918, belonging to the Hertfordshire County Council WAC, reveals that a request for thirty-five PoWs had been sanctioned for Braughing, but the scheme still awaited accommodation to be found on 8 May 1918. It had the TA Priswarian: Braughing (ADM 1/8506/265–120667).

A 16-year-old boy regularly escorted the work detail, consisting of eight PoWs, to their work placement in the morning, and back again in the evening. This camp was active in the second phase of internment camps when PoW labour was being utilised into work programmes.

It was reported in the *Hertfordshire Mercury* (5 July 1919) that a local man was fined £2.8s for assaulting one of the PoWs. He had lost two sons in the war.

BRECON: Old County Prison (OS: SO 035 282). Brecknock Museum can confirm that the old county prison was used as an internment camp during the First World War. Set up as an agricultural depot, it had the POWIB (1919) code Fg (Bre) (IWM: Facsimile K4655) and supported five agricultural groups: Aber Llown House; Aberglasney; Llanafan; Llandybie; and Talgarth. Its TA was Priswarian: Brecon (ADM 1/8506/265–120667). It was also cited by the FPHS (1973).

On a visit of inspection to Brecon in the spring of 1919, Dr A. de Sturler and Monsieur R. de Sturler created a report that is held at the National Archives at Kew (FO 383/506).

BRETBY (OS: SK 301 225). The POWIB (1919) cite there was an internment camp at Bretby Hall in the First World War; its code was Bro (Brt) (Bry) (IWM: Facsimile K4655). A HO document provides the camp's location as the stables, citing its TA as Priswarian: The Stables, Bretby Hall, Burton on Trent (ADM 1/8506/265–120667). Bretby, Staffs is cited by the FPHS (1973). The camp was a satellite of Burton upon Trent according to the list compiled by the POWIB (1919).

The Derby Daily Telegraph (10 July 1918) goes some way to dating when the camp was set up, by stating it was one of several already set up.

The Earl of Cardigan was in residence at the hall for at least part of the First World War. Bretby Park stands on the Derbyshire–Staffordshire border and was once the property of the Stanhope family. It dates back to *c.*1650 and for many years the hall, and its grounds, was used as a hospital: today it has been turned into luxury flats.

During March 1919, Dr A. de Sturler compiled a report on his visit of inspection to Bretby Hall. It is held at the National Archives at Kew (FO 383/507).

BREWOOD (see Somerford Hall).

BRIDGE OF EARN (see Kintillo).

BRIDGWATER (OS: ST 30- 27-). Minutes of the Somerset WAC show fifty-five PoWs were transferred from Sandhill Park to Dulverton, Bridgwater, Thorloxton, Kingston Seymour and Clavelshay in equal numbers. Five remained at Sandhill Park, and were being billeted in cottages on the estate.

Although the location is unknown the timeframe for this camp being active would be in the second phase of internment camps when PoW labour was being utilised into work programmes.

BRIGHTWELL GROVE FARM (OS: SU 568 930). The camp was listed as being at Brightwell Grove by the FPHS (1973). The POWIB (1919) describe it as an agricultural group attached to Cholsey AD and gave it the code Dor (Cho) (Bri) (IWM: Facsimile K4655).

In a study of the Oxfordshire wildlife and landscape written in 2004 it was suggested Brightwell Baldwin was a typical example of a rolling agricultural landscape that is characterised by country houses set in ornamental parkland and dispersed farmsteads. One of those farmsteads was cited as Brightwell Grove.

BRIXWORTH: The Grange (OS: SP 746 708). A HO document cites this camp, and gives its TA as Priswarian: The Grange, Brixworth, Northampton (ADM 1/8506/265–120667). This camp would probably have been active in the second phase of internment camps when PoW labour was being utilised into work programmes. It was a working camp, and had the POWIB (1919) code Pa (Brx) (IWM: Facsimile K4655). The FPHS (1973) cites it too.

BROAD MARSTON: The Priory (OS: SP 143 462). Described by the POWIB (1919) as a working camp, it was based at The Priory, Broad Marston; its code was cited as Dor (B M) (IWM: Facsimile K4655). It is also cited by the FPHS (1973).

This camp would probably have been active in the second phase of internment camps when PoWs labour was being utilised into work programmes. Its TA was Priswarian: Broad Marston (ADM 1/8506/265–120667).

BROCKENHURST (OS: SU 29- 02-). A working camp, it had the POWIB (1919) code Dor (Brc) (IWM: Facsimile K4655). It is also cited by the FPHS (1973). Its TA was Priswarian: Brockenhurst. No physical evidence has been found to suggest that this camp existed, which would have been in the second phase of internment camps that put PoWs into work programmes around the country.

BROCTON ARMY CAMP (OS: SJ 984 192). Brocton Army Camp was opened in 1914 as a centre for training raw recruits. It was built on land donated by the Earl of Lichfield, which was near to his family's ancestral home, Shugborough Hall. A letter to the Earl, from the Northern Command, based at York, expresses thanks for his 'very kind offer to allow troops to be located on his property on Cannock Chase'. From humble beginnings it grew into two vast army camps with the capacity to hold some 40,000 soldiers. The second camp took its name from the township of Rugeley. These camps had their own power stations, water supplies, sewage plants, shops, post offices, and railway infrastructures.

The arrival of the first PoWs to Brocton is not known, but they were put into the section nearest to Brocton Coppice, described by Whitehouse and Whitehouse (*A Town for Four Winters: Great War Camps on Cannock Chase*, 1987) as Lines 'A' to 'D'. These were converted into separate compounds with a barbed wire perimeter fence with guard towers. The first to be interned in the camp may have been civilians.

The guard consisted of men declared unfit for active service, taken from several regiments. Many would have sustained wounds at the front. Their commandant was Lieutenant Colonel Sir Arthur Grant. The internees disliked Grant intensely. Grant had his men search the belongings of the internees as they entered the camp. As a result of these searches many leather items were confiscated. There were claims that he purposely held back food rations, particularly potatoes, and that he and his junior officers intimidated anyone that tried to speak out. When the Swiss legation visited the camp, he personally escorted the visitors around the camp. Complaints, investigated by the Swiss, were not upheld. Major Meyer, from Kegworth, was appointed to look into how the camp was run. Evidence from German sources state there was a compound, cited as 'E Lager', suggesting there were at least five compounds. A compound generally held 1,000 men.

According to the Peak Dale History Group's *More Than Just Dust*, the Brocton camp became the parent camp for the satellite work camps and this is borne out in the directory produced by the POWIB (1919). It is estimated 1,500 wooden huts were erected on an exposed area.

Photographs survive of life in the camp. Some show an amateur theatrical group, run by the PoWs, in rehearsal for a production. Fifteen members of the camp guard appear in another. The Imperial War Museum holds documents relating to PoWs, and to the camp in general.

After the war the camp stood unused for several years, before being dismantled. Many of the huts were sold to local farmers at auction and most of the land returned to forestry. Today, some of the filter beds from the sewerage system survive. A scale model of Messines Ridge, constructed in concrete in 1918 by some of the PoWs, has become obscured by gorse.

In the late 1950s the Federal Republic of Germany sought a place to re-bury its war dead from both World Wars. Because Cannock Chase's pine covered slopes are very reminiscent of parts of Germany it was chosen, in 1959, to be the Deutscher Soldatenfriedhof (German War Cemetery). The cemetery contains 2,143 and 2,786 graves, respectively, of those that died in both world wars. Nearby is the smaller Commonwealth War Cemetery, containing the graves of many ANZAC troopers that died whilst on active service and based on the Chase, many as a result of the flu pandemic of 1918.

The camp's POWIB (1919) code was Bro (IWM: Facsimile K4655), and its TA Priswarian, Brocton (ADM 1/8506/265–120667). The parent camp at Catterick began its life as a satellite of Brocton. Brocton Army Camp, the camp's hospital, and Brocton Hall, are all cited by the FPHS (1973).

DKF 16: Der Vizefeldwebel der Reserve und Offiziersaspirant Emil Heisel, Reserve-Infanterie-Regiment Nr. 261, berichtet über Brocton (Februar 1918): Vom Recht der Beschwerde an die Schweizer Gesandtschaft, welche die Rechte der deutschen Kriegsgefangenen wahrzunehmen übernommen hat, können weder der von Lagerinsassen gewählte Ausschuß noch irgendein Gefangener Gebrauch machen, da selbst ordnungsmäßiger Beschwerde Strafandrohung in offener oder versteckter Weise, Einschüchterungsversuche oder sogar Strafe durch den englischen Lagerkommandanten Grant erfolgt.

Heisel bemerkt ferner, daß bei Besichtigungen durch neutrale Kommissionen der Kommandant mit seinem Stabe die Delegierten begleitet und nur die Räume zeigt, die er zeigen will. Wenn ein Kriegsgefangener einmal eine Beschwerde anzubringen weiß, so lenkt der Kommandant ab, verdreht die Tatsachen, Bestreitet glattweg den Sachverhalt oder schüchtern durch drohendes Verhalten den Beschwerdeführer derartig ein, daß er seine Beschwerde einschränkt oder gar widerruft.

Es wurde so weinig Heinzmaterial geliefert, daß das Essen nicht genügend gekocht werden konnte. Auch dir Heizung war gänzlich unzureichend.

Der Adjutant trat im Juli 1917 einen Mann, weil dieser, wie er sich äußerte, nicht schnell genug beim Antreten lief. (Nach dem bericht des Schweizer Delegierten vom 18 Juni 1917 war Captain W.G. Egerton 2nd in command, also vielleicht der, der von Heisel als Adjutant bezeichnet wird.)

Der damals in der Schweiz internierte Jäger Meibes, Otto, Jäger-Bataillon Nr. 11, machte Februar 1918 Angaben, die zu Beeiden er bereit ist: In einer Nacht wurden die Bewohner einer Baracke, sämtlich Feldwebel, plötzlich aufgeweckt und bekamen den Befehl, die Baracke sofort zu verlassen. Als einige sich notdürftig ankleideten und dieses dem Kommandanten zu lange dauerte, schlug er mit dem Reitstock um sich, ohne darauf zu achten, wohin er traf. In eisiger Kälte, bei schneidendem Wind, mußten die Betreffenden über eine halbe Stunde im stehen, bis die Revision, von der sie erst später erfuhren, beendet war.

Dieselben Zustände in diesem Lager schildert der Gefreite Sieber, 3. Batterie der Kaiserlichen Schutztruppe Deutsch-Südwestafrika.

Der in Holland, Rotterdam, Hotel Vereenigung, internierte Sargeant Alf. Jocham berichtet in seinem Schreiben an seine Angehörigen am 12. Februar 1918: ... Ich glaube, England wurde nie mehr verwünscht und beschimpft als im Broctonlager Dasselbe ist bei alles Kriegsgefangenen als das schlechteste und am meisten hungerleidende bekannt. Wir lagen in Baracken, 18 Grad Kälte, keine Kohlen, das Wasser lief an den Wänden herab, dazu Hunger wie ein Löwe. Von 20 Unzen Kartoffeln, die uns zustanden, bekamen wir nur 6 Unzen pro Kopf. So hat uns der englische Kommandant in der kurzen Zeit um 25 Zentner Kartoffeln betrogen und unterschlagen. Ebenso 550 Pfund Margarine pro Baracke. Von den anderen Sachen will ich gar nicht sprechen, denn die Briten haben selbst nix. Nun streiken die Arbeiter im Nebencamp, weil sie so wenig zu essen bekommen und sie keine Kohlen haben zum Kleidertrocknen, denn es regnet, und sie mußten öfters am Morgen nasse Kleider anziehen. Der Englische Kommandant ließ das ganze Camp heraustreten und im Hofe kompagnieweise antreten. Die ganze Wache wurde alarmiert und alles umstellt. Da kam der englische Kommandant in Begleitung zweier englischer Sargeanten und frug verschiedene: Wollen sie Arbeiten? Nein, Schwupp einen Schlag ins Gesicht, und so verschiedenen. So standen wir von morgans um 8 Uhr bis es dunkel war. Keiner durfte austreten, um seine Not zu verrichen. Da stank es wie die Pest. Unser deutscher Kommandant, der Mame ist mir entfallen, machte dem Englische Kommandant Vorstellungen und sagte, er verbätesicheineslche Behandlung, sie wären keine Hunde, die Schlägebekämen, sondern ehrliche Soldaten. Der Englische Kommandant: Was, Sie wollen auch noch was? Ihr seid doch noch schlimmer als Hunde und Schweine, und bauf, bum wurde er verhauen und auf Befehl des Englische Kommandanten in dir Zelle gesperrt mit dem Vermerk, das deutsche Schwein gründlich zu verhauen, und das haben zwei englische Sergeanten gut getan. Alles steht dabei und kann nichts machen ... Alles wurde uns abgezogen und bekamen fast nichts mehr, zumleben zu wenig und nicht einmal zum sterben zu viel. Was wir durch einen Posten einschmuggeln konnten, mußte alles mit dem doppelten und dreifachen Preis bezahlt werden.

Wenn wir nur eine Zigarre hatten und sich den Bauch voll Rauch pumpen konnten. Um die Kartoffeln und Abfälle wurde sich geschlagen, Hunger tut weh.

In einen Bericht vom 26 Januar 1918 aus Rotterdam bestätigt der Fähnrich im Feldartillerie-Regiment Nr. 45 Münchemeyer die Angaben über Brocton, indem er besonders die Mißhandlungen, verübt durch den Kommandanten Grant, hervorhebt und mitteilt, daß

Beschwerden an die Schweizerische Gesandtschaft vom Kommandanten zurückgehalten werden.

Bei der englischen Regierung wurde gegen die obengeschilderten Zustände im Lager Brocton und gegen das Verhalten des Kommandanten nachdrücklichst Einspruch erhoben und die englische Regierung aufgefordert, daß der Kommandant mit Weisungen versehen werde die eine Weiderholung für die Zukunft ausschließen.

Ein Bericht des deutschen Lagerführers, Vizewachtmeisters Kreitner, 1 Bayerisches Feldartillerie-Regiment, 8 Batterie, der von verschiedenen im selben Lager gefangenen älteren Unteroffizier en beglaubigt ist, schildert die Vorfälle im Lager Brocton genau so; er selbst ist bei der Arbeitsverweigerung mißhandelt worden durch der Kommandanten. Eine Stellungnahme der in Holland internierten Unteroffiziere fügt diesen Darstellungen noch hinzu, daß großere Mengen von Lebensmitteln den Gefangenen vorenthalten wurden. In der Zeit vom 15 December 1917 bis zum 15 Januar 1918 wurden etwa 1200 Gefangenen 23,740 englische Pfund Kartoffeln zu wenig geliefert. Dabei hatte die Schweizerische Kommission erklärt, daß jede Unze weniger als die offizielle Ration Hunger bedeute. Zahlreiche weitere Briefe von in Holland internierten deutschen Kriegsgefangenen erhärten die oben über Brocton gemachten Angaben.

In einer eidesstattlichen Versicherung berichtet der Unteroffizier Georg Obel, Infanterie-Regiment Nr. 64, 12 Kompagnie, über die Verpflegungsverhältnisse im Austaushlager F zu Brocton. Die Erklärung ist vom 26 Februar 1918 aus Dieren datiert, es heißt darin: Das tägliche Quantum war nunmehr wie folgt: Weißbrot 5 Unzen, Hartbrot 4 Unzen, Margarine 1 Unze, Käse 1 Unze, Marmelade 1 Unze, Kartoffeln 20 Unzen, Fleisch (Fett und Knochen) 6 Unzen (in der Woche Zwie Fleischlose Tage), Herring mit Maden an fleischlosen Tagen pro Tag 10 Unzen, Zucker 1 Unze, Gemüse, Bohnen, Erbsen oder Kohl 4 Unzen, Kaffeemehlersatz und Gewürze.

Der Kommandant kürzte noch vor Weihnachten angeblich auf Befehl der War Office die zugestandene Ration. Er begründete die Kürzung damit, nicht genügend Vorräte zu haben ... Gekürzt wurden 16 Unzen Kartoffeln, Margarine, Käse, und Marmelade fiel etwa 7 Tage vollständig fort. Letzteres ist teilweise nachgeliefert, Kartoffeln bis zum 20 Januar nicht.

Eine Beschwerdekommission des F-Lagers, bestehend aus drei Herren (folgen Namen) wurde nicht Vorgelassen. Eine Beschwerde an den Schweizer Gesandten hatte der kommandant unterschlagen, wie selbst der Herr Vertreter der Gesandtschaft vermutetc, welcher infolge einer durchgeschmuggelten Privatnachricht endlich Mitte Januar eintraf. Die Lagerverwaltung erhielt den Auftrag, dem Herrn Vertreter am 26 Januar eine belanglose Beshwerde zu senden, um zu ergründen, ob die Beschwerden absichtlich unterschlagen würden ... Der Hunger war so heftig, daß Küchenabfälle, halbverfaulte Zwiebeln, Kartoffelschalen und Kohlabfälle fleißig gesammelt wurden, moglichst, ohne Verlust gereinigt und auf der Hütte gekocht wurden. Der Unterzeichnete hat wiederholt mitgegessen; keine Probeportionen, sondern stramme Portionen, um dem Hungergefühl zu begegnen ... in der Kantine wurden Lebensmittel nicht verkauft.

Der Mitte Oktober 1918 nach Holland ausgetauschte Unteroffizier der Reserve, Offizieraspirant Karl Ottoweber, berichtet unter dem 19 Oktober 1918, daß die Zustände in Brocton jeder Beschreibung spotten. Die Ernährung ist vollkommen unzureichend. Das Essen besteht gewöhnlich aus gänzlich verfaulten Katoffolen und Rüben und nahezu ungenießbaren grünen Bohnen.

Die Unterbringung ist auch skandalös, da es durch die Baracken teilweise regnet und außerdem trotz der kalten und nassen Witterung keine oder doch nur sehr wenige Kohlen geliefert werden, so daß sich die Leute genötigt sehen, in den kalten Räumen zu sitzen und sich den ganzen Tag in ihren Decken einzuwickeln.

Die Schutzmacht wurde durch eine Note auf die obererwähnten Zustände hingewiesen mit dem Bemerken, daß die Zustände in Brocton seit dem letzten Besuch des Vertreters der Schweizerischen Gesandtschaft in London wieder erheblich schlechter geworden sein müssen. Es wurde ersucht, daß Lager baldigst wieder durch einen Delegierten besuchen zu lassen, und die Erwartung ausgesprochen, daß die Schutzmacht mit allen Mitteln bei der englischen Regierung auf Besserung etwaiger Mißstände (unzureichende Ernährung, mangelhafte Heizung der Unterkunftsräume) dringt.

Major Meyer (Lagerältester in Kegworth) richtete am 5 Juni 1918 einen Bericht an die Schweizerische Gesandtschaft in London: Deutsche Soldaten, die als Ordonnanzen von Brocton nach dem Offizierslager Kegworth gekommen waren, berichten, daß jeder deutsche Gefangenen, der nach Brocton kam oder von dort wegging, nur zwei Taschentücher, zwei Hemden und zwei Unterhosen im Besitz haben durfte; gleichgültig, ob die Dinge deutschen oder englischen Ursprungs waren, wurde, was mehr war, weggenommen.

Am 10 Juni 1918 berichtet Major Meyer an die Schweizerische Gesandtschaft in London: Neuangekommene deutsche Ordonnanzen aus Brocton berichten, daß auch Lederkoffer, Stiefel, in Leder gebundene Notizbücher, die alle aus Deutschland stammten, weggenommen wurden, und zwar nicht nur bei solchen, die nach Holland ausgetauscht wurden, sondern auch bei denen, die in ein anderes Lager in England kamen. Die Sachen wurden von englischen Unteroffizieren in Gegenwart von Offizieren weggenommen.

Am 10 Juni 1918 schreibt Oberleutnant Picot, Lagerkommandant von Kegworth, an Major Meyer, daß das Schreiben weitergereicht ist, daß er aber der Meinung sei, daß Meyer nicht berechtigt ist, sich mit den Interessen in Brocton internierten Deutschen zu befassen. Der Brief geht an den Hauptzensor, gemäß Verfügung des Army Council Erlasses, weil die duetsche Regierung ein Abkommen über solche Gesuche gebrochen habe.

Am 14 Juni 1918 schreibt Major Meyer an den englischen Lagerkommandanten, daß er noch keine Bestätigung hat, daß seine beiden Schreiben bei der Schweizerischen Gesandtschaft eingegangen sind. Er bittet um Bekanntgabe der Army Council Instructions. Am 15 Juni erfolgte diese. Die Verfügung ist datiert vom 19 Februar und besagt, daß die deutsche Regierung solche Bittgesuche der Zensur unterworfen habe; deshalb soll dasselbe in Zukunft auch durch die britische Regierung getan werden.

Am 11 Juli 1918 teilt die Schweizerischen Gesandtschaft mit, daß die englische Regierung die Anschuldigungen betreffend Wegnahme der Kleidungsstücke untersucht habe und mitgeteilt habe, daß diese Angaben unwahr seien.

Major Meyer vernimmt die duetschen Gefangenen nochmals, Aussagen: Musketier Theodor Kammering, Infanterie-Regiment Nr. 190, gibt an: Dem Unteroffizier Bode wurde eine eigene deutsche Militärhose weggenommen, ebenso ein Paar Lederhandschuhe, deutschen Ursprungs.

Infanterist Conrad Lenz, Bayerisches Infanterie-Regiment Nr. 7, gibt an: Ich sah, daß in Brocton bei der Untersuchung von Sanitätsmannschaften, die nach Deutschland kamen Ledersachen abgenommen wurden, deutschen Ursprungs. Speziell erinnere ich mich eines Koffers, der eine duetsche Firmenplatte trug, ich selbst mußte den Koffer in den Storeraum schaffen. Auch eigene Wäsche wurde abgenommen.

Friedrich Frost, Reserve Infanterie-Regiment Nr 79, gibt an: Es sind den Mannschaften in Brocton bei ihrer Überführung von dem E-Lager in das A-Lager folgende Bekleidungsstücke, ganz gleich, ob englischen oder deutschen Ursprungs, abgenommen worden: Uniformhose, Hemden, Unterhosen, Strümpfe, Stiefel, sobald mehr als zwei Stück vorhanden waren.

Diese Gepäckrevisionen und Wegnahme sind auch später auf alle Personen, die von oder nach Brocton gingen, ausgedehnt worden. Ich bezeuge, daß ich die Überführung der den Sanitätsmannschaften in März abgenommonen Sachen in den Storeräumen persönlich gesehen habe.

BROCTON HALL (OS: SJ 965 198). Whitehouse and Whitehouse (*A Town for Four Winters: Great War Camps on Cannock Chase*, 1987) do not cite the hall in their in-depth study of the army camps on Cannock Chase during the First World War. It is included, along with Brocton, in the lists published by the FPHS (1973) as being a British prison camp. The clubhouse of Brocton Hall Golf Club now occupies the site of the former Brocton Hall. The original hall was erected *c.*1611, and was vacated by 1850. A new hall was built *c.*1760 according to Pevsner (1974). The *Staffordshire Advertiser* (22 March 1922) reported that the picturesque clubhouse, which had been erected twenty-three years earlier, was gutted, together with an adjoining cottage. It was described as being two-storeys high and brick built, with cement cladding. The roof had been made of thatch from Norwegian rushes. After the fire only the two chimneys stood, exposed.

The golf club's centenary publication described that the club managed to survive the war years despite the irritation of having a single-track railway line being laid across the fifth hole. The opening holes, too, were subjected to a lot of wear and tear as they lay in the direct route from the nearby army camps to the Barley Mow pub. The railway line was removed in 1918. They make no reference to PoWs being billeted at the hall. It is believed the hall may have been some kind of medical facility or an officers'mess.

Prior to the Second World War, there was another fire at the golf club.

BROMFIELD (OS: SO 48- 77-). A satellite of Leominster, it is described as an agricultural group with the POWIB (1919) code Shrw (Lmr) (Bfd) (IWM: Facsimile K4655). Its address is cited as 42 West Street, Leominster. Its TA is cited as Priswarian: Leominster (ADM 1/8506/265–120667). Bromfield is also cited by the FPHS (1973).

The *Border Counties Advertiser* (24 April 1918) reported that the Salop WAC had received reports of work done by PoWs at Bromfield, and Wem, and had agreed to request 200 more. The *Border Counties Advertiser* (1 May 1918) stated that the 200 additional PoWs had been requested, and it was hoped to have them in small camps of fifteen to twenty, or in groups of up to three on single farms if the farmer could accommodate them.

It was alleged by the internees that because of the carelessness of the camp's sergeant they did not receive their full entitlement of rations on several days.

DKF 35: In Bromfield haben die Gefangenen mehrere Tage lang nicht ihre vollen Rationen erhalten durch die Nachlässigkeit eines Sergeanten.

BROMYARD: The Workhouse (OS: SO 670 542). An agricultural group, its POWIB (1919) code was Shrw (Lmr) (Byd) (IWM: Facsimile K4655); its address is cited as 42 West Street, Leominster. Its TA is cited as Priswarian: Workhouse, Bromyard (ADM 1/8506/265–120667).

Bromyard Union Workhouse stood on the south side of the A44. Built to the specifications of George Wilkinson, who also designed Weobley, Leominster and Ledbury workhouses, the workhouse was built in 1836 to accommodate up to 120 inmates. It followed the typical cruciform shape with an entrance wing at the front with four separate accommodation wings that led off from a central corridor. The workhouse was to become Bromyard Hospital, before being converted into a care home (Miranda Greene, 2003 in http://htt.herefordshire.gov.uk/698.aspx).

In 1893 there was an outbreak of smallpox, and a small cottage at Burley, 0.5 miles from the workhouse, was turned into an isolation hospital (SO 673 531). The hospital, which had been the joint responsibility of the urban and rural district councils, was taken over by the Birmingham Regional Hospital Board on the advent of the National Health Service. They decided to sell the hospital in 1949. The site has become residential dwellings.

There were allegations made by the internees that this Leominster satellite had nowhere to cook hot meals and, sometimes, they had to supply their own food.

DKF 35: In Bromyard, haben die Gefangenen keine Kochgelegenheit, um sich aus eigenen Vorräten Speise zu bereiten.

BROOM HALL STABLES (OS: TL 175 42). Listed as Broome by the POWIB (1919), it is described as a working camp with the code Pa (Boo) (IWM: Facsimile K4655). Had the spelling been correct, then the camp would, most probably, have been in Norfolk (OS: TM 344 914), but there is evidence that suggests a different location.

The Bedfordshire County Record Office has an extracts of documents relating to a camp at Broom (WW1/AC/PW/1&2). Between October 1918 and July 1919, the names of nine PoWs, along with their guard, are recorded on a time sheet showing they were being employed at Broom. This evidence is supported by a HO document, which gives its TA as Priswarian, Broom Hall Stables, Broom, near Biggleswade.

BRYNKIR: Brynkir Hall (OS: SH 521 436). The camp was identified as Brynker, Caernarvon, by the FPHS (1973). A HO document also cites this camp, and gives it the TA Priswarian: Brynkir Hall, Garn Dolbenmaen (ADM 1/8506/265–120667). A report of a visit of inspection to Brynkhir Hall by Dr A. de Sturler and Monsieur R. de Sturler during June 1919 is held at the National Archives at Kew (FO 383/508).

BUCKFAST ABBEY (OS: SX 734 672). When war was declared, a substantial proportion of Buckfast Abbey's monastic community was German. Because they were male subjects of military age, there was a lot of resentment to the latitude bestowed to them by the authorities. So, rather than let them return to Germany, it was thought more prudent to allow them to remain at the abbey with conditions attached to their movements and behaviour.

There was still an element in the upper echelons of society that repeatedly insisted that a cordon should be placed around the abbey, to monitor the monks' activities. If this was merely a small religious community, why, one has to ask, was the extra security necessary? Were not the French or Belgian monks in the abbey capable of monitoring the German monks impartially? It has been suggested the resentment emanated from the fact that this monastic community was Roman Catholic, and had very little to do with the war at all.

The Chief Constable of Devon, Captain H.R. Vyvyan, drafted a letter on 15 May 1916, to the Abbot, the Very Reverend Anscar Venier, explaining the restrictions put on the monks. He wrote:

> Having been in communication with the Home Office on the subject of the Monks at your Abbey, I am directed to inform you that it is not at present contemplated to disturb the Community, provided the following conditions are

carried out; that the Alien enemy Monks at the Abbey be entirely confined to the grounds – save in the case of the three who go to the farm and wood and that these latter, whenever they go outside the Abbey grounds, will be accompanied by one of the French Monks or a British subject.

Bro Gregory Miller (n.d.)

Concerns were also expressed about the difficulty of putting this community into internment, as there was an understanding with other nation-states that there would be no interference with priests or persons from belligerent states qualifying to become priests. Lieutenant Wilde was drafted into the abbey to monitor the daily activities of the ecclesiastic community. He found many of the monks were engaged in restoration work.

On a visit by J. Willcocks, the Labour Exchange Controller, on 14 March 1918, a scheme was proposed to send the younger clerics to work in a quarry, at Trusham. However, they could not be sent until proper accommodation was found, and not before the Chief Constable of Devon had sanctioned it. On a subsequent visit, on 11 April 1918, Willcocks was content to suspend the scheme, even though the nuns at Oakland would have undertaken to provide board and lodging at £1 per head a week, on top of the vegetables, butter, eggs, etc. the Abbot had promised.

BUCKNALL (see Bardney).

BUCKMINSTER (see Stainby).

BUGTHORPE (OS: SE 77- 57-). Bunthorope appears as an entry by the FPHS (1973). Neither it nor Bunthorpe exist according to a British Gazetteer. What may have been suggested was Bugthorpe. However no camp has been traced to this locality.

BULFORD (OS: SU 189 438). A civilian working camp, it had the POWIB (1919) code Dor (Chi) (IWM: Facsimile K4655). Bulford had the TA Priswarian: Bulford (ADM 1/8506/265–120667). It was also cited by the FPHS (1973).

Crawford (*Wiltshire and The Great War: Training the Empire's Soldiers*, 1999) cites a War Department list, dated November 1917, which mentions two prison camps in Wiltshire, at Larkhill and Perham Down: and a camp for interned aliens at Bulford. The internment camp at Bulford closed on 15 September 1918.

BUNGAY COMMON (OS: TM 335 895). Norfolk WAC minutes cite a camp was sought for Bungay Common on 29 June 1917. Some urgency was required in setting up this camp, as the PoWs were required for drainage work on the River Waveney, beginning on 25 August 1917 (C/C10/15–19).

Bungay Common covers an area of some 400 acres, a part of which is marshland. Today, there are no visible remains of the camp being on the common, which suggests the camp may have been tented. Local knowledge states the PoWs cleared the river of reeds, and the banks of their weeds.

The higher ground has recently been the centre of an ownership dispute.

Shipmeadow is nearby.

BUNNY (OS: SK 58- 29-). According to the minutes of the Notts County WAC there was a migratory gang at Bunny. No physical evidence has been found to support this claim. It may be the camp was near to Bunny Hall, built by Sir Thomas Parkyns *c.*1720. The contents of the hall were sold in 1910.

BUNTINGFORD: Bradbury House (OS: TL 391 301). There were plans to send PoWs to Buntingford as early as 21 February 1917, but this scheme was aborted. However, by 1 October 1918, thirty-five PoWs had been established at Bradbury House, Hare Street. A scheme intended for Newsells Bury was also abandoned, recorded by a minute of the Hertfordshire County Council WAC (19 June 1918) in favour of one to be set up at Hare Street.

The local newspaper reported that four PoWs from the Hare Street Camp had volunteered to dig and tidy up a 20-rod allotment belonging to a 78-year-old widow. The task, done in their own time, took two Saturday afternoons to complete, after their eight-hour shift at a farm.

After the war the house was bought and renovated. It was painted white, and is now referred to as The White House.

A working camp, its POWIB (1919) code was Pa (Bg) (IWM: Facsimile K4655). It is also cited by the FPHS (1973). Its TA was Priswarian: Hare Street, Great Hormead (ADM 1/8506/265–120667).

BURES (OS: TL 906 342). Bures appears on the list produced for the FPHS (1973). Its TA was Priswarian: Bures (ADM 1/8506/265–120667).

There was a tannery at Bures. Until 1909 the finished animal hides would have been transported down the river to Mistley, before being taken to London. When the yard closed the machinery was moved to Ipswich. The main building of the former tannery has been converted for residential use and is now known as Tannery House. The drying shed was dismantled in 1985 and replaced by Bridge House. During the First World War the drying shed was used as a dormitory for German PoWs. Until the shed was dismantled in 1985 the names of the PoWs could be seen on small white cards above the places where their beds had been.

One PoW drowned whilst diving off the road bridge. The fatality, reported in the local press on 25 June 1919, occurred as the men were bathing. An unnamed PoW had got into difficulties at the Jump, and was brought to the bank and given artificial respiration by his escorts and comrades. It was then discovered that Karl Volker was missing. His body was recovered some time later. The *Western Daily Press* (19 & 20 June 1919) cited both men were part of a bathing parade, and that Volker had drowned.

On a tour of inspection to Bures, Dr A. de Sturler and Monsieur R. de Sturler wrote a report of their visit during April and May 1919 which is held at the National Archives at Kew (FO 383/507).

BURGH HALL: Racquets Court (OS: TG 214 269). It was resolved by the Norfolk WAC to inform the Local Government Board that accommodation at Colonel Kerrison's Racquets Court, at Burgh Hall, could be provided for internees to carry out drainage work on the River Bures (C/C10/15–19).

BURGH-Next-AYLSHAM (OS: TG 22- 25-). E.T. Learner's barn at Burgh-next-Aylsham was cited by the Norfolk War Agricultural minutes as a place that could accommodate PoWs to work on the River Bures (C/C10/15–19). The barn is not cited on contemporary maps.

BURNHAM GREEN: Sunnycroft (OS: TL 264 164). A HO document cites the TA of this camp as Priswarian: Sunnycroft, Burnham Beeches, Maiden (ADM 1/8506/265–120667). No information on this camp is known, however Burnham Green also appears on a list produced for the FPHS (1973). Any PoWs sent to Sunnycroft would have been part of a work programme implement in the second phase of internment in Britain.

BURNHAM MARKET (OS: TF 825 434). On 14 July 1917, the Docking District Committee of the Norfolk WAC made a request for PoWs. It was recommended that two camps be set up; one was destined for Burnham Market, and the other for Heacham. The Quartering Committee was instructed to acquire the Maltings at Burnham Norton on 26 October 1917. Its POWIB (1919) code was Pa (Burn) (IWM: Facsimile K4655). The camp's TA was Priswarian: Burnham Market, Norfolk (ADM 1/8506/265–120667). On 7 September 1918, this camp was transformed into an agrarian based group.

The obituary of a King's Lynn solicitor stated that Captain E.M. Beloe had been commandant of several internment camps in Norfolk.

A report by Dr A. de Sturler and Monsieur R. de Sturler, of their visit of inspection to Burnham Market in the spring of 1919, is held at the National Archives at Kew (FO 383/508).

BURTON HALL: Burton by Lincoln (OS: SK 957 745). There are numerous towns and villages the length and breadth of England and Wales called Burton, of which a number have country houses bearing the name Burton Hall. This agricultural group, however, was near Burton by Lincoln. Sir Thomas Monson, *c.*1610, built the original hall. It was partially rebuilt in 1769 by the 2nd Lord Monson.

The camp was one of the satellites belonging to Bracebridge and it had the POWIB (1919) code Bro (Bbe) (Bt) (IWM: Facsimile K4655). Its TA was Priswarian: Burton Hall, Lincoln (ADM 1/8506/265–120667). The FPHS (1973) also include Burton Hall on their list.

PoWs billeted here would have been utilised into a work programme in the second phase of British internment during the First World War.

BURTON UPON TRENT (OS: SK 238 225). According to the POWIB (1919), despite having five satellite camps described as agricultural groups, Burton upon Trent was cited as a working camp. Its five satellite camps were Bretby Hall, Sudbury, Willington, Etwall, and Ilkeston. According to the *The Derby Daily Telegraph* (10 July 1918) it was ready to receive PoWs.

Stuart (*The History of Burton Upon Trent*, 1977) noted that new industries came to Burton upon Trent during the First World War:

> A machine gun factory, owned by the *Enfield Company*, was built by *Thomas Lowe and Sons* using German prisoner-of-war labour, in Burton Road, Branston, although the factory had not been completed when the war ended …

Stuart's statement is later refined to state that the PoWs were in fact employed to construct a perimeter wall. Part of the wall is still evident today. Local legend states that one of the Germans etched his name onto a brick, but according to retired local journalist, David Stacey, with the passage of time, its whereabouts is lost. The factory was completed too late to go into full armament production.

Before the Artificial Silk Company took over the factory, the site became known as the home of Branston Pickle, though in fact its makers, Crosse and Blackwell, had returned to their London roots within a short period of moving north.

In the Second World War, the site became an Ordnance Depot, and in the firemen's pay dispute in the 1970s, Green Goddess fire engines, belonging to the military, were stationed there as a precautionary measure.

The PoWs were interned in the Crown Maltings in Anglesey Road. Under the surveillance of a British Officer on horseback, they were marched to and from the factory site each day to their work place. Company records of Peach Leisure Ltd state the maltings, which were then owned in a partnership between Worthington's Brewery and R. Peach & Co. Ltd, were requisitioned in the First World War by the War Office to accommodate PoWs. It is said the PoWs constructed some houses too, adjacent to the factory, which are distinctive by their decorative twisted brickwork columns, a feature indigenous to a region of Germany from which at least one PoW, a proficient bricklayer, must have emanated, if this was the case.

A Faculty application made by the War Graves Commission to exhume German war dead, dated 21 November 1961, sought to have one PoW grave exhumed in Burton upon Trent Cemetery and re-interred at Cannock Chase.

During March 1919, Dr A. de Sturler compiled a report on visits of inspection to the PoW camps. One of those visited was Burton-on-Trent. They are held at the National Archives at Kew (FO 383/506).

Burton upon Trent is also cited by the FPHS (1973).

BUXTON (see Peak Dale).

BUXTON MILL (OS: TG 238 228). A proposal was put forward to the Local Government Board for PoWs to be put to clearing parts of the River Bures. Minutes of the Norfolk WAC suggest either Lamas Hall or Burton Mill could be used as an internment camp (C/C10/15–19). The latter does not exist in East Anglia, but Buxton does, and it has a mill. It was not noted which, if any, site was chosen. Any PoWs sent to either site would have been in the second phase of camps set up during the First World War.

BWLCH (OS: SO 14- 22-). Bwlch is cited by the FPHS (1973). Reports on visits of inspection to PoW camps at Blandford, Milldown, Louds Mill (Dorchester), Stowell, Glastonbury, Itton, Usk, Abergavenny, Hermitage (Crickhowell), Llangenny, Bwlch, Brecon, Talgarth, Abbeydore and Churchdown by Dr A. de Sturler and Monsieur R. de Sturler, during March and April 1919 are held at the National Archives at Kew (FO 383/506).

BYGRAVE (see Baldock).

C

CAERNARFON (OS: SH 48- 63-). This camp was only cited by the FPHS (1973). The obvious place for it would be the castle or its grounds, but although its location remains a mystery, it would have been active in the second phase of internment in Britain during the First World War.

CAERSWS: Workhouse (OS: SO 041 922). The POWIB (1919) entry for this camp cites its code as Fg (K N) (Csw), and attaches it, as an agricultural group, to Kerry Newtown AD (IWM: Facsimile K4655). The FPHS (1973) entry for this camp reads Caeresws (sic), Montgomery. Visits of inspection to camps in Wales by

Dr A. de Sturler and Monsieur R. de Sturler during June 1919 show Caersws was one of them. Their reports are held at the National Archives at Kew (FO 383/508).

A new union workhouse to accommodate up to 350 inmates was designed by Thomas Penson of Oswestry. It opened on 1 September 1840. The workhouse is cited in a HO document that gives its TA as Priswarian: Workhouse, Caersws, Mont. (ADM 1/8506/265–120667).

With the advent of the National Health Service the former workhouse became the Llys Maldwyn Hospital. It closed in 1960. Initially it operated as a children's hospital and provided care for patients with learning difficulties. The buildings were given Grade II listed status in 1994.

CAOLASNACON: nr Ballachulish (OS: NN 145 609). The POWIB (1919) directory states this camp's code as Stbs (Cs) (IWM: Facsimile K4655). Its TA was Priswarian: Caolasnacon, Kinlochleven (ADM 1/8506/265–120667). There is an entry for Caolas-na-Con in the list produced by the FPHS (1973).

Taking its name from a ferry station to the west of Kinlochleven, the internment camp at Caolasnacon is thought to be the first of the two internment camps established in this area. It was opened to accommodate conscientious objectors put to work of 'national importance'. In their case, this was building a road between Ballachulish and Kinlochleven. The construction of the road proved unsatisfactory and the project was abandoned. Amongst the objectors sent to Caolasnacon was Manny Shinwell. The importance of this road was to gain better access to the local aluminium smelter, but of course the local community would also have profited from its construction as all transport in and out of Kinlochleven was by boat.

Local belief suggests the departure of the conscientious objectors opened the door to civilian internees of 'professional status' and German officers. But the use of officers to do manual work would have contravened the Hague Convention.

A letter written by the District Surveyor indicated the PoW camp was about to become operational in the early part of 1918. By then the PoWs across Loch Leven were constructing the pipeline to Blackwater Reservoir (Herbert, per. comm., 10 October 1999).

Kinlochleven's population then was estimated to be around 1,000, and had become very much dependent on the British Aluminium Company's plant for their livelihood; it opened in 1909. When a second camp was established on the other side of Kinlochleven it brought the total number of PoWs to around 1,200, approximately the same total as the local populous of the day (Sosnauski, per. comm., 27 August 1998).

At an auction sale in 1923, the particulars included a sentry box that was sited approximately 1.5 miles east of Caolasnacon. A second lot, located nearer to Kinlochleven, included a large sectional hut, 60ft by 20ft, with beds and furnishings, a sentry box, smithy, motor house, etc. (MacDonald, per. comm., 28 August 1998 & 7 September 1998).

CADOXTON-JUXTA-NEATH (OS: SS 75- 98-). Cited by FPHS (1973), no further evidence has been found to support the claim that the camp existed.

One possibility for the site of a substantial camp could be the Vale of Neath Brewery. Established in the 1830s in Cadoxton-juxta-Neath the business was initially successful, but economic difficulties and a fire, in 1843, resulted in the business being sold in 1850 to Evan Evans (1791–1871). Acquired by Messrs Whitbread (Wales) Ltd, from Sir David Evans Bevan in 1967, the brewery closed in 1972.

The Rheola Estate may have also provided the PoWs with accommodation, and gainful employment. A villa created by John Nash *c.*1812 adorns the site. The gardens were enhanced later in the nineteenth century.

CAMBERLEY (OS: SU 88- 61-). A picture appears in *The Illustrated War News* (9 September 1914) showing an electrified barbed-wire entanglement surrounding tents at Camberley. The caption states it was to prevent German prisoners escaping, but one could argue it was equally for their protection. It may have been the same camp sited at College Town. The FPHS (1973) cites Camberley as a British Prison Camp.

CAMBRIDGE: Newmarket Road (OS: TL 473 594). A minute of the Cambridgeshire WAC (27 May 1918) cites large maltings on Newmarket Road, opposite the Gas Works, were available to accommodate a number of PoWs in Cambridge. A working camp, its POWIB (1919) code was Pa (Cam) (IWM: Facsimile K4655). There is a single entry for Cambridge made by the FPHS (1973). Blackamoor Head Yard, Cintra Road, The Hippodrome, and part of Westminster College are also cited in minutes of the Cambridgeshire WAC as having PoWs.

Today, Cambridge Airport stands near to this site. In December 1927, the Cambridge (East) Town Planning Scheme came into force. It included land in Newmarket Road now used by Messrs. Marshall as a flying school and aerodrome. The area of the existing aerodrome is about 66 acres. It may be PoW labour was used in clearing the original land for a runway.

CAMBRIDGE: Blackamoor Head Yard (OS: TL 447 589). The Cambridgeshire WAC minutes (27 May 1918) record that the large stables in Blackamoor Head Yard, in Bridge Street, were deemed suitable to be used to accommodate PoWs. Cintra Terrace, Newmarket Road, The Hippodrome, and part of Westminster College are also cited.

CAMBRIDGE: Cintra Terrace (OS: TL 456 576). The minutes of the Cambridgeshire WAC (27 May 1918) record that several houses in Cintra Terrace, Hills Road were deemed suitable to accommodate PoWs. Blackamoor Head Yard; Newmarket Road; The Hippodrome and part of Westminster College, were also deemed suitable venues.

CAMBRIDGE: The Hippodrome (OS: TL 460 588). The Cambridgeshire WAC minutes of 27 May 1918 record that The Hippodrome in Auckland Road was deemed to be suitable to accommodate PoWs. Blackamoor Head Yard; Cintra Terrace; Newmarket Road and part of Westminster College, are also cited in these minutes.

CAMBRIDGE: Westminster Theological College (OS: TL 443 590). Westminster Theological College has its origins in London, at Exeter Hall from 1844 to 1859, when it moved to Queen's Square. Work began on what is now a Grade II listed building in Cambridge, designed by Henry T. Hare, on 25 May 1897. The college moved in 1899. The college is situated within easy walking distance of the city's centre in 2 acres of ground at the junction of Madingley Road and Northampton Road. Part of the college is in St Margaret Road. The most significant event in the life of the college is its part in the formation of the United Reformed Church in 1972.

The Cambridgeshire WAC (CWAC) minutes of 27 May 1918 record that a portion of Westminster College was deemed to be suitable to accommodate PoWs. As it is known that the college housed refugees at that time, doubts have been cast about the PoWs being there too.

Blackamoor Head Yard; Cintra Terrace; The Hippodrome; & Newmarket Road, are also cited as places used to intern PoWs in the First World War, in minutes of the CWAC.

CANTERBURY (OS: TR 145 585). Neither list produced in 1937 or 1971 for the FPHS (1973) cites Canterbury as a British Prison Camp; but in an edition, produced in 1996 by Neil Russell, the camp is cited. A HO document cites the TA of this camp as Priswarian: Hanover Place, Canterbury, and that the camp closed on 15 November 1918 (ADM 1/8506/265–120667).

CARLISLE: Blackwell Grandstand (OS: NY 405 519). Carlisle Racecourse, at Blackwell, opened in 1901. In the First World War, when Lord Lonsdale raised a regiment, the racecourse was used as an army camp. Towards the latter stages of the conflict, part of the army camp, including the racecourse's grandstand, became an internment camp.

The first encounter between German PoWs and the citizens of Carlisle was reported in the *Carlisle Journal* in October 1915. It was when 350 internees passed through the city on their way to the newly established internment camp at Stobs in Scotland. News of their journey north had leaked out and a large crowd gathered at the station, but nothing could be seen of them as the blinds were down on the windows of the train. The crowd did not know how to react. Some hooted as the train left.

John Gregg (per. comm., 5 May 1999) recalls in his youth the course manager was called Mr Martin. As a young man in the 1960s, John said he was instructed by Mr Martin to remove whitewash from the police cells under the stand and in the grandstand's dining room. His endeavours in the cells exposed graffiti left by errant British squaddies of the day. In conversation, Martin had told him he too had worked at the racecourse in his youth during the First World War. He had been instructed to cut the hair of the PoWs interned in the camp at the racecourse. Quartered in wooden huts, they could often be seen foraging in the nearby wood for kindling for their pot-bellied stoves. They were well liked by the locals, and used bicycles donated to them to get to their work on the surrounding farms each day.

A book of the history of the 11th Battalion of the Border Regiment states they used the racecourse for an army training camp, but there is no indication that PoWs were interned there.

A photograph exists of British soldiers standing on a locomotive, whilst PoWs stood on the platform at Port Carlisle. It was taken *c.*1917 by Mr Canwell, a railway photographer. The locomotive was thought to belong to the Caledonian Company and would therefore have been 'foreign working' over a North British branch line. The distance between Port Carlisle and Carlisle is approximately 12 miles. The now defunct line was laid over the route of a pre-existing canal.

The minutes of the Cumberland WAC cite the Labour Officer's Report of 22 April 1917, when it was stated that he was awaiting a report from the Quartering Committee to approve the use of the grandstand to intern PoWs (CC1/39/1–2).

CARLTON (OS: SK 800 641). According to the POWIB (1919) directory there was an agricultural group attached to Kelham, based at Carlton, its code being Bro (Kel) (Ct) (IWM: Facsimile K4655). The FPHS (1973) cite both Carlton and Carlton on

Trent in their *List of British Prison Camps*. Both are in Nottinghamshire, and they are approximately 20 miles apart.

CARLTON ON TRENT (OS: SK 81- 64-). Cited in a HO document, its TA was Priswarian: Carlton on Trent, Sutton on Trent (ADM 1/8506/265–120667). The FPHS (1973) cites this camp, and the one at Carlton.

Stan Hough (per. comm., 30 August 1999) believes the PoWs were billeted in the Malt Kiln at Carlton on Trent, and put to work on rebuilding dykes and improving the banks of the surrounding watercourses. The locals regularly saw them marching down Carlton Lane, to Sutton on Trent. Today, only the bottom row of ventilators is still visible from the original red brick building. The upper part has since been converted into a workshop.

During March 1919, Dr A. de Sturler compiled reports on visits of inspection to PoW camps. One of those visited was Carlton on Trent. They are held at the National Archives at Kew (FO 383/506).

CARMARTHEN (OS: SN 41- 20-). Cited as being an agricultural depot, it had the POWIB (1919) code Fg (Crm) (IWM: Facsimile K4655). It supported three agricultural groups: Ruthin, Ciliau Aeron, and Lampeter. It was also cited by the FPHS (1973). The actual location of the camp is unknown. There is a reference made to a camp captain going to Llandybie, from Carmarthen, once a week although the camp was not one of its satellites, according to the POWIB (1919).

The Western Times and *The Liverpool Echo* (both 23 May 1918) carried reports of the re-capture of Franz Sander in Swansea who had escaped from Carmarthen.

CASTLE BROMWICH (OS: SP 144 912). Not far from Castle Bromwich Railway Station stood Berwood Hall, and its estate. The hall has now been demolished.

Bateson (*A History of Castle Vale*, 2005) states the land was flat and devoid of trees when the decision was made to create a sewage treatment plant there. But before this could happen, the existing field hedges had to be removed. These were ancient field boundaries that enclosed Round Moor, Long Close, Rough Coppice, Orchard Meadow and Brook Piece. Plants Brook, which trickled across the latter, had to be diverted. Today, these fields are remembered in the names of the nearby streets.

As the population of Birmingham and its environs grew, new methods of treating the growing demands put on sewage disposal were required, and in 1898 a revolutionary filtration method designed by Dewar and Hawksley saw raw sewage pass through a series of filters that then only required a fraction of the land previously used. Some of the former land at Home Farm, which stood near to the crossroads at Tyburn House, was retained. The rest of the land was leased out or sold.

John Boyd Dunlop had invented a pneumatic tyre in 1888. In 1916, the Dunlop Rubber Company obtained some of the land for a new factory. Smaller manufacturing concerns began to appear too. One of these was The Guanogen Fertiliser Company (which reclaimed sewage) and the Toro Soap Works. These, together with a glue factory and the sewage farm, did not do much to enhance the value, or image, of this area!

However, except for Home Farm and the semi derelict Berwood Hall Farm, which was built around the core structure, the former medieval hall, there was nothing standing on the central rectangle of land. In 1909, some 250 acres of this land was leased to the Housing Reform and Open Spaces Association, and in 1913 a further

33 acres was taken up by Birmingham Corporation Parks Department to permit sixty football matches to be played there simultaneously.

Construction of the compact filter beds continued into the period of the First World War. Loss of men to the front meant that the vital construction work was continued by women and by conscientious objectors and, when they became available, some German PoWs.

A large section of the playing fields had become a private aerodrome in September 1909. In 1911, passenger flights were being offered in a Bleriot monoplane flown by Bentfield C. Hucks.

When The Midland Aero Club established itself, a hangar was built for storing planes. It became a stopping place during early air races.

In 1914, the War Office requisitioned it for use by the Royal Flying Corps. The first active squadron at the Castle Bromwich airfield was No. 10 Squadron. Initially the pilots were accommodated in tents in a corner of the airfield; their mess was a large marquee. Later, some of them were billeted in Erdington, or at the jockeys' quarters at the nearby racecourse. As their numbers increased, the Old Hall farmhouse was turned into the officers' mess, new rooms were built, and a line of huts was erected as billets for the other ranks. More German PoWs were brought in to create the infrastructure, constructing roads, etc. They were housed in a corrugated iron shed on the airfield.

Huge corrugated buildings that were used to store the aircraft next to Castle Bromwich's railway station, were later to house the British Industries Fair; an early forerunner of the National Exhibition Centre.

In the early 1960s plans were drawn up to create the Castle Bromwich Airfield Estate on the site, which was eventually designated the name, Castle Vale. Having opened in 1901, Castle Bromwich Railway Station closed in 1965.

Castle Bromwich is described as a working camp with the POWIB (1919) code Dor (Ca B) (IWM: Facsimile K4655); it is also cited by the FPHS (1973). Its TA was Priswarian: Castle Bromwich (ADM 1/8506/265–120667).

CASTLE DONINGTON (see Donington Hall).

CATTERICK ARMY CAMP COMPLEX (parent camp) (OS: SE 180 974). Commissioned on 12 August 1914, Henry Boot secured the contract to build the army camp at Catterick. Originally to be called Richmond Camp, it was re-named Catterick to avoid confusion with Richmond Barracks in Ireland and Richmond in Surrey in 1915. Lt-General Sir Robert Baden-Powell (later Lord Baden-Powell, founder of the Scout movement) had been instrumental in establishing this camp. On his recommendation, it was proposed that 2,000 huts should be built to accommodate some 40,000 men. In the first phase, a camp for 1,000 men was established.

Macpherson (*History of the Great War – Medical Services*, Macpherson, Horrocks & Beveridge, 1923) cited the PoW camp opened 12 April 1917, with accommodation for 4,000 men in huts. It was initially a working camp under Brocton. Reports suggest over 5,000 non-commissioned PoWs arrived at the Catterick Camp in 1916. They were interned in the areas of the camp then known as the Bapuame, Peronne, and Piave Lines. The officers who accompanied them were sent to Colsterdale.

The PoWs built the officers' club, which was then officially opened by the Duke of Connaught. It closed in 1964. They also built the road to the River Swale Bridge en route to Richmond.

In 1923 the camp was used for storing redundant war equipment, and large areas of the camp were derelict. Towards the end of that year a decision was made to make Catterick a permanent military centre again. New amenities were erected.

The Times (8 April 1918) reported that P. Butz had been re-captured. *The Derby Daily Telegraph* (12 August 1918) carried a report of Walter Kleinenberg and Herbert Weide being on the run, having escaped from Catterick. *The Times* (17 August 1918) then reported Kleinberg & Martinke had been recaptured. Was this a case of mistaken identity, or just the PoWs trying to mislead the authorities? *The Times* (20 August 1918) reported that Johannes von Greuber, 45 years old had escaped the day before. On 9 October 1918, the same newspaper reported he had been re-captured after being at large for seven weeks.

On 20 August 1918, a guard shot Karl Pliefke, a German prisoner with the rank equivalent of a sergeant major, who allegedly ignored warnings by the guard to stop, and walked over to the whitewashed perimeter fence. His fellow prisoners doubted the inquest's verdict and asked the Swiss Delegation to investigate the circumstances of his death, asserting that eyewitness testimonies were suspect because of where they said they had witnessed the event developing. An account of the shooting was published in the *Northern Star* of 23 August 1918. At the hastily convened inquest, the jury was informed that the prisoners had been told not to touch the wire on several occasions. The jury returned a verdict that the deceased was shot whilst disobeying lawful orders, given by Private Keen in the execution of his duty. The foreman of the jury went so far as to commend the soldier for doing his duty. The internees also cited that any NCO that refused to work was threatened with punishment, resulting in the withdrawal of privileges.

DKF 2- Lager Catterick (Yorkshire) Am 20 August 1918, nachmittags 5,45 Uhr, wurde Vize fledwebel K. Pliefke, Infanterie-Regiment Nr. 51, 8. Komp., P.W. Nr. 4942, im Lager Catterick (Yorkshire) von Posten erschossen. Kameraden bekunden übereinstimmend, daß Pliefke, die Hände auf dem Rücken, langsamen Schrittes mit gesenktem Kopfe, in einer Entfernung von ungefähr 2 m vom inneren Draht, spazieren ging, als der tödliche Schuß ihn traf. In der englischen Presse (Northern Echo, 23.8.1918) hat der Vorfall folgende Darstellung erfahren: Gestern wurde eine Untersuchung bezüglich des Vizefeldwebels Pliefke abgehalten, wobei der betreffende Posten aussagte, daß Pliefke am Draht entlang marschiert sei und die Hand auf den Draht gelegt habe. Ein anderer Engländer bestätigt diese Aussage. Die Untersuchung kommission sei zu dem Schluß gekommen, daß Pliekfe die betreffenden Vorschriften nicht befolgt, auf Anruf des Postens nicht reagiert und somit dem Posten Berechtigung gegeben habe, auf ihn zu schießen. Der Vorsitzende habe am Schluß dem Posten gesagt: Wir befehlen Ihnen, zu jeder Zeit Ihre Pflicht zu tun. Diese Darstellung ist unwahr; in Frage kommt folgende Vorschrift: Kriegsgefangene dürfen den weißen Innendraht nicht berühren. Pliefke hat diesen Draht nicht berührt, sondern hatte die Hände auf den Rücken gelegt. Die Entfernung Pliefkes vom Draht betrug ungefähr 2 m. Die Zeugen haben den Vorfall aus nächster Nähe, aus einer Entfernung bis zu 15 m, gesehen. Demgegenüber können etwaige englische Aussagen nicht ins Gewicht fallen, da die Straße, auf der sie gewesen sein könnten, 70 bis 80 m entfernt ist, tiefer liegt und das Gesichtsfeld durch den 5 m breiten Drahtzaun beeinträchtigt wird. Das Lager betrachtet den Vorfall als Mord. (Folgen Unterschriften der Zeugen.)

Catterick den 7. September 1918 gez. G. Kleine, Vizefeldwebel, Reserve-Infanterie-Regiment 86, 10. Komp. P.W. Nr. 4835. Die Schweizerische Gesandtschaft in London wurde gebeten, die englische Regierung zu einer eingehenden Untersuchung zu veranlassen und gegen die Ermordung wehrloser Gefangener nachdrücklich Einspruch zu erheben und die Bestrafung des in Frage kommenden Wachtpostens zu fordern. In seinem Bericht über das Lager Catterick bemerkt der Vertreter der Schutzmacht hierzu unter dem 10. Oktober 1918: Am 20 August 1918 t sich ein bedauerlicher Zwischenfall ereignet, bei dem der deutsche Kriegsgefangene Karl Pliefke erschossen worden ist. Auf Anordnung des das Reservezentrum befehligenden Generals wurde in Catterick am 22. August eine gerichtliche Untersuchung abgehalten. Das Gericht war der Ansicht, daß die Aussagen der deutschen Gefangene unzuverlässigseien und ferner, daß der Gemeine Keys den ihm erteilten Befehlen entsprochen habe, als er auf den Gefangenen schoß, nachdem er ihm zugerufen und durch Zeichen bedeutet hatte, daß ER sich vom Draht entfernen solle und ihm genügend Gelegenheit geboten hatte, seinem Zuruf zu entsprechen, ehe ER auf ihn schoß, und daß ihn kein Tadel treffen Könne. Es wurde zur Zufriedenheit des Gerichts festgestellt, daß diese Befehle veröffentlicht und den Gefangenen bekannt waren. Im Lager Catterick werden die Unteroffiziere, die sich nicht freiwillig zur Arbeit melden, von dem Lagerkommandanten schlecht behandelt. Die Schweizerische Gesandtschaft wurde ersucht, das Lager Catterick baldmöglichst durch einen vertreter besuchen zu lassen und bei der englischen Regierung wegen der Beschränkungen gegenüber nicht freiwillig arbeitenden Unteroffiziere nachdrücklich Einspruch zu erheben.

CATTERICK ARMY CAMP COMPLEX (agricultural depot) (OS: SE 180 974). Catterick appears to have been upgraded from that of an agricultural depot to that of a parent camp around the same time that the Blandford camp experienced a reversal in status, that of being downgraded from that of a parent camp to that of a working camp. Also see Catterick (parent).

CAWOOD: Foster's Flour Mill (OS: SE 575 375). Foster's Flour Mill was built in 1852. From its conception it was powered by generated steam. It remained in use until its owners went bankrupt. Left dormant for nearly a decade, it was then requisitioned by the War Office to serve as a working camp during the First World War. Its POWIB (1919) code was Cat (Caw) (IWM: Facsimile K4655). According to records held by the National Archives at Kew the camp closed on 22 February 1919. Bell (per. comm., 1998) believes up until the commencement of the Second World War the mill briefly produced chocolate, before being used to make animal feed.

During the Second World War the mill returned to being a place of internment for Germans leased out to local farmers. Italians and Turks may also have been interned there at this juncture in time.

With the end of hostilities the buildings were used as an agricultural store before lying dormant, again, for many years. The buildings, then derelict, became a haven for the local children until they were destroyed in a fire in 1980. Salvaged bricks were used to build the houses that now occupy the site.

The camp was cited by the FPHS (1973). Its TA was Priswarian: Cawood (ADM 1/8506/265–120667).

CAXTON (OS: TL 305 584). A minute from the Cambridgeshire WAC (13 May 1918) states that a payment to Mr F.J. Ferguson had been made for carting water to the Caxton PoW camp. He was then instructed to hand over his watercart and his implements to the camp. The committee members were informed on 8 July 1918 that confirmation had been received from the Board, informing them that Caxton Workhouse was thought suitable to accommodate PoWs, and that the guardians should be informed of their decision.

The workhouse was designed by William T. Nash and opened in 1836 on a site towards the northern end of Caxton village. It had its own infirmary and chapel.

London County Council took over the workhouse building in 1930 and it was converted into an old peoples' home called Hillside. Most of the buildings were demolished in 1970; what remain have been re-developed into private dwellings (www.caxtonhouse.org).

A working camp, its POWIB (1919) code was Pa (Cax) (IWM: Facsimile K4655). Its TA was Priswarian: Caxton (ADM 1/8506/265–120667). Caxton is also cited by the FPHS (1973).

CAYTHORPE (OS: SK 938 489). The only evidence that this camp existed is found in a document produced by the POWIB (1919). This states Caythorpe was an agricultural group, attached to Grantham. Its code is given as Bro (Gr) (Cay) (IWM: Facsimile K4655).

Caythorpe Hall or its grounds may hold the key. Built of stone in the classical style between 1824 and 1827, it stands near the site of a much older hall. The old hall was the seat of Sir Giles Hussey, the Earl of Surrey. Today, a park wall is all that remains of the earlier dwelling. Towards the end of the century, Major Lubbock, a banker, started to develop the site. During this period the new main residence was built, and the grounds re-organised. A stable capable of holding fifty horses was also created.

Within three years of its completion the complex passed into the hands of the wife of a prominent Lancashire brewer, Mrs Yerbrough. Upon her death, in 1946, her will stated that the estate should be sold for agricultural education. Currently, de Montfort University have their School of Agriculture there.

Caythorpe Court is a Grade II listed building. Its grounds also carry a Grade II listing on the Register of Parks and Gardens. There are plans afoot to establish a refugee centre there.

CHALGROVE (OS: SU 63- 96-). Chalgrove is only cited in lists produced for the Forces Postal History Society (1937, 1971 & 1996). It may be that this camp was at Charlbury, as there has been no evidence found to support the FPHS (1973) claim.

CHAPEL EN LE FRITH: Bank Hall (OS: SK 052 788). The internment camp was at Bank Hall, a large country estate on the outskirts of Chapel en le Frith. Originally referred to as Little Ridge, the site has had several owners. The first of these was Nicholas Browne (*c.*1618). On the death of Peter Gaskell, in 1718, his four daughters became joint owners of the Hall, and by marrying Ann Gaskell, Jasper Frith then bought the shares of other sisters. Their son, Samuel 'Squire' Frith (1780–1828), had the hall rebuilt. Hitchens (*The Warming Stone: Reminiscences of Early 20th Century Childhood in Chapel en le Frith, Derbyshire*, *c.*1998) cites Henry Constantine Renshaw, an absent landlord, also had the hall rebuilt. Twelve months after his death in 1894 the estate, now comprising of some 238 acres, was put on the market. It was not until 1897 that a buyer, Raymond Unwin, was found; he paid £11,000 for it. Until the grounds were turned into an internment camp there was a bridle path that was a public right of way across Bank Hall. On the departure of the PoWs the new owner was loath to restore this bridle path. *The High Peak Reporter* (2 April 1921) carried a warning telling the public that notices had been posted not to cross this land.

Chapel en le Firth is also cited in a list of places being prepared to accept PoWs in the *Derby Daily Telegraph (10 July 1918).* Previous to this report was one of

19 February 1918 that stated timber buildings were under consideration to house 'the considerable amount' of PoWs expected to work in the local quarries.

Cited by the POWIB (1919), its code was Bro (Pe D) (Cf) (IWM: Facsimile K4655). It is also cited by the FPHS (1973).

P Hildebrand (d. 4 April 1919), a German soldier, was buried in St. Thomas A-Becket Churchyard. Permission was granted, on 9 August 1961, to remove his remains to Cannock Chase.

CHAPEL OAK – SALFORD PRIORS – IRON CROSS (OS: SP 057 519). Chapel Oak only appears in the List of Prison Camps produced for the FPHS that was edited by Neil Russell in 1996. The POWIB (1919) cite Iron Cross, Chapel Oak as a location, and gave it the code Dor (Ev) (C O) (Ie) (IWM: Facsimile K4655). Salford Priors is cited in a HO document; Its TA was Priswarian: Salford Priors (ADM 1/8506/265–120667). Despite three entries by different organisations nothing of this camp can be traced. Park Hall may unlock the mystery that surrounds this camp.

CHARLBURY (see Chipping Norton).

CHARLTON KINGS (OS: SO 962 210). Only cited in a HO document, its TA was Priswarian: Charlton Kings (ADM 1/8506/265–120667). Its exact location is unknown. Perhaps Charlton House holds the key.

CHATHAM: Naval Detention Barracks (OS: TQ 762 692). Machray (*Great Britain's Humane Treatment of German PoWs*, Wilson & Hammerton, 1919) wrote it was common knowledge that Churchill had no love for the German submariners. He demanded that if any were caught they were not to be regarded as 'honourable prisoners' and would not be treated as normal PoWs. So when the news broke of three *U-Boot* crews being sent to the Naval Detention Barracks at Chatham Dockyards, it was not received well by the German authorities, who sought any excuse to fuel their propaganda in the war against Britain. However, on his inspection of the Chatham camp, Mr Page, the American Ambassador in London, wrote to his colleague in Berlin that the officers and crews were not being maltreated in any way, but were just being kept in isolation, away from the other PoWs. In June 1915, the British government said it had abolished this isolation policy, however; most interned crews of *U-Boote* were then sent to Dyffryn Aled in North Wales.

The FPHS (1973) list the camp as Chatham Detention Barracks.

CHEAM (OS: TQ 242 636). A working camp, its POWIB (1919) code was Fe (Che) (IWM: Facsimile K4655). PoWs held at Feltham were not sympathetic to the German cause, and so any PoW based in Cheam would most likely have been the same. Also cited by the FPHS (1973), its TA was *Priswarian: Cheam House, Sutton* (ADM 1/8506/265–120667). Cheam House stood on the west side of the Broadway, south of High Street and should not be confused with Lower Cheam House which stood in Gander Green Lane.

Cheam survived as a rural village until the end of the First World War when the character of the village changed in the 1920s as the buildings along the southern end of Malden Road were cleared when the road was widened. Only one building has survived: this was a small late medieval timber framed cottage, which was dismantled and re-erected on a new site. The area around High Street and the cross roads where Cheam House stood was also cleared and re-developed. The fields around the village changed even more dramatically as they became overrun with suburban streets and houses. By 1939 most of Cheam was built up and the place had assumed its modern form.

CHELMSFORD (OS: TL 719 071). A working camp, its POWIB (1919) code was Pa (Chfd) (IWM: Facsimile K4655). Chelmsford is cited by the FPHS (1973). Its TA was Priswarian: Chelmsford (ADM 1/8506/265–120667).

A possibility that Chelmsford's workhouse, or its grounds, was used to accommodate the PoWs sent here cannot be dismissed, although there is no evidence to support this notion. It may have instead operated from the prison, where some PoWs that transgressed the rules of internment were detained.

CHELMSFORD DETENTION BARRACKS (OS: TL 719 071). Jackson (*The Prisoner 1914–1918*, 1989) cites, at the end of 1915, forty-two detention camps had been set up across the country. But these were not special units created for those that had transgressed the rules of their internment – such as trying to escape – but were camps set up to detain, mostly enemy alien civilians, arrested under the powers of the Defence of the Realm Act. However, there was also a need for special units to be put in place to detain those that transgressed the law. Segregated units of civil and military prisons were designated as detention centres.

For attempting to escape from the camp at Dyffryn Aled in 1915, a military court – presiding at Chester Castle – sentenced Oberleutnant Hans Werner von Helldorf, and Kapitans Heindrich George von Henning and Herman Tholens, to eighty-four days imprisonment. They went to Chelmsford's Detention Barracks. These three Germans had escaped and attempted to rendezvous with two *U-Boote*, sent to pick them up, at Great Orme Head. But the submarine commanders decided only one boat would go to the rendezvous point and the other would hunt for ships to sink. The awaiting boat failed to see their signal from the shore and sailed away. The three escapees were caught when an improvised alternative plan did not succeed. Helldorf gained cult status when he was put into solitary confinement at Chelmsford Prison. He described his cell as small, with bars on the windows, set high up in the walls.

Oberleutnant Heinz Justus was sentenced to fifty-six days at Chelmsford Prison for attempting to escape. Whilst being transferred from Wakefield, under escort, he jumped off the train that was taking him to Maidenhead.

On 26 May 1917 Leutnant Lehmann actually escaped from Chelmsford Detention Barracks. His escape and re-capture were cited in *The Times* (28 May 1917). He was caught at Basildon. Chelmsford Detention Centre had the POWIB (1919) code C D B.

DKF 68: Oberleuntnant von Helldorf verbüßte diese Strafe in Helmford (sic) *bei London, wo er in einer gewölbeartig Zelle in Einzelhaft gehalten wurde. Die Zelle etwas großes nur 6 qmses, notwendiger heizbar und hatte nur bei hoch-gelegenem schwer-vergittertem Fenster.*

CHELTENHAM (OS: SO 94- 22-). Cheltenham is probably better known for its young ladies' finishing school and its racecourse, rather than having a PoW working camp there in the First World War. The camp had the POWIB (1919) code Dor (Ch) (IWM: Facsimile K4655). It is also cited by the FPHS (1973), but no physical evidence has been found to suggest where this camp existed, although racecourses were often used, and that may hold the key.

CHEPSTOW (see Beachley and Chepstow Shipyards).

CHERITON BISHOP (OS: SX 773 930). Cheriton Bishop had the POWIB code Dor (Ce). It was described as a working camp. The HO had the TA Priswarian Cheriton Bishop for it.

Pitton Cross was suggested as a place to house PoWs sent to the area. Areas proposed for the deployment of PoWs were Cheriton Cross, Dunsford, and Tedburn St Mary (because it was not suitable for tractors) as recorded in the *Western Times* (8 January 1918).

CHERTSEY (OS: TQ 030 660). Internees sent to Chertsey may have been billeted at the town's workhouse which was built in 1836 at Ottershaw on the south side of Murray Road. By 1914, many of the outbuildings had been replaced. When the Local Government Act of 1929 abolished the Poor Law functions the workhouse became the property of Surrey County Council, who renamed it Murray House on 10 October 1930. On 16 June 1932 the premises were handed over to the Council's Mental Hospitals Committee, and it became the Murray House Certified Institution for Mental Defectives, an annexe of the newly established Botley Park Hospital. In 1948, along with its parent hospital, it became part of the South West Metropolitan Regional Health Authority. Murray House closed in 1984; most of the former workhouse and hospital buildings have been demolished, but the entrance block, which is Grade II listed, and the chapel survive, both having been converted to residential use (www.ezitis.myzen.co.uk/murrayhouse).

Reports of visits of inspection, held at the National Archives at Kew, to PoW camps in the UK, by Monsieur Corragioni d'Orelli during June 1919, include Chertsey (FO 383/508).

CHESTERTON (OS: TL 464 606). A letter from the Commandant of the PoW camp at Chesterton, seeking answers, was read out to the Cambridgeshire WAC on 8 March 1919. He had raised concerns as to the treatment of PoWs involved in the repair of the breach to the Soham Lode, and of the subsequent removal of the floodwater. A later minute, dated 19 April 1919, sought 100 PoWs for Chesterton's PoW Camp. It was described as a working camp, with the POWIB (1919) code, Pa (Che) (IWM: Facsimile K4655). Its TA was Priswarian: Chesterton, Cambridge (ADM 1/8506/265–120667). Chesterton is also cited by the FPHS (1973).

CHEVINGTON (OS: TL 784 596). Chevington was a working camp with the POWIB (1919) code, Pa (Chv) (IWM: Facsimile K4655). Its TA was Priswarian: Chevington, Suffolk (ADM 1/8506/265–120667). The location of this camp is not known. Perhaps Chevington Hall may hold the key.

CHICHESTER: Blairfield (OS: SU 858 042). Cited in a HO document, its TA was Priswarian: Blairfield, Chichester (ADM 1/8506/265–120667).

Blairfield is recorded as being the private residence of Miss Bramwell in *Kelly's Trade Directory* for Sussex of 1911. It stood near the junction of Whyke Lane and Whyke Road, near to The Crown. The Ordnance Survey Map of 1880 does not show the house, but later editions (of 1899 and 1913) show it, as Blairfield. Later maps record the house as Whyke Grange.

CHIGWELL: Belmont Park House (OS: TQ 437 937). A second internment camp was established in the Chigwell area, at Belmont Park House, the other being at Fox Burrows Farm. The POWIB (1919) directory recognised this as an agricultural group, its code being Pa (Chg) (Bn) (IWM: Facsimile K4655). Its TA was Priswarian: Belmont House, Chigwell (ADM 1/8506/265–120667).

CHIGWELL ROW: Fox Burrows Farm (OS: TQ 480 929). Fox Burrows Farm had the POWIB (1919) code Pa (Chg) (IWM: Facsimile K4655). It is cited by the FPHS (1973). Its TA was Priswarian: Foxburrow Farm (sic), Chigwell Row (ADM 1/8506/265–120667).

Minutes of the War Agricultural Executive Committee for Essex (12 February 1917) reveal PoWs 'should be placed at Fox Burrows Farm in Hainault Forest'.

On 20 September 1918 the *Derby Daily Telegraph* and the *Coventry Evening Telegraph* carried reports that three of the five PoWs had been recaptured after escaping from a farm at Hainault.

Reports on visits of inspection to PoW camps at Rainham, South Ockenden, Fox Burrows Farm, and Chipping Ongar are held at the National Archives, Kew (FO 383/506).

A satellite was established at Belmont Park House, Chigwell.

CHIPPING NORTON: Hillside House, Charlbury (OS: SP 358 191). Chipping means market, and the one at Norton, for a considerable time, was the leading commercial centre for wool in the Evenlode Valley. As the industry grew, the town also grew in stature as it became an important meeting place for merchants. The town was granted its Royal Charter by King John, to host an annual fair to sell wool.

A photograph exists of thirty-eight PoWs, in their uniforms, posing outside a house at Chipping Norton. This is thought to be Hillside House, where PoWs were interned. A modern map places this house at Hixet Wood, Charlbury. It is described as a working camp with the POWIB (1919) code Dor (C N), and had a satellite at Brailes (IWM: Facsimile K4655). A HO list of camps (May 1918) cites its TA as Priswarian: Chipping Norton. It is omitted from a later list (April 1919), which cites a camp at Chalbury, and gives its TA as Priswarian: Charlbury (ADM 1/8506/265–120667). Both Chipping Norton and Charlsbury (sic) are cited by the FPHS (1973).

CHIPPING ONGAR (OS: TL 554 035). Described by the POWIB (1919) as being an agricultural depot, it had the code Pa (Ch O) (IWM: Facsimile K4655). Based at Bowes House, its TA was Priswarian, Chipping Ongar. Abbots Roding was its satellite. Its TA was Priswarian: Chipping Ongar (ADM 1/8506/265–120667), and it is also cited by the FPHS (1973).

The internees were critical of the camp's canteen. Reports on visits of inspection to PoW camps at Rainham, South Ockenden, Fox Barrows Farm (Chigwell), and Chipping Ongar are held at the National Archives, Kew (FO 383/432).

In the Second World War, the house was used to accommodate officers of the American forces based in the UK. Previously it had been a private school. Originally called Shelley House, it is still standing today, having in more recent times been converted into flats.

DKF 33: Aus den Berichten des Schweizerischen Delegierten vom September und Oktober 1917 geht hervor, daß in den Arbeitslager in England noch immer Mißstände herrschten. In Hemel Hempstead (Herts) und Chipping Ongar (Essex) fehlten die Kantinen, in South Ochendon (Essex) (sic) *die Öfen.*

CHIPSTEAD – NETHERNE: Surrey County Lunatic Asylum (OS: TQ 296 563). PoWs worked in the market garden at Netherne Hospital, near to Chipstead. No evidence has been found to suggest any PoW was a patient.

> In 1898, Surrey County Council selected Netherne as the site for a new psychiatric hospital to relieve an overcrowding problem at nearby hospitals … a 960

patient hospital opened on 1 April 1909. The majority of patients suffered from stress, senility, melancholia or other mental handicaps. The aim was to re-integrate patients into society, but for many, Netherne became a permanent home – a 'place of sanctuary' … During World War 1, Netherne had to handle large numbers of patients from neighbouring hospitals, which had been taken over by the military. Food from the market garden contributed to national supplies and convalescent soldiers and German PoWs were bought in to assist.

CHIRK: Hendre, Glyn Ceiriog (OS: SJ 196 376). Its TA was Priswarian: Hendre, Glyn (ADM 1/8506/265–120667). The camp is cited by the FPHS (1973), and should not be confused with Rockfield, The Hendre, another cited camp. A slate quarry existed at Hendre, near Glyn Ceiriog, and this is could be where this pool of labour was utilised.

CHISELDON (OS: SU 185 795). Described as a working camp, it had the POWIB (1919) code Dor (Chi) (IWM: Facsimile K4655). Cited by the FPHS (1973), it had the TA Priswarian: Chiseldon (ADM 1/8506/265–120667).

Crawford (*Wiltshire and The Great War: Training the Empire's Soldiers*, 1999) states according to *The North Wilts Herald* (14 September 1914) that contracts for the barracks had been awarded to W.E. Chivers of Devises to build timber buildings with corrugated iron roofs at a cost of £15,000–£16,000. Land south of Chiseldon belonging to the Calley Estate and the Stratton Brothers was requisitioned, and the first troops to arrive slept under canvas. The camp eventually accommodated some 5,000 men, including two satellite sites near Wroughton. These satellites had tented accommodation.

In 1920, the camp was scaled down considerably with much of the equipment being sold off, as South Africans, Australian, and New Zealanders waited to be repatriated from there.

In the latter part of 1917, according to Bailey (*The Story of Chiseldon Camp 1914–1922*, 1998) the PoWs were accommodated in 'H' Line of Chiseldon army camp. Their principle activity was agricultural work, combined with some routine maintenance work within the army camp itself. Some PoWs worked on clearing the locks on the Kennet and Avon Canal.

As time went on, it was agreed that individual farmers could apply for a small group of internees to work on their farms without the presence of guards. The farmer was required to provide a secure place for them, and the authorities would supply their food. It was reported that PoWs sent to Draycot Farm were given bread, clandestinely, by Arthur and Albert Long, whose father was employed on the farm. They recall, during their school holidays, tying loops in string for the PoWs to use when gathering in the harvest. The Germans slept in the barn, and in the evenings they could be heard singing. The camp closed on 1 November 1918. The camp's hospital was also used to treat PoWs.

CHOLSEY (OS: SU 58- 86-). An agricultural depot, its POWIB (1919) code was Dor (Cho) (IWM: Facsimile K4655). It had three agricultural groups attached to it, at Cumnor, Brightwell and Watlington. It is also cited by the FPHS (1973). Its TA is Priswarian: Cholsey (ADM 1/8506/265–120667). The exact location of the camp is unknown, but it may have had links with the county lunatic asylum (Maudsford), where it is known two internees from Newbury were sent in November 1914 (D/H10/A4/9).

CHORLEYWOOD: Glen Chess Stables (OS: TQ 045 944). The FPHS (1973) cites Rickmanworth and Glen Chess in their *List of British Prison Camps*. The HO cites this camp as being in Loudwater, and gave it the TA Priswarian: Glen Chess Stables, Loudwater (ADM 1/8506/265–120667).

In 1848, Herbert Ingram, proprietor of the *Illustrated London News*, bought Loudwater Mill because he wanted to manufacture his own paper. Subsequently, he built a house which he called Glen Chess. The house stood alongside the mill which, due to legal action taken against it for polluting the River Chess, closed in 1885.

Hertfordshire County Council WAC minutes state, on 1 October 1918, a camp was being prepared to take forty PoWs.

CHURCHDOWN (OS: SO 886 189). Located at Chosen House, Churchdown, this working camp had the POWIB (1919) code Dor (Cd) (IWM: Facsimile K4655). Its TA is Priswarian: Churchdown (ADM 1/8506/265–120667). Churchdown was visited during a tour of inspections by Dr A. de Sturler and Monsieur R. de Sturler. Their report, written during March and April 1919, is held at the National Archives at Kew (FO 383/506).

CHURT (OS: SU 85- 38-). A working camp, it had the POWIB (1919) code Dor (Cu) (IWM: Facsimile K4655). It is also cited by the FPHS (1973). Its TA is Priswarian: Churt (ADM 1/8506/265–120667). The exact location of the camp is unknown.

The Coventry Evening Telegraph, *The Liverpool Echo* (both 19 December 1918) and *The Derby Daily Telegraph* (20 December 1918) all reported four PoWs were killed when the lorry they were travelling in, from Churt to Farnham, left the highway and turned over as it hit a tree on Tilford Road. The driver of the vehicle, three other PoWs and their guard were flung free. It was reported all four had died at the scene, crushed by their cargo.

CILIAU AERON (OS: SN 506 228). Cited as being at Cilian Aeron (sic) by the POWIB (1919), the camp had the code Fg (Car) (C A) (IWM: Facsimile K4655). It was a satellite of the camp at Carmarthen. Cited as being at Manachdy House (sic), its TA was Priswarian: Ciliau Aeron (ADM 1/8506/265–120667). This was probably at Monachty. Like a lot of Welsh place names, attempts to anglicise them result in variations in spellings at different points in time.

The Cistercian Abbey of Strata Florida was founded in 1164. Soon after, some 30 miles to its north, the hospitium at Monachty was built. Travellers on their way to the abbey could stop for the night and pay for their hospitality according to their means. These establishments were where not only hospitality started but being allowed a break from walking blisters could abate, creating the first hospitals. At the time of the Dissolution (1536), the abbey and its lands were passed to the Crown.

The Mynachty estate was granted to Richard Devereux before passing into the hands of John Stedman, of Chelsey. The house then came into the possession of the Gwyn family before passing to the Gwynne family. In 1805, Lewis Gwynne died leaving no direct heir and the estate passed to his cousin, the Reverend Alban Thomas Jones, of Tulgyn. Local legend says Gwynne left a considerable fortune, and a horse struggled to pull a sledge laden with gold when it was removed from Monachty to be taken to Tulgyn. As the new lord of the manor, the reverend became instrumental in rebuilding the pier and improving the harbour at Aberaeron in 1807.

The reverend's son, also forenamed Alban, extended Aberaeron but only allowed houses built to a set plan, that had been produced by his architect Edward Haycock. Unlike his father, he resided at Monachty, and built a new wing. Records then show the estate back in the Gwynne name, until a solicitor from Coventry, Albert Henry Jarrard, bought it in 1936.

A sale catalogue of 1936 describes the house as being of 'Georgian character', comprising on the ground floor: entrance hall with stone paved floor, morning room communicating with a small winter garden drawing room, dining room, smoking room, domestic offices, store room, butler's pantry, servant's hall, kitchen, scullery, fine oak staircase, cellars. On the first floor: five bedrooms, day nursery, night nursery, and linen cupboard. On the second floor: three large rooms for servants. To the rear of the house, extensive buildings, yard, larders, store-room, coach house, laundry, boot room, stables, etc., walled garden, three greenhouses for peaches and nectarines, and farm buildings.

Jarrard re-sold the mansion and some land to a trustee for Ivor Jones in 1937. On his death it passed to his son Nigel Symons-Jones.

There are no records to prove the house or its grounds were used as an internment camp.

CIRENCESTER: The Old Vicarage (OS: SP 022 022). Cirencester had a working camp with the POWIB (1919) code Dor (Cir) (IWM: Facsimile K4655). It is also cited by the FPHS (1973). Its TA is Priswarian: Cirencester (ADM 1/8506/265–120667). The camp was located at The Old Vicarage on Thomas Street.

CLAVELSHAY (OS: ST 25- 31-). Mark (per. comm., various dates) cited minutes of the Somerset WAC that showed fifty-five PoWs were transferred from Sandhill Park to Dulverton, Bridgwater, Thorloxton, Kingston Seymour and Clavelshay in equal numbers. Five were being retained at Sandhill Park, and were being billeted in cottages on the estate.

CLAYPOLE: Manor Farm (OS: SK 87- 47-). Cited by the FPHS (1973), its TA was Priswarian, Manor Farm, Claypole (ADM 1/8506/265–120667). Contemporary maps show a Manor Farm at Dry Doddington. Its present incumbents were unaware of PoWs being utilised at this farm during the First World War.

CLAYWORTH (OS: SK 72- 88-). Although the minutes of the Notts County WAC (28 January 1919) record a migratory gang being at Clayworth. Its exact location remains a mystery.

CLEADON (see East Boldon).

CLEE HILL DHU (OS: SO 63- 73-). The Clee Hills are famous for their basaltic dhu-stone, a mineral much sought after for its road building qualities. The area also once supported numerous coalmines, which were sunk through the very hard rock of the area. The coal in turn supported brickworks and iron making.

Today, there are very few traces of the coal shafts to be seen, as most have been filled in, or forgotten.

Clee Hill Dhu was a working camp; its POWIB (1919) code was Shrw (Cle) (IWM: Facsimile K4655). The exact location of the camp remains a mystery, although a question raised in the House of Commons may provide a key. When the Member of

Parliament for Ludlow asked why PoWs at Hard Hill had the 'luxury of being idle and smoking', he was probably referring to Hardmans Hill, near Milson (*Hansard*, 1917).

CLENT (OS: SO 92- 79-). An agricultural group attached to Northfield AD with the POWIB (1919) code Dor (Nfd) (Cln) (IWM: Facsimile K 4655), its TA is Priswarian: Clent, Stourbridge (ADM 1/8506/265–120667). No physical evidence has been found to suggest where this camp was actually located. Perhaps Clent House, now demolished, which was built *c.*1710, holds the key to this camp's location.

CLEOBURY MORTIMER (OS: SO 67- 75-). In the early twentieth century, a hard basalt dhu-stone was mined on the Brown Clee, which was brought down to Ditton Priors below, on an incline railway, and then taken onwards by light railway to Cleobury Mortimer. Whether any PoWs sent to this area were employed in this activity is not known, but an agricultural group, attached to Leominster was established here. Its POWIB (1919) code was Shrw (Lmr) (Cb) (IWM: Facsimile K 4655). The FPHS (1973) list this camp as Cleobury, Salop. These entries are the only evidence that a camp existed here.

Cleobury Mortimer Poor Law Union adopted the existing parish workhouse that could accommodate up to 150 inmates. It stood in an isolated position, approximately 0.25 miles from the town near Doddsplatt, off Catherton Road. In August 1932, the buildings were adapted into a youth hostel that became known as Styper House. The hostel closed on 30 September 1936. Today Glen Park Caravan Park occupies the site.

CLIFTON (Gang No. 1) (OS: TL 16- 38-). Employment time sheets, held by the Bedfordshire County Record Office (WW1/AC/PW/1 & 2) that were created between January and May 1919, cite the names of nine PoWs, and their guard, that comprised Gang No. 1, at Clifton. The names of the PoWs were: Gerling; R. Hoppe; Jandt; Katzwinka; A. Konkel; Kuchta; P. Kulessa; Kuscherka; and Kutcher. The guard comprised Privates R. Malins and E. Maxwell. They are also named as assisting the foreman at Clifton's No. 2 Gang.

CLIFTON (Gang No. 2) (OS: TL 16- 38-). Employment time sheets held by Bedfordshire County Record Office (WW1/AC/PW/1 & 2) record a second gang existed at Clifton. Privates R. Malins and E. Maxwell are named as assisting the foreman of both gangs. No PoWs were named in this gang.

CLIFTONTHORPE: Old Parks (OS: SK 362 188). On 16 January 1918 a letter was requested from the chairman of the Leicestershire WAC to inform John Gilles Shields that the asking price of £100 per annum, to rent Old Parks on the Southwood Estates to intern PoWs, was too high. The minute of Wednesday 30 January 1918 states there was a request to expedite the supply of PoWs for Old Parks, suggesting the cost of renting had been resolved (DE 1841/1). *Kelly's Trade Directory* (Leicestershire, 1913) cites Shields was a Justice of the Peace, owning farm property at Isley Walton, and as the land agent, acted for the Gretton family at Donington Hall.

COAL ASTON: Little Norton (OS: SK 361 818). The camp took its name from the Derbyshire village of Coal Aston, but the camp was nearer to Little Norton, in South Yorkshire. The camp appears on a *List of PoWs Camps in England and Wales*, compiled on 1 January 1918, in the section for working camps. Its TA is cited as being Priswarian: Dronfield (ADM 1/8506/265–120667).

Those interned at Coal Aston were concerned that the British were exploiting them and that many of them were not used to the nature of work being asked of them.

The Norton History Group (1995) states it did not bode well to be seen fraternising with the PoWs. They make reference to a Sheffield man being sentenced to six months imprisonment on 19 October 1917, for selling six loaves of bread to PoWs. A man from the Boscombe area suffered a similar experience for selling cakes to PoWs in Wiltshire, and a woman was fined for passing on a letter to a German PoW on 3 April 1918. They also recall local boys stealing carrots from the surrounding fields and crossing the Meadowhead to push them through the wire for the prisoners.

The camp stood near Birch Farm, at Little Norton, at the corner of Greenhill Lane and Chesterfield Road. The area was covered with huts in which the PoWs were kept, and each morning the PoWs were marched to the opposite side of the field, to their place of work, where they erected buildings for the airfield. He suggests it was surrounded by barbed wire to keep people out, rather than to keep people in. The camp was where a garage stands today. Local legend states the prisoners could often be seen marching down to the tram terminus at Chantrey Road, to go to work in other areas. Robertson (*Bases of Air Strategy Airlife, Higham*, 1998) includes Coal Aston amongst his aerodromes and air bases that were established in the First World War to combat German Zeppelin raids.

Reports on visits of inspections to PoW camps at Coal Aston (Sheffield), Monks Abbey (Lincolnshire), Peak Dale Quarries (Derbyshire), and Sproxton Moor (Yorkshire) are held at the National Archives at Kew (FO 383/432). Coal Aston is cited by the FPHS (1973).

The camp closed on 20 May 1918, and the site was put up for sale in March 1922. Since then there has been substantial redevelopment to the area, and it now embraces the Jordanthorpe housing estate.

DKF 31: Auch in Lochen Doon, auf der Insel Raasay, in Newlandside, Ceal Aston (sic), *Sutton Veney* (sic), *Bowithick, Netheravon, Yatesbury, Rovrah* (sic), *Port Clarence, und Hayrmyres* (sic) *werden die Leute zu sehr ausgenutzt.*

DKF 32: In Coal Aston sind die Kriegsgefangenen den Roheiten der Zivilunttemehmer preisgegeben, was unbedingt abgestellt werden muß.

COCKERMOUTH: 14 MAIN STREET (OS: NY 121 308). Main Street is famous for containing the house that William Wordsmith was born in, and has a museum dedicated to papermaking and printing; industries the town is famous for. A lesser known fact is that PoWs were billeted there in the First World War as cited by surviving minutes of the Cumberland WAC (CC1/39/1–2). They were expected to clear out watercourses in the area.

COCKERMOUTH: TWEED MILL (OS: NY 125 302). The mill stood in what is Tweed Mill Lane today. It is cited as being a billet for PoWs in the First World War in a minute of the Cumberland WAC (CC1/39/1–2). They were expected to clear out water courses in the area.

CODSALL: Wrottesley Hall (OS: SJ 850 018). In 1976, Wrottesley Hall was transformed into three luxury self-contained executive homes. They stand on the site of the first hall that dates back to the twelfth century, which was destroyed in 1897 by a fire that ravished the house and its treasures. In 1923 a second, smaller, hall was built on the site. For a brief period, prior to its present day arrangement it was used as a country club.

As a child, Mrs Ray MBE, who lived in Middle Lane, Oaken, recalled seeing PoWs walking to and from the stables at Wrottesley Hall. They worked on local farms in the Oaken and Codsall Wood areas. Two young English soldiers, with rifles, escorted each working party as it marched along the roads to and from the farms. The Germans often sang as they marched. Each week a large barrel of herrings was delivered to the PoW Camp from Codsall Station (Davies, per. comm., 2005).

Near to Codsall, Wrottesley Hall is recorded as being an agricultural group by the POWIB (1919), its code being Bro (Et) (Wro) (IWM: Facsimile K4655). It was a satellite of Ettingshall. Its TA was Priswarian: Codsall (ADM 1/8506/265–120667).

COLESHILL (OS: SU 954 958). A documentary showing a former water tower, near to Coleshill, being converted into habitable accommodation that was screened by Channel 4 (*Grand Designs*, 1999) cited that PoWs in the First World War had worked on its construction. But there was no mention made about where their camp was located. Perhaps Coleshill House, built by Jacob Pleydell Bouverie (*c.*1650) to designs set by Inigo Jones, may hold the answer.

COLLEGE TOWN (see Frimley).

COMBE FLOREY (OS: ST 151 31). Combe Florey is a small village that lies, off the main A358, approximately 6 miles north west of Taunton, about 1 mile from Bishops Lydeard. Amongst some of the most beautiful and unusual houses in England stands the Elizabethan Gate House at Combe Florey. The house, built in the local red sandstone, was constructed for John Francis, whose family were the lords of the manor. The building which used to be the main entrance to Combe Florey House has the most amazing archway. It was built by Thomas Francis in 1665. The Gate House is now a private dwelling.

According to Mark (per. comm., various dates) minutes of the Somerset WAC (18 October 1918) cite the Gate House at Combe Florey was approved as winter quarters for those PoWs being interned at Sandhill Park. Later minutes suggest there had been attempts to requisition Combe Florey House (29 October 1918). However, after the owner protested, it appears that approval was not given and instead the PoWs were distributed to Dulverton, Clavelshay, Thurloxton, Bridgwater and Kingston Seymour, with five remaining at Sandhill Park.

COLSTERDALE (OS: SE 152 814). When Leighton Reservoir was created in 1908, a construction camp was erected at Breary Banks to house the workers required to build it. At the outbreak of war in 1914, the dam had not been completed, and the work was suspended. The huts of the construction camp were then taken over by the army, and the first new occupants were a section of the West Yorkshire Regiment. They arrived by train at Masham, on 22 and 25 September 1914 and had to march the 5 miles to the Breary Banks camp. It was around this time, according to War Office documents, that the camp was identified and referred to as Colsterdale. An early account says there were three rows of navvies' huts, supplemented by three rows of tents, when the 1st Battalion arrived, but more huts were built in the following month. It finally comprised of fifty wooden buildings, which included a hospital, mission, recreation rooms and married quarters. Today, there is a monument to the 'Leeds Pals' at the site. The 1st Leeds Pals occupied the camp until June 1915, when they moved to Ripon. Other units had replaced them when the decision was made to transform the camp into an internment camp for officers in August 1917.

The FPHS (1973) also cites Colsterdale, Yorkshire in its listings. It is cited the PoW Camp was opened in August 1917 with hutted accommodation for 700 officers and 200 servant men.

The Times (18 March 1918) cites an escape of six officers from Ripon. The date of this escape pre-dates the date that camp opened. The six escapees were Frank Kaars, Augustus Hiller, Rudolf Schneider, Lorenz Hellselder, Helmuth Reinsvorss and Fritz Spraub, who may have absconded from Colsterdale.

The *Deutsche Kriegsgefangene in Feindesland* (1919) cites a Nordlager (North Camp) being at Colsterdale but this Nordlager could have been at Ripon, where there was a North Camp.

The Times (24 August 1917) cited von Grota and Lage had escaped. The same paper (29 August 1917) reported their re-capture near Whitby. *The Police Gazette* (28 August 1917) offers supporting evidence of their escape as it states Thomas von Grote, 35, and Heinrich Emil Matthies, 30, both of the navy, along with Willi Brossmann, 24, and Fritz Laue, 28, both of the army, had escaped from the Leyburn area on or around 21–23 August 1917. It is not uncommon for reports of foreign nationals to have their names misspelt. And in an attempt to confuse the authorities false names were often stated. And, in attempts to confuse the authorities, false names were often stated or written down incorrectly (FO 383/432). The news of the escape was reported in the *Daily Express* according to a newspaper cutting held by the Imperial War Museum (IWM 95/14/1). It named the four officers that had escaped from Colsterdale, and of another missing from the camp at Cove Heights, near Aldershot. The newspaper cutting had previously been in the possession of Miss Rees, a translator at the POWIB.

Dr Schwyzer and Dr Vischer inspected the camp on behalf of the Swiss Legation on 26 June 1918. It was stated that the roofs of some huts were leaking (FO 383/432).

The camp had the POWIB (1919) code CTD (IWM: Facsimile K4655). Its TA was Priswarian, Colsterdale (ADM 1/8506/265–120667).

When Oberleutnant Heinz Justus attempted to abscond from Colsterdale, he changed into a skirt and a hat with veil. The attire had been smuggled into the camp, sent in parcels from Germany. His inability to disguise his voice led to him being re-caught before he could buy a railway ticket to London. He was committed to Chelmsford Prison for thirty-five days. In another bid for freedom, he attempted to get away as he was being transferred from Maidenhead to Wakefield. Unsuccessful on several occasions, he admitted the poor success rate of escapes from Britain was due to the 'splendid isolation' of it being an island.

Sachsse & Cossman (*Kreigsgefangenen in Skipton*, Reiinhardt 1920) cite when a Swiss inspection team arrived to visit the camp in 9 October 1917, around 150 officers complained to them of the cold and wet conditions, and sought a move. The majority of them, around sixty in number, had recently been captured at Cambrai (late 1917). They asked to be transferred for health reasons into another camp in a warmer part of England. It is unclear if they took their servants with them when they left for the 'sunnier climate' of Skipton, in January 1918.

A diary was kept by Johannes Rienau, who was billeted in Hut 5 with nineteen others. He tells of his mundane life at the camp.

Werner Fürbringer was sent to Colsterdale after his command, *UB110* was sunk, on 19 July 1918 off the Yorkshire coast. According to his autobiography (*Fürbringer Fips: Legendary U-Boat Commander*, 2000) he had commanded several other boats in the Flanders flotilla before this.

Another *U-Boot* commander, Robert Wilhelm Moraht was also transferred to Skipton in January 1918. He had commanded *U64*.

An internee's envelope, addressed to Fritz Schilling of München, bearing a censor's adhesive label, sent from Colsterdale on 26 May 1918, exists, stating, 'Opened by censor: PW 640'.

H.M. Thompson served as a clerk with the 162nd Company, The Royal Defence Corps. He was based at Colsterdale from July to September of 1917, before moving on to Brocton where he stayed until February 1919.

After the war the camp reverted to being a construction camp. Leighton Reservoir was completed in 1924.

DKF 24: Aus dem Bericht des Schweizerischen Delegierten Dr Schwyzer und Dr Vischer vom 26 Juni geht hervor, daß die Dächer einiger Baracken undicht waren, daß noch zehn deutsche Sanitätsoffiziere in Colsterdale zurückgehalten wurden und daß die Ordonnanzen trotz ihrer schweren Arbeit nur die Rationen für Nichtarbeiter empfingen. Durch Vermittlung der Schweizerischen Gesandtschaft wurden bei der englischen Regierung Vorstellungen erhoben. Aus dem Bericht des Schweizerischen Delegierten über das Offizier-Gefangenenlager Colsterdale vom 9 Oktober 1918 geht hervor, daß die klimatischen Verhältnisse in Colsterdale eine Unterbringung der befindlichen Offiziere in Holzbaracken (besonders im Nordlager) für den Winter als nicht ausreichend erscheinen lassen. Nach Ansicht des Delegierten lassen verschiedene Räume hinsichtlich der Bequemlichkeit und Behaglichkeit zu wünschen übrig, und das Leben in Colsterdale weist besonders bei kaltem und feuchtem Wetter viele Mängel auf. Aus vorstehendem geht hervor, daß Aufenthalt im Lager besonders während des Winters den Anforderungen nicht entspricht, welche namentlich in gesundheitlicher Beziehung billigerweise gestellt werden müssen. 50 bis 60 kriegsgefangene Offiziere des Lagers haben gebeten, aus Gesundheitsrücksichten in ein anderes Lager in einem wärmeren Teil Englands verlegt zu werden. Der Delegierte selbst befürwortete in mehreren Fällen diesen Wunsch. Nach dem Bericht werden für den Burschendienst in Colsterdale vielfach solche Kriegsgefangene herangezogen, die für die ihnen zufallenden Arbeiten körperlich untauglich sind. Dem Berichterstatter ist eine Anzahl

Burschen vorgestellt worden, die er selbst als ungenügend bezeichnen und deren ärztliche Behandlung bzw. Rücksendung ins Stammlager er befürworten mußte. Gegen die obenaufgeführten Mißstände wurde Protest erhoben und Abhilfe gefordert.

COMPTON: Roden House (OS: SU 523 801). For a great number of years the chalk downs of Berkshire have been used to train racehorses. Amongst the successful trainers and owners that lived at Roden House are John Dawson, Richard Ten Broeck and William Stevens. Roden House (a.k.a. Stokes Manor) dates back to 1664, but now has a fine Queen Anne frontage. During the First World War it was cited as an agricultural depot, with its POWIB (1919) code Dor (Cmp) (IWM: Facsimile K4655). It had three agricultural groups attached to it: at Lambourn, Wantage and Faringdon. It is cited by the FPHS (1973) too. Its TA is cited as Priswarian: Roden House, Compton, Berks. (ADM 1/8506/265–120667).

CONVETH MAINS FARM: Laurencekirk (OS: NO 722 722). As a boy, his father told Arthur Bruce of Laurencekirk stories of PoWs working on the local farms during the First World War. There was an internment camp at Conveth Mains Farm; those that worked on nearby farms walked to their workstations, those further afield were taken on a lorry belonging to a local garage. Local gossip says because there were no men available to drive the vehicle, that John Gouk, a local lad of around 13 years of age, ferried the PoWs to and from the outlying farms (Bruce, per. comm., 14 August 1998).

When a sheep was found to be missing, the investigation ended with the discovery of a sheep's carcass in the PoW camp. The animal apparently had been stripped of anything that was edible. An inquiry into the theft proved nothing; but it is said that the internees had full stomachs for a while.

David Henderson purchased the farm after the war, and the farmhouse was only recently demolished. Henderson was to become the first resident of the new residential home, named Burnside Home, built on the site, replacing the farmhouse (Diane M. Henderson (Dr) (*Scots at War Project*), per. comm., 15 September 1998).

CONINGSBY (OS: TF 22- 57-). Though cited by both the POWIB (1919) and the FPHS (1973), nothing of this camp's whereabouts is known. A satellite of Bracebridge, it had the code Bro (Bbe) (Con) (IWM: Facsimile K4655). The FPHS (1973) also cite this camp. Its TA was Priswarian: Coningsby (ADM 1/8506/265–120667).

COPT HEWICK HALL (OS: SE 346 718). John Iles, of Copt Hewick Hall (per. comm., 20 September 1998), wrote there is evidence to show the army used Copt Hewick Hall as a training ground in the Second World War. Dummy and live shells are being constantly unearthed in the grounds. He was unaware that the Hall, or its grounds, had been used as an agricultural group for PoWs during the First World War. Its POWIB (1919) code was Cat (Th) (Cp) (IWM: Facsimile K4655). Its TA was Priswarian: Copt Hewick Hall, Ripon (ADM 1/8506/265–120667).

Chadwick (per. comm., 20 September 1998) tells that local legend suggests the PoWs billeted in the area worked on local farms in the First World War, and were employed on land reclamation and drainage work. They are fondly remembered for making an illegal distilled spirit to drink, which was very potent.

CORBY (OS: SP 885 894). Corby is cited as a civilian working camp, and it had the POWIB (1919) code Pa (Cor) (IWM: Facsimile K4655). The FPHS (1973) cite it too. The camp was located on Getton Lodge Road.

It was usually the local economy that brought the early railway companies to a place, but at Corby this was not so. Whilst constructing a line through a swath of Northamptonshire countryside south of the village of Corby in 1875 vast ironstone deposits were discovered. The Cardigan Ironstone Company was quickly set up to extract the ore. Lloyd's Ironstone Company then absorbed the company in 1881. This in turn became Stewart & Lloyd when it amalgamated with the Scottish tube makers in 1903. It became a part of the British Steel Corporation in 1967 and also traded as Corus.

In June 1917, Lloyd's Ironstone Company employed 117 civilian internees that had voluntarily transferred from a camp at Knockaloe on the Isle of Man to work there. Its TA was Priswarian: Corby, Northamptonshire (ADM 1/8506/265–120667).

On at least two occasions, men interned at Corby undertook to make good their escapes. The first attempt saw the quick recapture of two absconders, but according to *The Kettering Leader* (25 May 1917), a seaman who escaped proved to be a more elusive character. From the resulting inquiry, it was ascertained that the man had been in a party of men sent to work in the ironstone pits. During the morning in question the internees were being moved to another position, which meant for a time they had to walk single file through a thicket. It is thought that this was where he made good his escape as he was briefly out of sight of the guard. Alphonso Griem, aged 26, was not missed until mid-afternoon, when the authorities were alerted.

CORFTON HALL (OS: SO 492 849). The camp, an agricultural group, is cited as a satellite of Leominster. Its POWIB (1919) code was Shrw (Lmr) (Cof) (IWM: Facsimile K 4655). The address is given as 42 West Street, Leominster. The FPHS (1973) cite it only as Corfton. It is known that the hall was used as a hostel for Land Girls during the Second World War.

CORK BARRACKS (IGR: W 675 725). *The Lancaster Observer* (4 September 1914) recorded a number of seamen had been taken from an unnamed German ship at Castletown Berehaven, and had been placed under arrest. They were then marched in batches, under guard, to the military barracks in Cork. *The London Gazette* (3 October 1914) cited the *Excelsior* (GRT: 14 07) and the *Odessa* (GRT: 30 46) had been detained at Castletown Berehaven. Both ships were German owned. The fate of their crews and passengers is not recorded but possibly they were also taken to the barracks at Cork to be processed.

In 1916 the barracks were to hold an internee: this time it was Thomas Kent, who was held there briefly before being executed by firing squad for his part in the Easter Rising.

The British Fleet used Berehaven as a naval base since 1602. It has been described as having good anchorage and sufficient capacity to contain all the ships of Europe. Until 1938, Bere Island and Berehaven had a British Navy and Army base. When America eventually entered the First World War its ships used Berehaven Harbour as a base.

CORTON (OS: ST 93- 40-). Cited by the FPHS (1973), it is thought that the PoWs may have worked at a quarry, where they complained of having to wash at three troughs, standing in the open. They said they lived in tents that were poorly lit. They also complained their kitchens were unhygienic.

Crawford (*Wiltshire and the Great War: Training the Empire's Soldiers*, 1999) makes no mention of PoWs being at Corton where it is known an artillery unit had been deployed. Their camp was given over to the Australians in 1916. There was also an army veterinary hospital close by. A diary of the 38th Mobile Veterinary Section of the 26th Division, notes that it left Corton, bound for France, on 21 September 1915.

DKF 33: In Upavon, Milldown, Corton (Dorset), und Hendon (Middlesex) waren die Gefangenen noch weiterhin in Zelten untergebracht. In Milldown und Hendon war die Beleuchtung mangelhaft, in Corton fehlte sie ganz. Für die in Bergwerken beschäftigten Gefangenen im Lager Corton sind die drei Wannen Gänzlich unzureichend, die Wannen stehen im Freien.

DKF 34: In Milldown und Upavon war die Wasserzufuhr unzulänglich. Die in den Lagern Upavon, Milldown und Corton als Küchen benutzten offenen Schuppen waren durchaus unhygienisch.

COSTESSEY HALL (OS: TG 163 113). Norfolk WAC minutes (27 January 1917) record it was resolved to inform the Local Government Board that accommodation had been found at Costessey Hall, so that the internees could carry out drainage work on that part of the River Wensum (C/C10/15).

Queen Mary granted permission for the hall to be built for Sir Henry Jerningham. The hall has since been demolished.

COTTAM (OS: SE 993 648). Extracts from a diary of the General Post Office for Driffield (1901–45) show mail intended for PoWs was being handled at Driffield. An entry showed two bags of parcels had arrived at the Post Office on 7 September 1918. One was addressed to the NCO in charge of the PoW gang at Cottam and the other for the NCO in charge of the PoW gang in the care of Mr Beal at Cowlam. There was also, on 17 September 1918, special mail from the Catterick camp, with parcels for those PoWs working at Cottam.

COTTENHAM (OS: TL 455 674). Minutes of the Cambridgeshire WAC (19 April 1919) record there was a tented internment camp at Cottenham, where it was agreed to allocate 100 internees to work on the River Ouse. No evidence has been found to suggest where this camp was located.

COVENTRY. There were two camps in Coventry: one known as Radford Hutments and one as Whitley Abbey House.

RADFORD HUTMENTS (OS: SP 325 805). Today, Radford is a housing estate in the suburbs of Coventry. During the First World War, at what is now Villa Road, Radford Aerodrome was being developed alongside the Daimler and Standard motor companies that were there. Aircraft were test-flown from there before delivery to the military. It fell into disuse once the military contracts were completed, and by 1935 plans were in existence to turn it into a housing estate. The last known landing was when, in 1935, an RAF aircraft was forced to land there and collided with a goal post on one the football pitches that then graced the site.

Initially, it was civilian internees that were housed there, in tents. They were utilised in the construction of houses in Engleton Road. Later, wooden huts were erected that became known locally as the Radford Hutments.

There were complaints about how the canteen was being looked after at Radford, and that the half-covered kitchen was unhygienic.

The POWIB (1919) cite the camp's code as Dor (Rad) (IWM: Facsimile K4655). Radford is also cited by the FPHS (1973). Its TA was Priswarian: Radford, Coventry (ADM 1/8506/265–120667).

WHITLEY ABBEY HOUSE (OS: SP 349 842). Terry Reeves (per. comm., 19 February 2000) revealed this was the site of a large house, parts of which dated back to the seventeenth century, that stood next to Whitley Abbey. It is not clear whom the house was originally built for, but Lord Hood enlarged it *c.*1808, to designs created by Sir John Soane. After a fire in 1874, the house was partly rebuilt and altered by E.H. Petre.

At the onset of the First World War, it is known Belgian refugees were accommodated in it. In 1920, the Petre family sold the house to the Armstrong Whitworth Co. The house then stood empty for a number of years. Becoming derelict, it was demolished in 1953, and replaced by the school that today bears its name. The school, which partly surrounds a lake, stands next to Coventry Zoo.

Panayi (*The Enemy in Our Midst: Germans In Britain During The First World War*, 1991) cites Whitley Abbey House held some 200 Germans that worked at shed building, road making, drainage, etc. for Messrs. McAlpine & Sons for the Road Board.

It is believed most of the two camps' civilian occupants moved voluntarily to Knockaloe. Although it is known the internees were used in the house-building programme, it is not known if they were employed in the construction of the airfield's infrastructure too.

The Diocesan Registrar was able to show a Faculty, granted on 23 November 1961 to the Commonwealth War Graves Commission, to have the remains of H. Edmunds exhumed (d. 4 December 1917), from the graveyard on London Road, Coventry. He was re-interred at the new German War Cemetery at Cannock Chase (Rotherham & Co., Coventry (Solicitors)).

The FPHS (1973) also cite Whitley Bay.

DKF 30: In den Lagern von Rosyth, Eastgate, Uppingham, Belton Park, Ternhill, Bee Craigs, Hadnall, Sutton Veny, Larkhill, Fovant, Withley (sic) *und Radford sind die Kriegsgefangenen in Zelten untergebracht.*

DKF 31: Der im Lager von Sutton Veney (sic) *als Küche benutzte offene, jedum Witterungseinfluß zugängliche Schuppen und die nur halb gedeckte Küche in Radford, sind durchaus unhygienisch.*

DKF 31: Die Kantinen in Sproxton Moor und Radford sind schlecht versorgt, und auf der Insel Raasay werden in der von den Bergwerkunternehmern unterhaltenen Kantinen zu hohe Preise gefordert.

COWLAM (OS: SE 996 655). Extracts from a diary of the General Post Office for Driffield (1901–1945) show mail intended for PoWs was being handled at Driffield. An entry shows a bag of mail to the NCO in charge of the PoW gang in the care of Mr Beal at Cowlam, was being re-directed to Malton.

CRANLEIGH (OS: TQ 065 385). Thirty PoWs went on strike at Cranleigh because two of their number had part of their wages stopped for twenty-eight days, for disobeying orders and leaving their place of work on the land. Their grievance apparently emanated from the recent change of guard.

Described as a working camp, its POWIB (1919) code was Pa (Crg). The camp was at High Park. Its TA was Priswarian: Cranleigh (ADM 1/8506/265–120667). Cranleigh also appears as an entry on the list produced for the FPHS (1973).

CRAWFORD (OS: NS 955 204). The POWIB (1919) had the code Stbs (Cra) for this working camp that was at Crawford (IWM: Facsimile K4655). Its TA was Priswarian: Crawford, Lanarkshire (ADM 1/8506/265–120667). An entry also appears in the list compiled by the FPHS (1973).

For the County of Lanarkshire, *The 3rd Statistical Account of Scotland* (1960) states:

> The hill streams in the parish (of Crawford) help to provide water for the towns in the large industrial belt of North Lanarkshire. At Camps there is Lanarkshire County Council's extensive reservoir, built about forty years ago, at the construction of which German prisoners of war assisted ... In the burying ground at Kirkton there lies one of these German prisoners, his grave is marked by a German military cross, which was sent from his native land.

The account also states the old churchyard, beside the Clyde at Kirkton, had closed some years ago. Local knowledge confirms there was a Roman camp, near the ruins of Castle Crawford, where Camps Water enters the River Clyde. It was this camp that gave its name to the reservoir, and not the PoW camp, whose actual location is not known, but was near to Camps Reservoir, which is approximately 4.5 miles east of Crawford. A photograph exists, showing what is believed to be a PoW working party at the reservoir.

Crawford had a railway station, and one must assume that the authorities made great use of transporting the PoWs in and out of an area by rail. When setting up many camps the army tended to name them after the nearest railway station, and this may have been the case here.

The Western Times (18 October 1917) and *The Times* (18 October 1917) both reported the escapes of Karl Konrad and Arnold Pranzon. The next day's edition of *The Times* reported Konrad had been recaptured. He had been apprehended in Carlisle, along with someone called Granger, presumably the other escapee. It was a common occurrence for PoWs to provide their captors with wrong details to confuse, and prolong searches, thus tying up resources.

CREATON: Hollowell Grange (OS: SP 695 724). Located near to Creaton, this working camp had the POWIB (1919) code Pa (Hw) (IWM: Facsimile K4655). The FPHS (1973) cite the camp as Hollowell Grange. No further evidence has been found to confirm that this camp existed. It is uncertain that these internees were engaged in work connected to Hollowell Reservoir, as were those billeted at Guilsborough.

CRICHEL (OS: ST 995 083). A working camp, its POWIB (1919) code was Dor (Ci) (IWM: Facsimile K4655). No further evidence has been found to suggest this camp existed, but Crichel House or its estate may hold the key.

Crichel House is a modern mansion, which *Contemporary Biographies Wilts and Dorset* (Dorling, 1906) cites was built in the Classical style, and consists of the main building and a smaller wing. It stands in a park some 162 hectares in size. It stands on the site of a previous Tudor house, owned by the Napier family, which was burned to the ground in 1742. Shortly after, Sir William Napier had a new house built, which was greatly enlarged by Humphrey Sturt when he inherited it. To enhance his view he had the village of More Crichel moved to a location he called New Town. It took some forty years for the bricks and mortar to be re-located to what is still called New Town. BBC period costume productions take place there.

There were also camps at Milldown and at the nearby Blandford naval base.

CRICKHOWELL. Crickhowell is only cited once by the FPHS (1973). However the HO issued two TAs for Crickhowell: Priswarian, Crickhowell and Priswarian, Hermitage Camp, Crickhowell (ADM 1/8506/265–120667). The POWIB (1919) cite two locations: these are Crickhowell, working camp with the code Fg (Cri) and the Hermitage, with the code Fg (He C (IWM: Facsimile K4655).

THE HERMITAGE (OS: SO 229 251) and TY MAWR FARM: Cwm Rhos (OS: SO 189 247). Orinda Williams (per. comm., 21 December 1999) states The Hermitage was a shooting lodge belonging to the Glan-Usk estate. It stands derelict near to Tal-y-Maes Farm. Orinda states the Crickhowell camp was at Ty Mawr Farm at Cwm Rhos. There are no physical signs of the camp today, which was in a field on the left-hand side as you enter the lane adjacent to the Kestrel Inn.

When the US Embassy in London inspected the camp at Leigh, on 8 September 1916, one of the reasons stated for the reduction in numbers from a previous visit was the fact that men had gone out in working parties. They had gone to Crickhowell and Ampleforth, to participate in forestry work, and to Rowrah for quarry work. It was cited 200 men had gone Wales.

Reports on visits of inspection to PoW camps at Blandford, Milldown, Louds Mill (Dorchester), Stowell, Glastonbury, Itton, Usk, Abergavenny, Hermitage (Crickhowell), Llangenny, Bwlch, Brecon, Talgarth, Abbeydore and Churchdown by Dr A. de Sturler and Monsieur R. de Sturler, during March and April 1919 are held at the National Archives at Kew (FO 383/508).

The FPHS (1973) also has an entry for Hermitage, Bucks.

CROFT-ON-TEES: Monk End Farm (OS: NZ 248 106). In an advert for holiday accommodation at Clow Beck House, David Armstrong stated that his great grandfather and grandfather purchased 70 acres of land, including the farmhouse that was part of an estate for sale, near to Croft on Tees. They were also instrumental in the purchase of another 20 acres of adjoining glebe land (www.clowbeckhouse.co.uk).

When they erected a covered yard at Monk End Farm, it was done with the help of PoW labour that was employed on the farm between 1917 and 1920. Armstrong's grandfather, James William Fell, had the highest respect for Otto Hahn, one of the German prisoners who worked on his farm.

CRONDALL (OS: SU 795 485). Described as being a working camp by the POWIB (1919), its code was Dor (Cr) (IWM: Facsimile K4655). It is also cited by the FPHS (1973), although it was mis-spelt as Corndall. Its TA was Priswarian: Crondall (ADM 1/8506/265–120667). Any PoWs sent to Crondall may have been housed in the school attached to the workhouse.

Farnham and Hartley Wintney District School was built at Crondall, in 1856, to accommodate 200 children (www.pastscape.org.uk). Prior to then it had occupied the former Gilbert Union workhouse in Aldershot. The school was approximately 2 miles south of Crondall village. Girls were put into the east wing and boys into the west. Gradually additional buildings including a laundry, a chapel, stables and a large infirmary were added. In 1948, the school, then known as Wimble Hill District School, was adopted by the National Health Service and became Wimble Hill Hospital. In 1979 the site was redeveloped as several of the main buildings were demolished. Those buildings that survived were converted into private residential use.

CROXTON (see Warren Wood).

CROXTON PARK (OS: SK 824 275). Croxton Park, occupying some 777 acres, lies 2 miles south west of Croxton Kerrial. The mansion was built in 1735, and by 1912 this had been partly pulled down. Pre-war the Old Hall was occupied by Mrs F. Dent. Before the First World War horse racing took place in the park and mounted units of the army also carried out training exercises there.

Minutes of the Leicestershire WAC, of 15 August 1917, state that thirty-five PoWs were expected to arrive in the village soon. Instructions to the local farmers, advertising the conditions under which these men could be employed, were to be made available (DE 1841/1–3).

A second minute, of 17 October 1917, recommended continuing with this camp. On 24 October 1917 a letter arrived from the War Office stating if they wished to keep these prisoners then they must find alternative accommodation by 31 October, as it was no longer acceptable to keep these men under canvas. As the camp is not included in the lists issued by the HO after October 1918, it must be assumed it closed.

Croxton Park is cited by the POWIB (1919): its code was Bro (Cro) (IWM: Facsimile K4655). Camps at Thorpe Satchville, Long Clawson, and Wymondham, were its satellites. It had the TA, Priswarian: Waltham, Leicestershire (ADM 1/8506/265–120667). The FPHS (1973) also cite this camp.

CUDDINGTON (OS: SH 454 725). During the First World War a number of German PoWs were interned on the Delamere estate. They were employed in the transporting of timber to the saw mill, near Cuddington Railway Station.

It was described as a working camp, with the POWIB (1919) coding Hfth (Cdg) (IWM: Facsimile K4655).

Delamere House stood for around 200 years as testimony to the almost baronial power of the Wilbraham family which owned and controlled thousands of acres of land and farms around Cuddington and the neighbouring villages. It survived until just before the Second World War when Delamere Manor was built nearby. After the demolition of the old house the grounds became an army transit camp, first occupied by British troops and then by thousands of Americans prior to the D-Day invasion. After the war the former army huts were used to house local people.

The estate today has been turned over for residential housing (www.cuddington andsandiway.co.uk).

CULGAITH (OS: NY 60- 29-). The *Carlisle Journal*, in the *Cumberland News* (7 November 2003) had cited migratory gangs had been set up at Langwathby and Culgaith during the First World War. These were similar to the one set up at Kirk-oswald, where two tents had been erected to house ten PoWs who had been brought from Rowrah to do harvest work.

CUMNOR: Swinford Farm (OS: SP 465 045). An agricultural group attached to Cholsey AD, its POWIB (1919) code was Dor (Cho) (Cm) (IWM: Facsimile K4655). It is also cited by the FPHS (1973). Swinford Farm was at Lower Whitney. The PoWs worked the land. The camp's TA was Priswarian: Cumnor (ADM 1/8506/265–120667).

In his formative years, the son of the farmer remembers seeing the PoWs marching through the town as they left his village for the last time. He believes they were well liked by the locals, and local legend says many of the villagers were known to have shed a tear as they left.

During March 1919, Dr A. de Sturler compiled reports on visits of inspection to the PoW camps in Britain. Cumnor was one of those visited. His report is held at the National Archives at Kew (FO 383/506).

D

DALMELLINGTON (see Loch Doon).

DALTON-IN-FURNESS (see Stainton Sidings).

DARLEY DALE (OS: SK 26- 63-). The report in *The Derby Daily Telegraph* of 10 July 1918 is the only evidence to suggest the existence of a camp at Darley Dale.

DARTFORD (OS: TQ 568 528). At the start of the First World War anti-German feelings ran high in Dartford and there was a great deal of concern in and around the Dartford area that German spies were operating locally. Rees (*Dartford and the Great War*, 1999) and Burne (*Dartford's Capital River*, 1989) tell of attacks by anti-German mobs on the houses and shops of anyone suspected of being of German or Austrian descent. In local schools, teachers were criticised for continuing to teach the German language, and bands and orchestras were discouraged from playing German music. The few German and Austrian families not forced out of the area were eventually rounded up and sent to a special internment camp for enemy aliens, sited near Darenth Hospital.

DARTFORD: Gore Farm (OS: TQ 571 723). A working camp, it was established at Gore Farm with the POWIB (1919) code Pa (Go) (IWM: Facsimile K4655). It had the TA: Priswarian: Gore Farm (ADM 1/8506/265–120667).

In a town that had various sites used for internment purposes, Gore Farm is cited as a working camp attached to Pattishall, but it was also a hospital, with grounds where patients were employed on its farm as part of their recovery.

DARTMOOR: HM Prison (OS: SX 609 751). Dartmoor Prison was designed by Daniel Asher Alexander and constructed, between 1806 and 1809, by local labour, to hold about 5,000 prisoners of the Napoleonic Wars, in five two-storey buildings. The conditions were appalling. The buildings were unheated and had no lighting. Even though the windows had no glass, the ventilation was inadequate and with very rudimentary sanitation, it is quite amazing how any of them survived. From 1812, the numbers held there increased when around 6,000 American prisoners from the Anglo-American War were put there. In part of the prison's macabre history, seven prisoners were shot and killed and thirty-one were wounded on 6 April 1815 as their guard opened fire at the behest of the allegedly drunken officer in charge, who thought that they were attempting to escape. When the last French and American PoWs left, the prison closed. Around 1,400 PoWs are buried at Princetown Church, which was built by PoW labour. When the policy of transporting convicts to the colonies was abandoned the prison re-opened, in 1851, as a civilian prison. It was closed again in 1917.

McConville (*Irish Political Prisoners, 1848–1922: Theatre of Wars*, 2005) states Eamon de Valera and sixty-four other Irishmen were incarcerated in Dartmoor for their parts in the Easter Rising of 1916. Singled out as an instigator for the disruption caused by the Irishmen, de Valera was transferred to Maidstone. Eventually all the insurgents were moved to the former naval prison in Lewes, and Dartmoor was converted into a Home Office Work Centre for conscientious objectors granted release from other prisons; cells were unlocked, inmates wore their own clothes, and could visit the village in their off-duty time. It was to re-open again as a civilian prison in 1920 and now holds some of Britain's most serious offenders (www.dartmoor-crosses.org.uk/princetown).

DAWYCK (OS: NT 248 411). Situated in the Scottish Borders, near to Stobo, Dawyck Botanical Gardens and Arboretum are specialised out-gardens of the Royal Botanical Gardens of Edinburgh. Sir James Naesmyth created them in 1691. William Burn was then commissioned to build a new house on the estate, which was completed by 1832. In 1897 the property, on some 25 hectares, passed into the Balfour family until it was given to the nation, in 1979, to become part of the Royal Botanical Gardens.

This camp had the POWIB (1919) code 'Stbs (Da)'. It also appears in the list produced for the FPHS (1973). Its TA was Priswarian: Stobo (which should not be confused with Stobs, the main administration centre in Scotland, near to Hawick) (ADM 1/8506/265–120667).

Two newspaper cuttings that survive, held by the Scottish Borders Library, relate to Drummelzier Church. The first, dated September 1916, states:

> Great interest has been taken in the arrival of the soldiers guarding the German prisoners who are working at the timber on Dawyck estate. At the request of

> Lieutenant Laidlaw, I have held services at the Camp at 10.00am on Sundays, and in my absence in August, the Rev. Mr. Dewar has kindly taken my place.

The second cutting, dated March 1917, cites a morning service that was inaugurated by Mr Somerville being continued during the winter months by the Moderator, as Chaplain to the Guard.

The PoWs may have been accommodated at the Peebles Combination as it was placed at the disposal of the military authorities during the First World War. The poorhouse was around 10 miles north of the Dawyck estate. In 1919, the Peebles Combination was dissolved. The poorhouse stood on Rosetta Road, to the north of Peebles, and was demolished in the early 1930s to be replaced by council offices.

Horne (*The German Connection – The German Newspaper 1916–1919*, 1988) cites there were work camps at Dalmellington, Kinlochleven, Glendevon, Crawford, Dawyck, Lentran, Nethy Bridge, Raasay, Hairmyres, Penstone (sic), Inverkeithing and Bee Craigs, all in Scotland, and Grantham, Port Clarence and Catterick, in England.

DEDDINGTON: nr Stoneleigh (OS: SP 46- 31-). An agricultural group attached to Banbury, it had the POWIB (1919) code Dor (Ba) (Dd) (IWM: Facsimile K4655). Its TA was Priswarian: Stoneleigh, Deddington (ADM 1/8506/265–120667). Its location has not been traced. During March 1919, Dr A. de Sturler compiled reports on visits of inspection to the PoW camps. One of those visited was Deddington. This is held at the National Archives at Kew (FO 383/506).

DEGANWY (OS: SH 77- 79-). Some internment camps were attached to army camps, and although there is no evidence to show this was the case at Deganwy, there certainly was an army camp there during the First World War. The camp is cited by the FPHS (1973). In June 1919, Dr A. de Sturler and Monsieur R. de Sturler carried out visits of inspection to PoW camps. Their report of Deganwy is held at the National Archives at Kew (FO 383/508).

DENBY (OS: SK 386 472). *The Derbyshire Times* (8 June 1918) reported that there were proposals to bring more PoWs into Derbyshire; amongst the sites being proposed at this time was a camp at Denby. Frayar (*Some Chapters in the History of Denby*, 1934) states that from 20 August 1917 until the end of the war 100 German PoWs were interned in a camp at Denby (Ordnance Survey 1914, Field No. 575). The PoWs were employed at the tarmacadam plant near to the camp. Some were utilised by local farmers, too. In Denby today, many locals do not know how Camp Field (No. 575), situated off Rykneld Street near the crossroads, got its name.

Miles (*Recollections of Fred Miles*, unpublished, 1984) provides further proof of the Germans being in Denby:

> During the 1914–18 war there was a prisoner-of-war camp at Denby crossroads. The occupants were German prisoners and they worked during the day making tarmacadam; next to Denby Coal and Iron Works. There is now a school on this site. There was a dentist in a house at the bottom of Grosvenor Road; my father, Mr A.L. Miles. He became the PoW camp dentist. Patients were brought up to Ripley under guard, and the two soldiers did sentry duty outside the house whilst the patients were attended to. The Camp Commandant was an officer named Slichmann. At one stage, he wanted to know why one of the men wanted so much dental treatment. He was given a truthful answer, 'Because he is a very good piano player.' After that, the Commandant often came with the party.

The daughter of G.H. Salmon, a local farrier, remembers seeing their wooden huts, gathered around a standpipe from which they drew their water. Constantine (per. comm., 27 January 1998) cites fuel for their pot-bellied stoves was gathered from the side of the railway line which served the coal mine in the town. Some of them had worked on the farms in the area, and when it was time for them to go home in 1920, many of them still in their mid to late teens did not wish to leave Denby. The huts were taken over by homeless people for a time. One later became a chicken house.

Three PoWs were interred at Denby St Mary Church. The Flamstead History Group makes reference to their deaths, as did Frayar (1934). Memorial stones, made from fine slag and cement, were erected by their fellow prisoners. The dead were: Xavier Winter (d. 7 December 1918), Johannes Schlichting (d. 9 October 1918), and Hermann Thieroff (d. 30 November 1918).

The Dean of Derby granted permission for their transfer to Cannock Chase in the 1960s. For many years, whilst their graves were in Denby, a Mrs Cresswell tended their graves, placing fresh flowers on their graves every week. The camp had the POWIB (1919) code Bro (De), and is described as being a working camp (IWM: Facsimile K4655).

DEVIZES (OS: SU 017 623). In 1918 German PoWs arrived in the town. Their camp was located at Fairview in London Road. It was described by the POWIB (1919) as being an agricultural depot, its code being Dor (Dvs) (IWM: Facsimile K4655). It had two agricultural groups attached to it: at Wootton Bassett and Chippenham. It was also cited by the FPHS (1973) and had the TA Priswarian: Devizes (ADM 1/8506/265–120667).

The verdict of accidental death was recorded by the Mid Wilts coroner at the inquest into the death of Job Usher Greenhill of Common Farm that was reported in *The Western Times* (7 August 1918). In a macabre chain of events a PoW working at the farm, clearing a whey tank, got into difficulties, and a second went to his aid. He too, was overcome by the fumes, as did Job when he tried to rescue them. All three died from asphyxiation due to the presence of carbonic acid gas given off by the fermenting whey.

DISS (see Billingford Maltings).

DOLYHIR – KINGTON – OLD RADNOR (OS: SO 29- 56-). According to the POWIB (1919) this camp was located at Dolyhir; its code was Shrw (Doy) (IWM: Facsimile K4655), and its address was given as Dolyhir, Kington, Herefordshire. An entry cited in a list of war camps in England and Wales, produced by the HO, gives its address as Dolyhir (Old Radnor) and provides its TA as Priswarian: Dolyhir, Kington (ADM 1/8506/265–120667). The FPHS (1973) cite Old Radnor and Kingston (sic), Hereford separately amongst its entries.

DOLWILYM (OS: SN 170 261). The Carmarthenshire Archive Service hold The Administrative and Biographical Content Statement to the Protheroe-Beynon Additional Papers Collection which state Dolwilym Mansion was rebuilt in 1818. Amongst papers, it states the mansion was used for German PoWs during the First World War, the house then deteriorated (GB 0211). The camp was cited in a HO document that states its TA is Priswarian: Efailwen, Llanglydwen (ADM 1/8506/265–120667).

DONCASTER). There were two camps in the Doncaster area: Green Lane Farm at Hatfield and Warmsworth Hall.

GREEN LANE FARM (OS: SE 636 070). One of the most common names in England for a thoroughfare is Green Lane. There are at least nine recorded in the Doncaster postcode area today: at Askern, Barnburgh, Belton, Cantley, Dunsville, Hatfield, Scawthorpe, Skellow, and at Woodlands.

Green Lane Farm had the POWIB (1919) directory code Cat (P B) (G F), which would have made it a satellite of Pateley Bridge (IWM: Facsimile K4655). The distance to Doncaster from Pateley Bridge is approximately 50 miles; too great for this attachment to be viable.

The site of Green Lane camp remained a mystery, with its TA being Priswarian: Green Lane Farm, Doncaster, until a Foreign Office document, found by Graham Mark, citing a new camp was to open at Hatfield, near to Green Lane Farm, helped pinpoint it. Records show there was a farm, near Park Lane Grange, Hatfield, which bore the name of the lane it stood in, Green Lane (ADM 1/8506/265–120667).

WARMSWORTH HALL (OS: SE 547 005). The camp's TA was Priswarian: Warmsworth Hall, Doncaster (ADM 1/8506/265–120667). Warmsworth Hall, Doncaster is listed by the FPHS (1973). The POWIB (1919) directory lists the Hall as being an agricultural depot, but it had no agricultural groups attached to it. Its code was Cat (War) (IWM: Facsimile K4655). *The South Yorkshire Topic* (April 1987) has an article about PoWs being interned at Warmsworth Hall, near Doncaster, during the First World War. What connection it had to Sheffield agricultural depot, if any, has not been identified.

DONINGTON HALL: Castle Donington (OS: SK 421 269). Olsen (*Donington Hall: The History of an Ancient Family Seat*, 1990) says the present hall, built for the Hastings family in 1790, is the third to stand on the site at King's Mill, near to Castle Donington. On 24 October 1901, Frederick Gretton bought the hall, but it is believed he never lived in it. It was left to his land agent, John Gillies Shields to welcome those that wanted to hunt and fish there.

In February 1915, the War Office purchased the hall for £13,000 (including £4,000 for its contents). When announced it was to be used for interning around 300 German and Austrian officers, it was proclaimed to be the model for all future PoW camps in the UK.

Speed (*Prisoners, Diplomats, and the Great War: A Study in the Diplomacy of Captivity*, 1990) cites the camp opened on 10 February 1915 with a capacity to hold 174 prisoners who would all be housed in the building. In the ensuing period eight barrack huts were erected to take fourteen prisoners per hut. The camp in the early phase was never more than half full.

The New York Times (11 February 1915) states the officers were to be served with their food by German waiters, and shaved by German barbers, all selected from the lower ranks.

Stories abounded that those interned were playing snooker or card games all day long, in luxurious conditions whilst British soldiers were being subjected to the harshest of conditions in the trenches. Reports of British internees being mistreated in Germany only exacerbated the situation. On Tuesday, 27 June 1916, questions were asked in the House of Commons by Mr G. Faber, the Unionist Member of Parliament for Chapham, seeking to find out the manner in which these internees were being kept. Lord Charles Beresford asked the Prime Minister whether it was time to inform the German government that unless British PoWs and civilians interned received better treatment than they did at present, steps should be taken to treat

German PoWs in Britain in a less tolerant manner than at present. *The Daily Mail* cynically reported:

> One must suppose that the War Office has really at heart. The idea of reforming the Prussian Officer, by letting him soak in the suggestion of beauty and peace, and showing him the difference between the kultur that watched Louvain burn, and the kultur inspired by the sunset in the valley of the Trent.

When arrested in Gibraltar, Kapitan-Leutnant Gunther Plüschow, a pilot of the German Air Service, was taken, by ship, to Portsmouth where he was sent to Dorchester to be processed. He was then transferred to Holyport, before finally being moved to Donington Hall. Plüschow said of this seventeenth century Hall that the furnishings were basic and functional and that stories of them living in luxurious conditions were not true. He denied they had the use of snooker and card tables, but expressed a view that, because of the space available, the recreational facilities at Donington Hall were vastly superior to those he had left behind at Holyport.

A translation of a document held by the Austrian State Military Archive (Osterreichisches Staatsarchiv: Kriegsarchiv) states the internment camps, for officers taken PoW, had been selected in healthy places, in attractive areas.

The *Leigh Chronicle* (5 March 1915) carried a story of two German sergeant majors being transferred from Donington Hall to Leigh by train. Another report (9 April 1915) states about forty German PoWs had left Leigh destined for Donington Hall to act as orderlies.

Plüschow (*My Escape From Donington Hall*, 1921) states he and fifty-six prisoners were taken from Holyport, under escort, to a then unknown destination by rail. From the railway station they were marched through a village to a large country house. Only later, by duping their guard, were they able to ascertain they had been brought to Donington Hall. He describes how he, and Ober-Leutnant Trefftz, escaped on 4 July 1915. Navigating the perimeter wire, the pair walked to the train station in Derby. It had been their plan to separate there and make their own way to London, but by chance they ended up sharing the same compartment on a train en route to the capital. Again they went their separate ways. At Blackfriars Station, Plüschow changed his clothes to resemble those of a dockyard labourer. After several attempts, he finally managed to get on board a ship destined for the Netherlands. From there, he made it back to Germany, where he was awarded the Iron Cross. Trefftz was caught at Millwall Docks and, after forty-eight days in detention, was returned to Donington Hall.

Several attempts to escape from the Hall took place. Thelens and Keilhack, two German Air Officers, successfully tunnelled for more than seventy yards from the cellar, under the drawing room, until they were clear of the perimeter fence. They tried to stow away on a Dutch ship, but were re-caught and returned to the Hall. Three more fugitives were caught on the run because of their poor command of the English language. One escape was thwarted when the tunnel collapsed just 10 feet short of the perimeter fence. Getting rid of their extracted soil without it drawing attention was a problem, yet creating a great mound of extracted earth in the middle of a compound was never challenged by the guard.

Some of the PoWs at Donington had come from Llansannan. Its primary function was to hold officers taken from *U-Boote*.

When, at the end of the war, 150 naval officers that had brought the sequestrated vessels of the German Grand High Seas Fleet over to Scapa Flow, for internment, and then scuttled the fleet, were interned at Oswestry's Park Hall, before being sent to Lofthouse Park. They arrived at Donington Hall in 1919, and stayed until they were able to leave the country. One estimate suggests there were 1,000 officers interned at the hall at any one time, with another 300, selected from the lower ranks, acting as their valets.

Dr F. Schwyzer, Dr A.L. Vischer and Dr A. de Sturler compiled reports of their visits of inspection to the officers' PoW camps at Ripon, Skipton, Lofthouse Park, Kegworth and Donnington Hall during February and March 1919.

Thirty-four German internees were buried at Castle Donington's cemetery. They had been held at the Hall or had come from the Kegworth camp at Sutton Bonington. Their remains were exhumed in 1962 and transferred to the German War Cemetery at Cannock Chase.

Local photographer W.W. Winter was permitted to take photographs of the officers and their orderlies, dressed in their various uniforms, when he visited this camp, and the one at Sutton Bonington.

The camp's POWIB (1919) code was Dgn. It was also cited by the FPHS (1973). The camp had the TA Priswarian: Castle Donington.

After the war, the hall was returned to the Gretton family, who in turn sold it to their agent, John Gilles Shields, who opened it to the public. Between the wars, with Fred Craner's inspiration, the famous racing car circuit was created.

In the Second World War, the War Office requisitioned the hall once more, but this time as a transport depot. The hall was purchased by British Midland Airways in 1983, and extended, to become their corporate headquarters.

DORCHESTER. There were two camps in Dorchester: Louds Mill and Poundbury. The latter is better known. It was one of the first camps to open, and was in place for the duration of the war. It became a parent camp when PoWs were sent out on work projects. Louds Mill may not have been given recognition for events that are attributed to have occurred in Dorchester.

LOUDS MILL (OS: SY 710 903). Louds Mill, Dorset, is also cited in a HO document, which states its TA was Priswarian: Louds Mill (ADM 1/8506/265–120667). It was cited by the FPHS (1973). It was cited as being one of the camps inspected by Dr A. de Sturler and Monsieur R. de Sturler, during March and April 1919. Their reports are held at the National Archives at Kew (FO 383/506).

POUNDBURY (OS: SY 685 910). The barracks for the Royal Horse Artillery was located at Poundbury, on the northwest edge of Dorchester. Within hours of the Aliens Restriction Act being introduced on 5 August 1914, part of the camp was being converted to hold some of the first civilians to be put into internment in Britain. The new legislation updated the Aliens Act of 1905.

Four companies of Royal Scots had arrived at the barracks (*Dorset County Chronicle*, 13 August, 1914) to act as guard. They had little time to settle in as the first internees reported to have arrived were eighteen men from Falmouth. They arrived on the 10 August 1914. These new arrivals may have been those cited by *The Western Morning News* (14 August 1914) as being the passengers and crews from two German ships, held at Falmouth Harbour. Later that day larger groups arrived from Southampton and London. *The Western Morning News* (11 August 1914) cited two internees had arrived at the camp the previous day, where it was believed there were now 250 detainees. *Dorset County Chronicle* (20 August 1914) cited ninety-three internees arrived from Devonport just after noon on Sunday (16 August 1914). They were the crews taken off German merchant ships. On the Monday a further nineteen internees had arrived from Exeter, with others being brought in, in small groups of no more than two or three, by the police. *The Dorset County Chronicle* (27 August 1914) cited there were now around 1,000 being detained at Dorchester.

The Times (27 August 1914) reported that PoWs from Dorchester were helping with the harvest. This was at a time when combatants in internment in the UK were not made to do manual work. Interned civilians were not required to work either. However, many chose to, as they had no means to support their families.

The Western Morning News (3 September 1914) reported that Austrian internees had been moved to Dorchester, from Truro. *The Western Morning News* (11 September 1914) cited thirty internees were repatriated from Plymouth; they were men over the military age and they embarked on the *Hollandia* bound for Amsterdam. The men had come from the Dorchester camp.

The Times and the *Yorkshire Evening Press* (both 11 September 1914) reported that a carrier pigeon was shot at Dorchester. It was found to be carrying a message in German.

Dorset County Chronicle (10 December 1914) stated huts were being erected on the green of the Artillery Barracks in Dorchester, and shortly the 1,000 civilian internees currently being detained would be dispersed to make way for double this number of military PoWs.

The Times (14 December 1914) cited Otto Köhn had escaped. Arrested on board the SS *Potsdam* at Falmouth, he was being interned at Dorchester. He hid in a wooden crate that contained the baggage of the over-age men leaving Dorchester to be repatriated. He was taken to Tilbury Docks before he was discovered. *Essex County Chronicle* (Friday, 18 December 1914) stated, on the previous Saturday, that he had been discovered as the crates were being loaded on to a Dutch ferry, the SS *Batavier V*, at Tilbury. For his bravado, Köhn earned himself the nickname, 'the box man'.

Dorset County Chronicle (17 December 1914) reported the civilian internees were moved out. Fifty-eight men, all above the age for military service, were sent to Tilbury for repatriation. The younger men were to be sent to Handforth. The first batch of 352 left on the Friday by train. On the Sunday, a second batch of around 290 also left for Handforth. This left around 300 ship's officers and the 'better class' at Dorchester. They were taken to Ryde and put on board the HMT *Canada*. When the US inspection team visited the ship on 2 February 1915 these men stated they were not pleased with their transfer.

The first batch of about 500 military PoWs arrived at Poundbury on the Tuesday. They came from Frimley. A German report (20 January 1915) stated the men at Dorchester were sleeping twelve men to a tent initially; and there were 100 tents. After three weeks, however, the men were moved into the barracks. During this transition, the writing and receiving of letters was suspended. It was also stated there were only two interpreters for the 1,200 PoWs in the camp (CAB 37/123/37).

The Times (21 January 1915) cited Köhn, the box-man, after two weeks punishment, was transferred to the HMT *Canada*, moored off Ryde.

Dorset County Chronicle (21 January 1915) referred to the departure of the civilian internees. They had left before Christmas, and been replaced by a greater number of military PoWs. The paper also cited Major Henry O'Brien Owen had taken over the commandant job, as Colonel Block had resigned.

John Jackson's visit on behalf of the US Embassy in London (4 February 1915) noted the camp had previously contained a mix of interned civilians and combatants, but was now exclusively military. At the time of his visit there were 909 soldiers and twenty-five sailors, plus nine German boys brought from a reformatory in Belgium. Huts were being erected, which when completed would expand the camp's capacity to around 2,500 places. Labour to erect the huts had to be brought in to Dorchester, as local labour conditions made it impossible to employ the PoWs. New water closets and baths were installed. Whilst a large field adjoining the camp was being prepared to serve as an exercise ground, the internees were permitted to go on escorted marches in the countryside. The cooking was done entirely by Germans, and there were no complaints about food. Offizier-Stellvertreter and NCOs had separate rooms whilst the men were housed in the stables, lofts and other rooms of the barracks. Several severely wounded PoWs were hoping to be exchanged soon. Jackson noted the men were amongst the most content of any camp he visited and the commandant was a particularly popular figure with the internees. *The Times* (5 February 1915) cited a report written in the Danish press about the splendid treatment of those detained in camps in Britain.

It was around this time that Gunter Plüschow was brought to Dorchester. He had been arrested at Gibraltar and was held briefly in Portsmouth before being taken to HMT *Andania*. Plüschow was transferred to Holyport at the end of March 1915, before being moved on to Donington Hall.

The Times (17 March 1915) reported 1,000 PoWs taken at Neuve Chapelle passed through Southampton, en route to Dorchester.

The Times (1 September 1915) cited the funeral of Bernhard Schneider, an internee.

The Times (18 September 1915) reported five PoWs, Joseph Strautmann, Walther Iven, Edwin Bergmann, aged 20, Hans Heyn, aged 21, and Walter Volker, 30 years of age, had escaped.

The Manchester Evening News (18 September 1915) cites Volker and Strautmann were caught on a train bound for Waterloo as it passed through Southampton (West). In their possession were ticket stubs purchased in Moreton. The *Aberdeen Journal* and *Hull Daily Mail* (both 18 September 1915) cite Iven and Strautmann had been re-captured. The others were still at large according to *The Police Gazette* (21 September 1915). Bergmann and Heyn were apprehended in West Hartlepool; both were sentenced to six months hard labour, according to *The Times* (25 September 1915).

Mr Edward Lowry visited the camp on 1 December 1915 on behalf of the US Embassy in London. He noted there were 3,447 detainees, which were NCOs and lower ranks of the German Army. The camp at that time comprised of forty-five rooms capable of sleeping two to thirty men per room in part of the Artillery Barracks. Above in two lofts was accommodation for another 200 men, plus 113 wooden huts on the parade ground, capable of sleeping thirty men in each. There were twenty patients in the infirmary, which had beds for up to sixty. At the time of the visit there were no patients in the isolation hospital (FO 383/507).

According to *The Times* (16 December 1915), as a result of an escape, despite the four absconders being back in custody, Major Owen stood down as commandant.

A member of the Dutch press visited the camp, according to *The Times* (20 December 1915).

The Times (3 February 1916) cited the escape of two un-named PoWs the previous day. *The Police Gazette* (4 February 1916) named them as Ernst von Schweineher, aged 22, and Gohmer, aged 23. *The Police Gazette* (11 February 1916) reported they had been re-captured. Schweinher was sent to Woking Prison for five months for absconding. He returned to Dorchester. Gohmer's fate is unknown.

On 5 April 1916, it was stated a batch of 750 PoWs had been sent from Poundbury to Rouen, France, to be PoW labourers. On 10 May 1916 it was cited a further batch of 750 PoWs was sent, with thirty of the first batch returning as they were labelled unfit for work.

On 1 June 1916, an inspection team from the US Embassy in London visited the camp. It cited Lt-Colonel H.C. Bulkeley had been appointed as the camp's commandant on 16 December 1915. It was referred to as the Prince of Wales Camp, and it was noted that there were 1,779 internees, all German, in the camp: 1,771 soldiers, seven sailors and one civilian. Making mailbags was their principal occupation, 37,000 having been made.

The Times (8 August 1916) cited the proposed use of PoW labour to construct a new coastal road in Dorset.

The Times (26 October 1916) cited a man, later reported in the *Police Gazette* (26 October, 1916) as Frederick Gretten, 28 years old and a waiter from the Charing Cross Hotel, had escaped.

The Times (3 April 1917) reported men (PoWs) were available for work, but because there was no suitable accommodation outside of the camp, they could not be gainfully employed, except locally on a week-to-week basis.

Western Gazette and *Northampton Mercury* (both 8 August 1919) cited a ceremonial parade took place at Dorchester on Wednesday for a German prisoner's gallantry. Private Bruckmann was presented with a silver watch and a gift of money in recognition of the gallantry he displayed in extricating a British officer from a crashed and burning aeroplane on Salisbury Plain. Granted a free passage to his home, he was repatriated on the Sunday.

The Times (8 September 1919) reported W. Holling had been re-captured.

The Times (11 November 1919) and the *Dorset County Chronicle* (20 November 1919) cited all the PoWs left. The *Chronicle* reported they had been taken out clandestinely and repatriated, stating they left in large batches during the night. When they had all gone, the plateau was then opened to the public as a recreation ground.

Dorset County Chronicle (22 July 1937) printed a long account of a visit to Dorchester by a group of former internees. The account stated there had been forty-eight deaths in the camp.

Gosling (*Dorchester in Old Photographs*, 1994) reveals a railway line dissected the camp. The track allowed the lower portion of the camp to be initially fenced off with barbed wire, and with the erection of elevated sentry posts it created a detention area for civilian internees. The internees were housed in wooden huts identical to those used by the army, with each hut capable of billeting thirty men.

Draper (*An Illustrated History*, 1992) shows PoWs, watched by an armed guard, sweeping Dorchester's High East Street. The caption states:

> . . . up to 3,000 Germans were housed there [Poundbury]. Some were hired out to work in the sandpits at Moreton, to laying electricity cables in Dorchester, or doing general manual work around the town. Thomas Hardy paid 6d an hour for some of them to work in his garden – of which they only got 1d. The prisoners came 'with guards, rifles, interpreter, and all complete'.

Belfield (1920) noted that those internees engaged in the production of glass eyes at Dorchester were excused heavy labour tasks. At the height of their production, each week around 300 artificial 'vivid blue' eyes were being produced. However, these coloured eyes were not popular, and the line was discontinued. The PoWs also produced around 300 thermometers for the dairy industry every week.

Puddletown baker William John Barnes was fined £50, at Dorchester, for selling bread to German PoWs working on a nearby farm.

The camp's TA was Priswarian: Dorchester. It had the POWIB (1919) code Dor. Dorchester is listed by the FPHS (1973).

DORKING: Ranmore Common (OS: TQ 150 504). Ranmore Common is a few miles from Dorking. An entry for the camp appears in the *List of British Prison Camps*, first produced for the FPHS (1973) by F.J. Carter. Its TA is cited as Priswarian: The Fort, Ranmore Common, Dorking (ADM 1/8506/265–120667). Nearby is The Denbies, thought locally to be the actual location of the camp. The fort is near St Barnabas Church on Ranmore Common.

Thomas Cubitt built The Denbies in 1854, on the site of a house once owned by William Joseph Denison. The Denbies was demolished in 1953. Much of the estate is now Bradley Farm where there is a vineyard, with a winery and restaurant, appropriately called 'The Denbies'.

DOUGLAS, Isle of Man (OS: SC 388 773). Looking for a new site to place civilians deemed to be a threat to the national security of Britain, in September 1914, Sir William Byrne and Mr Sebag Montefiore of the Civilian Internment Camps Committee visited the Isle of Man to investigate the possibility of accommodating internees there. They choose Cunningham's Holiday Camp at Douglas, and before the first batch of 200 alien civilians arrived there on 22 September 1914, barbed wire fences were speedily erected. Gas and electric standard lamps were introduced for lighting the compounds at night, various guardrooms were built, and other alterations were made. Lt-Colonel H.W. Madoc was the Chief Constable of the Isle of Man, and was selected to be camp's commandant. His second in command was named as Captain F.C.C. Bland, and Dr Robert Marshall was appointed as the camp's Medical Officer.

The Times (24 October 1914) stated 200 internees moved from Frith Hill to Isle of Man. As Knockaloe was not yet available, those interned must have been sent to Douglas. It was estimated at that time there were 2,600 internees in the camp, guarded by the Isle of Man Volunteers. But, in order to assist in relieving congestion in temporary places of internment in London and elsewhere, a temporary increase to 3,300 prisoners was authorised. By February 1915 the number interned was reduced to 2,400, a figure set by the Destitute Aliens Committee, and this was maintained for the rest of the war.

Those interned there slept in tents and messed in a large permanent building. Later, huts superseded the tents, as the camp was divided into three sections: (1) The Privilege Section, (2) The Ordinary Section, and (3) The Jewish Section.

To qualify for the Privilege Section, a prisoner had to pay a weekly subscription, which entitled him to better accommodation, better meals, and a prisoner servant. However, as a result of food shortages arising in the country, these internees were rationed to the same as those in the Ordinary Section, and the privilege of making purchases of food in the town, through the medium of the Order Office, was withdrawn. Members of the Jewish Section were provided with kosher food and were given facilities for celebrating Jewish festivals.

There had been disaffection in the camp for some time when, on 19 November 1914, five internees were shot by the guard for rioting. At the inquest, held on the 20 and 27 November by the High-Bailiff of Douglas (the coroner for inquests), before a jury, it was recorded 'that the five deaths were caused by justifiable measures, forced upon the military authorities by the riotous behaviour of a large section of internees'. *The Times* (23 November 1914) confirms the riot took place, and reported on 3 December 1914 that a sixth internee had died from the wounds he sustained.

As a result of the riot cited in *The Times* (24 November 1914), Mr Chandler Hale of US Embassy in London was to visit the camp.

The Times (28 November 1914) cited the inquiry into the riot at Douglas had begun. Madoc, the camp's commandant, told the court that there had been signs of unrest for several weeks in the camp. He cited there were some 3,000 interned in accommodation only suitable for 2,400. On the day in question warning shots were fired, as some internees at the end of lunch began to throw plates. When a group of internees made a dash to the kitchens the guards blocked their path with their rifles. Despite attempts to repel the protesters it became necessary to fire into the approaching mob. Around thirty-four shots were fired. The jury agreed that all the deaths resulted from the justifiable measures forced upon the military authorities by the behaviour of a large section of the internees. The jury found the riot was partly blamed on overcrowding. The riot was blamed on the frustration of being in captivity, and being separated from friends and families. Poor food was another factor. Kurt Vausch was arrested for incitement, presumably as the ringleader. The dead were buried at Douglas Borough Cemetery.

The Times (16 December 1914) and the *Yorkshire Evening Press* carried similar reports of Otto Lutz and Kurt Vausch being tried in the Military Court. Lutz was charged with writing in invisible ink and writing under a stamp. Vausch was charged with incitement which led to the riot on 19 November 1914.

The Times (30 December 1914) cited the findings of a US Report, stating the camp was overcrowded – there were 2,000 Germans and 1,300 Austrians in the camp. To alleviate many of the camp's problems it was envisaged that around 1,000 internees were to be transferred to Knockaloe shortly. The paper also reported the trial of Herman Blass had taken place, for writing to Austria in lemon juice. *The Times* (12 January 1915) reported Blass was sentenced to two months in prison.

In the Isle of Man, the Lieutenant Governor was appointed the authority to convene military courts and to confirm the proceedings of such courts. Those sentenced to imprisonment were transferred to HM Prison, Douglas or sent to Liverpool. Just over one quarter (28.5 per cent) of the 345 secured convictions were for escaping or attempting to escape from the two camps on the island.

On 9 February 1915, a delegation from the US Embassy in London, led by Mr John Jackson, visited the camp. It concluded that there were about 2,400 prisoners, mostly housed in barrack huts. There were up to 120 men to a hut. There were however still some in tents, though this was by choice as it gave them more privacy. Captains had either a separate room or a tent to themselves. Within some huts cubicles for small numbers had been built and occupants paid a moderate sum for their use. Jackson believed there was more being done to provide occupation for prisoners than at any other camp he had visited. The canteen was adequate, and the washing, bathing, and WC arrangements were good. There was electric light; a swimming pool; a large hall for recreation, music and dancing. As exercise space was limited, route marches (walks outside the camp) were arranged. The original owners of the camp provided cooks, including women, so complaints about the preparation of food were few. Regulations as made by Captains of Companies were included in the report, as was the 'Daily

Dietary'. Besides the tents there was a large pavilion used as a dining room and recreational area. Later huts replaced the tents.

The Times (21 April 1915) reported three German sailors, Carl Hass, George Sudmann, and Ernst Frach, had escaped. *The Times* (26 April 1915) described it as 'a summer holiday camp for young men at a guinea a week'.

Liverpool Daily Post (27 April 1915) carried a plea from the Jewish authorities to allow all interned Jews on the island to be allowed to move to Douglas, the only camp where kosher food was being provided. The same paper also reported Hass, Sudmann, and Frach had been recaptured 5 miles to the southwest, at Kirksanton. The three had escaped on Tuesday.

The Times (29 April 1915) printed a letter referring to the *Camp Echo*, and stated how liberally we treated the internees, compared with our German counterparts. The paper was published by those interned at Douglas.

The *Liverpool Daily Post* (22 May 1915) stated an un-named internee was sentenced to two months hard labour for writing a letter in another's name. He claimed that this was a common practice.

The US Embassy's delegation re-visited the camp on 1 May 1916. It noted there were 2,744 internees in the camp, of whom 1,968 were German, 759 Austrian, 14 Turks and 3 others. A considerable number were of the Jewish faith. The camp was now split into an upper and lower camp with each having compounds. Both camps had a mixture of hut and tent accommodation.

The Lower Camp was the privileged camp where 'an officer class' of more wealthy internees paid extra to improve their food supply. 12s.6d (62.5p) bought their board and a half-share of a tent, 10/- (50p) for board and a third-share of a tent, 12/- (60p) for board and a third-share of a hut. For £1 a week they could have exclusive use of a hut or tent. There were approximately 500 places in the Lower Camp. Around 100 servants came from the Upper Camp to cater for them.

The Upper Camp had two compounds: one was described as the Ordinary Camp, and the other, the Jewish Camp, where kosher food was served. About 100 internees were employed outside the camps as gardeners and farm labourers.

The US Embassy delegation's visit of 19 June 1915 noted there were 2,429 internees in the camp, some 560 lived in tents, with the remainder in huts. A new playing field meant route marches were given up at the beginning of May. Although the camp had been described as a 'happy camp', the delegation was informed that there had been two deaths due to tuberculosis since February.

The Times (30 June 1916) reported that Georg von Streng had been re-captured as he tried to escape. The next day's edition cited he had attempted suicide.

The Times (14 December 1916) reported that a statement produced by Douglas Town Council alleged PoWs had luxuries.

The Times (1 March 1917) reported that three internees had escaped; they were named as Georg von Streng, who had escaped twice before, Otto Leikes and George Wigar. All three were reported re-captured in the next day's issue.

The Times (17 March 1917) cited von Streng had escaped again. It was in fact von Streng's fourth recorded attempt to get away. He was reported to be back in custody on 20 March 1917.

The Times (12 August 1917) reported Benno Lippchutz, 32 years old, a seaman, had escaped. The *Derby Daily Telegraph* (26 August 1918) noted that he was still at large, having escaped from a camp on the Isle of Man a fortnight earlier. He had absconded whilst returning from the brush-making factory to the camp. Belfield (*Report on the*

Directorate of Prisoners of War, 1920) wrote in his report that by May 1917 some 1,000 internees mainly from Knockaloe and Douglas did some kind of reclamation or agricultural work. The internees at Douglas made pipes, watches, and brushes. By August 1918, 734 internees were employed at a factory, set up by a contractor to make brushes (HO 45/11025/68577).

The Times (31 July 1917) reported Otto Rohreig and Jan Voight had escaped. They were re-captured on 6 August, and a woman from Ramsey was charged with harbouring them. She was sent to prison for one month and fined £1.

Isle of Man Examiner (25 May 1918) reported Fred Kroft had escaped and that a butcher, making deliveries, with his dog, had recaptured him at Ballaughton.

The Times (4 June 1919) reported the camp was cleared of detainees.

With hindsight, Belfield (1920), in his report, was sceptical about no one ministry having overall control of internees during the war. An Army Council Instruction (1090), of 1917, stated staffing levels did not apply to Home Office camps such as those at Douglas and Knockaloe, as they came directly under the umbrella of the Home Office.

The Home Office cited endeavours were made throughout the war to organise camp industries, but there were only three distinct successes recorded. One of these was brush making at Islington and Douglas, where contractors installed the necessary machinery, instructors were engaged, inmates taught and the output was sold through the contractors to government departments and the public. The enterprise was financially successful as the two plants gave continuous employment to about 600 interned aliens, but was criticised by the Brush Makers' Association. They were paid ordinary rates and were allowed to retain their earnings, less a deduction for maintenance.

Belfield (1920) cited around 900 men, from both Knockaloe and Douglas, were employed on quarrying and roadwork activities outside the camps. Most returned to their respective camps each night, but some temporary work camps existed around the island. He also cited the River Sulby was canalised with PoW labour.

After the war Douglas Detention Camp reverted to being a holiday camp, predating the opening of the first Butlin's camp at Skegness by many years.

DOVERDALE (see Droitwich).

DRIM WOOD, Llawhaden (OS: SN 066 176). Cited as being at Drim Wood, this working camp had the POWIB (1919) code Fg (Dr) (IMW: Facsimile K4655). The camp's TA is cited as Priswarian: Llawhaden (ADM 1/8506/265–120667). Its location has not been verified. The camp closed on 29 January 1919. Drim Wood is cited by the FPHS (1973).

DROITWICH (OS: SO 90- 63-). Droitwich had a working camp with the POWIB (1919) code, Dor (Dro) (IMW: Facsimile K4655). Its TA is cited as Priswarian: Droitwich (ADM 1/8506/265–120667). Doverdale only appears on the list produced for the FPHS (1973). Where the PoWs were billeted is not known. They may have been put into the workhouse in Union Lane, Droitwich; built in 1837 to the designs of Sampson Kempthorne, it could accommodate up to 200 inmates.

DRUMBUICH, nr Methven (OS: NO 002 278). Cited incorrectly by the POWIB (1919) as Drumbuach; it stands near Methven. It is described as a working camp, with the code Stbs (Du) (IMW: Facsimile K4655). Its TA is also cited incorrectly; it is stated as Priswarian: Drumburgh, Methven (ADM 1/8506/265–120667). The FPHS

(1973) listings do not cite Drumbuich, but state an entry for Methven. There is an entry for Keillor made by the FPHS (1973), which may be the same camp. Drumbuich Wood, at South Ardittie, is approximately 10 miles to the west of Perth. Nearby is the village of Drumbauchly.

Harding (*On Flows The Tay*, 2000) cites Canadian lumberjacks were based at South Ardittie.

DUBLIN. As a result of the Easter Rising three centres in Dublin were used to intern the insurgents. A number were taken to the British mainland, and those believed to be the leaders were executed. The three prisons were Arbour Hill Military Prison, Kilmainham Gaol, and Richmond Military Barracks.

ARBOUR HILL MILITARY PRISON (IGR: O 160 350). Dublin's Arbour Hill Military Prison was built in 1835 to the designs of Jacob Owen. It was then rebuilt in 1845 to plans of Sir Joshua Webb and it was the smallest of Dublin's Victorian prisons with only twenty-five cells.

Shelley (*A Short History of the 3rd Tipperary Brigade*, 1996) cited when Pádraig Pearse was arrested for his part in the Rising of 1916, he was sent to Arbour Hill. When he arrived, there were already around 125 co-conspirators being held there. Pearce, as a ringleader, was one of those put in a cell. Others, for their parts in the Rising, were kept in the old gymnasium in the prison yard. Arbour Hill was deemed the worst billet for those interned there, as brutality was a commonplace occurrence. In addition to the internees, soldiers found guilty of indiscipline and infractions of army rules were housed in it. Many prisoners allegedly had to endure semi-hangings and mock crucifixions. Hosings were a frequent punishment. The collective spirit of resistance, which prevailed elsewhere, was generally absent.

Pearse along with Thomas Clarke and Thomas MacDonagh was court-martialled at Richmond Barracks on 2 May 1916, and on being found guilty they were sentenced to death and transferred to Kilmainham Gaol that evening. They were executed in the early hours of the next day, and buried at Arbour Hill Barracks.

On 20 June 1916, Laurence Ginnell asked the Under-Secretary of State for War, Harold Tennant, if any doctor, other than the military doctors, had been allowed to inspect the unsanitary conditions in which prisoners were being kept at Arbour Hill, Dublin. Ginnell also inquired if he was aware that a number of men had been taken there from Galway and that they were being confined to one room with defective ventilation and insufficient beds, where vermin and filth was rife. Tennant replied that the prisoners were under the care of the military doctor at the prison, and the sanitary conditions were the responsibility of two sanitary officers that paid close attention to the needs of their prisoners, and there were no grounds for the imputation of want of care (*Hansard*, 1916).

HM PRISON KILMAINHAM (IGR: O 160 350). Built in 1792, Kilmainham Gaol closed in 1924. Its official name was the County of Dublin Gaol, but it was better known as the New Gaol to distinguish it from the old one it was intended to replace. Its 132 years played an important part in Ireland's history. Conditions were very poor, with no segregation of sexes; men, women and children were incarcerated, up to five in each cell, with only a single candle for light and heat; most of their time was spent in the cold and the dark. In its early years, many public hangings took place at the front of the gaol. Then, for nearly 100 years, very few hangings, public or private, took place at Kilmainham.

Many leaders of Irish rebellions were imprisoned within its walls, including those from the 1916 Easter Rising. After being tried before a military court and found guilty, fourteen conspirators were shot in Kilmainham gaol's courtyard. They were: Patrick Pearse, Thomas Clarke, Thomas MacDonagh, Joseph Plunkett, Edward Daly, William Pearse, Michael O'Hanrahan, John MacBride, Eamonn Ceannt, Michael Mallin, Con Colbert, Seán Heuston, Seán MacDiarmada, and James Connolly. Connolly was brought from the Castle's hospital for execution. Others were also sentenced to death, but had their sentences commuted to various terms of imprisonment; amongst them was Eamon de Valera. De Valera was sent to Dartmoor Prison.

The prison was abandoned by the government of the newly formed Irish Free State in 1924. Following lengthy restoration, it now houses a museum on the history of Irish nationalism.

RICHMOND BARRACKS (IGR: O 160 350). Dublin's Richmond Military Barracks, that dominate the skyline of Inchicore, were used to contain many of those that had taken up arms for their cause to free Ireland, at Easter 1916, from what they saw as British domination. When Pearse surrendered to General Maxwell, Maxwell decided to take a hard line with its leaders.

When arrested, many of the insurgents had been marched to the gym to be detained overnight and interrogated; others had gone to Arbour Hill Gaol or Kilmainham Gaol. Those not executed went to prisons in Scotland and England. Many eventually were transferred to Frongoch in North Wales.

Today, the names of the most prominent leaders are displayed on the walls around the building; Thomas Clarke, Padraic Pearse, Eamon Ceannt, Thomas McDonagh, James Connolly, Sean McDermott, Joseph Mary Plunkett, Liam Thomas Cosgrave, Sean Francis Lemass and Noel Lemass, with others. Descriptions of their maltreatment still exist.

During the Easter Rising, the Barracks had been taken by the insurgents and re-named the McGan Barracks. But, with the insurgency quelled, the Barracks returned into the hands of the British, and once again they became known by their former name. When the Irish Free State was established, Dublin's Richmond Barracks was taken over by the Irish Army and re-named Keogh Barracks. In 1927 it was decided to close them. The three storeys high buildings then passed into the possession of Dublin Corporation, who used the soldiers' quarters as accommodation for families on their housing waiting list. The Order of Christian Brothers, whose school occupies part of the site today, believe the Richmond Barracks was built in 1885. The Brothers purchased the gym, the officers' mess and the library/reading room and had them fitted out as classrooms. In September 1929 the first pupils took their places in their 'nearly new' school. During recent restoration work, bullets, knives and batons were found hidden under the floor of the gym.

DUFFIELD – RADBOURNE (OS: SK 34- 43-). An article appeared in the *Derby Daily Telegraph* (14 March 1918) citing thirty-five PoWs had been sought for Radbourne in Derbyshire. What connection to the arrival of PoWs to Duffield is not known by the same newspaper of 10 July 1918.

DULVERTON (OS: SS 915 285). HO documents show the Dulverton camp was located at Barle Combe House and had the TA Priswarian: Dulverton (ADM 1/8506/265–120667). It is described as being an agricultural depot, by the POWIB (1919), which gives it the code Dor (Dlv) (IWM: Facsimile K4655). South Molton and Tiverton are cited as its satellites. It is also cited by the FPHS (1973).

Kelly's Trade Directory (1914) shows Edward Bagnall occupied Barle Combe House prior to the First World War.

Minutes of the Somerset WAC (18 October 1918) show fifty-five PoWs that had previously been at Sandhill Park were transferred to Dulverton, Bridgwater, Thorloxton, Kingston Seymour and Clavelshay in equal numbers with some being retained Sandhill. A second minute (15 April 1919) cited the PoW Horse Depots at Axbridge, Dulverton and Shepton Mallet had been closed, and arrangements were being made for the early closure of Hallatrow.

DUNCANNON (IGR: S 750 005). According to the records of the Volksbund Deutsche Kriegsgräberfürsorge, Kassel (per. comm. 19 February 1997) the remains of Walter Richter (d. 9 August 1917), a German internee, were exhumed from Drumcannon's (sic) Old Graveyard in County Waterford, in the 1960s, and taken to the newly created German War Cemetery at Glencree, for reburial. He was a machinist by trade, so presumably a non-combatant.

Duncannon is in County Wexford and no camp has been traced there. No camps were traced in County Waterford either, so there is no plausible explanation for him being interred in Duncannon, although it was the custom of the day to bury those that died in internment close to where they died.

Duncannon is over 250 miles from Oldcastle, where no record of him escaping has been found.

DUNMOW: Union Workhouse (OS: TL 634 213). Minutes of the Cambridgeshire WAC record on 12 February 1917 that it was decided to place PoWs at the Union Workhouse, in Dunmow. It was a working camp, with the POWIB (1919) code Pa (Dun) (IWM: Facsimile K4655). Dunmow is also cited by the FPHS (1973). It had the TA Priswarian: Dunmow (ADM 1/8506/265–120667). The workhouse (a.k.a. The Close) was in Chelmsford Road. It was built in 1840 to the designs of Sir George Gilbert Scott and William Bonython Moffatt. A separate infirmary, designed by Fred Chancellor, was erected to the south of the workhouse in 1871.

Reports of the conditions at the working camps at Dunmow and Sutton Veny are held at the National Archives at Kew (FO 383/432). The internees complained to the Swiss Delegation that the building was inappropriate and that their supplies were inadequate, and of poor quality. Appropriate working apparel, too, was a concern of those internees that were expected to work on the watercourses.

The Chelmsford Chronicle (7 November 1919) reported 250 combatant PoWs had left the workhouse. They cheered as they were marched to the railway station to leave on a special train.

Today, the workhouse buildings have been converted to residential use.

DKF 33: Laut Bericht des Schweizerischen Delegierten Dr Schwyzer vom 3 September 1917 herrschen im Arbeitslager Dunow (sic), *Essex folgende Mißstände: Die zur Unterkunft der Gefangenen bestimmten Gebäude scheinen zweckentsprechend zu sein, doch wären die nötigen Öfen unbedingt alsbald aufzustellen und ausreichendes Heizmaterial zu liefern. Der als Küche benutzte Schuppen ist unzweckmäßig und zweifellos im holen Maße unhygienisch. Abhilfe erscheint dringend geboten. Die Zahnpflege liegt sehr im argen. Statt Brot wird zuweilen noch der harte Zwieback geliefert, was be idem Zustand, in dem sich die Zähne der Leute befinden, besonders unangebracht erscheint. Dir gelieferten Bohnen sind schlecht. Die Zustellung der Postsenddungen geht sehr langsam vor sich.*

DUNSTAN (see Newbold).

DURHAM: HM Prison (OS: NZ 273 422). A minute of the South Shields Council shows, in 1914, the Chief Constable of Durham sought recompense for expenses incurred by his police force in executing the provisions of the Aliens Restriction Act:

> As they (enemy aliens) were subsequently made PoWs, upon discharge from prison the Durham City Police having received and conveyed them, under the direction of the military authorities, to internment camps, the Chief Constable of the City of Durham has been in communication with the Home Office upon the subject of payment of the expenses incurred, and the Home Office reply that the Durham City Police Authority should be reimbursed by the Authority where prisoners were registered.

A Durham City Police Report Minute (1914) revealed the costs involved in dealing with 180 offences against the Aliens Restriction Act. It was revealed that 699 prisoners had been conveyed to HM Prison, Durham in 1914. 'The cost of maintenance before committal or discharge was £51.11s.7d; this included the cost of subsistence, but another £127.17s.4d was required for conveyance charges.' An insight into the work it was compelled to do showed the force conducted over 9,000 inquiries for other Services in 1916, including those for the Army Authorities. This figure did not include the many inquiries it undertook under the Aliens Restriction Orders.

McConville (*Irish Political Prisoners, 1848–1922: Theatre of War*, 2005) alludes to details of those interned for their involvement in the Easter Rising of 1916 being vague. Apart from the leadership most ended up in Frongoch. For their parts in the subsequent German Plot in 1917, individuals were sent to prisons in Scotland and Ireland. They were then, except for the leadership, moved to the Naval Prison at Lewes. Due to the disruption caused by the prisoners, they were separated into small groups and dispatched to prisons so that they could be managed properly. Some were briefly held in Durham Prison.

DUXFORD (OS: TL 472 460). This airfield dates back to the First World War. In 1914 aviation was still an untested method of warfare, but its potential usage saw the inauguration of the Royal Flying Corps and the ambitious scheme to expand its service from around 160,000 to nearly 300,000 men by 1917.

Located a few miles north-west of the village of Duxford in Cambridgeshire it was one of the sites chosen to train RFC aircrews; 238 acres of land, the main road from Newmarket to Royston bisected its northern perimeter.

In the summer of 1917, P. & W. Anderson, a Scottish civil engineering company, was given the contract to develop the site and the work, to cost an estimated £90,000, began that October. The buildings on the airfield site were mostly of brick and timber, but those on the north side of the road for domestic use were mainly constructed from timber. Four permanent timber-trussed hangars were built, consisting of three double bay and one single-bay Belfast types, with wooden concertina-type doors at each end.

The work had not been fully completed when Duxford became operational, in February 1918. German PoWs had constructed some of the buildings.

On 1 April 1918 the world's first fully independent air force was created when the Royal Navy Air Service and the Royal Flying Corps merged to become the Royal Air Force. In July that year, 35 Training Depot Station opened at Duxford to train pilots. RAF Duxford was opened officially in September 1918. The first resident RAF unit to be based there, in 1919, was No. 8 Squadron. From 1 April 1923 it became the home of No. 19 Squadron.

Three double bay hangars are still in use today, and have been listed as buildings of special architectural and historic interest. The single-bay hangar was destroyed by fire during the making of a film.

DYFFRYN ALED (see Llansannan).

E

EARDISTON (OS: SO 69- 68-). Described as a working camp by the POWIB (1919), its code is cited as Dor (Ear) (IWM: Facsimile K4655). It had the TA Priswarian: Eardiston (ADM 1/8506/265–120667). On 31 December 1917, when Eardiston was commanded by 2nd Lieutenant W.G. Richardson, there were twenty PoWs in the camp. The camp also appears on the list produced for the FPHS (1973), but the camp's actual location remains a mystery. Eardiston House is a Grade II listed farmhouse building which may hold the key. Today the building has been converted into flats.

EARTHAM: Slindon (OS: SU 963 118). A working camp, Slindon had the POWIB (1919) code Pa (Ert) (IWM: Facsimile K4655). The FPHS (1973) cite it too. The camp was situated at the bottom of Nore Hill and West Gumber Gate and its TA was cited as Priswarian: Eartham (ADM 1/8506/265–120667).

Close by was one of the largest Canadian Lumber Camps in Britain. Official papers from Canada cite there were around 300 PoWs at Eartham employed on various tasks. It is believed they may have worked on the construction of an aerial ropeway 7 miles long that would take the felled timber to a factory making cordite. Others worked on an airship station or on local farms and nurseries when required. They managed to supplement their diet by growing their own vegetables. At night Canadian troops guarded the camp perimeter.

EASINGWOLD: The Workhouse (OS: SE 535 704). Easingwold AG had the POWIB (1919) directory code Cat (Th) (Eas) (IWM: Facsimile K4655). This camp was in the town's workhouse. It had the TA Priswarian: Workhouse, Easingwold (ADM 1/8506/265–120667).

The workhouse was erected in 1837 on Oulston Road to the designs of John and William Atkinson. A twenty-bed infirmary was erected to the north of the workhouse in 1869. In 1934, the former workhouse was converted to become Claypenny Colony, to provide care for up to 200 people with learning disabilities. In 1948, it came under the umbrella of the National Health Service and the name Claypenny Hospital was adopted in 1952. It closed in 1993. The surviving buildings have now been converted to residential use.

EAST BOLDON (OS: NZ 385 624). At a meeting held at the Cottage Homes in Cleadon, on 11 November 1914, the Superintendent reported that the military authorities had taken possession of Woodbine Cottage from 7 November 1914 until further notice. Then, a report of the War Savings Special Committee meeting, held on 17 September 1915, indicated that the Children's Home was to be vacated shortly, for use by the military. Arrangements for transferring the children elsewhere were in the hands of a special sub-committee and, in batches of fifteen, in the care of foster mothers, the children transferred to Ponteland, Shotley Bridge, Lancaster or Stockton.

The first internees to arrive were probably civilians. There was an airfield at Cleadon, which opened in 1916. Any PoWs sent to Cleadon may have been employed there.

A newspaper article recorded by Smith (*The German Prisoner of war Camp at Leigh 1914–1919*, 1969) recounts a letter of Alfred Just whose father, at the turn of the century, was the gardener at Cleadon House, which refers to PoWs being billeted in the village. The article states:

> Outside the grounds [of Cleadon House] proper, over to the west ... patches of boggy ground in the area formed ideal training grounds for the army, which was stationed on Cleadon Hills during the First World War ... Later, many German prisoners were marched down Sunniside. Billeted in wooden huts adjoining the Cottage Homes, their job now was to dig trenches for our possible future defence.

The Leigh Chronicle (9 February 1917) states, 'About eighty German PoWs, from the Leigh Camp, left Leigh on Wednesday morning, by the 07.35 train for the county of Durham.' Their final destination may never be realised, as the county had several internment camps during this war.

The Borough Engineer of South Shields reported that he had been in touch with the Army Disposal Officer in regard to the hutments for sale at Boldon and Cleadon, and it was resolved by the town's Planning Committee to buy them for temporary housing purposes.

Woodbine Cottage is the only building that remained of the former Children's Home. It became part of Oakleigh Gardens School which catered for approximately fifty pupils with profound learning difficulties. As the building was not deemed Equality Act compliant, in December 2009 it was earmarked to close, to be re-located to a purpose built centre in Hebburn by 2012.

The Shields Gazette (n.d.) has a reference to the grave of a German PoW that was buried in East Boldon Cemetery.

A report of a visit of inspection to East Boldon (near Sunderland) by Dr A. de Sturler and Monsieur R. de Sturler during June 1919 is held at the National Archives at Kew (FO 383/508). The FPHS (1973) has two similar entries, East Bolden (sic) and Bolder East (sic), in their *List of Prison Camps*. The former is probably the entry for East Boldre in Wiltshire, where it is known an airfield existed. The latter is probably a misspelling of this location.

EAST BOLDRE (East Bolder) (OS: SU 368 011). East Boldre was first used as an aerodrome in May 1910, when William McArdle and J. Armstrong Drexel set up their New Forest Aviation School, using a small Bleriot monoplane. Unfortunately, a lack of interest in the facility saw its closure in December 1911.

In 1912 the site was considered, and rejected, by the Royal Flying Corps as a training school. However, as a result of the demand for basic pilot training to cover the Allied Western Front in Northern France and Flanders, the RFC did take occupation of part of the site in November 1915. In 1917 the airfield was extended to include the whole of the original 1911 airfield, with the addition of new hangars and barracks.

When the war finished, the East Boldre airfield became redundant, and the RAF moved out in 1919.

A Grenade School was created at Bolton's Bench, Lyndhurst, and there was a War Dog Training School in Matley Wood. Timber was extracted: around 2,000 acres were felled, and charcoal burning was done to provide absorbers for gas masks. Inevitably the forest suffered from these activities.

The camp was cited by the FPHS (1973) as East Bolder. This camp should not be confused with a camp at East Boldon in the north-east of England.

EAST DEREHAM. There were two camps near to East Dereham. One was at Gressenhall and the other at Neatherd Moor.

GRESSENHALL (OS: TF 964 165). When the Mitford and Launditch Poor Law Union came into existence in 1836 it took over the existing Gressenhall workhouse. To comply with the legislation, internal dividing walls were erected to create separate yards for the different classes of inmates. In 1930, the workhouse became Gressenhall Institution. The workhouse closed in 1948 and then provided accommodation for the elderly and emergency accommodation to homeless families, until 1974. In 1976, the buildings were converted into a rural life museum known as Gressenhall Farm and Workhouse: Museum of Norfolk Life (www.museums.norfolk.gov.uk).

It would appear from the Guardians' minutes that the military had taken up some accommodation at the workhouse from 25 October 1915. At a meeting of the Norfolk WAC (24 February 1917), it was recorded that if the main building was vacated of its inmates, then the workhouse could be adapted to accommodate PoWs instead. Extracts of the Guardian's minute books suggest the Infirmary wing on the east of the complex was then used to accommodate PoWs.

Its POWIB (1919) code was Pa (E D) (IWM: Facsimile K4655). Its TA was cited as Priswarian: East Dereham, Norfolk (ADM 1/8506/265–120667). It was cited by the FPHS (1973). Reports on visits of inspection to PoW camps in Norfolk include one to Gressenhall, conducted by Dr A. de Sturler and Monsieur R. de Sturler, during April and May 1919 which is held at the National Archives, at Kew (FO 383/507).

Minutes of the Guardians of the Workhouse (8 September 1919) cite inmate Mabel Bowman committed an indiscretion with a PoW. No proceedings were taken against her, but the matter was reported to the colonel in charge of the PoW camp, with regard to the laxity of the guard (NRO C/GP/14/45 & 47). Records indicate the military were ready to vacate the workhouse by October 1919, with recompense being sought by the Guardians for damages to the Infirmary wing in the period of occupation.

NEATHERD MOOR (OS: TF 984 125). In October 1917, Neatherd Moor, East Dereham, along with Belaugh Park and Elmham Park, were suggested as future locations for internment camps, according to minutes of the Norfolk WAC. It was resolved to apply for 150 PoWs for each venue. Gressenhall Union was also cited as an internment camp.

EAST GRINSTEAD (OS: TQ 390 386). According to the POWIB (1919) there was a working camp located at 218 London Road, East Grinstead. Its code was Pa (E G) (IWM: Facsimile K4655). This would put the camp near to Garland Road. It was also cited by the FPHS (1973). Its TA was Priswarian: East Grinstead (ADM 1/8506/265–120667). What this group did is not known.

EAST HARSLEY (OS: SE 42- 99-). Its TA is Priswarian: East Harsley, Ingleby Cross (ADM 1/8506/265–120667). Nothing is known of this camp. Harsley Hall or Morton Grange may hold the key to this camp's location or alternatively it may be that the camp only took its name from the fact the village had a railway station, and the camp was somewhere close by; a common practice used by the military minds of the day.

EAST HARLING (see Uphall).

EAST LEAKE (OS: SK 549 279). The 13th minute of the Notts County Agricultural Committee for 28 January 1919 states the total number of PoWs engaged on agricultural work in the County was 598. They were distributed among the following permanent depots: Retford, Tuxford, Ranskill, Laneham, Cuckney, Plumtree, Papplewick, Woodborough, Langar, East Leake, Kelham, Halam, Ossington and Carlton. There were also nine migratory gangs of ten PoWs: at Blyth, Wiseton, Clayworth, Walkeringham, Misson, Bunny, Ruddington, Shelford and Gotham.

The POWIB (1919) cite the camp as being an agricultural group attached to Loughborough agricultural depot. Its code was Bro (Lo) (Ek) (IWM: Facsimile K4655). The camp was at Hetchley Plaster Pit, with its TA being, Priswarian: East Leake (ADM 1/8506/265–120667). During March 1919, Dr A. de Sturler compiled reports on visits of inspection to the PoW camps. One report was of East Leake. It is held at the National Archives at Kew (FO 383/506).

It is believed the PoWs worked on the land.

An unsubstantiated story exists that some of PoWs were abusing pit ponies. The Hague Convention however did not permit PoWs to work underground.

EAST PRESTON – ANGMERING (OS: TQ 070 028). Described as a working camp, its POWIB (1919) code was Pa (E P) (IWM: Facsimile K4655). The camp was cited by the FPHS (1973), as was nearby Angmering. Its TA was cited as Priswarian: Angmering (ADM 1/8506/265–120667).

The War Office leased Preston Place, from 1 January 1918, from Admiral Warren and his brothers. Around seventy-five PoWs were interned there after alterations were done (Ron Standing, per. comm., 2004). The exact date of their arrival is recorded in a letter sent to Frank Standing at the 'Front', which states:

> 29 March 1918. We all went for a little walk this afternoon after I came home, and we saw some of the prisoners who came here yesterday. We saw a little group of them standing smoking outside the front door up Preston Place, and several walking about the grounds.

The PoWs worked on farms and nurseries in the area. They did not leave Preston Place until nearly a year after the Armistice, their number having swollen, by then, to around 160. Photos exist of their stay, as do some paintings done by P. Seifert, one of the internees.

EAST RUDHAM (OS: TF 825 286). The Eastern Command was informed, according to a minute of the Norfolk WAC (11 June 1917) that a camp for seventy-five PoWs was needed at East Rudham (C/C10/15).

EASSIE (OS: NO 33- 46-). Not far from Glamis Castle is the village of Eassie, probably better known for its Pictish Stone than the PoW camp that was established there in the First World War.

The Forfar and Strathmore Advertiser (2 August 1918) reported that the WAC agreed to accept a scheme 'providing for the establishment of camps at different centres'. The same newspaper (30 August 1918) does not make any specific reference to an internment camp being at Eassie, but there are references to PoWs being put to work on several unnamed farms in the Forfar area. *The Dundee Courier* (n.d.) provided some more details. Lieutenant Main, the National Service Sub-Commissioner for Agricultural Labour, told the Forfarshire WAC he had requested up to 2,000 soldiers to bring in the harvest in Forfarshire and Perthshire but the War Office replied they were unable to release any. Therefore he proposed to bring in PoWs instead from Auchterarder. The Board of Agriculture allowed groups of around twenty-five to fifty PoWs to be sent to suitable centres and to work in groups of no more than four or five on farms within a 3-mile radius of the centre, or in parties not exceeding three under the control of the farmer employing them.

Alistair Kidney provides proof that there was a camp at Eassie. His grandfather, John Kidney, was a CSM in the Cameron Highlanders. Wounded, he did not return to active service but instead became a member of the guard at the Eassie camp. In the Special Remarks Box in Kidney's discharge papers, it states:

> This Warrant Officer performed the duties of Quartermaster at the PoWs Camp, Eassie, from November 1918 to March 1919 in a very satisfactory manner. He contributed very greatly to the smooth running of the camp.
> (Signed) Lt-Colonel H. Richard (Commanding)
> Prisoner-of-war Camp, Stobs.

The Dundee Courier (9 January 1919) and *The Forfar Herald* (10 January 1919) reported four German PoWs had been found guilty of stealing a sheep from a field belonging to local farmer Thomas Wedderspoon, of Castleton, on the night of 5 December 1918. In their defence, the PoWs stated they stole the beast to make up for the shortages in their rations. Each was given a three month prison sentence. Wedderspoon stated to the court that his field, at Castleton, was about 1 mile from the camp.

Crawford (www.railscot.co.uk) mentions the station at Eassie, which stood on the Newtyle, Eassie & Glamiss Railway. There is no entry for Eassie in the POWIB (1919) listings but it does appear in the list produced for FPHS (1973). The camp's TA was Priswarian: Eassie: these records show the camp closed on 28 February 1919 (ADM 1/8506/265–120667).

EASTCOTE (OS: TQ 104 884). The camp was situated at Eastcote Lodge, in High Road, Eastcote. It had no connection to Eastcote House, Pattishall. It was an agricultural group with the POWIB (1919) code Fe (D L) (Ea) (IWM: Facsimile K4655). The camp, a satellite of Denham Lodge, had the TA Priswarian: Eastcote (ADM 1/8506/265–120667).

The Lodge was built *c.*1888 for Lawrence Ingram Baker and his bride Helen Peto. It was demolished in 1963 to make way for Flag Walk. It was the second building to have graced the site. John Baker had occupied the original building, until his death in 1886. Both buildings stood between the Black Horse and Flag Cottages.

Local legend suggests the PoWs worked on local farms and were well known customers of the Black Horse. It has been suggested that its occupants were German officers, but this does not correlate to it having an agricultural group's code.

Also in the town is Eastcote Place, built for a Miss M.A. Bevan in 1897. The house stands in Azalea Walk. In the Second World War, these premises were used as an extension to the Government Code and Cipher School at Bletchley Park; it was established *c.*1943. Today, the house, which once had ten bedrooms, has been converted into flats.

EASTGATE: Rosehill Farm (OS: NY 938 389). The POWIB (1919) states the address for Eastgate working camp as Rosehill Farm and quotes the following code Cat (Ea) for it (IWM: Facsimile K4655). The camp had a TA Priswarian: Eastgate (ADM 1/8506/265–120667). It is listed also by the FPHS (1973) as Eastgate, Durham.

Along with many other camps in Britain, the Eastgate camp was tented. A photograph exists of PoWs working for The Weardale Iron Company, taken *c.*1917.

With an increased demand for limestone during the First World War, the output at Heights Quarry rose dramatically. To improve the transportation of the limestone from the quarry the German PoWs were engaged in speeding up the process by creating a better incline at Cambo Keels.

EASTON ON THE HILL (OS: TF 005 045). A working camp, it had the POWIB (1919) code Pa (Ean) (IWM: Facsimile K4655). Its TA was Priswarian: Easton (ADM 1/8506/265–120667). The camp closed on 11 February 1919. It was also cited by the FPHS (1973). There is no evidence to suggest PoW labour was used to create the airfield or its infrastructure, but the possibility cannot be ignored.

Goodwin (*Easton on the Hill*, 1991) cites Easton on the Hill airfield opened as a training camp, and as a satellite for Wittering, on 26 September 1917. It was created at a time when airfields had become more than just reasonably flat pieces of land. Their heavier usage necessitated well-drained surfaces, free of obstruction. Buildings on these sites were usually grouped together and consisted of wooden huts for administration and accommodation. There would be a large hangar for servicing and repairing of the aircraft, supplemented by canvas Berameau Hangars for storage.

A corrugated structure, 70 feet by 25 feet, referred to locally as 'the Bloody Hut', was erected on the south side of New Road, at the corner of Stamford Road to be used for recreational purposes. As it was also intended for Sunday evening church services, the Bishop of Peterborough performed the opening ceremony on 3 February 1918.

After the war, the hall was given to the Church Army as a social centre. Other buildings, when no longer required, were dismantled and sold.

ECKINGTON (OS: SK 42- 79-). The village of Eckington, with others, is listed by *The Derby Daily Telegraph* (10 July 1918) as awaiting the arrival of PoWs, to work on the land. Minute No. 11 of the Derbyshire WAC (21 December 1918) expresses concerns about not completing the harvest in proper time, mainly due to the weather and the shortage of skilled men. The minute concluded that thirty German prisoners, in five gangs, were following threshers in the Chesterfield area (D331/1/27).

EDINBURGH. There were two camps in the Edinburgh area. One was in the castle and the other in army barracks at Colinton.

CASTLE DETENTION HOUSE (OS: NT 251 735). The current military presence at Edinburgh Castle could not confirm the castle was used to intern PoWs in the First World War. However, the Member of Parliament for the Dunbartonshire Burghs between the wars, David Kirkwood, provides evidence in his autobiography that the castle was used to intern German and Austrian officers when he wrote of his own internment in Edinburgh Castle. Arrested for allegedly inciting Clydeside's workers to strike for better conditions during the war, he was found guilty and agreed to be exiled from Scotland's west coast industrial belt for the rest of the war. He went to reside in the City of Edinburgh. He often went back clandestinely to Glasgow for visits, and his stays eventually became longer, which resulted in him being re-arrested for breaking the provisions of his release. He was taken back to the capital, and locked up in the castle.

Kirkwood (*My Life of Revolt*, 1935) describes his new environment, thus:

> My new habitation was a vault far below the ground, into which the only light entered from a small grated window high up near the roof. Above my vault were

> the Guard's Quarters, occupied by German and Austrian officer-prisoners. They were a noisy crew, singing, shouting, and scrapping day and night. They seemed to want for nothing. I thought it strange that I, who was innocent of any offence, should be in a dungeon while captured enemy should be so cheerfully housed up above. I was a done man.

It may be that those locked up above him were absconders awaiting trial, or convicted escapees. Kirkwood's internment began in mid-January 1917.

The use of the castle as a place to intern civilians and military lasted through the war.

The Times (15 April 1915) reported eight Germans were taken to Edinburgh Castle. They had been taken from a Norwegian barque, at Kirkwall, bound for South America. Presumably these were civilians.

Von Tirpitz's son, along with others, was sent to the castle from Redford Barracks for attempting to escape. He was eventually sent to a camp in North Wales.

The use of the castle's hospital is supported by an entry in the diary of Lady Kate Courtney. Her entry of 12 September 1915 states she met Mrs Campbell of Dunstaffnage on a train journey to the capital. In conversation with her, she learned of a dying German sailor that Mrs Campbell had visited at the castle.

Edinburgh Castle's Detention House had the POWIB (1919) code EDN (IWM: Facsimile K4655). The hospital had its own code, ECH. Edinburgh Castle is cited by the FPHS (1973) and by the OSt.

REDFORD BARRACKS: Colinton (OS: NT 226 686). Situated in the Colinton district of Edinburgh, it is the largest military installation built in Scotland since Fort George was created 150 years earlier. Built between 1909 and 1915, it was primarily a cavalry barracks. It is still used by the army today.

PoWs were held there in the early months of the war, in tented accommodation to the south of the main camp buildings. Horne (*New Evidence on Stobs Internment Camp 1914–19*, Manz, 2003) cited Redford Barracks functioned as the central collection camp for Scotland. From there, internees were dispatched to camps all over Britain. From around the end of the 1914, it appears to have been replaced, by the castle, to act as the main distribution centre in Scotland.

Although listed in a German Red Cross report of December 1915 as a PoW camp, and mentioned in the press several times, very little is known about this camp. A hand stamp mark exists, stating 'Redford Detention Camp–Colinton' dating from October 1914.

Jackson (*The Prisoners 1914–1918*, 1989) cites, in the early stages of the war, the first batch of PoWs to arrive at Stobs came from Edinburgh. It was probably to the barracks he was referring. Again, when the *Camberley News* printed, in October 1915, that a large number of civilian internees were being dispatched to Edinburgh, with the remainder going to Wakefield and Stratford, the exact location in the Scottish capital was not divulged.

Both the *Western Morning News* (11 August 1914) and *The York Herald* (12 August 1914) were more precise in their reporting of fifty German seamen that were moved under escort to Redford Barracks from German ships docked at Leith.

Several reports in the *Edinburgh Evening News* describe the arrivals of internees into Redford Barracks in 1914. The first of them (5 August 1914) reported the arrival of twenty German reservists that had been arrested on trawlers in the North Sea. Prior to being dispatched into internment, they were taken to Inverness before being sent to

Edinburgh. There is evidence from Fort George to corroborate the fact that ninety-one fishermen were held there prior to being sent south. The edition of 14 August 1914 stated there was disquiet in the capital about the many German fishermen being gathered at Redford Barracks, from all over Scotland. Harding (*On Flows the Tay*, 2000) cites nineteen internees passed through the railway station in Perth without incident. They were being moved from Inverness to Redford Barracks.

A further report, *Edinburgh Evening News* (20 August 1914), stated another thirty or forty had arrived the previous day and that there were now hundreds of men being interned in tents at Redford. The conclusion of this article stated the men seem contented as they pursued sporting activities to pass away their time. The edition of 26 August cited yet another thirty to forty internees were brought to Redford, again from Inverness.

Accounts of PoWs taken from the SMS *Mainz* on 31 August 1914, in *The Times*, *The Scotsman*, *The Liverpool Daily Post* and the *Edinburgh Evening News* give conflicting numbers landed at Leith. It appears around eighty to ninety internees, including the son of von Tirpitz, were put on a train to Redford. Ten to sixteen were wounded, some seriously, and were conveyed to Edinburgh Castle's hospital by motor vehicles. Shortly after being admitted, one of the wounded died. Tirpitz's son was one of about twenty that later tried to escape: when he and the others were re-arrested, they were sent to Edinburgh Castle.

The Scotsman (31 August 1914) reported four Germans, one a wounded German officer, were landed at Queensferry on the Firth of Forth. They were taken to Redford Barracks and the Castle Hospital, respectively.

The Scotsman (3 September 1914) reported eight German officers, including von Tirpitz, were removed from Redford and sent to the south. They were escorted discreetly to Slateford Station by charabanc. From there they travelled to the Caledonian Railway station in Edinburgh. Rumours the eight had tried to escape were denied, but a story appeared in *The Liverpool Daily Post* (4 September 1914) stating that at night about twenty internees, including von Tirpitz's son, had tried to break out of Redford Barracks, but were stopped, and arrested. They were taken to Edinburgh Castle, and the guard was increased. Tirpitz junior was later taken to Dyffryn Aled, in North Wales. A registered envelope, from him, addressed to Harrods, can confirm this.

The York Herald (16 September 1914) reported many aliens were arrested in Scotland. They were taken to Redford Barracks, presumably to be processed, and distributed. *The York Herald* (24 September 1914) and *The Yorkshire Gazette* (26 September 1914) cited similar reports of 300 Germans, including 70–75 sailors, leaving Redford Barracks, Edinburgh. From Edinburgh they were taken to Leeman Road in York. One wounded was taken to hospital in Fulmar Road.

The *Edinburgh Evening News* (2 November 1914) reported that nearly 500 prisoners were removed from Redford that evening. They were taken under guard to Georgie Station, and from there entrained south to England.

The Scotsman (3 November 1914) reported the first German prisoners to be interned at Stobs Camp had arrived the previous afternoon. They were taken by special train from Edinburgh and were accompanied by a strong military escort. The opening of Stobs meant the end for Redford as a place of internment. Included in a German report (20 January 1915) on internment camps in the UK, it was noted that men previously held at Redford, where conditions were bad, were now at Stobs whilst John Jackson's US Embassy in London's report of February 1915 stated 'the camp at Redford, near Edinburgh, had been closed for some time'.

EGGESFORD STATION (OS: SS 682 113). Described as a working camp by the POWIB (1919), its code was Dor (Eg) (IWM: Facsimile K 4655). It is also cited by the FPHS (1973). The camp had the TA Priswarian: Eggesford (ADM 1/8506/265–120667). Any PoWs sent to this area may have been billeted on the estate of Eggesford's Barton House, once the main farm for The Earls of Portsmouth.

ELLESMERE (OS: SJ 39- 34-). A satellite of Leominster, it was described as an agricultural group by the POWIB (1919); its code was Shrw (Lmr) (Ee) (IWM: Facsimile K 4655). Its address is cited as 42 West Street, Leominster. It is also cited by the FPHS (1973). The camp's TA was Priswarian: Ellesmere (ADM 1/8506/265–120667). A report on a visit of inspection to the PoW camp at Ellesmere, by Dr A. de Sturler and Monsieur R. de Sturler during April and May 1919 is held at the National Archives at Kew (FO 383/507).

ELLON (Boddam) (OS: NJ 955 305). There is no conclusive proof that this camp existed. The FPHS (1973) and the POWIB (1919) both cite a camp at Elton. The former places it in Aberdeenshire while the latter puts it in Huntingdonshire. Elton does not exist in Aberdeenshire and no camp has been traced to the other. Boddam appears in the FPHS (1973) list.

A newspaper article in *The Dundee Courier* (21 April 1917) only adds to the confusion. It seeks placements for PoWs to work on the land in Aberdeenshire (Kincardineshire was part of Aberdeenshire WAC).

The camp may have stood near Stuartfield, where it is known a camp existed in the Second World War. During the First World War, conscientious objectors were sent to nearby Dyce, to break stone.

The Formantine and Buchan Railway had a branch line running from Ellon Station to Boddam. On this branch line, which closed in 1945, stood Cruden Bay, where the bricks used in the construction of RNAD Lenabo originated. The airship base was constructed in 1915, too early for the PoWs to be employed in its construction.

ELMSWOOD PARK (see North Elmswood).

ELMSWELL: Eastwood Farm (OS: TM 001 654). The autobiographical *Memories of George Russell* (n.d.) produces the only reference found to this camp. Born in 1913, his father ran the Lion Inn, and was called up for military service, causing George to move with his mother and siblings to Eastwood Lane, about 2 miles from the centre of Elmswell. In recalling his early memories, he mentions PoWs worked on the land at Eastwood Farm. The government had requisitioned the farm as an experimental airfield. Imprinted in his mind is a field with army horses, and in the field next to them were bi-planes. They belonged to 75 Squadron of the Royal Flying Corps. The airfield was first used in December 1916 and closed in 1956. The Lion Inn was previously called The Swan and is sometimes cited as The Red Lion.

ELTON (OS: TL 084 935). A working camp, its POWIB (1919) code was Pa (El). Its TA was Priswarian: Elton, Peterborough (IWM: Facsimile K 4655). Its location remains unknown. A listing for a camp of this name was made by the FPHS (1973), but cites it as in Aberdeenshire.

ELY: nr Cardiff (OS: ST 142 764). The camp's TA was Priswarian: Cardiff (ADM 1/8506/265–120667). The location of this camp is unknown. There is evidence to show racecourses and workhouses were used to intern PoWs in the First World War at other locations, but no such evidence has been found to confirm either Ely Racecourse or the former Industrial School was used as a place of internment.

Ely Racecourse, Glamorgan, was first used as a racecourse around 1855. From 1895 to 1939 it was the home of the Welsh Grand National. The last race to be run at Ely was on 27 April 1939. Prior to then horse racing had been held at nearby Heath Farm. In 1953, facilities for playing soccer, rugby, hockey, cricket and baseball were established there, making it then Cardiff's biggest sports and recreation centre. On parts not used for sport, housing was built.

A workhouse was built on Cowbridge Road, Canton, Cardiff, in 1839. It was rebuilt in 1881 and enlarged several times. From 1863, the children had been accommodated separately, at the Industrial Schools at Ely, where they were taught trades. By 1901, the buildings had been extended and a separate hospital block was erected to the south-west. A change in policy saw most children accommodated in 'Scattered Homes' in different parts of the union. Those that remained at Ely were put in new 'Headquarters Homes' which were built on part of the Industrial Schools site. By 1903, the original Industrial Schools buildings were no longer being used for children and were adapted for use as an auxiliary workhouse for adults, especially the aged, infirm and 'mental defectives'. This became Ely Lodge in 1914, and the name of the main workhouse, in Cardiff, was changed to City Lodge. In 1930, City Lodge and Ely Lodge were taken over by the Public Assistance Committees of Cardiff City Council and Glamorgan County Council. City Lodge was transferred to the NHS in 1948, becoming St David's Hospital. Ely Lodge became Ely Hospital and provided accommodation for the mentally ill and as a hospice (www.archiveswales.org.uk).

The hospital closed in 1996.

A report on a visit of inspection by Dr A. de Sturler and Monsieur R. de Sturler during June 1919 to PoW camps in South Wales includes that of Ely that is held at the National Archives at Kew (FO 383/508).

ELY, ISLE OF (OS: TL 538 800). The PoWs may have occupied the same site as No. 26 Camp that stood in Barton Field in the Second World War. Contemporary maps of the First World War show Militia Barracks on Barton Road. Alternatively, the PoWs may have been billeted in a workhouse situated on Cambridge Road on the other side of the fields from the medieval hospital. Many workhouses were underutilised because of the constraints of the Mental Deficiency Act of 1913. It was built *c.*1837 to accommodate 300 inmates to the designs of William Donthorn. Ely Union Workhouse went through a period of transition, becoming Ely Poor Law Institution, then Ely Public Assistance Institution in 1930, before it became Tower House Hospital in 1948. The hospital closed in 1993. The site was sold for redevelopment, some buildings were demolished and some refurbished. It is now private housing under the name of Tower Court (www.cambridgeshire.gov.uk).

ENFIELD: Clay Hill Lodge (OS: TQ 314 989). The POWIB (1919) directory cites Enfield as a working camp and gives it the code Fe (En) (IWM: Facsimile K4655). Its address was Clay Hill Lodge. This was a large house on Strayfield Road, and it is currently a market garden centre. According to *Kelly's Trade Directory* the house was occupied by William James Freer in 1917 and a later edition states the house as unoccupied in 1921.

The PoWs could have been employed on the Hertford Loop, which passes close to the Lodge. When the war began the line north of Cuffley was still under construction. It opened in 1918 for freight purposes. The Enfield to Cuffley section opened to passenger traffic in 1924. The Horns Mill Viaduct at Hertford and the Ponsbourne Tunnel at Bayford could have both benefited from this pool of PoW labour. Alternatively, they simply worked on the local farms and market gardens in the area.

ENSTONE (OS: SP 37- 24-). Cited by the FPHS (1973), the camp location is not known. It had the TA Priswarian: Enstone (ADM 1/8506/265–120667). Enstone is included in a report of visits of inspection to PoWs camps done in March 1919, by Dr A. de Sturler. It is held at the National Archives at Kew (FO 383/506).

EPPING: Coopersale House (OS: TL 475 022). A working camp, its POWIB (1919) code was Pa (Epp) (IWM: Facsimile K 4655). It is also cited by the FPHS (1973). The camp is cited as being at Coopersale House and had the TA Priswarian: Epping (ADM 1/8506/265–120667).

There has been a building of some substance on the site of Coopersale House since the time of Agincourt. The Archer family had lived there for around 200 years. Then a marriage with Jacob Houblon created the double-barrelled name of Archer-Houblon, starting a branch of the family lasting until 1908. The contents of the house were sold in 1908 and the estate in 1914. Brown cites a religious order owned it during the First World War. In 1920 the house was sold to Mr H.E.J. Camps. Mr Dudley Ward owned it from 1936 until 1944. He, in turn, sold it on to Countess How. In 1946, Mr Jocelyn Hambro acquired it. More recent owners have been Rupert Murdoch and Mr Gerald Scott OBE. In 2002 it was empty and under renovation.

ESHER: Mill Meadow (OS: TQ 133 658). OS maps reveal an area described as Mill Mead next to Royal Mills, on the opposite side of Sandown Park to Esher. This is probably the place listed as an internment camp, described as being at Mill Meadow in the HO documents of 1918 and 1919 (ADM 1/8506/265–120667).

G.B. Greenwood's Account of Royal Mills at Esher state, according to the Domesday Book there was no mill at Esher when the survey was conducted. But from other sources it is known industrial activity had taken place at this spot for many generations. Jacob Momma and Daniel Demetrius opened a water-powered mill on the River Mole in 1670. The following year there is a letter written by William Lilly stating the inclement weather might stop his corn being milled there. However it has been cited that Momma was making products from brass, at Esher, from 1649.

In 1691, the mill complex was leased to William Dockwra to make products from brass. Copper was smelted at Esher and turned into brass wire and pins that were made on production lines. The top pin-makers could produce 24,000 pins a day.

ETTINGSHALL (OS: SO 924 953). Designated by the POWIB (1919) as having the code Bro (Et), this camp is cited as having two satellite camps attached to it, those of Somerford Hall and Wrottesley Hall. The HO gave its TA as Priswarian: Wolverhampton (ADM 1/8506/265–120667). Neither organisation gave the camp's actual location. This camp has been very difficult to place, as the area at that time comprised mainly of collieries, foundries, and iron works. However the camp may have been at Ettingshall Park Farm, which stood to the west of Ettingshall. The FPHS (1973) cites a camp at New Bilston (sic), Rugby and a camp at Ettingshall, Staffs

There is a grievance recorded in German archival material that states wages, still owed for work undertaken by PoWs at Ettingshall, that were then dispatched to Northern France, still had not been paid to them.

DKF 32: In Ettinghall (sic) *befindlichen Leuten ist der Lohn für in Nordfrankreich geleistete Arbeit noch ausbezahlt worden.*

ETWALL: The Ashe (OS: SK 261 325). The POWIB (1919) cite that PoWs were accommodated in Etwall, a satellite of the camp at Burton upon Trent. Its code was Bro (Brt) (Ew) (IWM: Facsimile K4655). The camp had the TA Priswarian: The Ashe, Etwall (ADM 1/8506/265–120667. Etwall is included in a report of visits of inspection to PoWs camps done in March 1919, by Dr A. de Sturler. It is held at the National Archives at Kew (FO 383/506). It is also cited by the FPHS (1973).

The Derby Daily Telegraph (10 July 1918) reported that PoWs were being sent to nearby Ash, where there were several large houses that could have been annexed for this purpose. Today, The Ashe is a Buddhist Centre.

EVESHAM: Bengeworth Brickworks (OS: SP 074 437). *The Evesham Journal* (21 July 1917) reported that another 100 prisoners were to arrive in Evesham, on Tuesday, to be accommodated under canvas in the brickyard. This seems to have been a temporary arrangement as on 3 November 1917, the brickyard camp was reported closed. The 200 PoWs there were transferred to the Drill Hall in Evesham or to Craycombe House in Fladbury in equal numbers.

EVESHAM: Bengeworth Drill Hall (OS: SP 074 436). Described as an agricultural depot with the POWIB (1919) code Dor (Ev) (IWM: Facsimile K4655), the camp's TA was Priswarian: Evesham (ADM 1/8506/265–120667). Chapel Oak is described as its satellite. Evesham is cited by the FPHS (1973).

The Evesham Journal (10 March 1917) reported that eighty PoWs from Ashchurch were to be billeted in Evesham's Drill Hall. The Drill Hall was part of the Barracks. It was described as providing meagre rations, and the PoWs documented evidence that there was no canteen facility there.

A photo exists of German PoWs helping the Martin family to pick plums. The Martin's orchard was in Bengeworth. The caption suggests Mr Martin got on well with his charges and that he frequently disregarded the rules by feeding them regularly. They had a mutual respect for each other.

In May 1918, there was a report in the local newspaper that stated three prisoners, from the Drill Hall Camp, had escaped whilst working at Langdon Hill. They were re-captured by a Badsey man, Harry Kelland, who came across the three taking a rest in a spinney, near Wormington.

One of the camps in Evesham was recorded as having forty-one PoWs billeted there on 31 December 1917 when Major J.J. Forbes-Pelloxfen was in command.

DKF 31: In Joice Green (sic), *Dartford, Linton, Sutton Veney* (sic) *Fovant, und Evesham bestehen Keine Kantine. Die Ausführung der Bestellungen der Kriegsgefangenen durch den Profoß Sergeanten, kann nicht als genügender Ersatz betrachtet werden.*

EVESHAM: Hampton House (OS: SP 028 435). In February 1918, *The Evesham Journal* informed its readers that 100 prisoners had been moved to the Badsey Manor House, making a total of 420 prisoners now in the area. Others were at Hampton House or Craycombe House.

A photograph showing a party of German PoWs filing past a sentry at a gate, to be counted out, exists, with the caption, 'German prisoners at Evesham, where a party of eighty are employed in various agricultural operations, leaving their quarters under armed guard to start work.' This gate is part of a high red-bricked wall.

Its TA was Priswarian: Hampton, Evesham (ADM 1/8506/265–120667). Great Hampton's POWIB (1919) code was Dor (Hmp) (IWM: Facsimile K4655). It was cited by the FPHS (1973).

EXETER (OS: SX 925 932). Exeter became the first provincial town to take refugees, when 120 Belgians arrived. By the end of October 1914, over 800 had arrived in the town. The city also received twenty Germans who were arrested in Torquay, and brought to Exeter for internment.

The Western Morning News (12 August 1914) cited forty-six Germans from the area around Plymouth had been arrested and put into internment at St Sidwell's School, in Exeter; further batches were expected. Two days later, the same paper reported most of those arrested had been paroled back into the community. It does not comment however on the fate of those not paroled.

The Taunton Courier (30 January 1918) cites PoWs were wanted to perform a variety of tasks in various parishes around Exeter. The request was again cited on 13 February 1918.

The Times (11 February 1918) cited there were 2,000 PoWs in Somerset; they were to be offered 5d (2p) per man, per hour for their labour.

EYE (OS: TM 252 732). A working camp, its POWIB (1919) code was Pa (Eye) (IWM: Facsimile K4655). It is also cited by the FPHS (1973). The camp was cited as being in the Old Workhouse at Hoxne, and it had the TA Priswarian: Eye (ADM 1/8506/265–120667).

The Hoxne Union Workhouse opened soon after the Union was formed in June 1835. The building was designed to accommodate up to 300 inmates. Built at Barley Green, near Stradbroke, it was based on the popular cruciform plan. The neighbouring Hartismere Poor Law Union erected their workhouse at Castle Hill, in Eye, the same year. In 1907, the Hoxne and Hartismere Unions merged.

The Hoxne workhouse had closed in 1871 and stood empty for many years before it was used as a PoW camp during the First World War (www.onesuffolk.co.uk/HoxnePC/History). The main building was demolished in the early 1920s. Only the single-storey entrance ranges and the fever block at the rear, which have been converted to residential use, survive.

F

FALMOUTH WORKHOUSE (OS: SW 789 334). Walter Goerlitz was a German national. He had been arrested on a ship in Falmouth's harbour in August 1914 along with thirty-one other enemy aliens. He sent a letter to the *New York Times* about his experience in internment in the United Kingdom. He wrote they had been detained in a grain store for about a week. The conditions there were poor: for instance, they had no mattresses to sleep on, and they had to improvise with freshly cut grass stuffed into sacking. However, he did praise their guard, which attempted to make their brief stay bearable. He was then transferred to Newbury.

The Western Morning News (14 August 1914) cited the workhouses at Falmouth, Redruth, St Columb and Truro were being used to hold passengers and crews from two German ships, held at Falmouth Harbour. Presumably, Walter Goerlitz was one of them.

Falmouth Poor Law Union was formed on 13 June 1837. The new Union kept and utilised the former parish workhouses until they were replaced *c.*1852 by a new building erected at Budock, about 2 miles to the north-west of Falmouth, at the east side of what is now Union Road. Designed by Fred William Porter, it was intended to accommodate up to 320 inmates. In 1933 the establishment had become Falmouth Public Assistance Institution, and was later called Budock House. Following the inception of the National Health Service in 1948, it became Budock Hospital. In 2001, the former workhouse buildings were lying disused but have now been demolished and the site has been redeveloped as a housing estate.

FARINGDON: Pidnell House (OS: SU 287 986). Meaning 'fern-covered hill', Faringdon was granted a Royal Charter in 1216 to hold a weekly market that still survives today. The camp was at Pidnell House. It had the TA Priswarian: Faringdon (ADM 1/8506/265–120667). An agricultural group attached to Compton AD, its POWIB (1919) code was Dor (Cmp) (Fdn) (IWM: Facsimile K4655). It is also cited by the FPHS (1973).

FARNBOROUGH – COVE HEIGHT (Blackdown Camp) (OS: SU 911 587). Based at Blackdown Camp, it was described as a working camp with the POWIB (1919) code Dor (Cve) (IWM: Facsimile K4655). Its TA was Priswarian: Farnborough (ADM 1/8506/265–120667). Cove is also cited by the FPHS (1973).

An undated newspaper cutting that had been in the possession of Miss Rees, a translator at the Prisoner-of-war Information Bureau, concluded, '*The Daily Express* yesterday gave the names of four officers who had escaped from the Colsterdale Camp, Yorks., and of a prisoner missing from the camp at Cove Height, Aldershot.' *The Times* (24 August 1917) carried a report of an internee that had escaped from Cove Heights. He was not named.

Messers Mielitz, Sahm, Zuker and Habel, escaped from Cove Heights according to *The Times* (4 December 1917). They were reported re-captured, near Odiham on 7 December 1917.

FELTHAM: HM Prison (OS: TQ 105 734). According to Bird (*Control of Enemy Alien Civilians in Great Britain 1914–1918*, 1986), Feltham was commandeered in the spring of 1916 to house a different kind of civilian internee from those being held at other camps in Britain. *The Times* (19 February 1916) cited the Borstal Institution at Feltham closed the previous day and it would re-open shortly, to house enemy aliens. It was envisaged they would cultivate the 90 acres of pastureland, which surrounded the buildings.

Reports of Danish soldiers being detained at Feltham are not strictly true, as Denmark was deemed to be neutral in this conflict. However, the Danish National Archive confirms around 6,000 Schleswiggers (German derivative) died, and many more were taken prisoner by the Allied Powers during the war, as many fought for the German cause. Slesvig (Danish derivative) had been annexed to Germany in 1864 at the London Conference.

In the plebiscite of 1920, the northern part of the state chose to return to Danish sovereignty.

These internees were deemed enemy aliens by the British authorities, but they had no love for Germany. They were Alsatians, Poles, Schleswig-Holsteiners, Czechs, etc. whose national aspirations could only be fulfilled by the Allies. They were screened before being sent to this special camp. They were treated like any other PoW, except they were permitted to converse openly in their own tongues, express political opinions, and seek the counsel of a national representative. As a group, they could select a captain to represent them. Many that would have qualified to come to this camp hesitated in fear of reprisals on family members back home.

Macpherson, Horrocks & Beveridge, (*History of the Great War – Medical Services*, 1923) cites the camp opened on 14 February 1916 for 1,500 men.

A report, emanating from the HO, cites why Feltham was set up:

> . . . since many of the cases were too doubtful, a separate camp was established at Feltham, in which those of them whom it was thought desirable to intern were collected. This had the double advantage of removing the genuine men from the German camps, where they were unpopular and sometimes ill-treated, and of enabling the authorities to get a better idea of their real sympathies, which, in the German camps, they did not dare to express. Feltham proved a success and it was found possible to liberate a number of the men after they had been sufficiently tested there. Combatants and civilians were located there.

The US Embassy in London sent a delegation to visit the camp on 17 May 1916. Their report stated that the place had been remodelled so that the feeling of prison confinement had been done away with. The commandant was Major L.W. Johnson. The internees comprised of 380 prisoners, of which 319 were German, fifty-five were Austrian, with six other nationalities. 201 were military, four naval and 175 were civilians. Some ships' masters were amongst the prisoners.

Later, under a re-organisation of the internment system, this establishment was also to become a parent camp for combatants. But the original internees were to object vehemently at being interned with 'full' Germans or Austrians, in fear of reprisals taking place aimed primarily at their family members back in their homelands.

The Times (18 October 1917) reported Leon Beeib had been recaptured. He had escaped two days earlier.

The Times (17 March 1919) reported that the 300 Schleswiggers/Slesviggers interned at Feltham had been released and that they had gone to Copenhagen.

The Times (7 November 1919) cited a prisoner, about to be released, had escaped. He was not named in the report.

The Middlesex Chronicle (18 August 1923) reported the Bantested Memorial being erected to the four Slesvigers (Christian Lund, Peter Andreas Petersen, Andreas Jakobsen, and Konrad Christensen) who died whilst interned at Feltham:

> An impressive ceremony recalling, in a pathetic way, the days when the Borstal Institution at Feltham was used as a camp for the internment of PoWs during the great world conflict of 1914–1918 took place at that institution on Wednesday afternoon. The captives, who came under the charge of Lieutenant-Colonel L.W. Johnson and his military force at the Feltham camp, consisted for the most part of what may be described as non-German people who were at the same time German subjects but really friendly aliens forced to fight on the side of the Kaiser.

The Slesvigers were not the only deaths that occurred at Feltham during the First World War:

Slesvigers still interred at Feltham:

Christian Lund	d. 24/11/1918
Konrad Christensen	d. 05/12/1918
Peter Andreas Petersen	d. 15/12/1919
&	
Andreas Jacobsen***	d. 01/12/1918

Germans moved to Cannock Chase (Nov. 1962):

Franz Chudak*	d. 20/12/1916
Leo Shipkowski	d. 10/08/1918
Stanislau Polezynski	d. 19/11/1918
Franz Chimelnik	d. 22/11/1918
Stephen Woischikowski	d. 22/11/1918
Anton Marciniak	d. 04/12/1918
Martin Warot	d. 30/11/1918
Wenzel Kubina	d. 22/06/1919
&	
Michael Jaskolski**	d. 30/11/1919

*Chudak was originally cited as Martin Hudak

**Jaskolski's name was included in those to be left at Feltham, but he is interred in Block 17, Plot 315 at Cannock Chase.

***Although his name appeared on the list of those to be transferred to Cannock Chase, Jacobsen's remains are still at Feltham.

The Volksbund Deutsche Kriegsgräberfürsorge notified the Imperial War Graves Commission that it was no longer willing to maintain the graves of those still interred at Feltham (IWGC, 1922).

In 1918, Feltham became a Polish military centre. The British military authorities allowed combatant PoWs detained at Feltham to enlist in the Polish Army. After assessment, they were drafted to France in considerable numbers.

A HO document cited, mid to late 1919, Feltham contained only a few civilian PoWs, all of whom claimed to be of friendly races. On 1 May 1919 it was cited only twenty-five internees were still there.

Feltham had been built in 1869 as the Middlesex Industrial Reform School, as part of the borstal system. After the war, it reverted to its intended usage as a borstal, and the internment camp's commandant Lieutenant-Colonel L.W. Johnson became its governor. Today, a modernised Feltham is still an integral part of the judicial system for dealing with young offenders.

Feltham's POWIB (1919) code was Fe, and its TA was Priswarian: Feltham (ADM 1/8506/265–120667). The FPHS (1973) have an entry for Feltham, Middx. It is also cited in the Osterreichisches Staatsarchiv's *Behandlung der Deutschen und Oesterreichischen Offiziere Kriegsgefangene im Vereinigten Koenigreiche, Wein*, June 1917.

FELTWELL (OS: TL 704 905). Situated on Shrub Hill Farm, it appears in the minutes of the Norfolk WAC when a proposal was put forward that the PoWs based at Feltwell should carry out 'southern drainage work' (C/C10/15–19).

FERNHILL: Gobowen (OS: SJ 311 335). *The Border Counties Advertiser* (3 December 1919) cites striking German PoWs secretly posted up an appeal of their plight in the yard of The Hart and Trumpet, in Gobowen.

The Times (17 November 1919) stated the Henlle and Fernhill camps had now been dismantled.

The FPHS (1973) cite Little Fernhill. There is a hall known as Little Fernhill on the outskirts of Guildford, but there is no evidence to prove this was this camp's location. Fernhill, near to Gobowen, where it is known that PoWs alighted from trains, and were marched to Park Hall for internment, is a more likely location.

FLADBURY: Craycombe House (OS: SP 000 474). The *Evesham Journal* (3 November 1917) gives an account of 100 PoWs being transferred to Fladbury when the brickyard camp at Great Hampton closed. Fladbury was described as a working camp with the POWIB (1919) code Dor (Fla) (IWM: Facsimile K 4655), and its address was quoted as being Craycombe House. Craycombe House appears in the list produced for the FPHS (1973). It had the TA Priswarian: Fladbury, Pershore (ADM 1/8506/265–120667).

Built in the eighteenth century by George Byfield, it was cited as having magnificent cellars, a walled kitchen garden, and an orangery; surrounded by pleasure gardens and a small park.

FLAT HOLM ISLAND (OS: ST 218 650). Flat Holm is an island consisting of about 70 acres. Its only population is its colony of sea birds. With an average height above sea level of 100 feet and its strategic position in the Bristol Channel, along with fortifications on Brean Down, Steep Holm and Lavernock Point, it made the ideal position to repel any French attacks on the ports of Bristol, Cardiff and Newport. It was fortified during the 1860s. In 1881, a 9 × 7-inch RML Mk III gun was housed there.

It was reported in the *Western Morning News* (11 August 1914) and the *Yorkshire Herald* (12 August 1914) that eighty-five men were being detained under guard in temporary accommodation in Rutland Street School in Swansea until a permanent camp was made ready. Flat Holm Island was proposed for this camp, but it is believed the idea never came to fruition.

FORGANDENNY (OS: NO 084 185). Like Forteviot, Forgandenny was a satellite of Auchterarder. Its POWIB (1919) code was Stbs (Au) (Fg) (IWM: Facsimile K 4655). It was cited by the FPHS (1973). Approximately 11 miles to the east of Auchterarder, this camp may have been at a railway yard, to the south-west of the railway station. The station opened in 1848 and closed to passengers on 11 June 1956. The station house is now a private residence.

FORT ELSON (OS: SU 599 029). *The Western News* (11 August 1914) cited 120 Germans were taken off an un-named German steamer at Gosport the previous day and marched to Fort Elson. Their fate is unknown.

FORT GEORGE (OS: NH 764 568). Fort George stands near to Ardersier and is a prominent landmark on the shores of the Moray Firth. It was created in 1769 as the base for around 1,600 Hanoverian soldiers of George III. Its purpose was to suppress any further resistance by the followers of Charles Edward Stuart (Bonnie Prince Charlie) after the rout of his Jacobite army at Culloden Moor in April 1746. It covers some 42 acres of land.

In the nineteenth century it became, for a brief time, the property of the Home Office, and was used as a prison. Then, as a result of the First World War, its military links were restored (Henderson, D.M. (Dr, Research Director of the Scots at War Project), per. comm., 15 September 1998).

The Highlander Regimental Magazine (*The Story of Fort George in The Great War And Its Aftermath*, 1992) states:

> As well as the main task of processing recruits, the Depot at Fort George housed a wide variety of other wartime 'birds of passage'. These were arrested deserters, conscientious objectors, PoWs, members of the Labour Corps, which supplied

men for agricultural work, and recruits of low category destined for Labour Units in France.

Fairrie, the author of this article, confirmed (per. comm., 7 August 1995) to the best of his knowledge that the only PoWs interned at Fort George were ninety-one German fishermen, men and boys, held there for a short period in August 1914, before being moved south. *The Times* (14 August 1914) confirms that around 100 Germans were taken off trawlers in the North Sea and taken to Fort George.

Harding (*Onward Flows the Tay*, 2000) cited from his father's diaries that foreign seamen, under guard, passed through Perth's railway station without incident in the early stages of the war. They were being transferred from Inverness to Redford Barracks, Edinburgh. These were probably the German or Austrian nationals noted by Fairrie.

The Times (23 June 1919) reported 200 Seaforth Highlanders were stationed at Fort George. They were sent to the Scottish Command's convalescent camp at Nigg, to act as temporary guard for 1,400 German sailors that were taken there from the scuttled interned ships that had been anchored in Scapa Flow, before their crews were transferred to other camps in the south.

Jackson (*The Prisoners 1914–1918*, 1989) cites it as a temporary camp. Today, Fort George still has military connections, and has a visitor's centre incorporating a museum to the Highland Regiments, once based there.

FORTEVIOT (OS: NO 049 177). Forteviot is approximately 9 miles to the east of Auchterarder.

Until 1926, Forteviot had become another sleepy backwater that previously played a significant role in shaping Scotland into the nation it is today. Around 843 Kenneth Macalpin moved his capital from the clan's ancestral capital at Dunadd in Argyllshire to a purpose-built wooden palace at Forteviot to be near to the monastery at Dunkeld. Four years earlier Macalpin, the king of the Dalriadan Scots, seceded to the throne of the Scottish Picts, too. Macalpin was slain in Forteviot, c860, and his body was taken for burial to Iona.

In 1926, John Alexander, the First Baron of Forteviot, had the village rebuilt in the style of an English garden city.

Like Forgandenny, it was a satellite of Auchterarder. Forteviot is listed by the FPHS (1973); its POWIB (1919) coding was Stbs (Au) (Ft) (IWM: Facsimile K4655). The actual location of the internment camp remains a mystery. Any PoWs sent to Forteviot would probably have worked on the land.

FOVANT (OS: SU 00- 29-). Although Crawford (*Wiltshire and The Great War: Training the Empire's Soldiers*, 1999) cites quarters of the Royal Engineers, near West Farm, were turned into a compound for PoWs. He also states the PoWs worked on local farms. Evidence from Germany suggests, at some stage, some of the PoWs were accommodated in tents.

It was, however, described as a working camp by the POWIB (1919), who cited its code as Dor (Fo) (IWM: Facsimile K4655). Its TA was Priswarian: Fovant. It was also cited by the FPHS (1973).

There were complaints registered by the PoWs that there was no canteen. They also complained of having nowhere to hold church services and felt decisions affecting them were not being made at a high enough level.

Crawford (1999) states that on 13 September 1917 three soldiers and two sailors escaped. Three were re-captured quickly, and the other two were caught a day or so later.

The camp closed on 19 January 1919. A catalogue, dated 21 March 1921, exists from the auction of the hospital's huts and surplus stores.

DKF 30: In den Lagern von Rosyth, Eastgate, Uppingham, Belton Park, Ternhill, Bee Craigs, Hadnall, Sutton Veny, Larkhill, Fovant, Withley (sic) *und Radford sind die Kriegsgefangenen in Zelten untergebracht.*

DKF 30: In Joice Green (sic), *Dartford, Linton, Sutton Veney* (sic), *Fovant, und Evesham bestehen Keine Kantine. Die Ausführung der Bestellungen der Kriegsgefangenen durch den Profoß Sergeanten, kann nicht als genügender Ersatz betrachtet werden.*

DKF 32: Gottesdienst: Die Seelsorge der Kreigsgefangenen ist auf vielen Plätzen sehr vernachlässigt. In den Lagern von Joice Green (sic); *Dartford; Hadnall; Peak Deal* (sic) *Quarries bei Buxton; Sutton Veney* (sic); *Larkhill; Netheravon; Codford; und Fovant hat noch kein Gottesdienst stattgefunden.*

DKF 34: In Fovant, Sutton Veney (sic) *und Larkhill sind trotz früheren Protestes keine Verbesserungen erfolgt.*

FOXHILL (OS: TQ 016 565). Recorded as being at Foxhill Round Bridge Farm, its TA was Priswarian: Old Woking (ADM 1/8506/265–120667), no details survive of how many, or when, the PoWs were there.

FRAMPTON on SEVERN (OS: SO 74- 07-). Frampton on Severn is cited as a working camp with the POWIB (1919) code Dor (Fra) (IWM: Facsimile K4655). Also cited by the FPHS (1973), no evidence has been found to suggest where this camp was. Its TA was Priswarian: Frampton-on-Sea (ADM 1/8506/265–120667).

FRANCE (Working companies in France). By the beginning of October 1916 there were over 12,000 prisoners serving in twenty-nine PoW companies in France, and Lt-General Sir George Henry Fowke, the Adjutant General at General Head Quarters of the British Expeditionary Force estimated a need for at least another twenty companies. By early 1917 the number of companies employed had risen to forty-seven. The number then rose dramatically: in November 1918 there were 343 PoW companies that comprised of 1,032 officers and 180,000 other ranks.

By early 1918 PoWs were being held in France, rather than being transferred to Britain. They were processed through holding cages, and sorted into trades. PoW labourers, orderlies, tailors and shoemakers were all paid 4d a day, and 6d per day for NCOs and interpreters. Cooks, sanitary men and others employed on camp routines were not paid, so those jobs had to be rotated on a daily basis. Later it was permitted to employ cooks on a long term basis, and they were then paid out of canteen profits. Canteens, managed by the prisoners, were set up in every camp, which were supplied from the Expeditionary Forces Canteen.

In 1918, metal tokens were introduced into the camps for the PoWs to spend in the canteens. Tokens equivalent to 1 franc, 50 centimes and 10 centimes were issued. On leaving the camp for whatever reason a PoW had to hand in his tokens and the paymaster credited his account with an equivalent sum for the next camp.

The POWIB (1919) (*List of Places of Internment*, 1919) had an entry for Working Companies Numbers 1–372, of which twenty-seven (Nos 1, 2, 7, 18, 29, 32, 40, 43, 44, 45, 55, 57, 61, 66, 76, 79, 81, 127, 134, 135, 138, 140, 141, 145, 147, 149, 150) had closed. Some numbers were re-used, and numbers greater than that stated in this list are known to have existed too.

FRANSHAM (OS: TF 895 135). Only cited in the minutes of Norfolk WAC when permission was sought to turn Crudds Hall in Fransham into an agricultural depot (C/C10/15–19).

FRIMLEY – FRITH HILL (OS: SU 901 587). The earliest report of the camp, under construction, comes from *The Yorkshire Herald* (12 August 1914), which cited 'a 40-acre camp was being constructed by the Royal Engineers at Blackdon (sic) a few miles from Aldershot.'

Bird (*Control of Enemy Alien Civilians in Great Britain 1914–1918*, 1986) cites in the early weeks of the war civilian internment camps were set up in London's Olympia and in a variety of other accommodations in Frimley, Douglas, Newbury, Stratford, Lancaster, Queensferry, Stobs, Handforth, York, Wakefield, Southampton and Hayward's Heath (the latter may have been Horsham).

The Frimley camp was at Frith Hill. The camp was one of the first locations in Britain to be made ready to take civilians arrested under the newly introduced Aliens Restriction Act. The camp was situated 2 miles to the east of Frimley, on a plateau, known to the locals as the Frimley Fuel Allotments, which stretched from Colony Gates to Frith Hill Reservoir. The camp remained tented throughout its usage, although a few huts graced the site too.

Aldershot News (18 September 1914) stated that in the past week many more PoWs arrived, and estimated that there were now well over 2,000 internees at Frith Hill. Among them were eighty Uhlans that had arrived in two batches on the Saturday and the Monday, with a batch of hairdressers and waiters arrested in Hastings. On the Tuesday, 392 German soldiers came from Southampton, and more civilians arrived from Bristol, Shrewsbury and Manchester. There were two compounds at the time, each capable of housing 2,800, and a third was planned to hold a further 5,000. The paper also stated the commandant was Major F.S. Picot of the Wiltshire Regiment, who had considerable experience of being a commandant of a detention barracks.

The Times (19 September 1914) cites there were two compounds at Frimley: one for civilians, and one for soldiers. It estimated there were 900 soldiers and rather more civilians being accommodated in tents and some iron buildings. But when Frith Hill opened, it was reported, Uhlans, still in their riding breeches and spiked helmets, infantrymen in blue-green uniforms, and sailors in their navy tunics, were intermingled with civilians. The civilians were still in the same attire they had been wearing when arrested; some were in dinner jackets. This scene must have been merely a temporary arrangement.

The Times (24 September 1914) cited 1,500–1,600 German PoWs from the Battle of the Marne arrived during the week. The prisoners had marched the 2 miles from the railway station at Camberley to the camp. Wellard (*200 Years on the Frimley Fuel Allotments*, 1995) states:

> The first intention was to house foreign internees there, together with some PoWs. But the arrival of 1,300 Germans, captured at the battles of Aisne and Marne in September, just one month later, led to plans being altered, and the transference of all (civilian) internees to the Isle of Man, and on to ships at Portsmouth and Southend. Accommodation was in the vast tented camp, surrounded by a barbed wire fence. Prisoners arrived by train at Frimley station and then

marched to the camp, through the village and along the Chobham Road under armed guards supplied from Blackdown Barracks …

He also stated that there were at least three compounds created at Frimley during its use as a PoW camp. The first two compounds were between Blackdown Barracks and the Brompton Sanatorium. A later extension was created to the west.

MacDonagh (*In London during the Great War*, 1935), a journalist, cited when he visited Camberley on 23 September 1914 he witnessed half a dozen officers and a couple of hundred other ranks arriving at the railway station and then marched to Frith Hill, 'where they are being lodged in hutments, behind barbed wire'.

The Times (29 September 1914) cited a further sixty arrivals at the camp. It was reported the authorities intended to construct more compounds to hold a further 10,000 internees at Frimley.

Hampshire Herald (Saturday, 3 October 1914) cited the previous day about 100 prisoners from Frimley were transferred to Longmoor, where 'it is understood they will be employed making a rifle range' near the camp. A special compound had been prepared for them on the Downs, near Longmoor.

The accidental death of Landwehrmann Josef Gilles was reported in *The Times* (16 October 1914). He was buried on 19 October 1914.

On 23 October 1914, Sir Edward Grey wrote to the US Ambassador stating that at present the combatant prisoners were, in the main, interned at Frith Hill Camp, Frimley.

The Times (24 October 1914) cited an army of waiters and hairdressers, 800–900 strong, had arrived at Frith Hill. They replaced 200 civilians that had just been moved to Isle of Man along with 400 military personnel that had gone to the Richmond Barracks at Templemore. It was estimated there were now about 8,000 at Frith Hill; the *Liverpool Daily Post* (24 October 1914) carried a similar report.

Only those civilian internees that could afford to pay had been allowed to stay on at Frimley when the decision was made to send the rest to HMT *Saxonia*, moored in the Thames Estuary, off Southend-on-Sea.

Aldershot News (30 October 1914) reported PoWs were arriving as civilians and being moved out to Shrewsbury and to the Isle of Man, in batches. Those bound for Shrewsbury left in two batches; one of 100, and one of 50. 400 went to the Isle of Man.

From the movement of PoWs in and out of Frith Hill, it appears that it was being used as a reception centre. In October 1914, *The Camberley News* had reported that 'although a couple of hundred of the Kaiser's soldiers had been removed there had been a number of casual arrivals every other day.' An account states 200 combatants had left on Monday, by special train, bound for Ireland; it was understood they were to be incarcerated by themselves.

The Times (12 November 1914) reported Geminer Wilhelm Schneips had died of septic poisoning. He was buried on 16 November 1914.

The Scotsman (13 November 1914) reported the visit of a delegation from the US Embassy to the camps. John B. Jackson, an aide to the American Ambassador in Berlin, inspected the internment camps in Britain and Ireland. He was informed that the German and Austrian prisoners did their own policing inside the camps, and the British guarded only the external perimeter, and so had very little contact with those on the inside. At Frith Hill, he was told the non-commissioned officers ran their 'own little republic' inside the wire, even to the extent of having their 'own secret police'.

Camberley News (28 November 1914) stated all civilian internees had been moved out, to the Isle of Man. The newspaper printed several reports about the arrivals and departures from Frith Hill. Batches arrived over several days to Frimley Station. The civilians that had arrived via London's Waterloo Station were then dispatched to Edinburgh and Wakefield. Curiously, some went back to London, to Stratford.

The Times (16 December 1914) stated the camp closed. With the onset of winter it was discovered that the allotments had been a poor choice as the site was poorly drained, and in late December 1914 the camp was evacuated. The civilian prisoners had been moved to the Isle of Man, and the military and naval PoWs had gone to the ships at Southend-on-Sea. The *Yorkshire Evening Press* (16 December 1914) stated the last batch of internees, some 700 men, had gone to Southend-on-Sea for the winter months. It would appear from an article in the *Dorset County Chronicle* (17 December 1914) that 500 combatant PoWs had gone to Dorchester: they arrived on the 15 December 1914.

Mr Jackson, on behalf of the US Embassy in London, visited the ships at Southend-on-Sea on 30 January 1915. He cites some civilians that had previously been at Frith Hill were on board the HMT *Saxonia*. One complaint they had was that the food had been better on shore than on the ship. In his report of visits to various camps he stated that he had been informed the Frith Hill camp had been closed for some time.

The Times (14 April 1915) cited the Frimley camp was to re-open, and around 300–400 Germans PoWs were expected. *Aldershot News* (16 April 1915) states it had not been intended to use this camp again. But that decision was reversed, and it re-opened for military and naval PoWs only. A total of 1,530 internees had arrived over three days from the ships at Southend-on-Sea.

A US Embassy visit of 29 April 1915 cited there were 1,637 PoWs, mostly ex HMT *Ivernia*, in the camp. A further thirty-two had arrived the day before, from Neuve Chappelle and 'Hill 60'. The report stated the tents had wooden floors; twelve privates, eight corporals, or four sergeants per tent. There were also new latrines, and showers with cement floors. As a consequence of the sinking of the RMS *Lusitania*, many enemy aliens that had not been seen to be a threat to the nation's security had to be taken into custody for their own protection.

The Camberley News reported the arrival of civilian internees in May 1915. *Yorkshire Post* (17 May 1915) cited 500 civilians went to Frith Hill on the Saturday. *The Times* (6 July 1915) cites a letter was published in the German press, describing the conditions as good in the camp.

The Times (31 August 1915) cited an unnamed airman had escaped, the first from this camp. *The Police Gazette* (31 August 1915) named him as Ernst August Junght. There is no report of him being taken back into custody.

Correspondence between the War Office and the Foreign Office (30 September 1915) suggests the civilians had been removed 'some time ago' and the place would be abandoned as a place of internment within the next few weeks.

On 5 November 1915 the *Leigh Chronicle* cited thirty-nine PoWs that had been captured at the Battle of Loos, arrived at Pennington Station on the previous Thursday evening. They had come from Frimley, 'in the charge of a guard of twelve soldiers of the Northamptonshire Regiment'.

When the work programme for PoWs was introduced in Britain, internees from Frith Hill assisted to extend the local railway line. Wellard (1995) states:

> With the rapid expansion of the Army and more and more men being called to the Colours, the Aisne Barracks were built at Blackdown. The Bisley railway line was extended from the barracks at Pirbright camp to Blackdown in order to

transport the thousands of troops, which were to pass through during the war years. Germans were utilised to help with its construction.

Other prisoners, not involved in the railway, were utilised to load and unload barges at Frimley Wharf, on the Basingstoke Canal.

Nottingham Evening Post (26 September 1916) states five men had escaped from Frimley. They had been working on the railway, at Deepcut. *The Times* (27 September 1916) cites four of them as sailors, Brune, Michaelski, Schmidt & Mathlesen, and the other as an airman, Mohr. The same newspaper of 28 and 29 September 1916 stated Brune, Schmidt & Mohr had been re-captured at Esher the next day, with Michaelski and Mathlesen being re-captured at Wokingham the following day. *The Camberley News* (30 September 1916) also reported their re-captures.

Again, according to German sources, the camp was evacuated in October 1916.

It was reported on 22 March 1918 that there were 5,000 men interned there still in tents. A common complaint made by the internees was that this time there were no boards in their tents, and many did not even have the luxury of a paillasse to sleep on. Overcrowding was another of their grievances. It had been calculated that each PoW was permitted to have around 17 square feet of personal floor-space, but from the reports (*Deutsche Kriegsgefangene in Fiendeslands*, 1919) this was contended and that the space was measured to be no more than 10 square feet.

People living in close proximity to the Frith Hill camp were not happy with this camp being on their doorstep. Not only did they suggest that they lived in fear for their safety, but also they were unhappy about the poor sanitary arrangements at the camp. Correspondence exchanged between the Army and the local council revealed the blame lay with a contractor. Brompton Hospital, the nearest to the nuisance, suffered worst from the unpleasant odours emanating from the site.

A Home Office document cites that Alexandra Palace was required for other purposes by the government. As there was insufficient room in other camps, relatively close to London, Frith Hill again came back into use in 1919. The movement of men, back to a tented camp again, raised a storm of protest from internees, their families and friends and from Swiss and Swedish diplomats. With the Armistice in place, applications for release were being approved. The commandant at Frith Hill was instructed not to release more than 100 internees per day, in order not to attract too much attention. The camp was finally closed on 22 September 1919 and the remaining 150 men were moved to Islington.

The POWIB (1919) cite its code as F Hi (IWM: Facsimile K 4655). It was also cited by the FPHS (1973). Its TA is cited as Blackdown Camp, Frimley (ADM 1/8506/265–120667).

Frith Hill is cited in a document produced for the Hadifogoly Magyarok (Budapest, 1930) (Szijj, Jolan (Dr) Honvédelmi Miniszrérium, per. comm., 23 July 1997).

Of the post and censor marks that survive from the mail delivered to PoW camps, three survive from the Frimley camp and are illustrated by Carter (Russell, 1996).

Today, four holes of the Pine Ridge Golf Course and its clubhouse stand on the former fuel allotment site.

DKF 14: Herbst 1914 war das Lager mit deutschen Kriegsgefangenen Belegt, wurde dann geräumt wegen der Unzuträglichkeit des Klimas; der Boden war feucht, zur Unterbringung standen nut Rundzelte zur Verfügung, die zu eng belegt waren. Das Lager wurde im Mai 1915 erneut mit Kriegs- und Zivilgefangenen belegt und Ende Oktober 1915 weiderum geräumt. Trotzdem sich das Lager also als für die Gefangenen völlig ungenügend und gesundheitsschädlich herausgestellt hatte, wurde es im Sommer 1916 wieder belegt. Irgendwelche Verbesserungen in der Einrichtung des Lagers waren nicht getroffen worden. Am 28 Oktober 1916 wurde Frith Hill wiederum geräumt. Am 22 März 1918 wurde Frith-Hill als Lager für 5000 Mann eröffnet. Nach dem Bericht des Vertreters der Schutzmacht waren die Gefangenen noch in Rundzelten untergebracht. Die vorhergesehene Belegung war viel zu eng, für den einzelnen blieben im besten Fall 17 Quadratfuß, meist nur 10 Quadratfuß. Das Kampieren in den Zelten wird erneut als höchst gefährlich in gesundheitlicher Hinsicht bezeichnet. Die Holzböden fehlen, an ihre Stelle treten wasserdichte Gummidecken Strohsäcke fehlen.

DKF 67: Am 12 Dezember 1914 kamen Dr Farber, Unterarzt meines Regiments, und ich mit dem Transport von Frith Hill an Bord HMT *Ivernia.*

FRITH HILL (see Frimley).

FRODSHAM (OS: SJ 52- 77-). Like so many other places of internment, the actual location has not been clearly identified. However, in correspondence between Mrs Park-Yates and her land agent, concerns were expressed about the placing of an internment camp near Ince House, at Thornton-le-moors. It intimated that hopefully, there would be better consultation with local people about its placement than there had been at the siting of the Frodsham camp at the Marshes.

In a letter dated 16 August 1918, the land agent wrote, 'I have a letter from a Captain Clapham, the Officer who was instructed to arrange for the Camp at Frodsham ...' The letter does not reveal the camp's location (DD/GR/388).

The Times (12 September 1918) reported PoWs employed on drainage works near Frodsham went on strike. Some of their team had been lent to farmers for the harvest and were being paid more. Instead of getting the higher allowances the strikers sought, they were put on a bread and water diet.

A Home Office document cites the camp closed on 2 November 1918, but a Foreign Office document contradicts this by citing the camp was visited in June 1919. Possibly, this may have been a tented seasonal camp that had been struck for the winter.

It was cited by the FPHS (1973), and its TA was given as Priswarian: Frodsham (ADM 1/8506/265–120667). Frodsham is included in a report of visits of inspection to PoWs camps done in June 1919, by Dr A. de Sturler and Monsieur R. de Sturler which is held at the National Archives at Kew (FO 383/508).

FROME: The Tannery (OS: ST 775 471). The internment camp at Frome had the POWIB (1919) code Dor (Fr) (IWM: Facsimile K4655). It is also cited by the FPHS (1973). Cited as being at The Tannery, its TA was Priswarian: Frome (ADM 1/8506/265–120667). Minute 3239 of the Somerset County WAC (21 May 1918) recorded approval was being sought for premises for PoW Depots at Keyford, Priston, Queen Camel, Glastonbury, Wookey, Hinton St George, and another near Yeovil.

FRONGOCH (OS: SH 903 395). Because of the peaty land and the good water of the Trywaryn valley, R.J. Lloyd-Price and Robert Willis chose Frongoch to create a distillery to produce whisky. Their plant opened in 1897. In an astute marketing ploy, both Queen Victoria and the Price of Wales (later Edward VII) were presented with barrels of their produce, allowing them to call their produce Royal Welsh Whisky. From the beginning, their venture had problems with the local Calvinistic church, which frowned on the making and consumption of alcohol. To preserve their anonymity the various carriers had to make their deliveries, and take out the produce, at night. In 1900 the company went into liquidation and the site was sold for £5,000 in April of that year. The buildings were taken over by the War Office in 1914.

When John Jackson conducted his survey of camps in the UK on 27 February 1915 it is stated he had not visited the camp at Frongoch as it was not open at the time of his arrival in England. The camp was cited to have opened on 25 March 1915. Macpherson (*History of the Great War – Medical Services*, 1923) claims when it opened it was expected to accommodate around 1,000 men.

The Wilmslow, Alderley & Knutsford Advertiser (9 April 1915) reported that PoWs had been transferred from Handforth to Frongoch. This seems to coincide with the transfer of Captain Kenneth Crause Wright to Frongoch as, according to *The Leigh Chronicle* (9 April 1915) he was transferred to Frongoch. He had been the first commandant of the camp at Leigh. A later report by the same newspaper stated he had been promoted to Major.

A visit by a delegation from the US Embassy was conducted on 26 June 1915. It stated that at that time there were 997 internees held there, of which five were sailors. The internees were housed in six dormitories and four huts. There had been one death at the camp: a wounded PoW died, as a result of contracting pneumonia. Five patients were recorded as being in the hospital – none serious. For exercise they had a play area of some 2.5 acres, or daily morning route marches for groups of up 200 at a time. A third visit was made by the US Embassy, on 31 March 1916.

The Cambrian News (21 April 1916) cited four PoWs had been spotted, and finally caught by a search party of the 2nd Royal Welsh Fusiliers at Llandegla, near Wrexham. They had escaped from Frongoch a few days earlier. Between them they had £10 in cash and a small supply of food, along with a compass and an accurate line drawing map. When caught, despite wearing German field uniforms with blue PoW patches sewn into them, they gave Welsh surnames. They even stopped at a pub for food and drink, openly stating that they were German prisoners working on a local farm, and were duly served! Their plan was to cross the mountains to find and join a neutral ship at Liverpool. They were Corporal Heinrich Brinkmann (aged 24), and Privates Wilhelm Arenkens (aged 23), Hans Schonherr (aged 21) and Julius Barnard Koch (aged 22). One was a Bavarian, one a Saxon, and the other two from Westphalia.

The Cambrian News (2 June 1916) reported the German PoWs leaving Frongoch to move to southern England. A few soldiers were remaining to guard a few sick PoWs who were not fit enough to travel.

In June, Frongoch was to become the main centre to hold dissident Irishmen. The authorities did not want them tried in Irish civil courts, fearing any juries made up of their peers would not be impartial. However, they could not be tried under civil law in England, as their offences had been committed in Ireland. A new regulation of the Defence of Realm Act was created and applied, which allowed the detention of persons of hostile origin or associations.

As a result of the Easter Rising, in April 1916, the first batch of Irishmen to be interned arrived at Frongoch on 9 June 1916. O'Mahony (*Frongoch: University of Revolution*, 1987) wrote that 2,519 Irish were deported to British jails in May and June of 1916 and Whitmore (*With the Irish in Frongoch*, 1917) cites some 650 were released within the first few weeks and the remainder were sent to Frongoch.

The Commandant was Lt-Colonel F.A. Heygate-Lambert, better known to the Irishmen as 'Buckshot'. He had previously been Commandant at Stratford. When it was realised the Irish were fraternising with the few sick German PoWs left behind, he quickly arranged for them to be moved out.

The Frongoch camp now comprised of two sites. The North Camp comprised of the disused distillery, with its adjoining buildings. This was sited on higher ground. The main distillery building was divided into dormitories and the other buildings into the hospital, the censor's office, coal depot, a jail comprising of six cells, the cook-house, the dining room, and workshops. There were also four wooden huts. Three of the dormitories held approximately 250 men in each, and two held 150 each. The greatest number of internees recorded at any one time in the camp was 936.

Across the road, what had been a recreation field was the South Camp. It had thirty-five wooden huts in two rows. Each hut could accommodate up to thirty-two men, making the overall capacity of 1,100 detainees; during the internment of the Irishmen the highest number recorded was 896. During their first month they laid paths and roadways because the underfoot conditions were very wet. This camp had its own cookhouse plus latrines, wash-houses, drying rooms, etc.

The Irishmen appointed their own commandants, adjutants and barrack captains to run the internal affairs of the camp. For commandants the Irish chose J.J. O'Connell for the South Camp and M.W. O'Reilly for the North Camp. In July, thirty of the Irish ring-leaders were rounded up and moved to Reading Jail. It was thought this would make the remainder easier to manage. From time to time as new leaders emerged, further removals had to be made. In July 1916 a committee was set up under Lord Sankey to review their cases. The hearings were held in London, which resulted in the internees being moved in batches to either Wormwood Scrubs or Wandsworth prisons whilst their cases were heard. As a result of these hearings, many were released, and by mid-August only about 600 Irishmen remained at Frongoch. All the remaining internees were then housed in the South Camp, as the North Camp was phased out.

On 1 September 1916 the Irishmen were offered quarry work at 5½d per hour, but subject to deductions for their daily train fares and 17s.6d (62½p) a week for board and lodging. They turned this, and one for agricultural work, down. The internees that remained pleaded to be allowed to go to North Camp. This was approved on 21 October 1916. The South Camp was then only used for punitive measures.

On 14 December 1916 *The Times* reported the death of the camp's Medical Officer, Dr Peters. Intimidated and overworked by the camp authorities, particularly by 'Buckshot' Lambert, he took his own life.

On 21 December 1916, the House of Commons announced that all 628 Irish prisoners held in detention in Britain were to be released, unconditionally. The first batch of 130 internees was released the following day. The last batch of twenty-eight, which included those held at Reading Jail, arrived in Dublin on the eve of Christmas.

Frongoch did not lie dormant very long. German PoWs were to return early in the New Year. Blaenau Festiniog Police Station Occurrence Book (14 February 1917) shows Wilhelm Jensen, a naval warrant officer, and John Rastenbolz, a sergeant major had been apprehended the previous evening on the Talsarnau and Harlech road, at 10.15pm. It recorded they had escaped from the internment camp at Frongoch. Both were lodged in the cell at Harlech for the night and handed over to a military escort at 2.15pm, the following day (ZH/5/11/4).

Both the *Leigh Chronicle* (17 April 1919) and the *Leigh Journal* (30 May 1919) reported that 400 PoWs had left the Leigh camp on Saturday, to be taken to a camp in

North Wales, 3 miles north of Bala. Another 500 were being transferred from Leigh to Frongoch that Monday.

The last batch of PoWs to leave Frongoch, according to *The Times* (24 November 1918), numbered around 2,000 men.

Today, except for one hut that is used by the Frongoch and District Women's Institute, the North Camp has been completely dismantled. There is nothing to show that a whisky distillery once stood there. The railway line from Bala to Blaenau Ffestiniog has been dismantled and the station has long gone. On the site of the former camp now stands Ysgol Gynradd Bro Tryweryn (Tryweryn Valley Primary School). On 29 June 2002, a plaque (Plaque Marks Frongoch internment camp, McKeane 2002) was unveiled to the 1,800 Irishmen that were interned, in 1916, without trial. According to academics who study the history of the republican movement in Ireland, Frongoch's internment camp was labeled the 'University of Revolution', as many of its future plans originated from those who were interned there.

German archive material suggests the sergeant major at Frongoch had a sadistic streak. He hit a German NCO, in his charge, in the face as he was smoking a pipe, breaking his tooth. The same document also stated that the commandant, who was not named, was no better by denying the internees their mail for fourteen days for no reason, resulting in food parcels going off.

Frongoch PoW camp was visited by Dr A. de Sturler and Monsieur R. de Sturler during June 1919. The report is held at the National Archives at Kew (FO 383/154, 164 & 508). The camp's POWIB (1919) code was simply Fg (IWM: Facsimile K4655). The FPHS (1973) cites Frongoch, Merioneth, and the camp's TA was Priswarian: Bala (ADM 1/8506/265–120667).

G

GAINSBOROUGH (OS: SK 81- 89-). The only reference to Gainsborough having an internment camp is suggested by the FPHS (1973). No evidence has been found to suggest where this camp was.

GAMLINGAY. The POWIB (1919) directory cites one code for Gamlingay, Pa (Gg) (IMW: Facsimile K4655). Minutes of the Cambridgeshire WAC (27 May 1918) record two locations as being available for accommodating PoWs; these are Castle House and Montagu House. The FPHS (1973) only has one entry, that of Gamlingay.

CASTLE HOUSE (OS: TL 235 523) and MONTAGU HOUSE (OS: TL 235 523). Today Castle House is known as Charnock's House (30 Church Street) and is currently used for commercial purposes. It stands near to The Cock Inn public house (25 Church Street). Montagu House supposedly stood on the same side as the Cock Inn, but its location is not known.

GARGRAVE (OS: SD 93- 54-). Cited in a HO document, the only thing known of this camp is its TA, Priswarian: Gargrave, Leeds (ADM 1/8506/265–120667). This address suggests it was not a camp for officers.

The Leeds and Liverpool Canal, opened *c.*1777 to provide a cheap means of transport for bringing coal into the area to fuel the lime kilns and smelt mills, and taking away lead and manufactured goods. Five separate wharves were built at Gargrave that resulted in large warehouses being constructed. Perhaps it is to one of these warehouses that PoWs sent to the area were billeted.

GAYTON (OS: TF 724 195). The Norfolk WAC (27 January 1917) resolved to inform the Local Government Board that accommodation at Gayton Workhouse could be provided for PoWs to carry out drainage work on the River Wensum (C/C10/15). The camp's TA was Priswarian: The Workhouse, Gayton (ADM 1/8506/265–120667).

Freebridge Lynn Poor Law Union Workhouse was erected in 1836, near Gayton, to the designs of W.J. Donthorn, to accommodate up to 150 inmates. The workhouse had a cruciform plan. From 1904, to protect them from disadvantage in later life, birth certificates of those born in the workhouse gave its address just as 1 Old Swaffham Road, Gayton. Additional buildings, designed by L.F. Eagleton, were added in 1905 and 1907. With the exception of the south east wing, which was demolished, the site was redeveloped in 2007 for residential dwellings (www.pastscape.org.uk).

Gayton appears on the list produced by the FPHS (1973). Gayton PoW camp was visited Dr A. de Sturler and Monsieur R. de Sturler, during April and May 1919. The report is held at the National Archives at Kew (FO 383/507).

GELDESTON MILL (OS: TM 387 918). A minute exists proposing to the Local Government Board, by the Norfolk WAC, that PoWs could be based at Geldeston Mill to carry out drainage work on the River Waveney [C/C10/15–19]. The four storey high mill stood near the lock. Little is known about it. It was demolished between 1860 and 1870 (Jonathan Neville, *Norfolk Mills*, 2004)

GILLINGHAM (OS: ST 80- 26-). The arrival of the railway, in the 1850s, saw an upturn in the town's prosperity. Industries such as brickmaking, printing and soap manufacture began augmenting the traditional ones of butter and cheese making. Towards the end of the century there was a plant making petrol engines in the community.

There was an agricultural depot at Gillingham with the POWIB (1919) code Dor (Gil) (IMW: Facsimile K4655). Beaminster, Bradford Abbas and Stowell were satellites of this camp. Its TA was Priswarian: Gillingham, Dorset (ADM 1/8506/265–120667). It is also cited by the FPHS (1973). No further evidence has been found to suggest where this camp was located.

GISBURN (OS: SD 83- 48-). Gisburn had the POWIB (1919) directory code Cat (P B) (Gi) making it a satellite of Pateley Bridge (IMW: Facsimile K4655). No further evidence has been found to suggest where this camp was, but it was described as agricultural group No. 19 in a HO document. Its TA was Priswarian: Gisburn (ADM 1/8506/265–120667).

GLASTONBURY (OS: ST 50- 39-). It was cited by the FPHS (1973). It had the TA Priswarian: Glastonbury (ADM 1/8506/265–120667). Minute 3239 of the Somerset County Council WAC (21 May 1918) approved premises for PoW Depots at Keyford, Priston, Queen Camel, Glastonbury, Wookey, Hinton St George, plus another near Yeovil.

GLANGRWYNEY (Llangenny) (OS: SO 24- 16-). This camp appeared on the FPHS (1973) list as Llangowyney (sic), Brecon. The actual location of the camp is unknown, but perhaps Glangrwyney Court, located just off the main A40 to Brecon, may hold the key. This Georgian mansion dates back to 1825 and is set in 4 acres of beautiful gardens and surrounded by parkland. Nearby, the former Beckwith and Company's papermaking mill is an alternative. Jones (*A History of the County of*

Brecknock, 1911) cites the mill was established in 1850 and took its water from the River Grwyne. Because of the purity of the water, the mill became famous for its production of brightly coloured paper for the grocery trade. Taken over in 1888, it traded under the mantle of the Usk Paper Works and abandoned its production of grocery papers, for rope browns. Lofts were installed for the air-drying process as the mill was renovated. Turbines replaced the old water wheels, as steam-power was introduced in 1900.

Usk PoW camp was visited Dr A. de Sturler and Monsieur R. de Sturler, during March and April 1919. The report is held at the National Archives at Kew (FO 383/506).

GLASGOW: HM Prison Barlinnie (OS: NS 635 661). McConville (*Irish Political Prisoners 1848–1922: The Theatres of War*, 2005) cited that on 20 May 1916, Irish men and women were arrested and detained for offences committed under Section 14b of the Defence of the Realm Act, for their parts in the Easter Rising of that year.

The ringleaders were expediently executed. Those that escaped execution, 197, were brought to the mainland of Britain and locked up in prisons, including Barlinnie, throughout Britain. Mainly men, they were only detained for a short term before being released again. Those not released were transferred to Frongoch in Wales.

GLEMSFORD (OS: TL 833 484). Glass (*A Short History of Glemsford*, 1962) wrote that the horsehair industry was introduced to Glemsford in 1844 when Messrs. H. Kolle & Sons built a factory in Bells Lane for the processing, curling and weaving of horsehair. The Victorians used a great deal of horsehair and for a number of years this factory employed a large staff. In 1907, Arnold and Gould set up a factory in a disused silk mill.

Ted Hartley recalled going down Mill Lane to Arnold & Gould's Horsehair Factory where they too employed a large number of people. During the First World War, part of the factory was used as a prison camp. That area is still referred to as the 'Camp'. The German prisoners used to write messages to the young women. They would put them in matchboxes, and throw them out through holes of the barricaded windows.

Leicestershire Record Office has evidence to show that the commandant of Glensfield (sic) Prisoner of war camp, Lieutenant Jesse Gibson, is buried in St. Paul's Churchyard, Woodhouse Eaves. His gravestone shows he was member of the Royal Defence Corps and states he died on 17 March 1919, aged 56. Prior to the war, Gibson had been the headmaster of the school in Woodhouse Eaves (Barnard, per. comm., 5 May 2005).

There is a report on a visit of inspection, by Dr A. de Sturler and Monsieur R. de Sturler during April and May 1919, held at the National Archives at Kew. The FPHS (1973) cite this camp. It had the TA Priswarian: Glemsford (ADM 1/8506/265–120667).

A photograph exists, thought to been taken in a field near to Long Melford, showing a man in civilian clothing standing with eight PoWs. Each PoW is holding a spade or a fork. It was probably a work party, possibly from Glemsford.

The Haverhill Echo (9 November 1918) reported that Mr and Mrs Pearl from Cavendish were involved in an accident in Water Lane, as they were returning from Glemsford. Mr Pearl pulled onto a bank overturning his trap when confronted by a motor car in which were a lot of German prisoners being driven back from work. It seems that the bright lights from the car dazzled him as they turned a nasty corner. Mr and Mrs Pearl received some small cuts.

GLENDEVON: nr Dollar (OS: NN 995 044). A working camp with the POWIB (1919) code Stbs (Gle) (IMW: Facsimile K4655). Glendevon is situated at the foot of the Ochil Hills in an area noted for its special beauty; but this Perthshire camp did not come up to the expectations of one German PoW. The disillusioned scribe wrote in *Stobsaide*, a newspaper produced by the internees at Stobs:

> If you have read one or two works by Sir Walter Scott, then you are all too likely to have a picture of Scotland's 'romantic' mountains, abounding with massive woods and ravines, bubbling streams and delightful lochs, cliffs, and caves – beautiful countryside. But I have never come across any of that, at least not in the part of the country that I have got to know ...

It would appear that the men were employed in the construction of Lower Glendevon Reservoir. Work building the dam started before the war, and it was completed in 1922. Two houses at Frandy, now demolished, were set aside to house officers. These presumably were British officers as any German officers sent to Glendevon would be under no obligation to work, as stated under the terms of the Hague Convention of the day.

The camp at Glendevon was amongst several criticised for their lack of washing facilities.

The *People's Journal for Perth and Dundee* (4 & 11 May 1918) recorded six sailors escaped from Glendevon on Sunday night. All were quickly caught. Two were caught on Tuesday, near to Kippen, and the other four the next day, near to Gleneagles. William Rowe, the workman who reported the position of the last group, was sent a letter of commendation from the Chief Constable of Perthshire, which included the sum of one pound, awarded by the War Office. Their escape was also cited in the *Dundee Courier* and *The Western Times* (both 2 May 1918).

Another bid for freedom was thwarted as Paul Lubke, a stoker, was caught hours after escaping from Glendevon, according to the *Glasgow Herald* (4 September 1917).

A bid for freedom by Paul Heymann and Max Radnutz from the Glendevon camp was reported in *The Dundee Courier* (3 October 1917). The two had absconded on 29 September. *The Times* (4 October 1917) also cited their re-capture.

There were at least five deaths at Glendevon. Men with the rank equal to a private of the 1st Prussian Guards were victims of the flu pandemic. They were: Gustov Leirman (d. 5 March 1919); Michall Dorsch (d. 6 March 1919); Karl Nuderstrasser (d. 7 March 1919); and Josef Brener (d. 9 March 1919); all had worked at the Little Frandy Reservior. They had been transferred to Perth War Hospital, where none recovered. They were buried in Jeanfield cemetery in Perth. Another victim also from the Glendevon Camp was Johan Zelasni (d. 21 June 1918).

The Court of Sessions granted authority for the exhumations of these five men. They were exhumed on 16 August 1962 and transferred to Cannock Chase. In Scotland, the channel to have the bodies exhumed is through the courts whereas in England it was a Church matter.

An entry for the camp appears in the list produced by the FPHS (1973). The camp's TA was, Priswarian: Glendevon, Muckhart (ADM 1/8506/265–120667).

GLENDON (OS: SP 84- 81-). Glendon appears on list a produced by the FPHS (1973), and in a document produced by the Germans after the war.

Despite attempts to make sure internees would be billeted in warm, dry premises during the winter months those interned at Glendon were still living under canvas at the end of January 1917. Complaints of not having clean clothes are cited.

Perhaps Canon Tonks served their spiritual needs better. He was appointed a parish priest at St Edward's in Kettering, in 1896. He stayed for twenty-eight years before moving to work in Bedford. During the First World War, he served three PoW Camps: Glendon, Rothwell and Corby. In Kettering, he was a chaplain for the military hospitals.

DKF 34: Aus den Berichten der Schweizer Delegierten aus dem Ende des Jahres 1917 über die Arbeitslager in England geht hervor, daß die Zustände in einigen dieser Lager sich gebessert hatten und daß in manchen dementsprechend das Leben erträglich war. Immerhin geben noch einige Lager zu berechtigten Klagen Anlaß. Trotz wiederholten Einspruchs der deutschen Regierung sind in der Lagern Wingland (Lincolnshire), Ordfordneß (Suffolk), West Tofts (Norfolk), Warren Woods (Norfolk), Glendon bei Keltering (sic), *Stratford on Avon, Kerry (Nord Wales), und Shirehampton (Gloucestershire) die Gefangenen immer noch in Zelten untergebracht.*

DKF 34: In Glendon fehlt außerdem jede Beleuchtung mit künstlichem Licht, auch haben die Kriegsgefangenen keine Matratzen und Strohsäcke.

GLOSSOP (OS: SK 043 953). The grid ref for the Glossop Union Workhouse is stated. It may have been the location of this camp; another possibility was Glossop Hall.

The workhouse was built *c.*1833. It is believed vagrants sent to the workhouse had to work in the local quarries. *c.*1896, an infirmary block was added, and this was extended in 1927. In between, a new laundry was added in 1902 and the kitchens rebuilt in 1920. The site also included piggeries. It then became known as Glossop Public Assistance Institution, before becoming the Shire Hill Hospital under the auspices of the National Health Service in 1947.

The alternative, Glossop Hall, became the property of Lord Edward FitzAlan Howard, the second son of the 13th Duke of Norfolk. He was a Member of Parliament and the Vice Chamberlain to Queen Victoria. He was created Lord Howard of Glossop. The hall was demolished *c.*1924, when the estate was sold to the Town Council. It is now a public park.

Wherever this camp was situated, *The Derby Daily Telegraph* (10 July 1918) reported it as being ready and awaiting to accommodate PoWs, who were to work on the land.

GLOUCESTER: HM Prison (OS: SO 829 186). Originally built in 1782 as the County Gaol for Gloucester, it was designed by the architect William Blackburn. In 1840, the prison was substantially rebuilt. Today, it still functions as part of the penal system.

Tom Dillon (1884–1971) taught chemistry at Trinity College, Dublin. During the Easter Rising he had been acting as a chemical adviser to the Volunteers on the production of explosives and hand grenades. He had taken a room in the Imperial Hotel, opposite the General Post Office. His role was to have taken charge of chemical works that the rebels intended to commandeer. But no chemical factories were taken. Dillon escaped immediate arrest, but when he was eventually imprisoned, he was taken to Gloucester Gaol in 1918. He wrote:

> One May night of that year, I was served by the Chief Secretary of Ireland, Mr Shortt, with a notice, which, in my case he did not take the trouble to sign,

> that, whereas I was suspected of behaving, or being about to behave, in a manner prejudicial to the defence of the realm, he therefore ordered that I was to be detained during His Majesty's (or somebody's) pleasure. In the small hours of the morning, I found myself on a sloop of the British Navy in Kingstown (as it then was) Harbour with a goodly company. We were soon on our way to English gaols, where those of us who did not escape, or die in the 'flu epidemic, remained until the end of the following March.

Eamon De Valera was also sent to Gloucester Prison. However, he was transferred to Lincoln Jail, from where he successfully escaped, in 1919.

On his release Dillon began a distinguished academic career. He was to be appointed to the Professorship of Chemistry at University College, Galway.

GOSPORT GROUP – THE SOLENT SQUADRON (OS: SU 600 045). The Gosport Group originally consisted of three ships: the *Ascania*, the *Lake Manitoba*, and the *Scotian*. When the Ryde Group was assigned other duties the Gosport Group took their place at Ryde. The *Uranium* then replaced the *Lake Manitoba*. When this group was re-assigned other duties the *Uranium* joined the Leigh Squadron, off Southend on Sea:

HMT *ASCANIA* (GRT: 9,111. Passengers: 1st = 200, steerage = 1,500). The *Ascania* was built by Swan, Hunter, & Wigham Richardson, of Newcastle upon Tyne. McCart (1990) cites it was the intention to name her the *Gerona* for the Thompson Line, but when she took to the water on 3 March 1911, it had been named the *Ascania*, and painted in the Cunard Line's colours. It regularly plied the Atlantic.

When the First World War began, it conveyed Canadian troops in its third class dormitories to Britain. Mark (*Prisoners of war in British Hands during WW1*, 2007) cites the ship was then sent to Portsmouth Harbour to anchor alongside the *Lake Manitoba*. Access to and from either ship was possible by a connecting gangway. Both ships were instructed to move to Ryde on 22 February 1915. The *Ascania* is also mentioned in Killeen (*World War One – 1914–1918 The Great War, The Prisoner of War Ships*, June 1993).

John Jackson visited the ship on behalf of the US Embassy in London. On 1 February 1915 he noted there were 1,003 civilian internees on board. He stated they had relative freedom of the ship until 7 pm, when they were then locked in, below decks.

It was amongst the ships cited by the *New York Times*, as still having 1,400 PoWs on board, on 15 March 1915. She was released from her duties on 4 May 1915, cleaned up and then served as a hospital ship in the Mediterranean. It was to founder, after going aground off Cape Ray in the Breton Strait, Newfoundland, on 13 June 1918.

Carter (Russell, 1996) cites a Post Office was set up in the commandant's ship, in each of the three groupings of ships. The *Ascania* was the designated ship in this group.

Panayi (*The Enemy In Our Midst: Germans in Britain during the First World War*, 1991) states the *Ascania* was moored in the Solent, along with HMT *Scotian* and HMT *Lake Manitoba*. When the US Ambassador's representative made his inspection in 1915, the three ships collectively carried 3,600 prisoners.

HMT *LAKE MANITOBA* (GRT: 9,674. Passengers: 2nd = 350, steerage = 1,200). Built by Swan Hunter for Elder Dempster's Beaver Line, the *Lake Manitoba* was launched at their Wallsend on Tyne yard, on 6 June 1901. After being refitted in

1902, she saw her first military service in the Boer War, making two round trips transporting troops, before joining the Canadian Pacific Line.

The *Lake Manitoba* began her short career as a prison ship in December 1914. Mark (2007) cites the ship was initially at Portsmouth Harbour alongside the *Ascania*. Access to and from either ship was only possible by an inter-connecting gangway. *Lake Manitoba* and *Ascania* were instructed to follow the *Scotian* to Ryde on 22 February 1915. Holding 1,200 internees, the *Lake Manitoba* is cited by the *New York Times* as still being in service as a prison ship on 15 March 1915, but it was due to be released from this duty soon. Released by 17 April 1915 she went to Southampton for a refit to start life as a troop carrier, before returning to crossing the Atlantic again in August 1916.

Ljungström (per. comm., 3 December 2000) stated whilst engulfed in fire, at Montreal on 26 August 1918, she was scuttled. Re-floated that September and repaired, she made a few cross-Atlantic trips carrying only cargo before being sold to the Canada Steamship Line in 1920, and was renamed the *Iver Heath*. In 1923, Steeple and Leighton Ltd purchased it for the Crete Shipping Company, before it was broken up in 1924.

The US Embassy's report (8 May 1915) noted of that most of the internees on board the *Uranium* had previously been on the *Lake Manitoba*.

HMT *SCOTIAN* (GRT: 10,491. Passengers: 1st Class = 200, 2nd Class = 175, steerage = 1,000, crew = 220). Smith (*The German Prisoner of war Camp at Leigh 1914–1919*, 1986) states Dr Athelstane Nobbs was the President of the Wandsworth Division of the BMA; he also held a commission as a lieutenant in the RAMC. He wrote about his experience of being the Chief Medical Officer of Portsmouth Harbour when the *Scotian* was moored off shore, in the British Medical Journal. The *Scotian* had on board some 1,200 German soldiers and sailors.

Kludas (*Great Passenger Ships of the World: Volume One: 1858–1912*, 1975) explains it was built by Harland & Wolff, and launched in Belfast on 7 May 1898 for the Holland-America Line as the *Statendam*. Sold to the Allan Line on 23 March 1911, she was renamed the *Scotian*. Until this time she had plied the Atlantic routes, until becoming a troop transport ship in 1914.

Moored off Fareham Creek, in the Gosport/Portsmouth area of the Solent, the *Scotian* was used as a prison ship from 1 December 1914 until February 1915. It was then re-located to Ryde Harbour until April 1915. Holding 1,100 internees, the *Scotian* is cited in the *New York Times* as still being used as a 'prison ship' on 15 March 1915. Released from this duty, it was reported later that month that she was being used to transport PoWs captured at Neuve Chapelle.

Canadian Pacific shipping line bought the Allan Line on 1 October 1915. After a refit in 1919 *Scotian* returned to her past duties as a passenger liner, sailing between Montreal and Antwerp. Renamed the *Marglen* on 16 November 1922, in 1925 she was laid up at Southampton before being sold, on 30 December 1926, to D.L. Pittaluga of Genoa for breaking.

GRANTHAM: Belton Park (OS: SK 932 393). In an attempt to match the weaponry of the enemy, a gunnery school was created at Belton Park where thousands of men were brought together to be taught how to use the Vickers machine gun before being deployed to France. They were housed in wooden huts arranged in lines spread over the land that now houses a golf course.

The POWIB (1919) cites Grantham agricultural depot had five groups attached to it. These were at Caythorpe, Digby, Nocton, Timberland, and Temple Brener (sic). The depot's code was given as Bro (Gr) (IWM: Facsimile K4655). Belton Park, where internees were housed in tents, is cited by the FPHS (1973), and had the TA Priswarian: Belton, Grantham (ADM 1/8506/265–120667).

The Grantham camp closed on 20 February 1919. The gunnery school closed in 1922.

GRASSINGTON (OS: SE 00- 64-). What constitutes an internment camp? Contemporary Members of Parliament were confused, as can be gleaned in a question put to the Home Secretary, Sir George Cave, by Mr R. McNeill on 8 July 1918. McNeill asked whether there was an internment working camp for civilians at Grassington, near Skipton; and if so, how many enemy aliens were employed there. He also enquired whether any alien enemies were allowed outside the precincts of this camp when not at work, and did any military or civilian units guard them. He then sought clarification on whether they were rationed with regard to food; and, if so, what were the rations?

In reply, the Home Secretary stated there was no working camp at Grassington. But he conceded there was a party of twenty-one civilians who had been released on licence, for work of national importance, at the request of the Ministry of Munitions. Seventeen of these were Austrian subjects, and the rest were natives of Schleswig-Holstein. They worked under the supervision of civilians, and they were being housed together in quarters provided by their employers. In addition to other restrictions imposed on them they were confined to their quarters after 9.00pm. The same rationing restrictions applied to them as those imposed upon the general public.

In November of that year it was reported to the House of Commons that the internees had been seen drinking in a local public house (*Hansard*, 8 July 1918). Neither the premises they were employed at, nor the pub, have been traced.

GRAYS (OS: TQ 599 776). When men employed at Wouldham Cement Works, West Thorrock, embarked for the front many of their places were filled by their womenfolk. Then, when no more female recruits could be found and they needed to increase the production, 123 PoWs were brought in to fill the void. They were guarded by thirty soldiers, designated light duties, many having been wounded at the front. As the colder weather arrived those internees still sleeping under canvas were transferred to the company's stable block, within the plant. They were to remain billeted at the stables until their repatriation in 1919.

Grays is also cited by the FPHS (1973), and had the TA Priswarian: Grays (ADM 1/8506/265–120667). Cited by the POWIB (1919), its code was Pa (Ga) (IWM: Facsimile K4655).

GREATHAM: Longmoor Down (OS: SU 797 314). The *Hampshire Herald* (3 October 1914) cited that the previous day about 100 prisoners from Frimley were transferred to Longmoor, where it was understood they would be employed making a rifle range, near the army camp. A special compound had been prepared for them on the Downs, near Longmoor. The *Hampshire Herald* (10 October 1914) cited the internees brought to Longmoor the previous week were engaged, between Whitehill and Wolmer Pond, doing useful work of making the new rifle range. There were now around 200 internees held in a small compound on Longmoor Down, guarded by the Hampshire Battalion of the National Reserve. Parties were making the range, whilst others were diverting the railway line away from the line of fire.

The Longmoor Camp pre-dated the Boer War, but in 1901 a new camp was set up to house returning soldiers. One of its functions was to train men how to maintain a railway. The Woolmer Instructional Railway opened in October 1906. The Bentley-Bordon link had opened in 1905. The route ran from Bordon Station, through Longmoor Camp, and Liss Forest Station. The name was changed to the Longmoor Military Railway in 1935.

Hampshire Herald (26 December 1914) cites the interned Germans left Longmoor at the end of the week bound for Portsmouth where they were put on board one of the vessels lying off Ryde.

GREENWICH (OS: TQ 384 770). German seamen served on British merchant ships prior to the First World War. When hostilities were declared many were arrested as enemy aliens. Those on board German ships in British harbours were likewise arrested. Many were released, but could not leave the country. They could not find employment and many became destitute. Father Hopkins, a Benedictine monk, offered shelter for some of these destitute seamen and boys, at Beech Abbey. The first arrived on 10 August 1914. Up to 200 alien sailors were housed at Beech – the seamen lived in tents, officers in the nave of the church building, and the boys in a corrugated iron building. Other destitute seamen found sanctuary at Eastcote House in Northamptonshire.

To alleviate the problem of overcrowding at Beech around fifty seamen were housed at a daughter house in London. The address is cited as No. 38 Hyde Vale, Greenwich, which was run by Sister Frances. There, the seamen were documented and sorted according to where they were to be interned.

The cost of feeding and clothing these internees was borne by the British government.

GREAT BADDOW (OS: TL 72- 05-). A working camp, its POWIB (1919) code was Pa (G B) (IWM: Facsimile K4655). It is cited by the FPHS (1973) as Great Beddow (sic). The camp had the TA Priswarian: Great Baddow (ADM 1/8506/265–120667). No evidence has been traced to suggest the location of this camp.

GREAT COGGLESHALL (OS: TL 85- 22-). It is cited by the FPHS (1973) as Coggleshall, Essex. It was also cited by the POWIB (1919). Its code was Pa (Hst) (Gra), making it a satellite of Halstead (IWM: Facsimile K4655). Reports on visits of inspection to Coggeshall and other PoW camps during April and May 1919 are held at the National Archives at Kew.

GREAT HALE – HECKINGHAM (OS: TF 14- 43-). Great Hale is cited by the POWIB (1919). Its code was, Bro (Sl) (Gh) (IWM: Facsimile K4655). Nothing is known about this satellite of Sleaford.

As 90 per cent of the area was arable farmland, most of the population was directly or indirectly engaged in agricultural work and any PoWs sent to the area would have done farm work or cleared ditches.

GREAT OFFLEY (OS: TL 147 260). Offley Mansion is near to Hitchen. The POWIB (1919) directory cites Great Offley working camp, with its code being Pa (G O) (IWM: Facsimile K4655). Its TA was Priswarian: Offley (ADM 1/8506/265–120667). Offley Holes appears as a camp location on the FPHS (1973) listings.

A camp for forty PoWs was suggested for Offley on 2 January 1918, and a camp plan was submitted to that effect. The application was made on 20 March 1918. By 8 May 1918, forty PoWs were in place. By 1 October 1918, this number had risen to sixty.

GREAT PARNDON (OS: TL 442 093). This camp appears on a list produced by the FPHS (1973). Official documents state it was based at North Brook Farm. It had the TA Priswarian: Great Parndon (ADM 1/8506/265–120667).

GREAT STAMBRIDGE (OS: TQ 90- 91-). A photograph in the Liddle Collection shows PoWs working in a field. The provenance states the men were at Broomhills, a local farm near Great Stambridge.

GREAT WITLEY (OS: SO 775 654). *The Malvern News* (5 October 1918) refers to a PoW camp being at Hillhampton House. As Great Witley is in close proximity to Hillhampton, it is very likely that this would have been the location of this working camp. Its POWIB (1919) code was Dor (G W) (IWM: Facsimile K4655). It is also cited by the FPHS (1973), and it had the TA Priswarian: Great Witley (ADM 1/8506/265–120667).

GRINGLEY ON THE HILL – WALKERINGHAM (OS: SK 698 930). Gringley on the Hill is described as an agricultural group that was attached to Retford; its POWIB (1919) code was Bro (Ret) (Gn) (IWM: Facsimile K4655). It also appears in minutes of the Notts County WAC, but the camp's actual location is not recorded. It had the TA Priswarian: Walkeringham (ADM 1/8506/265–120667).

Walkeringham is also cited in a minute of the Nottinghamshire County's WAC as a migratory gang. An earlier minute of 1917 recorded PoWs were employed 'in large numbers' at Gringley and Everton Carrs to improve the drainage system.

Perhaps Gringley Hall could hold the answer to where the 'large numbers' were billeted. Located at the western edge of Gringley on the Hill, the hall stands opposite a vicarage. Built *c.*1800 by the Duke of Portland, it became a children's convalescent home at the turn of the twentieth century. Today, the hall has been transformed into a guesthouse.

The migratory gang may have been billeted in a different location.

The camp closed on 16 January 1919,

GOTHAM (OS: SK 53- 30-). A minute of the Nottinghamshire County's WAC of 24 April 1917 estimated at least 500 more men were required 'if cultivation was not to be diminished very seriously'. The release of 700 soldiers on agricultural furlough had been of great assistance, but the employment of PoW labour at that time was not being considered, owing to the difficulty in finding suitable housing accommodation for them and their guard.

However, when accommodation was found, as a further minute of the Notts County WAC cites a migratory gang at Gotham was set up. The location of the camp is not known, but the Manor Hall may hold the key (CC1/4/10 & 12).

GLENTHAM (OS: SP 99- 90-). Situated near to Market Rasen, this camp was a satellite of Bracebridge's agricultural depot. It had the POWIB (1919) code Bro (Bbe) (Ce) (IWM: Facsimile K4655). This code is somewhat unusual as it does not follow the usual pattern of POWIB (1919) coding, and may be a misprint. It is recorded as Glentham, Lincs. by the FPHS (1973). Its TA was Priswarian: Glentham (ADM

1/8506/265–120667). No evidence has been found to suggest the actual location of this camp.

GUILDFORD: Langton Priory (OS: SU 992 485). A working camp based at Langton Priory, it had the POWIB (1919) code Pa (Gfd) (IWM: Facsimile K4655). The FPHS (1973) cite Guildford. The camp's TA was, Priswarian: Langton Priory, Guildford (ADM 1/8506/265–120667).

Oakley (*Guildford in the Great War*, 1934) cites about forty internees 'arrived in Guildford for work on farms in the neighbourhood, and some of them were employed at the borough's sewage works'. They were billeted, from early in 1918, at Langton Priory in Portsmouth Road. There was no hostility shown towards the internees by the locals, though they 'were deemed a curiosity'. As for the internees themselves, 'they appeared to be content with their lot.'

The priory stands on Portsmouth Road. It was leased to Miss Elizabeth Rideal in 1951, and by 1972 was occupied by Southland Securities.

GUILSBOROUGH (OS: SP 674 735). Renton (*Records of Guilsborough, Nortoft, and Hollowell*, 1929) cites, having been closed for some nineteen years Guilsborough House School was renovated and re-opened in 1858 at a cost of some £1,700. It was to enjoy a period of prosperity as a grammar school until 1896, initially with around forty to fifty pupils. When the numbers dropped, in 1909, the Head, the Reverend F.W. Kingston, was asked to resign, and the school shut its gates for the last time. When war broke out, Belgian refugees were temporarily housed there. Then during the winter of 1917–1918, the school became a working camp for German PoWs; it had the POWIB (1919) code Pa (Gu) (IWM: Facsimile K4655). The FPHS (1973) cite it too. The internees were employed by Northampton Corporation to do work 'connected with the reservoir'.

In 1925, the old school buildings were refurbished and the bigger schoolrooms were transformed into the Village Hall.

H

HADDENHAM (OS: SP 74- 08-). Haddenham appears on the lists produced by the FPHS (1973). It had the TA, Priswarian: Haddenham, Cambridge (ADM 1/8506/265–120667).

The Ely, Haddenham & Sutton Railway opened on 7 April 1866 with intermediate stations at Stretham, Wilburton and Haddenham. Its stations were remotely sited from the villages they were supposed to serve resulting in most cases in a long walk to and from the village. The Haddenham station opened in 1906. The company was renamed the Ely & St. Ives Railway and was eventually taken over in 1898. As the First World War dawned passenger numbers, which had always been secondary to freight, began to dwindle at a time when there was an improvement in local roads. In 1919, the first local regular bus service was introduced. In 1922 the Great Eastern Railway was absorbed into the London & North Eastern Railway. In 1963, the station buildings were demolished. In 1987 a new station was opened in Thame Road, adjacent to the airfield. In 1941, RAF trainee glider pilots were temporarily billeted in Yolsum House, which was demolished in 1988 (www.buckscc.gov.uk/assets).

Perhaps any PoWs sent to the area in the First World War may have been billeted there too.

HADNALL (OS: SJ 52- 20-). Cited by the FPHS (1973), it was a tented camp. Very little is known about it, although the PoWs complained that there were no church services available for them to attend.

Perhaps the grounds of Hardwicke Grange, built by the 1st Viscount Hill, hold the key to where the camp was located.

DKF 30: In den Lagern von Rosyth, Eastgate, Uppingham, Belton Park, Tern Hill, Bee Craigs, Hadnall, Sutton Veny, Larkhill, Fovant, Withley (sic) *und Radford sind die Kriegsgefangenen in Zelten untergebracht.*

DKF 32: Gottesdienst: Die Seelsorge der Kreigsgefangenen ist auf vielen Plätzen sehr vernachlässigt. In den Lagern von Joyce Green; Dartford; Hadnall; Peak Dale Quarries bei Buxton; Sutton Veny; Larkhill; Netheravon; Codford; und Fovant hat noch kein Gottesdienst stattgefunden.

HAILSHAM (OS: TQ 591 094). The POWIB (1919) directory lists its code as Pa (Hail) (IWM: Facsimile K 4655). HO documents place the camp at Roseneath, George Street (ADM 1/8506/265–120667). Hailsham is also cited by the FPHS (1973).

It was reported to the Swiss Delegation (24 July 1918) that those interned at Hailsham were expected to work up to fourteen hours a day. This complaint apparently took even the interpreter by surprise.

Roseneath was the home of Dr Gould. Gould was instrumental in the building of the Pavilion Cinema which stands in George Street, which opened its doors in 1921.

DKF 35: Im Arbeitslager Hailsham mußten laut Bericht des Schweizerischen Delegierten A. de Sturler vom 24 Juli 1918 die Gefangenen zwölf, dreizehn, ja vierzehn Stunden täglich arbeiten. Der Dolmetscher gab selbst zu, daß dieses zu viel sei. Der Schweizer Delegierte wandte sich dieserhalb bereits an die englische Regierung.

HAIRMYRES: nr East Kilbride (OS: NS 607 539). Niven (per. comm., 26 September 1997) provided the history of the sanatorium built at Hairmyres. In May 1903, Lanarkshire County Council acquired land at Hairmyres, to erect an inebriate reformatory for women. It was formally opened on 1 December 1904. However, due to a lack of patients the Lanarkshire Inebriate Reformatory was to close in February 1911. Then, because of the high incidence of tuberculosis in the Clyde Valley, the Scottish Office and the Lanarkshire County Council took the decision to re-open it as a sanatorium. Conversion work began in 1914. The local workmen were then assisted by German PoWs to complete the project. The new hospital opened on 14 June 1919; the same day Alcock and Brown made their historic flight across the Atlantic.

The PoW camp closed on 20 July 1918. It appears in the list produced for the FPHS (1973). The camp's TA was Priswarian: East Kilbride (ADM 1/8506/265–120667).

Campbell (*Hairmyres – The History of the Hospital Lanarkshire Health Board*, 1994) cites George Orwell was a patient. He was admitted to Hairmyres on Christmas Eve 1946 under his real name, Eric Blair. Whilst convalescing, from tuberculosis in one lung, he penned *1984*.

On 1 April 1994 Hairmyres Hospital acquired trust status.

HALAM (OS: SK 674 545). Despite being cited in the minutes of the Notts County WAC and listed by the FPHS (1973), there is no evidence to show where this agricultural group, attached to Kelham, could have been. Perhaps the workhouse at Southwell may hold the key. The property is now owned by the National Trust.

During March 1919, Dr A. de Sturler visited Halam. His report is held at the National Archives at Kew (FO 383/506). Its POWIB (1919) code was Bro (Kel) (Hl) (IWM: Facsimile K4655). Its TA was Priswarian: Halam, Southwell (ADM 1/8506/265–120667).

HALESWORTH (OS: TM 439 762). A working camp, its POWIB (1919) code was Pa (Has) (IWM: Facsimile K4655). It is also cited by the FPHS (1973). It was cited as being at the Bulcamp Union, and had the TA Priswarian: Halesworth (ADM 1/8506/265–120667).

When the Blything Hundred Incorporation was dissolved, it was replaced by the Blything Poor Law Union, which officially came into existence on 25 June 1835. The new union took over the existing Bulcamp workhouse, which opened on 13 October 1766, and carried out modifications to make the two-storey red brick main building, designed by Thomas Fulcher, comply with the Poor Law Amendment Act (1834), which required strict segregation of the sexes. Previously, married couples could have their own bedrooms and keep their children with them.

After 1930, the workhouse site was renamed The Red House. In 1948 it became the Blythburgh and District Hospital and provided care for the chronic sick. In 1994 the site was redeveloped for residential use (www.blythburgh.net).

In 1917, sixteen bodies were pulled out of the wreckage of a Zeppelin brought down near Theberton by a lone pilot. The sole survivor was handed to the police. There is a memorial in Theberton Churchyard to those who died. Their remains would have been taken to the German War Cemetery at Cannock Chase in the 1960s.

Reports on visits of inspection to PoW camps were carried out by Dr A. de Sturler and Monsieur R. de Sturler. They visited Bulcamp during April and May 1919. The report is held at the National Archives at Kew (FO 383/507).

HALLING: Lee Cement Works (OS: TQ 711 640). Lee Cement Work housed PoWs as a working camp, according to the POWIB (1919); its code was Pa (Hlg) (IWM: Facsimile K4655). The FPHS (1973) incorrectly cite Halling, as being in Birmingham. Its TA was Priswarian: Halling (ADM 1/8506/265–120667).

During the nineteenth and early twentieth centuries a series of cement works grew up along the banks of the Medway, each with its own pits, railway tracks, workshops, wharfs and barges. The earliest of these was at North Halling, which began in 1799.

When Samuel Lee died in 1852, the company passed on to William Lee 'of Rochester' (www.snodlandhistory.org.uk/localhis/cement.htm). William Lee was born in 1801 and had been the manager of lime works at Burham since 1826. When he took over at Halling works there were only two kilns, but as the business expanded he took over as the owner. The title changed to Lee, Son & Smith when Alfred Smith of Rochester was appointed as a new junior partner. Smith had married Lee's youngest daughter, Sarah. Around 1876 his grandson Samuel Lee Smith joined the business and following William's death in 1881 another of his grandsons became a partner. William Henry Roberts (1848–1926) was a cavalry officer and a friend of the Prince of Wales (later Edward VII). The company was renamed William Lee, Son & Co. Ltd. When it went into liquidation in 1912 it was then acquired by the British Portland Cement Manufacturers Ltd. William Lee Henry Roberts (1871–1928) was the company's last managing director.

HALLATROW (OS: ST 63- 57-). One of the many camps that have disappeared from history, with nothing recorded about it. The camp had the POWIB (1919) code

Dor (Sh M) (Hall) (IWM: Facsimile K4655), making it a satellite of Shepton Mallet. It is also cited by the FPHS (1973).

A minute of the Somerset War Agricultural Council minutes (15 April 1919) cites PoW Horse Depots at Axbridge, Dulverton and Shepton Mallet had been closed, and arrangements were being made for the early closure of the depot at Hallatrow.

HALSTEAD: Workhouse (OS: TL 813 311). Described as an agricultural depot, its POWIB (1919) code was Pa (Hst) (IWM: Facsimile K4655); it had Great Coggleshall as its satellite. Records show the camp was at the Workhouse. Its TA was Priswarian: Halstead (ADM 1/8506/265–120667). It is also cited by the FPHS (1973).

Halstead Union Workhouse stood in Hedingham Road. It was designed by Thomas Nash. Its location was a bone of contention until part of Bois Field was accepted as the preferred site. The workhouse was constructed in 1838. It was closed in 1916, and was used in 1917 for billeting soldiers on the way to the war. PoWs working in the surrounding areas were billeted there from the summer of 1918 until late 1919. It then lay empty until it was demolished in 1922. Samuel Augustine Courtauld (1865–1953) was part of a benevolent family in Halstead. He erected the Homes of Rest on the site.

Dr A. de Sturler and Monsieur R. de Sturler visited Halstead PoW camp during April and May 1919. Their report is held at the National Archives at Kew (FO 383/507).

The Haverhill Echo (26 January 1918) reported that at an Essex Tribunal at Colchester, the national representative appealed against the decision of the Belchamp Tribunal to exempt from enlistment a 19-year-old the son of a farmer, Mr C.L. Stunt of Munt farm. The father had stated he was unable to do much as he suffered from gout to which Dr Simon replied, 'You'll get rid of that if the food difficulties go on.' Captain Howard asked if his son enjoyed his day out skating last week. Stunt replied he did not know. Mr Gray pointed out to the farmer that there was a PoW camp at Halstead and he had better get his name down for some prisoners. Stunt junior was told he had to enlist on 17 February 1918. *The Haverhill Echo* (24 November 1917) had previously reported that he had been granted deferment from being called up on condition he remained with his 73-year-old father.

HAMPTON IN ARDEN (see Berkswell).

HANDFORTH: Former Textile Dye Printing Works (OS: SJ 860 828). New premises were built, in 1910, for the Bradford Dyers Association at Handforth, but the project was shelved before the factory buildings were completed. When the *Manchester Courier & Lancashire General Advertiser* (19 March 1914) cited interest was being shown in the factories future it ignited a series of articles in various newspapers about synthetic rubber being produced there. Production had begun; the Lancashire Rubber Company was making samples. Then reports began to appear of the army using a vacant part of the site to train around 2,000 men of the 3rd and 4th City Battalions of the Manchester Regiment. *The Manchester Evening News* (17 September 1914) cited the Pals regiments were using the grounds for camping.

Then the War Office intervened, taking over the premises for the retention of internees instead. The local newspaper, *The Wilmslow, Alderley & Knutsford Advertiser* (9 October 1914), stated:

> Engineers are now transforming the interior of the buildings into habitable quarters, and then attention will be paid to external work necessary to keep the prisoners within bounds.

The Coventry Evening Telegraph (7 October 1914) had previously reported the former textile dying works were being prepared by the Royal Engineers to accommodate 'war prisoners'. The site stood about 0.5km south of the railway station, east of the railway viaduct, and on the south bank of the River Dean.

The Manchester Evening News (5 November 1914) reported the first batch of 500 internees had arrived. The same paper reported (25 November 1915) their numbers had been doubled by the arrival of 573 prisoners from the Cameroons. They had been brought in by train.

Edinburgh Evening News (23 November 1914) cited a press correspondent's visit to the Handforth factory. He described it as 'a huge red-bricked structure, very nearly a quarter of a mile in length' interning around 1,000 men.

The Manchester Evening News carried several reports of the camp during December. The first (3 December 1914) reported the sudden death of a man expected to be released. Then it cited (14 December 1914) that a further 300 prisoners had arrived. Presumably this would have been those reported in the *Dorset County Chronicle* (17 December 1914) as having been moved from Dorchester to Handforth; and a second batch of around 300 followed them. Then a report (15 December 1914) cited a 'Notorious German at Handforth'. On 18 December a report of steps being taken to control the behaviour of the prisoners was printed.

On 15 January 1915 the *Manchester Evening News* reported the officers and the crew of the *Emden* were being interned at Handforth.

In early 1915 the figure had risen to approximately 2,000, including the 400 sailors that were kept separate. *The Wilmslow, Alderley & Knutsford Advertiser* reported that 115 National Reservists under the command of Major Lloyd were relieving the camp's guards, the King's Liverpool Regiment.

The same paper reported, on 27 November 1914, under the headline Life at the Camp, that:

> The prisoners of war are Germans, Austrians, and Czechs. They are divided into companies, with a 'Captain' over each one. Companies are then sub-divided into Messes. A 'Chief Captain' has a Secretary and an office. 'Officers' are appointed by votes. A Committee Meeting is held daily, and it is decided by vote whether to send any matters to the Camp Commandant. Captains of each Mess ensure fair distribution of supplies.

A delegation from the US Embassy in London, led by John Jackson on 12 February 1915, cited there were around 2,000 prisoners, including three soldiers and 400 sailors. The sailors, thought to be from the *Blücher* and *Gneisenau*, were in separate compounds from the civilians, under their own deck officers. The civilians were in several compounds, one of which was for the better classes. The report stated the building was sound, and the conditions inside were said to be good, roomy, airy and dry. There was an exercise ground and a football field was being prepared. The washing and bathing facilities were adequate. German cooks, some of whom had been working in London restaurants, ran a large, well-organised kitchen. In the hospital there were several wounded patients.

The *Manchester Evening News* (17 March 1915) reported a further 600 prisoners had arrived at Handforth.

Some 600 soldiers captured at Neuve Chapelle had arrived to an unostentatious reception. Only a few inhabitants watched them march past at a swift pace from the station to the camp. Bystanders were impressed by their excellent physique, sturdy fitness and well-clad appearance. Certainly they didn't look as though they had just survived an ordeal in the trenches. They were mainly aged 20–35 and marched with a light, strong step. While the column was forming outside the station, the men gossiped with great cheerfulness, and waved to a photographer they spotted at a cottage window. Their uniforms were in excellent condition and showed little sign of wear, apart from some mud.

The delegation found some discontent amongst the Germans. While others complained about their arrest and detention, and of the financial loss it caused, some complained it was only the Anglo-Germans that had been given the captains' positions. No meaningful work was provided, but some that had been caught gambling had been put to road making, as a punishment.

A second visit, in March 1915, by Mr Edward Lowry of the American Embassy in London, cited the camp commandant was Colonel Hugh C.C. Ducat-Hammersley. He was later to become the commandant of the camp at Shrewsbury. The number of prisoners under his control was again around 2,000 including those from the *Blücher*, which was sunk on 24 January 1915 as it allegedly sailed to shell Yarmouth.

The Times (7 April 1915) cites Herbert Greenwood, of the canteen staff, was charged with receiving letters meant for Herting, another PoW in the camp. Greenwood was imprisoned for three months.

The Wilmslow, Alderley & Knutsford Advertiser (9 April 1915) cites PoWs were transferred from Handforth to Frongoch.

The sinking of the *Lusitania*, by German *U-Boot* 139 on 7 May 1915, saw enemy aliens still at large on licence seeking internment for their protection, such was the unrest it had caused. Heusel (*Handforth through the Ages*, 1982) states a large contingent of those seeking internment came from Liverpool, the ship's homeport. On 15 May 1915, it was reported in *The Manchester Courier & Lancashire General Advertiser* that 150 individuals had been arrested and were waiting in police stations to be put into internment. The *Manchester Evening News* (19 May 1915) cited a large crowd watched as 1,000 prisoners were being moved to the Isle of Man. No sooner had they gone when others arrived to replace them.

It was a period of transition within and out of the camp. The US Embassy's delegation that visited Stobs on 15 June 1915 stated that sailors previously at Handforth in March were now at Stobs. When they visited Handforth on 29 June 1915 they stated 'no camp in the UK had shown greater improvement in the morale and general atmosphere.' They also noted the soldiers and sailors had been moved out, and all that remained were civilian internees. Craft classes had been set up, and a theatre company had been formed, as had an orchestra. The Jews amongst them had their own messing facility.

The Times (26 October 1915) recorded five unnamed PoWs were charged with looting from a canteen; their fate is unknown.

A complete change of detainees had occurred by the time of the next visit of the American inspection, in December 1915, as the camp was now being used to accommodate only military and naval personnel. The civilians had gone to the Isle of Man.

A PoW suspected of having leprosy was moved to a special unit in Dorchester in December 1916 (Hermann Herting, letters, 6 April).

On 16 March 1916 the *Manchester Evening News* cited there were 3,000 PoWs at Handforth.

A US Embassy visit of 1 April 1916 cited the commandant was now Lt-Colonel A.H.C. Kenney-Herbert. It was noted that the internees comprised a total of 2,713 prisoners, all German. There were 2,399 soldiers, 313 sailors, and 1 civilian, who was there as a concession, to allow him to visit his sick wife in Manchester.

The Times (8 May 1916) reported an Offizierstellvertreter Kahn of the Bavarian Artillery and Fahnrich-zur-See Johl of the SS *Blücher* had escaped and had been recaptured at Gorton. They were sentenced to six months at Woking Detention Barracks.

On 21 August 1916 the escape of Karl Reitz was reported in the *Dundee Evening Telegraph*. He was at large with two others thought to be Ernst Heyl and Joseph Hannes, from Handforth.

Stockport Advertiser (25 August–1 Sept 1916) reported three men had escaped. Two were recaptured at Bingley, and the third at Otley. Previously, *The Times* (22 August 1916) had named two escapers caught at Bingley as Lt Karl Reitz and Gefreiter Joseph Haneche.

The Times (29 September 1916) cited four sailors were found guilty of theft, at Wilmslow, and imprisoned for three months each.

The *Staffordshire Advertiser* (24 March 1917) cites that Ltzs Emil Lehmann, a PoW being transferred from the Isle of Man to Kegworth, escaped in Manchester. He was re-captured at Upper Elkstone, 5 miles northeast of Leek, on Sunday, 18 March 1917. He was seen in a local chapel and it appeared he had burnt some bibles. On Thursday (22 March 1917) he was brought to Handforth. Lehmann was also part of an unsuccessful attempt to escape from Kegworth in September.

On 19 April 1915, *The Manchester Evening News* reported the departure of prisoners from Handforth. They were moved by members of the Shropshire National Reservists. Another 1,500 were expected to follow.

The Liverpool Echo (3 August 1916) cited PoWs from Handforth were repairing main roads in Cheshire.

It would have been around this time that the camp was upgraded to that of a parent camp. Many of the surrounding camps that sprang up, classed as working camps or agricultural depots, would then have become its satellites.

The Times (14 August 1917) reported two more escapes had taken place. This time the absconders were named as Feldwebel (Army Sergeant) Richard Eber, 24 years old, and Albert Groensky, 31, of the navy. They had escaped on the night of 12–13 August, around the same time as another, unrelated, escape took place at Oldcastle. Reports on 17 August of the Handforth pair being re-arrested appear to be incorrect, and their capture was denied in a report that appeared in the press in August 1917. *The Police Gazette* (17 August 1917) cited the escapers were from Wilmslow. *The Times* (31 August 1917) reported they were at large, and believed to being sheltered by friends.

It was reported in *The Manchester Evening News* (18 October 1917) that a large number of prisoners were moved to a northern internment camp.

The Times (3 November 1917) reported five sailors had escaped. They were Wilhelm Otto, Emil Mandey, Georg Marienfeld, Heindrich Stold and Emil Stehr. Otto, Mandey and Marienfeld were recaptured at Stalybridge. The paper of 12 November cited Stold and Stehr were recaptured at Portsmouth.

A PoW died of exhaustion due to typhoid fever. He was 18 years old and named as Fauermann Martin.

The Times (3 June and 5 June 1918) cited a fatality had occurred at the camp. It named the deceased as Carl Liborius. Then it reported on 8 August 1918 an inquest into the death of William Schmidt had taken place at Manchester. It was stated Private John Taylor of the RDC had shot him accidentally, and a verdict of accidental death was recorded.

The Liverpool Echo (30 August 1918) praised the scheme to allow PoWs to work outside of their places of internment.

There were reports in September 1918, given to the Swiss Delegation by the internees, of dissatisfaction towards the rations they received.

The Times then cited the movement of PoWs. On 9 May 1919 it was reported around 1,000 PoWs had left the camp. On 27 May 1919 it cited they had gone to Leigh. It was cited on 11 November 1819 the remainder were expected to leave in a day-or-two.

The Times (15 November 1919) states the Handforth site was used for manufacturing. In the Second World War, the site became a tank depot and was still used as such in the early 1950s.

During March 1919, Dr A. de Sturler compiled reports on visits of inspection to Handforth. It is held at the National Archives at Kew (FO 383/506). The FPHS (1973) cite Handforth, Cheshire amongst its entries. Its POWIB (1919) code was Hfth (IWM: Facsimile K4655). The HO (1918) had issued the TA Priswarian: Handforth (ADM 1/8506/265–120667). A 1938 Ordnance Survey map shows the buildings as Handforth Works (disused).

DKF 14 In einen Brief des Fähnrichs zur See Rauber vom 12 April 1915 wurde mitgeteilt, daß die Unterbringung der Fähnriche sehr schlecht war. Schuppen mit vier Wänden, Strohsacke auf Pritschen, keine Bettwasche, kleiner Platz zum Gehen, voll von Leuten. Alles selbst zimmern und einrichten. Fenster nur in Decke. Furchtbarer Dreck und Staub.

Aus dem Bericht des Vertreters der Schweizerischen Gesandtschaft in London über das Lager Handforth vom 5 September 1918 ging hervor, daß die den Gefangenen geliefiten Räucherheringe, die an Stelle von frischen Heringen zur Ausgabe gelangten, durchaus ungeniessbar waren und fortgeworfen werden mußten, ohne daß den Gefangenen Ersatz dafur geliefert wurde.

Dies hatte zur Folge, daß die ohnehin auf das äußerste beschranken Lebensmittelrationen, die den Gefangenen seitens der englischen Behörde geliefert wurden, eine weitere Verminderung erfuhren, die von Gefangenen besonders hart empfunden werden mußte. Gegen dieses Verfahren der englischen Behörden wurde nachdrücklichst Einspruch erhoben und von der englischen Regierung gefordert, daß den Gefangenen die geringen Rationen, die ihnen neuerdings zustehen, in einwandfrier Beschaffheit geliefert werden.

HARBURY: Ladbroke Hall (OS: SP 415 586). The estates can be traced back to the Domesday survey. Robert Catesby, a leading member of the Gunpowder Plot, lived at Ladbroke Manor. It was acquired by Sir Robert Dudley *c.*1597, before Sir William Palmer bought the estates in 1633. It was he who created the park in *c.*1650. It is thought the original Ladbroke Hall dates back to around this time.

The high street bookmaker's chain, Ladbrokes, claims it took its name from the hall; the owners of the gambling chain apparently once lived there – as did Lord Rootes, the car magnate.

The minutes of the Warwickshire WAC record a PoW camp had been set up at Ladbroke by 20 April 1918. Cited as being near to Harbury, and although described by the POWIB (1919) as being a working camp, with the code Dor (Lad) (IWM: Facsimile K4655), Ladbroke Hall had an agricultural group attached to it, at Offchurch Bury. Both Ladbroke Hall and Harbury are cited by the FPHS (1973).

The Diocesan Registrar was able to show a Faculty, granted on 22 November 1961 to the Commonwealth War Graves Commission, to have the remains of B.F.J. Sprotte (d. 13 November 1918) exhumed from the graveyard at Southam. He was re-interred at the new German War Cemetery at Cannock Chase (Rotherham & Co., Coventry (Solicitors) (Diocesan Registrar)).

Today, the hall has been converted into flats.

HAREWOOD (OS: SE 321 451). Harewood AG had the POWIB (1919) directory code Cat (P B) (Hd) (IWM: Facsimile K4655), making it a satellite of Pateley Bridge. Described as being at the Harewood Arms, the camp's TA was Priswarian: Harewood (ADM 1/8506/265–120667). This camp would have been active in the second phase of internment.

LE HAVRE DOCKS (Quai de la Gironde) & SS *Phryne* (OS: n/a). Lord Kitchener insisted that Pows interned in Britain could be best utilised in labour camps in France, rather than being cooped up behind barbed wire doing nothing. Some 750 PoWs were sent to Rouen on 5 April 1916, before 700 were dispatched to Le Havre on 26 April 1916. There they worked in the ports unloading ships, but not munitions. A further 500 followed to Le Havre in early May. Besides port work the PoWs were employed in forests and quarries. With the demands on manpower for the Battle of the Somme in mid-1916, PoW labour in France was more extensively employed in quarries, on road works and in the lines of communication.

A delegation from the American Embassy visited the camp on 6 July 1916, and again on 7 December 1916. On one of the visits, they found twenty NCOs and 452 men of lower rank were being billeted on the SS *Phryne*. Others were being held in wooden barrack huts near the docks.

The *Phryne* had been involved in a collision with a German barque, the *Pangani*, on 26 January 1913. Twenty-six members of the German craft drowned. The 2,817-ton *Phryne* was badly damaged, according to reports carried in *The Advertiser* (Adelaide, SA) (27 January 1913), *The Toronto World* (29 January 1913), and *The Liverpool Mercury* and the *The Rijnbode* (Netherlands) (both 1 February 1913).

HARFLEUR BASE DEPOT COMPANY & HARFLEUR BASE DEPOT COMPANY No. 2 (OS: n/a). These camps were situated on the outskirts of Le Havre. Their POWIB (1919) codes were D & D2 (IWM: Facsimile K4655).

By 10 May 1916 over 2,000 PoWs had been dispatched to base camps in Rouen and Harfleur. Only a handful were sent back to Britain, declared unfit to work. The PoWs were employed in a variety of tasks, including roads, quarrying, forestry, and in ports unloading ships, but they were not permitted to handle munitions. In retaliation to this, German authority announced, on 10 May 1916, that 2,000 British PoWs would be put into labour companies in Poland and France (Misc.19 (1916), Cd. 8260).

HARLESCOTT PARK (OS: SJ 50- 15-). This camp is cited by the FPHS (1973). The only supportive evidence that this camp existed comes from a letter written by 2nd Lieutenant Albert E. Elsy of the Devonshire Regiment. In a letter sent to his wife he states he was about to be deployed to the PoW Camp Repair Depot at Harlscott from Buckminster where he was an interpreter. The letter was dated 12 November 1918.

HARPENDEN (OS: TL 127 157). The minutes of the Hertfordshire County Council WAC (8 May 1918) cite a scheme for thirty-five PoWs was agreed for Cootersend Farm, Harpenden.

HARPERLEY STATION (OS: NZ 174 534). During the First World War PoWs were sent to Fir Tree, Harperley, near Crook, in County Durham. They slept in tents at Low Harperley Farm until the permanent camp was opened on 16 September 1916. The new camp was at Shipley Moss, about 1 mile from the station and across the River Wear, from the farm. The POWIB (1919) cites this was a working camp with the code Cat (Har) (IWM: Facsimile K4655). Its TA was Priswarian: Hamsterley (ADM 1/8506/265–120667). All that remains of the camp today is a low circular brick wall, which was part of the filter bed.

The PoWs had to carry all their supplies up a hill, from the station to their camp. The men worked at Knitsley Fell Quarry, further up the hill. When the camp was visited on 18 June 1917 there were around 230 internees there. They were housed in eight dormitory huts, 60 feet long and 18 feet wide with wooden floors, asbestos lined walls, and roofs covered with tarred felt. Each hut slept twenty-eight, and had stoves to heat them. Each man was issued with four blankets. There was a separate dining hall. A separate hut, with hot and cold running water, provided twelve showers for washing, along with the latrines.

As a result of the influenza pandemic of 1918, twenty-seven of their number died. They were:

Balzke, Alfred Paul Alwin	d. 13 Nov 1918
Beck, Karl Edmund	d. 17 Nov 1918
Bedorf, Anton	d. 16 Nov 1918
Bertoldt, Fritz	d. 11 Nov 1918
Boog, Wilhelm	no date given
Braunigen, Kurt	d. 14 Nov 1918
Fink, Karl Edward Wilhelm	d. 12 Nov 1918
Fischer, Otto	d. 12 Nov 1918
Garling, Ernst Klaus Friedrich	d. 11 Nov 1918
Grassoff, Arthur	d. 15 Nov 1918
Hadla, Edward	d. 11 Nov 1918
Horwege, Willy Klaud August	d. 15 Nov 1918
Kaussmann, Hensonn Gustav	d. 17 Nov 1918
Kempe, Ernst	d. 14 Aug 1918
Kniesche	no date given
Krinn, Heinrich Max	d. 18 Nov 1918
Lange, Alfred Karl John	d. 11 Nov 1918
Lehmann, Richard	d. 12 Nov 1918
Meier, Rudolf Max Heinrich	d. 23 Nov 1918
Merkle, Ernst Heins	d. 13 Nov 1918
Rosnick, Otto Karl	d. 11 Nov 1918
Rudloff, Alfred Paul	d. 13 Nov 1918
Schneider, Kurt Gustav	d. 15 Nov 1918

Schwendler, Willy	d. 12 Nov 1918
Sternberg, Paul Ernst Friedrich	d. 7 Nov 1918
Walkowiak, Anton	d. 17 Nov 1918
Wloczyk, Felix	d. 8 Nov 1918

Initially, they were buried in the graveyard of St James Church, at Hamsterley. Their bodies were exhumed on 3 May 1963 and taken to the German War Grave Cemetery at Cannock Chase, in Staffordshire for re-burial (EP/Ham 28 & 82).

The FPHS (1973) does not cite this camp, but includes Harpurhey in its listings, which may be an incorrect reference to Harperley. Harperley Station stands to the west of Witton le Wear, in the Hamsterley Forest.

A camp existed in Harperley during the Second World War which, today, has been developed into a tourist attraction.

HARPURHEY (OS: SD 85- 01-). Harpurhey appears on the FPHS (1973); but as no camp of this name can be traced to the Manchester area during the First World War, it may have been an incorrect reference to the camp at Harperley. Alternatively, Harpurhey may have connections to Middleton Junction, which also appears on the FPHS (1973) lists.

HARWICH: Royal Naval Dockyard (OS: TM 259 328). Gibson & Prendergast (*German Submarine War 1914–1918*, 2002) describe the events on the day the German *U-Boote* were ordered into internment as part of the agreement that surface vessels sail to the Firth of Forth. On 20 November 1918, a squadron of submarines comprising of twenty boats sailed into British waters to be met by Rear-Admiral Tyrwhitt of the British Navy, on board HMS *Curacao*. The *U-Boote* were then escorted the 30 or so nautical miles to Parkeston Quay at Harwich. The navy had designated five light cruisers and twenty destroyers assisted by two airships, the *R26* and the *SR1* to make up the escort.

The *New York Times* (21 November 1918) reported the submarines were spotted at 7.00am, accompanied by the transport ships, the *Tibania* and the *Sierra Ventana*. As the ships entered the war channel the paravanes were hauled aboard. On reaching a point some 20 miles off Harwich the ships dropped anchor and Captain Addison went out on the warship *Maidstone*. British crews were then put on board the submarines to take them into harbour. With the exception of the engine staff, all the German sailors remained on deck. As the boats went through the gates a white signal was run up on each of them with the German flag underneath. The submarines were then taken through the gates of the harbour and the German crews were transferred to the transports and taken back to Germany. At the transfer, each German submarine commander was required to sign a declaration to the effect that his vessel was in running order, that its periscope was intact, that its torpedoes were unloaded and that its torpedo heads were safe.

On 21 November 1918 at 9.30am the surface craft were met off the Firth of Forth and taken to Scapa Flow. On this day, the second squadron, again of twenty submarines, was met and taken to Harwich. But the *U97* foundered on the way. For the exchange, a similar routine would have been followed. The third batch, comprising of twenty-eight boats, was met on 22 November 1918, and made it to Harwich intact. Three days later the fourth batch, comprising of twenty-eight boats, arrived. The last big batch to arrive at Harwich, twenty-seven boats, was met on the 27 November 1918.

At the beginning of December, eight more boats arrived, and thereafter only a trickle of craft declared fit to sail made the journey to Harwich. It has been widely recorded that those that sailed with the surface craft were interned with their ships. However, it appears the submariners were allowed to return back to their homelands despite Churchill's loathing for them.

HARWORTH (OS: SK 61- 91-). *The York Herald* (8 August 1914) cites sixteen employees of a German-English syndicate that sunk a mine at Harworth in North Nottinghamshire were arrested. As they were of military age, they were taken to East Retford for processing. Their fate is unknown.

Harworth is cited only in the *Sheffield Daily Telegraph* (19 October 1918), when the chairman of the local WAC stated that a camp was to be established there so that the PoWs would not have to travel daily from Cuckney.

HASLAND: Hasland Hall (OS: SK 397 691). An article published in *The Derbyshire Times* (15 June 1918), and another in *The Derby Daily Telegraph* (14 March & 10 July 1918) are the only proof that this camp existed. The former cites PoWs had been sought by the Chesterfield District WAC.

Perhaps the ideal choice of location for this camp may have been on the estates surrounding Hasland Old Hall.

A minute of the Derbyshire WAC (No. 11 of 21 December 1918) expressed concerns about not completing the harvest in proper time, mainly due to the weather and the shortage of skilled men. The minute concluded that thirty German prisoners, in five gangs, were following threshers in the Chesterfield area (D331/1/27).

HATFIELD. Four locations were identified in minutes of the Hertfordshire WAC Meetings. These were the Church Rest, Chantry House, New Town House, and the workhouse.

CHANTRY HOUSE (OS: TL 221 075). Chantry House was used in conjunction with the workhouse, the Church Army Rest, and New Town House to accommodate PoWs in Hatfield according to several minutes of the Hertfordshire WAC. One records at least forty-five PoWs were being sent to Chantry House. Their arrival, on 19 June 1918, took the total number of PoWs in Hatfield to 205.

CHURCH ARMY REST (OS: TL 224 075). Minutes of Hertfordshire WAC show several buildings were used to accommodate PoWs in Hatfield. Amongst them was the Church Army Rest.

NWE TOWN HOUSE (OS: TL 226 088). Minutes of Hertfordshire WAC show several buildings were used to accommodate PoWs in Hatfield. Amongst them was New Town House.

THE WORKHOUSE (OS: TL 226 088). Minutes of Hertfordshire WAC show several buildings were used to accommodate PoWs in Hatfield. Amongst them was the workhouse that stood on what was then Union Lane.

Which location was used when the first forty PoWs arrived on 3 October 1917 is not stated, but most likely it was to the workhouse the first PoWs arrived. There were plans to increase this number to seventy by 13 November 1917, but at the end of the year their number was still only forty. Minutes show the number of PoWs in Hatfield was then to rise sharply: by 13 February 1918 it stood at 134; and by 20 March 1918 it had risen to 160. It was also proposed at this juncture in time to send forty-five PoWs to Chantry House. On 10 February 1919 the number had dropped to 130 PoWs. When the New Town House and the Church Army Rest were used is not stated.

Small migratory gangs were sent from Hatfield to Stevenage and Knebworth to work.

Boys from the village, curious about the PoWs, used to creep up to the windows at night and peep in to see what the Germans were doing. The PoWs were often observed removing grain from their shoes, which they ate as they were so hungry.

Reports on visits of inspection to the PoW camps at Tonbridge, Marshmoor Sidings, and Hatfield in Hertfordshire, by Monsieur de Corragioni d'Orelli, during March 1919, are held at the National Archives, London (FO 383/506).

The original workhouse, situated in Union Lane, later to become Wellfield Road, was built in *c.*1788 as the Hatfield Parish Workhouse. It was run as such until 1835 when responsibility for relief of the poor was transferred. In 1929 Hertfordshire County Council inherited the site. The major part of the building was used as a Home for Elderly Women, with clinics in the rest. In 1948 the building was split up. The Local Authority became responsible for the Home for Elderly Women and the rest was adopted by the NHS. In 1983 the Home ceased to operate whilst the District Health Authority continued to operate the elderly care ward. In 1988 the site was sold by the North West Thames Regional Health Authority on the understanding that demolition of the home would take place and a new hospital would be built. The site was subsequently resold for housing development (www.wellfieldtrust.co.uk/history).

The camp's TA was Priswarian: Hatfield (ADM 1/8506/265–120667).

HATHERLEIGH: Fishleigh House (OS: SS 541 058). The POWIB (1919) directory cites Hatherleigh as a working camp with the code Dor (Ht) (IWM: Facsimile K4655). The FPHS (1973) also cite Hatherleigh. The internees were accommodated in Fishleigh House. It had the TA Priswarian: Hatherleigh (ADM 1/8506/265–120667).

The house is currently being renovated.

HATHERTON (OS: SJ 69- 47-). The only evidence that this camp existed is an entry in a list produced by the POWIB (1919). It states it was a working camp and had the POWIB (1919) code Hfth (Han) (IWM: Facsimile K4655).

Perhaps Hatherton Hall may hold the key. The present hall, rebuilt in stone in the Gothic style by Moreton Wallhouse in 1817, stands on the site of a previous hall, within its own parkland at the south-western periphery of Cannock Chase.

HATLEY ST GEORGE: The Rectory (OS: TL 284 515). Minutes of Cambridgeshire WAC (27 May 1918) cited a number of locations available for accommodating PoWs in the county; amongst them was an unnamed house in Hatley St. George. The POWIB (1919) directory cites The Rectory as being the premises in question, stating its code as Pa (Hs) (IWM: Facsimile K4655). The camp is also cited by the FPHS (1973). Its TA was Priswarian: Hatley St George, Gamlingay (ADM 1/8506/265–120667).

The Old Rectory was destroyed in the 1930s, and the land was sold for development.

HAUGHLEY (OS: TM 02- 62-). An agricultural depot, its POWIB (1919) code was Pa (Hgy). It had satellites at Claydon, Heveningham, Semer and Wilby (IWM:

Facsimile K4655). It is also cited by the FPHS (1973) and had the TA Priswarian: Haughley (ADM 1/8506/265–120667).

Haughley, once an important market town, has a castle that was one of the most significant edifices in East Anglia.

The Village Hall, built in 1907, which stands opposite Haughley House, is thought to have billeted a handful of German PoWs. Palmer (per. comm., 1 June 2009) says they apparently had come from Harwich. It is not known how long they stayed.

HAUXTON (OS: TL 434 525). Six months after the cessation of hostilities it was proposed to the Cambridgeshire WAC minutes (19 April 1919) that every endeavour should be made to get back the 300 PoWs withdrawn from the county in January. It was stated that accommodation for 200 of them was available at the Copralite works at Hauxton.

HAVERFORDWEST: Shoals Hook Farm (OS: SM 967 169). A working camp, it had the POWIB (1919) code Fg (Hf) (IWM: Facsimile K4655). The camp was based at Shoals Hook Farm and had the TA Priswarian: Haverfordwest (ADM 1/8506/265–120667). No details of this camp are known.

HAVERHILL (see Kedlington).

HAWICK (see Stobs).

HAWKESBURY UPTON (OS: ST 78- 87-). The camp has the POWIB (1919) code Dor (Hk) (IWM: Facsimile K4655). Its location is unknown, but the *Thornbury Gazette* (26 October 1918) cites that at a Farmers' Union meeting, the chair, Mr F. Minett, stated that it was anticipated that a permanent camp would be set up in Hawkesbury Upton, despite a migratory camp in the area being unsuccessful due to the ill feelings of local farm workers, against working beside German labour. The chair indicated any farmer could have up to three PoWs from the camp, if he could house and feed them.

HAYWARDS HEATH (OS: TQ 337 253). A Home Office report compiled by an unknown source cited there was a camp in Hayward's Heath at the start of the First World War. Also cited were London's Olympia, Frimley, Newbury, Stratford, Lancaster, Queensferry, Stobs, Handforth, York, Wakefield, Southampton and Douglas. Bird (*Control of Enemy Alien Civilians in Great Britain 1914–1918*, 1986) cites these too. It has not been proved that there was a camp at Hayward's Heath. It may have been erroneously entered at the expense of Horsham where it is known a camp was set up briefly at Christ's Hospital School (HO45/11025/410118/2).

A second camp set up in Hayward's Heath at a later stage of the war has provenance: it is cited by POWIB (1919), and also in a HO list. Its POWIB (1919) code was Pa (Hy) (IWM: Facsimile K4655) and had the TA Priswarian: Hayward's Heath (ADM 1/8506/265–120667). It is believed to have been at Summer Hill. Locally, it is thought any PoW sent to Hayward's Heath would have been employed at the reservoir, lying between Hayward's Heath and Ardingly, created around this time. It is known PoW labour was used on similar projects.

Hayward's Heath is also recorded by the FPHS (1973).

What is known is that there was a camp at Brook House, Ardingly in the Second World War, where a number of wooden huts were used to accommodate civilian internees. They did not work outside their camp.

HEMEL HEMPSTEAD: The Institute (OS: TL 055 073). The first internment camp at Hemel Hempstead was suggested when plans to send seventy-five PoWs to Buntingford and St Albans had to be aborted. A minute of the Hertfordshire County Council WAC (8 May 1918) cites the camp was to be at the Institute (The Old House), situated on Marlowes. By 3 October 1917, thirty-five PoWs were on site, and by 2 January 1918, that number had risen to seventy.

Five internees appear to have vanished by May 1918 as the minutes state that a further fifteen PoWs had been sent to this camp, 'making the total up to eighty'.

Hemel Hempstead was re-developed in the early 1950s. Marlowes, a tree-lined thoroughfare, became the main shopping centre for the new town, but retained some of its older properties. One of these older properties was a Grade II listed building two storeys high that once belonged to the Coombes family. Built in the seventeenth century, it had been a dower house, the home of a widow. Today, numbered 53, it is being offered as attractive office accommodation that maintains the original character of the building.

HO documents cite its TA as Priswarian, Prisoners of war Camp, Hemel Hempstead and that the camp closed on 16 June 1918 (ADM 1/8506/265–120667). The camp was cited by the FPHS (1973).

The internees were critical of the canteen during their stay.

A second camp opened on Cemaes Court Road.

DKF 33: Aus den Berichten des Schweizerischen Delegierten vom September und Oktober 1917 geht hervor, daß in den Arbeitslager in England noch immer Mißstände herrschten. In Hemel Hempstead (Herts) und Chipping Ongar (Essex) fehlten die Kantinen, in South Ochendon (sic) *(Essex) die Öfen.*

HEMEL HEMPSTEAD: Cemaes Court Road (OS: SU 051 074). The minutes of the Hertfordshire County Council WAC cite, from October 1918, seventy-five internees were being billeted at Hemel Hempstead, presumably at Cemaes Court Road. This figure was to drop to thirty on 10 February 1919. The minutes show another forty PoWs being sought on 25 July 1919.

The POWIB (1919) List of Places of Internment (January 1919) cites Hemel Hempstead as an agricultural depot, with the code Pa (Hem) (IWM: Facsimile K4655). The list shows it had a satellite camp, at Berkhamsted. The camp TA was recorded as Priswarian: Cemmaes Court (sic), Hemel Hempstead (ADM 1/8506/265–120667).

HEMPSTED: Newark House (OS: SO 818 173). Newark House, Hempsted was cited as a working camp with the TA of Priswarian, Gloucester (ADM 1/8506/265–120667). The camp closed on 18 May 1918. The camp also appears on the FPHS (1973) list.

An extract from *'Hempsted', A History of the County of Gloucester*, 1988, states:

> Some way north of the village by Hempsted Lane the large house called the Newark was established as a residence for the priors of Llanthony in the late Middle Ages. Newark Farm nearer the village was built by the owners of the Newark and Llanthony estate in the earlier 19th Century, probably soon after 1815 when the estate was reorganized at an inclosure (sic).

Any PoWs sent to Hempstead would most likely have been employed in agricultural work.

HENDON (see Mill Hill: Goldbeater's Farm).

HENDRE, GLYN (see Chirk).

HENFIELD (OS: TQ 21- 16-). A working camp, its POWIB (1919) code was Pa (Hn) (IWM: Facsimile K4655). It had the TA Priswarian: Henfield (ADM 1/8506/ 265–120667).

PoWs sent to Henfield were housed in tents in the milder weather, in a field on the north side of the now demolished windmill. Although the mill has now gone the Mill House is still there, just to the east of Mill Drive. In the winter months the prisoners were kept in the Assembly Rooms on the High Street; their guards stayed in the caretaker's cottage at the rear of the building. The shell of the Assembly Rooms survives today and has been converted into shops.

The PoWs most probably worked on the market gardens.

HENLLE PARK (see Preeshenlle).

HENTLAND (OS: SO 530 253). Its TA is cited as Priswarian: Hentland, Harewood End, Hereford (ADM 1/8506/265–120667).

The camp's location has been lost with the passage of time. However, the land adjoining Gillow Manor may hold the key. The Manor House had consisted of four ranges enclosing a courtyard, and was built *c.*1400. It has been restored at various times, but only the Gatehouse survives today. There are several large barns that stand around Hentland that may have sufficed.

HEREFORD: HM Prison (OS: SO 514 402). *The Times* (8 June 1915) cited an unnamed PoW had attempted to escape in a swill bin from the internment camp at Leigh. *The Leigh Chronicle* (11 June 1915) stated the man had almost suffocated. It was reported in *The Leigh Chronicle* (18 June 1915) that he had been sentenced to twenty-eight days in Hereford Gaol.

A new prison was to be built in Hereford on land known locally as The Priory. A Mr Blackburne was chosen to build it, but he died before its construction started. In 1791, the task was then given to Mr Hobson, but his plans were rejected and John Nash was then asked to submit his plans. Nash is famous for designing London's Marble Arch and Regents Park, as well as the Brighton Pavilion. He had also built prisons at Carmarthen and Cardigan.

The main buildings were constructed out of locally produced bricks, and were laid out in the popular cruciform shape of the period. A high brick wall surrounded it. The only entrance to the complex was from Bye Street Without, now known as Commercial Road.

The City Gaol and the County Gaol were both in Hereford. As a result of the Prisons Act (1877) they amalgamated. On 1 April 1878, they came under the auspices of the government, and over the next decade many alterations were made.

The last Governor of Hereford County Gaol was Henry Thomas Pearce. When it closed in 1915, he was responsible for overseeing the transportation of the prisoners to Gloucester Gaol. During the First World War deserters were housed there, as were PoWs. Hereford Goal finally closed in 1929. The County Council purchased the site in February 1930. Reclaimed materials were put up for sale in *The Hereford Times* (28 June 1930). Today the only surviving parts are the governor and deputy governors' houses, which were converted into offices, and toilets for the new bus station.

HERMITAGE (OS: SU 51- 73-). Hermitage, Bucks is cited by the FPHS (1973). However this is probably an incorrect reference to The Hermitage at Crickhowell.

HERSHAM (OS: TQ 118 647). The camp is cited as being at the Drill Hall which was located at 174 Molesey Road. Its TA is cited as Priswarian: Hersham (ADM 1/8506/265–120667). Reports of visits of inspection, by Monsieur Corragioni d'Orelli during June 1919, to PoW camps in the UK, are held at the National Archives at Kew. These records cite a visit to the camp at Hersham (FO 383/508).

HEVENINGHAM (OS: TM 33- 72-). This was an Agricultural Group attached to Haughley AD. Its code was Pa (Hgy) [Hv]. It is cited by the FPHS and its TA was Priswarian: Heveningham, Peasenhall. No further evidence has been found to show where this camp was actually located, but it did close on 18 February 1919.

HINCKLEY (OS: SP 434 939). At the 74th meeting (30 January 1918) of the Leicestershire War Agricultural Executive Committee it was recorded that depots were to be formed for PoW ploughmen at Hinckley, Loughborough, Market Harborough, North Kilworth and Long Clawson.

The Hinckley Times and Bosworth Herald (2 February 1918) reported local concern about German prisoners bring accommodated at the workhouse. Situated on London Road the workhouse was erected in 1837 and had room for 400 inmates. Work did not begin 'effecting the necessary repairs for their reception' until the Board of Guardians met and agreed. Mr Powers reminded the committee that Hinckley was a manufacturing district and there would not be sufficient work for German prisoners to do, because no one would take them on, and he would rather his land 'went out of cultivation' than employ this labour. In seconding Power's motion to desist employing PoWs, Mr Warner pointed out that the townspeople did not desire them in their midst, as over 3,000 Hinckley men were in the forces, and over 200 of them had fallen.

The Finance and General Purposes Committee reported that the army authorities, without the permission of the Hinckley Board of Guardians, had taken possession of a portion of the workhouse for the purpose of housing German prisoners to be employed on the land in the immediate neighbourhood, and the Clerk had been instructed to enter the strongest possible protest against such a proceeding and to ask the Local Government Board – if it was not too late – to take steps to have this arrangement cancelled.

The Hinckley Times and Bosworth Herald reported that The Honourable Gerald Walsh of the Local Government Board stated that fifteen Unions – out of forty-five in the area – had agreed to accept PoWs. The next edition (9 February 1918) reported that PoWs were being housed at the workhouse and misgivings of the Guardians were now being directed at the forty PoWs being housed in the workhouse, as they were fearful of the danger their close proximity to the community could cause.

Druzdz (per. comm., 30 July 1999) divulged that the Urban District Council had also felt that this was the wrong place to accommodate PoWs:

> Accommodation for them at the Workhouse would mean that they would have to pass through the streets of Hinckley daily as he (Mr Kinton) understood the police had made arrangements for their horses to be stabled at the George Hotel, and from the expressions he had heard in the town he was afraid the presence of Germans would lead to unpleasantness ... suggesting Normanton Hall, an isolated residence right in the midst of agriculture would be a lot more suitable and had stabling on the spot.

There were no further reports of the PoWs by the newspaper, but Normanton Hall is listed as being an agricultural group under Loughborough agricultural depot by the POWIB (1919).

HINTON ON THE GREEN (OS: SP 02- 40). The only reference to this camp comes from Frank Green, the Town Clerk (per. comm., 2000). He cites local legend suggesting around six PoWs were billeted in a house in the Hinton on the Green area.

HINTON ST GEORGE (OS: ST 42- 12-). A minute of Somerset County Council WAC (21 May 1918) gave approval for depots for ploughman gangs at Keyford, Priston, Queen Camel, Glastonbury, Wookey, Hinton St George, plus another near Yeovil. The location of the depot is unknown.

HITCHEN: Gangs No. 1 & No. 2 (OS: TL 180 300). K.C. Simpson (*Hertfordshire Countryside* Vol. 14, 1974) cited the compound at Bearton Green Army Camp was used for German PoWs during the First World War. The accommodation used to house them was typical of army accommodation – raised huts constructed of wood. The internees decorated the walls with silhouettes of their companions. Working parties, wearing their distinctive little round forage caps with a red band, were often seen being marched down Bearton Road. On their backs were blue circular patches of cloth.

The minutes of the Hertfordshire County Council WAC record two migratory gangs (numbered 1 & 2) being at Bearton Road.

HOGSTHORPE (OS: TF 53- 72-). This camp was a satellite of Wainfleet; the POWIB (1919) gave its code as Bro (Wai) (Hog) (IWM: Facsimile K4655). Its TA was Priswarian: Hogsthorpe, Alford (ADM 1/8506/265–120667). The FPHS (1973) cite it too.

The location of the camp is unknown. However the key to finding the camp may lie in the Dennett family's ice cream making promotion (www.dennetts.co.uk). A passage reads:

> At the beginning of the First World War, the army took over his (Arthur Dennett's) stables. So Mr and Mrs Dennett moved to Hundleby in 1914 where they worked hard to develop their dairy business.

At the start of the war the army requisitioned horses in large numbers for the front. But if they had also taken over his buildings, it is possible that they could then have been used to accommodate PoWs, when they were organised into labour gangs, post 1916.

HOLBEACH (OS: TF 37- 24-). Nothing is known about this camp, other than it was an agricultural group with the POWIB (1919) code Bro (Wgl) (Hol) (IWM: Facsimile K4655). It was a satellite of Wingland and had the TA Priswarian: Holbeach, Lincs (ADM 1/8506/265–120667). Perhaps the grange at Wingland was used, which in more recent times has gained some notoriety as an adult entertainment centre.

Dr A. de Sturler and Monsieur R. de Sturler visited Holbeach PoW camp during April and May 1919. Their report is held at the National Archives at Kew (FO 383/507).

HOLMBURY ST MARY (see Shere).

HOLSWORTHY: Thuborough House (OS: SS 355 105). HO documentation cites this camp was at Thuborough House and it had the TA Priswarian: Thuborough House, Holsworthy (ADM 1/8506/265–120667). Thuborough is situated some 6 miles to the north of Holsworthy, near to Sutcombe. Nothing is known about this camp other than that HO entry.

HONING (OS: TG 32- 27-). The only evidence to show this camp existed comes from a report of a visit of inspection to the camp by Dr A. de Sturler and Monsieur R. de Sturler, during April and May 1919. It is held at the National Archives at Kew. The grounds of Honing Hall may hold the key to the camp's location (FO 383/507).

HOOK NORTON (OS: SP 35- 33-). This camp is cited by FPHS (1973). It had the TA, Priswarian: Hook Norton (ADM 1/8506/265–120667). Reports of visits of inspection by Dr A. de Sturler during March 1919 to PoW camps in the UK are held at the National Archives at Kew. These records cite a visit to the camp at Hook Norton. (FO 383/506).

HORSHAM: Christ's Hospital School (OS: TQ 149 286). Christ's Hospital School, near to Horsham, was used as a temporary camp for civilian internees. These were mainly men of German or Austrian origin that were arrested whilst travelling as seafaring passengers in British territorial waters. Some were students; others were young men that worked in the catering industry. A few sailors belonging to the German navy were also taken there. A report in *The West Sussex County Times and Standard* of Saturday, 8 August 1914, stated:

> In the early hours of Thursday morning the fine block of schools at Christ's Hospital, which has accommodation for about 1,000 scholars, was taken over by the military authorities for the detention of German PoWs. As a result of naval operations in the North Sea, a large number of Germans have been landed at Sheerness and placed under the custody of the West Kent Regiment, by whom they are being guarded. Brigadier General Anderson is in charge of the arrangements.

Under a sub-heading 'PoWs at Christ's Hospital' it continued:

> At about seven o'clock last evening a batch of twenty-two prisoners arrived at West Horsham from Dover, in the charge of an officer and a detachment of the Royal Sussex Regiment. They reached Horsham town station by motor train from Three Bridges and changed into the Brighton train for Christ's Hospital, being locked into carriages with their armed custodians.

The school's minutes cite four houses were used to accommodate the internees.

Thirty-three sailors, taken from the sunken minelayer *Konigin Luise*, were the third batch to arrive at the school. They had been taken into custody on Monday, 3 August 1914, and had come from Harwich by Great Eastern Railway, under guard by members of the 5th Essex Regiment. The article ended by stating, 'when the paper went to print that there were about 150 Germans being detained in there.'

The same paper reported that on the Monday (10 August 1914), a fourth batch of 219 prisoners, consisting mainly of waiters from the Folkestone area, arrived on a special train, under escort from the Royal Irish Fusiliers. Later that day, at 5.50pm, seventy-two German reservists arrived from Dover, and four more internees arrived at 7.44pm under an escort with fixed bayonets. These arrivals had created some excitement amongst the townspeople. More internees arrived on each of the following days, until there were around 550 incarcerated at the school. They were mainly young reservists who had failed to get back to their own countries before the ports were closed to prevent them leaving. Colonel Hamilton, with a detachment of the West Kent Regiment, was in charge of the camp. 'Whilst they are under close surveillance, exercise is allowed within limits, and it is understood that they are not prevented having daily papers and so on ... Only those to whom "permits" have been issued are allowed to call at the hospital in connection with matters of supply, etc. Each prisoner is allowed one pound of meat daily; and it presumed that those who have what may be termed luxuries or extras have means of paying for them. It is quite possible that a canteen will shortly open on the estate.' The article concluded with another sub-heading, Prisoners Leave For Chester, which stated that 200 PoWs were to be transferred to Chester Castle, via Queen's Ferry, on Thursday, 13 August 1914. They probably went to Queen's Ferry, via Chester instead.

Dr Upcott, the headmaster of Christ's Hospital School, refuted the allegation that German PoWs were 'living off the fat of the land'. This was carried by a London evening newspaper, under the sub-heading 'False Report'. He told his congregation at Itchington Parish Church that they were receiving identical rations to those of their guards: members of the Royal West Kent Regiment. Reports, too, of internees defacing school property, or of them playing football all day, were also denied. They were permitted to use the Great Dining Hall, but only under strict supervision. One hour per day was allowed for exercise, again under guard. The article concluded with an account given by an Austrian who had briefly been at the Hospital School, to a correspondent of the *Manchester Guardian*:

> The Austrians, I was told, started out for Austria on the day after the declaration of war, believing they had twenty-four hours grace in England. They were however seized at Folkestone, and conveyed to Shornecliffe, and then to Horsham. The prisoners were as diverse a body as could be imagined. They included many prosperous businessmen, some waiters, hairdressers, shopkeepers, many students, and musicians, some rather rough Polish miners, who had arrived from America, a few doctors, and one priest. They were prisoners of war because they were all of military age, and were trying to leave the country. The only way they could be released was by an approved English householder becoming surety for their behaviour, and by their taking an oath not to leave the country or to commit any act helpful to the enemy. This gives them a release upon parole, and they are given a permit sealed by the left thumb mark.

Curiously, Bird (*Control of Enemy Alien Civilians in Great Britain 1914–1918*, 1986) makes no reference to this camp. He does, however cite Haywards Heath, where no evidence has been traced to support the existence of an early camp in the First World War.

School minutes state there were initially 630 PoWs at the school. They were shipped out to other destinations to enable the new term to begin on time. A further 200 that arrived were billeted at a temporary camp set up at Sharpenhurst Hill.

A third camp was established in Horsham later in the war.

HORSHAM: North Road (OS: TQ 170 305). For the third time, the citizens of Horsham had internees in their midst, but this time they were not interned at the nearby Christ's Hospital School, or at Sharpenhurst Hill, but in the town itself. Horsham's historical magazine, *The Causeway* (No. 12) states:

In 1918, some 125 German PoWs were held in Horsham for work on the land, and were kept in a disused brewery premises near the corner of Worthing Road and the Bishopric.

Barnes and King, a brewing firm once owned the now disused premises at 25 North Street. This camp's POWIB (1919) directory code was Pa (Hsm) (IWM: Facsimile K4655). The FPHS (1973) cited Horsham only the once. The camp is also cited as having the TA Priswarian: Horsham (ADM 1/8506/265–120667).

HORSHAM: Sharpenhurst Hill (OS: TQ 137 282). The minutes for Christ's Hospital School state that some of the later internees destined for the school were instead accommodated at a camp at Sharpenhurst Hill. Because the school was required for its intended usage, the occupied buildings had to be evacuated by 4 September 1914. As the internees at the school were being moved out, a further batch of around 200 civilian internees joined them at Sharpenhurst Hill. The new site would probably have been an enclosed barbed wire tented site, as it seems to have been used for a brief time. A newspaper report cited fencing being erected.

Later in the war combatant PoWs were sent to Horsham, to be billeted in the former brewery building in North Street.

HOUGHTON (OS: TF 924 354). It was intended to use the stables at Houghton Hall as winter accommodation for internees, but on 2 November 1917, it was reported to the Norfolk WAC (1 February 1918) that the stables would not be available. In February 1918, a further application was made to use them, to house forty PoWs, but no decision was recorded in further minutes, until on 6 July 1918 it was reported that forty PoWs were billeted at Houghton Hall's stables. It was requested on 4 January 1919 that the PoWs be withdrawn from the stables (C/C10/17, 18 & 19).

The camp closed on 13 January 1919. It had the TA, Priswarian: Haughton, Norfolk (ADM 1/8506/265–120667).

HOUGHTON REGIS (OS: TL 015 246). A working camp, its POWIB (1919) code was Pa (Hi) (IWM: Facsimile K4655). It was also cited by the FPHS (1973). This Bedfordshire camp was based at Grove Farm and had the TA Priswarian: Grove Farm, Houghton Regis (ADM 1/8506/265–120667).

HOUGHTON ON THE HILL (OS: SK 663 023). There is a reference to PoWs being at Houghton on the Hill provided by the FPHS (1973). According to the POWIB (1919) there was an agricultural group at Haughton Lodge (sic), with the code Bro (M H2) (Hh) (IWM: Facsimile K4655). This was one of five camps in the Market Harborough area during the First World War. The others were Market Harborough (Nos. 1 and 2), Illston on the Hill and North Kilworth.

HOVE (OS: TQ 283 049). A working camp, its POWIB (1919) code was Pa (Hov) (IWM: Facsimile K4655) . Its address is cited as Brooker Hall, Hove. The FPHS (1973) cite it as Brocker Hall (sic).

Designed, in the very popular Italian style of the day, by Thomas Lainson, Brooker Hall was built for John Oliver Vallance in 1877. Vallance named the house after his father, John Brooker Vallance. It stood in 4.5 acres of land. Vallance died in 1893, but his widow continued to live in the property until her death in 1913. In 1915, the unoccupied house was adapted for use as a fund-raising venue for injured servicemen.

A letter published in the *Brighton Society* of 7 February 1918, signed, 'yours faithfully, Sarcastic', provides a possible clue as to the date when the house became an internment camp. It read, 'I was glad to notice the company of German prisoners being brought into our town and was further gratified to notice that they are being housed in one of Hove's mansion houses.'

A diary belonging to Miss Gladys Austen, a local schoolteacher, suggests the arrival of the PoWs to the Hove area may have been earlier than that suggested by 'Sarcastic'. Her entry for August 1917 cites German PoWs were working in a field, under the supervision of a British soldier with a fixed bayonet. Those seen by Miss Austen may be the ones known to have marched up Sackville Road to work in the orchards.

Apparently, the presence of PoWs in Hove was the result of a need to shift an enormous accumulation of clinker and ash from the local gasworks. Around 50–60 internees were marched daily, under armed guard, between the Brighton and Hove Gas Company's plant at Portslade, and Brooker Hall.

The last of the PoWs left Hove in November 1920. By now, Brooker Hall had gained a searchlight on its roof, manned by men from the 1st Volunteer Battalion, The Royal Sussex Regiment.

Hove Corporation purchased the Hall in 1925 for £4,000. It was to become the town's museum and art gallery, and was formally opened on 2 February 1927. Still used for this purpose today, its surrounding land has been swallowed up in the town's development.

HUNTON BRIDGE (OS: TL 08- 00-). The POWIB (1919) cite a camp at Hunton Bridge, and gives it the code Pa (H B) (IWM: Facsimile K4655). It was also cited by the FPHS (1973). The minutes of the Hertfordshire County Council WAC cite a camp was set up that serviced Hunton Bridge, Langleybury, and Watford districts. On 8 May 1918, an application was made for thirty-five PoWs to be sent to Hunton Bridge, and by 1 October of that year, the camp was operational. It had the TA Priswarian: Hunton Bridge (ADM 1/8506/265–120667).

I

ILCHESTER & LANGPORT WORKHOUSE (OS: ST 434 274). A minute of Somerset County Council's WAC (15 November 1918) recorded the PoWs at Ilchester had been now moved to the Langport Workhouse. This was in a response to an earlier minute (8 November 1918) stating the Quartermaster General had asked for all canvas camps to be struck by 31 October 1918.

The POWIB (1919) only cites Ilchester, recording its code as Dor (Ih) (IWM: Facsimile K4655). Its TA was Priswarian: Ilchester (ADM 1/8506/265–120667). Both Ilchester and Langport are cited by the FPHS (1973).

Langport Poor Law Union Workhouse was opened in 1839, at Picts Hill. It was erected on Sampson Kempthorne's hexagonal plan. It was used as a poultry farm and egg-packing facility but was then left derelict. When the site was put out to tender for residential use in 2004 there were plans to retain the facade of the main building of the workhouse. It was to become Hamdown Court. However the facade fell, which delayed the completion of the project, as accusations were made as to whether this was done on purpose or not. The project has now been completed (per. comm., 22 February 2013).

ILKESTON: Oakwell Colliery Buildings (OS: SK 462 412). Recorded as a satellite of Burton upon Trent, its code was Bro (Brt) (Il) (IWM: Facsimile K4655). According to the POWIB (1919), buildings of the former Oakwell Colliery were transformed into an internment camp.

The Ilkeston Colliery Company was established *c.*1872 and produced coal until it was forced to close in 1913. Most of its coal went to Stanton after a rail link was established in 1883.

As a result of a major fire underground, the owner Lord Belper put the site and that of the adjoining brickworks up for sale. The Oakwell Red and Blue Brick Company went into liquidation in 1930. Thomas Ward of Sheffield was hired to demolish the colliery buildings, according to newspaper reports. Oakwell Dairy acquired the pit's stable area on Derby Road, where it houses its milk floats; beside it stands a filling station, and a car dealership.

The camp was cited by *The Derby Daily Telegraph* (10 July 1918); it had the TA Priswarian: Ilkeston (ADM 1/8506/265–120667).

A minute of the Derbyshire WAC cites the depot at Ilkeston opened on 1 July 1918, with thirty-one prisoners. This number increased to forty-three on 24 September 1918. The last three months of that year recorded that the men on the Day Work Scheme had worked practically 1,000 hours, which equated to each man working four and half days per week. During this period, twenty men, on average, were living out on farms under 'Scheme B'. In that year, partly due to the dead time of the year, a total of 295 days of work had been completed under 'Scheme A' by fifteen men, with twenty men still being away on the farms. Some men had been withdrawn and sent to Ockbrook.

Local legend says two PoWs, not wishing to return to Germany after the hostilities, stayed on in Ilkeston. They continued to work on the farm they had been seconded to as PoWs. It is believed they are both buried in the town's Park Cemetery.

ILLSTON ON THE HILL: The Grange (OS: SP 700 981). *Kelly's Trade Directory* for Leicestershire, 1912, cites Illston-on-the-Hill as being a pleasant village, township and chapelry in the civil parish of Carlton Curlieu. The site of this PoW camp was known to have been at The Grange, which, according the Directory, was a handsome mansion of red brick, commanding some fine views of the surrounding country. Lt-Col. Frederick David Murray Baillie was in residence.

One PoW, probably from the camp at Illston, was interred at Carlton Curlieu (St. Mary) Churchyard in November 1918. He and others buried in Leicester (Welford Road), Loughborough, Market Harborough, Ashby de la Zouch, and North Kilworth, had their remains exhumed and taken to Cannock Chase in the 1960s.

It was correctly cited by the FPHS (1973), but the POWIB (1919) cited it as Illeston. The POWIB (1919) gave it the code Bro (M H2) (Ie) (IWM: Facsimile K4655).

INGWORTH (OS: TG 19- 29-). A minute of Norfolk WAC records G. Dunham's farmhouse, at Ingworth, was an acceptable place to accommodate PoWs working on the River Bures (C/C10/15–19). Dunham's farmhouse is not named as such on contemporary maps.

INVERKEITHING (see Rosyth).

INVERLAIDNAN (see Seafield: Carrbridge).

IRON CROSS (see Chapel Oak).

ISLEWORTH (OS: TQ 149 753). A working camp, its POWIB (1919) code was Fe (Isw) (IWM: Facsimile K4655). It had the TA Priswarian: Isleworth (ADM 1/8506/265–120667). The camp is thought to have been on Warton Road. Local knowledge suggests, during the First World War, the PoWs worked on the Osterley Estates, off Jersey Road.

ITTERINGHAM (OS: TG 15- 29-). The Norfolk WAC informed the Local Government Board that a barn belonging to G. Hawkins, at Itteringham, could be utilised to facilitate PoWs destined for drainage work on the River Bures (C/C10/15–19). There is no named barn belonging to Hawkins on contemporary maps.

ITTON. In their reports on visits of inspection to PoW camps Dr A. de Sturler and Monsieur R. de Sturler, during March and April 1919, cite they visited Itton, but there were two camps, both on farms. One was at Cottage Farm and the other at Howick Farm. They are cited by the Home Office. Itton was omitted from the list produced by Alan J. Brown for the FPHS (1973), but it was included in the lists of Carter, 1937 and Russell (ed.), 1996.

COTTAGE FARM (OS: ST 486 951) and HOWICK FARM (OS: ST 502 955). Their respective TAs were, Priswarian: Cottage Farm, Itton, Chepstow, and Priswarian: Hewick Farm (sic), Itton, Chepstow (ADM 1/8506/265–120667).

Only Cottage Farm is cited by POWIB (1919). A satellite of Leominster, it had the code Shrw (Lmr) (It) (IWM: Facsimile K4655).

IVER HEATH: Black Park (Langley Park) (OS: TQ 024 834). Capability Brown landscaped Langley Park in 1764. A house was built, *c.*1603, for Sir John Kederminster. 'Stiff' Leadbeater converted the house into a hunting lodge for the 3rd Duke of Marlborough in 1758. It received a face-lift in 1860 and according to *Kelly's Directory* of 1914, the owner of the house was Sir Robert Grenville Harvey, who died in 1931.

Page (*Parishes: Iver in A History of the County of Buckingham*, 1925) suggested the northern portion of Langley Park was given over to firs, surrounding a 27-acre lake, planted by Thomas Greening for the Duke of Marlborough. This part became Black Park. Today Black Park is separated from Langley Park by a main road.

It would appear that the internees were based at Black Park, and its TA was Priswarian: Black Park, Iver Heath, Uxbridge (IWM: Facsimile K4655). The camp closed on 10 August 1918. It may be they assisted the Canadians that felled timber, for it is known 150 officers and men of the Canadian Forestry Corps were encamped on the verge of the parish in 1917. It was cited as an agricultural group attached to Denham Lodge agricultural depot; its POWIB (1919) code was Fe (D L) (Lgy).

Black Park and Iver Heath are both cited by the FPHS (1973).

Heatherden Hall is in Iver Heath. It is where the ratification of the agreement for the formation of the Irish Free State took place in November 1921.

IVYBRIDGE: Lee Mill (OS: SX 634 565). A working camp, apparently at Lee Mill, it had the POWIB (1919) code Dor (Iv) (IWM: Facsimile K4655). It is also cited by the FPHS (1973). Contemporary maps show there was an isolation hospital on Beech Road, which may hold the key to where this camp was. Today a mental health unit, known as The Cottage stands on this site.

IWERNE MINSTER (OS: ST 86- 14-). A working camp, its POWIB (1919) code was Dor (Iw) (IWM: Facsimile K4655). Nothing is known of this camp.

Perhaps Clayesmore School may hold the key, once a Manor House, built for Lord Wolverton in 1878 to the designs of Alfred Waterhouse. The estate passed to James Ismay in 1908, a great benefactor to the village. During the First World War he organized food production and also distributed news locally of the conflict. Following his death in 1930 the Manor House became Clayesmore School (www.iwerneminster.info/history).

J

JERSEY: (Blanches Banques). The camp at Blanches Banques on Jersey closed to lower ranks and re-opened to house non-commissioned officers.

MEN'S (OS: n/a). The War Office asked the Jersey government, in August 1914, if they were prepared to accept PoWs temporarily onto the island. The only readily available site they found was the Royal Jersey & Horticultural Grounds, at Springfield. Alterations were completed within a month, but the 4th South Staffordshire Regiment occupied the site instead. A second proposed site to take German officers, at Brighton Road School, was adapted instead to become a military hospital.

In December 1914, the War Office again requested a site on the island for a PoW camp, to accommodate 1,000 male internees. Problems with supplying water made it difficult to provide a suitable location until Blanches Banques (or Quennevais/White Banks), a site previously used for army manoeuvres, was chosen.

With no idea of how an internment camp should look, forty army-styled huts were purchased from Messrs Browne & Lilly of Reading and brought to the island. Local contractors, C.J. Le Quesne, N.H. Harris and T.R. Blampied carried out most of the construction work. Boulton & Paul of Norwich constructed the hospital.

Each hut was heated by an enclosed coal burning stove, and lit by electricity supplied by a generator installed on the site. Ancillary buildings consisted of a bathhouse, a cookhouse and wash-ups, a drying house, ablution and latrines, an office block, a company office and store, quarters for the clerical staff, the guard, the officers, and a hospital and isolation unit. The enclosed area, around 300 yards square, contained most of the buildings. Eight sentry towers backed up a 10-foot high barbed wire perimeter fence that provided the security of the camp.

Naish (*Historical Note on the German PoWs Camp at Jersey during the Great War 1914–1918*, 1920) cites the camp opened on 20 March 1915, with a small intake of internees. A second group arrived two days later, to take the total to 1,000. A third batch arrived on 7 July 1915 to bring the number of PoWs held there up to 1,500, requiring more huts to be built. Of those interned on the island were groups that came from the German navy, with *Könige Luise* and *Mainz* being prevalent names on their headwear.

The guard's strength was estimated to be 130. Around sixty PoWs worked on improving facilities at the St Peter's Barracks. The PoWs erected a recreational hut, donated to the camp by the American YMCA.

Dr Gerhard Günzel spent around two years in internment at Blanche Banques before being moved to Brocton. He was an internee between the autumn of 1914 and September 1919.

In April 1917, 1,200 of their number were transferred to the British mainland to be utilised in work programmes as the Jersey farmers refused to take them. The remaining 300 were employed at St Helier harbour to load potatoes onto ships bound for

England. These were then split into two groups and they departed from the island on the 13th and 16th of February 1917 respectively.

The camp closed on 29 August 1917. It was to re-open again in April 1918, as a camp for NCOs.

Mark (*Prisoners of war in British Hands during WW1*, 2007) cites there were several attempts to escape that all ended unsuccessfully. One PoW tried to escape by cutting the perimeter fence wire. One tunnel was discovered before it could be used; and in July 1917, in another attempt, the tunnellers were re-captured before they could leave the island.

Eight deaths occurred in the camp.

NON-COMMISSIONED OFFICERS (OS: n/a). In 1917, it was decided to remove all the lower ranks on the island, except for 300, back to mainland Britain. They left in two parties on 13 February and 16 February 1917. Those PoWs that remained helped with the potato harvest, by loading ships in St Helier. On the completion of the potato season this party also left the island, on 29 August 1917.

On 12 April 1918 the camp re-opened, this time to accommodate 1,000 NCOs sent to the island. They arrived in batches. Under the Hague Convention, non-commissioned officers were not compelled to work, which was strictly observed by the British Prisoners of war Department.

The camp finally closed on 6 October 1919. According to the *Guernsey Weekly Press* (11 October 1919), around 900 PoWs were put aboard the German steamship *Melitta*, on 5 October 1919, to sail directly to Germany. The rest left the following day.

Naish (1920) cites there were in all six commandants of the camp. These were Lt-Colonels Gregory Sinclair Haines and Ludovic Seymour Gordon-Cumming, Majors Arthur Carew Richards, W.A. Stocker, E.P. Allpress, and Owen Pulley. Except for Haines and Gordon-Cummings, who already held that rank, the rest were all given the temporary rank of Lt-Colonel whilst commanding the camp.

Only one camp is cited as being in the Channel Island's by the POWIB (1919), its code was Jer. Jersey is also cited once by the FPHS (1973) and in a document held by the Osterreichisches Staatsarchive (GZ 9815/0-KA/97).

In the Second World War, when it was known the Germans were about to invade the Channel Islands, all records deemed to be useful to the new administration not taken to mainland Britain were destroyed. It is believed documents relating to Jersey's former internment camp were amongst them.

Note: During the First World War, the Defence of the Realm Act did not apply to The Channel Islands.

JUSTINHAUGH (OS: NO 457 572). An entry for Instinhaugh appears in the listings of the FPHS (1973). However this should have read Justinhaugh, a village lying west of Oathlaw in the County of Angus. Described as a working camp by the POWIB (1919), its code was Stbs (Ju) (IWM: Facsimile K4655). Newmilns of Craigeassie is cited in its address.

K

KEDINGTON: The Institute (OS: TL 703 470). Described as a working camp, its POWIB (1919) code was Pa (Kedn) (IWM: Facsimile K4655). The camp had the TA Priswarian: Kedington (ADM 1/8506/265–120667). Nearby, Haverhill is cited by the FPHS (1973).

Minutes from August 1917 of the Guardians of the Union Workhouse state that a number of PoWs with a guard of thirty-five were billeted in the grounds of Risbridge Union Workhouse, near Kedington. It is believed the PoWs worked on the land.

In 1856, a new building was erected at Kedington, to designs of J.F. Clark. Sometime prior to the beginning of the First World War its name was altered to The Institute. Today, the site is occupied by a housing estate and geriatric care home.

Sir William E. Cuthbert Quiler asked Harold Tennent, the Under-Secretary for War, whether it was proposed to take over the Kedington workhouse as a hospital for soldiers suffering from a contagious disease – and was he aware of the objections of its Guardians. Tennent replied it had been proposed to take over this institution as a hospital, but as the local authorities had objected, other arrangements had been made (*Hansard*, 1 March 1915).

The Times (3 October 1917) cited Wilhelm Buhler absconded from Kedington and was re-caught at Swaffham the following day. *The Haverhill Echo* (14 December 1918) reported that on the Monday morning, Private Harry Coyne of the Royal Defence Corps was proceeding along the road, towards Hundon, with a party of German prisoners when he saw one of his comrades, Private John Hooker lying beside the road, dead. He sent word to his sergeant, and the body was conveyed to the PoW camp at Kedingdon. Coyne said at the inquest that they saw the deceased lying beside the road, 200 yards on the Hundon side of the Plough Inn. It was concluded he had died of heart failure.

KEGWORTH: Sutton Bonington (OS: SK 505 261). The Midland Dairy Institute was opened at Kingston-on-Soar, Nottinghamshire, in 1895 and became the Midland Agricultural and Dairy Institute in 1902. Three years later, its status was upgraded to that of a college and its name was altered again to reflect this. In 1913, as the college grew it was decided to create a new campus at Sutton Bonington, to augment the original college at Kingston-on Soar. The work was completed at the onset of the First World War, and within a few days of all the fittings and machinery being delivered to the new campus, it was taken over by the War Department to serve as a PoW camp for German and Austrian officers. The camp closed on 17 February 1919 and the Sutton Bonington site returned to its intended academic usage. With extensions and renovation, it is now an integral part of the University of Nottingham. The original Kingston-on-Soar campus closed in January 1928.

The PoW officers at Sutton Bonington stayed until the spring of 1919. The college magazine, *Agrimag*, reported:

> The removal of the large number of huts and fixtures – the camp contained as many as 600 prisoners sometimes – and the cleaning and painting was quite a formidable piece of work, but it would have been possible to open the College at the beginning of October (1919) had not the railway strike supervened.

By the time of the First World War, it was becoming common practice for the military to name many of their camps after the nearest railway station, which was not always the nearest township. The camp at Sutton Bonington is a prime example of this. Sutton Bonington is in Nottinghamshire, and was the actual location of the camp. A few miles away stands Kegworth, then the nearest point of embarkation from the railway system to the camp; it was in Leicestershire, but on the border of Derbyshire.

A letter sent from the Chief Constable of Nottinghamshire to the Under Secretary of State at the Home Office, of 1 October 1917, reported that 'At 4.30 in the morning of the 25 September 1917 Sergeant Richards and his men had re-captured three escaped PoWs. Of the twenty-two officers that had escaped that night, eighteen had been captured by the evening of 28 September 1917; the remaining four were arrested in Chesterfield two days later.'

Leutnants Lutz, aged 33, Lehmann, aged 23, and Landsberg, aged 29, were the first three to be caught by Richards and his men. They were caught in the West Bridgeford area of Nottingham. On being taken into custody, they had the following individual property with them:

Lutz, Gustave (aged 33) £7.13s.7d	Lehmann, Emil (aged 23) £1		Landsberg, Erich (aged 29) 5d	
1 purse	1 pair kid gloves	1 compass	1 purse	1 key
1 pipe	1 pair mittens	4 handkerchiefs	1 manicure set	1 knife
1 tin tobacco	1 pencil	1 pipe	1 pot Vaseline	2 pipes
1 local timetable	1 tobacco pouch	3 handkerchiefs	1 pair gloves	1 watch
1 dark kit bag containing:	1 pair scissors		3 tins tobacco	
1 toilet case	3 pairs of mittens		1 bag with scissors	
1 shirt	1 knife		1 pair cuff links	
2 pair socks	1 brush		1 cigarette case	
1 pocket-handkerchief				

Also, in their possession was a suitcase containing:

12 tins of sardines	2 packets of bacon	a number of German sausages
7 tins of milk	8 packets of dried toast	a large quantity of biscuits
1 tin of cheese	4 × 2lb bags of prunes	several packets of cheese
1 tin of rolled ham		& excellent handmade maps

Nottinghamshire's Deputy Chief Constable visited the scene and was able to see how the twenty-two escapees had absconded through a narrow tunnel, which they dug underneath the barbed wire enclosure. Later, it was established that, over a period of time, the internees were able to put the soil from their excavations into the tiered-floor section of an upper floor classroom in the main building, now designated Lecture Room One. When the Chief Constable reviewed the incident, he was dismayed at the security system employed at the facility. He found the camp's commandant had no overall control. It was customary, inside the perimeter, for the internees to police themselves. The military only patrolled the exterior. He was highly critical of having soldiers on guard duty as, in his opinion, they had no formal training for doing the 'job of gaolers'. He found too, the camp's canteen, inside the compound, was run by an independent civilian organisation.

Lehmann had previously escaped, in Manchester, whilst being transferred from the Isle of Man to Kegworth; according to the *Staffordshire Advertiser* (24 March 1917) he was caught near Leek.

Karl Friedrich Max von Müller was accredited as the leader of that escape plan. Von Müller had been the captain of the SMS *Emden* which was forced to run aground at North Keeling Island after being severely damaged by gun-fire from the HMAS *Sydney* of the Australian navy. Along with the rest of the crew rescued from that ill-fated ship, von Müller was taken to internment in Malta. Separated from his crew on 8 October 1916, von Müller was brought to Sutton Bonington. A victim of malaria, he was eventually sent to the Netherlands for treatment as part of a humanitarian prisoner exchange programme. In October 1918 he was repatriated to Germany.

Many who had been detained at Kegworth were later to be transferred to Shropshire. Anecdotal evidence states they were transferred to Oswestry as snow lay on the ground. The internees had to make improvised sleds to take their belongings the mile or so to the railway station. There they had to stand, in the open, in wind and rain for an hour whilst their transport arrived. On reaching their destination, they then had to trudge through thick mud to reach the Park Hall camp.

Early photographs of the college exist, as do some of the internees, taken by the Derby firm of W.W. Winter (see plates). One of photographs has not been fully explained. It clearly shows a man in a dress naval uniform, with one chevron on his arm. He was not an officer, but someone with the rank of Obermatrose of the Kaiserliche Marine. *Unterseeboote* can be visibly read from his cap's headband. As the photograph was taken of him standing in a vegetable patch, he may have worked in the kitchens, or acted as an orderly to the officers, which was permitted.

Dr F. Schwyzer, Dr A.L. Vischer and Dr A. de Sturler compiled reports of their visits of inspection to the officers' PoW camps at Ripon, Skipton, Lofthouse Park, Kegworth and Donnington Hall during February and March 1919 (FO 383/432). The camp's POWIB (1919) code was simply Keg (IWM: Facsimile K4655). It had the TA Priswarian, Kegworth (ADM 1/8506/265–120667). The camp is also cited in a document by the Austrian War Archive dated June 1917 (Egger, Rainer (Dr) (Osterreichisches Staatsarchiv, Wein), per. comm., 30 May 1997).

DKF 19: Major Meyer (Lagerältester in Kegworth) richtete am 5 Juni 1918 einen Bericht an die Schweizerische Gesandtschaft in London: Deutsche Soldaten, die als Ordonnanzen von Brocton nach dem Offizierslager Kegworth gekkommen waren, berichten, daß jeder deutsche Gefangene, der nach Brocton kam oder von dort wegging, nur zwei Taschentücher, zwei Hemden und Unterhosen im Besitz haben durfte; ob die Dinge deutschen oder englischen Ursprung waren, wurde, was mehr war, weggenommen.

DKF 19: Am 10 Juni 1918 schreibt Oberstleutnant Picot, Lagerkommandant von Kegworth, an Major Meyer, daß das Schreiben weitergereicht ist, daß er aber der Meinung sei, daß Meyer nicht berechtigt ist, sich mit den Interessen der in Brocton internierten zu befassen.

DKF 24: Das neben dem Mannschaftslager gleichen Namens errichtete Offiziers-Gefangenenlager Oswestry wurde im September 1918 eröffnet. Zu Beginn des Jahres 1919 wurden einige Offizierlager in England – Kegworth; Margate; Dyffryn-Aled – aufgelöst, um ihren ursprünglichen Zweck (Landwirtschaftliche Schulen usw.) zurückgegeben zu werden.

KEILLOR (OS: NO 270 402). Shrouded in mystery, it is only listed by FPHS (1973) as being the location of an internment camp. The villages of Keillor and Keillour are both in Perthshire some 30 miles apart. Keillor only appears in a list produced by the FPHS in 1973. There are several camps also cited close by. Keillour is not named, but is close to Methven, which is named; and to a camp at Drumbauch (not found in British Gazetteers), which could be Drumbauchly.

KELHAM (OS: SK 743 556). The POWIB (1919) shows this camp as being at Kelham Brickfields, Kelham, Newark, Notts. Its code was Bro (Kel) (IWM: Facsimile K4655). Carlton and Tuxford are cited as its satellite camps. The camp's TA was Priswarian: Kelham (ADM 1/8506/265–120667). It is also cited by the FPHS (1973).

Two days after two PoWs escaped from Kelham, *The Western Times* (5 July 1918) reported their re-capture. *The Times* states they escaped on 1 July 1918.

The Nottinghamshire County WAC minutes recorded German prisoners, using Food Production Department horses and implements, working under British soldier ploughmen.

Another minute (30 July 1918) cited seventeen, unnamed, locations for PoW centres in the county; six were already working, and the others were nearing completion. Proposals for 636 PoWs to complete various tasks in the county were accepted.

During March 1919, Dr A. de Sturler compiled reports on visits of inspection to PoW camps including Kelham, which are held at the National Archives at Kew (FO 383/506).

By 28 January 1919, the number of PoWs working in the area had dropped to 598; by 31 December 1918 that number had dropped by another forty, as the migratory gangs at Bunny, Gotham, Ruddington and Shelford, became redundant. The men were returned to the parent camp at Brocton.

On 28 October 1919, the county's War Agricultural Executive Committee reported the demand for PoWs had fallen off. Seven depots had been closed, and only 229 PoWs remained in the county. The Northern Command then served notice to withdraw the remainder, as a programme of repatriation had started (CC1/4/11–12).

KENDAL (OS: SD 51- 92-). The only known reference to this camp is in a report on visits of inspection to PoW camps. In a document held at the National Archives at Kew, Kendal is cited as being inspected by Dr A de Sturler and Monsieur R. de Sturler in June 1919 (FO 383/508).

Nothing appears to have been recorded as to where the PoWs at Kendal were housed. One possibility was the workhouse on Stricklandgate, at the bottom end of House of Correction Hill, on what is now Windermere Road. It has now been converted for residential use and is known as Strickland Court (www.pastscape.org.uk).

KENILWORTH (OS: SP 284 698). Kenilworth had an agricultural depot with the POWIB (1919) code Dor (Ke) (IWM: Facsimile K4655). It is also cited by the FPHS (1973). Cited as being at Little Woodcote, its TA was Priswarian: Kenilworth (ADM 1/8506/265–120667).

KENNINGHALL (see Uphall).

KERRY – NEWTOWN (OS: SO 154 866). The Cambrian Railway Company upgraded the sidings at Kerry Station in 1917, to take twenty waggons of standard gauge. PoWs from the internment camp, 'above Black Hall in the Rhos Dingle', were used to carry out the work. The depot was then used to take away the timber felled on the Naylor Estate, some 6,000 acres, at Kerry. Christopher Naylor had built the original narrow guage line to remove felled timber from the family's estate, and to take it to their sawmills for cutting.

On their rest day, Sunday, the PoWs were permitted to take a walk around the district, accompanied by two guards. However those PoWs manning the locomotive engine were allowed more freedom and often were permitted to go to the engine shed unaccompanied. Among them was a blacksmith who was willing to repair household utensils, and even fashioned rings from shillings. They were generally liked by the locals, who attended functions run by the PoWs in the summer months, although a photograph (Ray George Collection) of the Black Hall camp exists showing some circular thatched huts that could have belonged to a bygone era and which concerned to the German government. By the summer of 1916, the PoWs were housed in wooden huts equipped with stoves. When visited by the Swiss Delegation at the end of January 1917 they noted conditions had improved.

Kerry-Newtown was an agricultural depot according to the POWIB (1919) directory. Its code was Fg (K N) (IWM: Facsimile K4655). There were satellite camps at Caersws and Welshpool.

The site of the camp was on land belonging to the estate's agent for Brynllywarch Hall. A lane, which was the primary access route to most of the Kerry Forest, dissected the camp. When the camp closed the site was allowed to return to pasture land. It was cited by the FPHS (1973) as Kerry Newton (sic), Mont., and it had the TA Priswarian: Kerry (ADM 1/8506/265–120667).

DKF 34: Aus den Berichten der Schweizer Delegierten aus dem Ende des Jahres 1917 über die Arbeitslager in England geht hervor, daß die Zustände in einigen dieser Lager sich gebessert hatten und daß in manchen dementsprechend das Leben erträglich war. Immerhin geben noch einige Lager zu berechtigten Klagen Anlaß. Trotz wiederholten Einspruchs der deutschen Regierung sind in der Lagern Wingland (Lincolnshire), Ordfordneß (Suffolk), West Tofts (Norfolk), Warren Woods (Norfolk), Glendon bei Keltering (sic), *Stratford on Avon, Kerry (Nord Wales), und Shirehampton (Gloucestershire) die Gefangenen immer noch in Zelten untergebracht.*

DKF 34: Die Versorgung der Gefangenen mit genügender Kleidung und Wäsche ist verschiedentlich sehr mangelhaft. Hauptsächlich in den Lagern Warren Woods, West Tofts, Orfordneß und Kerry wird hierüber geklagt.

KETTLEBURGH (OS: TM 266 610). A working camp, its POWIB (1919) code was Pa (Ket) (IWM: Facsimile K4655). It is cited by the FPHS (1973) as Kettleborough (sic), Suffolk. The camp was cited as being in the Rectory, and had the TA Priswarian: Kettleburgh Rectory (ADM 1/8506/265–120667). Kettleburgh was inspected by Dr A. de Sturler and Monsieur R. de Sturler, during April and May 1919. Their report is held at the National Archives at Kew (FO 383/507).

The rectory and its adjoining farmhouse have been Grade II listed since 1951.

KEYSTON (OS: TL 044 754). Keyston was an agricultural group attached to Oundle; its POWIB (1919) code was Pa (Ode) (Ky) (IWM: Facsimile K4655). It was also cited by the FPHS (1973). Its TA is cited as Priswarian: Keyston, Raunds Station (ADM 1/8506/265–120667).

KIDBROOKE (OS: TQ 414 764). No evidence has been found to support the FPHS (1973) listing. Perhaps Kidbrooke Park, an estate conceived in 1724 may hold the key. A mansion was built in *c.*1734 for William Nevill, the 13th Lord Abergavenney when his main residence at Eridge Park, Kent, was destroyed by fire. It was to remain in the family until the 1790s when they returned to Eridge Park. In 1802, after some neglect, the then Speaker of the House of Commons, the Rt. Hon. Charles Abbot purchased the estate and engaged the services of Humphry Repton to landscape the parkland. In 1874 Henry Ray Freshfield bought the property from the 3rd Lord Colchester and it was in his period of ownership that the house was extended. Sir James Horlick occupied it from 1916 to 1921 with the last private owners being financier Olaf Hambro and his wife Winifred. Large parts of the land have been turned over to provide housing. Some parts have been used in the past by the RAF.

KILBURN: Kilburn Hall (OS: SK 377 458). The Flamstead Community History Group in their publication *Kilburn Hall* show two photographs of Germans gathered in the grounds of the Hall.

A minute of the Ilkeston District of the Derbyshire WAC, dated March 1919, records a Depot was established at Kilburn Hall for the joint use of the Derby District and themselves. It was also stated that it had been very useful to farmers 'on this side of the district'.

During March 1919, Dr A. de Sturler inspected Kilburn Hall. The report is held at the National Archives at Kew (FO 383/507).

A report in *The Derbyshire Times* (8 June 1918) states this camp had been set up, with others. Kilburn Hall is cited by the FPHS (1973), but Denby is not. The camp had the TA Priswarian: Kilburn, Derbyshire.

KIMBOLTON CASTLE (OS: TL 094 674). Scottish architect William Burn was commissioned to build the stable block at Kimbolton Castle in the late 1860s for the 7th Duke of Manchester.

It is cited by the POWIB (1919) as being the location of this working camp; its code was Pa (Kim) (IWM: Facsimile K4655). Kimbolton is cited by the FPHS (1973), as is Stoneley Grange, which is thought to be Stonely Grange.

The castle was converted into a private school in 1950, and the stables were converted into the school's dining hall and music school.

KIMPTON: The Hyde (OS: TL 138 176). The minutes of 8 May 1918 of the Hertfordshire County Council WAC record thirty-five PoWs were based at 'The Hyde', Bower's Heath, Kimpton. The minutes also cite PoWs, designated as agricultural workers, were allocated to Mill Hill from there.

KINGS LYNN. There were three locations used in King's Lynn: Estuary Road, Lynn Recreation Ground, and St James's Hall.

When Dr A. de Sturler and Monsieur R. de Sturler, completed their report of their tour of inspection during April and May 1919 they cited they had visited King's Lynn (FO 383/507). The National Archives has a report of another visit (FO 383/432). The FPHS (1973) cite King's Lynn. Its TA was Priswarian: King's Lynn.

ESTUARY ROAD (OS: TF 61- 21-). A newspaper clipping survives showing internees being escorted from the docks. The nearest location known to have housed PoWs closest to the docks was Estuary Road. The POWIB (1919) cite a working camp with the code Pa (E R) (IWM: Facsimile K4655).

LYNN RECREATION GROUND (OS: TF 626 199). The Library Service in King's Lynn hold a sketch showing Lynn Recreation Grounds during the First World War with tents on it. It is believed to be a PoW camp.

ST JAMES'S HALL (OS: TF 617 198). The POWIB (1919) cites a camp at St James's Hall, King's Lynn; its code was Pa (K L) (IWM: Facsimile K4655). It had a satellite camp at Aldborough.

An obituary to a local solicitor supports the POWIB (1919) claim that there was an agricultural depot based in, or near, St James's Hall. Carried by *The Lynn News* of 16 February 1922, part of it read:

> In the Great War, Mr Beloe was in command of a detachment of the National Reserve Guard, which was quartered in St James's Hall, Lynn. Subsequently, he was transferred to Hunstanton, and during the last two years of the war he was Commandant of the Prisoners of war camps at Burnham Market, Houghton, Snettisham, Summerfield and elsewhere.

This camp closed on 6 January 1919.

KINGSBRIDGE (OS: SX 73- 44-). A working camp, it had the POWIB (1919) code Dor (Kg) (IWM: Facsimile K4655). It is also cited by the FPHS (1973). Its TA is cited as Priswarian: Kingsbridge, Devon (ADM 1/8506/265–120667).

The location of the camp is unknown. However any PoWs sent here may have been billeted in the workhouse which stands on the north side of the town. Built in 1837, it was designed by Thomas Ponsford to accommodate up to 350 inmates. In the 1930s it came under the control of the Devon County Council, and was known as the Public Assistance Institution before becoming Homelands.

In January 1959, the central part of the buildings was severely damaged by fire. The buildings were then used as a furniture store, agricultural engineering workshops, and flour and corn store. The surviving buildings are today used by various small businesses (www.southhams24.co.uk).

Alternatively the PoWs may have been housed in the former grammar school in Fore Street.

KINGSBURY EPISCOPI (OS: ST 43- 21). Described as being a working camp, it had the POWIB (1919) code Dor (Ks) (IWM: Facsimile K4655). There is an entry for Kingsbury in the FPHS (1973) listings. The camp's location is unknown.

KINGSTON SEYMOUR (OS: ST 22- 29-). Minutes of the Somerset WAC show fifty-five PoWs were transferred from Sandhill Park to Dulverton, Bridgwater, Thorloxton, Kingston Seymour and Clavelshay in equal numbers. Five remained at Sandhill Park, and were being billeted in cottages on the estate, but it is unknown where those sent to Kingston Seymour were housed.

KINGSTON UPON HULL (OS: TA 098 285). To hold, and detain, those arrested as enemy aliens at the start of the war two ships moored in the docks at Kingston upon Hull were sequestrated. They were the SS *Borodino* and the SS *Calypso*.

SS *BORODINO* (GRT: 1,970. Passengers: 1st = 27). The *Hull Daily Mail* (Saturday, 8 August 1914) reported that about 170 Germans had turned up to register themselves with the police the previous evening, in response to the government's new edict that they should do so. About half of them had been interviewed and released, but the remainder, which included some sailors, liable to service in the German Navy, were detained. They were taken to the SS *Borodino*, which was standing in the dock. The court was also removed to the ship so that the magistrates could hear cases. *Hull Daily Mail* (Wednesday, 12 August 1914) stated the crew of a ship were taken away from Parliament Street Police Station in a motor charabanc, probably to the *Borodino*, where other Germans were being kept prisoner. *Hull Daily Mail* (Thursday, 20 August 1914) cited there were now over 300 Germans and Austrians under detention at Hull, mostly Germans. The paper reported that until the previous day they had been held on the *Borodino*, but they had now been transferred to the *Calypso* in the Albert Dock.

Built in Hull in 1911 by Earles Shipbuilding & Engineering Company, for the Wilson Line, the SS *Borodino* was, at around 1,970 tons, intended for the Baltic trade. Along with a refrigerated cargo space for mainly eggs and butter, it could also carry twenty-seven first class passengers. She was requisitioned in December 1914 as Merchant Fleet Auxiliary No. 6, a stores ship, and after being refitted in London, was stationed at Scapa Flow and operated by Junior Army & Navy Stores Ltd until release in February 1919. She was requisitioned again in 1939, and, along with the *Atlantic Guide*, was sunk as a block-ship at Zeebrugge on 27 May 1940.

SS *CALYPSO* – HMS *CALYX* (GRT: 2,876. Passengers: 1st = 45, 2nd = 46, steerage = 200). SS *Calypso* was built in 1904 for The Wilson Line, as a Scandinavian immigrant ship. It also had three refrigerated cargo holds that could be modified as additional accommodation for 570 passengers.

In August 1914, whilst standing in the Albert Dock at Hull, she was commandeered to serve briefly as a prisoner of war ship. Some Germans previously held aboard the SS *Borodino* were transferred to her at the beginning of August 1914, before being taken to Lancaster at the end of the month. *The Lancaster Observer* (28 August 1914) cites a party of internees had arrived at Lancaster from Hull.

Weighing some 2,876 tons it was taken over by the Admiralty in November 1914, and renamed HMS *Calyx*. It was fitted with eight 4.7-inch and two 3-lb guns at Hull, and employed as an Armed Merchant Cruiser from December 1914 until March 1915. She was de-commissioned and returned to the Wilson Line in June 1915. En route from London to Christiania, with general cargo, she was torpedoed by *U53* in the Skagerak, off Jutland, on 10 July 1916. The master and all thirty members of her crew were lost.

The William Wright Dock, built in 1873, could only be accessed through Albert Dock until 1910, the latter being built in 1869. In the 1950s, both docks underwent redevelopment. They were then closed to commercial traffic in 1972. Today the docks are open for the fishing industry, general cargo and ship repairs.

KINGTON (see Dolyhir).

KINLOCHLEVEN (OS: NN 291 632). The second of the two camps that was built on one of the few areas of flat ground situated in the Leven valley alongside the River Leven, it measured some 720ft by 320ft, and took its name from the village of Kinlochleven. A plan of the camp shows thirteen huts and ancillary buildings (laundry, washrooms, latrines, kitchen, theatre, workshops, and a hospital). Other features included a parade ground, a detention block, a sergeants' mess, and the guard and officers' quarters, which overlooked the general area. A railway line ran through the camp, which terminated at the 'Temporary Factory'.

Ciaran Water lies to the east of Kinlochleven, which supports the notion that these men worked on the pipeline from Loch Eilde to the Blackwater Reservoir. Evidence suggests that to get to work each day the PoWs walked along the pipeline to an old railway track, then crossed a bridge. This camp can be reached by walking on the north side of the river, up the Ciaran Path. The construction of the pipeline was a result of the smelter's need for a hydroelectric power supply. The intended source of water, Blackwater Reservoir, proved insufficient and was to be supplemented by drawing more from Loch Eilde, some 5 miles away. The construction was done by Balfour Beatty and took two years to complete. A letter written by the Lorn District Surveyor, in January 1918, suggests PoWs should be set to work on the Kinlochleven stretch of road immediately, as their work on the reservoir's pipes was almost completed. He saw no reason for waiting until the Caolasnacon camp had become operational again. The new road would provide better land access to the village that was previously best served by bringing supplies by boat up Loch Leven. It became known locally as the German Road and today is registered as the B863.

No date for the opening of this camp is known, but German archival material states three PoWs were killed at Kinlochleven when huts were blown over on the night of 14 October 1916; twenty-five more were injured as the storm raged. Originally, the men slept under canvas. Some tents, erected in the path of a dormant mountain stream, were washed away in an incident that occurred prior to the fatalities. Records held by the Regional Council suggest the PoWs were buried in Duror Cemetery, and the German War Graves Commission were able to confirm twenty-eight graves were transferred from there to Cannock Chase in the 1960s. A likely scenario is that the PoWs themselves built the camp, under the supervision of Balfour Beatty staff, whilst they were being accommodated in tents.

The kitchens at Kinlochleven did not meet with the approval of the internees, and according to the same documentary source, there was never enough fuel to heat their food. Despite this, the villagers and internees were on friendly terms and there are suggestions of concerts taking place at the Lagern Theatre, and PoWs doing 'odd jobs' for the townsfolk. The conscientious objectors were never given this respect. Although food rationing in the area was severe, the locals still managed to donate parcels to those interned. It was said the internees insisted on paying and in return would manufacture rings from silver coins or make wooden toys that were given to local people. But this fraternisation has to be tempered against the revelation that PoWs on their arrival into these camps were told that to cross a wire set around the inside perimeter, known as the 'Death Line', would only be to their detriment. This paradox of human nature is further compounded when some of the internees settled in the area after the war. One PoW, Arnold Mayer, stayed on in Kinlochleven, married a girl from Glencoe, and worked at the aluminium plant.

The Times (16 August 1918) reported Karl Konig and Daniel Schneider had escaped the previous day. There is no report of their capture. *The Dundee Courier* (16 August 1918) also reported their escape.

This camp, a working camp, had the POWIB (1919) code Stbs (Ki) (IWM: Facsimile K4655). There is also an entry for Kinlochleven in the list produced by the FPHS (1973). Its TA is cited as Priswarian: Kinlochleven (ADM 1/8506/265–120667).

KINTILLO: Bridge of Earn (OS: NO 135 175). The village of Kintillo is the oldest known recorded surviving village in Scotland today, close to Bridge of Earn; it dates back to at least 1260.

The internment camp is believed to have stood at Kintillo Farm, which has now gone to make way for a housing estate. Described as a satellite of Auchterarder, the camp's POWIB (1919) code was Stbs (Au) (Ki) (IWM: Facsimile K4655). Kintillo is approximately 14 miles to the east of Auchterarder. The FPHS (1973) cites Bridge of Earn in its *List of British Prison Camps*.

KIRKBY STEPHEN (OS: NY 777 089). In 1810, the Gilbert Union took over a cotton mill to the north of St Stephen's church in Kirkby Stephen for use as a workhouse. When the East Ward Poor Law Union came into being on 31 October 1836, it took it over, and enlarged the site. The entrance was on the southern side of the site with receiving wards to its east and stores to its west. At the south-west corner were the board-room, master's office, and a nursery. The kitchen with a dining room was to its north. Female vagrants' wards were at the south east, with male vagrants' wards and the infirmary at the north-east. The main building lay to the north-west, with the ground floor accommodating able-bodied women and old men. After 1930, the workhouse became Eden House Public Assistance Institution. The buildings no longer exist, and the site has now been redeveloped for housing.

In July 1918, it was reported that no British soldiers would be available for farm work that year, but German PoWs prisoners would be available instead from about the second week in August. The *Carlisle Journal* reported that provision had been made for accommodating thirty PoWs and six guards at the workhouse at Kirkby Stephen. Similar arrangements were made at Wigton that the authorities would pay 3d per head, each day from 15 August 1918.

Kirkby Stephen has a station on the Settle to Carlisle Line that belonged to the former Midland Railway Company.

KIRKOSWALD (OS: NY 55- 41-). The *Carlisle Journal* cited two tents at Kirkoswald were used to house ten PoWs that had been brought from Rowrah to do harvest work. Similar gangs had been despatched to Langwathby and Culgaith. An editorial in the *Carlisle Journal* reported there had been complaints about the degree of freedom allowed to these men. But the editor had a 'good word for German labour, especially those selected for farm work'.

In September 1918, the migratory camp scheme was reported in the *Carlisle Journal.* Gangs of ten German prisoners, with two guards to each camp, had been established in twenty-five camps in Cumberland. All were operating very satisfactorily.

Kirkoswald shared a railway station with Lazonby on the Settle to Carlisle Line.

KNEBWORTH (OS: TL 25- 20-). A minute from the Hertfordshire County Council WAC, dated 22 July 1918, cited a migratory gang, consisting of ten PoWs and a guard, had been approved for Knebworth. A later minute, dated 10 January 1919, indicated had Knebworth had closed. These minutes also state PoWs previously allocated at Hatfield had been engaged in agricultural work in the Stevenage and Knebworth areas of the county.

KNIGHTWICK – MARTLEY (OS: SO 75- 59-). Formerly known as Knightwick, this was a working camp with the POWIB (1919) code Dor (Mrt) (IWM: Facsimile K4655). Both Martley and Knightwick are listed by the FPHS (1973). The camp had the TA Priswarian: Martley (ADM 1/8506/265–120667).

No physical evidence has been found to suggest where this camp was. Perhaps The Noak, purchased by James Nash *c.*1665 and rebuilt in 1853, holds the key. Worcestershire historian, Reverend Tearaway R. Nash, once owned this house.

Records show 2nd Lieutenant C. Sprague commanded the camp, and it had twenty-five PoWs billeted there, as of 31 December 1917.

KNOLL HILL (see Twyford).

KNOCKALOE: Peel (OS: SC 240 820). Seeking to open more places of internment, the HO's Civilian Internment Camps Committee visited the Isle of Man on 24 October 1914 to seek suitable sites to supplement the camp at Douglas, which was operating at the time of their visit. The site they chose was beside a farm on Knockaloe Moor, 2.5 miles southeast of Peel. It was a site used by the Territorial Army as a camping ground. It was envisaged the camp would hold 5,000 internees. The supply of fresh water required for such a camp could be provided by tapping into the mains that supplied Peel. However, the surface water that accumulated on the site due to the heavy clay could be problematic and so it was believed that by laying an abundance of cinders the problem should be cured and permanent pathways could be maintained. They also chose to raise the hutments from the ground to allay any possible objections to the choice of the site.

The camp initially opened as a tented site in November 1914, and once established it was then to become the principal camp in Britain for the internment of enemy alien civilians during the First World War. Eventually the camp would cover an area of approximately 7 square miles, and it was estimated that around 700 miles of barbed wire was required to enclose it. A railway spur, from Peel, was added to serve the camp.

The first commandant of the camp was Lt-Colonel John M. Carpendale. Under his command, the first internees to be transferred to Knockaloe were a batch that came from the Frith Hill camp.

Chandler Hale, on behalf of the US Embassy in London, visited the camp on 24 November 1914, investigating reports of a riot caused by unrest in the camp. On the day of his visit he noted there was still considerable discontent amongst the internees. As part of his investigation he was informed food, previously available to order by post from London and elsewhere, had been stopped. This was because a German newspaper had been smuggled into the camp in a sausage. All sausages in future had to be purchased from the camp's canteen. Even cigars were cut open for examination. In an attempt to reduce the tension, British newspapers were to be permitted. Hale noted there were two separate compounds, interning some 2,000 men in total. In each compound were blocks of huts. Each block comprised six 30ft by 15ft huts grouped together that were capable of housing 180 men. The bunks were organised three high against a central partition, and two high around the longer walls. Tables and benches occupied the spaces between. Each hut was equipped with a stove for heating, and was lit by electric light. The showers were in a separate building. The food, prepared by the Germans, was stated to be generally good. There was also ample hospital accommodation. He described the camp as being in a hollow, on clay soil. Attempts to lay cinder paths on the mud had not been successful. Wooden planks were being used for a road surface. Within the enclosures there was little space for exercise, and there was no work available except for camp duties. Marches, under guard, were allowed, but in the inclement weather most internees preferred to stay in their huts, reading, playing cards, etc. No deaths had been reported at the time of his visit.

With the passage of time, and the need to intern more civilians, it was decided to create more than one camp at Knockaloe. The eventual population would grow to around 23,000, detained in five camps. Each of these camps consisted of between five and seven compounds. Compounds generally held 1,000 men. John Jackson of the US Embassy in London wrote that because of time constraints he did not visit the camp on 9 February 1915, when he published his findings on visits to other camps.

The Times (2 March 1915) cited 500 civilians were moved from ships moored off Southend on Sea to the Isle of Man. The article said the use of the ships had been a temporary arrangement until more suitable accommodation could be found. A few of the civilian internees from the ships had gone to London, but the majority were split between the camps at Knockaloe and Douglas. A statement, read in the House of Commons at this time, cited there were 2,587 internees at Knockaloe, with a similar number being interned at Douglas.

Cohen-Portheim (*Time Stood Still: My Internment in England*, 1931) states, from the end of May 1915, he was interned at Knockaloe for two months. He described the compound he was allotted to as 'a dozen or more long, low wooden huts, each of which housed about forty men'. The facilities had not been completed when he arrived. There were too few latrines and washing facilities. Apparently the plan had been to build a camp, and then intern the aliens. However the government was forced to give way to popular feeling after the sinking of the *Lusitania* in May 1915, after which the camp had virtually doubled in size. He was permitted to write, twice a week, on one page of glazed paper. However, he said, he and his fellow internees were forbidden to mention either the war or conditions in the camp; and all letters had to pass a censor. He was eventually moved, with sixty others, to Wakefield.

A second delegation, led by John Jackson of the US Embassy in London, visited the camp on 9 February 1915. At the time of the next US Embassy visit, on 19–20 June 1915, it was reported that there were now 8,470 internees on site. They were all civilians. Some 2,000 had arrived the previous week and it was envisaged that more would arrive in the ensuing weeks in groups of around 1,000, until all five sub camps were full. A playing field of 22 acres had been added for around 2,000 internees to use each day. It was noted that 510 men were still living under canvas, but they would be moving into wooden huts. Since the last visit there had been three deaths.

In August 1915, an internee described the conditions at Knockaloe as no better or worse than those at Newbury or Douglas.

Another visit from an US Embassy-led delegation (September 1915) noted the reduction in overcrowding in three of its camps. Camp IV was half full. However, a further intake of internees, estimated to be around 2,000, was envisaged.

The Times (4 October 1915) cited Sir William Byrne of the Home Office had revisited the island in connection with more to be interned. Byrne had been instrumental in setting up the camp at Douglas.

The Times (24 October 1915) reported that K. Buda, an internee, was given a two months custodial sentence for the unlawful wounding of P. Oswild, the Assistant Postmaster. He had been caught stealing letters addressed to other PoWs.

With the onset of winter that year, the weather had deteriorated and complaints began to be heard about the poor weatherproofing of the huts, and of the stoves being inadequate to provide heating. The mud was everywhere and there was a lack of dry clean clothing to wear. Twenty-eight deaths were recorded.

At the time of the US Ambassador's inspections on 8 January 1916, there were 21,387 men being interned at Knockaloe.

The Times (15 January 1916) cited four unnamed sailors had escaped on the Isle of Man. They were recaptured at Peel harbour according the paper two days later. Named as W. Druschke, E. Muller, R. Wilcher and W. Pederson, they had tunnelled out from under the floor of the theatre in Compound 1 of Camp II, a distance of 89 yards.

The Times (3 March 1916) reported the Manx gaol was too small to hold convicted German internees and military offenders; therefore some prisoners had to be transferred to Liverpool.

Lieutenant-Colonel Francis William Panzera, a Boer War veteran, who had previously been the commandant at Libury Hall, succeeded Carpendale as commandant in February 1916. Panzera died on 4 June 1917, and had to be replaced by Lieutenant-Colonel Bertram Metcalfe-Smith.

On 16 April 1916, an incident occurred in Camp IV which resulted in three internees being shot. An internee had sought refuge with a guard after being chased by other internees. When a crowd gathered, and refused to disperse, shots were fired. As a result August Uccusie, who later sought compensation from the British government, and two others, were wounded.

A delegation from the US Embassy in London again visited Knockaloe. Their visit lasted three days, from 29 April to 1 May 1916. Their report stated that there were 20,563 men interned at Knockaloe. The breakdown, per camp was:

Location	*Sub-Commandant*	*Previous Visit January 1916*	*This Visit April/May 1916*
Camp I	Major A.B.R. Kaye	5,749	5,627
Camp II	Major H.N. Fyfe-Scott	4,423	4,622
Camp II	Major J. Quayle-Dickson, DSO	4,640	4,846
Camp IV	Major A. Nodin	6,148	5,873

Of these 16,936 were Germans, 3,382 Austrians, 101 Turks, and 144 other nationalities.

Thomas (*St Stephen's House: Friends Emergency Work in England 1914–1920*, 1920) had described four sub camps, divided into compounds of 1,000 men. She also stated the hospital was on the upper slopes, attached to Camp III, but the embassy team cited each camp had its own hospital. There were 192 patients in hospitals at the date of their visit. There was also an isolation hospital, which may have been the hospital cited by Thomas. The number of reported deaths in the camps was now forty-two. Burials had taken place at Patrick Church, which stood close to the camp. It was also noted two internees were in the cells.

By May 1916 some 30 acres of land outside the camp had been turned over to growing vegetables. Civilians were never forced to work, but many volunteered, either to make some money to send home to their families, or just to escape what became known as 'barbed wire disease'. About 72 per cent of the internees at Knockaloe were now employed as bootmakers, tailors, joiners, cap workers, plumbers, woodworkers, gardeners, latrine men, police, coal and railway workers, quarry workers, post office and parcel post workers, etc.

The Isle of Man Examiner (26 May 1916) wrote of fears that men from Ireland involved in the earlier uprising had been brought to Douglas by steamer, to be interned at Knockaloe. But these were the internees from Oldcastle, recalled by Murphy (per. comm., 1997), that had been put on a train one Sunday afternoon watched by the townsfolk who cheered them off. One of the last big batches to arrive at Knockaloe came from the Stobs Complex at Hawick, in July 1916.

The Times (8 August 1916) commented on a letter of praise, published in the German press, for the commandant, Lt-Colonel Panzera.

The Times (15 August 1916) cites an apparent escape of a man named Kanopa. He is found in the camp two days later. Another statement from the House of Commons revealed the camp's population was now 22,435. This figure included 2,500 men over the age of 45.

The Times (19 October 1916) reported a tunnel had been discovered. When the captain of that compound was arrested, the other captains resigned in protest. At a meeting to nominate new captains, one speaker tried to dominate the proceedings and was arrested. A riot then ensued, where the captains were attacked and beaten. The arrested man was taken out of the camp. According to *The Isle of Man Weekly News* (28 October 1916) a military court was convened where three of the internees, A. Beirich, W. Wunderle and O. Kohler, were all charged with mutiny and assault.

As the numbers of internees grew, so did the need for more men to police the external perimeter. The solution was to merge the guard from both the Knockaloe and Douglas camps. On 24 February 1917, Brigadier Edward A D'Arcy-Thomas,

CMG, was appointed the Area Commandant. He was based in Douglas and had a pool of 2,500 guards at his disposal, to cover the whole island.

When the Americans severed their relations with the Central Powers, they relinquished their role as neutral observers and were replaced by Swedes and the Swiss. In London, the War Office amended its scale of rations to be given to each PoW; issued on 22 February 1916, it was to come into effect on 2 March 1916. Unrestricted submarine warfare, by the Germans, was the reason given for the change, as it was having a detrimental effect on the amounts of imports into the country, especially of grain. The calorific level of the new rations was questioned, and was found to be wanting, by the Swiss. The change to the diet was reported in *The Times* (9 March 1917). A new scale of rations was issued by the Manx government, which was again challenged as being inadequate by Dr Taylor, from the University of Pennsylvania. He calculated that a non-working internee needed at least 2,400 calories a day. It was later calculated that Britons in internment in Germany, between June and October 1916, were receiving between 1,750 to 2,050 calories per day.

The Times (10 March 1917) reported the escape of five internees two days earlier. These were W. Brinkmann, J.P. Cullsen, F. Harris (all seamen), L. Oezvick (a stoker) and A. Ahlers (a clerk). All five were recaptured, in a small cove on the west coast of the island. *The Times* (12 March 1917) reported two more had escaped three days earlier. They quickly were recaptured, but not named.

The Times (18 April 1917) reported eleven Germans had been charged with various charges, mainly for theft and breaking into stores.

In May 1917, Dr A.L. Vischer, a Swiss observer, inspected the camp. He noted, and informed the Home Office, that depression was rife in the camp. He advised more could be done for those less than 20 years of age. Although segregated, he thought they needed better mentoring. A delegation that visited on behalf of Sweden concluded a much more relaxed regime would be better for all the internees on the island (FO 383).

Around the middle of 1917 about 1,000 internees on the Isle of Man had volunteered for agricultural work, whilst another 900 worked in quarries or on road building schemes. Some internees went to Corby. Work gangs were set up at Regaby and Ballaugh. In 1916, a gang of around 200 had set about canalising the River Sulby. They were augmented by a further 100 men in 1917. Interned civilians were not required to work, but many did to support their families, who relied on charity with the loss of their breadwinner.

A series of escapes on the Isle of Man was reported in *The Times*: on 15 May 1917, it was reported that Wojesch Kazakewics had escaped; on 25 May 1917, that Joseph Isher, Otto Muller and Heinrich Agathen had been taken back into custody after escaping four days earlier. Again, *The Times* (28 August 1917) reported Freidrich Sherberth and Hermann Gross had escaped five days earlier. It was reported on 8 September 1917 that they were back in custody. A second report stating von Verman had escaped was refuted in the edition of 29 September 1917.

The Times (9 November 1917) cited PoWs employed in road-making in Monmouthshire had been transferred to the Isle of Man.

The Times (21 November 1917) stated five unnamed internees from Knockaloe were imprisoned for between six and nine months for breaking into a store.

In November, it was noted by the Swiss observer that the under 21s had been moved to Compound 8, in Camp IV. The person in charge of this unit changed several times, and finally the trial was aborted and the young men were re-distributed to various areas of the camp by the end of that year.

Belfield (*Report on the Directorate of Prisoners of War*, 1920) cited around 900 men, from both the Knockaloe and Douglas camps, were employed in quarrying and road-work activities, outside of their camps. Most returned to their respective camps each night, but some temporary work camps existed around the island. He also cited the River Sulby was canalised with PoW labour. During December 1917, the internees at Knockaloe were encouraged to produce furniture. The scheme was then recommended to the Home Office by the Civilian Internment Camps' Committee. It was to be sponsored by a distress fund, run by the Society of Friends (HO 45/11025/68577).

Baily (*Craftsman and Quaker: The Story of James T. Baily 1876–1957*, 1959) wrote that James Baily, a Quaker, watched as the last 175 internees marched out of the camp, under escort, en route to freedom. He had been their supervisor when they produced many useful articles, as well as souvenirs and knick-knacks. Under his supervision the internees made furniture to special order, as well as pre-fabricated housing and flat-pack furnishings for the homeless in the devastated areas of northern France and Belgium.

Within the camp, internees published various newspapers. Two titles produced were the *Knockaloe Lager-Zeitung* and *Lager Echo*.

The Times (23 March 1918) cited that three half-hour visits per quarter for non-resident visitors and one half-hour visit per two weeks for IoM residents were allowed on the Isle of Man.

The Isle of Man Examiner (6 April 1918) reported that Alfred Clague, William Christian and Phillip Killey had been charged with illegally trafficking with PoWs. Apparently cigarettes, margarine, bacon and sausages were found on the prisoners when they were searched on their return from working in a quarry.

The Times (11 April 1918) reported six internees from Knockaloe had escaped. They were cited as Freidrich Schmidt, August Stander, Carl Schlander, Victor Ehlerb, Paul Stoffel and Baron von Theodar Jugenfeld. The *Isle of Man Examiner* (20 April 1918) reported they had been recaptured at Port Erin on Saturday night (the 14th).

The Isle of Man Examiner (4 May 1918) cited Albert Czoborn and Heindrich Vogler were respectively convicted of stealing flour and breaking into a warehouse. Each was sentenced to two months in prison. Ferhand Mustapha was sent down for twelve months for wounding a fellow PoW. The suicide of Friedrich Charles Brandauer, a manufacturer of pens, was also reported; he poisoned himself with veronal.

Carl Herman Diderich Melloh was reported missing and suspected of escaping on Friday 24 May 1918, but he was found hiding in the camp on the Saturday.

The Isle of Man Examiner (1 June 1918) reported that around 500 aliens had arrived at Douglas by steamer on the Sunday evening (26 May 1818) and were taken by train to Knockaloe. Rumour of their pending arrival from Dublin prompted speculation that they were Irish Nationalists. But this was unfounded. They were probably the internees from Oldcastle that Murphy (per. comm., 1997) recalled leaving on a train one Sunday afternoon, with the townsfolk lined on both sides of the railway track, waving and cheering them off. It was also noted at this period of time that forty-eight internees suspected of having criminal backgrounds were to be kept in isolation in Compound 4 of Camp 3. They had previously been held at Brixton Prison. The government stated they had been moved at their own request. These could have been Irishmen, as there is no record of German nationals being interned at Brixton.

The Times (14 September 1918) cited Karch, Lassen and Gey were charged with altering records to enable men to be released quicker. Working as clerks in the camp's Post Office they falsified the ages of internees on their records, because priority for release was given to men over 45 years of age.

The Times (19 September 1918) stated Robert Peters had escaped whilst on parole from Knockaloe. He was visiting Oadby, in Leicestershire.

When the Lofthouse camp was to be closed for civilian use, the internees were transferred to Camp 4 at Knockaloe between 8 and 10 October 1918. Camp 4 then took on Wakefield's former status of being a privileged camp.

When the Armistice came in November 1918 it did not bring a quick release, as had been hoped, to those interned at Knockaloe. The expectation was they would be released quickly and allowed to return to their British homes, but they were to be disappointed because the Home Office attended to their travel arrangements in a very lackadaisical way. By February 1919 there were some 16,000 still in internment on the island. The last 278 internees at Knockaloe were to be moved to Islington on 25 September 1919, but a railway strike further delayed their transfer.

Knockaloe closed at the end of September 1919. The wooden buildings of the camp were dismantled and re-used all round the island as British Legion huts. The site of the camp became an experimental farm.

There were approximately 130 graves of civilian internees buried in Kirkpatrick's Holy Trinity Churchyard. Most of these were exhumed and taken to Cannock Chase in 1962, to the German War Cemetery. Of the graves that remained, new headstones were erected, the majority of which bear Turkish names.

KNUTSFORD: HM Prison (OS: SJ 751 784). This camp was cited by POWIB (1919), and had the code Hfth (Ku) (IWM: Facsimile K4655). It was also cited by the FPHS (1973).

The gaol was built in 1818 to plans drawn up by the architect, George Moneypenny, standing on what is now Stanley Park. At least seven executions took place inside the prison before it was used first as a military prison at the end of 1914. In the months of May and June 1916, it has been suggested 599 Irishmen that took part in the Easter Rising were sent to Knutsford Prison.

On 1 June 1916, Pierce McCan, an activist in the campaign to free Ireland from British rule was brought to Knutsford from Ireland. On 10 June, he and four others were placed in solitary confinement on orders that emanated from the War Office. Why is not exactly clear, but they were leaders of the insurgency. Early in July, McCan was transferred to Reading Jail along with Darrell Figgis, Thomas MacCurtain, Terence MacSwiney, Ernest Blythe, Arthur Griffith, Eamon O'Duibhir, Seamus Robinson and Con Deere.

At the start of the war, it is thought civilian internees were detained in the gaol.

The gaol is known to have held Conscientious Objectors. Referred to as 'Peculiar People' in many quarters of society, they were transferred to Knutsford from Wormwood Scrubs, to reduce overcrowding there. The *Knutsford Guardian* (7 December 1917) cited the librarian and caretaker had exceeded their authority when COs had been turned away from the library and reading room on 17 and 24 November 1917. When the matter was discussed in Council, the chairman, Reverend G.A. Payne, stated that he had no sympathy with the views of the COs; but they had all expressed themselves willing to do work of national importance, and they had already been punished. Doctor Fennel confessed he disliked them intensely, but did not think they

wo photographs taken almost eighty years apart. (*Left*) The photograph of the three German officer risoners of war standing in that elusive doorway at the Kegworth Camp. (*Right*) Stan Cramer tanding in that same doorway at Sutton Bonington.

an-Henri Dunant, *c.*1860 (see pp. xv–xvi).

Winifred Carney, *c.*1912 (see p. 11).

The former Upper Strathearn Combination Poorhouse as it looks today (see p. 9).

Helena Moloney (see p. 11).

Countess Constance de Markievicz (see pp. 11–12, 191 & 304).

:empshott House (see p. 16).

'rottesley Hall (see pp. 61–2 & 99).

Barle Combe House as it is today, originally home to Dulverton camp (see pp. 86–7).

Ex-PoW camp on 25 North Street, Horsham. At the time of the war the building was a disused brewery (see pp. 144–5).

Brooker Hall, Hove (see pp. 145–6).

Kilburn Hall (see pp. 155–6).

Lewes Naval Prison became a place of internment for German PoWs in 1916 (see p. 178).

Nocton Hall, pictured in 1999 before the fire (see p. 219).

Nocton Hall as it looks today after the fire of 2004 left the building decimated (see p. 219).

Ragdale House, *c.*1900 (see p. 246).

Ragdale House, how it looks today (see p. 246).

Beoley Hall as it is today. The building has now been converted into flats (see p. 248).

The Bull Inn at Rippingale, as pictured in 1926 (see p. 253).

The Hendre country house, *c.* 1900 (see pp. 254–5).

Sandgate working camp, Storrington, *c.*1900 (see p. 288).

Temple Bruer Preceptory as it stands today (see p. 293).

ichmond Barracks, Templemore, *c.*1914, showing troops on drill (see pp. 293–4).

Halton Park, as it looks today. The house is now an officers' mess for RAF Halton (see pp. 313–14).

Cambridge Military Hospital, 1891 (see pp. 331–2).

Bedford General Hospital, formerly Bedford Military Hospital (see pp. 332–3).

1st Birmingham War Hospital, *c.*1900 (see p. 333).

2nd Birmingham War Hospital at Hollymoor (see p. 333).

Wounded troops recovering at Brighton's 2nd Eastern General Hospital in 1915 (see p. 333).

Dover Military Hospital (see p. 338).

King Edward VII Hospital in 1914, known as Cardiff's 3rd Western General Hospital during the war (see p. 334).

)ublin's King George V Hospital, pictured just before the First World War (see p. 339).

'he site of the former Edinburgh Castle Military Hospital (see pp. 339–40).

HMHS *Lanfranc*, which was torpedoed by *UB-40* on 17 April 1917 (see p. 341).

Cannock Chase German Military Cemetery (see p. 360).

deserved to be refused admission to the library. Member of Parliament, Alan Sykes, protested about the COs being in Knutsford, and had a reply from the Home Office that the men would be employed in useful work and 'kept hard at it ... they are however not prisoners and they will have a small amount of personal liberty. They are working on mail bags and 100 are weaving cloth for uniforms.' Their basic diet had been supplemented by buying goods in the town but shopkeepers were refusing to serve them so some were receiving parcels. Local shopkeepers wanted them to wear badges, and many put up notices saying they would not be served.

An anonymous Scot, signing himself 'An unwilling resident of Knutsford' (17 December 1917), wrote there were errors in the recently published report which stated one of the industries being undertaken by the COs was the weaving of cloth, for uniforms: 'No weaving of any kind is being undertaken.' He continued:

> With reference to the general agitation for our removal from Knutsford, one is inclined to wish for more power to the elbows of the agitators. Nothing would please us more, especially for those of us from north of the Tweed. Of the 400 men currently interned, only a handful were engaged on productive work of any kind. Experienced teachers, farmers, businessmen, etc., are being employed teasing out fibre, and filling it into prison bedding.

He sarcastically ended his letter by saying he would drink a flowing pint of cocoa to the success of agitation for the removal of COs from Knutsford. After the conscientious objectors were released, the gaol was used as a test school for prospective Church of England ordinates. The Prison was demolished in 1934.

L

LADBROKE HALL (see Harbury).

LAIRA (see Plymouth).

LAKENHAM (OS: TG 234 062). It was resolved, by the Norfolk WAC, to inform the Local Government Board that accommodation at Old Lakenham Mills could be provided to carry out drainage work on the River Wensum. However Mrs Croft of Old Lakenham Hall objected to PoWs being interned at the mill. Her objection was read out at the committee meeting of 31 August 1917 (C/C10/16).

Lakenham was inspected by Dr A. de Sturler and Monsieur R. de Sturler, during April and May 1919. Their findings are held at the National Archives, at Kew (FO 383/507). The camp had the POWIB (1919) code Pa (Lk) (IWM: Facsimile K4655). It had the TA Priswarian: Trawse (ADM 1/8506/265–120667). The FPHS (1973) cite Lakenham, Suffolk in their lists of British Prison Camps.

LAMAS HALL (OS: TG 244 235). The minutes of the Norfolk WAC minutes state the choice of Lamas Hall or Burton Mill (sic) was put to the Local Government Board to house PoWs that were to be put to clearing the River Bures (C/C10/15–19). The original house at Lamas was replaced by the Lubbock family, *c.*1740. It was not known which site was chosen. The mill was at Buxton.

LAMBOURN (OS: SU 343 797). An agricultural group attached to Compton AD, its POWIB (1919) code was Dor (Cmp) (Lmb) (IWM: Facsimile K4655). It is also cited by the FPHS (1973). It is cited as being based in The Chestnuts, with the TA Priswarian: Lambourne (sic), Berks. (ADM 1/8506/265–120667).

LAMPETER (OS: SN 577 483). A satellite camp of Carmarthen, it had the POWIB (1919) code Fg (Car) (Lam) (IWM: Facsimile K4655). It is cited as being in the Drill Hall, and it had the TA Priswarian: Lampeter (ADM 1/8506/265–120667).

LANCASTER CASTLE (OS: SD 473 618). There appears to be no connection between the two camps that were in Lancaster. The first was a short-lived camp set up early in the war at the former waggon works in Caton Road. The second opened at the former county gaol when the second phase of camps had been established.

It had the code Lgh (La C) (IWM: Facsimile K4655). The camp had the TA Priswarian: Lancaster (ADM 1/8506/265–120667). Only one entry is cited for Lancaster by the FPHS (1973). Cited by the POWIB (1919), this camp is described as a working camp attached to Leigh. Latterly used as the County Gaol, the last execution took place there in 1910 and, due to the decrease in the number of prisoners nationally, it closed in 1916. Then it re-opened to hold German prisoners of war. The castle dates back to the Middle Ages and allegedly saw the trial and subsequent executions of the 'Lancashire Witches' in the early seventeenth century. In the Victorian era, it was a debtors' prison, then as a female penitentiary until its closure in 2011.

A document exists in the county's archive requesting PoWs to widen Caton Road.

LANCASTER WAGGON WORKS (OS: SD 484 633). Bird (*The Control of Enemy Alien Civilians in Great Britain 1914–1918*, 1986) cites disused buildings in Lancaster were used for the purpose of internment during the First World War. Potter (*Reflections of Lancaster*, 1992) cites buildings in Caton Road on the outskirts of Lancaster belonged to The Lancaster Railway Carriage and Waggon Co. Ltd. The company was formed in 1863, and had a reputation for producing work of a very high standard for the rail industry. The workshops however were closed in 1908, when the business changed ownership and all the work was transferred to Manchester. In August 1914, the War Office requisitioned the empty premises and they became the home of the 5th Battalion of the King's Own Royal Lancaster Regiment. The buildings were then prepared for an influx of some 2,000 internees. A Company of Royal Welsh Fusilier Reserves was deployed to act as guard. *The Lancaster Observer* (28 August 1914) reported that the first batch arrived by train from Liverpool on 24 August 1914. Later that day, another batch arrived from Hull. *The Lancaster Guardian* (29 August 1914) confirmed this, stating the first batch of Germans and Austrians arrived on Monday. The work of transforming the buildings into a camp was completed on the Saturday, prior to their arrival, and the internees were conveyed directly into the wagon works by train. Further batches arrived during the week bringing the total to about 380.

Colonel Hugh C. Cholmondeley was chosen to be the camp's first commandant. However, he moved to Shrewsbury in September, and was replaced temporarily by Major William de Bathe-Hatton. Before the end of the year, Colonel John H. Ansley had replaced Bathe-Hatton.

Panayi (*The Enemy In Our Midst: Germans in Britain during the First World War*, 1991) cites the camp was operational by 5 September 1914 when forty-three Manchunians were arrested, as enemy aliens, and sent to the newly opened internment camp in Lancaster. *The Times* (7 September 1914) confirmed forty to fifty enemy aliens were arrested in the Manchester area and sent to Lancaster for internment.

The Lancaster Guardian (19 September 1914) stated there were approximately 1,700 internees in the camp. New arrivals had come from as far afield as Hanley, Newcastle and Carlisle. Its following edition of 26 September stated the guard was being changed to National Reservists, from Manchester. It also reported that four prisoners were locked up in the police cells at the Town Hall for three days in solitary co-finement for squabbling.

The Lancaster Guardian (21 November 1914) reported that some internees had broken through the roof and caused damage amounting to about £30. It was not clear as to whether this was an attempted escape or a raid on the stores. An internee reportedly claimed conditions in camp good, in contrast to German allegations of maltreatment.

The Times (3 December 1914) reported no one was seriously hurt in a riot at the camp. It was not reported on locally, but the *Yorkshire Evening Press* (4 December 1914) commented that there had been a serious conflict between the PoWs in the camp, that resulted in one prisoner receiving a knife wound. The commanding officer, Colonel Ansley, denied the report, saying 'there was not a word of truth in it'. Apparently booing had begun when a few Alsacians were being released. The atmosphere within the camp had been tense, due to the events that had previously taken place at Douglas.

When John B. Jackson for the US Embassy in London's party arrived to inspect the camp on 12 February 1915, the former waggon works held around 1,800 men and 200 boys. It was understood that the boys were being concentrated at Lancaster, with a view to quickly repatriating them back to Germany. There were also a considerable number of men over fifty-five. Some of the interned were Poles and there were Hungarians too. Many of the boys were 17 years of age, or younger, taken from fishing boats that had come into British Territorial Waters and had their crews arrested, or itinerant musicians. The American delegation was informed that conditions for the internees were constantly being improved as monies became available. The floor was being concreted over and the leaky roof repaired. Gymnastic equipment was being ordered and a boxing ring set up. Arrangements for the education of the young, and volunteers, were in place. The commandant was commended for his attitude. The delegation found the heating satisfactory, but the lighting poor. The kitchens, though small, seemed to be satisfactory and the canteens adequate. The medical facility, full of ex-African patients, was well arranged. There was a separate isolation unit for venereal cases.

Thomas (*St Stephen's House: Friends Emergency Work in England 1914–1920*, 1920) described the factory floor as originally having been constructed of wooden blocks, with many were missing, leaving the earth exposed. Her remarks have been challenged as unfair criticism, as there had been attempts, when funds were available, to patch these holes with concrete. She also cited around 700 civilians, of all classes, were herded together for the winter of 1914/15 in the factory, without heat or artificial light, and with no proper bedding or furniture of any kind. Sanitary conditions were wretched, as water for washing was hard to obtain. Conditions at Lancaster, according to Thomas, were deplorable.

The US Embassy's inspection of 16 June 1915 reported there were 2,097 enemy aliens interned at Lancaster. This visit had been preceded by a party from the House of Commons, which was cited in *The Times* (26 April 1915). They were impressed 'with the complete confidence which the prisoners seemed to have in the authority's sense of justice and fair play'. The US team noted around 200 of these were boys under the age of 17 and were housed separately. The roof had been repaired and the floor was in the process of being concreted over. A technical school, staffed by the prisoners, was operating, but route marches had to be postponed due to public hostility generated by the sinking of the *Lusitania* on 7 May 1915. A lack of recreational space was noted.

A minute of the Durham Joint Meeting of the Women's Relief Committee (21 January 1915) resolved to give Alien Relief to the wives of two Germans who had been sent into internment at Lancaster. The committee noted that as the women were not British born, half of any money they received could be claimed back from the government.

When exactly the camp closed is uncertain, but the premises were used, later in the conflict, to manufacture torpedoes. An indicator to when the camp closed may be that the commandant, Colonel John H. Ansley, is cited as being the commandant at Pattishall in 1916. The site became dormant again until 1922, when Morton Sundour Fabrics, a Carlisle firm, purchased it.

According to the POWIB (1919), a second camp opened in Lancaster. Cited as a satellite of Leigh, it was a working camp based at the Castle. Only one entry, for Lancaster, is quoted in the FPHS (1973) listings.

LANCING: Sompting (OS: TQ 17- 04-). Sompting appears on the list produced for the FPHS (1973). Its TA was Priswarian: Sompting (ADM 1/8506/265–120667).

At a meeting in Shoreham that took place in January 1917, the East Lancing Sea Defences Committee was told that soldiers who were to be employed on sea defence work were no longer available, as they were required elsewhere. Instead, they were informed prisoners of war could be made available for the task. They were also told that some forty barrows and seventy shovels had been purchased for this work. When the committee next met (27 February 1918) it considered Lord Leconfield's suggestion that German prisoners should be obtained, and instructed the Clerk to apply for twenty, or so, PoWs for the task in hand.

PoWs sent to Sompting were accommodated in tents. They complained to the Swiss Delegate (16 October 1917) about their conditions, the main one being there was nowhere to dry their clothes.

The camp, consisting of three compounds, was in the vicinity of Rectory Farm Road, Dankton Gardens, Dankton Lane, and Millfield Road. There is a reference to this camp being called Lancing. The POWIB (1919) gave it the code Pa (Lc) (IWM: Facsimile K4655).

DKF 34: Nach dem Bericht des Schweizer Delegierten A.L. Vischer vom 16 Oktober 1917 waren die Leute im Arbeitslager Sompting, Sussex am 11 Oktober noch in Zelten untergebracht. Die Gefangenen haben alle nur ein Hemd, so daß sie nicht in der Lage sind, noch dazu bei dem herrschenden feuchten Herbstwetter, nach der Arbeit die Wäsche zu wechseln.

LANEHAM (OS: SK 81- 76-). The top floor of an empty warehouse belonging to a malt kiln at Church Laneham was converted into an internment camp during the First World War. The malthouse stood at the top of a steep slope where barges that serviced it were moored below to a pier-like structure that stretched out into the River Trent below, for loading and unloading purposes.

Murals, drawn on the walls by the internees, were lost when renovations of the property took place, but photographs of the drawings taken in the 1960s by Robin Minnett survive.

Minnett's father often spoke of the most senior internee at the camp. He was of a rank equivalent to that of a sergeant major. It transpires he escaped one night and was never heard of again.

Laneham was an agricultural group attached to Retford; its code was Bro (Ret) (Lh) (IWM: Facsimile K4655). This camp also appears in the minutes of the Notts County WAC. Its TA is cited as, Priswarian: Laneham, Dunham on Trent (ADM 1/8506/265–120667).

LANGLEY PARK (see Iver Heath).

LANGPORT (see Ilchester).

LANGWATHY (OS: NY 56- 33-). Citing a past edition of *The Carlisle Journal*, the *Cumberland News* (7 November 2003) cited migratory gangs had been set up at Langwathby and Culgaith. These were similar to the one set up at Kirkoswald, where two tents had been erected to house ten PoWs that had been brought from Rowrah to work on the harvesting.

LARKHILL (OS: SU 126 439). Larkhill became a vast army complex that embraced a number of camps, including those at Fargo and Rollestone. The Larkhill camp had thirty hutments, each capable of holding up to 1,000 men. Its railway system was laid in 1914, and comprised of some 10 miles of track, some of which served airfields. Lines 8 and 9 sat very close to Stonehenge. It was described by the POWIB (1919) as being a working camp with the code, Dor (La) (IWM: Facsimile K4655).

Crawford (*Wiltshire and The Great War: Training The Empire's Soldiers*, 1999) cites a War Department list, dated November 1917, that mentions two prison camps in Wiltshire, at Larkhill and Perham Down, and a camp for interned aliens at Bulford. In June 1918 the number of camps in the county was quoted in the newspapers as five.

> … at one time or other prisoners are recorded at most military bases (in Wiltshire), probably constituting small groups working on local farms and lodged in secure accommodation rather than large concentrations of men confined in the popular conception of a PoW camp.

In May 1917, Scotland Yard announced three Germans had escaped from a camp on the eastern side of Larkhill, near sheds of the former British and Colonial Aircraft Company. They had been dressed in their uniforms when they absconded, but these were found discarded.

Most escapees appear to have been recaptured quickly; however, Otto Homke and Conrad Sandhagen, two German sailors escaped from Larkhill on 17 April 1918. They remained at liberty until early May, when they were caught trying to take a boat on the south-east coast with the aim of crossing to Zeebrugge. They were dressed as civilian sailors, in blue serge clothes and high boots, and between them had an Australian shilling and nearly £1 in English silver coins. A mile from where they were caught they had hidden two bags containing biscuits, bread and other food, clothing, razor, shaving brush and knife. The men looked robust and well fed and one had a large bottle of water.

The FPHS (1973) entry cites Larkhill as being in Lancashire. They also cite an entry for Fargo, which the POWIB (1919) cites as Fargo Rollestone Military Hospital. Larkhill had the TA Priswarian: Larkhill (ADM 1/8506/265–120667).

DKF 30: In den Lagern von Rosyth, Eastgate, Uppingham, Belton Park, Ternhill, Bee Craigs, Hadnall, Sutton Veny, Larkhill, Fovant, Withley (sic) *und Radford sind die Kriegsgefangenen in Zelten untergebracht.*

DKF 32: In Wackerley (sic), *Sproxton Moor, Port Clarence und Larkhill fehlen Plätze bzw Räume zur Erholung der Kriegsgefangenen.*

DKF 32: Gottesdienst: Die Seelsorge der Kreigsgefangenen ist auf vielen Plätzen sehr vernachlässigt. In den Lagern von Joyce Green, Dartford; Hadnall; Peak Dale Quarries bei Buxton; Sutton Veny; Larkhill; Netheravon; Codford; und Fovant hat noch kein Gottesdienst stattgefunden.

DKF 34: In Fovant, Sutton Veney (sic), *und Larkhill sind trotz früheren Protests keine Verbesserungen erfolgt.*

LAUNCESTON. The only reference to this camp comes from the *Western Times* (19 January 1917). A reply from the Cornwall WAC to the Board of Governors at Launceston were informed German PoW labour could only be supplied in groups of a hundred men. They could only accommodate a working party of just ten, but after discussion it was proposed to write seeking a party of twenty.

LAURENCEKIRK (see Conveth Mains Farm).

LAWFORD HEATH (OS: SP 45- 73-). A working camp with the POWIB (1919) code Dor (L Hth) (IWM: Facsimile K4655), it is also cited by the FPHS (1973). The minutes of the Warwickshire WAC record a PoW camp had been set up at Lawford Heath by 20 April 1918 (CR 73/1–2). It had the TA Priswarian: Lawford Heath, Rugby (ADM 1/8506/265–120667).

LAYSTON FARM: nr Woodside, Perthshire (OS: NO 185 381). Layston Farm is approximately 13 miles to the north of Auchterarder.

Both the entries of the POWIB (1919) and FPHS (1973) incorrectly cite this camp as Leystone.

A spokesperson for the Perthshire branch of the National Union of Farmers for Scotland suggests the farm was near Woodside in Perthshire, and like so many of the farms from that era it no longer functions today as such, having either been abandoned, or absorbed into a larger combine, or undergone redevelopment.

A satellite of Auchterarder, its POWIB (1919) code was Stbs (Au) (Ly) (IWM: Facsimile K4655).

Crawford mentions the Scottish Midland Junction Railway and a station serving Woodside & Burrelton (see Strathord).

LE HAVRE DOCK (see Harfleur).

LEADENHAM: Glebe Farm (OS: SK 924 529). It had the TA Priswarian: Glebe Farm, Leadenham (ADM 1/8506/265–120667). What kind of work they were engaged in is not known. Perhaps they were employed in work connected to RFC Leadenham (OS: SK 960 520). The air station opened in 1916, and closed at the end of the war.

LEASOWE CASTLE: Moreton (OS: SJ 265 918). Do not go to Leasowe Castle expecting to see a fortress on a hill, surmounted by tall towers and surrounded by a moat. Castellation and turrets it may have, but there the likeness to a fortress ends. Situated on the sands of Liverpool Bay, Leasowe Castle was built in 1593 as New Hall by Ferdinando, 5th Earl of Derby. The castle has a colourful history and several theories exist as to why it was erected. The one proffered by Ormerod seems the most plausible. This suggests that it was built to be prepared for any eventuality 'which the disturbed times rendered possible'. It lay empty towards the end of the seventeenth century, becoming derelict, and acquiring the pseudonym Mockbegger's Hall. Transformed into a farmhouse, it then was occupied by the Egertons of Oulton who possibly gave it the name Leasowe Castle. It was sold in 1786 to Robert Harrison, and then to Margaret Bode in 1818, before passing to Sir Edward Cust, who turned it into an unsuccessful hotel. Cust built the perimeter wall and the entrance. He also had a library fitted out in oak timbers taken from the nearby, submerged, forest at Meols. Panelling was brought from the original Star Chamber at Westminster, and it was fitted into his dining room. Cust died in 1878. In 1891, another attempt to turn the castle into a hotel, by Cust's descendants, failed. The Trustees of the Railway Convalescent Homes bought it in 1910. Children of railway workers were cared for there up until 1970, and then for twelve years it lay empty again. In 1982, after undergoing substantial renovation it was again turned into a hotel. Throughout its chequered history, several of its owners added new wings and outbuildings to enhance the property. Many of these additions had extra turrets and towers built on to them.

During the First World War, it was used to accommodate German prisoners. Smith (*The German Prisoners of war Camp at Leigh*, 1986) quotes from the *Leigh Chronicle*, 'Fifty German PoWs left Leigh on Friday morning for Leasowe near Birkenhead ...'

The camp's POWIB (1919) code was Hfth (Lea) (IWM: Facsimile K4655), and its TA was Priswarian: Wallasey (ADM 1/8506/265–120667). The entry by the FPHS (1973) gives its address as Leasowe Castle, Cheshire.

LEDBURY (OS: SO 709 381). The camp was situated in the workhouse, where the camp commandant believed that there was insufficient accommodation for all the internees being sent there.

When Ledbury Poor Law Union was formed, on 2 June 1836, a new union workhouse was commissioned to house 150 inmates. It was built to the northwest of the town on what became Union Lane (now Orchard Lane). The architect was George Wilkinson who also built the workhouses at Leominster, Bromyard and Weobley. After 1930, the workhouse became a Public Assistance Institution. After 1948 it became an old people's home known as Belle Orchard House. The building's central hub and inner cross-ranges have been demolished, and the surviving sections are now used for residential accommodation.

Described as an agricultural group, its POWIB (1919) code was Shrw (Lmr) (Ldy) (IWM: Facsimile K4655). Like many of the camps attached to Leominster, its address was cited as 42 West Street, Leominster. The camp's TA was Priswarian: Ledbury (ADM 1/8506/265–120667). It is also cited by the FPHS (1973).

In the Second World War there was another camp in Ledbury. Opened initially to hold Italian PoWs it was known locally as Tin Town. It was later used to intern German PoWs. John Masefield School now occupies that site.

DKF 35: In Ledbury sind, wie vom Lagerkommandanten selbst bestätigt wurde, die Unterkunftsräume nicht ausreichend.

LEIGH: Etherstone Street (OS: SJ 653 997). New weaving sheds, in Etherstone Street, Pennington, had not been completed or used by the Lilford Weaving Company Limited when they were requisitioned by the War Office and transformed into an internment camp. Both the *Leigh Chronicle* and *Leigh Journal* carried reports, from 30 October 1914, that PoWs were being interned at the weaving sheds, until the camp was last mentioned on 3 June 1919.

The *Leigh Chronicle* (18 December 1914) cited the commandant as Captain Kenneth Crause Wright. He however had gone to take charge at Frongoch, and was replaced temporarily by Captain Lindsey, as cited in *The Leigh Chronicle* (5 February 1915).

The *Leigh Chronicle* (31 December 1914) contained a photograph of the officers of the guard that had arrived at the camp. Their senior officer was Colonel H. Hawkins. The guard then comprised of 200 reservists.

In his report of his visits to various camps in the UK, in February 1915, John Jackson, on behalf of the US Embassy in London, stated he did not go to the camp at Leigh as it was not then open at the time of his arrival in England on 26 January 1915. Macpherson, Horrock & Beveridge (*History of The Great War: Medical Services*, 1923) suggest the camp opened on 28 January 1915, with accommodation for 1,785 internees.

According to the press, the PoWs began to arrive, between 29 January 1914 and 19 February 1915, in five batches of approximately 360 men. *The Leigh Journal* (5 February 1915) cited the first prisoners had arrived at Leigh Station and were marched from the station to the mill site. They had come from Templemore Barracks in County Tipperary, via Dublin and Holyhead. In all 1,885 were transferred; they were mostly soldiers, with some sailors. With them had come their commandant at Templemore, Major George G. Tarry, and he took over the reins at Leigh from 7 April 1915.

The *Leigh Chronicle* (9 April 1915) reported that Major Tarry had arrived at the camp two days earlier to take up the position of commandant. This coincided with some forty PoWs being sent to Donington Hall to act as orderlies. *The Times* (12 April 1915) cited there were now 2,000 prisoners at Leigh, both military and naval. It also reported that an interned soldier, named Freidrich Schwenke, had escaped. He was later found at Salford Docks and returned to the camp. His military hearing took place in Leigh. According to the *Liverpool Daily Post* (28 April 1915) Schwenke was said to have ruined his uniform deliberately, and had been supplied with overalls and a jacket from other parties. He had escaped by walking out with contracted workers, with a toolbox slung over his shoulder. When arrested he was taken to Manchester's London Road Police Station. The *Leigh Chronicle* (30 April 1915) confirmed he had been taken to London Road.

The Times (8 June 1915) cited an unnamed PoW had attempted to escape in a swill bin. The *Leigh Chronicle* (11 June 1915) reported the man almost suffocated. The *Leigh Chronicle* (18 June 1915) states he was sentenced to twenty-eight days in Hereford Gaol.

The Times (26 June 1915) cited sixty invalids daubed 'ambulance men' left Leigh for Germany, to be exchanged for British personnel. This was part of an exchange scheme to allow disabled PoWs and medical orderlies to be repatriated.

A visit by a delegation from the US Embassy in London took place on 28 June 1915. They reported that there were 1,688 soldiers and 39 sailors being interned at the time of their visit. The camp had six dormitories, the smallest of which held the Feldwebels and other NCOs, a total of 80 men. The largest dormitory held 519 men. All had their own beds, with a paillasse, and three blankets. A hut for recreational purposes had been provided by the YMCA, which also provided classes that had been organised for the internees.

The Times (26 July 1915) cited fifty PoWs had arrived by train from Shrewsbury.

The Leigh Chronicle (28 July 1916) carried an article, written by George Leach for the *Manchester Guardian*, in which he said he had visited the Leigh camp. He commented on the dietary scale of the private soldier:

Meat:	0.5 lb		Vegetables (fresh):	8 oz
Salt:	0.5 oz		bread:	1.5 lb
Sugar:	2 oz		Rice or pulses (peas, beans, lentils):	2 oz
Pepper:	0.0015 oz		Tinned Milk:	0.05 lb
Margarine:	1 oz			
Tea:	0.5 oz	or	Coffee:	1 oz

(flour could be drawn in place of bread, at the rate of 0.75 lb: 1 oz)

The Leigh Chronicle (27 August 1915) cited Colonel Hawkins had left the camp to join the 7th Manchester Regiment.

On 16 October 1915, fifty men of the Shropshire Light Infantry arrived to strengthen the guard.

The Leigh Chronicle and *The Times* (both of 29 October 1915) cited internee Wilhelm Hofschild had died, apparently of heart failure.

The Leigh Journal (15 September 1916) reported on a White Paper, published on Wednesday, 21 February 1916, containing reports from visits by officials from the American Embassy in London, as to the conditions being afforded to the PoWs held at twenty-three internment camps throughout the UK and Ireland. On their inspection they noted the humane treatment of internees was acceptable to them, although they had received complaints relating to the monotony of the diet. The inspection, carried out in March 1916, stated there were 1,770 prisoners (1,732 military and 38 naval) being detained. The report stated 'this camp seemed to me to be noteworthy, on account of its great neatness and cleanliness ... It is conducted on strict military principles, but the men, being soldiers, seemed to understand this.' The commandant was stated to be Colonel Henry John Blagrove.

On the day of the visit, there were seventeen in-patients in the hospital. A further twenty-seven were being treated as outpatients. One patient had recently come from Frongoch. He was being treated for TB and was isolated from the others. It was hoped he would be sent to Switzerland as part of the medical transfer scheme that existed. A local dentist frequently visited the camp, and an internee was also a qualified dentist. The delegation was told some of profits from the canteen were spent for the benefit of the PoWs. Church services were available on Sundays for those that wanted to attend.

The Times (15 March 1916) reported the death of Ernst Heindrich Rabbow.

A visit by a delegation from the US Embassy in London on 8 September 1916 concluded that there had been a reduction in the number of men currently held in the camp. It was explained that around 500 internees had gone to do forestry work at camps at Crickhowell, Harperley and Ampleforth-Sproxton Moor, and a further 165 to work in a quarry at Rowrah. Those that went to Rowrah complained their luggage was not forwarded to them. Twenty-six men also commuted daily to work at the pithead at Atherton Colliery. There are also reports of PoWs being sent out to work around the country. Some 180 – 250 men went to Abergavenny, and two batches of around 200 each went to the camps at Harperley and Eastgate in County Durham.

The *Leigh Chronicle* (19 October 1917) cited Ernest Bolt, a sailor, and Norbet Ahrens, a soldier, escaped on or around 12 October 1917. They had been re-captured in the Manchester area on 15 October. *The Times* (15 & 16 October 1917) carried similar reports.

The *Leigh Chronicle* and the *Police Gazette* (both of 26 October 1917) cite Bernhard Henschkel aged 26, Fritz Willi Renessler aged 27, and Herman Brunte aged 24 had escaped two days earlier. *The Times* (25 October 1917) reported only Bunte and

Roesser had escaped. *The Leigh Chronicle* (24 November 1917) states they had been recaptured at Aughton, near Ormskirk.

The *Leigh Chronicle* (16 November 1917) reported that Gustav Kockrich, a sailor, working on the surface at Abram Colliery, had escaped on 12 November, and that he had been recaptured at Croston, near Preston, the next day.

Colonel John Henry Ansley, previously at Lancaster and Pattishall, replaced Blagrove as the camp's commandant on 23 Nov 1917. The *Leigh Chronicle* (30 November 1917) then reported that Lieutenant Jones left Leigh for the Penmaenmawr PoW camp.

On 6 December 1916 it was reported that there were 1,474 PoWs, all German. Of these 33 were naval personnel, the rest were army. The 200 previously stated to have gone to Crickhowell, had returned due to the inclement weather. However, they were expected to return to Wales in around ten days, when better shelter could be made available.

The *Leigh Chronicle* (25 January 1918) cited four sailors: Joseph Weingartner, Hermann Ren, Emile Wertsch and Heindrich Stoldt, had escaped on 19 January. Weingartner and Ren were recaptured at Grimbsy the following day, and the other two were recaptured in Gloucestershire on 24 January 1918. Corroborative reports to their escapes and recaptures appeared in *The Times* (21 and 28 January 1918).

The *Leigh Chronicle* (11 April 1919) cited around 100 arrived on Wednesday and Thursday.

The *Leigh Chronicle* (17 April 1919) cited around 400 PoWs were transferred to Frongoch on Saturday, 12 April 1919.

The Times (27 May 1919) cited 1,000 internees had moved from Handforth to Leigh. However the men had gone the opposite way, as cited in *The Leigh Journal* (27 May 1919), which stated two batches of internees, totalling 800, moved to Handforth on Sunday (25 May), and the next day a further 500 went to Frongoch. It stated:

> The German soldiers and sailors, who have for over four years been PoWs at the camp, of which the Lilford Weaving Sheds forms the buildings, have, with the exception of a few kept for cleaning up purposes, left Leigh for good, and the camp will be closed on 1 June (1919). There was little excitement, and the event caused very little interest to the inhabitants, who have got used to seeing German working parties going backwards and forwards on foot and tramcar.

Of the working parties that used the tramcar daily, a group went to a depot in Fair Hill Road, Irlam, where the PoWs sorted old boots into matching pairs. Moody-Stuart compiled a report on 24 June 1918 that mentions some of the work being undertaken by the internees: three of them were engaged in repairing damaged stitching, another forty graded them, and fourteen more pulled a truck that ran on a steep gradient. Their working day was barely seven hours. The depot was set up on a site intended to manufacture soda. Today the Irlam site no longer exists. Many of the old buildings were demolished as part of Greater Manchester's urban renewal initiative.

In all there were thirteen reported deaths in the Leigh camp. One had been shot attempting to escape, a further six died during 1915–16, and the rest in the flu pandemic of November–December 1918.

The camp's POWIB (1919) code was Lgh, its TA being Priswarian, Leigh (ADM 1/8506/265–120667). The camp officially closed on 30 May 1919.

There was a camp in Worcestershire, Leigh Court that had the POWIB (1919) code Dor (Lei) (IWM: Facsimile K4655). Both these camps were recorded by the FPHS (1973).

DKF 32: Die Rovrah (sic) *beschäftigten Leute haben ihre im Lager Leigh zurückgelassenen Koffer immer noch nicht erhalten.*

DKF 36: Inder Note Nr 11202 12 18/p vom 13 September 1918 hat die britische Foreign Office erklärt, daß Irlam keine Arbeiter mehr beim Entladen von Roheisen beschäftigt werden und daß geeignete Maßnahmen getroffen sind, daß einer Wiederholung der Strafmethode, wie sie in Stanhope angewandt wurde, vorgebeugt wird.

LEIGH CHANNEL SQUADRON (see Southend on Sea).

LEIGH COURT (see Worcester).

LEIGHTERTON (OS: ST 824 924). Cited as Leighterton, Tetbury, it appears in the FPHS (1973) listings. It was a working camp, with the POWIB (1919) code Dor (Lig) (IWM: Facsimile K4655). Its TA was Priswarian: Leighterton, Tetbury (ADM 1/8506/265–120667). The camp, at Leighterton Aerodrome, closed on 23 January 1919. Later that year one of the huts described as being timber framed with corrugated iron cladding, which held some German PoWs, was purchased by the Amberley Scouts. It moved to Jackdaw Quarry, near Culver Hill.

LEIGHTON BUZZARD (OS: SP 925 255). Contradictory information was cited in the directory produced by the POWIB (1919). Their entry for Leighton Buzzard designates it as a working camp with the code Pa (L B) (IWM: Facsimile K4655), however the entry for Bletchley cites it was an agricultural group attached to Leighton Buzzard agricultural depot, and qualifies this with the appropriate coding. The entry for Leighton Buzzard suggests this camp was based at 20 Market Square.

The names of eighty-eight PoWs that worked at Leighton Buzzard between February 1918 and May 1919, along with their guard, are recorded in an extract taken from the employment time sheets of the PoWs held by the Bedfordshire Record Office.

The camp's TA was Priswarian: Leighton Buzzard (ADM 1/8506/265–120667).

Today, Huckleberry's hairdressing salon, occupies Nos 18 and 20 Market Square.

In the Second World War, the town's former workhouse, in Grovebury Road, was used as an internment camp.

LENTRAN (see Beauly).

LEOMINSTER (OS: SO 495 590). The POWIB (1919) cites sixteen satellite agricultural groups attached to this depot, which was the most satellite camps to be attached to any one depot during the war. Its code was Shrw (Lmr) (IWM: Facsimile K4655). Although its address was not stated, many of its satellites had the address 42 West Street, Leominster. Its satellites were Abbeydore, Abergavenny, Bromfield, Bromyard, Cleobury Mortimer, Corfton Hall, Ellesmere, Itton, Ledbury, Llandinabo, Llanmartin, Stoke Edith, Thing Hill, Wem, Weobley and Usk (IWM: Facsimile K4655). It is also cited by the FPHS (1973).

Situated in the middle of Leominster this site underwent redevelopment during the 1960s. In more recent times, Echo, a craft shop, has occupied the site.

LEWES: Royal Naval Prison (OS: TQ 416 104). Contemporary maps show this to be a different establishment than the one used to hold civilian lawbreakers. The architect was William Blackburn and it functioned from 1789 until it was no longer required by the navy, and was demolished in 1967. Records show it had been enlarged in 1814. Originally built as a House of Correction, it replaced an earlier establishment that stood on Cliffe High Street that dated back to 1612.

A House of Correction was built in Lewes in 1793. It was built by 300 PoWs from the Crimean War (1853–1856). They are cited as Finnish in some documents and as Russians in others. Finland, then was part of Russia. There is a plaque on Brighton Road to commemorate this. The prison was demolished in 1981. During their stay the Finns formed a bond with local people still remembered in a popular Finnish folksong.

Described as a working camp, with the POWIB (1919) code Pa (Le) (IWM: Facsimile K4655) it is cited as being in North Street. Standing at the corner of Lancaster Street, it is now the site of North Street Car Park. Lewes is also cited by the FPHS (1973). It had the TA Priswarian: PoW Depot, Lewes (ADM 1/8506/265–120667).

During the First World War it became a place of internment for Eamon de Valera, Harry Boland, Thomas Ashe and Frank Lawless. On 27 April 1916, the British government's reaction to the Easter Rising had been to appoint Major-General Sir John Maxwell as the commander-in-chief of the troops in Ireland and he was given the remit to restore public order at any cost, and to punish those responsible for the insurgency. Maxwell's methods only alienated Irish public opinion further. So determined was he to crush this militant nationalism that in a nationwide sweep he had 3,430 men and 79 women arrested; of these 1,841 were sent to England without trial, to be interned. Most were released by early August 1916. Kilpatrick (*Harry Boland's Irish Revolution, 1887–1922*, 2004) reveals those believed to be behind the insurrection were tried in Ireland. The court's verdict in ninety cases was execution. For varying reasons Ashe, de Valera, Boland and Lawless had their sentences commuted to life imprisonment, and they were sent to the prison in Lewes. The rest were dispersed to different prisons around Britain.

Then, at a time when most prisons were under-utilised, it was decided to bring all those arrested in the Easter Rising to Lewes. McConville (*Irish Political Prisoners, 1848–1922: Theatres of War*, 2005) cites de Valera then organised a campaign to cause as much disruption as possible, and in June 1917, the internees were transferred in small groups to Parkhurst, Maidstone and Pentonville prisons. A fourth group remained at Lewes. Then, as part of a general amnesty in August 1917, they were all to regain their freedom. Whilst in Lewes, Ashe wrote 'Let Me Carry Your Cross for Ireland'.

LEYSDOWN-ON-SEA (OS: TR 03- 70-). The first Royal Naval Air Station created, RNAS Eastchurch, was on the Isle of Sheppey in Kent. It was where pilots went for their basic flight training. As early as 1910, the Royal Aero Club at Eastchurch emerged as a centre of excellence for civil flying. The Short Brothers, well known for manufacturing balloons, set up a factory nearby when they branched out into aircraft manufacture. In February 1911, the Admiralty was offered the use of two Shorts aircraft, so that naval officers could learn to fly. In December 1911 the navy established their own flying field, which was called the Naval Flying School Eastchurch.

In 1912, the Royal Flying Corps was formed from the combined air wings of the army and navy, but kept apart because there were differences expressed on how it should be run as a single identity. The Naval Wing officially became the Royal Naval Air Service on 1 July 1914.

A Gunnery School was established at Eastchurch on 1 May 1916, composed of the Bomb Flight, Gun Flight, and Miscellaneous Flight. Newly qualified pilots would be posted to the school to obtain instruction in combat techniques, bombing practice, target practice from the air, and even mock combat situations.

On 1 April 1918, upon the transition of the RNAS base to that of an RAF one, the Naval Flying School Eastchurch became 204 Training Depot Station. In April 1918, the gunnery school at Eastchurch was split up when a second school, known as the Aerial Fighting and Gunnery School, was set up at nearby Leysdown-on-Sea. Leysdown-on-Sea is cited by the FPHS (1973) as a British Prison Camp.

It may be these new premises engaged a gang of PoWs in its construction, although there is no evidence to prove it.

The base at Eastchurch was disbanded in March 1919.

LINCOLN: HM Prison (OS: SK 991 719). This camp varies from the norm in that there were no known Germans interned in Lincoln Gaol. But it does qualify as a place of internment because three Irish political prisoners were detained there during the First World War. The most famous of them was Eamonn de Valera.

Although he was born in New York in 1882, he had a passionate love of Ireland. He hated what he considered to be its domination and control by England so he joined *Sinn Féin*. As a battalion commander for The Irish Volunteers he fought at Boland's Hill in the Easter Rising of 1916. He was captured, put on trial, and sentenced to death. On account of the fact that he was born in America his sentence was commuted to imprisonment. He was sent to Lewes Prison in Sussex.

When the *Sinn Féin* adapted an abstentionist policy in 1917, de Valera was elected its president. De Valera was released from prison under the General Amnesty a year later and returned to Ireland, where he immediately started to resist the rule of London and consequently was arrested again. This time he was sent to Lincoln Gaol.

With the help of Michael Collins, de Valera, Sean Milroy and Sean McGarry escaped from Lincoln Gaol. *Freeman's Journal* (5 February 1919) cited de Valera had escaped and managed to get to America. He spent eighteen months there, on a fund raising tour, before being arrested for subversive activities and put in prison in New York's Toombs Prison.

LINGFIELD (OS: TQ 38- 43-). The fact that other racecourses were used as places of internment does not conclusively prove that the Lingfield course was used, but no other location in Lingfield has been found to suggest otherwise. Lingfield is cited in the list of camps produced by the FPHS (1973) as a British Prison Camp.

LINLITHGOW (see Bee Craigs).

LINTON (OS: TL 559 472). Callard (www.linton.info/lintonnews: March 2006) cites there was huge excitement, mixed with a tinge of apprehension, in the village of Linton, when the old yard at the workhouse in Symonds Lane had been surrounded by barbed wire and a garrison of thirty-five armed guards prepared for the arrival of sixty-five German PoWs. They arrived by train from Cambridge on 18 May 1918 and by late June their number had increased to 100.

A shortage of male farm labourers meant that farmers competed to employ them. Renowned for their hard work, they were marched out under close escort for their eight hour working day on the local farms. They remained in Linton until October 1919.

Cambridgeshire County Council inherited the former workhouse in 1929 when it became Linton Public Assistance Institution. It then became Linton Hospital in 1948. It was turned into a residential home for elderly people in the 1960s. There had been plans to move the facilities at Linton to Maidstone in November 1985. Today the impressive workhouse facade remains as the modernised buildings are still used as a private care home.

France (www.linton.info/lintonnews: February 2007) wrote the brick and flint building was based on a standard workhouse design – a large rectangle divided into four squares with the Master's house at the centre. From his tower he could keep an eye on each quarter housing the different divisions: the women and very young children, the men, the boys and the girls. A part of the workhouse was known locally as The Spike where unmarried girls who became pregnant were sent to have their babies.

Prisoner Leo Schmidt died whilst billeted at Linton. He possibly succumbed to the influenza pandemic that was prevelant at that time. He was buried on 3 April 1919 in Linton cemetery in an area designated by the War Graves Commission. On 9 April, Stephen Cottage of the Suffolk Regiment, discharged from the forces in July 1917 on medical grounds, died at his home in the Horseheath Road. He was buried next to Schmidt. Three days later the body of another German PoW, Karl Strauss, was placed on the other side of Stephen's grave. Letters began to appear in the press as the War Office was pressurised to remove the two German bodies. A gesture of true compassion followed. The Reverend Edwards informed the public that Stephen's father had no objection whatsoever to the two German soldiers lying at rest next to his beloved son. In 1965 the interred remains of the two German soldiers were exhumed at the bequest of the West German government. They were taken for re-burial to the German War Cemetery at Cannock Chase.

It was pointed out to the Cambridgeshire WAC on 27 May 1918 that some of the PoWs accommodated at Linton Prisoner-of-war Camp had been working in Essex, and others had been utilised by the Road Surveyor, therefore denying local farmers the use of their services. It was proposed to get these men recalled to Linton, along with those working for the Committee at Balsham. At the next meeting Lieutenant Atkins was asked to investigate if it was desirable to increase the number of PoWs at the camp.

At a subsequent meeting a letter was read out (24 June 1918), from Mr Luddington of Ashdon, expressing his concerns that the PoWs employed on drainage work on his farm would be recalled for other duties before the work was completed. It was resolved to allow him to keep the men, who had previously been at Balsham. It was further reported, on 19 April 1919, that the commandant of the Linton PoW Camp had attended a committee meeting. He indicated that the date set by the parent camp, Padishall (sic), to discontinue charging for prisoners employed on the Barway breach, was different from that issued by the Food Production Department. Pending inquiries, the matter was to be resolved later (R67/012).

The internees cited that the canteen facilities at Linton were inadequate.

It was a working camp, the POWIB (1919) had given it the code Pa (Lin) (IWM: Facsimile K4655). It is cited by the FPHS (1973). The camp's TA was Priswarian: Linton, Cambs. (ADM 1/8506/265–120667).

DKF 31: In Joice Green (sic), *Dartford, Linton, Sutton Veney* (sic) *Fovant, und Evesham bestehen Keine Kantine. Die Ausführung der Bestellungen der Kriegsgefangenen durch den Profoß-Sergeanten, kann nicht als genügender Ersatz betrachtet werden.*

LITTLE BALBROGIE (OS: NO 24- 42-). A working camp, created near to Ardler, its POWIB (1919) code was Stbs (Lt) (IWM: Facsimile K4655). The army often chose to name a camp from the nearest railway station, and this may be the case here. Its TA was Priswarian: Ardler Station (ADM 1/8506/265–120667). Keillor, cited by the FPHS (1973), may be another reference to this camp.

LITTLE GRANSDEN (OS: TL 275 554). Little Gransden appears on a list produced by the FPHS (1973), but no further evidence has been found to confirm or suggest where this camp was located.

LITTLEPORT (OS: TL 565 865). A working camp, its *POWIB* code was Pa (Lp). It is also cited by the *FPHS*. The camp's TA was Priswarian: The Grange, Littleport.

The Grange on Ely Road was built *c.*1855 by Canon Sparke of Ely, and was later occupied by the Hope family. During the First World War it was initially used to house Belgian refugees before being turned into an internment camp for German prisoners of war. In 1920 it was purchased by the Transport and General Workers' Union to be a convalescent home. During the Second World War it became an RAF hospital. Today it is a care home. (R. B. Pugh (Ed.) *Ely Hundred: Littleport: A History of the County of Cambridge and the Isle of Ely*, in Volume 4*: City of Ely; Ely, N. and S. Witchford and Wisbech Hundreds*, 2002, pp. 95–102).

LLANAFAN: Grogwynion House (OS: SN 685 726). The POWIB (1919) directory cites Grogwynion House, near Llanafon (sic) was used to intern PoWs. Its code was Fg (Bre) (Lf) (IWM: Facsimile K4655), making it a satellite of Brecon. Its TA was Priswarian: Grogwynion House, Llanafan (ADM 1/8506/265–120667).

The only information available about a house of this name comes from the census returns of 1891. This records John Owen, the agent for the local mine, his family and one servant girl, resided at Grogwynion House. Today, the exact whereabouts of the house is not known, but it is thought to be have been near to the Grogwynion Mine.

As the silver and lead mines were generally worked out by the time of the First World War, an alternative suggestion for the prisoners' employment, if they were not utilised by local farmers, could have been forestry work.

LLANBEDR: Pen-yr-allt Hall (OS: SH 592 275). The POWIB (1919) cites this camp as being at Penyalt Hall (sic), Llanbedr, with its code Fg (Ty) (Lla) (IWM: Facsimile K4655). Located near Llanbedr is Pen-yr-allt Hall. The camp had the TA Priswarian: Penyrallt Hall, Llandebie (ADM 1/8506/265–120667). All knowledge of its use as an agricultural group attached to Tywyn however has faded with time. A possible use of their labour could have been connected to the infrastructure of creating an airfield at Llanbedr during the First World War.

LLANDYBIE: Lime Firms Ltd (OS: SN 615 171). According to *The Illustrated Journal* (1989), the Ministry of National Service commissioned an inspection of internment camps in Britain; amongst them was the Llandybie camp based at Lime Firms Ltd. The article cites that the PoWs were working fifty-one hours per week in a quarry. This was two and half-hours less than the civilians employed there. The reason for the difference was that the time 'was lost' when the prisoners had to be marched back to their camp for their dinner. The report also stated that a Camp Captain came over once a week from Carmarthen.

The camp was attached to Brecon and had the POWIB (1919) code Fg (Bre) (Llb) (IWM: Facsimile K4655). The entry made by the FPHS (1973) states Llandebie (sic), Carn. Its TA was Priswarian: Llandebie (sic) (ADM 1/8506/265–120667).

LLANDINABO (OS: SO 517 285). An agricultural group, its POWIB (1919) code was Shrw (Lmr) (Lb) (IWM: Facsimile K4655); its address is cited as 42 West Street, Leominster. Because this area of Herefordshire is mainly agricultural and rural in nature, finding further evidence that this camp existed, or where its actual location was, has been difficult.

LLANENGAN (OS: SH 295 270). Cited as being at the National School in Llanengan, its TA was Priswarian: Llanengan, Abersoch (ADM 1/8506/265–120667). The camp at Llanengan was inspected by Dr A. de Sturler and Monsieur R. de Sturler during June 1919. Their findings are held at the National Archives at Kew (FO 383/508).

LLANERCHYMEDD (OS: SH 424 847). Llanerchymedd was a satellite of the agricultural depot at Penmaenmawr. It is cited as being in the workhouse, and its POWIB (1919) code was Fg (Pen) (Ll) (IWM: Facsimile K4655). The camp's TA was Priswarian: The Workhouse, Llanerchymedd (ADM 1/8506/265–120667).

The first workhouse built on Anglesey was opened *c.*1870, at Llanerchymedd. Its completion was delayed for a number of years due to escalating costs. When it was completed additional expenditure was incurred to make the building waterproof as it transpired that inferior quality bricks were used to reduce the overheads. These had been brought from Tal-y-Foel. The workhouse could accommodate up to seventy inmates at any one time.

LLANFARIAN: Aber Llown House (OS: SN 587 773). The entry in the POWIB (1919) directory cites this camp was in Aber Llown House, Llanfarian; it had the code Fg (Bre) (Ab) (IWM: Facsimile K4655), indicating it was attached to Brecon. The camp's TA was Priswarian: Llanfarian (ADM 1/8506/265–120667).

LLANMARTIN: Pencoed Castle (OS: SO 408 893). An entry by POWIB (1919) for Penycoed Castle (sic) directs you to Llanmartin, which cites an agricultural group with the code Shrw (Lmr) (Llan) (IWM: Facsimile K4655). Its address is given as 42 West Street, Leominster. The camp's TA is Priswarian: Penhow (ADM 1/8506/265–120667). Penycoed (sic) is cited by the FPHS (1973).

Situated in rolling farmland Pencoed Castle is a Tudor manor house, built in the sixteenth century, by Sir Thomas Morgan, on the site of a former Norman castle. In 1914, Lord Rhondda bought the property and began to restore it, but the work apparently ceased with his death in 1918.

The Derby Daily Telegraph (7 November 1918) cited two Austrians sent here, one a smelter, the other a waiter. They were sentenced to nine months imprisonment with hard labour at Hereford Assizes for assaulting a 15-year-old girl, whilst working on a farm at Pencoyd (sic).

LLANRWST. Three regional newspapers reported the imprisonment of Annie Seiser. *The Liverpool Echo* (3 January 1916) was the most detailed. It is not known what circumstances led to her being in the workhouse, or where her husband was being interned. Both *The Manchester Evening News* (3 January 1916) and *The Dundee Courier* (4 January 1916) cite her as Annie Seisu.

LLANSANNAN: Dyffryn Aled (OS: SH 948 670). Dyffryn Aled was a stately home built *c.*1777, by Joseph Turner, for the Wynne family, near to Llansannan in North Wales. Translated, the name means 'Beside the water of Aled'. It became a private mental sanatorium in 1893, before being requisitioned by the War Office in 1914.

Macpherson, Horrock & Beveridge (*History of The Great War: Medical Services*, 1923) cite the camp opened on 2 September 1914, with accommodation for ninety officers and thirty servants. When it opened, the camp boasted it had the best security system of any internment camp in Great Britain. There were four searchlights on its perimeter, and six sentries were deployed instead of the usual two. Garrett (*PoW: The Uncivil Face of War*, 1981) stated the number of roll-calls taken daily was twice that of any other British internment camp. This was because the men sent here were crew-members of German *U-Boote*. Many had previously been kept in detention centres, such as Chatham Naval Barracks. It was common knowledge that Churchill disliked them intensely, and it has been alleged they were treated differently because of this.

Amongst the detainees sent to Dyffryn Aled was Captain Schlagintweit of the German Consulate in Manchester. The *Hull Daily Mail* (24 August 1914) and the *Liverpool Daily Post* (25 August 1914) both state he was arrested at his home in Whalley Grange. No specific charges were cited, but the matter was put into the hands of the military authorities. The *Lancaster Guardian* (29 August 1914) cited he was fined for contravening the Aliens Restriction Act by travelling outside the 5-mile limit. He was reported to be in charge of mess supplies and purchases when the camp was visited in February 1915. *The Times* (4 March 1915) stated he was one of twelve consular officials exchanged in early 1915. Another internee held at Dyffryn Aled was the son of German Admiral Von Tirpitz. He was captured after his ship, the light cruiser SMS *Mainz*, was sunk in the Battle of Heligoland on 28 August 1914. He had first been detained in Edinburgh.

The Scotsman (13 November 1914) cited the US Embassy had visited the camp. John Jackson's team visited the camp on 11 February 1915. The report stated there were ninety-one officers in the camp plus twenty civilian servants and cooks that had been transferred from Queen's Ferry. He noted the windows were barred, but assumed this was from the buildings previous usage as an asylum. He also noted the lighting in the rooms was poor. Outside, one large field was enclosed and a further field was being enclosed, for recreational purposes. Walks in the woods and surrounds took place, escorted by British officers. There were also several rooms in the house set aside for recreational purposes. A billiard table was on order at the time of his visit. There were single rooms for the most senior officers, and no more than six shared the other rooms.

The house lacked many modern amenities, and was described in *The Times* (26 April 1915) as being inaccessible, gloomy and mildewed-looking.

The Times (6 April 1915) noted two internees had escaped. They were named as Ober-Leutnant Hans Audler of the navy and Leutnant Hans Freidrich Rudolf von Sanders Leben from the army. A reward of £10 leading to their arrests was offered. *The Police Gazette* (9 April 1915) cited the surname of the seaman as Andler. Subsequent editions of *The Times* confirmed they were still looking for the two absconders. The edition of 12 April 1915 stated the pair had been re-captured 33 miles from Llansannan, at Llanbedr, 3 miles south of Harlech. They appeared before the magistrates in Festiniog, and were remanded to Denbigh. At their hearing the camp's commandant, Lt-Colonel Cottell gave evidence. A full report of their court martials, at Chester, appeared in *The Chester Chronicle* (24 April 1915). *The Times* (3 May 1915) stated both were sentenced to twenty-eight days detention. The Occurrence Book, Blaenau Festiniog Police Station, Sunday, 11 April 1915 cites:

> PC Nathaniel Davies reports apprehending at 3.00pm this day, near Pensarn Railway Station, the two German Officers, Lts Hans Andler and Rudolf von Sanders Leben, who escaped from the military camp at Llansannan a week ago (4 April). They were brought to Blaenau Festiniog lock-up the same afternoon by Inspector Stephen Owen. 1.00pm (12 April) – before a full bench of magistrates they were ordered to be handed over to an escort from Llansannan. Owen received a wire from the Commandant at Llansannan to hand the prisoners over to an escort of the Denbighshire Constabulary. (J. Jones Morris showed me a telegram from the Home Office ordering the prisoners to be handed over to a military escort.) After consulting with the Chief Constable, on the phone, I handed the prisoners over to Superintendent Worlam and Sergeant Evans, of Denbigh, at 4.00pm.

Another US Embassy delegation visited the camp on 25 June 1915. There were sixty-nine officers interned in the camp of which forty-three belonged to the army and twenty-six to the navy. They also had twenty-nine servants. The senior German army officer was Major Ritter, and Captain Wallis was the senior naval officer. At the time of the visit it was reported there was a water shortage due to the drought. Subsequently the latrines were not working.

Despite the additional security measures in the camp it did not deter Korvetten-Kapitan Tholens, and Leutnant-Kommander von Henning (both of the German Naval Service) and Leutnant von Heldorf (Army) from escaping from it. It is believed a fellow prisoner, who was being sent back under the exchange of prisoners scheme, carried a message to the German High Command arranging for coded messages sent from 'friends discussing an impending wedding' to be sent to Tholens giving details for their escape. *U-Boote 38* and *27*, captained by Max Valentiner and Bernd Wegener respectively, were despatched to pick them up from the beach at Great Ormes Head, on the night of 14/15 August 1915. Thinking it to be a simple task *U38* rendezvoused at the designated beech, whilst *U27* went off after British shipping instead. Unfortunately a rock obstructed the transmitted beacon from the shore and the rescue attempt failed. The three escaping men then split up, with Tholens making for London. An alert policeman apprehended him as he was getting on a train at Llandudno Station. *The Times* (16 August 1915) and *The Liverpool Daily Post* (16 August 1915) reported their escapes. It was assumed they got out through a window. They had been observed on the road going north, by two women, and were also re-captured at Llandudno. *The Liverpool Daily Post* (18 August 1915) stated Tholens was arrested in Llandudno Railway Station. As it was raining heavily that day, Henning and Heldorf took a taxi in Llandudno. The driver of the cab, suspecting who they were, drove them to the headquarters of the London Welsh Battalion instead. *The Times* (20 August 1915) indicated they had been taken to Chester Castle. At their court martial they were sentenced to eighty-four days each, at Chelmsford Jail.

That September, Lt-General Sir Herbert E. Belfield, who was in charge of overseeing the internment of PoWs, was called to the Admiralty to explain their escapes and their consequences. Procedures for the internment of submarine crews were revised and it was agreed to make Dyffryn Aled the main camp for detaining submarine officers. Plans were instigated for forty to fifty additional submarine officers to be sent there, but these could not be implemented until all non-submariners had been re-located.

The US Embassy in London received a letter dated 5 October 1915, sent from a PoW in the camp, stating it took a lot of time to make the house habitable. He stated the roof leaked, and that the house had been neglected. It was in want of fittings and facilities. Windows and doors were ill-fitting and caused drafts and smoke problems from fireplaces. He also stated the windows were barred and fire escapes had been removed. Another visit by a delegation from the US Embassy in London on 30 March 1916 reported there were seventy-eight prisoners (sixteen army officers, thirty-six naval officers, with twenty-one soldiers, one naval servant and three civilian servants). The commandant was cited as Lt-Colonel W. Selwood Hewett.

The head teacher of Denbigh School recorded in the school's log of 7 January 1916:

> A holiday is given this afternoon owing to the Officers and men of the Manchester Regiment, forming the Guard at the German internment camp at Dyffryn Aled, treating the scholars to tea …

The Times (3 June 1918) reported the escape of another two officers. According to the following edition Leutnant W.J.E. Petersen and Leutnant (Ing) H.F. Burkhardt were recaptured at Llanfyndd, 5 miles north-west of Wrexham.

The Times (24 October 1918) cited Leutnant Franz Laue, another escaped PoW, was re-captured two days later at Caernarfon. A second report carried by *The Police Gazette* (8 November 1918) cites he had escaped from Abergele.

The camp closed on 10 December 1918. Those interned at Dyffryn Aled were transferred to either Donington Hall or Oswestry to await repatriation. It was later found that Dyffryn Aled had structural damage, reputedly caused by the clandestine activities of the PoWs in the camp. Consequently the house was demolished in 1920.

The camp was cited by the FPHS (1973), and the Osterreichisches Staatsarchiv, Kriegsarchiv (Wein, 1919). It had the TA Priswarian: Llansannan (ADM 1/8506/265–120667).

DKF 24: Das neben dem Mannschaftslager gleichen Namens errichtete Offiziers-Gefangenenlager Oswestry wurde im September 1918 eröffnet. Zu Beginn des Jahres 1919 wurden einige Offizierlager in England – Kegworth; Margate; Dyffryn-Aled – aufgelöst, um ihren ursprünglichen Zweck (Landwirtschaftliche Schulen usw.) zurück gegeben zu werden.

LLANTHONY (OS: SO 28- 27-). Cited by the FPHS (1973), this entry is the only evidence that a camp existed here, as its exact location is unknown. Perhaps the site of a ruined priory built in the first quarter of the thirteenth century as a hermitage by William de Lacy may hold the key. After the Dissolution of the Monasteries, the site was sold for about £160, and left to decay. Except for its early English arches, little remains of the cloistral buildings of the priory. There is a parish church and farm buildings. It could be to these buildings that the PoWs were directed.

LLANVIHANGEL GOBIAN (OS: SO 34- 09-). Cited as being at 'The Huts', its TA was Priswarian: The Huts, Llanvihangel Gobian (ADM 1/8506/265–120667). Nothing is known about the camp, that would have been active in the second phase of camps that opened.

LOCH BROOM – BRAEMORE (OS: NH 069 305). Very little is known about this camp and its location. The POWIB (1919) records it as being a working camp attached to Stobs, with the code Stbs (Bra) (IWM: Facsimile K 4655), but then erroneously cites its location. It should have read Loch Broom, Ullapool and not Loch Doon as stated. A distance of some 270 miles separates them. Its TA was Priswarian: Braemore, Loch Broom (ADM 1/8506/265–120667).

Local knowledge states the Government Timber Supply Department bought a portion of the Braemore Forest and began to harvest the trees, employing internee labour, brought into the area for that purpose. Minutes of the Railway Committee of 11 June 1918 suggest the creation of the Garve and Ullapool Railway would bring prosperity to the region by cutting production costs of timber, as well as enhancing transport in and out of Ullapool. Despite attempts to exploit the ideal harbour and anchorage at Loch Broom, which would bring the existing naval stations of Ross and Cromarty into closer touch with the west coast of Scotland, the line was never built.

The FPHS (1973) wrongly cites Braemore as being in the County of Aberdeenshire, perhaps getting it confused with Braemar.

LOCH DOON – DALMELLINGTON (OS: NX 492 973). In its entry for Braemore working camp the POWIB (1919) incorrectly states Loch Doon in its address for the camp. A more likely stretch of water for that camp is Loch Broom, as Loch Doon lies near to Dalmellington, some 270 miles to the south of Braemore.

The FPHS (1973) cites Loch Doon, as does the twelfth edition of *Stobsaide*, a newspaper published and printed under licence by the PoWs at Stobs.

A PoW sent to work at Dalmellington said that it had a distinct advantage over life at Hawick. He expressed this opinion:

> On the way to and from work we come briefly into contact with the local traffic, which we all enjoy, particularly when we can see women out for a drive or a walk. Our fellow soldiers at Stobs certainly envy us this advantage …

In the autumn 1916, because of Loch Doon's remoteness and the physical attributes provided by Craigenclon and Cullendoch Hills, it was selected for the School of Aerial Gunnery. It was based on an idea developed, at Cazaux, by the French, to train airmen in the art of firing at targets from simulated moving aircraft. Despite concerns being expressed by the farmer who sold the land to the government that Loch Doon was not an ideal location for such a project, the scheme began on 16 September 1916. Doubts expressed about the viability of this site by Lt-General Sir Spencer Ewart of Craigcluech, who said the loch could freeze over in the winter months, and the boggy ground would attract thick mists, and therefore restrict the flying time for the students, were ignored. Lt-Colonel Louis Arbon Strange of Almer was appointed to command the school. The Royal Engineers, who also expressed fears about the site, commenced draining the bog.

In April 1917, with the scheme behind schedule, Robert McAlpine & Sons, who had been represented at the original meeting at the lochside on 5 September 1916, was engaged as the main contractor, to complete the work. McAlpine's first task was to construct a rail link, as the existing unmetalled road was inadequate for the traffic it was exposed to. But he was not permitted to complete the line from Dalmellington to the school at Lambdoughty, because the cost of tunnelling through the intervening hills was thought to be too expensive. Instead, for the last miles a new road was built from Dalfarson to the lochside. A weir was also constructed, as was an outlet channel, and sluices to regulate the water level. Some 1,000 PoWs augmented a 1,400 civilian workforce, supported by detachments of Royal Engineers and Royal Defence Corps.

The gunnery range consisted of a Blondin Aerial Ropeway along which the gunnery cadets were propelled whilst firing at huge Telfer Targets, mounted on rails that were gravity-fed on the hillside opposite. A second target was mounted on a railway track, next to the loch. A seaplane station was constructed along with a dock for motorboats. A power station was built on the hilltop to supply the village below with electricity. A small village was created, with its own cinema that could seat up to 400 people.

McAlpine employed a civilian workforce of 1,400, mainly of Irish origin, and detachments of Royal Engineers. Later, around 1,000 internees, guarded by members of the Royal Defence Corps, augmented the civilian workers.

An airfield at Bogton was also incorporated into the scheme. When the costs of the scheme soared over its intended budget, it attracted the attention of the government's auditors. The programme was suspended until a visit of the site took place in January 1918. A report issued at the time stated:

> At that time the whole situation ought to have been reviewed and the Authorities should then have acknowledged the mistake that had been made and stopped the work. Had this been done a great part of the waste of money, which has occurred, would have been obviated. We consider that the failure to do this was even less excusable than the original error in the selection of the site. The actual work was well carried out, but practically no limit was placed on expenditure.

The first batch of PoWs arrived in March 1917. They were billeted in a large camp just north of Lambdoughty. Altogether around 3,000 men worked on the ill-conceived project, estimated to cost £150,000. Had the project been allowed to carry on to completion, it is believed that improvements in aircraft technology that were being established, enabling planes to fly faster, would have made the slow moving targets obsolete and the gunnery school redundant before it could have become fully functional. The camp closed on 21 August 1918. Another project, set up near to Montrose, replaced the shambolic Loch Doon project.

The internees criticised the kitchen amenities at Loch Doon.

Dalmellington, Ayrshire is listed by the FPHS (1973). The camp's TA was Priswarian: Dalmellington (ADM 1/8506/265–120667).

DKF 31: In Loch Doon sind die Kessel zu klein, oft herrscht sogar Mangel an Heizmaterial; auch in Kinlochleven fehlen oft die zum Kochen notwendigen Kohlen.

DKF 31: Auch in Loch Doon, auf der Insel Raasay, in Newlandside, Ceal Aston (sic), *Sutton Veney* (sic), *Bowithick, Netheravon, Yatesbury, Rovrah* (sic), *Port Clarence und Hayrmyres* (sic) *werden die Leute zu sehr ausgenutst. Die Heranziehung der Einäugigen zu schwerer Arbeit in Loch Doon und der dreistündige Arbeitszwang für die vom Arzt krank geschriebenen Leute in Kinlochleven, müssen unbedingt abbgestellt werden.*

LONDON. Many locations in London were used to detain both combatants and non-combatants during the First World War. It is also where trials were held of persons charged with spying.

ABBEY MILL: West Ham (OS: TQ 392 834). Eight watermills were recorded on the River Lea, at Stratford, within the Manor of Alestan (West Ham) in the Domesday Book (of 1086). William de Montfitchet established an abbey at Stratford Langthorne around 1134, near a mill, 'using the power of the Lea'. This mill or a successor could be then known thereafter as Abbey Mill, and it survived the dissolution of the monasteries in 1539. The function of the mill is uncertain, but it probably produced flour. Records show it stood in Abbey Row. The area began to become known as Abbey Mill, especially after a pumping station that plays an integral part in taking the sewage away from the capital was created bearing that mantle. In 1914, West Ham Borough Council bought the area from Christ's Hospital. The hospital, on the outskirts of Horsham, was one of the first places used to intern German and Austrian businessmen living in Britain when war was declared.

The address cited by the POWIB (1919) for this working camp was Abbey Mill, Manor Road, Canning Town; giving its code as Pa (We H) (IWM: Facsimile K4655). The FPHS (1973) incorrectly cite Abbey Mills, Lancs in its lists.

ALEXANDRA PALACE (OS: TQ 295 901). Alexandra Palace is in North London. It was converted to be the last civilian enemy alien internment camp to be opened in the early stages of the First World War. The 'cultural and entertainment centre' had begun its war service as a refuge for Belgians in September 1914. It then lay dormant from March 1915 to 7 May 1915, when a barbed wire perimeter fence was erected and guards put in place to accept internees. When prison ships were being phased out, many civilians then held on the HMT *Royal Edward* and HMT *Saxonia* were transferred there. The Palace's trustees charged the government £225 per week to lease the premises.

At its peak, some 3,000 men were held there. It has been calculated that around 17,000 civilians passed through its doors by the time it closed in May 1919. True to military parlance, each of the three large halls, which housed around 1,000 each, were called Battalions. Each of these was subsequently divided into companies. They elected their own company captain to act as a spokesman. In June 1915, Rudolf Rocker was sent to Battalion 'B'. Panayi (*The Enemy In Our Midst: Germans in Britain during the First World War*, 1991) describes these battalions as having thirteen companies, with each unit comprising 80–100 men.

The Times (28 September 1915) cited that around 1,000 aliens living in London were rounded up. Some 600 of their number went to Alexandra Palace, with the remaining 400 going to Stratford in London's East End. Eventually combatants were also sent to Alexandra Palace.

Returned to the trustees after the war, Alexandra Palace was briefly used by the British Broadcasting Corporation to make programmes. It was partially destroyed by a fire in the 1960s, and today it stages both national and international events.

The camp's POWIB (1919) code was Ax P (IWM: Facsimile K4655). Its TA is cited as Priswarian: Alexandra Palace, London (ADM 1/8506/265–120667).

HM PRISON BRIXTON (OS: TQ 305 742). Mark, Graham (per. comm., various dates) cites that Leutnant Matthias Peterson was detained at Gibraltar and brought to Britain for internment. When he attempted to escape from Southampton on 23 March 1915, he faced a court martial at Southampton on 8 April 1915. He was sentenced to three years imprisonment, but this was commuted to four months, which was served at Brixton Prison. He also provides details of Ober-Leutnant Flieger, a German Naval officer, who wrote to the American Embassy from Brixton Prison, on 7 May 1915, disputing his trial by court martial for attempting to escape from Dyffryn Aled on 23 April 1915. He stated such proceedings contravened Article 8 of Chapter 11 of the Hague Convention. In their defence the War Office stated Section 22 of The Army Act covered the offence of escape. Mark cites other sources have named this officer as Andler.

Hans Andler and Hans Friedrich Rudolf von Sander Leben both escaped from Denbigh on 5 April 1915. According to *The Liverpool Echo* and *The Manchester Evening News* (both 23 April 1915) and *The Post* (2 May 1915), they appeared in court on charges relating to their escape.

On 13 June 1918, the Swiss authorities forwarded a letter from Berlin. It asked why about forty-eight Germans had been held in Brixton Prison before being moved to Compound 4 in Camp III, on the Isle of Man. The Foreign Office replied that they had been transferred to Knockaloe from Brixton at their own request. It was further cited that 'all in that compound had criminal antecedents or were of character such that it was in the best interest of the other prisoners to keep them separate.'

Brixton Prison was also used to detain at least one of those convicted of espionage before they were taken to the Tower of London for execution. On 21 June 1915, Carl Frederick Muller had his appeal rejected and the following day he was taken in a London taxi cab, from Brixton Prison to the Tower of London, to be executed. On the way to the Tower the cab broke down. Muller eventually reached his place of execution in a second hired taxi.

ISLINGTON NORTH: St Mary's Institute (OS: TQ 302 867). This camp was set up in the former workhouse that stands on Cornwallis Road, in Islington, London.

Islington's first workhouse was set up in a rented house, *c.*1726, at Stroud Green. Around five years later a new workhouse was set up on Holloway Road, near Ring Cross. As time passed, and the need for more places grew, more property was rented. Then the Poor Law in England was restructured. As a result of this restructuring, the West London Poor Law Union was formalised on 13 December 1837. In 1864, the union erected a new T-shaped workhouse for 500 inmates at the west side of Cornwallis Road. Its architects were Searle, Son and Yelf. The administrative offices and the master's quarters were at its hub. The male accommodation was in the southern wing, with the female section in the north. The dining-hall, with the chapel above, lay to the rear. The West London Union was absorbed into the City of London Union in 1869. The workhouse then became known was The St. Mary's Institute. It was to here that the internees were sent in 1914.

The POWIB (1919) cites this institute was in Cornwallis Road. The camp's TA was Cornwallis Road Institution, London N19 according to a HO document (ADM 1/8506/265–120667). The camp's POWIB (1919) code was Isl (IWM: Facsimile K4655).

It was one of the few camps run by the Home Office. It was estimated that 700 civilians were detained there at any one time. They were all from the London area, and all deemed enemy aliens. Most were Germans that had settled in the UK and were married to British born women. Most would have posed no threat to national security and were detained for their own protection. The external guard comprised of four police constables and a sergeant. An elected committee ran the internal affairs of the camp. The camp was inspected by a delegation of the American Embassy in London on 1 March 1916. Panayi (1991) notes the camps at Islington and Hackney Wick shared the same commandant, Major Sir Frederick Halliday.

Islington remained operational until November 1919. When Knockaloe closed in September 1919, its last 278 internees were transferred to Islington as it was being used to house those seeking exemption, to Mr Justice Younger's committee, from repatriation.

On 31 July 19, the Home Secretary had been asked by Sir John Butcher how many Germans were in the UK, and whether he intended to deport them, unless they obtained exemption from the Advisory Committee presided over by Mr Justice Younger. Edward Shortt informed him that there were 5,785 males and 5,965 females not being interned, and 3,256 Germans still under internment in this country, and he proposed to deport those who were not recommended for exemption by Mr Justice Younger's committee.

A censor's mark, showing the date 31 August 1915, is included in Carter's (Russell, 1996) postal history book.

Islington, London is the entry made by the FPHS (1973). It was also cited in a document held by the Osterreichisches Staatsarchiv (GZ 9815/0-KA/97).

The workhouse site has been redeveloped and is now occupied by housing.

LEWISHAM: 2 Belmont Grove (OS: TQ 385 757). *The Times* (16 March 1918) stated this camp, and four others, had been set up as a retaliatory measure to the Germans putting their PoWs near to the front. The British denied this was the case in a reply sent to the Swiss on 26 July 1918.

The camp was for forty officers and ten servants that had been moved from Philberd's House, near Maidenhead. The new camp was described as being in a mansion house, built *c.*1850. It was at 2 Belmont Grove, Lewisham. According to Macpherson, Horrocks & Beveridge (*History of the Great War – Medical Services*, 1923) the camp opened on 23 April 1918, and closed on 10 January 1919.

During this short lifespan there was one escape attempt that made the press. *The Times* (4 July 1918) reported that Lt Walter Tarnou, of the German Air Service, got away, and that he had been re-captured some 30 miles away. Apparently, according to the *Kentish Mercury* (5 July 1918) he was trying to steal an aircraft from an airfield at Farnborough.

Lewisham is also cited in a HO document that gives Priswaroff: Lewisham as its TA (ADM 1/8506/265–120667).

HACKNEY WICK: Gainsbourgh Road (OS: TQ 364 851). Bird (*Control of Enemy Alien Civilians in Great Britain 1914–1918*, 1986) cites that Hackney Wick was created for internees 'with a knowledge or aptitude for mechanical work'. Adept civilians with good engineering skills were gathered together at a disused part of the workhouse in Hackney Wick to produce tools, fixtures and gauges for making sewing machines, with the equipment supplied by Messrs. Vickers Ltd. The Gainsborough Road Casual Ward functioned from 1898 to 1904, offering overnight accommodation for vagrants, who also had to work in return for their accommodation. It was also a 'labour test' site, where non-residential able-bodied paupers performed daytime work in order to gain poor relief. With reception rooms, bathrooms, sleeping cells, work cells, workshops, a laundry, water tower, and administrative offices designed by William A. Finch, they were taken over by the Home Office in 1916.

The first parts produced at the workhouse left the assembly line in autumn 1917.

Like Islington, this camp came under the umbrella of the Home Office, and was guarded by the police force. The commandant however was a soldier. Major Sir Frederick Haliday was also the commandant at the nearby Islington North camp.

A delegation from the US Embassy in London visited the workhouse on 10 October 1916. A report produced by them states the camp opened on 1 June 1916. There were fifty-seven Germans and eight Austrians interned at the time of their visit: but more were expected. The men slept on the two upper floors. The kitchen, canteen, dining area and admin were on the ground floor. Outside, there was a vegetable garden, a skittle alley, and a recreational area. There was no hospital ward at the workhouse;

any patients were taken to the German Hospital in Dalston (1.5 miles away) for treatment. Visits from families were permitted, twice a week for two hours. The men were paid for the work they produced. Their weekly gross wages ranged from 13s.5d (67p) to £3.2s.4d (£3.12p). Disputes arose, as the authorities clawed back part of their earnings for board and lodgings; they were also expected to pay tax too.

When a delegation from the Swedish Legation in London visited the camp in December 1917 it was reported there were 116 Germans, fifty-nine Austrians, and seven Hungarians being interned. In the New Year, a further twenty internees arrived, requiring five wooden huts that could sleep up to twenty men in each to be erected to augment the main building (FO 383/306).

With the Armistice in place, in December 1918 the internees requested they be allowed home visits, on parole, at least once a month. This was in line with an announcement in the House of Commons suggesting internees might be allowed out on parole for good conduct and industry every 2½ to 3 months (*Hansard*, 1918).

The Times (4 June 1919) reported the Hackney Wick camp had been vacated. Mark (*Prisoners of war in British Hands*, 2007) believes the site was developed as Hackney Baths before being lost under a motorway.

It was listed by the POWIB (1919) and had the code Hny. It was also cited by the Osterreichisches Staatsarchiv (GZ 9815/0-KA/97).

HM PRISON HOLLOWAY (OS: TQ 306 859). When Countess Markievicz was interned for a second time, she, along with Edith Maud Gonne MacBride and Kathleen Clarke, for their roles in The German Plot, in May 1918, were put in Holloway Prison.

McConville (*Irish Political Prisoners, 1848–1922: Theatres of War*, 2005) states many considered Clarke's plight particularly distasteful. The British had executed her husband, Tom, and her brother, Ned Daly, and was now separating her from her five children without producing any charges whatsoever. After a time, the women were allowed to associate and have food, clothes, books, newspapers and painting supplies sent in. For one day in August 1918 the women were joined by Hannah Sheehy-Skeffington, who was also arrested under the Defence of the Realm Act, but only detained for twenty-four hours.

MacBride, whose husband James was executed along with James Connolly, was the founder of *Inghinidhe na hÉireann* (Daughters of Ireland). In May 1914, it was to merge with the newly-formed *Cumann na mBan* organisation. MacBride was released to a nursing home in London in October 1918. The health of Clarke, who was also a member of *Cumann na mBan*, was considered to be even worse than that of MacBride and she was released in February 1919. The Countess was released on 10 March 1919.

The German Plot was a rationale given by the British authorities for a mass round-up and internment of Irish nationalists in May 1918. But no reliable evidence ever came to light to give credence that the *Sinn Féin* leadership was planning to open a military front in Ireland with German help. The resulting imprisonment of moderates within the *Sinn Féin* leadership allowed Michael Collins to consolidate his control of the organization and to give focus to a more militant footing. At best, the plot is seen as a mistake by the British, based on flawed intelligence. Attempts to validate the 'plot' and link it with an earlier Indian-German conspiracy are entirely unproven.

OLYMPIA EXHIBITION HALLS (OS: TQ 243 790). Many males of military age of Austrian or German descent, living in Britain when war was declared in August 1914, were arrested under new legislative powers that had been quickly drafted and passed through parliament. Bird (*The Control of Enemy Alien Civilians in Great Britain 1914–1918*, 1986) cites the following locations were all used to intern civilians in the early weeks of the war: Olympia, Frimley, Haywards Heath, Newbury, Stratford, Lancaster, Queensferry, Stobs, Handforth, York, Wakefield, Southampton and Douglas. According to him the majority were interned near to where they lived; 'they were housed in an assortment of accommodation, ranging from disused factories and workhouses to tents and ships.' They became known as enemy aliens.

Bishop (*The Illustrated London News – Social History of the First World War*, 1982) suggests these new powers resulted in the Olympia Exhibition Halls, in London, becoming a place of internment, and some 300 enemy aliens residing in the Home Counties were sent there. Rocker (*The London Years*, 1956) cited the centre also held merchant seamen of German and Austro-Hungarian origins, taken from ships that had been confiscated in British territorial waters. A German anarchist residing in Britain, he was amongst those taken there. His wife, Millie, was put into Aylesbury Prison. He arrived at the Olympia on 3 December 1914, and was met by the camp commandant, Lord Lanesborough, whom he described as 'a pleasant old gentleman'. On his arrival he was informed that for one pound a week he could stay in the restaurant where he could expect better conditions than in the other parts of the camp, which were the exhibition halls. The two exhibition halls were sub-divided into twelve sections, with up to 150 internees in each. Each section was segregated from its neighbour by a heavy rope and to move between sections permission had to be sought from a guard. Rocker described the whole place as being 'sad and hopeless'. He wrote that he felt better once he had been moved to a prison ship moored in the Thames Estuary, off Southend-on-Sea.

As a result of being stopped and questioned in Stoke Newington, 17-year-old German student Karl Wehner became one of the first internees of the war; after being held in a local police cell for one night, he was taken to Olympia. Wehner, according to Gillmann (*Collar the Lot: How Britain Interned and Expelled its Wartime Refugees*, 1980), described the conditions at Olympia as 'somewhat rough and ready'. Those interned had to sleep on damp straw paillasses spread throughout the hall. They used the hall's public lavatories, and at first could do so in relative privacy; but after an attempt to escape through one of the toilet windows, all the cubicle doors were removed. A guard was then positioned outside the toilets to regulate the queue, barking at each internee as he approached, 'Piss er a shit?' Wehner was sent to HMT *Royal Edward*.

By early November there were 1,500 men interned at Olympia. Bird (1986) cites Olympia ceased to be an internment camp when it was required for another use. Olympia is listed by the FPHS (1973).

HM PRISON PENTONVILLE (OS: TQ 307 846). Roger David Casement was born on 1 September 1864. He had gained notoriety for his report, published in 1904, that led to a major reorganisation of Belgian rule in the Congo. Then for a similar report about the conditions in the Putumayo River Region of Peru in 1912 he was knighted. When ill-health had forced him to retire, he went back to Ireland. He then helped the Irish National Volunteers, and in July 1914 he travelled to New York City to seek aid for their cause. Casement was party to obtaining a cargo of rifles and ammunition brought to Howth Harbour on 26 July 1914. He had acquired the weapons from a dealer in Antwerp. It was done in response to the Ulster Volunteers landing a shipment of guns at Larne on 24 April 1914.

Jackson (*Home Rule: An Irish History 1800–2000*, 2004) cites when the First World War broke out in August, Casement went to Berlin to ask the German government for help. The Germans realised the potential that an uprising in Ireland could have but they were still unwilling to risk an expedition to Ireland, or to loan army officers to lead an Irish rising. In the end Casement only succeeded in securing a token gesture of arms that were dispatched aboard the SS *Libau*, which was disguised as a Norwegian merchant ship named the SS *Aud Norge*. It sailed around the north of Scotland to the agreed rendezvous point of Inishtooskert, County Kerry. After failing to make contact with the shore party it moved offshore again, only to be intercepted by HMS *Bluebell* who ordered the ship to follow them into Queenstown. Unknown to her escort, charges were set to scuttle the craft, as the crew put on their German naval uniforms. The German Ensign was hoisted as the charges were detonated, off Daunt's Rock. All the crew surrendered as the ship and its cargo went to the seabed. Meanwhile, Casement had been to Limburg Lahn Prison Camp to try to persuade the Irish prisoners to form a brigade that would fight in Ireland against Britain. Only sixty were recruited.

On 12 April 1916 Casement was put ashore near Tralee from a German submarine, and was arrested twelve days later to be taken to London and put in the Tower. He was tried at the Old Bailey on 29 June 1916. Found guilty of treason, he was sentenced to death and was hanged at Pentonville Prison on 3 August 1916. In 1965, Casement's remains were returned to Ireland and buried in Glasnevin Cemetery in Dublin.

STRATFORD: Carpenters Road (OS: TQ 384 840). Panayi (1991) cites a camp opened on 20 December 1914 in Stratford, London. According to Bird (1986) it was one of the first internment camps to be opened in the UK during the First World War. *The Borough of West Ham, East Ham & Stratford Express* (28 November 1914) cited a camp was being prepared in Carpenters Road, Stratford, for internees, which until a few years previously had been a jute works. The premises to be used had belonged to William Ritchie & Son. Jute spinners, their factory had opened in 1864. They had around 1,000 employees, mainly women, by 1876. The mill closed in 1904, and its production of making jute sacks was transferred to Caxton Street North, in Canning Town. The refurbishment of the dormant factory took over 100 men three weeks to complete. *Essex County Chronicle* (4 December 1914) cited an internment camp was being established at Stratford, in premises taken over by the authorities. This was a large unoccupied factory, near to Stratford Market Station. *The East and West Ham & South Essex Mail and the Stratford Express* (both 18 December 1914) reported the first batch of German prisoners for internment at the jute factory had arrived at Stratford on Tuesday (15th), five days earlier than that cited by Panayi (1991).

The *Stratford Express* (2 January 1915) stated there were now around 100 internees at the camp. There was also a report of a Christmas service held by a Lutheran Minister. Prisoners had a Christmas tree and gifts 'from German ladies'.

The Times and the *Stratford Express* (both 29 January 1915) reported that a concert had taken place at the former jute works to celebrate the Kaiser's birthday.

Mr John Jackson visited the camp on 28 January on behalf of the US Embassy in London. He cited the camp opened in mid-December. At the time of his visit there were approximately 400 men being interned, however the actual numbers were always in a constant state of flux as new men came in and others left for other destinations. The number of internees at the camp rose in January 1915, from 400 to 740 by May of that year. A year later the number had dropped to 174, before rising again to 260 that

December. Internal policing was done by a group of internees that enjoyed its own messing, sleeping and other privileges. The rest slept in one large hall on wooden beds with straw mattresses. There was steam heating and electric light, but these were used sparingly in the mornings and switched off at 9.15 to save expense. The cement floor was dry. The internees ate in a different part of the hall to where they slept, but in inclement weather it had to be used for exercise. In good weather the men could go outside, though exercise was not compulsory. There was little opportunity for occupational therapy. There were only the camp chores and local improvements, like for example making paths or shoe repairs, to occupy their time. Jackson also noted that a single barbed-wire fence, then a 'danger zone' and finally a high wire fence surrounded the camp. The guard had orders to shoot anyone in the danger zone. Occasional parole was permitted and visits were allowed, including from female members of families. The internees had organised their own post office and circulating library, with an ex-chef from the Trocadero in charge of the kitchens. There was a canteen available but no alcohol allowed to be sold. A concert – they had a piano – had been organised for the Kaiser's birthday. No deaths had been reported in the camp, but two patients had been sent to outside hospitals for treatment. A number of cases of venereal disease had been found and individuals concerned were being isolated, as far as possible, using separate baths and WCs. There were also punishment cells, but they lay empty at the time of Jackson's visit. Twenty-four hours on bread and water was the maximum punishment given.

The *Stratford Express* (6 March 1915) reported that around 400 PoWs were marched to the station, among them several Turkish officers, to be transferred to the Isle of Man.

The *East Ham Echo and Stratford Express* (both 15 May 1915) carried reports of riots and looting taking place in the wake of the sinking of the RMS *Lusitania.*

A visit on behalf of the US Embassy in London on 22 May 1915 cited there were 740 prisoners which was almost the total number recorded on the previous visit by John Jackson on 28 January 1915. Many of the internees had come from Cameroon, or South West Africa.

The South Essex Mail (25 June 1915) reported, over 500 internees were marched out of their camp on Friday, and were taken to the railway station. It was the second batch of 500 to leave the camp that week.

Richard Noschke, who kept a diary, was one of those interned. He wrote he was sent to Ritchie's Works in Carpenters Road, Stratford on 23 July 1915. German by birth, he had married an English woman and had been living in Britain happily for twenty-five years, before his arrest. After his arrest he noted an acute change of attitude from his in-laws and family friends, which greatly saddened him. There were already 400 men billeted at Carpenters Road when he arrived. In the days ahead, many internees came and went: many to more permanent places, whilst others awaited their repatriation. It made it hard to strike up friendships. *The Times* (28 September 1915) cited around 1,000 aliens living in London had been rounded up. Some 600 had gone to Alexandra Palace, with the remaining 400 going to Stratford. Noschke made several negative comments about the state of the camp. He wrote the food was poor. He also cited the roof leaked, and the drains were inadequate. The YMCA had provided a tent but it could only take 200 men. He also noted the recreation area, measuring some 50 × 80 yards, was not big enough for the needs of the 750 men being interned in the camp. He also noted that a stable had been converted to serve as the hospital. He was appalled at the treatment meted out to his countrymen when the *Lusitania* was sunk. However, conditions did improve. He was at Stratford for only nineteen months when he applied for a transfer. In February 1917 he was moved to Alexandra Palace, where he became a camp gardener.

Other inmates also cited the accommodation as poor and the administration as intolerant. The commandant was cited as the Marquis de Burr. He kept the five punishment cells well occupied with men on bread and water. At the end of October 1915, 500 men were transferred to the Isle of Man. Early in the spring of 1916, de Burr left and was replaced by Heygate-Lambert who, it was stated, was even worse than his predecessor. Lambert was very strict about the internees' letters. He denied Noschke the opportunity to lodge an appeal for release. In July 1916, Heygate-Lambert was moved to Frongoch, and replaced by Colonel Haines. Haines was 'a perfect gentleman in every way' and conditions began to improve under his command. But soon he too was moved on, and was succeeded by Colonel Lushcombe, and the bad old days were quickly reinstated (*An Insight into Civilian Internment in Britain during WW1*, AGFHS, 1998).

Paul Cohen-Portheim was taken off a Dutch ship. He passed through Stratford on his way to Knockaloe. He reported it as being worse than anything he could have had imagined. Because there was such a high turnover of internees that never stayed very long, no community spirit ever developed amongst the internees (Cohen-Portheim, *Time Stood Still: My Internment in England 1914–18*, 1931).

The Times (30 December 1916) reported that 25-year-old Emile Schmidt (a.k.a. Revosa), a ship's steward, had escaped.

The *Stratford Express* (2 May 1917) reported that Isaac Judah Hannar, an Austrian aged 37, had been charged with maliciously wounding Frederich Rauchstadt, a German.

Thomas (*St Stephen's House: Friends Emergency Work in England 1914–1920*, 1920) cited the building was not suitable for prolonged internment of men. Declared unsuitable, because the building was deemed draughty and unhealthy, it closed in 1917.

Belfield (*Report on the Directorate of Prisoners of War, 1920*) cites:

> Civilian prisoners began to move to the island's [the Isle of Man] camp from the ships in the Spring of 1915, leaving, eventually, only three camps for civilians in England – at Wakefield; Stratford, SE; and in the Alexandra Palace – and one at Oldcastle in Ireland.

In addition to this camp, there was another camp, for combatants at Stratford upon Avon cited by the FPHS (1973). A new camp, for officers, was created in October 1918, at Nos 11 & 13 Watery Lane, Stratford, according to a HO document. It closed on 11 December 1918.

STRATFORD: Watery Lane (OS: TQ 394 847). A new camp opened in Stratford, for officers, according to a HO document. It cites Nos 11 & 13 Watery Lane, Stratford were used for this purpose in October 1918 (ADM 1/8506/265–120667).

Macpherson Horrocks & Beveridge (*History of the Great War – Medical Services*, 1923) cite this camp had opened on 23 April 1918. They suggest the camp, for forty officers and ten servants, was in a mansion house.

The HO recorded the camp closed on 11 December 1918. It was one of a number of camps set up as reprisal camps. The officers were purposely moved into areas that were being bombed as the Germans were holding Allied prisoners near to the front line.

The Times (11 June 1918) cites three officers escaped from Water Lane (sic), Stratford. They were recaptured two days later.

THE TOWER OF LONDON (OS: TQ 243 790). On 3 August 1916, Roger Casement was hanged for treason at Pentonville Prison. Eight others, also found guilty of spying, were executed in the Tower of London. All had been tried in a military court for offences committed against the Defence of the Realm Act (1914), for an offence that carried the death penalty. Their arrests and subsequent convictions were the culmination of the work of MO5, the predecessor of MI5. All are buried in East London Cemetery, Plaistow. They were:

Name	*Date executed*	*Place*
Karl Hans Lody	6 November 1914	Miniature Rifle Range
Carl Frederick Müller	23 June 1915	Miniature Rifle Range
Haicke Petrus Marinus Janssen	30 July 1915	The Ditch of the Tower
Willem Johannes Roos	30 July 1915	The Ditch of the Tower
Ernst Waldemar Melin	10 September 1915	Miniature Rifle Range
Augusto Alfredo Roggen	17 September 1915	Miniature Rifle Range
Fernando Buschmann	19 October 1915	Miniature Rifle Range
Georg Traugott Breeckow	26 October 1915	Miniature Rifle Range

(*The King's Council: The Life of Sir Henry Curtis-Bennett*, Wild, 1938)

Lody had been sent to Britain to observe and report back ship movements of the Royal Navy. Given a substantial amount of money, an American passport, and the alias Charles A. Inglis during his stay in Edinburgh, he regularly sent messages to his contacts in Stockholm. His correspondence was being monitored by MO5 who were monitoring all mail sent abroad. On a trip to Dublin he sent an un-encrypted letter describing the ships in Liverpool's docks, and conversations that he had overheard. As its content revealed real military value to the Germans, he was arrested on 2 October 1914. Lody was tried in public and the case was widely reported in the press; he was found guilty.

Müller was fluent in Russian, German, Dutch, Flemish and English. He was on a trip to Germany to pick up mechanical engines, from Antwerp where he had been living, when he was recruited into the German Secret Service. Like Lody, postal censors were routinely monitoring his mail. Müller was arrested on the 25 February 1915. An acquaintance of Müller, John Hahn, who owned a baker's shop in Deptford, was persuaded to write a letter to which Müller then added messages, written in invisible ink, in-between the lines written by Hahn. Hahn, naively, sent the letter to Müller's contact putting his address on the back of the envelope. It was intercepted, and Special Branch detectives went to Hahn's home on 24 February 1915 where they found a pen and a piece of lemon. They also found a piece of paper with Müller's Guildford Street address written on it, in invisible ink. Both were tried at the Central Criminal Court (Old Bailey) on 2–4 June 1915. Hahn pleaded guilty and was sentenced to seven years imprisonment. Müller pleaded not guilty but was found guilty.

Janssen and Roos arrived in Britain within twenty-fours of each other. Janssen came via Hull on 12 May 1915. Roos had come in through London a day later. Both claimed to be cigar salesmen from Amsterdam. Janssen went to Southampton on 22 May 1915. A telegram sent by him was intercepted and he was arrested on 30 May 1915, suspected of being a spy. When his belongings were searched, they found a letter stating he was an employee of Dierks & Co. The search revealed Janssen had been in Edinburgh on 18 May 1915, staying in a hotel near the Port of Leith, a port being used by vessels of the Royal Navy. Roos alerted the security services when he sent a postcard of HMS *Indefatigable* to Dierks. He was arrested on 2 June 1915. In his belongings incriminating material was found. Janssen and Roos were interviewed separately at New Scotland Yard on 3 June 1915. Roos admitted knowing Janssen. They were tried separately at Middlesex Guildhall. Janssen presented no defence and made no statement. He was found guilty on 16 July 1915. The following day Roos was also found guilty and both were sentenced to death by shooting. Roos's sanity was questioned, but it called for no modification to his sentence. They were executed within ten minutes of each other.

Melin was a Swedish national. When the First World War broke out, he was living in the Russian town of Nikolaieff, where he worked in a shipbroker's office. After the loss of his job he travelled to Hamburg, to stay with friends. At his father's suggestion he contacted a man called Gerdes, who introduced him to several German friends. It was suggested to him that he travel to Antwerp, to meet Dierks. Melin took lodgings in London on 12 January 1915 and stayed for two weeks. He returned to Holland and reported on the various interesting items he had seen. It was agreed that he would return to England on 26 February 1915. Under the radar of the British security services Melin was arrested. He was tried 20–21 August 1915 at Middlesex Guildhall. Found guilty, he was sentenced to death by shooting.

Roggen was born in Montevideo. His father was a German who had become a Uruguayan citizen. Roggen arrived in Tilbury Docks on 30 May 1915 from Rotterdam, where he told the authorities he was an agricultural salesman intending to travel to Scotland on business. He went to Edinburgh on 5 June 1915. He sent two postcards to Holland. Both were intercepted by the British security services because they had been sent to addresses known to them. Under surveillance, Roggen booked into the Tarbet Hotel at Loch Lomond on 9 June 1915, stating he was going fishing. That area however was in a restricted zone, used for testing torpedoes, raising concerns about his movements. He was arrested on 9 June 1915. Unwilling to explain the postcards or the Browning revolver with fifty rounds of ammunition that were found, Roggen was tried at Middlesex Guildhall on 20 August 1915. He gave no evidence and made no statement in his defence. Found guilty, he was sentenced to death by shooting. Because the Uruguayan Ambassador sought clemency the date for his original execution was postponed.

Buschmann was French by birth and educated in Austria. His parents had moved to Brazil where he began an import/export business importing commodities from Europe and exporting bananas and potatoes in return. Experiencing difficulties because of the anti-German feeling in Britain during the war Buschmann had travelled to Hamburg to tidy up his business dealings before coming to London. In London, Bushman met Emil Samuel Franco, an employee of Messrs Bolus & Co., who had stopped shipments from his company in Brazil. On 23 April 1915, Buschman went to Southampton. The following day he received a telegram from Flores Dierks & Co., which alerted the security services. On the morning of 5 June 1915, Buschman was arrested. He denied sending telegrams to Dierks, and was unable to satisfactorily explain why they were so interested in a new employee to transfer him money, via telegram. Buschman's trial took place on 29–30 September 1915, at Middlesex Guildhall. Pleading not guilty, he presented evidence on his own behalf. Found guilty, he was sentenced to death by shooting. His request that he be allowed to have his violin, to keep his mind occupied in his last hours, was granted, and the night before his execution he played through the night. It is stated that before leaving his cell in the

Tower, Buschman picked up his violin and kissed it, saying, 'Goodbye, I shall not want you any more.'

Breeckow was born in Germany, but had become an American citizen, before returning to Berlin on 28 May 1914 to work for the Bureau of Foreign Affairs. He made several requests to be allowed to return to the USA, but was persuaded to wait until they were sure of the situation regarding American-German relations. When Breeckow was informed he could return, he had to travel to Holland to meet a Mr Dierks to arrange his business cover. He was to be given a new passport in the name of Reginald Rowland, because his own had been stamped in Berlin. Breeckow arrived at Gravesend on 11 May 1915 and went straight to London to make contact with Lizzi Emily Vertheim, who had been recruited by German intelligence. They travelled to Britain together.

As instructed, Breeckow sent a package to H. Flores in Rotterdam. As Flores was being monitored by the British security services, the package was intercepted as were letters he sent, with his address on the back of the envelopes. Breeckcow was arrested on 4 June 1915, as was Vertheim on 9 June 1915. They were tried together at the Old Bailey on 14 -17 September 1915. Both pleaded not guilty. Breeckow admitted a great deal in an attempt to protect Vertheim, but the jury took just eight minutes to decide they were both guilty. Vertheim was sentenced to ten years imprisonment, and Breeckow was sentenced to death by shooting. Vertheim was initially sent to Aylesbury Prison, but in 1918 she was certified as insane and transferred to Broadmoor Criminal Lunatic Asylum, where her behaviour and general medical condition worsened. She died of pulmonary tuberculosis on 29 July 1920.

Ries was an alias; his real name has never been disclosed. On 4 July 1915, after arriving from New York via Liverpool, he travelled to London, claiming he was a sales representative for the hay and corn business. He travelled to several cities in the UK, before, on 9 August 1915, going to the American Embassy in London to obtain a visa for his passport, stating he wished to travel to Rotterdam. When his passport was examined it was noted that it was a forgery, and the British police were informed. He was arrested on 10 August 1915. Ries was tried at Middlesex Guildhall on 28–29 September 1915. At his trial he pleaded not guilty. He refused to provide details about his birth, apart from saying that his father was Dutch and his mother was Scottish. He was found guilty. It was reported Ries shook hands with each of his executioners and said, 'You're only doing your duty, as I did mine.' He was reputed to have refused to give his real name to protect his parents from knowing how he met his death.

Meyer claimed he was a Danish citizen working in the catering industry in Hamburg, Seville and Pamplona, prior to arriving in the UK during June 1914. He continued to work in that trade, before seeking permission to travel to Copenhagen, via Flushing and Germany, on 22 March 1915, which was granted. He returned to the UK during May 1915 and married Catherine Rebecca Godleman at St Pancras Registry Office. The ever vigilant security services intercepted a letter destined for a suspicious address in The Hague, and incriminating evidence written in invisible ink, was found giving information about the locations of ships, and describing ways men were being coerced into enlisting. Late in August 1915, Meyer and his wife were arrested. She was cleared of any involvement and was subsequently released. Meyer was tried at Middlesex Guildhall on 5–6 November 1915. He was found guilty and sentenced to death by shooting. The Danish Embassy denied that Meyer was a Danish subject, and he may have been either German or a Turk.

Zender was Peruvian. He came to Europe in August 1914, claiming to trade in paper, handkerchiefs and various food products. He arrived in Glasgow via Bergen, Oslo and Copenhagen. During late May 1915, the British security services started intercepting telegrams sent to an address in Oslo, which they knew was acting as a collection point for the German intelligence services. Zender had sent all the telegrams, which were signed in his own name and stated his address as 59 Union Street in Glasgow. Unaware the police had circulated his details when he arrived back in Newcastle on 2 July 1915 from a trip to Bergen, he was immediately arrested. In his possessions were found various hotel bills, which suggested that he had been in Norway, Denmark and Germany, and a covering letter stating that he was ordering sardines and other tinned fish for shipment back to Peru. However it was not the correct season for sardines. His trial was delayed due to him requesting evidence from Peru, which took around twenty-eight days to reach the UK. The Peruvian Embassy in London also requested to speak with Zender, which was approved. He was tried on 20–22 March 1916, at Caxton Hall Westminster, where he pleaded not guilty. He was found guilty and sentenced to death by shooting.

HM PRISON WORMWOOD SCRUBS (OS: TQ 222 812). Robert Rosenthal was 23 years old when he arrived in Britain from Copenhagen on an American passport. *The New York Times* (7 & 9 June 1915) reported that he was arrested in May 1915 and charged with forging passports. Under arrest, he reputedly confessed to the British security services that the German government had the perfect equipment for manufacturing American passports. In his confession he wrote he had been employed to come to Britain to report on naval and military movements. The US Ambassador in Berlin, James W. Gerrard, pleaded for information about Rosenthal from the German government but they refused to comply with his wishes, although Rosenthal was a German citizen. He was tried on 6 July 1915 and on being found guilty was sentenced to death by hanging. He was hanged on 15 July 1915 at Wormwood Scrubs (WO 94/103).

LONDON COLNEY: Cotlands (OS: TL 174 075). Minutes of the Hertfordshire County Council WAC cite two camps in St Albans, those of Cotlands and St Michael's Rural CP. According to the minute of 1 October 1918, the smaller of these two camps was the Cotlands site. Not strictly in St Albans, it had thirty-five PoWs billeted there. The St Michael's camp had at least fifty men interned there.

The POWIB (1919) listed two locations in St Albans. The first was a working camp, with the code Pa (S A) (IWM: Facsimile K4655). Presumably this code covered both camps cited in the War Agricultural minutes. The second entry was for Napsbury War Hospital (its code was Np H). Cotlands is listed by the FPHS (1973). Its TA is Priswarian: London Colney (ADM 1/8506/265–120667).

LONG CLAWSON (OS: SK 735 277). The address for Long Clawson's agricultural group is cited by the POWIB (1919) as being at The Hall. Its code was Bro (Crx) (L C) (IWM: Facsimile K4655), making it a satellite of Croxton Park. The camp's TA was Priswarian: Long Clawson (ADM 1/8506/265–120667).

Kelly's Trade Directory of 1912 indicates there was a Hall at Long Clawson that was occupied by Major Gerald W. Hobson.

The 74th meeting (Wednesday, 30 January 1918) of the Leicestershire War Agricultural Executive Committee recorded that Depots were to be formed for PoW ploughmen at Hinckley, Loughborough, Market Harborough, North Kilworth and Long Clawson.

LOUGHBOROUGH (OS: SK 531 199). The 74th Meeting of the Leicestershire War Agricultural Executive Committee (Wednesday, 30 January 1918) accepted the need for depots for German prisoners to be formed at Hinckley, Loughborough, Market Harborough and Long Clawson. *The Hinckley Times and Bosworth Herald* (2 February 1918) cites the Unions of Loughborough and Market Harborough had granted permission or at least indicated that they would accept PoWs into their institutions. Part of this agreement stated that the PoWs would work within a 3-mile radius of the workhouses.

Accounts of PoWs being in Loughborough are recorded in the borough council's minute book of 1917–18. The first account, taken from a minute of the Sanitary Committee meeting of 20 February 1918, states:

> A suggestion was made that for the extra labour required on the Sewage Farm, application should be made to the Leicestershire War Agricultural Executive Committee for German PoWs to be employed on such work, and the Borough Surveyor was requested to communicate with the Agricultural Committee on the matter.

A month later, on 20 March 1918, the Chairman of the Committee was able to report (Minute No. 10) that several German PoWs were now employed at the Sewage Farm as per authorised by LWAEC. On 17 April 1918, a third minute informs us that there were four Germans engaged at this farm.

Loughborough agricultural depot's address is given as being in the workhouse by the POWIB (1919). Its code was Bro (Lo) (IWM: Facsimile K 4655). It records that it had five agricultural groups attached to it. These were Ashby de la Zouch, East Leake, Normanton Hall, Narborough, and Ragdale Hall. It is also cited by the FPHS (1973). The camp's TA was Priswarian: Loughborough.

This Union Workhouse was built in 1838, and was Loughborough's second (and last) workhouse. The four-storey building, which stands empty today on Derby Road, was once capable of housing 350 residents at any one time. Used as a hospital after the First World War, it was converted, in 1977, into Hastings House, a home for the elderly.

During March 1919, Dr A. de Sturler compiled a report on the PoW at Loughborough. It is held at the National Archives at Kew (FO 383/506).

The Leicestershire Record Office was able to provide further evidence of PoWs being in the area as two of their number were buried in Loughborough's Leicester Road Cemetery in 1918, before being exhumed and removed to Cannock Chase with others in 1961.

LONGBRIDGE DEVERILL (see Sutton Veny).

LUDGERSHALL: Perham Down (OS: SU 258 492). Crawford (*Wiltshire and The Great War: Training the Empire's Soldiers*, 1999) cites a War Department list dated November 1917 that cites three 'prison camps' in Wiltshire, at Larkhill, at Perham Down, and at Bulford. In June 1918, the number of camps in the county is quoted in the newspapers as five.

> ... at one time or other prisoners are recorded at most military bases [in Wiltshire], probably constituting of small groups working on local farms and

lodged in secure accommodation rather than large concentrations of men confined in the popular conception of a PoW camp.

Before the war, thousands of Britons had flocked to see the military splendour in the Grand Reviews of 1913 and 1914 at Perham Down.

Perham Down was a working camp and was cited by the POWIB (1919) as Dor (Prm) (IWM: Facsimile K4655). The camp's TA was cited as Priswarian: Perham Down (ADM 1/8506/265–120667).

Situated 1 mile from Ludgershall Station, the army camp grew from a campsite established in 1898. In early 1915, wooden huts were erected to accommodate some 5,000 men; by February 1919 these huts were in bad condition. Crawford (1999) cites a PoW camp was established at the camp, but gives no further details of it.

Just as a local man was caught selling food to PoWs at Coal Aston in South Yorkshire, Richard Bright was charged, and tried by the magistrates at Salisbury, for selling cakes to internees whilst they were being escorted in the Boscombe area. He was fined £3. The Chairman on the Bench, Mr L.M. Swayne, reckoned that the prisoners were being paid too much if they could afford this luxury. The PoWs were employed on a road construction project.

After the war the Anti-Aircraft Artillery School was based at Perham Down, as was the Royal Tank Corps, with brick buildings replacing the wooden huts.

LUNCARTY (see Strathord).

M

MACHYNLLETH: Park Common (OS: SH 760 001). The Camp's TA is cited as Priswarian: Machynlleth (ADM 1/8506/265–120667). An agricultural group, it had the POWIB (1919) working code Fg (Ty) (Mc); its parent camp being at Tywyn (IWM: Facsimile K4655). It was on Park Common, which is to the east of the town.

Park Common Lodge stands near to where copper has been extracted in the past.

Machynlleth was inspected by Dr A. de Sturler and Monsieur R. de Sturler during June 1919 (FO 383/508).

MAIDENHEAD: Holyport, Philberd's (OS: SU 894 774). Philberd's House was a large eighteenth century house, built to replace the former Manor of Philibert that had been destroyed by fire. The original building, erected for Roger de St. Phylybert, dated back to 1208. In 1860, Charles Pascoe Grenfell purchased the house from the Dean of Windsor. Reverend Edward H. Price then turned the house into a school. When he retired, his son, also named Edward, succeeded him. Around the turn of the century the school took on a military focus. The headmaster from 1908 was Mr E.G.A. Beckwith. He had founded the Army School at Stratford-on-Avon before becoming head of Imperial Service College, Windsor.

In 1914, the War Office requisitioned the school buildings, which had not been used since the pupils at Philberd's had transferred to Windsor, on the merger of the two schools. It served as an internment camp, initially for civilians, then for officers. The figures interned, suggested by Macpherson, Horrocks & Beveridge (*History of the Great War–Medical Services*, 1923), seem high compared to other contemporary reports. They cite the camp opened 14 October 1914, with maximum accommodation for 500 officers and 160 servants in the house, plus the huts. More conservative figures suggest there was accommodation for 100 officers and forty other ranks that acted as their servants. The camp was guarded by a territorial unit from the Devonshire Regiment. The *Maidenhead Advertiser* (2 December 1914) states, on 25 November 1914 about forty officer PoWs were the first to arrive at Philberd's. When they arrived, they were taken to the camp from Maidenhead station by taxis. Two days later a batch of rank and file soldiers arrived to be their servants. They had to march the 3 miles from the station.

The *Maidenhead Advertiser* (15 January 1915) reported some survivors of the Battle of the Falklands arrived. Numbers at the camp had reached over 100 officers and about fifty orderlies. Devonshire's National Reserve provided the guard, and the camp's first commandant was Major Hon Eustace H. Dawnay. Captain Armstrong was named as the Adjutant/Quarter Master.

The *Maidenhead Advertiser* (27 January 1915) reported a Norwegian visitor gave a favourable report on conditions, which *The Times* (29 January 1915) repeated when Mr John Jackson from the US Embassy in London inspected the camp. Jackson's report stated the camp opened on 24 November 1914. He noted there were 140 officers present, so the place was overcrowded. To try to alleviate the congestion, forty officers had already gone to Donington Hall in Derbyshire. There were also around forty soldier servants in the camp. The senior German officer was Korvetten-Kapitan Pochhammer, of the SMS *Gneisenau*. He had a room to himself, but the rest had to share, sometimes as many as fifteen to a room. The building had not been used for some time, and the ground floor rooms were damp and some attic rooms draughty, but repair work was being done. The house and its immediate grounds were enclosed by barbed wire, but the football field was outside the enclosure, so guards were posted on the perimeter when it was in use. Some colonials present complained of their treatment upon arrest, before their transfer to the UK, and reservists complained they had not been paid. English cooks prepared the meals, with German assistance. Jackson also commented on a swimming tank, which was empty at the time of his visit.

Early in 1915 the prisoners suddenly took to gardening in an unprecedented way. Eventually the Adjutant, Captain Armstrong, became suspicious and called in workmen to lay unneeded drainpipes. *The Times* (7 April 1915) cited that whilst they were digging with their picks they exposed a 2-foot-square tunnel, approximately 9 yards long. Its walls were encased in wood and had pads for resting your elbows on. The tunnellers had cut through the concrete foundations of a high wall and would probably have escaped had it not been for the vigilant Armstrong.

A delegation from the US Embassy in London visited the camp, again, on 27 April 1915. It was reported there were 100 officers and men in the camp. The Germans were stated to be cooking the meals themselves, having replaced the English cooks. The swimming tank was full of water and was in regular use. The commanding officer was ordered to send fifty prisoners to Donington Hall. He sought volunteers, but in the end he had to decide whom to send.

The *Maidenhead Advertiser* (22 September 1915) stated there were now around eighty PoWs in the camp.

The Times (20 December 1915) stated a Dutch newspaper reporter had visited the camp.

Maidenhead Advertiser (22 December 1915) reported on an article in *The New York Herald*, which stated there were now 125 officers and forty-seven orderlies at Holyport. The commandant was now Colonel Sir John Gladstone.

The Times (1 February 1916) reported a tunnel had been discovered. The *Maidenhead Advertiser* (9 February 1915) cited Leutnant Thelen of the German Air Service and Leutnant Keilbach of the navy were sentenced to nine months each at Chelmsford Detention Barracks for attempting to escape. Both had previously got away from Donington Hall.

The *Maidenhead Advertiser* (12 March 1916) and *The Times* (15 March 1916) reported Naval Leutnant Freiherr von Grote was caught trying to dig his way out. He was sentenced to nine months detention at Chelmsford.

Another inspection was carried out by a delegation from the US Embassy in London. It took place on 25 May 1916. The commandant was Colonel J.R. Harvey, who had recently been appointed. The roll call was eighty-nine army officers, twenty-nine naval officers, forty-seven orderlies and three civilians (two cooks and one barber), all German. The camp was described as being in a large house with twenty-three rooms. Huts supplemented the house. Initially there were three provided by the War Office but there were now seventeen although not all were in use.

Up to twenty-five PoWs at a time were allowed to take country walks under the supervision of a British officer and an orderly. *The Maidenhead Advertiser* (16 November 1916) cited these walks caused annoyance to the clientele of the Eagle Public House in Holyport Street, which was close to the camp. Its sign bore a Prussian eagle, and when the prisoners passed it they saluted. Infuriated, the landlord changed the name of his establishment to the Belgian Arms.

There was then a spate of escape attempts recorded in the press. *The Times* (9 December 1916) cited two escapees had been re-captured near Old Windsor. Two days later the same paper carried a report of an enquiry which stated they hid in waste paper. One was Leutnant Thelen, who had just returned from his detention at Chelmsford, and the other was Leutnant Anton Cmentek.

The Times (27 August 1917) stated two pilots had escaped. *The Maidenhead Advertiser* (29 August 1917) also reported the escape. They were named as Flink and von Scholtz. Their intention was to steal an aircraft and fly it back to Germany. *The Times* (29 August 1916) cited they had been re-captured at Beckenham, in Kent.

The Times and *The Maidenhead Advertiser* (both 26 September 1917) cited another escape attempt. Leutnant Henvard had attempted to pedal his way to freedom by bicycle.

The Times (12 November 1917) and *The Maidenhead Advertiser* (14 November 1917) cited Leutnant von Nassau and Leutnant Burkhardt had escaped. Both papers (19 and 21 November 1917, respectively) reported their recapture, at Bath, on the London to Bristol train.

May 1918, Colonel C.H. Colvin CB DSO was stated to be the camp's commandant. The guard was the 253 Company, Royal Defence Corps, and their commanding officer was Major Barnett.

It must have been to Philberd's House that Ober-Leutnant Heinz Justus was referring to when he recounted his second attempt to escape. Whilst being transferred from Maidenhead to Wakefield by train, under escort, he managed to jump off as it was moving slowly through a station near Doncaster. Wearing rough and ready-made civilian clothes, he made his way to Doncaster where he caught a train to London. From there he went to Cardiff, hoping to get out of Britain on a ship. Had he not caught the flu, and was obliged to give himself up at a police station, he would probably have successfully got away. After medical treatment, he was sentenced to fifty-six days at Chelmsford Prison. *The Sheffield Daily Telegraph* (26 October 1918) cited

Heinz Heinrich Ernst Justus had escaped from Wakefield. Whilst on the run he sent a parcel, containing his uniform and Iron Cross, to the commandant at Holyport. As to his personal comfort whilst at the Berkshire camp, Justus described it as being the best camp he had been at. However, Gunther Plüschow, who was to successfully escape from Donington Hall, in his brief stay at Holyport, complained of a lack of recreational space. Plüschow was one of the fifty transferred out, in March 1915.

On a more sombre note, the deaths and burials of three PoWs from Philberd's were cited. *The Times* (14 November 1918) stated the funeral of Leutnant Mahn had taken place. Next day Leutnant Mannhausen and Uffz Matuszak were buried. All three had died as a result of contracting flu. They were buried at Bray churchyard.

When the Armistice began the local newspaper, *The Maidenhead Advertiser* (1 January 1919), carried this report of the Christmas festivities held in the camp:

> Loosened from the severities of wartime disciplines, the men of the 73rd Company, Royal Defence Corps, in charge of the prisoners' camp at Holyport were permitted to indulge in a new style – or rather, the old style – form of Christmas celebration ... During the meal Colonel Colvin CB., DSO, Commandant of the Camp, and Major Lorainne, Assistant Commandant, accompanied by officers of the guard, visited the hall (the recreation hut) and were given a loyal reception.

Badly damaged during its time as an internment camp, Philberd's was demolished in 1919. In October 1919, the War Office advertised the sale of posts from the fencing around the house. The buildings were demolished shortly afterwards. Part of a wall and a moat are all that is visible today.

The camp had the POWIB (1919) code Hlt. The FPHS (1973) cite Holyport, Berkshire in its listings.

MAIDSTONE: HM Prison. Maidstone Prison stands close to the town centre in County Road. It was built between 1811 and 1818 to the designs of Daniel Alexander to accommodate 229 male and 68 female inmates, with capacity for a further 128 if required.

The prison was to accommodate Harry Boland, who along with brothers Gerry and Ned, participated in the Easter Rising of 1916. Harry was sentenced to ten years penal servitude for his role. After a brief spell at Dublin's Mountjoy Prison, he was shipped to Dartmoor Prison in England, before being moved to Lewes Prison. During this time the idea arose of putting some of the imprisoned men forward as candidates in the upcoming by-elections in Ireland. Opinions differed on whether or not to do this, with Michael Collins, Boland and Thomas Ashe in favour of it and Eamon de Valera and others opposed to it. He was also an active participant in seeking prisoner of war status for those imprisoned for their role in the Rising. As a result, Harry was identified as one of the ringleaders and was transferred to Maidstone Prison along with de Valera and several others.

MALDON (OS: TL 85- 07-). Apart from its POWIB (1919) code, Pa (Mal) (IWM: Facsimile K4655), and its TA, Priswarian: Maldon, nothing is known about this camp, other than it was a working camp with no satellites (ADM 1/8506/265–120667). It is cited by the FPHS (1973).

MALLDRAETH MARSH (OS: SH 479 715). The HO cited this camp was near to Gaerwen, which is reflected in its TA, Priswarian: Gaerwen (ADM 1/8506/265–120667). The FPHS (1973) entry for this camp reads Malltraeth Marsh (sic),

Anglesey. Maltreath Marsh (sic), was inspected by Dr A. de Sturler and Monsieur R. de Sturler during June 1919 (FO 383/508).

MANCETTER (see Atherstone).

MARCHAM (OS: SU 45- 96-). A working camp, it had the POWIB (1919) code Dor (Ma) (IWM: Facsimile K4655). It is also cited by the FPHS (1973). No further evidence has been found to suggest the whereabouts of this camp, but perhaps Denman College or its grounds may hold the key. The college stands in private land within the village of Marcham.

MARGATE (OS: TR 356 709). If the national press is to be believed, Margate was prone to air attacks, but according to Wilde (*A Short History of Margate College*, 1970) this was played down by *Our News*: a contemporary local newspaper. The paper had made the following comment, 'There was never a more preposterous legend than this idea that Margate, and its immediate neighbourhood, have received special marks of Teutonic favour.' Jackson (*The Prisoners 1914–1918*, 1989) however supports the national press's comments, and cites that Margate was deliberately chosen to house PoWs as a retaliatory measure to British PoWs being moved nearer to the war zone by the German authorities. The basis of his argument was that boys boarding at Margate College were moved out, in 1917, to what had formerly been a convalescent hospital at Hale, and German officers were then moved in.

The college had opened as a preparatory school for boys in 1873. By 1886, it had moved to Hawley Square, and was still being used as such until 1917. McPherson, Horrocks & Beveridge (*History of the Great War – Medical Services*, 1923) cite the camp opened on 20 March 1918. The PoWs are believed to have come from Taunton. Their senior officer was Captain Fischer. In reply to a parliamentary question, it was answered on 7 May 1918 that there were eighty officers, with twenty-five servants, being interned in Margate. Similar numbers had been dispatched to Southend and Ramsgate. The question had been asked by Joynson-Hicks on 11 April 1918. *The Isle of Thanet Gazette* (20 April 1918) reiterated Joynson-Hicks's request.

The internment camp closed on 6 January 1919, and the site was returned to its former usage as a college. The students returned from Hale. *The Thanet Times* (10 January 1919) reported the closing of the camp.

Ironically, the college received a direct hit in the Second World War, obliterating a comment, being preserved under glass, that had been made by a former internee. He had carved into a wall of Dormitory IV, 'Gott strafe England.'

The camp had the TA Priswaroff: Margate (ADM 1/8506/265–120667). Margate is also cited by the FPHS (1973).

MARKHAM (see Marksham).

MARKET HARBOROUGH. There were two camps in Market Harborough. One was a parent camp and the other a working camp attached to it. Strangely the senior camp was numbered 2. They may have both been housed in the local workhouse. From a newspaper report we know at least one of them was in the workhouse that stood in Leicester Road.

This was the town's second workhouse, built in 1836 to house around 300 inmates at any one time. It had replaced premises that stood in Adam and Eve Street, built in 1723. Like so many of these institutions its role changed throughout its lifetime. By 1930 it was council-run. It closed with the introduction of the National Health

Service in 1948. The Council then used it to house the temporary homeless until the 1970s, when it was partly demolished. The site now houses St. Luke's Hospital.

The Hinckley Times and Bosworth Herald (2 February, 1918) cites that the Unions of Loughborough and Market Harborough had indicated they would accept PoWs into their institutions. It was agreed that any PoW billeted at the workhouse would work within a 3-mile radius of the camp.

A directory produced by the HO in 1919 only gives one TA, that of Priswarian: Market Harborough (ADM 1/8506/265–120667). Market Harborough is listed only once by the FPHS (1973).

At Northampton Road Cemetery, the grave of a German was exhumed, *c.*1960, and relocated to Cannock Chase (Leicestershire Record Office, per. comm. (L355P), 4 September 1996).

AGRICULTURAL GROUP (M H) (OS: SP 726 882) and AGRICULTURAL DEPOT (M H2) (OS: SP 726 882). Both the agricultural group and the agricultural depot were cited by the POWIB (1919). The code for the agricultural group was Bro (M H2) (M H), and for the agricultural depot it was Bro (M H2) (IWM: Facsimile K4655). The Depot had three more satellite camps attached to it, those of Haughton Lodge, Illston, and North Kilworth.

MARKS TEY (OS: TL 91- 23-). Described as a working camp, its POWIB (1919) code was Pa (M T) (IWM: Facsimile K4655). It is also cited by the FPHS (1973). The camp's TA was Priswarian: Marks Tey (ADM 1/8506/265–120667). Marks Tey was inspected by Dr A. de Sturler and Monsieur R. de Sturler, during April and May 1919. Their findings are held at the National Archives at Kew (FO 383/508).

MARKSHALL (OS: TG 23- 08-). The location of this camp is unknown. An entry made by the FPHS (1973) for Marksham may be incorrectly stated, and it may be a second reference to a HO document that gives the camp the TA Priswarian: Markshall, Norfolk (ADM 1/8506/265–120667). Alternately it may be Markham was the incorrectly stated location.

MARKSHAM (OS: SO 16- 01-). The FPHS (1973) cite a camp at Marksham, for which no place in the UK can be found. Markham cannot be completely ruled out as a location of this internment camp, but the most likely site for this camp was Markshall, in Norfolk (OS: TG 230 088), where there is evidence of a camp in a HO document (ADM 1/8506/265–120667).

MARSDEN: Frenchman's Fort (OS: NZ 384 660). An article appeared in the *Shields Gazette* on 6 August 1914 praising the 'business like' way in which the country was handling the arrangements for the great struggle ahead, in comparison to the muddle and disorder that had characterised the Boer War. It stated:

> Everything seems to have been carefully thought out beforehand, and there have been no improvisations of expedients and stopgaps at the last moment. Overnight, a grassy plot near Frenchman's Fort sprouted tents and an enclosing barbed wire fence. Here were accommodated German and Austrian prisoners, mostly seamen from captured ships.

After making his inspection of the camp a reporter from the local *Gazette* said that the enemy was 'tolerably well fed and well housed, had plenty of fresh air, and was able to enjoy the picturesque scenery'.

Frenchman's Fort does not appear on contemporary maps but there was a coastal defence battery constructed in 1900 that was built by Durham Artillery Volunteers, at Trow Point, near Frenchman's Bay according to Beamish (*Defence Review*: The Modern Defence Heritage and the National Trust Annual, 1999). The Fort took around five years to complete. But even before the First World War began its two 64-pdr rifled muzzle loading guns were obsolete. The area was instead used by the Volunteers to train, with land adjacent being used as camps. The First World War saw hurried re-equipping of Frenchman's Fort and implementation of fieldworks to prevent beach landings, and with it, a place to intern merchant seamen, and those civilian internees arrested under the powers of the Defence of the Realm Act of 1914. An anniversary edition of *The Shields Gazette* (7 August 1964) re-iterated the events of the day (DJ/NP/L13).

MARSHMOOR SIDINGS: North Mymms (OS: TL 235 057). When the First World War began, there was no railway station at Marshmoor, but an ambitious parish council of the day rectified this.

A PoW working camp was established near to North Mymms with the POWIB (1919) code Pa (Msh) (IWM: Facsimile K4655). The POWIB (1919) cite its address as Marshmoor Sidings. The camp stood opposite to where the railway station stands today. The camp's TA was Priswarian: Marshmoor Sidings.

Kingsford (*North Mymms People in Victorian Times*, www.brookmans.com) reported there were strong objections made by the local council to German prisoners, working at the siding, drawing water from the well as they could not be 'trusted from committing filthy nuisances or any other spiteful damage'. Ambrose (*During the Great War*, www.brookmans.com) counters this by stating that when the Germans learned of the plight of a local cripple boy, whose only method of transportation was an old box on wheels, they decided to raise enough money to buy him a proper wheelchair. With the help of the camp's guard, they staged concerts that were well attended, and soon reached their goal.

Pinder (www.brookmans.com) cites Welham Green lies between Hatfield and Potters Bar. During the 1914–18 war, there was a German prisoner of war camp opposite where the railway station is today. Pinder's father was a builder in the village and he had to build a brick silo for Mr Crawford at Potterells Farm. Two of the German prisoners from the camp helped him. They learnt quite a lot of English, and it was great fun listening to them.

Reports on visits of inspection to the PoW camps at Tonbridge, Marshmoor Sidings, and Hatfield in Hertfordshire by Monsieur de Corragioni d'Orelli, during March 1919 are held at the National Archives, London (FO 383/432).

Several of the PoWs at North Mymms died, many from the influenza pandemic in the winter of 1918.

MARTLESHAM HEATH (OS: TM 25- 47-). Situated at Martlesham Heath, Woodbridge it was a working camp with the POWIB (1919) code Pa (Mar) (IWM: Facsimile K4655). The camp's TA was Priswarian: Martlesham, Woodbridge *Martley* (ADM 1/8506/265–120667). Martlesham is cited by the FPHS (1973). The camp closed on 20 March 1919. On 20 March 1924, the RAF established the Aeroplane and Armament Experimental Establishment at Martlesham Heath.

MARTLEY (Knightwick) (OS: SO 75- 59-). A working camp with the POWIB (1919) code Dor (Mrt) (IWM: Facsimile K4655). The directory cites it had formerly been known as Knightwick. Both Martley and Knightwick are listed by the FPHS (1973). The camp had the TA Priswarian: Martley (ADM 1/8506/265–120667).

No physical evidence has been found to suggest where this camp was. Perhaps The Noak, purchased by James Nash *c.*1665 and rebuilt in 1853, holds the key. Worcestershire historian, Reverend Tearaway R. Nash, once owned this house.

Records show 2nd Lieutenant C. Sprague commanded the camp, and it had twenty-five PoWs billeted there, as of 31 December 1917.

MARTON (see Stow Park).

MARYPORT (OS: NY 03- 36-). Several sites in the county were recommended for quartering PoWs. The Cumberland WAC was informed on 22 April 1918 that the report on the suitability of these locations was expected soon. It had been suggested in a former minute of 18 February 1918 that Maryport would make an excellent site to test out the capabilities of PoW labour by cleaning out the local ditches. The sites proposed by the committee were the Agricultural College in Aspatria; The Noble Temple, also in Aspatria; the Tweed Mill and 14 Main Street, both Cockermouth; the Blackwell Grandstand at Carlisle Racecourse; Wasdale Head, and Maryport (CC1/39/1 & 2).

MAYLAND (OS: TL 915 014). PoWs were held at Henry Samuel Hall on Steeple Road, Mayland. It is described as a working camp by the POWIB (1919), its code being Pa (May) (IWM: Facsimile K4655). It is cited by the FPHS (1973), and had the TA Priswarian: Mayland. Its postal address is cited as 'Commandant, Prisoners of war Camp, Mayland, Maldon (ADM 1/8506/265–120667).

On 16 August 1919, *The Guardian* reported that Joseph Holmischmather and Ernst Koltman, two Germans who escaped from the Southminster camp, had been recaptured. *The Times* (12 August 1919) cited them as Harnischmacher and Rottman.

The POWIB (1919) also cite a camp at Maldon.

MELBOURN (OS: TL 38- 44-). The only evidence this camp existed comes in a request that was made from a Cambridgeshire WAC sub-Committee meeting (26 August 1918), which states six PoWs from the Melbourn camp have been placed at the disposal of the Hertfordshire County Council, for work on roads at Royston. The request was recommended.

MELCHBOURNE (OS: TL 024 656). A working camp, its POWIB (1919) code was Pa (Me) (IWM: Facsimile K4655). The camp's TA was Priswarian: Melchbourne (ADM 1/8506/265–120667).

The names of ten PoWs that worked at Melchbourne, between October 1918 and December 1918, along with their guard, are recorded in an extract, taken from PoWs employment time sheets held at the Bedfordshire Record Office (WW1/AC/PW/1&2).

MEPPERSHALL (OS: TL 13- 36-). The location of this camp remains a mystery, though the evidence suggests a farm was involved. Only the names of two soldiers that assisted the foreman are recorded in an extract, taken from the PoWs employment time sheets of October 1918 to February 1919 for Meppershall, to show this camp existed. They were Sergeant W. Bridges and Private P. Jeanes (WW1/AC/PW/1&2).

DKF 24: Das neben dem Mannschaftslager gleichen Namens errichtete Offiziers-Gefangenenlager Oswestry wurde im September 1918 eröffnet. Zu Beginn des Jahres 1919 wurden einige Offizierlager in England – Kegworth; Margate; Dyffryn-Aled – aufgelöst, um ihren ursprünglichen Zweck (Landwirtschaftliche Schulen usw.) zurückgegeben zu werden.

MELDRETH (OS: TL 386 469). A working camp, its POWIB (1919) code was Pa (Mel) (IWM: Facsimile K4655). It is also cited by the FPHS (1973) and had a TA too, Priswarian: Meldreth (ADM 1/8506/265–120667).

The exact location of this camp has not been confirmed. It may be the work carried out by those sent to Meldreth may have been connected to one or both of the town's cement works.

Wright (*A History of the County of Cambridge and the Isle of Ely*, 1982) states the Cam Portland Cement Company was operational *c.*1896. It was located by the railway line at the north-eastern edge of the parish. In the 1930s, as the Cam Blue Lias Lime and Cement Company, it was still burning lime and making cement. These works went out of use between 1948 and 1953.

The Meldreth Portland Cement and Brick Company began life in 1897, situated to the west of the village, on Whaddon Road. By 1901 a tramway had been built connecting the works with the railway station. In 1911 the premises were offered for sale as the Meldreth Lime and Cement works, capable of producing 350 tons of lime and cement a week. They may have closed for a short time in the late 1920s before being taken over and expanded by the Atlas Stone Company, which manufactured asbestos cement.

In 1977, when it was part of the Eternit Group, it was the largest employer in the parish, with around 360 staff. In the 1930s, Ritagen manufactured disinfectants at Meldreth, perhaps using the by-products of the lime works there.

METHVEN (see Drumbuich).

MIDDLESBOROUGH (see Port Clarence).

MIDDLETON JUNCTION (OS: SD 88- 04-). An entry for Middleton Junction, Lancashire appears in the FPHS (1973) listings. However, no evidence has been found in the area for this camp that was also cited in lists produced by the HO. These state its TA as Priswarian: Middleton Junction and that the camp closed on 12 December 1918 (ADM 1/8506/265–120667).

Parts of the Middleton Junction and Oldham Branch Railway, Middleton Junction East and Middleton Junction West are now closed. According to Wright, all that remains now are the Vitriol Works signal box and the new Castleton East Junction (www.signalbox.org).

Another camp, only cited by the FPHS (1973), at Harpurhey, may be linked to this camp.

MIDHURST (OS: SU 887 220). A working camp, it had the POWIB (1919) code Pa (Mid) (IWM: Facsimile K4655). The FPHS (1973) cite it too. It is cited as being in North Street, its TA being Priswarian: Midhurst (ADM 1/8506/265–120667). It is believed around fifty PoWs would have been employed by local farmers and used to do road maintenance work. Letters of protest to the council survive.

A possibility for the home of this camp is the former Midhurst Grammar School that stood on North Street. Founded in 1672, it had a long and proud history. Amongst its former students were Charles Lyell and H.G. Wells. Capron House had its frontage on North Street. The school closed in 2008 to become Midhurst Rother College. A new hub for the community is scheduled to open in the north wing of

Capron House to become a base for people associated with the South Downs National Park.

MILDENHALL (nr Tuddenham) (OS: TL 689 778). Any PoWs sent here were most probably engaged in forestry or agricultural work. The ancient parish of Mildenhall covers 17,000 acres and was the largest in Suffolk. Much of the land was of little value until the fens were drained. Mildenhall is described as a working camp, its POWIB (1919) code was Pa (Mil) (IWM: Facsimile K4655). It is cited as being in Beck Row, and had the TA Priswarian: Mildenhall (ADM 1/8506/265–120667).

The Sycamores may hold the key to this camp's location.

The FPHS (1973) cite a camp at Tuddenham. Unfortunately, the list makes no distinction as to which Tuddenham, in Suffolk, they were referring to. One is near Mildenhall (OS: TL 735 715), whilst the other is near to Ipswich (OS: TM 194 484).

MILL HILL: Goldbeater's Farm (OS: TQ 210 916). The entry for Hendon in the POWIB (1919) directory directs you to Mill Hill. The latter is described as a working camp, with the code Pa (M Hi) (IWM: Facsimile K4655). The PoWs were kept at Goldbeater's Farm, near to Mill Hill, and they worked on improving an access road to Hendon Aerodrome. PoWs based at Kimpton were allocated to Mill Hill for agricultural work. Mill Hill is cited by the FPHS (1973). Its TA is cited as Priswarian: Mill Hill, Hendon (ADM 1/8506/265–120667).

On 13 February 1918, it is recorded that a ploughing section of forty PoWs, the first of its kind in Britain, was established at Mill Hill. Its sole purpose was to be actively engaged in agricultural work.

Complaints about the poor standard of the camp's illumination were lodged, in what was a tented compound.

DKF 32: In Upavon, Milldown, Corton (Dorset) (sic), *und Hendon (Middlesex) waren die Gefangenen noch weiterhin in Zelten untergebracht. In Milldown und Hendon war die Beleuchtung mangelhaft, in Corton fehlte sie ganz.*

MILNTHORPE (OS: SD 49- 81-). Of the many industries in and around the town, none was so important than that of papermaking, which was established some 200 years ago on the banks of the River Bela.

The status of the Milnthorpe camp, attached to Stainton Sidings, was that of an agricultural group with the POWIB (1919) code Lgh (St S) (Mi) (IWM: Facsimile K4655). Milnthorpe was inspected by Dr A. de Sturler and Monsieur R. de Sturler during June 1919. Their findings are held at the National Archives at Kew (FO 383/508). Milnthorpe was also cited by the FPHS (1973), and had the TA Priswarian: Milnthorpe (ADM 1/8506/265–120667).

Nothing appears to have been recoded as to where the PoWs at Milnthorpe were housed. One possibility was the workhouse, erected in Milnthorpe in 1813, situated at the east of Kirkgate Lane.

During the Second World War, an internment camp was established, *c.*1942, at Milnthorpe to intern, firstly, Italian and then later German PoWs. When the last of the 600 Germans had gone, it was then used to accommodate displaced persons of Polish and Ukrainian origins, until 1951. It was then transformed into an open prison. In 1974 the prison, which stood on 23 acres of land, was closed, and the thirty-four houses from the prison staff in the area, were offered to the local council.

MILTON ERNEST (OS: TL 021 551). Cited by the FPHS (1973), no further evidence has been found to suggest where this camp was. However, it is known that the grange, built for Henry Curtis in 1906, was used by the military in the First World War. Between the wars it was a private school, before the military occupied it again in the Second World War. In 1950 it was sold and turned into flats. In the 1990s the building became a residential home. During the First World War, Lord and Lady Ampthill occupied Milton Ernest Hall. It is known that two of King George V's children stayed at the hall in that decade. It, too, is now a residential home (www.galaxy.bedfordshire.gov.uk).

MISSON (OS: SK 61- 87-). Minutes of the Notts County WAC (28 January 1919) cite a migratory gang at Misson, although there has been no evidence forthcoming to suggest where the camp was located.

MONK'S ABBEY (OS: SK 989 713). This camp is cited as a working camp. Its TA was Priswarian: Monks Abbey, Lincoln (ADM 1/8506/265–120667). The National Archives at Kew holds reports on visits of inspections to PoW camps at Coal Aston (Sheffield), Monks Abbey (Lincolnshire), Peak Dale Quarries (Derbyshire), and Sproxton Moor (Yorkshire) (FO 383/432). It is not known what PoWs based here did.

Only the ruins of the chancel of Monk's Abbey remain today. They stand on Monks Road relatively close to the Lincoln County Hospital.

A German account (*Deutsche Kriegsgefangene In Feindesland*, 1919) cited the camp's German Medical Officer had repeatedly referred a fellow PoW for hospitalisation, but each time his request was refused by his British counterpart. Eventually, the patient, suffering from tuberculosis, had to be sent to the hospital in Lincoln.

DKF 65: Einen Mann mit schwerer Lungentuberkulose schickte ich mehrmals zum Arzt, der ihm immer wieder als arbeitsfähig bestimmte, bis der Betreffende schließlich kaum mehr bis zum fünf Meilen entfernten Hospital in Lincoln transportfähig war.

MORTON (OS: TF 09- 23-). Morton is cited by the POWIB (1919); its code being Bro (Sl) (Mo) (IWM: Facsimile K4655). It was a satellite of Sleaford. It had the TA Priswarian: Morton, Bourne, Lincs. (ADM 1/8506/265–120667). A second camp, cited as Morton Fen, existed.

MORTON FEN (OS: TF 14- 23-). Its TA was Priswarian: Morton Fen, Morton, Bourne. It was a satellite of Sleaford (ADM 1/8506/265–120667).

MUNDFORD – WEST TAFTS (OS: TL 804 934). A working camp, its POWIB (1919) code was Pa (Mun) (IWM: Facsimile K4655). The camp had the TA Priswarian: West Tafts, Mundford, Norfolk. The FPHS (1973) cite Tafts West.

The Swiss delegates were informed by the Germans that West Tafts, with other camps, was a tented affair. Internees sent there complained that there was no proper laundry service at the camp, and consequently the few clothes they had were not being cleaned, nor were they being offered replacements.

DKF 34: Aus den Berichten der Schweizer Delegierten aus dem Ende des Jahres 1917 über die Arbeitslager in England geht hervor, daß die Zustände in einigen dieser Lager sich gebessert hatten und daß in manchen dementsprechend das Leben erträglich war. Immerhin geben noch einige Lager zu berechtigten Klagen Anlaß. Trotz wiederholten Einspruchs der deutschen Regierung sind in der Lagern Wingland (Lincolnshire), Ordfordneß (Suffolk), West Tafts (Norfolk), Warren Woods (Norfolk), Glendon bei Keltering (sic), *Stratford on Avon,*

Kerry (Nord Wales), und Shirehampton (Gloucestershire) die Gefangenen immer noch in Zelten untergebracht.

DKF 34: Die Versorgung der Gefangenen mit genügender Kleidung und Wäsche ist verschiedentlich sehr mangelhaft. Hauptsächlich in den Lagern Warren Woods, West Tafts, Orfordneß und Kerry wird hierüber geklagt.

N

NARBETH (see Drim Wood).

NARBOROUGH (OS: SK 53- 97-). This was an agricultural group attached to Loughborough agricultural depot, and should not be confused with another similarly named camp in Norfolk.

The actual location of this camp is not cited, but perhaps Narborough Hall, or its grounds, may hold the key. Built in 1907, it was the home of William E. Briggs in 1912.

The alternative could have been the old asylum at Humberstone, or to give it its full name, the Leicestershire and Rutland Lunatic Asylum. Built in 1860, it lay empty in 1914, and was taken over by the military to become the 5th Northern General Hospital. It closed in 1919 and was then bought by Thomas Fielding Johnson and gifted for use as a University College. It is now the Fielding Johnson Campus of the University of Leicester.

Another possible site is the new asylum, built in Narborough in 1904. It changed its name in 1914 from the Leicester Borough Lunatic Asylum to the Leicestershire and Rutland Mental Hospital. In 1939 it was changed again to Carlton Hayes Hospital. When the hospital closed, the site was bought by Alliance and Leicester Building Society to be their headquarters in 1995.

During March 1919, Dr A. de Sturler compiled reports on visits of inspection to the PoW camps. Narborough in Leicestershire was inspected. His findings are held at the National Archives at Kew (FO 383/506). The camp's POWIB (1919) code was Bro (Lo) (Nb) (IWM: Facsimile K4655). Narborough was also cited by the FPHS (1973).

NARBOROUGH (OS: TF 744 125). This camp should not be confused with the Narborough agricultural group in Leicestershire that is cited by the POWIB (1919). This camp was situated in Norfolk.

It appears in the county's War Agricultural Executive Committee minutes. One such minute, dated 14 July 1917, suggests additional PoWs could be accommodated at Narborough, where there were already some being employed. A week later it was read out that eighty men could be sent out daily from the camp, if transport was made available. What duties these PoWs performed is not stated, but it would most probably have been linked to agricultural work as many PoWs were set the task of clearing watercourses (C/C10/15).

Evidence of where the camp was is provided in a newsletter published by the Defence of Britain Project, in which it states the PoWs were being held at the airfield. Opened in August 1915 as Royal Naval Air Station Narborough, it was one of several night landing grounds established by the Admiralty to attack Zeppelins as they came over the East Anglian coast. In April 1916, the War Office took control of anti-aircraft defences, resulting in Narborough becoming an operational training base for the Royal Flying Corps. By this time the airfield had acquired a line of six permanent hangars to house its Armstrong Whitworth aircraft; and a high wire fence to contain up to 100 German prisoners of war. The PoWs were transported daily to work on the land. It is believed the internment camp had closed down before the Armistice (*Defence Lines* (No. 5), Newsletter of The Defence of Britain Project, July 1996).

During the First World War, Narborough was the biggest airfield in Britain with over 100 buildings, standing on 908 acres. There were four large bases for airships. By 1918, nearly 1,000 service personnel were based there. The aerodrome closed in 1919 when the last units moved out. Today little remains of the original airfield structures; only the YMCA shed remains. One of the better known landmarks that had survived until recent times, known locally as the Black Hangar, succumbed to gales in 1976.

There were a few persistent escapees, but the Kings Lynn constabulary were always quick to round them up.

NETHERAVON (OS: SU 149 480). Netheravon's amenities were heavily criticised (*Vereinigung Wissenschaftlicher Verleger*, 1919) by those interned there during the First World War. When the Swiss Delegation visited the camp on 31 May 1917, they were informed by the internees that there were no beds in the tents and they had to sleep on the wooden floorboards, making do with four blankets each. They also complained of inadequate lighting. The medical unit was under canvas.

Netheravon Aerodrome is cited by the POWIB (1919) as the address of the camp, its code being Dor (Na) (IWM: Facsimile K4655). It is also cited by the FPHS (1973). Its TA was Priswarian: Netheravon, Wilts. (ADM 1/8506/265–120667). The camp closed on 16 November 1918.

DKF 30: Im Arbeitslager Netheravon (Wiltsh.), sind die Kriegsgefangenen laut Bericht des Schweizer Delegierten in Zelten untergebracht, in denen sie zu neun beziehungsweise zehn Mann liegen, ein Zelt dient als Lazarett. Die Leute haben vier Decken und schlafen auf dem Holzboden. In den Zelten ist keine Beleuchtung. Eine Badeeinrichtung ist nicht vorhanden. Bericht am 31 Mai 1917.

DKF 30: In Netheravon müssen die Leute aus Mangel an Bettstellen sogar auf dem blanken Boden liegen.

DKF 31: Gesundheitliche Vorsorge. Die gesundheitlichen Vorkehrungen sind in mehreren Lagern sehr mangelhaft. In Glendevon, Uppingham, und Netheravon ist keinerlei Badeeinrichtung vorhanden. Die Kriegsgefangenen werden dort in Eisensteingruben mit Erdarbeiten und im straßen – und Schuppenbau beschäftigt, Arbeiten, bei denen häufige Reinigung des ganzen Körpers unerläßlich ist.

DKF 31: Auch in Loch Doon, auf der Insel Raasay, in Newlandside, Ceal Aston (sic) *Sutton Veney* (sic), *Bowithick, Netheravon, Yatesbury, Rovrah* (sic), *Port Clarence und Hayrmyres* (sic) *werden die Leute zu sehr ausgenutzt.*

DKF 32: Gottesdienst: Die Seelsorge der Kreigsgefangenen ist auf vielen Plätzen sehr vernachlässigt. In den Lagern von Joyce Green; Dartford; Hadnall; Peak Dale Quarries bei Buxton; Sutton Veny; Larkhill; Netheravon; Codford; und Fovant hat noch kein Gottesdienst stattgefunden.

NEW BILTON (OS: SP 49- 75-). The camp's TA is cited as Priswarian: New Bilton, Rugby (ADM 1/8506/265–120667). The exact location of this camp is not known. It would have been active in the second phase of internment camps that opened in Britain.

NETHY BRIDGE (see Seafield).

NEWBOLD (OS: SK 37- 73-). Along with other locations, the village of Newbold is listed by *The Derby Daily Telegraph* (10 July 1918) as awaiting the arrival of PoWs, to work on the land.

Minute No. 11 of the Derbyshire WAC (21 December 1918) expressed concerns about not completing the harvest in proper time, mainly due to the weather and the shortage of skilled men. The minute concluded that thirty German prisoners, in five gangs, were following threshers in the Chesterfield area (D331/1/27).

The FPHS (1973) cite a camp at Dunston. According to British place name gazetteers there are several places of this name, one of which is near Newbold.

NEWBURY (OS: SU 490 664). Newbury Racecourse opened on 26 September 1905. During the First World War the racecourse was requisitioned for various wartime activities, including an internment camp. Some of these activities worked in tandem with others. Initially, the course was occupied by troops before it became a Hay Dispersal Centre, a Munitions Inspection Centre and a Tank Testing and Repair Park. From the start the stables were used to house interned German civilians. At first it would have been local men that were of military age and were living in Britain when the war began. Then as others were brought in from further afield, tents supplemented the stables.

The Newbury Weekly News (3 September 1914) reported the 1st South Midland Mounted Brigade arrived on Sunday and Monday (30 and 31 August) under command of Brigadier General Wiggin. It was originally intended that they go to Churn Down (sic) to join up with the 2nd South Midland Mounted Brigade (Churchdown may have been their intended destination).

When reports began to appear in the press that plans were being pushed forward to accommodate German internees at Newbury it was expected that there would be accommodation for 300 men who would be guarded by three companies of the National Reserve. *The Newbury Weekly News* (10 September 1914) cited the first Germans had arrived. The first three arrived on the Friday, followed by 150 on the Saturday, 380 on the Monday, sixty on the Tuesday, and a few more on Wednesday. It reported they were mostly civilians and reservists arrested in this country, along with six PoWs and an officer. The *Hampshire Herald* (12 September 1914) cited 200 German internee prisoners had been conveyed by rail from London to Newbury Racecourse the previous Saturday.

The *Western Morning News* (15 September 1914) reported that about 100 PoWs from German vessels brought into Falmouth within the past few days had left by train for Newbury. Walter Goerlitz was possibly amongst them. Goerlitz sent a letter to the *New York Times*, which was published. He stated he was being treated well by his captors and that he had been arrested on board the SS *Gelbria* whilst posing as a steerage passenger. He was taken to Falmouth on 19 August 1914. There, he and thirty-one others were detained in a grain store for about a week. They were obliged to make their own mattresses from freshly cut grass, as there was no straw or hay available. The conditions, he stated, were poor, but their guards, in the circumstance, had tried their best to make their stay as comfortable as possible. They then travelled to Newbury by train; en route, they were allowed some latitude with their liberty. At Newbury Racecourse, they were put into horseboxes, in a closed building. Depending on its size, each horsebox housed six to ten men. The internees did their own cooking; some of those interned had been professional chefs at some of the finest hotels in Europe. Permission was granted for the internees to select 'captains' from their midst to act as intermediaries in disputes and to delegate duties. Panayi (*The Enemy in our Midst, Germans Living in Britain during the First World War*, 1991) cites the use of horseboxes was intended to be a short-term measure; but with no other suitable accommodation forthcoming, their stay was prolonged, without proper heating or light, into the winter of 1914. In total, 145 horseboxes were to be used.

The Newbury Weekly News (17 September 1914) stated there were 1,300 interned at the racecourse. They included Uhlans, sailors, stokers, spies and suspects.

The Newbury Weekly News (24 September 1914) cited a Berkshire Battalion of the National Reserve had taken over guard duties of a compound established on the northern side of the course. A Lancastrian regiment guarded the stables. *The Newbury Weekly News* (1 October 1914) states the Lancashires left for Plymouth, which only fuelled speculation about the internees being moved to the Isle of Man.

The Newbury Weekly News (15 October 1914) cites 386 internees had gone to the Isle of Man. They travelled by train to Fleetwood and then by the *Duke of Cornwall* to Douglas. They then marched the 2 miles to their new camp. Amongst the new arrivals at Newbury were first class passengers, taken from a German ship, and sixty uniformed soldiers. *The Newbury Weekly News* (22 October 1914) reported there were German PoWs coming in daily. When Jacob Hock, an Austrian, died, it was the first reported death at the camp. He was buried at Greenham, on Friday, 23 October 1914.

On 23 October 1914 a second compound was erected. This was a tented affair, with wooden boards deployed as walkways.

The Newbury Weekly News (28 October 1914) reported a further 400 internees had been sent away yesterday, and now none were left in the 'lower camp'. Some had gone to the Isle of Man. It stated that Newbury was now being used solely for the reception of PoWs.

An article appeared in the *British Medical Journal* (n.d.) entitled 'Germans in Concentration Camps'. It reported that Emil Seleke had made a series of charges, to the neutral observers, about conditions at Newbury. His main complaint was that there were eight or ten men, lying on old straw paillasses, sharing a horsebox. He stated there were 1,340 Germans at the training stable, and:

> ... there was no furniture and no light, so that at dusk they must all 'creep into their straw'. They had to cook their own food in the open air on a hearth consisting of a ditch and some bricks, on which stood saucepans, which had to be used alike for cooking tea and thin soup ... There were no sanitary precautions ...

A representative sent from *The Times* to investigate Seleke's claims reported that whilst it was true the men slept in the stables, they were well aired and clean, each man being provided with two blankets, a towel, a tin mug, and a knife and fork. When interviewed, several internees described the charges as nonsense, and a statement denying Seleke's allegations was signed by a majority of the 1,200 internees. *The Cologne Gazette*, which had first reported Seleke's claims, was therefore obliged to print a retraction to his unsubstantiated claims of 5 November 1914.

At the time the German newspaper was printing its retraction Maudsford Asylum is reported to have received two German PoWs, in November 1914, from the Newbury internment camp. The asylum's General Statement Book testifies to this, in an entry made by the Medical Superintendent. The men were not named; nor was the length of their stay recorded. He also commented on the fact that a further twenty internees were under observation in the camp.

The Newbury Weekly News (29 October 1914) stated that as a consequence of the government's policy to arrest of all male Germans and Austrians of military age, a great number of new internees were being brought to the camp at Newbury.

The Newbury Weekly News (5 November 1914) reported the German press had made comments on the treatment of PoWs at Newbury. The paper refuted the German paper's claim saying they were absolutely without truth. *The Times* (30 October 1914) broke the story. Mr Asquith visited the camp to see for himself the conditions at the camp. There were reports that there were now some 3,000 men being interned at Newbury.

The Newbury Weekly News (19 November 1914) cited the South Midland Mounted Brigade had left for Norfolk, again fuelling speculation that the open compounds were to be cleared. This time the internees were to be moved to ships, moored off the south coast.

The *Yorkshire Evening Press* (1 December 1914) reported the *Norddeutsche Allgemeine Zeitung* was dissatisfied with the US report on Newbury. It commented on the dismissal of the internees' complaints, asking why they were unfounded. The Germans sought to know why there was no comment made about the commandant's lack of rapport with the internees, and the resultant abuse. Nor, in their eyes, did it deal with the inadequacies of the camp.

The Newbury Weekly News (3 December 1914) reported that the men under canvas had left, and those in the stables would be following soon.

The Times (10 December 1914) cited the camp at Newbury was closing. This is supported by the *Newbury Weekly News* (10 December 1914), which concurred with its more illustrious national.

The Newbury Weekly News (17 December 1914) cited internees had been sent to HMT *Canada*, based in the Solent, off Ryde. This was confirmed in a report produced by the US Embassy in London, whose delegation visited the ship on 2 February 1915. Apparently the men from Newbury were pleased with their transfer. In his report, Jackson noted the Newbury camp had closed on 20 December 1914. In contrast, Goerlitz wrote that when the camp broke up, he started to send an address of thanks to Colonel Haines and wanted to collect signatures of other internees, but that it created unrest, because the men thought that the newspapers would use it extensively for propaganda purposes. His letter was dated 28 December 1914.

On 20 January 1915 a report published in Germany (CAB 37/123/37) recorded many of the internees at Templemore had previously been at Newbury. It stated when the men had been at Newbury they were housed, eight to a stall, in stables. It painted a bleak picture of these men, including them not having their straw changed for two months, of having no opportunity to air blankets, etc., and of having a poor diet.

The Times (8 February 1915) carried an article written by a former Austrian internee from Newbury, which countered the reports in the German press of the atrocious conditions at that camp. The man, on parole at the time of writing, said that he had been held there from 25 October until 13 December 1914. He was complimentary about the running of the camp, which he described as having three different compounds. He described them as Compounds I and II, which were tented, and the stable block. According to the author, the food was good, and the sanitary arrangements were adequate. He described the hierarchical arrangements of 'seniors' and 'captains' elected by the inmates for the internal administration. He also stated there were 4,000 internees at Newbury, and the commandant was Lt-Colonel G.S. Haines.

Panayi (*An Intolerant Act by an Intolerant Society: The Internment of Germans in Britain during the First World War*, Cesarani & Kushner, 1993) cited the camp had no heat or light, that the War Office was conscious of the poor conditions and it had intentions to close the camp before the onset of colder weather, but it remained open until the beginning of 1915.

Thomas (*St Stephen's House: Friends Emergency Work in England 1914–1920*, 1920) stated deep mud prevailed throughout the time the racecourse was used as a camp. Bird (*Control of Enemy Alien Civilians in Great Britain 1914–1918*, 1986) confirms that Newbury was used in the early stages to accommodate civilian internees and adjudged to be unsuitable for purpose and it was phased out early in the campaign.

It is known the War Office ceased its occupation of the racecourse on 6 April 1915, but the Ministry of Munitions, which had taken over certain areas of it, did not interfere with racing up to August 1916. After that meeting, the ministry used the whole racecourse for storing tanks. It was not released again for racing until early 1919 (D/H10/A4/9).

Carter (Russell, 1996) has two illustrations of letter stampings of the Newbury camp. One bears the date 20 November 1914 and is from the Commandant's Office; the other bears the inscription, Commandant's House. He also reproduced a disclaimer sticker stating the British censors were not responsible for the mutilation of any letters bearing an interpreter's mark from Newbury.

The camp was cited by the FPHS (1973).

NEWCASTLE UPON TYNE (OS: NZ 253 643). There is a reference to a camp in Newcastle in a memo dated 13 November 1914 sent by Sir Edward Grey. It stated, 'The American Ambassador asked me today whether the American Embassy would be allowed to send someone to visit the Germans interned in Newbury and Newcastle.' There is also a reference to a camp where Germans were working in the dock area of Newkastle (sic) (CD 7817 & 7857).

An article appeared in *The Times* (2 February 1917) reporting that Newcastle City Council were considering proposals that PoWs should be put to quarry working rather than working on roads. What the council resolved to do, was not known.

Mark (*Prisoners of war in British Hands during WW1*, 2007) makes reference to a postcard, sent from America, to the captain of a German ship seized at Blyth. Passing through the Chief Constable's office on 28 November 1914, it was addressed to the 'Concentrate Camp, Newcastle'.

Files held at Woodhorn Museum for the Northumberland Constabulary show male 'enemy aliens' between the ages of 17 and 45 were interned. A number were sent across the Scottish Borders, to Stobs Army Camp, near Hawick. Plans were then to be put in place for the repatriation of their wives and children (NC/3/46–NC/3/48).

During the First World War anyone living in Britain who was not British by birth had to be registered at their local police station. They were classed as 'friendly' (allies of Britain), or 'enemy' (against the allies) aliens. Women married to these foreigners took on their husband's nationality. When enemy aliens registered with the police, he, or she, was prevented from leaving their home between 9.00pm and 5.00am, unless they had a warrant allowing them to do so. Guesthouses and hotels also had to register any foreign guests. Sensitive areas of the country, which many parts of rural Northumberland were, were off-limits to many aliens. When British nurse Edith Cavell was executed by the Germans for allegedly helping allied soldiers to escape in 1915, the situation for many foreign nationals in the UK worsened, and many sought internment.

The FPHS (1973) cited Whitley Bay in its *Lists of Prison Camps*. Tynemouth Union Workhouse, lying between Newcastle and Whitley Bay may hold the key to where these camps were located.

NEWMARKET (OS: TL 644 635). The Victoria Hotel, Newmarket is cited by minutes of the Cambridgeshire WAC (27 May 1918) as being available to accommodate a number of PoWs. The Quartering Committee was instructed to make an immediate inspection of the Newmarket site with a view to filling an application for 100 PoWs. The Victoria had opened in the High Street as the Greyhound Hotel, *c.*1860. It changed its name to the Victoria in 1897 to coincide with Victoria's Diamond Jubilee. After the Second War it became the Carlton. It succumbed to redevelopment of the town centre, in 1977.

NEWLANDSIDE (see Stanhope).

NEWNHAM (see Tenbury Wells).

NEWPORT MINING GANG (OS: ST 31- 88-). This camp is only cited by the FPHS (1973). Newport is one of the commonest place names in Britain, which makes placing this camp extremely difficult. Only by assuming that the commodity being mined for was coal, can it be placed in South Wales. PoWs were not allowed to go underground, but there is evidence to show some worked at pit heads.

NEWPORT PAGNELL (OS: SP 875 434). Westbury House was built *c.*1865 for William Powell. It was requisitioned to become an internment camp in the First World War and the POWIB (1919) directory cites it as being the Headquarters. It was a working camp with the code Pa (N P) (IWM: Facsimile K4655). Its TA is cited as Priswarian: Newport Pagnell (ADM 1/8506/265–120667). The FPHS (1973) cite it too.

Westbury House was transformed into a maternity hospital in 1948, but has now been demolished to make way for a purpose-built nursing home, which still graces the site today.

NEWSELLS BURY (see Barkway).

NEWTON ABBOTT: The Institute (OS: SX 861 710). This was a working camp cited as being at the Institute: it had the POWIB (1919) code Dor (N A). It is also cited by the FPHS (1973). Its TA was Priswarian: Newton Abbot (ADM 1/8506/265–120667).

The institute may have been the one donated to Newton Abbott by John Passmore Edwards (1823–1911). He was a newspaper proprietor, MP and philanthropist who funded the creation of many institutions in Devon, Cornwall and London. Because his mother, Susan Passmore, had lived in the town, in 1843, he wanted to build a hospital, but found there already was one, so instead he gave a Library and Technical School. It was designed by Cornish architect Sylvanus Trevail, built on land then known as Harvey's Corner. It opened in 1904 and is now a Grade II listed building. After refurbishment it re-opened in 2012 as the Passmore Edwards Centre (www.devon.gov.uk//newabb).

NEWTYLE (OS: NO 30- 41-). Newtyle had the TA Priswarian: Newtyle (ADM 1/8506/265–120667).

In a rather flowery article, the *Forfar Dispatch* (16 May 1918) commented on the need to get replacements onto the land in Forfarshire (later to become the County of Angus), to replace those men that had been called to The Colours. It stated that until recent times, men and women had worked in equal numbers on smallholdings; and these times would have to come back. The article concluded:

> We shall presently see companies of WAACs – it would be ungallant to call them gangs of female conscripts – working hard the livelong day in the open air, and seeking the bustle and excitement of our streets and halls in the evening. The German prisoners will also be in evidence in some districts, perhaps in auld Forfar, and made to earn their keep at any rate. There must be many sons of the soil and labourers among them.

The Forfar Review and Strathmore Advertiser also reported from minutes taken on 29 July 1918 of the WAC for Forfarshire, stating that arrangements had been made for the utilisation of PoW labour in the county to be put into groups of from twenty-five to fifty men to be stationed at suitable centres. They could be available, in gangs of four or five, for service within 3 miles of their camp, or in groups of three, to be under the charge of the farmer employing them. The siting of PoWs in Newtyle was not to everyone's agreement. A complaint, with little Christmas sentiment, of 'a pampered German walked the Newtyle district like a free man', was printed in the *Dundee Courier* (23 December 1918).

It was then reported that seven centres – unnamed by the paper – were to be set up in Forfarshire for employing German PoWs to do harvesting work. Lieutenant Main, Sub-Commissioner for Agriculture Labour for the area, explained that it was never contemplated that farm workers should be asked to live with internees, but when the colder weather came on, arrangements might be made for the use of a large granary in which to house a detachment of the prisoners. The Forfarshire WAC agreed to adopt the scheme to establish a number of camps in the county.

The camp closed on 1 March 1919.

Prior to re-grouping of the railway companies in 1923 Newtyle's station was re-sited. At this time, several railway companies served Newtyle.

NOCTON (OS: TF 06- 64-). This camp is described as a satellite of Grantham, this agricultural group had the POWIB (1919) code Bro (Gr) (No) (IWM: Facsimile K4655). Nocton lies in the Witham Valley, where there was once a priory. No evidence has been found to suggest the location of this camp. Unless Nocton Hall may hold the key.

In 1945, at the end of the Second World War, Nocton Hall was chosen to be the RAF general hospital for Lincolnshire and several new buildings were erected on the site in 1946, with the hospital officially opening in 1947. It was to close in 1983, but was leased to the US Air Force. Thirty-five casualties of the Gulf War were treated. The hospital officially closed in 1994 and has stood empty. Repeatedly targeted by vandals, the house succumbed to a major fire in 2004.

NORMANTON (OS: SK 93- 06-). According to the POWIB (1919) there was an agricultural group based at Normanton; its code was Bro (Up) (N) (IWM: Facsimile K4655). The camp was attached to Uppingham. The camp's TA is cited as

Priswarian: Normanton, Carlton Scroop (ADM 1/8506/265–120667). The FPHS (1973) also cite this camp, but no evidence has been found to suggest where the camp was. It may be the camp was in Normanton Park, which was created for Sir Gilbert Heathcote, *c.*1700. There was a hall in the park that was demolished in 1925.

There was a camp at Normanton Hall near Thurlaston, in Leicestershire. Apart from having similar names, there is no connection between these two camps.

NORMANTON HALL (OS: SP 490 983). Normanton Hall agricultural group is cited by the POWIB (1919) as being attached to Loughborough, its code being Bro (Lo) (N Ha) (IWM: Facsimile K4655). It had the TA Priswarian: Normanton Hall, Leicester (ADM 1/8506/265–120667).

Several halls in England bear this name, but the most probable location for this internment camp would have been the one at Thurlaston in Leicestershire. It was described in *Kelly's Trade Directory* (Leicestershire, 1912) as the seat of Major William Worsley-Worswick; he was the principle landowner in the area. The hall, now demolished, is described as a fine mansion, and was situated in Normanton Park.

The Hinckley Times and Boswell Herald reported in 1918 that the Guardians of Hinckley Union were opposed to having PoWs in their midst. But, not seeking to appear to be hostile to the authorities they suggested an alternative site, that of Normanton Hall, stating its rural setting would be a better place to accommodate PoWs than the workhouse. As this suggestion was made at the beginning of 1918, it infers no PoWs had been placed at the hall before then.

During March 1919, Dr A. de Sturler compiled reports on visits of inspection to various PoW camps, including one at Normanton Hall. The reports are held at the National Archives at Kew (FO 383/506).

NORTH ELMHAM: Elmham Park (OS: TF 984 214). The fact that PoWs were in Norfolk and Suffolk during the First World War has been largely forgotten. Even in June 1919, hundreds of German prisoners were still doing valuable work in the community clearing the River Wensum. A report in the *Eastern Daily Press* (10 June 1919) cited that from the result of the work they did clearing the river, occupiers of land in the upper reaches of the river had greatly benefited. The article cited two main gangs working on the river clearance. The first were 110 men billeted at Elmham Hall. The other group consisted of 125 housed at Whitwell Tannery, with a small detachment from the army camp at Whitwell. Elmham Hall and its estates are to the south of North Elmham. North Elmham, Norfolk is recorded by the FPHS (1973).

The minutes of the Norfolk WAC (October 1917) suggested Elmham Park along with Neatherd Moor and Belaugh Park as future sites for internment camps. An application for 150 PoWs was envisaged for each venue.

Reports on visits of inspection to PoW camps by Dr A. de Sturler and Monsieur R. de Sturler during April and May 1919, held at the National Archives at Kew (FO 383/508), include North Elmham.

NORTH END (OS: SD 174 710). There was an airship station created on the Isle of Walney during the First World War. Today it is an airfield. No connection between the airship station and those interned at North End has been established. North End is cited by the FPHS (1973). Reports on visits of inspection to PoW camps by Dr A. de Sturler and Monsieur R. de Sturler during June 1919, held at the National Archives at Kew (FO 383/508), include Northend (Furness).

NORTH KILWORTH (OS: SP 615 834). The camp is cited by the POWIB (1919), and gives its code as Bro (M H2) (N K) (IWM: Facsimile K4655). Its address is quoted as The Hawthorns. The camp's TA is cited as Priswarian: North Kilworth (ADM 1/8506/265–120667).

The 74th meeting (Wednesday, 30 January 1918) of the Leicestershire War Agricultural Executive Committee recorded that depots were to be formed for PoW ploughmen at Hinckley, Loughborough, Market Harborough, North Kilworth and Long Clawson.

The FPHS (1973) does not cite North Kilworth as having a camp, but does refer to one at Kilworth, Co. Cork where it is known there was an army camp. There has been no evidence found to support the notion that this Irish location was used as an internment camp.

NORTHLEACH (OS: SP 11- 14-). Northleach is described as a working camp, and had the POWIB (1919) code Dor (No L) (IWM: Facsimile K4655). It is also cited by the FPHS (1973), and had the TA Priswarian: Northleach, Gloucestershire (ADM 1/8506/265–120667). No evidence has been found to suggest the location of this camp.

NORTH MYMMS (see Marshmoor Sidings).

NORTHALLERTON (OS: SE 37- 94-). The North Yorkshire County Record Office, based in Northallerton, can find no trace of an agricultural group in the town, or of any other internment camp in what was the North Riding of Yorkshire during the First World War.

The camp, Cat (Th) (No) (IWM: Facsimile K4655), could have been based at the workhouse, as it is known that it was given over to the military. The prison became a Military Detention Centre.

Northallerton's parish workhouse had been in the former Guildhall. William Bonython Moffatt and George Gilbert Scott were engaged in 1856 to design a new building on a site on the southern part of Friarage Fields, to accommodate around 120 inmates. In 1929, it became Sunbeck House Public Assistance Institution.

Ashcroft (per. comm., 1998) states in 1939, land adjacent to the Public Institution was purchased to provide a casualty clearing station known as the Emergency Medical Scheme Hospital in anticipation of bombing on Teesside. This consisted of eight wooden wards imported from Canada. It was extended in 1940, principally for the armed forces, and from 1943 it was taken over by RAF Northallerton. It closed in 1947. Then as part of the National Health Service both sites became Friarage Hospital, initially as an orthopaedic hospital for treating polio victims, then later becoming a general hospital under different regional bodies.

The camp's TA is cited as Priswarian: Northallerton (ADM 1/8506/265–120667).

NORTHAMPTON: HM Prison (OS: SP 755 609). *The Northampton Mercury* (13 November 1914) cited a group of around twenty Germans were being moved to Frimley, by train from Northampton. Prior to being in the prison they had been at the Eastcote camp. Eastcote at this time held destitute seamen. Whether these men had transgressed the law is not known.

NORTHIAM (OS: TQ 82- 24-). The camp in Northiam had the TA Priswarian: Northiam (ADM 1/8506/265–120667). Although it is known PoWs were brought in by train to fell timber in Plashet Wood, the location of a camp in Northiam is not known (northiam.east-sussex.co.uk). Like so many camps, it may have been a tented encampment used only in the milder weather.

During the First World War, Great Dixter House was utilised as a convalescent hospital for British soldiers. Bought in 1910 by Nathaniel Lloyd, author of books on brickwork and topiary, it had been restored by Edwin Lutyens.

In May 1944 four prime ministers gathered on the playing fields at Northiam for a final inspection of the troops of Southern Command before D-Day. Their names are recorded on gates erected by the parish to commemorate the visit.

NORTH LEW: Ashbury Court (OS: SX 505 982). Described as a working camp, it had the POWIB code Dor (N L). The camp's TA however is cited as Priswarian: Ashbury & North Lew Station. Amongst the listings of the FPHS are camps at North Lew and Ashbury Court.

A minute of the West Devon WAC (22 June 1918) provided by John Brunton (Senior Archivist, Devon County Council, per. comm., 30 November 1998) refers to a claim for damages, owing to the alleged bad work of the Ashbury prisoners, and other causes, by a Mr Palmer.

NORTHOLT: The Needles (OS: TQ 13- 84-). Surviving documents state the Needles was used to accommodate an agricultural group in Northolt. Mrs Freeman supports this evidence, when she cited, *c.*1956, that her father, F.W. Crieff owned Needles Farm, and that during the First World War some PoWs worked for him at the farm.

Contemporary maps do not show the Needles.

Soon after the creation of the Royal Flying Corps airfields were established on the fields belonging to Down Barne Farm, Northolt; Glebe Farm, Ruislip; and Hill Farm, Ickenham (www.ickenham.co.uk). The Northolt airstrip took over most of the meadows and grazing land of Hill Farm. As depots were required to service the RFC, No. 4 Stores (4MU) Depot was built on the pastureland of the adjoining Home Farm. High Road, Austins Lane and two railway lines bounded the depot. Local knowledge states, during the latter part of the war it was not unusual to see a schoolboy driving a pony and trap in which were some German PoWs being hired out to local farmers to help with the haymaking and other farm tasks. It is possible that PoWs sent here were involved in the creation of new infrastructure at the airfield.

The airfield opened in May 1915 for aircraft belonging to the Royal Flying Corps. It became an active base for RAF and Polish Air Force squadrons during the Second World War. The French, Canadian and American airforces all have had bases there between 1950 and 1980. Since then privately-owned aircraft, mainly corporate jets, have been allowed to access the runways. When Fairey Aviation had a factory in Hayes, it used the airfield for test flights of its company's products. Today, it is become an important airfield and the home of 32 (The Royal) Squadron. There are plans to relocate the offices of the British Forces Post Office (BFPO) to RAF Northolt.

Many early military establishments in the UK were named after the nearest railway station; in this case it was Northolt Junction, which is now called South Ruislip.

Northolt agricultural group had the POWIB (1919) code Fe (D L) (Nh) (IWM: Facsimile K4655). It was attached to Denham Lodge.

NORTON-CUCKNEY (OS: SK 576 715). The camp's POWIB (1919) code was Bro (Ret) (No), indicating it was a satellite of Retford (IWM: Facsimile K4655). The camp's TA is cited as Priswarian: Norton, Cuckney, Warsop (ADM 1/8506/265–120667).

As the Nottinghamshire villages of Norton and Cuckney lie close together, presumably, the camp lay somewhere between the two of them. Hatfield Grange may hold the key to the camp's location, but there is no evidence to support this notion.

The Sheffield Daily Telegraph (19 October 1918) cited a camp was to be established at Harworth, so that the PoWs would not have to travel daily from Cuckney.

During March 1919, Dr A. de Sturler compiled reports on visits of inspection to various PoW camps, including Norton-Cuckney. The reports are held at the National Archives at Kew (FO 383/506).

This camp should not be confused with Coal Aston, a working camp near Norton, in South Yorkshire.

O

OCKBROOK (OS: SK 423 359). A minute of the Derbyshire WAC (1 July 1918), cites a depot was open at Ilkeston for thirty-one prisoners. In the last three months of that year it was recorded that they had been working on farms. Some men were withdrawn and were sent to Ockbrook. To where they were sent in Ockbrook was not recorded.

OFFCHURCH BURY (OS: SP 35- 63-). This was an agricultural group attached to Ladbroke Hall; it had the POWIB (1919) code Dor (Lad) (Of) (IWM: Facsimile K4655). It is also cited by the FPHS (1973), and had the TA Priswarian: Offchurch (ADM 1/8506/265–120667).

A minute of the Warwickshire WAC shows a PoW camp had been established at Offchurch Bury by 15 August 1917. There were 610 internees designated to the camp, of which 465 were in the camp, eighty-nine were billeted out to farmers and the remaining fifty-six were allocated to migratory gangs (CR 73/1–2).

OLDCASTLE: Union Workhouse (IGR: N 555 805). Early in the First World War, according to Jackson (*The Prisoners 1914–1918*, 1989) Oldcastle's workhouse became an internment camp.

Con Farrelly says his father was a local carpenter employed to carry out maintenance work on the buildings, and states it was a former workhouse, dating back to 1842. It consisted of a front office enclosed by steel railings, a church, a laundry, and had various dormitories. Part of the workhouse complex stood on what are now houses numbeed 19–30 St Bridget's Terrace. The buildings were pulled down in the 1950s, and the date stone was re-located into a boundary wall opposite Nos 50 and 51 Mellows Road.

John Jackson's report of February 1915 stated that, because of the time constraints, he could not visit the camp, but in a statement read out in the House of Commons meanwhile, it was reported there were 304 internees at Oldcastle. A visit did take place later that year, in June. At the time of the visit there were 534 civilians including 99 Austrians housed in stone buildings, which were formerly a workhouse. Some of the internees were ships' captains and officers who had individual rooms or shared, two or three to a room. There was also a detached hospital ward, with no patients at the time of the visit. Four recreation yards and two playing fields, each about 2 acres, were available for exercise, and route marches lasting approximately two to three hours for about 100 men took place. The camp's commandant was Major Robert Johnston.

The Times (17 January 1916) reported August Bockmeyer and K. Graurnam had escaped, and according to the edition of 19 January they had been re-captured at Rathowen, Co. Westmeath.

A second attempt by Bockmeyer, in September of that year, resulted in his death. On 17 September 1916, at around 9.30pm, an alert guard shot August Bockmeyer whilst he was attempting to escape with another internee, identified only as Kruez. While Bockmeyer lay dying of his wounds in the camp's hospital, Kruez had managed to evade the guard, but was later re-captured. Could he have been the same fellow-prisoner Bockmeyer attempted to escape with in January, as German names were often difficult to understand and sometimes given incorrectly to confuse the authorities?

Written witness statements for the coroner survive. On 18 September 1916, the evidence was given before an inquest conducted in front of twelve local jurymen by Coroner John Brangan (*Coroner's Inquest Notes*, 18 September 1916). One statement, proffered by Dr Charles A. Kelly, indicated he had tended the wounded man soon after the shooting had taken place. He stated that Bockmeyer died early the next morning at the camp's hospital; the cause of death being from 'Haemorrhage shock as a result of a bullet wound to the abdominal area'. The doctor stated the bullet pierced his liver as it passed through his body.

Bockmeyer, a civilian, was buried in the workhouse's small cemetery, known locally as Bully's Acre. His thwarted escape and the re-capture of Kruez were reported in *The Times* of 22 September 1916. Bockmeyer's death was also reported in the *Meath Chronicle* (23 September 1916).

That same edition also carried an article on a visit to the Oldcastle camp on 10 June 1916, by Mr Edward Lowry, a special attaché to the German Division of the American Embassy in London. At the time of Lowry's visit there were 579 internees, all civilians apart from one, who was a sailor. One half had been living in Ireland when war was declared, and the rest merchant seamen taken from ships in Irish ports, of which 468 were German, 110 were Austrian, and one of another nationality. Lowry described the living conditions at the camp as good.

A representative of Oldcastle's historical society has stated:

> The workhouse opened in *c.*1841 to house the poor of the area. When war seemed inevitable, the Powers in London decided, for their safety, to relocate German and Austrian businessman – a predominately Jewish community – to the workhouse. As the workhouse could only house around 120 people at any one time, some internees were obliged to sleep under canvas or in wooden billets.

Farrelly's father maintained the internees were a most dextrous lot, and made ornamental jewellery. A letter from Jack Briody, which says the internees were very good with their hands, making rings, trinkets and broaches, etc. support this. Briody added they gave these to local people. The internees formed a band. They often played as they marched under escort to their place of work in the morning, and back again in the evening.

Bockmeyer and Kruez's attempt to escape was not the first to be attempted by those interned at Oldcastle. The *Meath Chronicle* (14 August 1914) reported an escape had taken place. The next edition (21 August 1914) reported the escapees had been apprehended. They were not named, but were most likely to be Carl Marlang, 25, and Alfons Grien, 24. Cited by *The Times* (13 August 1915) as being two ship's officers that had escaped, it was thought the absconders had been dressed as women. The next edition stated they had been recaptured in County Cavan. One of them was dressed as a clergyman. *The Times* (21 August 1915) stated Charles Fox was charged with aiding the two internees to escape.

Aloysius Duffner was a jeweller by trade; a German living in Tipperary, he was sent into internment at Oldcastle at the beginning of the war. Whilst interned he received several telegrams of mixed fortunes. One informed him his wife had given birth to a girl and that both were doing well. He replied to it on 5 February 1915, sending his heartiest congratulations. The second telegram he received, on 16 August 1915, stated his mother had died that day, at four o'clock. On his release, Duffner was issued with an identity book, dated 10 April 1920.

The Times (20 September 1915) stated Hans Christian Deichmann, aged 28, had escaped from Oldcastle; he was still at large. The *Police Gazette* (12 October 1915) cited Deichmann had been apprehended.

Because of fears arising from the troubles in the civil war that took place when the Post Office in Dublin and other prominent institutions were seized, Germans being interned in Ireland became a political hot potato. The *Isle of Man Examiner* (1 June 1916) reported that around 500 aliens had arrived at Douglas by steamer on the Sunday evening (26 May) and were taken by train to Knockaloe. It was rumoured they were Irish Nationalists from Dublin, but they were more likely to have been some of the interned Germans and Austrians that Murphy (per. comm., 20 January 1997) recalled were put on a train one Sunday. He cited the townsfolk lined both sides of the railway track, to wave and cheer the internees off. However rumours that the camp closed then are unfounded as it was to remain open for another two years.

The *Meath Chronicle* (13 January 1917) reported twenty-two internees were repatriated, amongst them was Count Stolberg, a well-known racehorse owner. The same paper (3 February 1917) carried news of another fatality at the camp when an internee received a blow to the head during a football match and died. This unfortunate man would have been Franz Seemeier who died on 30 January 1917 and was buried in the graveyard of Oldcastle's Roman Catholic Church.

The Times (25 August 1917) stated Gosh Loy Ehlers, a ship's officer, had absconded from a camp in Ireland. The same paper (27 August 1917) reported his re-capture.

The *Meath Chronicle* (17 November 1917) reported of a court martial taking place at the camp.

Jackson (1989) stated Oldcastle, by the autumn of 1918, had closed.

The *Isle of Man Examiner* (1 June 1918) reported that around 500 aliens had arrived at Douglas by steamer on the Sunday evening (26 May 1818) and were taken by train to Knockaloe. Rumour of their pending arrival from Dublin had prompted speculation that they would be Irish Nationalists. They may have been the internees last to leave Oldcastle. Murphy (1997) recounted that a batch of internees were put on a train one Sunday afternoon, with townsfolk lined on both sides of the railway track, waving and cheering them off.

The remains of the two dead internees were exhumed and transferred to the German War Cemetery at Glencree, in County Wicklow. Mullingar and Duncannon are also cited as having war dead that were transferred to Glencree (Volksbund Deutsche Kriegsgräberfürsorge, Kassel, per. comm. 19 February 1997).

The FPHS (1973) cites Oldcastle, Meath in its listings. It is also recorded in a document held by the Oesterreichisches Staatsarchiv in Vienna (GZ 9815/0-KA/97) and in Hadifogoly Magyarok Tortenete, (Budapest, 1930).

ORFORDNESS (OS: TM 425 495). Orfordness was used as secret military test site from 1914 until the mid-1980s. In an attempt to foil any missile attack from the USSR an early warning tracking system was created there.

Since 1993, the area has become a nature reserve, run by The National Trust and very little of the camp remains today. It was a working camp, and its POWIB (1919) code was Pa (Ofd) (IWM: Facsimile K4655). The camp was located at Town Marsh, near to the Trust's site office, some 12 miles northeast of Woodbridge. The camp is also cited by the FPHS (1973). It had the TA Priswarian: Orfordness (ADM 1/8506/265–120667).

A Swiss Delegation visiting camps was told that the internees were still being housed in tents at the end of January 1917. Similar complaints were made at Wingland (Lincolnshire), West Tafts (Norfolk), Warren Wood (Norfolk), Glendon, Stratford upon Avon, Kerry (Wales), and Shirehampton (Gloucestershire). The internees were also critical of the medical facilities at Orfordness, and complained of a lack of fresh clean clothes to wear.

DKF 34: Aus den Berichten der Schweizer Delegierten aus dem Ende des Jahres 1917 über die Arbeitslager in England geht hervor, daß die Zustände in einigen dieser Lager sich gebessert hatten und daß in manchen dementsprechend das Leben erträglich war. Immerhin geben noch einige Lager zu berechtigten Klagen Anlaß. Trotz wiederholten Einspruchs der deutschen Regierung sind in der Lagern Wingland (Lincolnshire), Ordfordneß (Suffolk), West Tofts (Norfolk), Warren Woods (Norfolk), Glendon bei Keltering (sic), *Stratford on Avon, Kerry (Nord Wales), und Shirehampton (Gloucestershire) die Gefangenen immer noch in Zelten untergebracht.*

DKF 34: In Orfordneß ist für Erkrankungfälle über keine Vorsorge getroffen.

DKF 34: Die Versorgung der Gefangenen mit genügender Kleidung und Wäsche ist verschiedentlich sehr mangelhaft. Hauptsächlich in den Lagern Warren Woods, West Tofts, Orfordneß und Kerry wird hierüber geklagt.

OSBOURNBY (OS: TF 07- 38-). Apart from being cited by the POWIB (1919) nothing is known about Osbournby other than it was a satellite of Sleaford. Its code was Bro (Sl) (Ob) (IWM: Facsimile K4655). It would have existed in the second stage of internment camps being set up in Britain.

OSSINGTON (OS: SK 761 652). Cited in a HO document as being at the stables of Ossington Hall, its TA was Priswarian: Hall Stables, Ossington, Sutton on Trent (ADM 1/8506/265–120667).

Minute 13 of the Notts County WAC, dated 28 January 1919, records the total number of PoWs engaged on agricultural work in the county was 598. They were distributed among permanent depots at: Retford, Tuxford, Ranskill, Laneham, Cuckney, Plumtree, Papplewick, Woodborough, Langar, East Leake, Kelham, Halam, Ossington, and Carlton, and in migratory gangs at Blyth, Wiseton, Clayworth, Walkeringham, Misson, Bunny, Shelford, Ruddington and Gotham.

During March 1919, Dr A. de Sturler inspected Ossington. His findings are held at the National Archives at Kew (FO 383/508).

OSWESTRY (OS: SJ 314 315). There were four camps at Oswestry and two hospitals. Oswestry had been the parent camp for the lower ranks farmed out into working parties prior to Shrewsbury taking over the role in 1918, around the same time as the fire that gutted the Hall. The four camps, with their known HO codes were:

PARK HALL OFFICERS (OW) PARK HALL WESTERN (OSW)
PARK HALL WORKING MENS PARK HALL EASTERN (OE)

Park Hall in Oswestry was described as being one of the finest Tudor mansions in England; a fine example of an Elizabethan timbered house, dating to around 1560. It stood about 1 mile to the east of Oswestry, near the junction of what are now the A5 and A495. Mrs Wynne-Corrie had purchased the estate in 1871. *The Times* (23 June 1913) reported she died in 1913 as a result of the lift in the house crashing to the ground when she was in it.

In 1914, the War Department took over the estate. According to the *Border Counties Advertiser* (November 1914), Major Wynne-Corrie had moved out of the hall and had gone to live in Shrewsbury. Despite the intolerable wet and miserable weather, over 900 labourers were engaged in constructing a camp to accommodate around 14,000 soldiers. The first arrivals, in July 1915, were around 4,000 men from the combined Royal Welsh Fusiliers and Cheshire Regiment. Men disembarked at Whittington Station and marched to the camp with the Fusiliers' mascot, a goat, taking the lead.

According to Macpherson (*History of The Great War – Medical Services*, 1923), the PoWs first arrived at Park Hall in April 1918. A HO document issued in October 1918 cites Oswestry as a parent camp. A later document cites Shrewsbury was the parent camp.

The *Border Counties Advertiser* (20 November 1918) cited there had been a fire in the generating station at Park Hall. Temporary lighting was being installed, but was considered to be a poor substitute. It would appear that this fire was not as devastating as the next one.

The Times (28 December 1918) reported the mansion burnt down. The report said that just before midnight, on Boxing Day, a fire started in the west wing, in an area near the chapel. It spread very quickly and attempts by both the Oswestry and Shrewsbury fire brigades were hampered by the lack of water. The cause of the fire was thought to have been faulty electrical wiring.

Some 700 German officers had arrived in September 1918, a few months before the fire. *Border Counties Advertiser* (1 January 1919) reported PoWs at Park Hall had assisted with the removal of rescued furniture and fittings and taken it to the remaining section of the camp.

Despite the Armistice being in place, internees were still attempting to escape. *The Times* (8 January 1919) reported Vingent had escaped. The next day's edition reported his re-capture. Again, *The Times* (24 March 1919) cited Lt Screinuller had escaped. There was no report of his recapture. *The Times* (11 April 1919) reported the escape of Waldhausen. He had been recaptured before next day's edition had hit the streets.

The *Border Counties Advertiser* (25 June 1919) cites German sailors from the scuttled ships at Scapa Flow had arrived by train at Gobowen, on Tuesday (24 June 1919). Amongst them was von Reuter, who was taken to the Park Hall Camp. Some men and officers were taken to Henlle.

Friedrich Ruge was a naval officer in the German Grand High Seas Fleet. He was instructed to be part of a ship's company that brought, as part of the Armistice agreement of November 1918, the German ships into internment. He maintained that it was never a part of the agreement that the crews were to be interned too, but they were. He was in a party of about fifty officers taken by HMS *Royal Oak* to Nigg, where they spent one night before being sent by train to Oswestry. He alighted at Gobowen, and walked for about half an hour to reach their destination.

Ruge (*Scapa Flow: The End of the German Fleet*, 1973) cites there were five large camps, each holding several thousands of NCOs and men. In his camp (which was probably the Eastern Camp) he states the compounds were numbered E1 to E5. Each compound contained around 500 men, most of which came from the army. He was put into E5 with about fifty other officers. According to him, the men were accommodated in tents, and the officers in wooden huts. The huts were very simply built, with only one room. Cynically, he stated, 'there was never a lack of oxygen' because at the end of each hut were a dozen large cut holes, and the wooden floorboards had spaces between them. He further claimed, despite felt on the roofs, they leaked. In the huts, on each side of a central walkway were a dozen beds, and in the walkway sat three long tables, surrounded by chairs. By each bed was a wall shelf, and a footstool; and at one end of each hut stood their one source of heat, a pot-bellied stove. Ablutions were done in wash huts, which he says, 'displayed no exaggerated luxury.'

The *Border Counties Advertiser* (25 June 1919) cited German seamen arrived in Oswestry.

The day before von Reuter's transfer the *Border Counties Advertiser* (2 July 1919) noted three German officers went, under escort, by car, to Oswestry to exchange a quantity of German paper money. But the bank manager refused to take the German money. When they were in the bank, word quickly spread that they were there, and as they left, a woman assaulted them. A youth was also seen throwing a cabbage at them. PoWs were forbidden to have British currency, and this may be why the bank manager refused to exchange the money. Instead of cash they were given tokens, which had no monetary value outside their camp. Instances of camps producing their own currencies, for the prisoners to use, are frequently commented on. In some camps, Spanish coins that had become worthless between their date of commission and their intended date of circulation, and never released by the Royal Mint, were over-stamped for their new usage as internal currency.

The *Border Counties Advertiser* (16 July 1919) reported the death of Willi Oster. He was a German PoW shot dead during disturbances at camp E2 on Saturday, 12 July 1919. This was a result of officers in the adjoining compound throwing parcels over the fence to the men. The sentry shot at random to drive away the PoWs who were throwing stones at him. Oster was on the roof of a building retrieving a parcel when he was shot. The Coroner's Court recorded a verdict of misadventure. It also reported Admiral von Reuter had been transferred to Donington Hall on 3 July 1919.

The *Border Counties Advertiser* (23 July 1919) cited some PoWs had plotted to burn down their huts. German officers were summoned to a meeting and told that if anything should happen along such lines no replacement accommodation would be provided.

The *Border Counties Advertiser* (13 August 1919) stated there had been reports in the German press of mistreatment of PoWs. A letter appeared in the *Hamburger Nachrichten* saying the internees had gone on strike at Park Hall, ie they refused to attend roll call, in response to the shooting of Willi Oster.

The *Border Counties Advertiser* (29 October 1919) reported that British units had left Oswestry to go overseas. The camp however would still continue to be used as a demobilisation centre for men returning from overseas. It also stated the Henlle Camp closed on Sunday, and the Fernhill Camp was to close in the coming week. The German PoWs were leaving Oswestry in batches of a few hundred at a time.

The Times (17 November 1919) stated that some of the crews from the interned fleet at Scapa Flow had been brought to Park Hall after the Henlle and Fernhill camps had been dismantled. At this time, German officers, including Ruge, were being transferred to Donington Hall, where they joined up with other officers who had previously been at Wakefield.

The *Border Counties Advertiser* (26 November 1919) stated that all the German PoWs have been sent home, and their guard had been dispersed. But *The Times* (28 November 1919) cited 20,000 internees had been repatriated, and that the property was to be sold. The following day's edition stated that around 1,600 men who had been brought from Scapa Flow were still actively engaged in clearing up the camps at Oswestry. When they became discontented and refused to obey orders, the guard had to turn out, with fixed bayonets, to get the work resumed.

The *Border Counties Advertiser* (3 December 1919) cited internees, still at Park Hall, were refusing to co-operate with the British authorities, resulting in their rations being withheld. They demanded to know why they were being forced to work, rather than being repatriated. The PoWs made an appeal to the British public. Two PoWs, not named in the article, had attempted to escape in the previous week. Both were re-captured locally. *The Times* (9 December 1919) denied reports in the German press of hunger punishment being carried out at Park Hall.

The Times (15 December 1919) cited the escape by Paul Simon from Oswestry. He was re-captured at Harwich.

The Times (30 January 1920) reported 144 officers and 1,640 other ranks left from Hull for repatriation. It is believed the officers came from Donington Hall and the sailors from Oswestry.

The *Border Counties Advertiser* (4 February 1920) advertised the sale of effects from Park Hall Camp, including huts, posts, duck-boarding, timber, barbed-wire etc.

The Times (17 April 1920) and *Border Counties Advertiser* (21 April 1920) noted the last PoW departed from Oswestry: an *U-Boot* commander, he left for Scotland under escort. No reason as to why he was so late in being released was given.

After the war the camp lay dormant until it sprang into life again in the Second World War. It finally closed in 1975. By then many of the huts had been vandalised and set alight. Much of the site returned to agricultural usage.

A total of 108 internees died whilst being interned at Park Hall. They were buried at Park Hall's Prisoner-of-war Cemetery. A Faculty, dated 21 November 1961, requesting their remains, with one other from Whittington Cemetery, be moved to Cannock Chase, is held at St Mary's House, Lichfield.

The FPHS (1973) record three sites at Oswestry, plus a working camp. They also recorded Harlescott, Tern Hill, Little Fernhill, and Henelle Park (sic). There is a report on a visit of inspection to the PoW camp at Oswestry by Dr A. de Sturler on 1 December 1918 (FO 383/507).

DKF 24: Das neben dem Mannschaftslager gleichen Namens errichtete Offiziers-Gefangenenlager Oswestry wurde im September 1918 eröffnet. Zu Beginn des Jahres 1919 wurden einige Offizierlager in England – Kegworth; Margate; Dyffryn-Aled – aufgelöst, um ihren ursprünglichen Zweck (Landwirtschaftliche Schulen usw.) zurückgegeben zu werden. Die dort untergebrachten Offiziere, die sich im Laufe der Zeit leidlich eingerichtet und mit ihrem Schicksal abgefunden haben wurden ganz plötzlich in das Lager Oswestry überführt. Die Überführung von Kegworth z. B. geschah in der Weise, daß die Gefangenen bei Schneesturn und Regen, bepackt mit ihrem Gepäck, zum Bahnhof ziehen mußten. Dort standen sie eine volle Stunde in Wind und Wetter, bis sie ein Extrazug aufnahm, der sie nach Oswestry überführte. Von der Station Oswestry bis zum Lager mußten sie wiederum ihr Handgepäck drei viertel Stunden lang durch den dicksten Schmutz schleppen.

Das lager Oswestry selbst spottete zur Zeit ihrer Ankunft jeder Beschreibung. Die Baracken, die früher für die Unterbringung von englischen Mannschaften verwendet wurden, waren in keiner Weise für den Empfang so vieler kriegsgefangener Offiziere vorbereitet. Die Schlaf- und Wohnräume entbehrten jeder Bequemlichkeit. Die Offiziere wurden zu zwanzig Personen in einem Raum untergebracht, indem lediglich Betten standen, außerdem befanden sich darin ein Tisch und eine viersitzige Bank sowie ein kleiner Ofen. Die Dächer der Baracken waren undicht, so daß der Regen freien Zutritt fand. Die Waschgelegenheit war außerordentlich mangelhaft. Es gab keine Komode, Keine Waschschüssel, geschweige denn Waschtisch; eine Petroleumstallaterne bildete die Beleuchtung. Zu Anfang wuschen sich die Kriegsgefangenen mit Schnee, bis mit Eintritt des wärmeren Wetters die Wasserleitung in Betrieb kam. Später gab es für je zwanzig Personen eine Waschschüssel. In den Baracken mußten ständig zwei Fenster offen stehen, angeblich aus Gesundheitsrücksichten. Als die Fenster von den Offizieren geschlossen wurden, um eine einigermaßen erträgliche Temperatur in den Räumen zu erhalten, wurden auf Befehl des Kommandanten je zwei Fenster ausgeschraubt. In den Wohnräumen, die zu Studienzwecken benutzt werden sollten, fehlte jegliche Beleuchtung, außerdem war die Heizung durchaus unzureichend. Die gelieferte Kohle genügte kaum für zwei Stunden täglich, so daß es bei den geöffneten Fenstern für die Gefangenen unmöglich war, sich genüend zu erwärmen. Infolge der schlechten klimatischen Verhältnisse von Oswestry war der Boden im ganzen Lager vollständig aufgeweicht, so daß die Gefangenen, die zum Apell, zum Wasschen sowie zur Verrichtung ihrer Notdurft die Baracken verlassen mußten, ständig unter nassen Füßen zu leiden hatten, da keine Gelegenheit war, das Schuhwerk zu trocknen. u diesem vollständigen Mangel an Bequemlichkeit jeder Art kam auch die wenig wohlwollende Haltung der Lagerbehörden hinzu, so daß Oswestry als ein Vergelungslager schlimmster Sorte erscheinen mußßte, obwohl für die englische Regierung nicht die geringste Veranlassung hierzu bestand, nachdem die englischen Gefangenen Deutschland bereits verlassen hatten. Auch heir muß angenommen werden, daß derartige unhaltbare Zustände nur eintreten konnten, weil Vergeltungsmaßregeln von deutscher Seite nicht mehr zu befürchten waren. Es gelang erst nach veilen Beschwerden seitens der Kreigsgefangenen sowie nachdrücklichsten Protesten durchdie deutsche Regierung und die Deutsche Waffenstillstandskommission eine kleine Besserung zuerzielen. Es liegt eine große Anzahl von Klagen deutscher kriegsgefangenen Offiziere vor, aus denen allen die Emmpörung über diese unverdiente schachvolle Behandlung spricht. Der nachstehende Auszug aus einem dieser Berichte illustriert am besten die Stimmung, in der sich die deutschen Gefangenen befinden:

Nach Ablauf des Waffenstillstandes wurden alle Lager aufgelöst und Gefangenen in völlig uneingerichtete Sammellager transportiert. Englische Offiziere sprachen bei Abtransport ihre Genugtuung und Freude über Verschlechterung unserer Lage unumwunden aus; Captain Finney Stratford: bis dahin hätten wir es gut gehabt, aber jetzt würden uns die Augen übergehen. Schlimmste Erwartungen sind durch Wirklichkeit noch weit übertroffen. Lager besteht aus fünf Abteilungen für je 700 Offiziere und Mannschaften auf kaum 120 zu 240 Meter, je 20 Mann in Baracke von 5 zu 17 Meter. Dezember und Januar fast keine Kohle und kein Licht, pro Baracke eine Stallaterne, die alle drei Tage einmal gefüllt. Wege verschlammt, Speisebaracken niemals geheizt, niemals Sonne, Betten verfaulen. Wasserleitung mit Hähnen ohne Becken zum Waschen in gesonderten offenen Schuppen meist eingefroren. Essen ungenügend. Pferdefleisch und für Bevölkerung verbotener, sicher versalpeterter Speck, trotz massenhafter anderer Vorräte im lande, einzige Fleischnahrung. Viele vor Hunger schwer überreizt. Verkehr mit Nachbarlagern verboten, man sieht Kameraden dort an, wie Tiere im Zoologischen Garten. Im Vergleich werden Zustände in den englischen Gefängnissen von bestraften Kameraden als paradiesisch geschildert. Über dem ganzen liegt öde Trostlosigkeit, die alle physisch und moralisch zugrunde richten muß. Das ist auch Zweck der Behandlung und die Absicht der maßgebenden englischen Behörden. Dazu kommt unsere Hilflosigkeit in Erledigung der heimatlichen Angelegenheiten, die schlechte und seltene Postverbindung, die Strenge der Zensur, die Ungewißheit über Dauer dieses Zustandes, die Sorge um die Angehörigen daheim und die Verhältnisse in Deutschland.

OTLEY (OS: SE 20- 45-). There was an Otley agricultural group that was attached to Wetherby agricultural depot. Its POWIB (1919) code was Cat (Wet) (Ot) (IWM: Facsimile K4655).

There was a workhouse in Otley, and this, or its grounds, may have been the site of this camp, although there is no tangible evidence to suggest this was so. It opened in 1873 as Wharfedale Union Workhouse, on Newall Carr Road, Otley, to the designs of C.S. and A.J. Nelson; it replaced the former parish workhouse. An infirmary block was added in 1907 to designs by W.H. Herbert Marten. Taken over by the West Riding County Council, it became known as Otley County Hospital in 1930. Seven hutted wards were added in 1940, which were used to treat and accommodate people from the nearby Prisoner of war camp. When adopted by the NHS in 1948 it was renamed Wharfedale General Hospital, and extended in 1957. In 2000 the main workhouse buildings acquired Grade II status. In 2004 a new hospital was built partly on the site of the workhouse and partly on adjacent land (www.pastscape.org.uk).

OXFORD: HM Prison (OS: SP 509 061). Pardoe (per. comm., 2000 & 2003) wrote that her grandfather, John Thomas Allen, was a sergeant in the King's Royal Rifles in the Great War. He was awarded the Mons Star (1914, Star with bar), the British War Medal and the Victory Medal. Because of injuries sustained he was transferred to the Labour Corps, and was stationed for a period at Tilbury, Essex. She also stated that he spent some time at Oxford Prison as a member of the guard, guarding German PoWs. She wrote 'they must have liked him as they made him several lovely hand carved items.'

OXTED (OS: TQ 392 519). A working camp, its POWIB (1919) code was Pa (Ox) (IWM: Facsimile K4655). It was also cited by the FPHS (1973). The camp's TA was Priswarian: New Oxted (ADM 1/8506/265–120667). Local knowledge suggests the camp was located at the quarry on Chalkpit Lane, where it is believed the PoWs worked. Chalk and limestone have been produced from the Oxted Chalk Pit for more than 150 years.

P

PANSHANGER (OS: TL 289 132). Near Welwyn Garden City is Panshanger Park, owned by Earl Cowper; it is thought to date back to *c.*1819.

De Soissons (*Welwyn Garden City: A Town for Healthy Living*, 1988) cites 'oak wood timbers being cut by local men for the war effort, especially from Sherrard's Wood. At Panshanger, this work was done latterly with German PoW labour.'

The camp was also cited in the minutes of the Hertfordshire County Council WAC. According to the minute of 10 February 1919, there were twenty PoWs billeted at Panshanger, engaged in agricultural work.

The camp had the TA Priswarian: Hertingfordbury (ADM 1/8506/265–120667).

PAPPLEWICK (OS: SK 54- 51-). The camp at Papplewick was a satellite of Plumtree. It appears in minutes produced by the Notts WAC and has the POWIB (1919) code Bro (Pl) (Pp) (IWM: Facsimile K4655). It had the TA Priswarian: Papplewick,

Hucknall Torkard (ADM 1/8506/265–120667). During March 1919, Dr A. de Sturler inspected Papplewick and his findings are held at the National Archives at Kew, London (FO 383/506).

A pumping station with twin beam engines, built by James Watt & Co., has existed at Papplewick since 1884, but it is unlikely the PoWs worked on it during the war. Instead, they probably worked on one or more of the many farms in the area.

Parish Councillor Mary Barker believes they were billeted at Papplewick Hall, which lay empty prior to the beginning of the First World War. It was built in 1787 for Frederick Montague, to replace the one left to him by Lady Colladon, his mother. According to *Kelly's Trade Directory* the hall was once the home of Francis Abel Smith, and was unoccupied in 1912. Between the wars, Arthur F. Houfton, described as a farmer, and Claude William Chadburn JP, were in residence. The latter bought the hall in 1925. Cicely James became the next owner when Chadburn's widow died in 1982. Today, the hall has been converted into an office block. Poets Thomas Gray and William Mason are buried in its grounds.

An alternative to the Hall is Papplewick Grange. This was a large mansion pulled down in 1932 to be replaced by Papplewick Lido. The lido was demolished in 1995, to be replaced by housing (www.papplewick.org/local/history/papgrange).

PAPWORTH ST AGNES (OS: TL 270 641). Papworth St Agnes appears on a list produced by the FPHS. The camp is cited as being at The Rectory, and had the TA Priswarian: The Rectory, Papworth St Agnes, Papworth Everard (ADM 1/8506/265–120667).

St John the Baptist Church was constructed in 1850, to the plans of the Reverend J.H. Sperling, who also built the adjacent Rectory, in 1848. In 1976, the church was declared redundant, de-consecrated and subject to a demolition order, but it was saved by residents of Papworth St Agnes. Enough money was raised to start renovation in 1980. It is now a focal point for the community.

PARKHURST: HM Prison (OS: SZ 491 910). Brothers Joseph Mary, George Oliver and John (Jack) Plunkett took part in the Easter Rising of 1916. For his role Joseph was shot by firing squad. For their roles, George and Jack were also sentenced to be shot, but these sentences were commuted to ten years penal servitude. Their sister Geraldine wrote:

> When the newspapers came out on Saturday the 6 May 1916 we saw that George and Jack had also been sentenced to death and the sentence commuted to ten years. Jack told me afterwards that he had been told first of the death sentence and that the officer had then paused for a whole minute before telling him it had been commuted. Jack and George were brought to Mountjoy Jail for a few days, and then brought in a cattle boat to Holyhead. They spent six months in Portland Prison before being moved to Parkhurst, on the Isle of Wight. I got some South African medal ribbon because it was green, white and orange and made it into a bow which I wore everywhere. A big policeman in Dame Street stopped me and said the tricolour would get me into trouble. I said, 'I have one brother shot and two brothers sentenced to death and my father and mother in jail. He said 'You're Plunkett, you can wear it.'

Both were released due in the 1917 amnesty and returned to Ireland.

PARTNEY (OS: TF 408 681). Partney is a satellite of Wainfleet, it was an Agricultural Group with the *POWIB* code Bro (Wai) (Py) (IWM: Facsimile K 4655). The camp's TA was Priswarian: Partney, Spilsby (ADM 1/8506/265–120667). The FPHS (1973) cites it too.

The Victory Hall opened in April 1921 as the Dalby and Dexthorpe Village Hall. The original wooden structure was replaced by the present hall in 1986. The hall was a memorial to those who served in the First World War. Built on the site of the old White Horse Inn, it was an area used as a German prisoner of war camp during the First World War (www.partneyvillage.co.uk).

PATELEY BRIDGE. There were two camps at Pateley Bridge that may have been open concurrently. One was an agricultural depot and the other an agricultural group attached to it. Pateley Bridge is cited only once by the FPHS (1973). Confusing entries exist in the POWIB (1919) listings and none more so than those for Pateley Bridge.

There is one for an agricultural group that has the code Cat, (Wet) (P B). No depot for Pateley Bridge appears on that list, but four separate entries for agricultural groups state they are attached to Pateley Bridge Agricultural Depot (IWM: Facsimile K4655).

One explanation to this anomaly is that it changed its status at some point. If not, they may have been together, in the workhouse.

AGRICULTURAL DEPOT (OS: SE 158 658) and AGRICULTURAL GROUP (OS: SE 158 658). Burgess (Nidderdale Museum: per. comm., 1 September 2000) informs us the PoWs were billeted in the workhouse which stood in King's Street, and opened in 1863. Following a refusal by the guardians to pay for improvements to the building demanded by the Local Government Board, the workhouse closed in 1914. The buildings were emptied of their patients and they were transferred to the workhouse at Ripon. PoWs were then billeted in the vacated workhouse.

Selina Dorothy Millward was the daughter of the Thomas Millward who was the Workhouse Master; they lived in the master's living quarters. In 1919, Selina had an illegitimate son named Edwin. His father was rumoured to be a German Prisoner of War who was billeted in the workhouse. Selina, who was a nurse at the workhouse, did not marry the father who is thought to have returned to Germany (www.family treemaker.genealogy.com).

Between the wars, the casual wards of the workhouse remained in use, providing vagrants with a staging post between the Ripon and Skipton workhouses. It also housed workers on the Scar Dam project. A part of the building is now Nidderdale Museum which opened in 1975. The former casual ward block is now King Street Workshops.

PATTISHALL: Eastcote House (OS: SP 675 544). Eastcote House stood near Blisworth, 7 miles southwest of Northampton. Unlike other internment camps it had been set up by neither the War Office nor the Home Office, but by a trade union. Pattishall PoW Camp occupied the ground between School Road and the top of Bird's Hill Road, in the village of Eastcote, near to a site marked by the planting of a chestnut tree for the Coronation of George V in 1911.

Before the war, the National Sailors' and Firemen's Union of Great Britain (NSFU) had purchased Eastcote House for £3,500, with the intention of turning it into a retirement home for its members. The site then comprised of a medium sized house, and 60 acres of agricultural land. As a result of the war many German and Austrian merchant seamen were being left destitute on the streets of Britain as their ships had been confiscated as prizes of war, or ship owners would not employ them (see also, Alton Abbey). Joseph Havelock Wilson was the General Secretary of the NSFU. He was a leading instigator in the setting up of the Destitute Aliens' Committee, which oversaw the project to convert Eastcote House into a refuge for sailors. The Home Office agreed to allow the house to be used to accommodate up to 1,000 seamen.

The Northampton Mercury (25 September 1914) cited there were fifty men at the camp, guarded by police and boy scouts. They were making preparations for others expected within a few weeks. It was expected that up to 1,000 men would be staying there. Towcester Rural District Council was concerned about its water supply and of its sewage disposal. *The Northampton Daily Echo* (23 September 1914) carried a similar article. *The Northampton Mercury* (2 October 1914) reported there were still fifty men there. A large marquee had been erected and served as the dining hall and an assembly room. Sleeping quarters were bell tents. *The Northampton Herald* (2 October 1914) carried a similar report, stating there were fifty bell-tents, each capable of sleeping eight men. Boatswains were to be appointed to be in charge of twenty-five men. Two German doctors, presently interned elsewhere, were to be transferred in to Eastcote to serve in the hospital that was being fitted out in two cottages.

The external perimeter of the camp was patrolled by nine police officers from the Northamptonshire County Constabulary, aided by local senior boy scouts. Internally, the inmates policed themselves, which was the common practice in other camps too.

The Northampton Mercury (30 September 1914) cited Alfred Stockhurst escaped from the camp. He was apprehended at Fosters Booth, 1 mile west of the camp. At his trial, in Towcester, he told the magistrate he wanted to join the British Army.

The Northampton Mercury (13 November 1914) cited a group of around twenty Germans that had been held at Eastcote had been moved to Northampton Prison. They were now being moved to Frimley, by train.

The Times (20 November 1914) cited a letter, printed in the German press, praising the standard of treatment at Eastcote. *The Northampton Daily Echo* (5 January 1915) printed the full text of the letter, as did *The Yorkshire Herald* (5 January 1915).

Mr Jackson's report for the US Embassy in London, of 27 February 1915, stated he did not visit the Eastcote camp. But there was a visit conducted by MPs at this time. The visit had taken place two days before the article that appeared in *The Times* (15 May 1915), which stated:

> 27 acres of land are enclosed in a high wire fence put up by the Home Office at a cost of £500. Huts and various buildings, both of brick and stone, have been erected by the inmates, who now number 779. It is said the union intends to make the place, in the end, a home for ancient mariners. The Government pays the union 10 shillings a head, a week.

However, the 'relaxed manner' in which these seamen were treated was too soon to alter. One of the treats the interned seaman had was their camp concert. On hearing of the sinking of the RMS *Lusitania*, Wilson cancelled the scheduled concert for that evening as he expected a sympathetic response to the news that some 500 of their fellow seamen had perished. Silence prevailed at the conclusion of his announcement, but as he left the concert hall stage, the *Watch on the Rhine* was heartily sung by his German audience. More patriotic songs followed, before cheering began. This incident went down very badly with Wilson and soured his opinion of the German seamen in his care, which resulted in the camp being turned over to the War Office.

One escape was mentioned in the report of 15 May 1915. The unnamed sailor was re-captured after three months of working on a British collier supplying the Royal Navy.

The camp, now functioning under the mantle of Pattishall, was extended to accommodate combatant PoWs too. A considerable expansion of the camp was undertaken, with new water supply, drainage and sewerage system. A new hospital and other installations were built. The accommodation was enlarged to hold up to 2,000, but Macpherson, Horrocks & Beveridge (*History of the Great War – Medical Services*, 1923), who did not give an opening date for the camp, stated there was accommodation for 4,000 internees in hutments.

The Northampton Mercury (13 August 1915) cited three internees that had escaped from a camp near Towcester were taken away to a military camp near Crewe.

The Times (14 September 1915) reported the escape of Wilhelm Wetzel and Hermann Yarus. They were re-captured at Northampton.

A delegation from the US Embassy in London visited the camp on 11 April 1916. It cited the commandant of the camp was Lt-Colonel J.H. Ansley. There was also a breakdown of the 1,559 internees: 705 were German soldiers; 749 were German civilians; and 105 other civilians. The military personnel were separated from the civilian population. Each compound had five barrack huts capable of accommodating 200 men each. At the date of the visit, buildings for workshops and a theatre/hall were almost completed (FO 383/507).

The Times (1 September 1917) cited the escape of seven. They were named as: Walter Heinrich Schultz, Hermann Harte, William Schutle, Arthur Kerst, Heinrich Müller, Wilhelm Gitzen and Max F. Ball. *The Northampton Mercury* (31 August 1917) also reported the escape. A press cutting held by the Imperial War Museum states, 'Scotland Yard announces that seven German prisoners escaped yesterday morning from the Pattishall Camp, Northants. This brings the number of prisoners who have escaped during the last fortnight up to seventeen, but nine of these had been recaptured ...' Descriptions of the seven are given, before the article concludes with the report of another escape attempt, this time from the camp at Rochford in Essex.

The Times (3 September 1917) reported the seven escapees had been re-captured at Denton. Again *The Northampton Mercury* (7 September 1917) covered their apprehension.

After the Armistice, men were still attempting to escape. *The Times* (11 August 1919) reported a man, later identified as Heinrich Schultz, had escaped from Eastcote, and, according to *The Northampton Mercury* (15 August 1919) he was re-captured at Wolverton.

The Northampton Mercury (22 August 1919) cited the commandant was Colonel O'Donnell Colley Gratton CBE DSO.

The Northampton Mercury (29 August 1919) cited Schultz was charged with burglary of a house at Castlethorpe. He appeared in court and was committed to quarter sessions, but does not appear to have come back to be tried. In a separate court case, regarding the theft of blankets and unserviceable clothing from the camp, Mr Darnell, appearing for the defence, stated that there were now no Germans left in the camp as reported by *The Northampton Mercury* (28 November 1919).

The Pattishall Parish Records show around thirty German military personnel were buried in Pattishall Churchyard, their deaths mostly attributed to the influenza pandemic. Their bodies have subsequently been exhumed, and moved to Deutsher Soldaten Hof (German War Cemetery), on Cannock Chase, in Staffordshire.

Those interned in the camp helped in the construction of a reservoir, dining hall and other amenities. Little physical evidence remains today to suggest this camp ever existed. The sale of 100 huts, building materials, etc., was advertised in *The Northampton Mercury* (5 March 1920).

The Northampton Mercury (20 November 1925) reported headstones for the graves of German PoWs were being put in situ.

The Northampton Independent (14 August 1953) cited the dining hall from the Eastcote site was re-used in 1925, as the garage of Abington Motors Ltd, Wellingborough Road, Northampton. Prior to that, it had been a *Palais de Danse*. The former guard room was utilised as the parish hall for many years after the last PoW left.

The camp's TA was Priswarian: Pattishall (ADM 1/8506/265 – 120667). Another camp, near Pinner, was called Eastcote Lodge. Both Pattishill (sic) and Eastcote, Northants are listed by the FPHS (1973), but the camp at Pinner was not recorded by them.

PEAK DALE: Buxton (OS: SK 097 768). At the onset of the First World War there was no immediate effect on the production of limestone in quarries around Buxton, North Derbyshire. But as the demand increased, it was found that there were not enough local men to extract it, as over 700 of their number had gone to answer the call to the Colours. To try and fill this void their places were taken by the womenfolk, but when no more could be found, PoWs were brought in. Each morning these PoWs were marched through the village of Peak Dale, near Buxton, to Wainwright's Quarry, returning the opposite way again each evening back to their camp. The officials of the camp stayed at the Midland Hotel in Peak Dale, which was near the quarry, which was also known as Peak Dale Works.

Storer (*More than Just Dust*, 1989) cites the local community and the internees appear to have been on friendly terms. Silver coins were often thrown to the internees for them to fashion rings and other pieces of jewellery. They were even challenged to play 'friendly' matches against the local football team that was dubbed the Rib Lifters, for their illegal use of the elbow. Jack Salt, the quarry manager, was presented with a framed photograph in appreciation of his fair treatment to the internees, which they didn't get in their football matches. The wooden frame was fashioned, by a PoW, from broken hammer shafts.

Records show that not all the PoWs were happy. There were complaints that the washing facilities at the camp were insufficient. This was a common complaint in camps where dirty or heavy work was being undertaken. It was also noted that church services were not provided regularly.

The Ashbourne News (2 November 1917) cited Chesterfield Fire Brigade apprehended three PoWs that had escaped from Buxton.

Between 29 September 1918 and 4 March 1919, eighteen PoWs died, most probably from the flu pandemic that was prevalent in Europe at that time. Their bodies were interred at Peak Dale Trinity Church Graveyard at Wormhill; and subsequently re-located to the German War Graves Cemetery at Cannock Chase in 1961.

Reports on visits of inspections to PoW camps at Coal Aston (Sheffield), Monks Abbey (Lincolnshire), Peak Dale Quarries (Derbyshire), and Sproxton Moor (Yorkshire) are held at the National Archives at Kew, London (FO 383/432).

According to a directory produced by the POWIB (1919), Peak Dale was an agricultural depot located at Doveholes, with the code Bro (Pe D) (IWM: Facsimile

K 4655). Peak Dale is also cited by the FPHS (1973). The camp's TA was Priswarian: Doveholes (ADM 1/8506/265 – 120667).

DKF 31: Auch in Sproxton Moor haben die bei den Waldarbeiten beschäftigten Kriegsgefangenen keine genügende Gelegenheit, zu baden Sehr empfindlich ist der Mangel an gutem und genügendem Wasser außer in Sproxton Moor, hauptsächlich in Peak Deal (sic) *Quarries bei Buxton, Belfon Park* (sic), *und Yatesbury.*

DKF 32: Gottesdienst: Die Seelsorge der Kreigsgefangenen ist auf vielen Plätzen sehr vernachlässigt. In den Lagern von Joyce Green; Dartford; Hadnall; Peak Dale Quarries bei Buxton; Sutton Veny; Larkhill; Netheravon; Codford; und Fovant hat noch kein Gottesdienst stattgefunden.

PEASMARSH: Rye (OS: TQ 87- 23-). Near to Rye, this was a working camp with the POWIB (1919) code Pa (Pea) (IWM: Facsimile K 4655). Rye is cited by the FPHS (1973), but no further evidence has been found to suggest where the camp was located.

PEMBREY (OS: SO 413 000). The isolated sand dunes of southern Cefn Sidan were ideal for explosives manufacture, and in 1881, the New Explosive Company of Stowmarket started producing gunpowder and dynamite near the village of Pembrey in Carmarthenshire. Around five years later it was taken over by the South Wales Explosive Company, a subsidiary of the Nobel's Explosives Company, of Glasgow, to produce TNT. The 62-hectare site consisted mainly of sandhills and sand dunes to provide some protection in the event of an explosion.

In 1914, in response to the need to drastically increase the production of shells, a new factory was built. The new site was one of the first purpose-built TNT manufacturing sites to be created in Britain. The factory was taken over by the Ministry of Munitions in 1917, and it became known as the National Explosives Factory, Pembrey. It produced 15,000 tons of TNT and 20,000 tons of propellant and was one of the largest of the 200 factories producing munitions during WW1. The site was now described as being some 304 hectares.

It closed in the early 1920s. The administration building became a convalescence home for children of unemployed miners. The water supply was taken over by Llanelli to supply the town with clean water.

The PoWs would not have been involved in activities in the ordnance factory, but from evidence gathered about other camps they may have helped create some of its infrastructure.

Dr A. de Sturler and Monsieur R. de Sturler inspected the PoW camp at Pembrey, among others, in June 1919. The report is held at the National Archives at Kew, London (FO 383/508).

During the Second World War a new factory, the Royal Ordnance Factory, Pembrey, with around 3,000 employees, was created for the Ministry of Supply, again to make explosives. It had its own railway system, linked to the main railway line at Pembrey, and its own power station. It was Britain's largest producer of TNT. After the war it continued to make TNT and tetryl, for military use; and ammonium nitrate, as a fertiliser for agricultural use (www.kidwellyhistory.co.uk).

ROF Pembrey closed at the end of 1965 and the majority of this site, 206 hectares, was taken over by the Forestry Commission to become Pembrey Country Park.

PENARTH (OS: ST 18- 71-). The camp at Penarth is cited by the FPHS (1973). Reports on visits of inspection to PoW camps by Dr A. de Sturler and Monsieur R. de

Sturler during June 1919 include Penarth. The reports are held at the National Archives at Kew, London (FO 383/508).

PENMAENMAWR (OS: SH 71- 76-). The FPHS (1973) and the POWIB (1919) both cite Penmaenmawr. The entry for the latter states it was a working camp with the code Fg (Pen) (IWM: Facsimile K4655). However, the same document also cites Llanerchymedd as being an agricultural group attached to Penmaenmawr Agricultural Depot giving its code as Fg (Pen) (Ll). The camp's TA was Priswarian: Penmaenmawr (ADM 1/8506/265 – 120667).

The Leigh Chronicle (30 November 1917) stated Lieutenant Jones, who had been at Leigh Military Camp for some time, had gone to take charge of the Penmaenmawr prisoner of war camp, in North Wales.

The Times (26 June 1918) cited the escape of Arthur Sabish from Graigboyd Quarries, whilst he was an internee at Penmaenmawr. He was re-captured quickly.

PENNERLEY (OS: SO 35- 99-). The camp's TA is cited as Priswarian, Minsterley (ADM 1/8506/265 – 120667). Reports on visits of inspection to PoW camps by Dr A. de Sturler and Monsieur R. de Sturler during April and May 1919 are held at the National Archives at Kew. They include Pennerley (FO 383/507).

PENHURST (see Bough Beech).

PENSTON (OS: NT 344 722). Details of this camp are scarce. It may be that the PoWs were involved in the creation of the infrastructure for an airfield at nearby Macmerry, which was constructed around this time, an activity known to have taken place at other locations. The alternative is that they worked on the surface at Penston Colliery, in an activity going back some 600 years. Or they worked on farms.

Horne (*The German Connection: The German Newspaper 1916–1919*, 1988) cited there were work camps at Dalmellington, Kinlochleven, Glendevon, Crawford, Dawyck, Lentran, Nethy Bridge, Raasay, Hairmyres, Penstone (sic), Inverkeithing, Bee Craigs, Port Clarence, Catterick and Grantham. Most were satellite camps of Stobs.

Snodgrass (*The Third Statistical Account of Scotland – The County of East Lothian*, 1953) along with Martine (*Reminiscences and Notices of the Parishes of the County of Haddington*, 1999) and Edmond (*Reflections on the Life and Times of the Edinburgh Collieries Company Limited*, 1981) divulge it was an area rich in mineral deposits. Coal, limestone, fireclay, ironstone, and freestone, along with brewing, milling, and agriculture, all created some kind of industry in East Lothian. Some of these may have been activities undertaken by the PoWs. At its peak there were twelve collieries in East Lothian. This allowed the black band iron ore to be smelted locally. At Penston, two of the three shafts had closed by the time PoWs were available for work. The last shaft closed on 12 March 1928 with the loss of approximately 150 jobs.

PENZANCE: Chyandour Barracks (OS: SW 475 311). Rees (*Old Penzance*, 1956) cited that by 10 August 1914, Chyandour Barracks was made ready to receive internees. On 16 August, seventy Germans were brought to Penzance, and interned at Chyandour. They possibly then joined others that had been removed from Falmouth, at Dorchester.

PEOPLETON (OS: SO 93- 50-). A working camp with the POWIB (1919) code Dor (Peo) (IWM: Facsimile K4655), it is also cited by the FPHS (1973). It had the

TA Priswarian: Peopleton (ADM 1/8506/265 – 120667). However, no evidence has been found to suggest where this camp was located.

Evidence records the camp was commanded by Lieutenant C.E. Withers, and on 31 December 1917, thirty-one PoWs were being billeted there.

PERHAM DOWN (see Ludgershall).

PERSHORE (OS: SO 94- 45-). Described by the POWIB (1919) as an agricultural depot, it had the code Dor (Per) (IWM: Facsimile K4655). There was a satellite at Stoulton. Also cited by the FPHS (1973), the camp's TA was Priswarian: Pershore (ADM 1/8506/265 – 120667). Sadly, the camp's exact location is unknown.

Alexander MacCallum Scott asked James Hope, the Member for Sheffield (Central Division) whether Pershore fruit-growers had applied for the services of forty prisoners of war for whom they guaranteed permanent work; and whether any steps had been taken in response to that application. In reply Hope said:

> Since the reconstruction of the Prisoners of War Employment Committee at the end of last year, no application from Pershore for the services of prisoners has been brought before them. All the prisoners who could be spared for agriculture were allotted by the Committee to the Board of Agriculture, who undertook the task of distributing them through the country in conjunction with the War Office. I understand that eighty of such prisoners were assigned to the WAC for Worcestershire.

In his follow up, Scott asked if the Committee was open now to receive requests for these prisoners? Mr Hope replied, 'No; application for agricultural employment must be addressed to the Board of Agriculture.' (*Hansard*, 19 March 1917).

PERTENHALL (OS: TL 085 655). The names of twenty-four PoWs that worked at Pertenhall between September 1918 and September 1919, along with their guard, are recorded in an extract taken from the PoWs' employment time sheets that are held at Bedfordshire County Record Office (WW1/AC/PW/1/2).

PERTH: HM Prison (OS: NO 118 223). With no facility readily available in Perthshire to receive the first enemy aliens arrested under the Defence of the Realm Act, seven individuals from Callender, St Fillan, Pitlochry, and Crieff were put into Perth Prison. Harding (*On Flows the Tay*, 2000) does not state into which institution they were placed, nor does he record if they were detained for any period of time. If not detained, they would have been released under licence back into their communities, and if detained they would most probably have been transferred to Edinburgh for processing.

Perth's City and County Prison was built in 1819, and stands behind the County Building on Tay Street. HMP Perth had been built seven years earlier under the supervision of Robert Reid, the King's Architect and Surveyor for Scotland, to house 7,000 French prisoners from the Napoleonic Wars; it is located to the south of the South Inch. In the 1830s it was used as an asylum, before being used in its current usage as a prison for civilians, from 1842.

McConville (*Irish Political Prisoners 1848–1922: The Theatres of War*, 2005) cites that on 20 May 1916, Irish men and women were arrested and detained for offences committed under Section 14b of the Defence of the Realm Act, for their parts in the Easter Rising. The ringleaders were executed and 197 were put into prisons on the mainland of Britain, including Perth and Barlinnie Prison in Glasgow. Many were only detained for a short term before being released. The rest were transferred to Frongoch in Wales.

PETERHEAD (see Boddam).

PLUMTREE (OS: SK 61- 33-). An agricultural depot cited by the POWIB (1919), its code was Bro (Pl) (IWM: Facsimile K4655); it also appears in the minutes of the meetings of the Notts County WAC. There were three satellites attached to it, at Barnstone, Papplewick, and Woodborough. The camp's TA was Priswarian: Plumtree (ADM 1/8506/265–120667). Although it is also cited by the FPHS (1973), there is no evidence to show the camp's actual location.

PLYMOUTH: SS *Urania* & Bull Point, Mortehoe (OS: SX 485 539). In order to protect the nearby Royal Ordnance Depot, barracks were erected at Bull Point, *c.*1858. This consisted of two blocks, one for officers and one for the lower ranks. The jetty was not constructed until 1898.

The *Western Morning News* (12 September 1914) cited eleven Germans were put into temporary internment on board the SS *Urania*, a four-masted barque that had been taken as a prize of war. It was moored in Plymouth Sound. Of the eleven, five had been crewmembers of the *Heathfield*, a British barque, and of the rest were five crewmembers and one passenger from the SS *Llanstephen Castle*, of the Union Line. Another report in the same newspaper (25 September 1914) cited four German soldiers, recovering from wounds, were being moved from the Fortress Hospital, Devonport to a compound at Bull Point.

Mark (*Prisoners of War in British Hands during WW1*, 2007) cites a letter from the Postal Censor (3 March 1915) showing that PoWs' mail for Bull Point, near Mortehoe (OS: SX 444 458) had to pass through Salisbury House for censorship.

PLYMPTON – WOODFORD – SALTRAM (OS: SX 526 568). A working camp, it was cited by the POWIB (1919): its code was Dor (Sa) (IWM: Facsimile K4655). It is recorded as being at Saltram, Woodford, Plympton. A HO document cites Woodford Camp, but states its TA as Priswarian: Plympton (ADM 1/8506/265–120667). Woodford and Plympton are cited separately by the FPHS (1973). Woodford Farm may hold the key to the location of this camp.

PODINGTON (OS: SP 940 620). A working camp, near Wellingborough, it had the POWIB (1919) code Pa (Po) (IWM: Facsimile K4655). The FPHS (1973) cite it too. No further evidence has been found to suggest the location of this camp. An airfield, dating back to the Second World War, existed at Podington (OS: SP 953 603).

PONTEFRACT (OS: SE 444 212). *The Yorkshire Herald* (9 August 1914) cited internees were being detained at the barracks in Pontefract. This was probably only a short-term measure. Their fate is unknown. They may have been released or transferred to another facility, possibly to York where it is known enemy aliens, as they were often referred to, were being detained.

PORT CLARENCE: Middlesbrough (OS: NZ 51- 21-). The POWIB (1919) directory cites Port Clarence as being a working camp, with the code Bro (Po C) (IWM: Facsimile K4655). Listed by the FPHS (1973), Port Clarence has the TA Priswarian: Middlesbrough (ADM 1/8506/265–120667).

In the nineteenth century Port Clarence was part of the docklands area of Middlesbrough. It was to become landlocked as a result of the industrial development that transformed the mouth of the River Tees.

However, there is an entry for South Cleatham in the same directory, which states it to be an agricultural group attached to Port Clarence Agricultural Depot. It is believed that PoWs sent to Middlesbrough may have worked for Isaac Bell, who, with his family, owned the major steel plant in the town. Bell, a Quaker, was a director of Brunner Mond, a firm that took over a Ministry of Munitions experimental plant at Billingham, where PoW labour was used to create internal pathways, and an access road to the plant.

Port Clarence's staff was cited as not being empathic of the plight of the internees in their charge as many of them were unaccustomed to hard physical work. The PoWs also complained that they were undernourished for the work that was asked of them (Vereinigung Wissenschaftlicher Verleger, 1919).

DKF 31: Diese 14 Lager müssen für die bevorstehende kältere und nasse Jahreszeit als durchaus ungeeignet bezeichnet werden. Unzureichend sind auch die Baracken in Port Clarence und Yatesbury, es sei denn, die Wände der Baracken baldmöglicht verstärkt werden.

DKF 31: Auch in Loch Doon, auf der Insel Raasay, in Newlandside, Ceal Aston (sic) *Sutton Veney* (sic), *Bowithick, Netheravon, Yatesbury, Rovrah* (sic), *Port Clarence und Hayrmyres* (sic) *werden die Leute zu sehr ausgenutzt.*

DKF 32: Auf der Insel Raasay ist die verlangte fünfzigstündige Förderund Ladezeit viel zu schwer. Die vielen vorkommenden ernsten Verletzungen sind ein deutliches Zeichen von Überarbeitung. Dies trifft auch auf Rovrah (sic) *und Port Clarence zu.*

DKF 32: Den Straßen -und Steinbrucharbeiten in Port Clarence fehlt genügendes Schuhwerk und Altrinchan (sic) *ausreichende Kleider bzw. Arbeitsanzüge.*

DKF 32: In Wackerley (sic), *Sproxton Moor, Port Clarence und Larkhill fehlen Plätze bzw. Räume zur Erholung der Kriegsgefangenen.*

PORT TALBOT (OS: SS 792 899). Described as a working camp, its POWIB (1919) code was Fg (Po T) (IWM: Facsimile K4655). It is also cited by the FPHS (1973). Its TA was Priswarian: Port Talbot (ADM 1/8506/265–120667).

It is believed that those interned were detained in a former celluloid factory. The factory had a very short life span; it opened in 1901.

A request to the local radio station (bbc.co.uk/wales/southwest/yoursay/topics/askalocal.shtm) by Debrunner (2005) seeking details of why the commandant of the PoW camp at Port Talbot, Viscount Melville, resigned in 1917, remains unanswered. But it did prompt these replies. Vance Broad (2008) stated:

> My grandfather, Walter Broad, was born in Capetown but was invalided to Port Talbot to recover after being gassed in France. In 1915, as a 15-year-old he was a horse soldier with Brandt's Greenpoint Kommando in German West Africa. He spoke Afrikaans, Dutch and German, which is why he was posted to Taibach in 1917 to take charge of a group of German PoWs who were building the Abbey Works at Margam. He died, aged 39, never fully recovering from the mustard gas. The prisoners at Goytre were most certainly German.

Others replied too, suggesting there had been a PoW camp at Port Talbot in both the First and Second World Wars. Chris from Porthcawl (2008) cites:

> There was a German First World War One camp near Goytre at the old celluloid factory near Glen Hafod colliery. In 1917, the Port Talbot Railway ran a

> workman's train for the use by PoWs from the Celluloid Sidings to Copper Work Junction, to construct blast furnaces for Baldwin's. The factory closed *c.*1910.

Thomas (2007) states:

> There was a prisoner of war camp at Goytre. My grandmother lived at Tyn-y-Ffrem Farm, just up the valley from the camp. One of the prisoners worked on the farm and made her a tablecloth.

PORTON (see Purton).

POTTERHANWORTH (OS: TF 05- 66-). The Society for Lincolnshire History and Archaeology (Lester, per. comm., 19 April 1998) suggests Potterhanworth may have had an internment camp, as buildings survive today that suggest this. However to which conflict these belong has not been confirmed. Bilsby, Brigg, and Usselby Hall were also suggested as sites by the Society.

POTTERS BAR (OS: TL 26- 01-). A working camp, its POWIB (1919) code was Fe (P Ba) (IWM: Facsimile K4655). This camp is also cited by the FPHS (1973). Its TA was Priswarian: Potters Bar (ADM 1/8506/265–120667). No further evidence has been found to suggest this camp's location.

POTTON (OS: TL 22- 49-). Described as a Working Camp, its POWIB (1919) code was Pa (Pot) (IWM: Facsimile K4655). Its TA was Priswarian: Potton (ADM 1/8506/265–120667). The FPHS (1973) cite a camp at Purton, which may be an incorrect reference to this camp.

In 1914 there was a German prisoner of war camp near Potton and many local woods were said to have been cleared by the prisoners (www.bernardoconnor.org.uk/Everton). Local knowledge suggests they were there for only a short period. It is believed that they were housed in the centre of the town, and were taken daily to Sutton Park.

Railways often played a vital role in transporting groups of PoWs. Potton's railway station may have seen the arrival and departure of many of them.

PREESHENLLE: Henlle Park (OS: SJ 304 355). Located to the south of Prees-gweene, on part of the Henlle Hall estate, it is thought to have been a satellite of the Park Hall complex of internment camps at Oswestry. It is cited by the FPHS (1973) as Henelle Park (sic), Salop.

The *Border Counties Advertiser* (28 January 1920) reported the suicide of Johann Beck, an interned ship's stoker. He died on 24 January 1920. At his inquest it was stated that he often took morphine to induce sleep while at the Henlle Camp.

The Times (17 November 1919) claimed the Henlle and Fern Hill camps had been dismantled, but Beck's suicide shows the former to have been operational again.

PRISTON (OS: ST 69- 60-). Approval was sought for premises for PoW depots at Keyford, Priston, Queen Camel, Glastonbury, Wookey, Hinton St George, and another near Yeovil according to minutes of the Somerset County WAC of 21 May 1918. Nothing is known about the location of this camp, or the numbers it held.

PURTON (OS: N/A). This camp appears in the list produced by the Forces Postal History Society. A gazetteer of British place names cites several possible locations, of which none has revealed evidence of the camp's location.

Purton	SO 67 04	Gloucestershire
Purton	SO 69 04	Gloucestershire
Purton	SU 09 87	Wiltshire
Purton	SU 48 77	Berkshire
Purton Common	SU 08 88	Wiltshire
Purton Stoke	SU 09 90	Wiltshire

The camp at Potton does not appear on the list produced for the FPHS (1973); their entry of Purton may therefore have been erroneously entered.

Details supplied by Crawford (*Wiltshire and the Great War: Training the Empire's Soldiers*, 1999) strengthen the argument against PoWs being located at Purton in Wiltshire. The hazardous nature of the work being carried out, and the need for secrecy would not have lent itself to having PoWs there. In the First World War the army tested explosives there.

Q

QUEEN CAMEL (OS: ST 59- 24-). A minute of Somerset County Council WAC recorded that approval of depots for Ploughman gangs at Keyford, Priston, Queen Camel, Glastonbury, Wookey, Hinton St George, plus another near Yeovil, was being sought on 21 May 1918. The location of the depot is unknown.

QUEEN'S FERRY (OS: SJ 331 679). Bird (*Control of Enemy Alien Civilians in Great Britain 1914–1918*, 1986) cites Queen's Ferry was used at the start of the war to hold civilian internees.

Anon (*The Industrial Architecture in Flintshire 1899–1901*, *c.*1962) reveals, on its completion in 1901, the front facade of the Willans & Robinson plant, near Queen's Ferry, had won worldwide acclaim for its designer, H.B. Cresswell. The new plant, which included a 90-foot tower, was located on the south side of the River Dee, between Queen's Ferry and Sandycroft. There are references to the camp being called Sandycroft in local sources.

Willans & Robinson's main plant was in Rugby, and produced water tube boilers for the navy. When business waned, the Queen's Ferry plant closed in 1911, and remained dormant until its conversion into an internment camp at the beginning of August 1914 (Lloyd, *Willans & Robinson Limited, Engineers & Boiler Makers, Queensferry*, 1959).

Photographs show enemy aliens being marched through Queen's Ferry; the accompanying caption states these to be 'German prisoners arriving at Queen's Ferry on 11 August 1914.' On closer inspection, the photograph reveals the marchers were in civilian attire and not military uniforms.

In September 1914 around 100 alien civilians were arrested in Manchester and brought to Queen's Ferry. At the time of John B. Jackson's inspection visit in early 1915, Queen's Ferry held 2,000 civilians; but it was then abandoned as a place of internment by May 1915, when many of the prisoners went to the new camp created at Alexandra Palace, London.

The West Sussex County Times and Standard (15 August 1914) reported that 200 prisoners were transferred on Thursday to Chester Castle, via Queen's Ferry, from Christ's Hospital School in Horsham. The following issue (22 August 1914) states the prisoners went to Queen's Ferry. A corridor train belonging to the London and North Western Railway Company took them and their escort, thirty men and an officer, of the 3rd West Kent Regiment. After the train departed, from Horsham at 10.30am, bread, meat, and cake was served.

The Chester Chronicle (Saturday, 15 August 1914) reported 500 internees had arrived in three batches by special trains on the evening of Tuesday, 11 August. Escorted by Lancashire Fusiliers, they were taken to the camp at Queen's Ferry to be met by Colonel T.A. Wynne-Edwards, the camp's commandant. The guard then comprised of the 5th Cheshire Regiment, under the captaincy of W.A.V. Churton. A week later The *Chester Chronicle* (22 August 1914) cited four hotel waiters working in Chester had been arrested and conveyed under military escort to the camp. The number of internees grew as more arrived from Christ's Hospital School, near Horsham. It was believed their number at Queen's Ferry was now around 1,000.

The Times (27 August 1914) stated there were 1,400 at Queen's Ferry.

The Chester Chronicle (Saturday, 5 September 1914) stated 200 men of the Royal Welsh Fusiliers replaced the 5th Cheshire Regiment.

The *Liverpool Daily Post* (22 September 1914) reported the moving of some 200 internees from Queen's Ferry to the Isle of Man. *The Chester Chronicle* (26 September 1914) surmised there were now over 2,000 at Queen's Ferry, and that accommodation was being taxed to the utmost. The 200 that had gone to the Isle of Man had been quickly replaced, as the same number was reported to have arrived on Thursday, 24 April 1914 under military escort.

The Scotsman (13 November 1914) cites the report of the visit by US Embassy staff was published.

A letter, dated 1 January 1915, from 250 internees billeted at Queen's Ferry, complained they were destitute. They were seeking their salaries from the German Colonial Office.

John Jackson led a US Embassy delegation to visit the camp. Their findings, dated 10 February 1915, concluded that at the time of their visit there were approximately 2,200 civilians and a small number of soldiers interned there. His impression was that the general atmosphere of this camp was the most depressing of all the camps he had visited as it had been occupied for about five months with little done to improve the buildings, which were an old machine shop, divided into two compounds. The floors were stone or cement; and the roof leaked. Some internees had built 'tents' around their beds to protect against leaks and draughts. As there was little opportunity to work, many of the internees were listless. The washing facilities were limited, but new kitchens were being built to replace the present one which was dirty and inadequate. The latrines were insufficient too. A lot of money was required to improve the plight of these internees. Two deaths had been reported. A third had died after being hospitalised for surgery. The dead were buried in Howarden Old Cemetery.

The Chester Chronicle (3 April 1915) suggested those interned at the former Willans & Robinson engineering works were to be transferred soon, as the plant was to be utilised for other purposes in connection with the war. The edition of 17 April 1915 stated many of the internees had been moved out recently; supposedly they had gone into internment on the Isle of Man.

The Queen's Ferry camp was cleared of its internees by 21 May 1915. Many of them had been taken to London. A US Embassy report cites the first arrivals from Queen's Ferry went to Alexandra Palace on 7 May 1915. Six Germans remained in Wales, though not at Queen's Ferry. They had been transferred to the North Wales Counties Asylum, near Denbigh, presumably on health grounds.

During the war, a munitions factory was opened on part of the site. It was to be one of the most important plants for manufacturing TNT in Great Britain.

The Times (25 April 1915) cited MPs made an unofficial inspection of the Queen's Ferry site. They noted the internees had a band, which played in fine weather as they walked about their compound.

Cheshire Corporation took over the plant's powerhouse in 1923, to supply electricity to the area; and in 1959, a joinery firm was based in the old munitions works.

R

RAASAY, ISLE OF (OS: NG 554 354). The camp on the Island of Raasay was a working camp. The POWIB (1919) directory cites its code as Stbs (Ra) (IWM: Facsimile K4655). Its TA was Priswarian: Raasay (ADM 1/8506/265–120667). Raasay also appears in the lists produced by the FPHS (1973).

Raasay's indigenous population was around 350, when in 1912, Messrs Baird & Company, Ironmasters of Coatbridge, bought a plot of land near to Suisnish, to extract iron ore. To entice miners to come and work on the island the company built houses at Inverarish. These houses were to incorporate the prisoner of war camp on the island. Company records (5 June 1916) show the first group of internees sent to Raasay were eighteen sailors rescued from the *Blücher*, but they were quickly returned to the mainland for security reasons. The exact number of internees sent to Raasay is unknown, but a ledger kept by a local suggests there were around 280 in total. Draper & Draper (*The Raasay Iron Mine: Where Enemies Became Friends*, 1990) state 'Because most of the local men had been called to the Colours, Baird arranged for German PoWs to work at the installation from 1916 onwards.' Currie (*Discover Scotland*, Horton 1990) suggests that the arrival of 200 German PoWs on Raasay meant that the 'newcomers' outnumbered the locals.

The internees were housed in two terraces of the Inverarish Houses. They had been segregated from the other dwellings by a high barbed-wire perimeter fence with a guard tower at opposite corners. Enclosed were nos. 17 to 32 and 49 to 64. The guard was accommodated at Nos 46 and 47. It is thought No. 45 served as the sick bay and its administrative centre. Lighting came from the powerhouse situated near to the pier. Each house comprised of two rooms and a kitchen, with one toilet shared between two houses. At its peak, possibly eight or nine PoWs shared a house. There were allegations that the prices charged by the mining company in their canteen were over-priced.

As well as working at the mine, small groups of prisoners were also gainfully employed on farms on the island.

With the signing of the Armistice of 11 November 1918, the need for steel waned and its priced dropped rapidly. As the quality of the ore extracted was poor, the mine at Raasay was one of the first extraction plants to suffer. Draper & Draper (*Der Anschnitt*, April 1999) state, by 30 April 1919, when Raasay's ore was no longer required, the PoWs were transferred to another location, to await being repatriated home.

A band formed by the internees often played for the locals as well as to the other camp members. How they came by their instruments or their Tyrolean outfits is not known.

Despite their country being at war, it did not stop friendships being made, and a mutual respect for each other resulted in gifts and food being exchanged in spite of the government's orders forbidding such exchanges. The Mining Engineer was presented with a cigar/cigarette box – inscribed under the lid PoW 1919 – and a hand crafted table, fashioned from scrap pieces of hard wood, which are still cherished by his descendants today. Yet we find there were complaints made by internees that they were being overworked, which they claim resulted in a number of serious injuries.

In June 1917 cases of scurvy were reported. It transpired that eighty-two men were taken ill due to the overcooking of their food, and a poor choice of available foods did not help, according to MacPherson, Horrocks & Beveridge (*History of the Great War – Medical Services*, 1923).

During their stay on Raasay fourteen internees died, most in the winter of 1918 when the flu pandemic swept across Europe. Two died whilst the war was actively going on, and a gravestone for them was fashioned by Corporal G. Duda, a fellow interned German stonemason. Paul Sosinka had died in an accident at the pit, for which an inquiry was held on 2 March 1917. Georg Kagerer died on 7 May 1917, in circumstances unknown to us today. All fourteen were originally buried on Raasay; their remains were taken to Cannock Chase between 18 and 20 July 1967, against the wishes of the islanders.

By 1919 the mine had become uneconomical to operate and was closed. The company houses at Inverarish lay empty for many years, but were gradually occupied by the islanders. The camp had closed by 21 March 1919. Evidence of the mine's workings are still visible today. Several photographs exist of the Germans at work on the island.

DKF 31: Die Kantinen in Sproxton Moor und Radford sind schlecht versorgt, und auf der Insel Raasay werden in der von den Bergwerkunternehmern unterhaltenen Kantinen zu hohe Preise gefordert.

DKF 31: Auch in Loch Doon, auf der Insel Raasay, in Newlandside, Ceal Aston (sic) Sutton Veney (sic), Bowithick, Netheravon, Yatesbury, Rovrah (sic), Port Clarence und Hayrmyres (sic) werden die Leute zu sehr ausgenutzt.

DKF 32: Auf der Insel Raasay ist die verlangte fünfzigstündige Förder- und Ladezeit viel zu schwer. Die vielen vorkommenden ernsten Verletzungen sind ein deutliches Zeichen von Überarbeitung.

RAGDALE: Ragdale House (OS: SK 680 210). The camp, a satellite of Loughborough, had the POWIB (1919) code Bro (Lo) (Rd) (IWM: Facsimile K4655); its address is cited as Ragdale Hall. However its TA is stated as Priswarian: Ragdale House, Grimston, Leics. (ADM 1/8506/265 – 120667).

Ragdale House was built as part of a retreat for his family in 1897 by Arts and Crafts architect Howard Van Doren Shaw. He named his retreat after Ragdale Hall, a Tudor mansion that stands a few miles away. Hayes (*Ragdale: A History and Guide*, n.d.) believed he chose the name because Ragdale, to him, meant meadows, woods, and hollow apple trees, and country vistas …

Today, it has just undergone refurbishment and is still a retreat for writers and artists.

During March 1919, Dr A. de Sturler compiled reports on his visits of inspection to the PoW camps. Ragdale was inspected and his findings are held at the National Archives at Kew (FO 383/506).

RAINHAM (OS: TQ 521 822). A Working Camp, its POWIB (1919) code was Pa (Rai) (IWM: Facsimile K4655). Its TA is cited as Priswarian: Rainham, Essex

(ADM 1/8506/265–120667). It was cited by the FPHS (1973) but its exact location remains a mystery. Close by is Wennington, also cited by them.

Russell (*A History of the County of Essex*, 1978) states Rainham Hall was built in 1729 for John Harle, a ship owner. Built in red brick in the Dutch Domestic style, it is a Georgian merchant's house with spectacular wrought iron gates. An alternative site could be Wennington House. Built *c.*1810, it was demolished in 1956 and replaced by twenty semi-detached houses called Kent View.

Reports on visits of inspection to PoW camps at Rainham, South Ockenden, Chigwell), and Chipping Ongar are held at the National Archives, Kew (FO 383/506).

RAMSBURY: Burney Farm (OS: SU 242 725). The address of this working camp is cited as Burney Farm; it had the POWIB (1919) code Dor (Ram) (IWM: Facsimile K4655). It is also cited by the FPHS (1973). Its TA was Priswarian: Ramsbury, Marlborough (ADM 1/8506/265– 20667). Day (per. comm., 23 November 2000) cited the camp was in the parish of Burney, on a farmstead 2 miles west of the village on an unclassified road that links Axford and Aldbourne.

RAMSGATE (OS: TR 381 653). Ramsgate is cited by the FPHS (1973). The camp's TA was Priswaroff: Ramsgate (ADM 1/8506/265–120667), suggesting it was a camp for officers.

The area was prone to attack from the air by Zeppelin and Gotha bombers. Jackson (*The Prisoners 1914–1918*, 1989) was of the opinion that Ramsgate's PoWs were put there as a retaliatory measure to British PoWs being held in war-zone areas on the Western Front.

Basford (per. comm., 22 October 2006) believes Chatham House School was emptied of its Canadian invalids to accommodate the PoWs from September 1917 until the camp closed on 19 February 1919.

RANSKILL (OS: SK 663 878). An Agricultural Group cited by the POWIB (1919) as being attached to Retford, it also appears in minutes produced by the Notts County WAC (28 January 1919). The camp's TA was Priswarian: Ranskill (ADM 1/8506/265–120667).

Allen (per. comm., 10 April 1999) was born in the village in 1914; she remembers her mother talking about the PoWs being billeted at the maltings on Blyth Road.

Today the site has been turned over to a housing development.

READING: HM Prison (OS: SU 721 735). Around 100 Irishmen, sympathetic to the German cause for their own agenda, were sent to Reading Prison during the First World War. They had previously been held in other secure units, but the Home Office, in consultation with the Prison Commission, decided to transfer them to one 'special' prison. The ordinary prisoners were moved out to accommodate the new arrivals. They mostly came from the prisons at Brixton, Birmingham, Leeds, Liverpool, Wakefield, Stafford and Manchester.

Liam Mellows was one of those taken to Reading. His name had come to light during the British government's inquiry into the Easter Uprising. He was arrested in 1915 for offences committed under the Defence of the Realm Act and had been interned for four months in Mountjoy Gaol. Wanted again, he went 'on the run', but was arrested in Galway. Transported to England on 2 April 1916, he was put in Reading Prison. Visited by his family during Holy Week, Mellows changed places with his brother, Barney, and escaped disguised as a priest, via Glasgow and Belfast, and returned to Dublin (www.searcs-web.com/mellows).

In 1917, about fifty of the Irishmen had become discontented and demanded an improvement in their conditions. The Home Office reacted by transferring them to Knockaloe, where they were separated from the rest of the internees.

Mellows was executed at dawn on 8 December 1922 in Dublin's Mountjoy Gaol by the newly formed Irish government for the shooting of TD Sean Hales at Dublin's Four Courts in June 1922.

Reading War Hospital was used to treat wounded Germans.

READING BARRACKS (OS: SU 690 730). *The Berkshire Chronicle* (1 January 1918) reported three German prisoners of war, Privates D. Schneider, H. Triebel and L. Müller, appeared before a military court at Reading Barracks, having been charged with a serious assault on a girl, aged 16. A fourth defendant Pte G. Weinburger of the Bavarian Reserve Infantry Regiment did not appear in court because he was seriously ill with pneumonia. The four were accused of dragging the girl into a barn, presumably to have unlawful sex with her. All four were acquitted of the charge. Their guards had stated when they saw the girl afterwards she was perfectly calm and normal and had made no complaint. Inspector Halfacre corroborated this. Triebel and Schneider admitted to a lesser charge of being outside their billet after curfew. Their billet is unknown.

Brock Barracks stands off Oxford Road. Built in 1881, it was named after General Sir Isaac Brock. During the First World War, men of the 2nd Battalion, Royal Berkshire Regiment, were stationed there. Now vastly reduced in size, its future is uncertain.

REDDITCH (OS: SO 062 702). Cited as being at Ichneild Street, Redditch, the camp's TA was Priswarian: Beoley Hall, Redditch (ADM 1/8506/265–120667).

Page (*A History of the County of Worcester*, 1924) cites Beoley Hall is a large H-shaped house three storeys high, built of brick. The present house was erected some time after the Restoration. In more recent times, Tapster Rock used part of the hall as its administrative centre. It has been a Grade II listed building since 1986. Today the hall has been converted into apartments.

REDHILL (OS: TQ 281 509). The camp's address is cited as 73 London Road, and its TA was Priswarian: Redhill (ADM 1/8506/265–120667). It was a working camp, with the POWIB (1919) code Pa (Rdh) (IWM: Facsimile K4655). Redhill also appears on the list produced by the FPHS (1973).

On 27 February 2012 a planning application was submitted for 73 London Road, Redhill. It is advertised as a new office development to replace the former Crown Buildings Inland Revenue office. The application was refused and new ones have been submitted. The buildings have been empty since 2007.

REDMIRES (OS: SK 261 857). Prior to the war, horse racing took place at Lodge Moor, on the outskirts of Sheffield. Racecourse Farm can still be traced to that area.

Norton History Group (*Wartime Norton History Group*, 1994) cites Redmires Reservoir was created by Sheffield City Corporation, *c.*1850, using local stone, to serve the needs of the people of Sheffield. Between 1861 and 1889 the Sheffield Artillery Volunteers practised firing their projectiles on the moor, probably ending the horse racing. When coastal ranges came into vogue, the less popular inland ranges became obsolete. Formed by two students from the University of Sheffield on 5 December 1914, Sheffield City Battalion (12 Battalion, The York and Lancaster Regiment), began by practising at Bramall Lane; but they were not popular with the owners of the club, as they ruined the playing surface. The city offered them the use of huts near Redmires Reservoir, where they became adept at digging trenches.

The POWIB (1919) cites Redmires as being an officers' camp and gives its code as Re (IWM: Facsimile K4655). Redmires is listed by the FPHS (1973).

MacPherson, Horrocks & Beveridge (*History of the Great War – Medical Services*, 1923) believe the camp opened in October 1918, with accommodation, in huts, for 650 officers and 156 servants, which marries up with the number stated in the local newspaper. The camp's commandant was cited to be Lt-Colonel Ernest Cooke in a report done of the camp's conditions. At the time of news of the Armistice being sought, the press also made reports about PoWs arriving at Redmires. *The Sheffield West Riding* (27 September 1919) reported that up to 900 PoWs were being detained at Redmires, fifty of which were doctors awaiting repatriation. Except for their orderlies, they were all officers.

The *Sheffield Daily Telegraph* (19 October 1918) cited that Emile Franke, with two other PoWs from Redmires, got out of the camp during the night to steal potatoes and turnips from Soughley Inn Farm. Franke was shot by the farmer and taken to Firvale Hospital suffering from gunshot wounds. The men had been engaged in preparing the camp for more arrivals. Karl Braun and Richard Kummeth, the two not wounded, were handed over to the Military authorities; according to the *Sheffield Daily Telegraph* (23 October 1918).

The Swiss visited the camp on 22 January 1919.

The process of allowing the internees to return to their homelands was slow. One reason offered for this is the fact that German ships were interned and the country had no money to employ other nations to bring them back. The last batch to leave for home, from Redmires, left in February 1920. Even as late as this, *The Times* (7 February 1919) cited Leuntant Plessing had escaped, but had been re-captured at York.

An internment camp was set up in the Second World War on Lodge Moor, near to where the earlier camp for officers stood. Cleared of its huts, today there is a council owned camp that was set up for travellers that stands partially on the site of the second camp.

Sheffield Library Service holds an artist's impression of the Redmires camp. Drawn from a photograph taken in 1915, it shows two lines of wooden huts in the foreground, supplemented by tents. In March 1920 these huts and other buildings were auctioned off. Pine trees now cover the site.

To the south-west of the Sportsman Inn, there are remnants of buildings believed to be from the earlier camp that are still visible today.

REDRUTH WORKHOUSE (OS: SW 688 416). A new workhouse was built, with stone from Carn Brea, to the designs of George Gilbert Scott and William Bonython Moffatt in 1838. It could accommodate up to 450 inmates. It stands in Barncoose Terrace. The workhouse was used to house ninety Germans that had been arrested, and interned, while trying to flee to America in August 1914. *The Western Morning News* (14 August 1914) cited the workhouses at Falmouth, Redruth, St Columb, and Truro were being used to hold passengers and crews detained from two German ships being held at Falmouth Harbour.

In 1918, in the House of Commons, Lord Cavendish-Bentinck asked Mr Hayes Fisher, the President of the Local Government Board, whether over 100 children were being maintained in the Redruth Workhouse; and what steps did he propose to take with regard to this union? Fisher said this was the case because of restrictions on capital expenditure during the War and so long as these restrictions were maintained these children must remain in the workhouse. A follow up question about why these children were not being boarded out was answered, 'I will make inquiries into that' (*Hansard*, 17 July 1918).

In 1935 it became the Redruth Public Assistance Institution and then in 1948 under the umbrella of the National Health Service it became the Barncoose Hospital. This remained the case until 1996 when it became the Camborne-Redruth Community Hospital. The workhouse was demolished in 1999, leaving only the 1897 infirmary.

RETFORD (OS: SK 712 814). Retford was an agricultural depot according to the POWIB (1919); its code was Bro (Ret). It had four satellites: Norton-Cuckney, Ranskill, Gringley on the Hill, and Laneham. The camp's TA was Priswarian: Retford (ADM 1/8506/265–120667). It also appears in the minutes of the Notts County WAC. Retford is cited by the FPHS (1973) too.

Joan Board (*The Great North Road*, 1992) suggests land donated to the Royal Flying Corps as a training ground, employed PoW labour in the construction of their airfield. The PoWs were housed in the workhouse.

Janet Landon of Thorpe House, Headon (per. comm., 18 March 1999 & 19 April 1999) was brought up on stories told to her by her mother, Phyllis Clark. Phyllis was born in 1910, and she remembered there were often internees working on her parent's farm at Greenmile. She believed them to be sociable, and they were invited to many of the village's functions. Extracts taken from Miss Clark's diary read:

> During the First World War about 30 acres [of her parent's farm] was used for an aerodrome, and that section was always called 'the Old Aerodrome' . . . In August 1939, a Government man came to look at the Old Aerodrome. The Government planned to take it for a training camp because there was going to be a war with Germany.

The airfield was later to become Ranby Army Camp, *c.*1940. Ranby Prison, which opened *c.*1970, now occupies the site.

The first person to be buried in the new part of Babworth All Saints Cemetery, according to Joan Board, was a German PoW named W. Enghardt. His remains were exhumed in 1960s and taken to Cannock Chase to the German War Cemetery.

REVESBY (OS: TF 30- 61-). The camp's TA is cited as Priswarian: Revesby (ADM 1/8506/265–120667). It is also cited by the FPHS (1973). No further evidence has been found to suggest where this camp was but the estate may hold the key.

Following Henry VIII's dissolution of the monasteries (1536–41) the land belonging to the abbey at Revesby was re-designated a country estate. Very little of the abbey is visible today. The Revesby Estate lies 12 miles to the north of Boston; it is a traditional sporting estate situated on the edge of the Lincolnshire Wolds and covers 6,000 acres of agricultural land and 450 acres of mainly mature woodland. The current house was built in 1845 by William Burn for James Banks Stanhope. The house, gardens and stables are currently in private ownership. The house is Grade I listed, and remains on the English Heritage at risk register.

RHOOSE (OS: ST 06- 66-). Cardiff Airport is 12 miles west of the city centre, at Rhoose. Its terminal is described as having all the amenities that a traveller could wish for, such as a food court, bars, and departure lounges. However this site was very different at the time of the First World War. From contemporary maps, Rhoose was a very isolated, rural place that consisted mostly of a few farms and a smithy.

Official documents place the camp at a hotel in Rhoose. Depending on which document you read it can be Kemey's or Stemey's Hotel, neither of which can be traced on those contemporary maps. However these maps do indicate there was an unnamed hotel at Rhoose Station, which stood to the south of the village on the former Vale of Glamorgan Railway (www.railscot.co.uk). Perhaps, it is this location that holds the key to the whereabouts of the camp.

RICHBOROUGH PORT (OS: TR 33- 61-). Richborough is cited by the FPHS (1973).

On 6 September 1917, the Swiss Delegation was reminded that the camp was located in an area prone to flooding. This resulted in many of the internees complaining of having rheumatic pains, as well as lice. There were also complaints that good drinking water, not contaminated by salt, was locked up during the day.

In *Deutsche Kriegsgefangene in Feindesland* (1919) the PoWs state the kitchens were unhygienic.

DKF 33: Nach einem weiteren Bericht vom 6 September 1917 waren die Zustände im Arbeitslager Richborough (Kent) geradezu unhaltbar. Das Lager liegt auf sumpfigem Boden, und eine Entwässerung ist undurchführbar, im Winter wird nach Ansicht des Delegierten das ganze Grundstück unter Wasser liegen. Die Leute sind sehr eng in Zelten untergebracht, in die das Wasser jetzt schon so stark eindringt, daß es an einigen Stellen sogar fast die Höhe der Zeltbretter erreicht. Die allgemeine Feuchtigkeit hat schon viele Rheumatismuserkrankungen zur Folge gehabt. Durch das Fehlen jeglicher warmer Bäder sind die Leute so wenig imstande, sich reinlich zu halten, daß Läuse in starkem Mäße vorhanden sind. Das Trinkwasser ist salzhaltig und nicht in genügender Menge vorhanden, es wird sogar nachmittags einige Stunden abgesperrt. Die unzureichende Badegeleggenheit in Verbindung mit der zu salzigen Kost haben bewirkt, daß viele der Gefangenen an Geschwüren leiden. Der als Küche dienende Schuppen ist unhygienisch. Beleuchtung und Heizung fehlen in diesem Lager Vollkommen. Alsbaldige Durchführung einer Zahnärztlichen Behandlung aller im Lager untergebrachten Leute ist dringendes Bedürfnis. Auch hier wird an Stelle des Brotes zuweilen der harte Zwieback ausgegeben. Auch hier sind die Klagen über zu langsame Postbestellung berechtigt.

RICKMANWORTH: Park Stables (OS: TQ 045 944). Rickmanworth Park House was completed *c.*1811. During the First World War its grounds initially were used for army training and then for detaining German PoWs.

A working camp, with the POWIB (1919) code Pa (Rk) (IWM: Facsimile K4655), Rickmanworth appears in the list produced for the FPHS (1973), as does Glen Chess. Glen Chess is at Loudwater.

According to minutes of the Hertfordshire County Council WAC the camp was open by 13 February 1918 and awaited the arrival of its first thirty PoWs on 22 February 1918. By 8 May 1918, the number working out of this site had risen to forty. Another minute confirming there were still forty PoWs in residence, dated 1 October 1918, suggests this camp was at the Park Stables.

The house was eventually sold to the Royal Masonic Institute for Girls, in 1926. Queen Mary officially opened the Royal Masonic School, originally intended for orphans of masons, on 27 June 1934 on the site.

RIDING MILL - SLALEY (OS: NZ 01- 61-). This was a working camp near to Slaley; its POWIB (1919) code is given as Cat (Rid) (IWM: Facsimile K4655), and its TA is quoted as Priswarian: Slaley (ADM 1/8506/265–120667). The FPHS (1973) cite a camp at Slaley. How many internees were detained there is not known, nor is what they were employed at. Perhaps Slaley Hall, which stands near a forest, or its grounds hold the key.

RINGWOOD (OS: SU 15- 05-). One of the many camps that have disappeared from history, with nothing recorded about it. It is cited by the FPHS (1973). Any PoWs sent to Ringwood would most probably have been engaged in agricultural work which would have been active in the second phase of camps that opened.

RIPLEY (OS: SE 283 606). *The Ripon Gazette* (10 October 1918) cited a letter stating that Ripley Town Hall was unsuitable for housing German PoWs. The letter then went on to complain of the little work done by this group, and the lax conditions of travel and of the guarding of the PoWs during their three months stay, whilst engaged in drainage work.

RIPON There were two camps at Ripon. They were in different sections of the vast army camp that almost engulfed the town. One camp was for officers and the other for the lower ranks.

As the numbers in khaki rose, so too did the number of places required to accommodate them. In December 1914, Lord Kitchener gave his consent for some 1,000 acres of land to the north and west of Ripon to be turned into an army camp. In the first month of the war navvies arrived to build two camps, designated as North and South Camps, spread over three sides of Ripon; from Littlethorpe in the south-west, travelling anti-clockwise through Red Bank and Studley Roger to Coltherholme in the north-west, making it a major garrison town in England. The work was completed in April 1915. The first soldiers to arrive were Leeds Pals, who had previously been at Colsterdale. In 1917 there were 70,000 soldiers at the camps, comprised mainly of Scots from the Highland Reserve Brigade.

MacPherson, Horrocks & Beveridge (*History of the Great War – Medical Services*, 1923) suggests the PoW camps at Ripon were opened in October 1918. They state there were huts, constructed out of brick, for 720 officers and their 216 servants; and more huts that could accommodate up to 1,200 other ranks.

The POWIB (1919) directory cites only one camp. This was No. 8, North Camp, and gives it an unusual code, that of Ni. A more fitting place for this code would have been Nidd, approximately 7 miles south of Ripon, and not far from Ripley, where PoWs were accommodated in the Town Hall. This unusual code also defines it as a camp with no administration links.

Mark (*Prisoners of War in British Hand during WW1*, 2007) cites the North Camp was for the other ranks. He believes the officers were in No. 3 Compound of the South Camp. This would tie up with the FPHS (1973) list, which states a Men's North Camp existed.

After the war, proposals to re-develop both sites were shelved. The War Office then decided to build 300 family homes on the site of the North Camp.

MEN'S CAMP (OS: SE 294 724). There was a consensus amongst internees brought from other camps to Ripon that this was the worst camp in the British Isles, especially in wet weather. Then, the camp was just a constant quagmire, and because of fuel being restricted for their huts, their clothes never dried out, including their footwear.

Accusations that their parcels were tampered with, and cigarettes and chocolate were taken from their luggage when they were being transferred, were cited. But the cold at night in their huts, coupled to the poor food rations they were given, was their biggest grievance at a time when the flu was prevalent. Promises to make playing fields available to them, outside the camp itself, were never kept by an administration described as not being sympathetic to them, especially to their sick. Because of the lack of recreational facilities books were a highly sought after commodity, but their availability was extremely curtailed due to an over-zealous camp censor, who even refused them toothpaste and nail clippers. There was a problem in the translation of many of the orders given out, and there was a suggestion that the senior British translator at the camp often transcribed the orders wrongly, on purpose.

NORTH RIPON: Officers (OS: SE 294 724)). A German document cites twenty-eight officers had to share huts designed to hold twenty-four. Some 700 officers and 300 orderlies were quartered in an area that measured about 300m by 200m: these are figures that concur with those stated by MacPherson. Complaints were expressed about overcrowding.

A TA for the officers' camp was stated to be Priswaroff: Ripon (ADM 1/8506/265–120667).

The Times (18 March 1918) cites an escape of six officers from Ripon, six months before the camp's opening date that was suggested by MacPherson. The six officers were Frank Kaars, Augustus Hiller, Rudolf Schneider, Lorenz Hellselder, Helmuth Reinsvorss and Fritz Spraub. *The Coventry Evening Telegraph* (19 March 1918) cites their re-capture. A solution to this conundrum is that the officers absconded from Colsterdale, around 12 miles away.

The Times (13 January 1919) cites two Zeppelin L33 crewmen were recaptured at Hull, and that an *U-Boot* officer named Boedt had escaped.

Dr F. Schwyzer, Dr A.L. Vischer and Dr A. de Sturler compiled reports of their visits of inspection to the officers' PoW camps at Ripon, Skipton, Lofthouse Park, Kegworth and Donnington Hall during February and March 1919. Ripon was inspected on 25 February 1919, where it was stated there were 675 officers and 219 orderlies, living in concrete huts. Lt-Colonel H. Sturgess is cited as the camp's commandant. The senior German officer was Major Claus. No reference is made to the men's camp.

The Times (4 June 1919) reported that Ripon's PoW camp had been vacated, presumably so that a reception centre for returning soldiers could be established in the South Camp. On 17 November 1917 the first contingent of repatriated British PoWs – 1,700 men – arrived at Ripon, via Holland and Hull. A further 2,500 men arrived the next day.

RIPPINGALE: Bull Inn (OS: TF 101 278). Apart from Rippingale being cited by the POWIB (1919), very little is known about this satellite of Sleaford. Its code was Bro (Sl) (Rip) (IWM: Facsimile K4655). It had the TA Priswarian: Rippingale, Bourne, Lincs. (ADM 1/8506/265–120667). Atkinson & Cottam (*Rippingale Village*, 1998) cite during the First World War twenty-eight PoWs were billeted in the clubroom at the Bull Inn. They worked on farms during the day.

RIPPINGALE FEN: Camp Farm (OS: TF 129 277). Cited by the POWIB (1919), Rippingale Fen is a satellite of Sleaford, its code Bro (Sl) (Rl) (IWM: Facsimile K4655). Atkinson & Cottam (*Rippingale Village*, 1998) cite during the First World

War twenty-eight prisoners of war were billeted in Camp Farm at Rippingale Fen. They worked on farms during the day.

ROBERTSBRIDGE (OS: TQ 73- 23-). There was a working camp at Robertsbridge; its POWIB (1919) code was Pa (Robs) (IWM: Facsimile K 4655). The camp's TA was Priswarian: Robertsbridge (ADM 1/8506/265–120667). Robertsbridge was also cited by the FPHS (1973). The location of the camp is not known.

The first successful Roman invasion of Britain took place at Robertsbridge.

ROCHFORD: The Union Workhouse (OS: TQ 875 906). Rochford Working Camp had the POWIB (1919) code Pa (Rch) and should not be confused with another working camp, operating out of Rochford House, Tenbury Wells, Gloucestershire. It was cited by the FPHS (1973) and had the TA Priswarian: Rochford (ADM 1/8506/265–120667).

In May 1916, the aged and infirm block of the workhouse was taken over by the military authorities for housing German prisoners of war. Minutes of the county's War Agricultural Executive Committee (12 February 1917) cite it was decided to place PoWs at the Union Workhouse in Rochford. This is supported by a Guardians' minute of 30 January 1917 stating seventy-five German prisoners, with thirty-five soldiers as a guard, were expected into the Rochford district to do agricultural work. *The Chelmsford Chronicle* (22 June 1917) reported thirty PoWs had arrived at Rochford.

The Times (1 September 1917) reported seven internees had escaped from Pattishall. Their names and descriptions were stated, before the article concluded with the report of an escape attempt at Rochford, in Essex. The details of this man were not published.

Ball (per. comm., 17 December 1998) confirmed that on 13 November 1917, a meeting of the guardians agreed to the patients in the Temporary Female Infirmary being transferred out to accommodate more PoWs. In June 1918, the guard was offered the use of the Female Mental Wards thus releasing more space for another intake of PoWs into the Aged and Infirmed Block. According to Dr David Reynolds that intake comprised of civilian PoWs. He noted in his diary the nurses had a social evening with the guard that year. The PoWs left the workhouse on 2 September 1919.

Horncastle (www.rochforddistricthistory.org.uk) cites Rochford Union Workhouse was built in 1837 to accommodate up 300 inmates. In 1930, the infirmary block was separated from the rest of the site and transferred to separate Public Assistance Committees. The workhouse became Rochford House. Under a series of regional titles it has cared for the old, the infirmed, the mentally deficient and children. It was called Southend Municipal Hospital and then Rochford Hospital, this time as a maternity Hospital. There is not much left of the original Rochford workhouse, but what is, is listed as buildings of historical and architectural importance. The boiler house built in 1933 was turned into flats. In 2009 a new Rochford Hospital was opened to treat the mentally ill.

ROCHFORD HOUSE (see Tenbury Wells).

ROCKFIELD (OS: SO 48- 14-). Cited in a HO document, its TA was Priswarian: Rockfield, The Hendre (ADM 1/8506/265–120667). No details of this camp are known. This camp should not be confused with the camp cited at Hendre, Glyn.

The Hendre was originally a shooting lodge, for John Rolls (1776–1837). From 1837 until 1872 the house and grounds were constantly being extended by a series of architects for the Rolls family. When Lord Llangattock died in 1912, his son Charles Stewart Rolls had predeceased him: one half of the founders of Rolls-Royce, he died in an aviation accident in 1910. When the heir died at the Somme in 1916, the barony became extinct, but the Hendre remained in the Rolls family until the 1980s. The mansion is presently the club house to The Rolls of Monmouth Golf Club.

ROCKLAND (see Attleborough).

ROMSEY (OS: SU 35- 21-). A working camp, it had the POWIB (1919) code Dor (Ro) (IWM: Facsimile K4655). It is also cited by the FPHS (1973), its TA was Priswarian: Romsey (ADM 1/8506/265–120667).

Romsey grew up around a Benedictine abbey. Its main industry was typical of the area, being wool and hop production. During the seventeenth century its wool industry declined, and new industries such as brewing, papermaking and sack making replaced it. In 1794 a canal was dug from Redbridge to Andover which passed through Romsey. The railway arrived in 1847. Thomas Strong purchased a brewery in 1858. In 1886, David Faber purchased three more for the company, and for nearly 100 years Strong's Brewery was a major employer in Romsey. It closed in 1981. Perhaps an under-utilised building of the brewery could have been used to accommodate any PoWs sent here.

ROSS-ON-WYE (OS: SO 60- 24-). The camp at Ross on Wye is listed as being a civilian camp, and it had the TA Priswarian: Ross-on-Wye, Herefordshire (ADM 1/8506/265–120667). The camp was cited by the POWIB (1919) as being an agricultural depot, with the code Shrw (R W) (IWM: Facsimile K4655). It had a satellite camp at Wigmore. It is also cited by the FPHS (1973).

The actual location of this camp was not stated in any of the above documents; however there was a workhouse in Ross-on-Wye that may hold the key to this camp. Built in 1872, its entrance was on Alton Street. The workhouse later became Dean Hill Hospital. Most of the buildings have since been demolished and replaced. In 1997 it became Ross Community Hospital.

The Brotherton Library at the University of Leeds has in its collection a photograph of two German officers posing for a studio portrait that is believed to have been taken in Ross-on-Wye.

ROSYTH: Inverkeithing (OS: NT 116 835). Before the First World War, had it not been for the Forth Bridge, Rosyth would have been the first choice as the base for the British North Atlantic Fleet; instead, Scapa Flow was chosen. However, the Rosyth dock was to be kept busy repairing many of the ships that were damaged at the Battle of Jutland.

The PoWs did not work in the dockyard. It is believed they assisted in the construction of temporary accommodation for the workforce required to create houses for the new accommodation required for the incoming workforce in the dock. Ironically the PoW labour was living in tents. The huts built by the PoWs were part of the site known locally as Bungalow City.

Horne (*The German Connection – The German Newspaper 1916–1919*, 1988) cites Inverkeithing in her list of work camps. The camp's POWIB (1919) code was Stbs (Ros) (IWM: Facsimile K4655). Its TA is cited as Priswarian: Inverkeithing

(ADM 1/8506/265–120667). There is an entry for Inverkeithing in the FPHS (1973) publication.

After the war, the dockyard was put on a care and maintenance basis. Ironically, it was to reopen when it was used to break up ships rescued from Scapa Flow that had been scuttled by the German Navy in 1919. The yard has seen many turbulent times, but is still in existence today, though its future role is always a bone of contention between the government and its workforce.

DKF 30: Arbeitslager: Unterkunft: In den Lagern von Rosyth, Eastgate, Uppingham, Belton Park, Tern Hill, Bee Craigs, Hadnall, Sutton Veny, Larkhill, Fovant, Withley (sic) *und Radford sind die Kriegsgefangenen in Zelten untergebracht.*

ROTHWELL. (OS: SP 815 815). A working camp with the POWIB (1919) code Pa (Rot) (IWM: Facsimile K4655); it should not be confused with the Ruthwell working camp in Dumfries-shire, Scotland. Its TA was Priswarian: Rothwell, Northamptonshire (ADM 1/8506/265–120667). The FPHS (1973) cite it too.

Royall (per. comm., 11 December 1998) wrote the camp was situated to the east of Rothwell, on the north side of the road to Glendon. The camp is thought to have been near a fallen stone wall that can be seen today. Local knowledge is divided on whether this wall was an integral part of the camp or not.

ROUEN DOCK (OS: n/a). Lord Kitchener insisted that those PoWs interned in Britain could be better utilised in labour camps in France rather than being cooped up behind barbed wire fences with nothing to occupy their time. Winning his argument, on 5 April 1916, 750 PoWs were transferred from British camps to Rouen. The Germans retaliated by putting British PoWs into Poland to work. The situation eased slightly when the Germans were promised that any PoWs sent to France would remain under British jurisdiction.

ROWLEY (OS: NZ 08- 48-). Rowley working camp is recorded as being near Healeyfield in Co. Durham, its POWIB (1919) code is Cat (Rwl) (IWM: Facsimile K4655), and its TA is cited as Priswarian: Castleside (ADM 1/8506/265 – 120667). It was also listed by the FPHS (1973). The location of the camp is unknown.

ROWRAH (OS: NY 05- 18-). *Cumberland News* (7 November 2003) carried an article about the camp at Rowrah during the First World War. It disclosed details that had been printed in the *Carlisle Journal* of 1918, when it was reported in March 1918 that there were 130 PoWs billeted and working at Rowrah.

They were there because conscription had brought about a lack of local labour in the area from 1916. The *Journal* reported that Westmorland County Council had pleaded with the government to make PoW labour available for road making or for work of other national importance. A local tribunal had favoured their use for farm work. When the US Embassy in London sent an inspection team to Leigh on 8 September 1916 they were informed 165 internees had been transferred to Rowrah, to work in a quarry.

In July 1917, the *Journal* reported, under the headline Employment of German PoWs, that the county's highways committee had asked the Arlecdon and Frizington councils to apply to the government for PoWs labour to improve the approaches to Rowrah Bridge.

It was reported that no British soldiers would be available for farm work, but that German prisoners in migratory camps would be available. In the latter part of August, provision had to be made for accommodating these gangs. It was reported in the *Journal* that Wigton Workhouse guardians would house thirty PoWs and six guards in its pauper ward. The authorities would pay 3d per head each day from August 15. Similar arrangements were made at the workhouse at Kirkby Stephen for PoWs on harvest work.

At Kirkoswald two tents were used to house a group of prisoners. The *Journal* said three groups of ten PoWs were being conveyed to Kirkoswald, Langwathby and Culgaith respectively from Rowrah to do harvest work. In an editorial, the *Journal* stated there had been complaints at the degree of freedom allowed to these men, especially from girls seeking familiarity with them. But the editor had a good word for German labour, especially those selected for farm work.

In September 1918, the migratory camp scheme was fully reported in the *Journal.* Gangs had been established in twenty-five camps in Cumberland and all were operating very satisfactorily because each group had been carefully chosen. The prisoners were all men that had been engaged in agriculture activities in Germany and had good disciplinary records. The *Journal* stated that farmers were prepared to escort these gangs to and from their camp each day.

Everything was going smoothly with rations distributed from Rowrah, but according to German sources, Rowrah was not alone in being criticised for the way in which it abused its internees. It was reported to the neutral powers that they had to work long hours, doing heavy work, which many of them were not accustomed to. There was a high incidence of accidents recorded at Rowrah.

The 165 internees from Leigh complained their belongings had not been forwarded on to them.

A working camp, with the POWIB (1919) code Lgh (Row) (IWM: Facsimile K4655), its TA was Priswarian: Lamplugh (ADM 1/8506/265–120667). It is also cited by the FPHS (1973). The camp at Leigh closed in May 1919.

DKF: Die Rovrah (sic) beschäftigten Leute haben ihre im Lager Leigh zurückgelassenen Koffer immer noch nicht erhalten.

RUDDINGTON (OS: SK 581 341). Although a minute of the Notts County WAC (28 January 1919) cites a migratory gang at Ruddington, no evidence has been found to suggest its exact location. Ruddington Hall or its grounds perhaps hold the key to the camp's location.

RUGBY: Stockton (OS: SP 43- 63-). The *List of British Prison Camps* produced by Carter (1937) cites Stockton as a place of internment. Russell's reproduction of the list (1996) cites Stockton twice; once as Stockton and again as Stockton, Rugby. Details of the former may be linked to Codford St Mary in Wiltshire, where it is known a camp existed. Nothing is known of the camp near Rugby.

RUSHDEN (OS: SP 955 663). This was a working camp based at Rushden House; it had the POWIB (1919) code Pa (Rus) (IWM: Facsimile K4655). The camp's TA was Priswarian: Rushden (ADM 1/8506/265 – 120667). The FPHS (1973) also cite a camp at Rushden.

Standing in some 25 acres of land, Rushden House was built in 1871 for the Currie family. It was purchased in 1901 by Mr Browning, who lived there, with his family, until he died in 1914. It was then bought by a Mr George Henry Lane, leather merchant of Kettering, who never lived in the house, but wanted to turn it into a lunatic asylum. In 1915, Lane allowed the house to be used as a prisoner of war camp.

It became known as Ploughmans' Camp and the name stuck until the PoWs were repatriated after the war finished. *The Northampton Mercury* (24 October 1919) reported all the internees at Rushden had left.

The house lay empty until the Northamptonshire County Council acquired it, treating tuberculosis. In September 1921 the first patients were admitted to Rushden House Sanatorium. Six huts were brought from Houghton Regis Army Camp. Gradually, purpose-built buildings were erected and the types of patient it treated broadened, and the name was changed to Rushden Hospital to reflect this. The hospital then had eighty-three beds. The hospital continued to change to meet the needs of the people it served. Part of the original house, in a joint funded venture with Social Services, became Cordwainers Day Centre and received its first patients on 10 November 1980.

Rowan J. Flack was a Clinical Nursing Officer at Rushden Hospital 1966–1990. From his archive, evidence of the Germans being at Rushden survives:

> Most of the British Guards were billeted in the town but the officers used a small portion of Rushden House and certainly Captain Winter also used certain rooms as office accommodation. The old stable yard was fenced off with barbed wire and a sentry box stood behind the great gates leading to the main drive. The prisoners were all housed in two long attics, one over the old coach house and the other over the stable and garage which once housed Mr Browning's large Daimler car. The yard is today much as it was then and initials carved into the ironstone still serve as a reminder of those days of Ploughman's Camp. (Extract taken from Flack's archival material – http://www.rushdenheritage.co.uk/war/GermanPrisonersOfWar.html)

RUTHIN: Bathafarn Hall (OS: SJ 148 579). The original hall is believed to have been built by John Wynn Thelwell in *c.*1632. Bathafarn Hall was put up for sale on 27 October 1919; the brochure (Particulars of Lot 24 – Sale of Bathafarn and Llanbedr Halls) describes the lot as an attractive country seat standing on 69 acres of land. The Rhuthun Local History Group (Broadsheet No. 28, 1991) cited the estate as again put up for sale in 1952, and today the house is divided into flats. The present building is believed to date back to the late 1800s or early 1900s. A watercolour by Moses Griffith shows the hall before subsequent remodelling took place (DRO: NTD 940).

In March 1919, Dr A. de Sturler and Monsieur R. de Sturler visited the camp on behalf of the Swiss Legation (FO 383/507). This camp was a satellite of Carmarthen, and had the POWIB (1919) code Fg (Car) (Ru) (IWM: Facsimile K 4655).

RUTHWELL: nr Annan (OS: NY 043 715). Lying between Dumfries and Gretna Green, Ruthwell has two claims to fame. Burke (*The Ruthwell Cross, in Horton*, 1990) discloses that the first savings bank was established here in 1810 by Reverend Henry Duncan. Its second claim to fame is its 16-foot high Pictish cross. A not so well known fact is that it was also the home to a prisoners-of-war camp in the First World War. The camp's POWIB (1919) code was Stbs (Rut) (IWM: Facsimile K 4655).

Although there is no evidence to show where or how those interned were utilised, it is believed locally that they built roads, and worked on the farms in the area. As Ironhirst Moss was an area where peat cutting was being undertaken during the First World War, they may have been deployed into this process too. A factory in the vicinity that processed the cut peat, closed in 1923. The moorland lies near to the

B724 and the village of Mouswald. Today, a caravan park stands near the site thought to be where this camp stood.

Its TA was Priswarian: Ironhirst, Ruthwell (ADM 1/8506/265–120667). The camp closed on 21 February 1919. Carter (Russell, 1996) cites Rithwell *(sic)*, Carlisle as the location of this camp for the FPHS (1973). Crawford mentions Ruthwell Station standing on the Glasgow, Dumfries and Carlisle Railway prior to re-grouping in 1923 (www.railscot.co.uk).

At nearby Gretna, during the war, the country's largest factory for producing cordite was constructed.

RYDE (OS: SZ 59- 36-). Szijj (*Honvédelmi Miniszrérium*, per. comm., 23 July 1997) provided evidence that suggests some internees, taken to and from the ships moored in the Solent, were detained at a camp at Ryde, on the Isle of Wight. This may however have just been a holding station, as internees were transferred on to, or off, these ships.

RYDE GROUP – THE SOLENT SQUADRON (OS : SZ 580 940). The Ryde Group comprised of three ships: The *Andania*, the *Canadian* and the *Tunisian*. They replaced the three ships moored off Gosport when those ships were assigned other duties. The *Uranium* was the seventh ship to join the Solent Squadron, replacing the *Lake Manitoba*, before moving to join the Leigh Squadron, off Southend on Sea.

HMT *ANDANIA* (GRT: 13,405. Passengers: 2nd Class = 520, steerage = 1,520). McCart (*Atlantic Liners of the Cunard Line from 1884 to the Present Day*, 1990) states before being used as a prison ship that the *Andania* was used to carry Canadian troops to Britain. She was moored off Ryde Harbour, alongside the HMT *Canada* and HMT *Tunisian*. She was allocated other duties around February 1915.

Built by Scott's of Greenock for the Cunard Line, the *Andania* was launched on 13 May 1913. Panayi (*The Enemy In Our Midst: Germans in Britain during the First World War*, 1991) states both military and naval PoWs were interned on the *Andania*. Representatives of the US Embassy in London inspected her at the beginning of 1915.

She was at Gallipoli by the summer of 1915. She had transported the Royal Inniskillen Fusiliers and the Royal Dublin Fusiliers to Cape Helles, before taking troops to Bombay, then returned to her cross-Atlantic sailings in 1916.

The name *Andania* does not appear on the list of prison ships published in the *New York Times* (15 March 1915) as it had begun other duties. The article reveals three of the ships that had been used had been vacated, and the rest would follow suit, by April.

On Friday, 26 January 1918 the *Andania* was struck by a torpedo from *U-Boot 46*, and listed. Nine hours later she rolled over onto her side near to the Altacarry Lighthouse, off County Antrim. There were seven casualties recorded.

HMT *CANADIAN* (GRT: 8,800. Passengers: 1st Class = 200, 2nd class = 200, steerage = 800). The SS *Canada* was built in 1896 for the Dominion Line, which was absorbed into the White Star Line in 1909. Built by Harland & Wolff in Belfast she regularly sailed across the Atlantic from Liverpool to Boston or Quebec/Montreal. From 1899 until 1902 she was used as a transport ship in the Boer War, before returning to her trans-Atlantic duties. Leased to the British government in 1914, she was moored in the Solent, off Ryde. According to Panayi (1991), there were 1,026 civilians on board, some of which had been transferred from Newbury racecourse. By late February she had been allocated other duties, and was not on the list of ships cited by the *New York Times* still being used to intern PoWs. Possibly used as a troop carrier until she returned to the White Star Line after the war ended, she remained in service until August 1926 when she was sold to Italian ship breakers.

HMT *TUNISIAN* (GRT: 10,576. Passengers: 1st class = 240, 2nd class = 220, steerage = 1,000). On lists compiled for the FPHS (1973) by Carter, the ship is incorrectly cited as the Yunisian. The ship was actually the *Tunisian* and held 795 civilian internees. She was moored in the Solent, off Ryde. She was not amongst the ships cited by the *New York Times* (15 March 1915) as still being used to intern PoWs.

Built at Alex Stephens & Sons on the Clyde for the Allan Line in 1900, the *Tunisian* plied the Atlantic as a passenger liner until 16 September 1914 when she was requisitioned by the government as Hired Military Transport, initially to intern PoWs. She then saw service taking troops to France Point in 1916. She was used as a troop carrier until she was released from military duty in 1917.

Bird (*Control of Enemy Alien Civilians in Great Britain 1914–1918*, 1986) cites that on his inspection tour on behalf of the US Embassy in London, Jackson noted conditions on this ship were 'generally depressing'. There had been numerous complaints about medical arrangements on board, and the food. Some internees had resorted to putting letters expressing their grievances into bottles and throwing them overboard.

The Allan Line was taken over by Canadian Pacific on 1 October 1917. The *Tunisian* returned to her owners after the war. In 1922 she was re-named the SS *Marburn*. She returned to trans-Atlantic crossings between various ports until being laid up in April 1928. She was sold to be broken up in Genoa by Soc Anon Co-op Ligure Demolitori Navi on 17 September 1928.

HMT *URANIUM* (GRT: 5,183. Passengers: 1st class = 80, steerage = 1,000). Carter (1996), Jackson (*The Prisoners 1914–1918*, 1989), Bird (1986), and Panayi (1991) all cite nine ships were used to intern PoWs in the early stages of the First World War. John B. Jackson mentions this figure when he made his inspection tour in February 1915. The *New York Times*, in March 1915, also cited nine vessels, but in fact a tenth ship was also used. Weekes (2002) explains:

> To alleviate the shortage of Internment and Prisoner of War camps at the outbreak of World War I the Government requisitioned nine passenger liners to act as temporary Prison Ships. These were anchored off Portsmouth, Ryde and Southend on Sea, from late October 1914 to May 1915. Some positional changes were made during this period, and a further liner, the *Uranium*, replaced one of the original liners in early 1915.

The *Uranium* was built by W. Denny & Brothers of Dumbarton, for British India Associated Steamers, as the *Avoca*, in 1891. She also briefly sailed under the name *San Fernando* when chartered, in 1896, by the Cia Transatlantic; but within the year she had reverted to her original name. Between 1899 and 1900 she made four voyages between India and South Africa as a troop carrier in the Boer War, and a fifth as a hospital ship. In 1903 she was transferred to the British India Steam Navigation Company. In 1907, the ship was bought by the Danish East Asiatic Company and sailed as the *Atalanta*. She was chartered as the royal yacht for King Christian's visit to Greenland, before being laid up at Copenhagen. In 1908, she was sold to the New York & Continental Line and reverted to her original name, *Avoca*.

In July 1908, after landing 300 passengers at the Hook of Holland, she collided with a German steamer at anchor. The captain was arrested. As a result of the costs incurred by the collision, the now insolvent company was forced to put her up for auction and she was bought by C.G. Ashdown. They in turn sold her on to the North West Transport Line.

In 1910 she was again named the *Uranium* having been bought for the Uranium Steamship Company. She made several Rotterdam–Halifax–New York voyages for her new owners. She went aground in thick fog on 12 January 1913 at Chebucto Head, near Halifax, Nova Scotia, whilst going to the aid of the *Carthaginian*, which was on fire. The *Toronto Daily Star* carried the story.

She was brought in to replace the *Lake Manitoba* as one of the prison ships anchored off Ryde. When the ship was inspected in May 1915 there were 743 men on board. At some point, she moved to join the Leigh Channel Squadron.

In 1916, she joined the Cunard Line and was to become the *Feltria*. She was torpedoed by *U-Boot 48* and sank, 8 miles off Mine Head, County Waterford, on 5 May 1917. Forty-five crew members including the captain perished.

RYE (see Peasmarsh).

S

SAFFRON WALDEN: The Union (OS: TL 551 386). A working camp, based at the Union, its POWIB (1919) code was Pa (Sf W) (IWM: Facsimile K4655). It is also cited by the FPHS (1973). The camp's TA is cited as Priswarian: Saffron Walden (ADM 1/8506/265–120667).

Saffron Walden Union Workhouse was built in 1836 to the designs of James Clephan to accommodate up to 340 inmates. Based on a cruciform plan, built of yellow stock brick, it stood off Radwinter Road. Above the entrance was a clock. In 1846, an infirmary, washhouse and laundry were added in the north-east yard and four fever wards were added in 1848.

In 1866, Saffron Walden General Hospital opened from a bequest from Quaker Wyatt George Gibson. It stood on London Road. During World War One twenty beds were placed at the disposal of the War Office. The General closed in 1988.

In 1930 the workhouse infirmary had become St James's Public Assistance Institution. And in 1948 it became part of the National Health Service, becoming St James's Hospital. When the General closed in 1988, the former workhouse hospital took on its mantle. When Saffron Waldron Community Hospital opened on an adjacent site, the former Grade II listed buildings of the former workhouse were converted into residential use (www.pastscape.org.uk).

SALFORD PRIORS (see Chapel Oak).

SANDHURST: College Town (OS: SU 859 609). Lieutenant W.B.P. Spencer did not record where he was when he wrote in his diary (IWM: 87/56/1), 'Yesterday after church parade I spent all day at the PoW Camp about 5 miles from here; there are about 2,200 German soldiers and many civilian prisoners.' The camp in question must have been the same one stated in a HO document which cites its TA was Priswarian: College Town, Sandhurst (ADM 1/8506/265–120667). The POWIB (1919) referred to College Town working camp, it was designated the code Dor (Cg) (IWM: Facsimile K4655). The FPHS (1973) cites Camberley as a British Prison Camp.

SAWLEY (OS: SE 222 658). Sawley working camp is cited by the POWIB (1919); its code was Cat (Sy) (IWM: Facsimile K4655). The entry recorded by the FPHS (1973) cites Ripon, Sawley. Local knowledge believes that the camp was near Klondyke

Quarry, Warsill. Any PoWs sent to Sawley may have worked at the quarry. Alternatively, they may have worked on farms. The camp's TA was Priswarian: Sawley, Ripon (ADM 1/8506/265–120667).

SCAPA FLOW (OS: HD 350 990). Facing defeat, the German High Command indicated to the American President, Woodrow Wilson, that they were prepared to accept his Fourteen Point Plan if he could convince the rest of the Allies to accept it too. This led to an inter-allied conference that met, in Paris on 25 October 1918, to discuss the proposals for an armistice with the Central Powers. This in turn led to an agreed armistice, to begin on 9 November 1918, that would last six months. The German army was instructed to surrender to Marshall Ferdinand Foch on 11 November 1918, at Compiégne. The German navy was also required to surrender, and plans were drawn up for designated ships to be interned in ports of neutral powers. Article XXIII of that plan required the named German ships to have their armoury dismantled before sailing into internment. The ports were to be appointed by the Allied Command. The Allied Naval Council insisted alternative ports should be considered. As the ships were being prepared for internment, on 15 November 1918 Rear Admiral Hugo Meurer of the German navy arrived in the Firth of Forth to receive his instructions. Both Spain and Norway, the Allied Command's choices, declined to accept the German fleet. This suited the British, as it was later mooted that there was never any real intention on the part of the British to let this German prize sail into internment in a neutral country where it could be usurped by the allies. With no other option available, Rear Admiral Ludwig von Reuter of the German High Seas Fleet was instructed to sail to a point near the Firth of Forth, off Scotland, where he would be met by the British Commander in Chief of the Grand Fleet, Sir David Beatty. German *U-Boote* had sailed the previous day to be taken to Harwich. Beatty assembled the British Grand Fleet at Rosyth. He left port at 08.30 hours on the 21 November 1918 on his flagship, HMS *Queen Elizabeth*, in a convoy of 250 ships of the Royal Navy to meet the seventy-three designated craft of the German High Seas Fleet. Ships of the French and American navies also accompanied Beatty's flotilla, making it 370 ships strong. When met, the German flotilla was described as a pitiful sight, with dirt everywhere, rusting engines, and, an apparent lack of discipline amongst its ranks. After being inspected, the German ships were ordered to Scapa Flow on 25 November 1914. A breakdown, given by Ruge (*Scapa Flow: The End of the German Fleet*, 1973) of the numbers and type of craft interned is listed below:

Eleven battleships × 175 men = 1,925	Five battle-cruisers × 200 men = 1,000	Eight light-cruisers × 60 men = 480
Baden	*Derfflinger*	*Bremse*
Bayern	*Hindenburg*	*Brummer*
Friedrich der Grosse	*Moltke*	*Cöln*
Grosser Kurfürst	*Seydlitz*	*Dresden*
Kaiser	*Von der Tann*	*Emden*
Kaiserin		*Frankfurt*
König Albert		*Karlsruhe*
Kronprinz Wilhelm		*Nürnberg*
König		
Markgraf		*were late arrivals*
Prinzregent Luitpold		

Plus fifty unnamed torpedo boat-destroyers × 20 men.

Missing were the *Mackensen*, a newly launched battleship, which was not yet deemed sea worthy, and the *Dresden* that was still undergoing repairs on the day of its intended departure. Nor had the *König* sailed that day because she had developed engine problems as she set sail. On 27 November 1918 seventy ships were in their appointed anchorage positions. On route the *V30* struck a mine and sunk with the loss of two crewmen. The *König*, the *Dresden* and a replacement torpedo boat (the *V129*, for the unfortunate *V30*) arrived on 6 December 1918. To complete the complement of interned ships, the *Baden* arrived as the late replacement for the *Mackensen* on 9 January 1919. 20,000 men brought the ships into British waters.

Like Ruge, who had commanded *B112*, they all expected to go home on completing the crossing. But Beatty, who had taken personal command of the exercise, had a different opinion and wanted 1,800 officers and a similar amount of crewmen to remain on board their ships, and the rest to be dispersed to land-based camps around Britain. The numbers of crew and officers left on board the ships anchored in Scapa Flow varies from account to account. In his official report von Reuter states there were 5,917 in total, which was higher than the set agreed level of 4,385. Van der Vat (*The Grand Fleet: The Sinking of the German Fleet at Scapa Flow in 1919*, 1982) cites the official level of 4,385 men remained on board their ships anchored in Scapa Flow. There is no record of the submariners at Harwich being detained, and it is reported they left immediately on two transport ships that came with them.

Beatty insisted the crews were not to be treated as prisoners, and permission for their return to Germany would be granted as soon as German transport facilities and circumstances generally permitted. When the SS *Sierra Ventana* and the SS *Grag Waldersee* arrived with supplies on 3 December, they took back some 4,000 crewmen with them. The SS *Burgermeister* and SS *Pretoria* arrived with more supplies on 6 December and departed with around another 6,000 crewmen. On 12 December 1918, the third and last two evacuation steamers, the SS *Batavia* and the SS *Bremen*, to bring supplies, left with around 5,000 crewmen. The latter took von Reuter home for some respite. On his return, on 25 January 1919, he contemplated moving his flag to several of the other ships, and on 25 March, he left the *Friedrich der Grosse* for the *Emden*. Von Reuter was becoming aware he was not popular amongst the crew-members of his fleet, anchored in the sound.

Brown & Meehan (*Scapa Flow*, 1968) state mail was distributed at Scapa by a British motor launch, which tossed the mail aboard the German ships as no contact was permitted between British and German sailors. However, there was contact and trade did develop in other ways. For those internees left on board their ships, the British supplied fresh water and British newspapers that were several days old when received. Fishing craft came alongside once in the morning and once in the afternoon to deliver and fetch official and private mail. Although the mail came pretty regularly to Scapa Flow it reached the crews very irregularly. That caused annoyance, as did the fact that the British censored the mail in London, despite written assurance to the contrary. Immediately after the peace conditions were announced the British intensified the censorship. Ruge (1973) stated von Reuter protested, but he was given no clarification as to the intensification of the censorship; but its existence generally increased the mistrust in the British.

Van der Vat (1982) states in March the British broached the subject of reducing the crews to those levels adopted for ships in the reserve of the Royal Navy (i.e. seventy-five crewmen for each battle cruiser; sixty per battleship; thirty per light cruiser; and a reduction in torpedo boats crews as the commanding officer saw fit). Von Reuter looked favourably on this request because it gave him the opportunity to remove many troublemakers from the crews on board his ships. On 16 June 1919 the SS *Badenia* and the SS *Schleswig* arrived to take the surplus 2,700 men home. They left Scapa Flow on 17 June 1919. The Armistice was due to expire at 19.00 hours on 23 June 1919; von Reuter had been informed of the new date. Vice-Admiral Sir Sydney Fremantle was convinced the Germans would scuttle their ships, and drew up a plan to seize them an hour or two before the deadline. However Fremantle was sent out on an exercise on 21 June 1919, leaving only two destroyers behind on guard duty. Fearing no amicable solution would be obtained and that Britain and others could use his ships against Germany, von Reuter seized this opportunity and ordered the ships be scuttled. A pre-arranged encoded signal was hoisted aloft on the *Emden* at 10.20am, ordering the ships to prepare to scuttle. After the order was given, by 1.00pm the German ships were foundering. As Fremantle rushed back towards Scapa, it was recorded by Kapitan Hermann Cordes, the commander of the German destroyers, that some of the British guard panicked and shot wildly at the defenceless crews of the sinking ships as they took to their lifeboats. Accounts vary, but it is thought six Germans were killed and ten more were wounded. A number never specified were declared 'missing' (von Reuter believed ten were killed and sixteen wounded, whilst Ruge (1973) cites nine dead and twenty-one wounded).

It has been mooted, though never proven, that the scuttling of the German ships was done with the knowledge of the British Secret Service, to maintain British supremacy of the oceans. Was Fremantle deliberately sent out of the way? After the scuttling on 21 June, many of the German crewmembers were taken on board HMS *Resolution* for two nights, and then transferred to the *Royal Oak*, which took them to Nigg, in the Cromarty Firth. There, the Seaforth Highlanders escorted them to a camp where they slept before, next evening, being entrained for Oswestry. Hoehling (*The Great War at Sea: a History of Naval Action 1914–1918*, 1985) states the surviving Germans were transferred to PoW camps on mainland Britain where they were held for the next six months.

The Times (24 June 1919) reported that 800 PoWs from Scapa Flow were taken into internment in Wales. In fact the crewmembers were taken to Oswestry. Ruge contends the crews of these ships were not part of the deal, but they were still taken into internment. This contrasts with the submariners that took their boats to Harwich, who were then allowed to go home again.

Ruge was taken with others to Park Hall, Oswestry, where he states the huts were very simply built, with only one room. The wooden roofs were covered with felt to waterproof them, but they still leaked. The wooden floors had spaces between the boards, and at each end of the huts were cut a dozen large holes, so 'there was never a lack of oxygen'. In each of the huts there was a dozen beds, and in the space between them sat three long tables with chairs. Beside each bed, there was a wall shelf and a footstool, and at one end of the hut stood a pot-bellied stove. Ablutions were done in wash huts, which 'displayed no exaggerated luxury'. The PoWs were forbidden to have British currency, and were given tokens to spend which had no monetary value outside of the camps. Von Reuter and two of his staff were sent, briefly, to Oswestry, then to Donington Hall before being sent to Lofthouse Park, Wakefield. Until a treaty was signed to officially end the war, a state of war still officially existed, and there could be no repatriation for those German PoWs still in British PoW camps. The Treaty of Versailles was signed on 28 June 1919, and ratified by the House of Commons on 22 July 1919, thus allowing the repatriation of German PoWs. The process of repatriation took some seven months to complete, and the last Germans were allowed to drift home from Britain on or about 30 January 1920. The last left from Hull. On 27 April 1921, the Allies claimed £6,650 million in reparation from Germany for the damage done by it during the war, thus crippling the German economy and sowing the seeds for the Second World War some two decades later.

SEAFIELD ESTATE (Strathspey). There were two camps on the Seafield estate; one at Inverlaidnan and the other at Nethy Bridge.

The Seafield estates are located in two areas in the north of Scotland: the lowland Banffshire area around Cullen on the Moray Firth, and at Strathspey where the higher land of the upper Spey valley has small agricultural units with sheep and cattle the predominant mix. The Seafield estate has grown timber for many generations and is famous for including remnants of the old Caledonian Pine Forests that used to cover most of Scotland. There was a steam-powered mill on the estate.

INVERLAIDNAN (OS: NH 861 214). Surrounded by spectacular mountains and moorland, this camp was located near to Carrbridge, on the Seafield Estates. The camp had the POWIB (1919) code Stbs (Ivl) (IWM: Facsimile K4655), and was also cited by FPHS (1973). The PoWs were sent here to fell timber. It is believed the camp, for around 400 internees, was 200 metres south-east of the present steading. The camp had the TA Priswarian: Inverlaidnan (ADM 1/8506/265–120667).

The Times (18 November 1918) cited three PoWs had been caught near Inverness. It is thought they escaped from Inverlaidnan.

Many of the internees at Inverlaidnan fell foul of the flu germ that spread across Europe in 1918, which resulted in a large number of fatalities. Those that died were initially buried locally, but their remains were exhumed and transferred, in the 1960s, to Cannock Chase.

NETHY BRIDGE (OS: NJ 024 193). Nethy Bridge was connected by rail to the Boat of Garten in 1866. With its dramatic backdrop of the often snow-capped Cairngorms and the prestigious Abernethy Forest, it became a great holiday destination of the Victorians.

The entry for Nethy Bridge in the POWIB (1919) list refers you to a second entry, that of Seafield. However no entry for Seafield was made. The FPHS (1973) cites Nethy Bridge. The Camp's TA was Priswarian: Nethybridge (ADM 1/8506/265–120667).

The camp was situated on the edge of the Seafield Estate, at Lettoch. Farmers have never cultivated the field where the camp stood because the foundations of the structures are still there today, still visible in the gravel. During the First World War, German PoWs constructed the original bridge at Lettoch Farm that spanned the Dorback Burn. They also built a tramline to transport the felled timber, on horse drawn carts, from Sliemore Wood to the village to the local railway station for distribution.

The Times (4 July 1917) reported Wilhelm Hom had escaped. The edition of 6 July reported he had been recaptured the previous day.

Castle Roy, one of the oldest fortifications in Britain stands near to the village's Old Kirk. Apparently, much to the annoyance of some of those interned at Nethybridge, church services were not always available.

DKF 32: Gottesdienst: Auch in Nethy Bridge fehlt regelmäßiger Gottesdienst.

SEALAND (OS: SJ 331 694). Prior to the Royal Flying Corps taking over the airfield near Sealand in 1916 for training and maintenance work, it had been a civilian airfield.

Today, it is home to RAF No. 30 Maintenance Unit, which was established in 1937, and is responsible for the third line repair of airborne avionic equipment for all three armed services. There is also a gliding school (No. 631, Volunteer Gliding School), which operates Viking TX1s out of the southern part of the airfield.

Described as a civilian working camp, it had the TA Priswarian: Sealand (ADM 1/8506/265–120667).

Internees were utilised at the airfield, and they were housed adjacent to Hawarden Bridge Station. When visited by a Swiss Delegation, in June 1918, there were 106 German, 22 Austrian or Hungarians, and 2 others, being employed building aeroplane sheds, or loading and unloading railway waggons (FO 383/360).

There were at least two unsuccessful attempts by the internees to escape reported in the newspapers. *The Times* (12 November 1917) cited Alfons Grium, Heinrich J.A. Gevers and Paul Salamon had absconded. These were all reported captured in the same paper two days later. Grium may also have attempted to escape whilst detained at Oldcastle in 1915. *The Western Times* (13 November 1917) cites six men had escaped. On 17 January 1918, *The Liverpool Echo* reported the escape of Wilheim Clersey and Hans Bottcher. *The Coventry Evening Telegraph* (22 January 1918) also carried news of their escape.

SEDGE FEN (see Belaugh Mill).

SEER GREEN (OS: SU 965 915). Seer Green appears in a list produced for the FPHS (1973). The camp's TA was Priswarian: Seer Green, Beaconsfield. The location of the camp was at Rawling's Farm (ADM 1/8506/265–120667).

SELBY: The Union Workhouse (OS: SE 611 319). Cited in a HO document, its TA was Priswarian: The Workhouse, Selby (ADM 1/8506/265–120667).

Webb (*From County Hospital to NHS Trust: The History and Archives of the NHS Hospitals In York*, 2002) states Selby's workhouse was built in 1837 to accommodate up to 170 inmates. It stood on the south side of Doncaster Road (now Brook Street). When the site was re-developed in 1892 a new larger infirmary block replaced the former one. It did not become part of the National Health Service in 1948, but was later converted into a care home for the elderly.

The Hull Times (4 January 1919) cited the vicar of Goodmanham, the Reverend G.A. Braund, was fined 3 guineas (£3.3s or £3.15p) for apparently raising his hat to PoWs, then going to the kiosk to buy cigars for them, and their guard, at Market Weighton station on 23 November 1918 while they were all in the station's waiting room. This incident took place twelve days after the Armistice began. The article does not state why the PoWs were at the station, and there is no evidence to suggest a camp nearer than the one recorded at Selby. Perhaps the PoWs were in transit and awaiting a connecting train as two routes belonging to the York and Midland Railway Company (Selby to Driffield and York to Beverley) met at the station.

SEMER: Cosford Workhouse (OS: TM 010 452). Described as an agricultural group, it was attached to Haughley AD. Its code was Pa (Hgy) (Sem) (IWM: Facsimile K 4655). It is cited by the FPHS (1973). A HO document cites the camp as being at Cosford Workhouse. Its TA was Priswarian: Hadleigh (ADM 1/8506/265–120667).

The House of Correction at Semer, which dated back to 1780, was taken over, in 1836, to become Cosford Union Workhouse. To comply with the segregation requirements of the Poor Law Amendment Act (1834) the buildings had to be modified, requiring additional yard walls to be erected and interconnecting doorways had to be sealed off. In 1869, the workhouse was extended to include an isolation hospital (www.pastscape.org.uk).

SEND (OS: SP 754 655). Pearson (per. comm., 7 February 2000) says there has been property built on this site in Send since *c.*1518. Originally known as Griggs, by 1820, after substantial rebuilding, the house was re-named Boughton Hall, after the family that occupied the house. Much of the present hall dates from Victorian times. It passed into the ownership of Robert Boughton Smith, a retired sea captain. In 1884, Abraham Walter Paulton occupied it. On Paulton's death, his widow Martha lived on in the house, until her death in 1908. The house then lay unoccupied until 1913 when there began a series of short tenancies.

During the First World War, it is thought locally that the house became a hospital. However, this does not relate to the evidence stating it was a working camp. Its POWIB (1919) code was Fe (Sen) (IWM: Facsimile K4655). Its TA was Priswarian: Send (ADM 1/8506/265–120667).

After the war, the house lay empty until it was bought as part of a marriage settlement. There then again began a series of short tenancies, culminating in the Hall becoming a private hotel, *c.*1980. In 1988 the house was converted and extended into a nursing home for fifty residents, and is still used for this purpose today.

SEVENOAKS: Rumshott Wood (OS: TQ 524 552). A working camp, its POWIB (1919) code was Pa (Rm) (IWM: Facsimile K4655). It was cited as Rumshott Wood by the FPHS (1973). The camp had the TA Priswarian: Rumshott Wood, Tubs Hill, Sevenoaks (ADM 1/8506/265–120667).

SHARDLOW: The Union Workhouse (OS: SK 429 305). The workhouse, originally known as the House of Industry, was established in Shardlow in 1812. The Reverend Robert Letheridge Farmer, *c.*1920, cited an Act of 1801 as his inspiration to use twenty-three cottages on Shardlow Road to house the poor of the district. In 1897 an annex, to care for children, known as The Grove was established on the opposite side of the road.

Kate Wyatt, the Hospital Administrator of The Grove (per. comm., 20 September 1998) wrote prior to the hospital's closure that in 1911, with the welfare reforms introduced, the workhouse and its grounds passed to the county council. Then came the war years, when at a meeting in June 1918, the Board of Guardians was informed that forty PoWs were to be billeted at their Union Workhouse. Satisfied with their inspection of the premises, the Clerk was then informed that the internees sent there would work on land within a 5-mile radius of the camp. In 1924, additional buildings were added to the workhouse, and the Grove eventually moved across the road onto the site of the workhouse. After extensive alterations, the former House of Industry site was put under the remit of the National Health Service. A change of name took place in 1948, when it became known as the Grove Hospital.

Until very recently it was still in use as a hospital, caring for the elderly. The buildings have now been demolished.

The Derby Daily Telegraph (25 June 1918) cites a camp being set up in Shardlow.

SHEFFIELD: Hyde Park Drill Ground (OS: SK 366 875). Designed by M.E. Hadfield, the drill hall was situated near to Hyde Park in Clough Road, and built for the 4th (Hallamshire) Battalion, Yorkshire and Lancashire Regiment. The 15th Duchess of Norfolk, Flora Fitzalan-Howard, laid the foundation stone on 25 September 1878. After some delays, the hall was formally opened on 2 June 1880. Following the national re-organisation of the volunteer corps in 1908, the hall became Crown property in 1910. It underwent refurbishment and was re-opened on 24 May 1912 by General Sir John French. In August 1914 the regiment moved to new premises at Endcliffe and the Clough Road premises were commandeered as a PoW camp.

Alfred Mißner, a PoW, complained that he had nowhere to write whilst interned at Hyde Park.

An audiotape of a local woman, held by Sheffield Archives, describes prisoners being marched into Bernard Street, towards Hyde Park. She said:

> My mother's sister used to live in Bernard Street at the top of Weigh Lane ... Often when I was in their house I used to see them marching German prisoners on Bernard Street and going up Weigh Lane, taking them to Hyde Park.

In both World Wars the building was used for military purposes. Hindmarch (per. comm., 4 July 1996) stated it was a base for a Royal Artillery unit. During the Second World War, the Home Guard had use of the hall too. Until 1967, it was the headquarters for the Artillery Volunteers. The building then lay empty for around twelve years.

Being one of the largest venues in Sheffield, the Drill Hall was in constant demand for events. It housed flower shows, Trades' Exhibitions, Ideal Home Exhibitions, and dances and recitals. There were a number of political meetings held in the building, including one by a Prime Minister: Balfour addressed an audience there on 10 October 1903. In 1906, suffragettes sabotaged a meeting. Several sporting events took place there too: from 1882, roller skating, boxing matches, and walking marathons were staged. Charles Blondin, the tightrope walker, appeared there in 1885.

The camp closed on 9 December 1918.

In 1979, the premises were purchased, and occupied by Clark & Partners, specialists in converting and repairing motor vehicles for the disabled.

This may have been the missing Sheffield agricultural depot, a satellite of Catterick, cited by the POWIB (1919) in its entry for Bolsover Castle (IWM: Facsimile K 4655). Hyde Park, Sheffield is listed by the FPHS (1973).

DKF 34: Aus dem Arbeitslager Hyde-Park, Zweiglager von Catterick, schreibt der Oberheizer Alfred Mißner, daß es eines der schlechtesten Lager in England sei, daß Schreibgelegenheit gänzlich fehle, und daß die Kriegsgefangenen ihre Briefe auf Knien schreiben müssen.

SHEFFIELD OFFICERS (see Redmires).

SHELFORD (OS: SK 66- 42-). Although the minutes of the Notts County WAC cites a migratory gang at Shelford, its actual location is unknown.

Drainage was a problem for the Food Production Board, and PoWs were used in large numbers to alleviate the problem on the River Devon and River Smite, as well as at Carr Dyke. Minute No. 7 of the Nottinghamshire WAC (29 October 1918) cites fourteen drainage orders had been served, requiring dykes to be cleaned. Another minute (28 January 1919) recorded PoWs were to be employed to clean dykes in the Bingham area after the harvest was brought in.

SHELSLEY WALSH (OS: SO 72- 62-). Shelsley Walsh is listed as a working camp in the POWIB (1919) directory, with the code Dor (Sh W) (IWM: Facsimile K4655). The camp was cited by the FPHS (1973), and had the TA Priswarian: Shelsley, Beauchamp (ADM 1/8506/265–120667).

Bernard (*A Tale of Two Villages*, 1995) states twenty-six PoWs were interned in a building opposite to the Court House, in Shelsley Walsh. As of 31 December 1917, it was commanded by 2nd Lieutenant T.R. Ramsey.

SHENLEY (OS: TL 19- 00-). On 22 July 1918, migratory gangs had been approved for areas in Hertfordshire that previously had not been served by PoW camps. Minutes of the Hertfordshire County Council WAC record a migratory gang at Shenley had been dispersed by 1 October 1918. The report stated that three gangs had been closed in the county, as the harvest was now complete. The gangs had been formed under Mr Uren (Shenley), Mr Taylor (Deeves Hall, Ridge), and Mr Clark (Tring). No further evidence has been found to suggest where the internees were kept.

SHERE – HOLMBURY ST MARY (OS: TQ 111 444). A working camp, its POWIB (1919) code was Pa (She) (IWM: Facsimile K4655). The camp's TA was Priswarian: Holmbury St. Mary (ADM 1/8506/265–120667). Both Shere and Holmbury St Mary are cited by the FPHS (1973).

Turner (per. comm., 7 April 2000) related the reminiscences of Beattie Eden which state that as a 6-year-old daughter of a farmer in 1916, she heard German soldiers being marched to the camp situated on the hill above Holmbury St Mary, during the night. She explained that the main task of the PoWs was to fell firs for timber. 'A sawmill was worked at the top of the Glade (on the bonfire site) and another beyond the old village school.' But one of their first tasks had been to build a set of steps up the hill to the camp. Off duty, the dexterity of these men, dressed in grey uniforms with their small round soft fatigue caps, was explained thus: 'a small piece of wood would quickly become an opening fan.' The internees stayed there for about two years. According to Eden, Primrose Cottage was outside the perimeter of the camp fence, but it was a part of the camp complex; it may have been the guards' quarters. Apparently, during the war the interest of local children was aroused when a balloon came down on the camp's cookhouse. Eden wrote it was the only time she really saw the camp: 'Nothing, and no one, would have stopped the local, very excited, children from ascending that hill in double quick time.' She had frequently seen the PoWs at her father's farm when they brought the old straw of their paillasses for the horses. Neither she, nor her younger sister, were permitted to speak to them. In her fifties, she reproduced a sketch of the camp's layout, which was typical to that of any army camp layout of the day.

A photograph of uniformed British soldiers taken *c.*1917 in a field with a building at their back exists. It is claimed to be the Holmbury St Mary PoW camp. However, there is no sign of a wire fence circumnavigating it, as shown in Beattie's sketch that also exists. Perhaps this is Primrose Cottage.

DKF 34: Im Arbeitslager Holmburg St Mary, Surrey (sic) *ist weder für genügende Beleuchtung noch für ausreichende Heizung Sorge getragen. Es fehlen ein weiterer Kochkessel, eine Kantine und die sehr nötige Badeeinrichtung.*

SHILLINGTON (OS: TL 12- 34-). The names of nine PoWs that worked at Shillington between May 1919 and October 1919, along with their guard, are recorded in an extract taken from the PoWs employment time sheets held by Bedfordshire

County Record Office. Although the workplace was not cited, one has to assume the men were engaged on a farm (WW1/AC/PW/1 & 2).

SHINGAY (OS: TL 30- 46-). A minute of the Hertfordshire County Council WAC recording a migratory gang at Shingay is the only record of this camp existing. Its location is unknown.

SHOTTERY: Drayton Manor Farm (OS: SP 189 546). A working camp cited at Shottery had the POWIB (1919) code Dor (Str) (IWM: Facsimile K4655). The farm is near to Ann Hathaway's Cottage, opposite St Andrew's School. According to an 1886 map of Warwickshire, Drayton Manor Farm virtually backed on to Shottery Rifle Range.

The FPHS (1973) cited Stratford upon Avon. The camp had the TA Priswarian: PoW Camp, Stratford-on-Avon (ADM 1/8506/265–120667).

According to the meeting minutes of 20 November 1916, the Warwickshire WAC recorded that discussions took place about employing PoWs on local farms. One of the places under discussion was a farm at Drayton that had lain derelict for some thirty-five years. The committee took possession on 15 August 1917. The farm was overgrown in hawthorn bushes, briars, anthills, silted up ditches, and had waterlogged fields. Rabbits, which were causing a nuisance to adjoining tenants, infested the place; so 100 PoWs were put to the task of getting the farm back into some kind of order. When the job of rectifying the years of neglect was complete, corn and potatoes were planted. Some of the PoWs were then moved on to the adjoining farms to reclaim more land for planting.

The minute of 14 January 1919 cites Drayton Manor Farm consisted of some 465 acres, of which 380 acres was arable and the remainder (85 acres) was pasture (CR 73 1–2).

According to the German PoWs (*Deutsche Kriegsganene in Fiendesland*, 1919) this camp, at the end of January 1917, was still a tented site.

A further minute of the committee (29 April 1919) recorded there were still 591 PoWs employed on farms in the county, exclusive of those working at Drayton Manor Farm. It was anticipated that on the signing of peace they would be repatriated.

There were also camps at Stratford, in the east of London, and at Stratford St Mary in Suffolk, which should not be confused with this camp.

DKF 34: Aus den Berichten der Schweizer Delegierten aus dem Ende des Jahres 1917 über die Arbeitslager in England geht hervor, daß die Zustände in einigen dieser Lager sich gebessert hatten und daß in manchen dementsprechend das Leben erträglich war. Immerhin geben noch einige Lager zu berechtigten Klagen Anlaß. Trotz wiederholten Einspruchs der deutschen Regierung sind in der Lagern Wingland (Lincolnshire), Ordfordneß (Suffolk), West Tofts (Norfolk), Warren Woods (Norfolk), Glendon bei Keltering (sic), *Stratford upon Avon, Kerry (Nord Wales), und Shirehampton (Gloucestershire) die Gefangenen immer noch in Zelten untergebracht.*

SHIPMEADOW (OS: TM 378 898). A telegram sent from Captain G. Harvey, an inspector from the Local Government Board, informed the Norfolk WAC that Wangford Union Workhouse near Shipmeadow was suitable to accommodate PoWs. This could have been the group that was employed at Bungay Common.

Like most workhouses in England, the one at Shipmeadow, built in 1767, began life providing relief and employment for the poor. It was set on an exposed hilltop, miles from the nearest town. Built in an H shape in red brick, it could accommodate up to

350 inmates. The workhouse purchased 40 acres of farmland, and erected outbuildings for livestock. A pesthouse was also built 300 yards from the main building. It was a two-storey building with attics, and used as an isolation hospital for up to thirty infectious patients, mostly with smallpox. On 25 June 1835, the Wangford Poor Law Union took over the buildings.

The camp's TA was Priswarian: Bungay (Beccles) (ADM 1/8506/265–120667). It is cited by the FPHS (1973)

SHIREHAMPTON (OS: ST 53- 77-). It was a working camp with the POWIB (1919) code Dor (Sh) (IWM: Facsimile K4655). It is also cited by the FPHS (1973). The camp had the TA Priswarian: Shirehampton (ADM 1/8506/265–120667).

Despite representations by the Swiss to the British government at the end of 1917, many internees were still being accommodated in tents at the onset of winter, Shirehampton amongst them.

DKF 34: Aus den Berichten der Schweeizer Delegierten aus dem Ende des Jahres 1917 über die Arbeitslager in England geht hervor, daß die Zustände in einigen dieser Lager sich gebessert hatten und daß in manchen dementsprechend das Leben erträglich war. Immerhin geben noch einige Lager zu berechtigten Klagen Anlaß. Trotz wiederholten Einspruchs der deutschen Regierung sind in den Lagern Wingland (Lincolnshire), Orfordneß (Suffolk), West Tofts (Norfolk), Warren Woods (Norfolk), Glendon bei Keltering (sic), *Stratford on Avon, Kerry (Nord Wales), und Shirehampton (Gloucestershire) die Gefangenen immer noch in Zelten untergebracht.*

SHOTLEY: HMS Training Establishment (OS: TM 229 341). In 1903, the Royal Navy had created a depot on the peninsula, 10 miles from Shotley. On 4 October 1906, new barracks were commissioned for a training establishment to be built there.

The Lancaster Observer (7 August 1914) reported that the crewmembers of the *Königin Luise* were being interned at the naval station at Shotley. From the evidence provided by an eye witness stationed there in 1917 we can assume it was a reception centre of some kind. Summers (*HMS Ganges: Boys Training for the Royal Navy*, 1966) states a cadet wrote that there were German prisoners, awaiting transfer to a prison camp, being accommodated in a hut at the bottom of the Long Covered Way.

Saunders (per. comm., 9 July 1998) stated that the Navy relinquished the base in 1976. For a time it became a sports complex, but today is utilised by the Home Office as a police training centre. A museum dedicated to HMS *Ganges* also stands on the site.

Reference to its time as an internment camp is recorded in the POWIB (1919) directory. The HM Training Establishment, Shotley, had the code Shy. The camp's medical facility had its own code, S S Q.

SHOULDHAM: Shouldham Hall (OS: TL 679 093). Minutes from the Norfolk WAC (2 November 1917) recommended that Shouldham Hall should initially accommodate forty PoWs (C/C10/17). Its POWIB (1919) code was Pa (Shm) (IWM: Facsimile K4655). Its TA was Priswarian: Shouldham (ADM 1/8506/265–120667). Shouldham was inspected by Dr A. de Sturler and Monsieur R. de Sturler, during April and May 1919. Their findings are held at the National Archives at Kew (FO 383/507). It was cited as Shouldham by the FPHS (1973).

Today the hall cares for the elderly. It is advertised to accommodate up to forty-eight residents in pleasant country surroundings.

SHREWSBURY: Abbey Works (OS: SJ 501 121). Macpherson, Horrocks & Beveridge (*A History of the Great War – Medical Services*, 1923) did not provide an opening date for the Shrewsbury camp, but stated it had accommodation for up to 500 men in 'buildings and railway works'. It is cited by the POWIB (1919) as being at Abbey Wood, but the local archivists believe this should have read Abbey Works. These were premises owned by the Midland Railway Carriage and Waggon Works. It was situated to the south of the abbey. Today the site is occupied by a Morrison's supermarket and its car park.

Thomas (*St Stephen's House: Friends Emergency Work in England 1914–1920*, 1920) described the use of the railway works as being undesirable for prolonged internment of men.

Described by the POWIB (1919) as a parent camp, its code was Shrw (IWM: Facsimile K4655); it had a number of satellites attached to it. It was simply recorded by the FPHS (1973) as Shrewsbury. It had the TA Priswarian: Shrewsbury (ADM 1/8506/265–120667), and was cited in a document held by the Osterreichisches Staatsarchiv (GZ 8915/0-KA/97).

The first date recorded for the use of Shrewsbury Concentration Camp is given by the *Liverpool Daily Post* (2 November 1914). The *Shrewsbury Chronicle* (Friday, 6 November 1914) carried a report of Ernst Koanig walking out the camp and going to visit his family in Liverpool. He then handed himself into the police and was sentenced to three months in jail.

The *Shrewsbury Chronicle* (18 December 1914) reported the War Office vetoed a concert to be given by the PoWs at Shrewsbury. A letter from Colonel Hugh Cecil Cholmondley, the camp commandant, was published in the paper. The *Shrewsbury Chronicle* (25 December 1914) cited the commandant had received various donations in lieu of the cancelled concert. The number of PoWs reported to be in the camp at this time was estimated to be 500 to 600.

When John Jackson was visiting the camps in February 1915, on behalf of the US Embassy in London, he did not go to Shrewsbury because he was informed officially that it was intended to close the camp. For whatever reason, the camp did not close at this juncture of time.

The Times (14 June 1915) cited the escape of B.J. Zimpel and O.R. Kirchner. They were re-captured at Welshpool.

A delegation from the US Embassy in London visited the camp on 30 June 1915. They reported it was not up to standard. They noted there were 493 internees (467 soldiers, 26 sailors). Eight civilians acted as officers' servants; they had previously been at Dyffryn Aled. The report said the roofs leaked, and that the flooring was poor. The recreational area measured around 1,000 sq yds. At the time of their visit there were nine in the hospital, some recovering from wounds. Again there are reports of the authorities contemplating abandoning it.

The Times (26 July 1915) cited fifty PoWs were taken to Leigh, by train, from the Shrewsbury camp. Also cited in *The Leigh Chronicle*, the PoWs belonged to the 107th and 242nd Regiments of Infantry.

Another US Embassy visit, on 18 March 1916, cited the commandant was Major H.C.C. Ducat-Hammersley; he previously had been the commandant at Handforth. They noted there were now 464 prisoners (411 soldiers, 46 sailors and 7 civilians), all German.

The Times (15 January 1917) reported the escape and re-capture of Ernst Boldt and Herman Bunte.

The Police Gazette (19 February 1918) cited the escapes of Otto Krueger (aged 24), Fassian Arthur Leo (aged 27), and Max Willi Laessig (also aged 27) on 12 February 1918. *The Times* (20 February 1918) reported Kreuger had been recaptured at Rotherham. *The Derby Daily Telegraph* (18 June 1918) reported that two escapees from Shrewsbury had been re-captured, presumably Leo and Laessig. The three PoWs had escaped by climbing out through a disused chimney shaft.

Complaints were made to the Swiss Delegation about the unhygienic state of the camp's hospital when they visited the camp in June 1917.

Trumper's *20th Century Shrewsbury* (1999) cites the PoWs were employed at Monkmoor Aerodrome. The airfield is about 1 mile north-east of the PoW camp, and was bounded on three sides by a loop of the river.

The Shrewsbury Chronicle (10 May 1918) cited Walter Henry Booton was charged with receiving a letter from a German PoW in Monkmoor Road, Shrewsbury. The letter apparently was intended for his daughter. He was sentenced to one month in prison.

The Times (19 June 1918) cited Bruno Sens and E.J.L. Clausnidzer had escaped and were recaptured at Tipton.

The *Shropshire Records & Research Service* hold photographs (Ref. B44 & B45) showing the cathedral's tower, visible through trees, in the background, with several interned PoWs in the foreground of what appears to be an exercise yard.

A HO list, issued in October 1918, omits Shrewsbury, citing instead Oswestry, the parent camp for the area.

Reports on visits of inspection to PoW camps by Dr A. de Sturler and Monsieur R. de Sturler during April and May 1919 are held at the National Archives at Kew (FO 383/507); they include Shrewsbury.

DKF 15 Der Bericht der Schweizer Delegierten Dr Schwyzer und Vischer vom 15 Juni 1917 über das Lager Shrewsbury stellt fest, daß dort Mißstände herrschten, die Grund zur Beschwerde gaben: Das Dach der Großen Halle war undicht trotz fortwährender Reparaturen. Ferner war der Spielplatz – angblich wegen Mangels an Wachpersonal – nur 1½ Stunden täglich geöffnet, obwohl gerade für die vielen im Lager untergebrachten Arbeitsunfähigen es Wünschenswert war, daß sie sich möglichst den ganzen Tag im Freien bewegen konnten. Das Lazarett entsprach den hygeinischen Anforderungen nicht. Nachts wurden daselbst Kübel als Aborte aufgestellt. Auch sonst wurde über das Lazarett geklagt. Die Zustände dort waren derartig, daß die Schweizer Vertreter selbst vorschlugen, daß jeder ernste Fall in ein modernes Lazarett verbracht würde.

Wegan der oben erwähnten Beschwerden wurde bei der englischen Regierung durch Vermittlung der Schweizerischen Gesandtschaft Vor Stellungen erhoben und die Schweizer Gesandtschaft ersucht, das Lager Shrewsbury baldigst wieder durch Delegierte besuchen zu lassen.

SIDBURY (OS: SY 13- 91-). Described as an agricultural depot, Sidbury had the POWIB (1919) code Dor (Sd) (IWM: Facsimile K4655). Honiton was a satellite of this camp. The camp's TA was Priswarian: Sidbury (ADM 1/8506/265–120667). The camp closed on 18 February 1919. No evidence has been found to suggest the location of the camp.

SINNINGTON (OS: SE 74- 85-). Sinnington was a satellite camp of Sproxton Moor, and is near to Castle Howard. It had the POWIB (1919) code Cat (Sp M) (Sin) (IWM: Facsimile K4655). The camp's TA was Priswarian: Sinnington, Yorks.

(ADM 1/8506/265–120667). No further evidence has been found to support the claim that this camp existed or of its location.

Perhaps Elmsall House or The Hall may hold the key to this camp's location. Alternatively, the camp may have taken its name from the fact there was a railway station there: a practice well known to the military mind.

SITTINGBOURNE (OS: TQ 87- 62-). Sittingbourne appears in the list produced by the FPHS (1973). A website produced by Bobbing Parish Council cites that during the First World War there was a German prisoner of war camp in Oad Street (www.bobbingpc.kentparishes.gov.uk/heritage.htm, 2007).

SKEFFINGTON VALES (OS: SK 740 017). This camp is only cited in a HO document, which states its TA was Priswarian: Skeffington, Billesden (ADM 1/8506/265–120667). It would have existed in the second phase of camps.

SKIPTON (OS: SD 984 525). Raikeswood Camp was a typically built army camp located between the hollow at the Girls' High School and the houses in Raikes Road in Skipton. It opened in November 1914 to accommodate the Bradford Pals Regiment. It was listed by the POWIB (1919) as being a camp for officers; its code was Skp (IWM: Facsimile K4655). Prisoners from Colsterdale were transferred to Skipton in January 1918. It was to house 546 officers and 137 other ranks. Doctors, F. Schwyzer, A.L. Vischer and A. de Sturler inspected the camps at Ripon, Skipton, Lofthouse Park, Kegworth and Donington Hall during February and March 1919 (FO 383/432). The FPHS (1973) cite Skipton, Yorkshire in its listings.

In 1919 the influenza pandemic hit the camp at Skipton. 105 PoWs were taken for treatment to Keighley Military Hospital, where a number died of the illness. Despite the high mortality rate, the prisoners were impressed with the quality of treatment provided (Eddon, per. comm., 11 June 1988).

The camp was closed on 24 October 1919 and the equipment was sold off. Rowley (*The Book Of Skipton*, 1983) states thirty-nine sleeping huts were sold for £117.10s.0d each, Bradford Corporation being the largest purchaser.

Two former PoWs, S. Sachsse and R. Cossman, wrote *Kreigsgefangenen in Skipton: Leben und Geschichte deutscher Kriegsgefangener in einem englischen Lager*, in 1920, their experience of being in the camp.

DKF 26: Der englische Kommandant erzählte daß im Lager Skipton 45 deutsche Offiziere gestorben seien infolge der Grippe.

DKF 39: Der ausgetauschte Hauptmann von Kühlewein sagte aus: Am 16 August 1918, gelegentlich des Transportes von Dartford zum Lager Skipton, der ein drei- bis viermaliges Umsteigen erforderlich machte, mußten Leutnant Jung (amputierter Fuß), Leutnant Hoßol (offene Genickwunde), Leutnant Langner (Lungenschuß), Leutnant Luerke (Gesichtverletzung), Leutnant Paschkewitz (Blasenleiden) und ich (Arm amputiert) ihr sämtliches Gepäck selber tragen, zum Teil schwere Stücke. Ein Dienstmann mit Wagen bot sich an, ebenso ein englischer Begleitsergeant, alle wurden vom englischen Begleitoffizier zurückgewiesen. Einmal mußten wir das Gepäck zur Freude der Zivilisten auf eine Gepäckkarre laden und selbst fahren.

SLALEY (see Riding Mill).

SLEAFORD (OS: TF 074 462). Sleaford agricultural depot had six groups attached to it. These were Folkingham, Great Hale, Morton, Osbournby, Rippingale, and

Rippingale Fen. The camp's POWIB (1919) code was Bro (Sl) (IWM: Facsimile K4655), and its location is cited as The Union, Sleaford. Its TA was cited as Priswarian: The Workhouse, Sleaford (ADM 1/8506/265–120667). Sleaford is also cited by the FPHS (1973).

Sleaford Union Workhouse was erected in 1838 to the design of William J. Donthorne to accommodate up to 180 inmates. It stood in East Street, opposite Cogglesford Mill. When the buildings were demolished in 1972 it was known as Slea View, the name it took in 1948. The buildings have since been demolished and the site redeveloped (www.pastscape.org.uk)

SLIMBRIDGE (OS: SP 073- 03-). As of 31 December 1917, the working camps at Evesham, Toddington, Peopleton, Leigh Court, Shelsey Walsh, Martley, Eardiston, and Slimbridge were to be put under the control of the Southern Command of the Royal Defence Corps. There would be thirty-five PoWs billeted at Slimbridge under the command of Lieutenant G.E. Melsome.

SLINDON (see Eartham).

SLOUGH (OS: SU 995 795). Cited by the POWIB (1919), its code is Pa (Slo) (IWM: Facsimile K4655). It also appears on the list produced for the FPHS (1973). The camp's location remains a mystery. Perhaps the PoWs were drafted in to help create the army's motor repair depot, built *c.*1918, to the west of Slough.

SNODLAND (see Halling).

SOBERTON: Down House (OS: SU 610 162). Listed as being a working camp by the POWIB (1919), its code was Dor (Sob) (IWM: Facsimile K4655). It is also cited by the FPHS (1973). A HO document cites its address as Down House, and gives its TA as Priswarian: Soberton (ADM 1/8506/265–120667).

SOLENT SQUADRON – GOSPORT GROUP (see Gosport).

SOLENT SQUADRON – RYDE GROUP (see Ryde).

SOMERBY HALL STABLES (OS: SK 960 335). This camp was attached to the agricultural depot at Bracebridge. Its TA was Priswarian: Somerby Hall Stables, Gainsborough (ADM 1/8506/265–120667). The FPHS (1973) also cite this camp.

Throughout history there have been several Somerby Halls in Lincolnshire, but the location of this agricultural group was the stable block of the hall near Old Somerby.

SOMERFORD HALL: Brewood (OS: SJ 902 820). Originally built for the Somerfords of Cheshire, the hall was rebuilt *c.*1780 by Charles Watkin John Shakerley. Today Somerford Hall, near Brewood, is in private ownership.

The camp was a satellite of Ettingshall. An agricultural group, it had the POWIB (1919) code Bro (Et) (Sm) (IWM: Facsimile K4655). Its TA was Somerford Hall, Brewood (ADM 1/8506/265–120667).

SOMPTING (see Lancing).

SOULDROP Bedford County Record Office holds extracts from timesheets of PoWs employed in the area. Two farms in the Souldrop area were recorded to have employed them. The location of one was Knotting Fox Farm and the other was Knotting Green Farm between October 1918 and June 1919 (WW1/AC/PW/1 & 2).

KNOTTING FOX FARM (OS: TL 006 622). Gang 1, based at Knotting Fox Farm.

KNOTTING GREEN FARM (OS: SP 987 623). Gang 2, based at Knotting Green Farm

SOUTH BRENT (OS: SX 697 604). The POWIB (1919) directory cites Coronation Hall was used to house internees during the First World War; its code was Dor (Su) (IWM: Facsimile K4655). Moore (Chairman, South Brent Parish Council, per. comm., 10 November 1998) states it stands on glebe land and is sometimes referred to as the Church Hall. It was built in 1911 by money raised by public subscription. In 1970 the Hall was purchased by the Parish Council to serve the local community as their village hall.

South Brent is cited by the FPHS (1973). The camp's TA was Priswarian: South Brent (ADM 1/8506/265–120667).

SOUTH CARLTON (OS: SK 965 771). South Carlton was the home of an airfield originally belonging to the Royal Flying Corps. It was situated to the north of Hallifers Plantation, near to Cliff Farm. Opened in November 1916, it trained pilots destined for the front. It eventually consisted of seven large canvas and brick hangars. PoW labour could have been employed on its infrastructure.

In July 1918 the airfield was designated as No. 46 Training Depot Station when it came under the auspices of the RAF (http://www.burton-by-lincoln.info).

Although it closed in 1920, several buildings still survive today, and are being used as farm stores. Of the two brick buildings that occupy the site today one is known as 'the old cinema', although this may date from the Second World War.

SOUTH CLEATHAM: nr Winston (OS: NZ 126 182). The POWIB (1919) directory cites an agricultural group being at South Cleatham that was a satellite of Port Clarence agricultural depot in Middlesbrough; it had the code Cat (Po C) (Sc) (IWM: Facsimile K4655). The camp's TA was Priswarian: South Cleatham, Winston (ADM 1/8506/265–120667).

SOUTH MOLTON (OS: SS 713 258). An agricultural group attached to Dulverton AD, its POWIB (1919) code was Dor (Dlv) (S M) (IWM: Facsimile K4655). It is also cited by the FPHS (1973). A HO document cites the camp and gives its TA as Priswarian: Unicorn Hotel, South Molton (ADM 1/8506/265–120667).

The National Archives hold a letter from A.H. Stevens of the Goose and Gander Hotel in South Molton saying that the name was changed from the Unicorn to the Goose and Gander in 1965 and that it was a prisoner of war camp during the First World War (B264/2/6, 1983).

SOUTH OCKENDON (OS: TQ 58- 81-). A working camp, its POWIB (1919) code was Pa (Ock); its address is cited as South Ockendon, Romford (IWM: Facsimile K4655). The camp's exact location is not known. The FPHS (1973) cite a camp at South Ockendon. Its TA was Priswarian: South Ockendon (ADM 1/8506/265–120667). Reports on visits of inspection to PoW camps at Rainham, South Ockenden, Fox Burrows Farm (Chigwell), and Chipping Ongar are held at the National Archives, Kew (FO 383/506).

Disturbingly, the Swiss Delegation, on their visit in October 1917, recorded that the stoves in the camp's canteen were missing.

DKF 33: Aus den Berichten des Schweizerischen Delegierten vom September und Oktober 1917 geht hervor, daß in den Arbeitslager in England noch immer Mißstände herrschten. In Hemel Hempstead (Herts) und Chipping Ongar (Essex) fehlten die Kantinen, in South Ochendon (Essex) (sic) *die Öfen.*

SOUTHEND ON SEA. With the limited number of viable places to intern the vast numbers of civilians being interned and the arrival to Britain of captured combatants the government hired passenger liners to bridge the gap. The German authorities complained of their use as Britain had a history of putting PoWs into old hulks in the past. The use of these ships was brief, mainly because of the cost involved in hiring them, and they were phased out as locations on land became available. The ships were known as the Leigh Channel Squadron.

Again, controversy surrounded officers being brought to Southend on Sea as a retaliatory measure to British officers being moved forward nearer the front line, or that it could stop the aerial bombardment of the south east coastal towns. The officers were billeted in a house in Victoria Avenue.

THE LEIGH CHANNEL SQUADRON. Initially there were three ships in the Leigh Channel Squadron, anchored off Southend on Sea. They were the *Ivernia*, the *Royal Edward* and the *Saxonia*. When both the Gosport and Ryde groups had struck anchor, the *Uranium* sailed to join this group.

HMT *IVERNIA* (GRT: 13,799. Passengers: 1st class = 164, 2nd class = 200, steerage = 1,600). Some reports wrongly record this ship's name as the *Invernia*. Panayi (*The Enemy in Our Midst, Germans in Britain during the First World War* 1991) claims the *Ivernia* was off Southend on Sea, holding, in March 1915, 1,575 internees. It has been suggested that it was mostly German soldiers, captured in France, that were sent to the *Ivernia*. Still holding 1,600 internees, she is cited by the *New York Times* as being in service as a prison ship on 15 March 1915, but was due to be released from this duty soon. *Ivernia* was part of the Leigh Channel Squadron until she was released for duties in April 1915.

Kludas (*Great Passenger Ships of the World: 1858–1912*, 1975) and McCart (*Atlantic Liners of the Cunard Line From 1884 to the Present Day*, 1990) confirm she was launched on 21 September 1899 by C.S. Swan & Hunter of Newcastle for the Cunard line. She crossed the Atlantic for many years, including taking troops to South Africa in the Boer War. On 24 May 1911, captained by Thomas Potter, the *Ivernia* struck the Daunts Rocks, at Queenstown's harbour and was holed. Repaired, she returned to cross-Atlantic sailings again until the outbreak of war. Killeen (*The Great War: The Prisoner of war Ships – A History, Together With Special Reference to the Postal History*, 1993) wrote that, having completed her return trip from New York, she was again hired as a troop-transport. Smith (Curator of the Museum of Transport, per. comm., 29 November 2000) wrote that on 1 January 1917, whilst sailing from Marseilles to Alexandria with 1,000 troops on board, under the command of Captain William Turner, who had captained the ill-fated *Lusitania*, she was torpedoed by German *U-Boot UB 47* off Cape Matapan in Greece. Within one hour of being hit, the *Ivernia* sank, with the loss of 36 crew and 87 troopers.

DKF 67: Am 12 Dezember 1914 kamen Dr Farber, Unterarzt meines Regiments, und ich mit dem Transport von Frith Hill an Bord HMT *Ivernia.*

DKF 67: Mitte Januar 1915 wollte ein Korporal dem in der Post-Office beschäftigten Oberjäger Möller, Jag 9, befehlen, angekommente Postsäcke an Bord der Ivernia zu schaffen.

HMT *ROYAL EDWARD* (GRT: 10,864 (11,117). Passengers: 1st class = 344, 2nd class = 210, steerage = 560). Built for the Egyptian Mail Steamship Company as the *Cairo*, she was launched at Fairfield of Glasgow in July 1907. She plied the Marseilles – Alexandria service until she was laid up in 1909. Bought by the Canadian Northern Steamship Company in 1910, she was refitted for service in the North Atlantic at Fairfield's yard before being renamed the *Royal Edward*.

The *Royal Edward* held 1,200 civilian internees, some of whom had come from camps at York and Olympia in London. Others had been arrested in Gibraltar, the Royal Navy taking men of military age off ships as they were making their way back to Germany or Austria.

Panayi (1991) states the *Royal Edward* was moored off Southend-on-Sea, and used as a 'prison ship'. Karl Wehner, who was a 17-year-old student living in Stoke Newington when war was declared, supports this claim. He was a German national arrested and taken into internment. His first night was spent in a police cell, before he was taken to the Olympia Exhibition Halls. After several weeks at Olympia, Wehner states he was transferred to the *Royal Edward* moored in the Thames Estuary, near Southend.

Bird (*Control of Enemy Alien Civilians in Great Britain 1914–1918*, 1986) cites that on his inspection tour John B. Jackson found a class system operated on several of these vessels. On the *Royal Edward*, 'the best appointed of the three internment ships moored in the Thames, internees were divided into three classes in which their ability to pay was more important than their social status'. Those that could afford it were allowed to join the 'Club Class', making their own catering arrangements. Of the rest, some were permitted use of the first class facilities, with the less affluent occupying the steerage accommodation and receiving standard PoW rations. These arrangements were not so visible on the *Saxonia* moored alongside.

Cited by the *New York Times* (15 March 1915) as still being in service as a prison ship, she was due to be released from this duty soon. As the 'prison ships' were phased out, many of internees from the *Royal Edward* went to Alexandra Palace. She was last used as a prison ship in April 1915, and on 14 August 1915 whilst serving as a troop carrier she was torpedoed by the German submarine *UB 14*, and sank in the Aegean Sea with the loss of 935 men.

HMT *SAXONIA* (GST: 14,281. Passengers: 1st class = 164, 2nd class = 200, steerage = 1,600). Panayi (1991) cites the Saxonia was based at Southend-on-Sea, carrying some 2,300 civilian internees. Some had come to the ship from Frith Hill, others were men of military age attempting to return to Germany to enlist who had been taken off ships as they docked at ports around the British Empire, such as Gibraltar.

The *Saxonia* was a sister ship of the *Ivernia*. Built on the River Clyde by John Brown for the Cunard Line, she was launched on Saturday, 16 December 1899.

For a time, she was used as a PoW accommodation ship in the Thames, before continuing in the company's service. Between May 1915 and October 1916 she made a dozen round voyages between Liverpool and New York.

Everyone sent to the *Saxonia* was treated as an equal, unlike those on the *Royal Edward*, moored alongside.

The Southend and Westcliff Graphic (20 November 1914) reported that 500 German prisoners, formerly interned at Olympia, were escorted by members of the 5th Battalion Royal Sussex Regiment, on Wednesday, through the High Street from the Midland Railway Station to the *Saxonia*, *Royal Edward* and *Ivernia*, which had been moored off Southend for some days.

Holding 2,800 internees on board, the *Saxonia* is cited by the *New York Times* (15 March 1915) as still being in service as a prison ship, but was due to be released from this duty soon.

When the prison ships were phased out in April 1915, many of the internees from the *Saxonia* went to Alexandra Palace. McCart (1990) states the *Saxonia* was taken over by the government under the Liner Requisition Scheme, and made numerous journeys between New York and Liverpool carrying both troops and supplies. In December 1918, along with other ships, she transported American soldiers back across the Atlantic. After a refit, she was ready to re-join Cunard and served for another five years before being sold in March 1925 to a Dutch breaker for £47,000.

HMT *URANIUM* (see Gosport).

VICTORIA AVENUE (OS: TQ 877 864). Jackson (*The Prisoners 1914–1918*, 1989) claims, in the latter stages of the war, German officers were transferred to Southend on Sea, which was under aerial attack by Gotha bombers and Zeppelins. Amongst the reasons he suggested for this move was a retaliatory measure to British officers being moved forward, nearer the front line, or that it could stop the aerial bombardment of the south east coastal towns. He states the PoWs were accommodated in schools and other buildings, many of which had formerly been used to treat the wounded of the Allies, but had to be transferred away from the potential bombing. Lockwood (*Somewhere Over Essex*, 2004) suggests air raids on Maldon, Heybridge, Southend, Braintree, and Harwich prompted the authorities to move German PoWs to Victoria Avenue in Southend on Sea and to other locations on the Kent Coast.

In her reminiscences, Barnwell (per. Comm.) recalls, as a child, she saw German officers – some with Iron Crosses – in their distinctive grey uniforms with high collars, in Victoria Avenue. They were imprisoned in a large house, which later became the Commercial School, situated near the Civic Centre (Martin per. *comm.* 8 January 1999).

The camp had the TA Priswaroff: Southend-on-Sea (ADM 1/8506/265–120667). It closed on 11 December 1918.

SOUTHAM (see Harbury).

SOUTHAMPTON. There were to two camps in Southampton. Both were reception centres; one for officers and one for the lower ranks. Both camps shared the same POWIB (1919) code, Spn. The ice rink and Bevois Mount House were cited separately by the FPHS (1973).

SHIRLEY ICE RINK (OS: SU 406 135). Reception Depot No. 1.

BEVOIS MOUNT HOUSE (OS: SU 422 134). Officer Transit Camp.

The TA of Shirley Ice Rink was Embarking: Southampton. Bird (1986) cites the skating rink was amongst those camps set up in the early stages of the war to hold civilians. There was also a camp near Shirley in Warwickshire.

In his report of 1920, Belfield emphasised the need to set up disembarkation ports at the beginning of any future war. He had two such facilities available to him in the Southampton area, which were a large private house and a skating rink. They had accommodation for 80 officers and 800 men respectively; but in an emergency, each could be pushed to hold another 25 per cent. In his report Belfield admitted these centres were never big enough for the demand put on them, and then conveniently states 'the limitations on numbers were precluded by local conditions.'

Described as a Reception Centre for officers, its POWIB (1919) code was Spn (IWM: Facsimile K4655). Its TA was quoted as being Priswarian: Southampton (ADM 1/8506/265–120667). It was to close on 12 February 1919. Bevois Mount is cited in a document held by the Oesterriechisches Staatsarchiv (GZ 9815/0-KA/98).

SOUTHILL PARK: Biggleswade (Old Warden) (OS: TL 15- 42-). A working camp, its POWIB (1919) code was Pa (So P) (IWM: Facsimile K4655). Several alternatives for this camp were cited by the FPHS (1973): these were Southill, Biggleswade, and Old Warden. The camp had the TA, Priswarian: Old Warden, Biggleswade (ADM 1/8506/265–120667).

Although it has not been proven, the Agricultural College at Shuggleworth would have made an excellent choice for this camp. The fact that similar colleges at Aspatria and Sutton Bonington were used for internment purposes is further evidence for this.

SOUTHPORT (OS: SD 300 120). In April 1918, Southport's Corporation Councillors were successful in their challenge to stop a PoW Camp being set up in the Hesketh Park district of the town, but they failed in their second attempt to block the camp being set up at Woodvale, Ainsdale according to *The Liverpool Echo* (10, 13 & 24 April and 1 & 10 May 1918).

There were no reports of activity at the camp in the press.

SOWERBY (OS: SE 429 818). A HO document cites the camp's TA was Priswarian: Sowerby, Thirsk (ADM 1/8506/265–120667). Where the PoWs were housed is not known.

ST ALBANS: St Michael's Rural CP (OS: TL 14- 07-). Minutes of the Hertfordshire County Council WAC reveal, when suitable accommodation could not be found for a camp at St Albans, by 21 February 1917, the proposed scheme was aborted in favour of Hemel Hempstead.

The St Michael's camp was reported in the minutes of 8 May 1918 when it was stated that fifty PoWs were working out of this camp.

Napsbury War Hospital was in the St Albans area.

ST COLUMB WORKHOUSE (OS: SW 917 637). *The Western Morning News* (14 August 1914) cited the workhouses of Falmouth, Redruth, St Columb and Truro were being used to hold passengers and crews arrested from two German ships being held at Falmouth Harbour. It is thought they were trying to get to America.

A new workhouse was built on a site north of St Columb Major, in 1840, to accommodate up to 150 inmates to replace the former parish workhouse. It was designed by George Gilbert Scott and William Bonython Moffatt. With the abolition of the poor law unions and the creation of public assistance institutions its management passed to Cornwall's County Council. In 1933, the workhouse closed for alterations to be turned into a home for mentally ill men. Its architect was S. Pool. Now known as The Retreat it re-opened in 1935. In 1988, it was given Grade II listed status. It closed in 1999 and was converted into residential housing.

In the Second World War, there was a PoW camp (No. 115) at Whitecross.

STAFFORD DETENTION BARRACKS (OS: SJ 923 238). Standley (*The High Sheriff of Staffordshire and the County Gaol*, 2005) provides an insight into life in an early English prison. He stated that in 1166 a decree demanded every shire in England was to have a county gaol. The details were vague but the county's first gaol was established soon after, at the end of Crabbery Lane, near to the Broadeye. By a charter of Edward II, Stafford Borough was also granted the right to have and maintain a Borough Gaol, which stood at the North Gate. How long both these establishments continued to co-exist is not clear, but when Elizabeth I passed through Stafford in 1575 only one gaol existed, and that was at the North Gate. Towards the end of the eighteenth century it was found necessary to replace the gaol. Significant overcrowding has been cited as one of the major contributory factors. The new prison opened on its present site in 1793.

With the outbreak of the First World War, the role of the prison changed, and felons were moved out of one section as it was commandeered to take civilian internees. By 1916, the number of civilian prisoners was drastically reduced as the prison was taken over fully by the military and was then known as Stafford Detention Barracks. It was not handed back to the Prison Commissioners until 1923, and by then its normal function had been absorbed by other establishments.

During the thwarted Easter Rising of 1916, Michael Collins surrendered to British forces outside Dublin's Grand Post Office. He was arrested and taken to the Richmond Barracks in Dublin before he and 487 others were marched to the docks and put on board a cattle boat bound for Holyhead on the British mainland. On his arrival, he and 288 of his fellow dissidents were put on the train for Stafford, the remainder going to Knutsford Prison. Collins remained at Stafford Detention Barracks for two months before being transferred to internment camp at Frongoch. When released from internment he returned to Ireland to begin his short political career.

Also detained at Stafford Detention Barracks were fifty-nine non-commissioned German officers found guilty of stealing from the Quartermaster's Stores at Catterick in March 1918. They were each sentenced to eighty-four days military confinement.

After the war, the prison remained inactive, until 1939 when war broke out once more. Again it took on a specialised role by relieving the strain put on other prisons. After the war Stafford Prison became a training prison and still continues this role today.

STAINBY (Buckminster) (OS: SK 89- 23-). The FPHS (1973) cites both Stainby and Buckminster in its *List of British Prison Camps*. Stainby is recorded by the POWIB (1919) as being a working camp, its code being Bro (Stby) (IWM: Facsimile K 4655). An HO document states its TA as Priswarian: Buckminster (ADM 1/8506/265–120667), and also provides evidence that this camp was for civilian internees. Unlike combatants, non-combatants did not have to work but many chose to because they still had dependants who would otherwise be left to seek help from charitable organisations.

There was an airfield created by the Royal Flying Corps near Buckminster in 1916. It was to become RAF Buckminster, before closing in June 1919. Any internees sent to this area may have worked on the airfield's infrastructure.

When the Armistice was declared in 1918, 2nd Lieutenant Albert E. Elsy of the Devonshire Regiment was an interpreter at the camp. In a letter home, sent from Buckminster, he states he was being deployed to the PoW camp at the Repair Depot at Harlescott. His letter was dated 12 November 1918.

There is a possibility that this camp may have been at Buckminster Hall. According to *Kelly's Trade Directory* of 1912, Captain Cecil Stone occupied the Hall. The description of the park states it consisted of some 230 acres, housing the mansion, which was a large handsome edifice in the Italian style, erected *c.*1798, by Sir William Manners Talmash.

Reports on visits of inspection to PoW camps at Stainby, Boston Docks, and King's Lynn are held at the National Archives at Kew (FO 383/432).

STAINTON SIDINGS: Dalton-in-Furness (OS: SD 248 725). Described as an agricultural depot, it had the POWIB (1919) code Lgh (St S) (IWM: Facsimile K4655). Dalton in Furness is cited by the FPHS (1973). The camp closed in May 1919. The camp's TA was Priswarian: Stainton, Dalton-in-Furness (ADM 1/8506/265–120667). The POWIB (1919) also state that the Stainton camp had a satellite at Milnthorpe.

STANDON: Hursley Park (OS: SU 423 254). Cited by the POWIB (1919) as Hursley Park, it was described as a working camp, with the code Dor (Hur) (IWM: Facsimile K4655). It was also cited by the FPHS (1973). The camp's exact location is unknown. Its TA was Priswarian: Hursley (ADM 1/8506/265–120667). There was also a camp near Ware, recorded as being at New Street Farm, Standon.

STANDON: New Street Farm (OS: TL 397 222). Cited in the minutes of the Hertfordshire County Council WAC the camp at Standon opened in 1917 with thirty-five PoWs in situ. Situated near to Ware, the camp was at New Street Farm, Kents Lane. Aslo cited by the HO, its TA was Priswarian: New Street Farm, Standon, Ware (ADM 1/8506/265–120667). The camp appears in lists produced for the FPHS (1973).

STANFORD-LE-HOPE (OS: TQ 68- 82-). A working camp, its POWIB (1919) code was Pa (Stn) (IWM: Facsimile K4655). Stanford le Hope was also cited by the FPHS (1973). No further evidence has been found to suggest where this camp was located, but perhaps St Cleres Hall or its grounds may hold the key. The majority of the hall was built in 1690 to designs of Robert Adams, for the Clerk of the Stables to King George I. In 1997, this magnificent old manor was converted into a clubhouse for a golf course that opened in 1994.

STANHOPE: Newlandside (OS: NY 976 376). The internment camp at Stanhope is also known as Newlandside; its POWIB (1919) code was Cat (Sta) (IWM: Facsimile K4655), and its TA was Priswarian: Stanhope, Co. Durham (ADM 1/8506/265–120667). It was listed by the FPHS (1973) as Stanhope, Durham.

The DKF cites that 560 internees at Newlandside were engaged in quarry work and there were complaints made about safe working practices being ignored. They were expected to work high up on steep sided faces without safety equipment. The quarry was approximately 0.75 miles south of Stanhope.

The camp, on 12 September 1916, consisted of tents that leaked, and the PoWs were expected to sleep on wooden floorboards. Interestingly, this document cites Handforth, and not Catterick as its parent camp. This was because Catterick was upgraded at a later date.

During the First World War, troops were garrisoned in the Town Hall, according to the War Office.

Two German PoWs, Karl Lux (d. 23 April 1918) and Michael Krebbs (d. 29 October 1918), were buried in Stanhope Cemetery. Their comrades had fashioned gravestones from the stone they quarried.

DKF 30: Unter dem 12 September 1916 berichtet der Gefreite Alfred Lutsche, daß die Gefangenen bei dem Steinbruchkommando Newlandside (zu Handforth gehörig) des Nachts unter undichten dünnen Zelten, durch welche es regnet, auf dem nackten Erdboden schlafen müssen, zu einer Zeit, als die Nächte schon empfindlich kalt waren. Auch Weihnachten 1916, hatten sich die Verhältnisse kaum gebessert.

DKF 31: Unzureichend sind auch die Baracken in Port Clarence und Yatesbury, es sei denn, daß Wände der Baracken baldmöglichst verstärke werden. Die Beleuchtung der Baracken in Newlandside und Yatesbury bedarf dringend der Änderung.

DKF 31: Auch in Loch Doon, auf der Insel Raasay, in Newlandside, Ceal Aston (sic) *Sutton Veney* (sic), *Bowithick, Netheravon, Yatesbury, Rovrah* (sic), *Port Clarence und Hayrmyres* (sic) *werden die Leute zu sehr ausgenutzt.*

DKF 32: Bei den Steinbrucharbeiten in Newlandside, wo die Leute an 20 bis 40 Yards tiefen Wänden arbeiten müssen, fehlen die notwendigen Sicherheitsvorkehrungen.

DKF 32: Die Bestellung der eingehenden Briefe und Pakete ist fast überall, hauptsächlich aber in Tern Hill, Newlandside und Rovrah (sic), *sehr langsam.*

DKF 36: Im Arbeitalager Stanhope sind 560 deutsche Gefangene mit Steinbrucharbeiten schwerster Natur bei ungenügender Ernährung beschäftigt.

DKF 36: In der Note Nr 11202 12, 18/P vom September 1918 hat die britische Foreign Office erklärt, daß in Irlam keine Arbeiter mehr beim Entladen von Roheisen beschäftigt werden und das geeignete Maßnahmen getroffen sind, daß einer Wiederholung der Strafmethode, wie sie in Stanhope angewandt wurde, vorgebeugt wird.

STANLEY MOOR – BURBAGE: Ludmanlow (OS: SK 044 715). Listed by the POWIB (1919) as a working camp, its code was Bro (St M) (IWM: Facsimile K4655). This camp was near to Ludmanlow, in Derbyshire. The camp was possibly near Burbage Reservoir, on Stanley Moor, which is close to the Derbyshire village of Ludmanlow. The FPHS (1973) cite a camp at Burbage. It had the TA Priswarian: Burbage, Derbys (ADM 1/8506/265–120667).

Derbyshire Record Office hold documents, dated 4 July 1961, citing two internees who died whilst interned at Burbage being interred in Christ Church's graveyard. Their bodies were exhumed and taken to the war grave cemetery at Cannock Chase. They were M. Geyer (d. 25 July 1918), and G. Schneider (d. 28 December 1918). The latter's death was after the Armistice began (D1372 API 65/75).

STANSTED MOUNTFITCHET (OS: TL 511 241). Nearby stands Stansted Airport, opened on 7 August 1943. It is now Britain's fourth largest airport. Taking its name from the nearby village of Stansted Mountfitchet its beginnings were much humbler before American engineers arrived to begin construction work in August 1942.

The PoWs may have been billeted at Mountfitchet High School and employed in the nurseries nearby. Wherever the camp was, it was cited as a working camp, with the POWIB (1919) code Pa (Std) (IWM: Facsimile K4655). The camp's TA was Priswarian: Stanstead (sic), Essex (ADM 1/8506/265–120667). It is also cited by the FPHS (1973).

STARCROSS (OS: SX 97- 81-). A working camp, it had the POWIB (1919) code Dor (Sr). It is also cited by the FPHS (1973). Its TA was Priswarian: Starcross (ADM 1/8506/265–120667). The location of the camp remains a mystery.

The Western Times (13 May 1919) reported around 200 PoWs were leaving Starcross.

STEEPLE BUMPSTEAD (OS: TL 679 406). A working camp, its POWIB (1919) code was Pa (Sp) (IWM: Facsimile K4655). It is also cited by the FPHS (1973). The camp is cited in a HO document, which gives its address as Bower Hall. Its TA was Priswarian: Bower Hall, Steeple Bumpstead (ADM 1/8506/265–120667).

The hall dated back to the sixteenth century and was lived in by the Bendyshe family. It was used in the First World War to intern German PoWs. Steeple Bumstead (sic) is cited as being inspected by Dr A. de Sturler and Monsieur R. de Sturler, during April and May 1919 according to the National Archives, at Kew (FO 383/507).

Bower Hall was demolished in 1926 and the materials sold off. Even its great staircase found its way to America (http://www.steeplebumpstead.co.uk/History/files/SBhistory.htm).

STEYNING (OS: TQ 228 060). A working camp, its POWIB (1919) code was Pa (Stg) (IWM: Facsimile K4655). Its TA was Priswarian: Steyning (ADM 1/8506/265–120667). Steyning is also cited by the FPHS (1973).

Evidence suggests the camp may have been in the workhouse on the Shoreham to Brighton Road where it is known that, in 1918, German PoWs cultivated 16 acres of the workhouse's gardens. The union had to pay 5 ¼d (2.2p) per hour for them and they were given tea, coffee, or cocoa at midday. The workhouse opened in 1901 on a twenty-three acre site at Kingston-by-Sea to replace the one built in New Shoreham in 1835. To protect those born in the workhouse after 1904 from disadvantage in later life, the address on birth certificates was given as 2 Upper Shoreham Road, Kingston-by-Sea. In 1906, four additional ward blocks, known as New Hospital, were opened. When Poor Law was abolished in 1930, the workhouse became Steyning Poor Law Institution until the inauguration of the National Health Service in 1948 and it was renamed Southlands Hospital. *The Argus* (7 August 2009) reported 200 new homes could be built. The site was sold in 2005 as part of a £320 million deal forged by the NHS Hospital Sites Programme and the Homes and Communities Agency (HCA). A spokesperson for the council said the development would keep some of the original workhouse buildings, including the refectory and entrance block, to be re-named the Refectory Building and West Lodge.

STOBS ARMY CAMP COMPLEX: nr Hawick (OS: NT 514 090). *The Jedburgh Gazette* (11 October 1902) reported the estate surrounding the ruins of Stobs Castle had been purchased for the country from the Eliott family; it had been in their family since 1583. In 1903, on land estimated to be some 3,600 acres, the military established a camp and then created the rail link, about 1 mile to the north, to new sidings at Acreknowe. These sidings were later extended into the camp itself.

The Hawick News (18 September 1903) reported that a further tract of land adjacent to Stobs was purchased for the War Office from the Duke of Buccleuch. Soldiers soon occupied this site, with the men initially 'under canvas'. Gradually huts replaced the tents. The number of troops that were there at any one time varied, as soldiers frequently came and went, and by the end of 1903 around 20,000 men had been stationed at Stobs.

During the war, the main part of the complex was used for preparing British troops for the front. Later in the conflict Canadian units also underwent training. Throughout the war the camp was used as a place of internment. From the beginning of

November 1914, only civilian internees were detained at Stobs. On 2 November 1914, the first batch of prisoners was brought from Edinburgh, by train. *The Scotsman* (3 November 1914) reported the first internees to arrive at Stobs came from Edinburgh by special train. A strong military escort accompanied them. *The Hawick Express and Advertiser* (14 October 1914) had announced PoWs were to be held in 100 newly built double huts (120ft × 20ft), erected at a cost of £50,000. The huts had concrete bases, with corrugated roofs that were asbestos lined. The first forty huts were built southwest of Winningtonrig. Each hut slept thirty prisoners, making the total capacity 6,000, when sixty more huts were to be put up on the north-eastern side.

In February 1915, John Jackson stated in his report on visits to internment camps in the UK on behalf of the US Embassy in London that they did not inspect Stobs, as 'such a visit would require time' for so few prisoners. Jackson had noted that there were 300 prisoners at the camp, none of which were combatants.

The Hawick Express & Advertiser (16 April 1915) reported that 780 internees were expected to arrive at Stobs, and that the guard was to be increased. The same paper (7 May 1915) stated thirty-six Germans captured in the North Sea were to be kept at Stobs. These were probably the crews of two torpedo boats (*A2* and *A6*) from the Flanders Flotilla that were sunk off the Dutch coast on 1 May 1915.

The Times (13 May 1915) then reported 150 internees arrived from Liverpool. *The Hawick Express & Advertiser* reported (21 May 1915) that 150 businessmen from the Manchester area, of German or Austrian origin, were now at the camp. Fearing a reprisal for the sinking of the RMS *Lusitania* by a German submarine on 7 May 1915, many had offered themselves up for internment. To deter sightseers, an order prohibiting the public from approaching any nearer than 0.25 miles to the camp was issued under the Defence of the Realm Act.

A second US inspection team visited Stobs in June 1915. They found there were 1,098 civilians, 783 soldiers and 496 sailors, totalling 3277, being interned. They were being held in four compounds, in huts designed to hold around sixty men in each. The average was thirty-three to a hut. A fifth compound was being erected, with the intention of increasing the total number of internees to 1,220. Some sailors had been transferred to Handforth in March. When the inspection team came back eight months later there was no mention of this fifth compound – but a hospital facility was reported. The civilian population was transferred from Stobs to Knockaloe in July 1916.

The Times (22 September 1915) reported that Karl Klein, a German sailor at Stobs, had hanged himself.

According to the *Carlisle Journal*, in October 1915, 350 PoWs passed through the city on their way to Stobs. News of their journey north had somehow leaked out and a large crowd gathered at the station, but nothing could be seen as the blinds were drawn on the windows of the train. Not knowing how to react some hooted as the train left.

On 19 October 1915, the *Hawick Express & Advertiser* reported that Gustav Geblin had absconded from the camp. On 29 October 1915 the same newspaper cited his re-capture three days earlier.

The Times (28 October 1915) reported three sailors, Alfred Joksch, aged 26, a boatswain's mate, Emil Stehr, also aged 26, a ship's officer, and Karl Villbrandt, had escaped from Stobs. Stehr and Villbrandt had been on the SMS *Blücher*. *The Police Gazette* (2 November 1916) reported that Joksch had been recaptured. Although there is no report of Stehr's re-capture, a PoW of that name is cited as escaping from Handforth in November 1917.

Carl Michalski, another sailor from the SMS *Blücher* was reported to have escaped (*The Times*, 6 January 1916) but he was recaptured two days later, according to the same newspaper of 8 January 1916.

On 13 April 1916, led by Boylston Adams Beal, the camp was visited for a second time for the US Embassy in London. Beal's team noted there were four compounds. Compounds 'A' and 'B' housed 1,102 and 1,098 civilians respectively. Compounds 'C' and 'D' housed 1,081 and 1,209 military and naval personnel respectively. All the interned were housed in wooden huts. The inspection team noted three soldiers in Compound 'D' and four non-combatants from Compound 'B' were from the Alsace region. A further nine internees were in cells, six of which had been charged with pilfering the contents of parcels belonging to fellow internees. The total number of internees was 4,592, comprising of 1,821 soldiers, 502 sailors, all German, and 2,269 civilians. The latter comprised of 2,089 Germans, 178 Austrians and two Turks. In the eighteen months the camp had been opened, there had been twelve deaths. On the day of the inspection there were sixty-five patients being treated in the camp's infirmary, staffed by four doctors and twenty-eight hospital orderlies recruited from the compounds. If a surgeon was required, one would come down from Edinburgh. Beal noted 500 prisoners were engaged in road making, whilst others were employed in shoemaking and tailoring. Some made use of the workshops to do woodwork. In 'C' Compound was a bakery, which baked bread for the whole camp. The commandant was Lt-Colonel H.J. Bowman, late of the Nottinghamshire & Derbyshire Regiment (HMSO, 1916).

Horne (*The German Connection: The German Newspaper 1916–1919*, 1988) cited a school was set up in the camp. A hut was set aside, and around seventy students at any one time could use the facility. It is estimated a total of 3,500 pupils passed through the school, which was staffed by sixty-seven teachers, themselves PoWs. Subjects on offer included commercial subjects, motor engineering, architecture, interior design and languages. The inspection team's report cited the internees published their own newspaper. The most plentiful editions produced were called *Stobsaide*, but there were others papers, the *Neue Stobser Zeitung* and the *Neu Stobsische Zeitung*. The civilian internees had started the paper, and when they were transferred to the Isle of Man in July 1916, military personnel continued the process. Twenty-five issues of *Stobsaide* were published. One was produced every three weeks from October 1916 until January-February 1919. The prisoners did the typesetting themselves, and after being approved by a censor, it was printed in Hawick. For reasons unknown, issue No. 23 did not meet the censor's approval and was suppressed. Early 'civilian issues' of the paper are very scarce.

Wihelm Jensen, Max Ammerlich, Walter Dusselmann, Emil Schultz, Paul Butz and Bernhard Haak, escaped on 25 August 1917. According to Belfield (*Report on the Directorate of Prisoners of War*, 1920) they stole a boat, but were picked up in the North Sea, around 7 miles from the shore, and thereby produced a legal conundrum as to whether they had actually escaped from British jurisdiction or not. But as they had not been able to re-join their units, they were, in his eyes justifiably, taken back into captivity. *The Hawick Express* (21 September 1917) cited the six men were captured by a British naval patrol in the North Sea. They had made their way across the hills and moors from the camp, making for Newbigging Point, where they hoped a boat would be in readiness for them. At Amble they succeeded in buying provisions, before getting to the small fishing village of Cresswell. There, in desperation, they stole a boat. Out at sea, a trawler spotted their stolen craft and passed on their bearings to a destroyer. Amongst the escaping boat crew were two submariners. Some of the six had revolvers, and two of them were recipients of the Iron Cross (HO 45/11025/ 68577). Their recapture provoked reaction as it was claimed these men when taken into custody were in international water. *The Glasgow Herald* (4 September 1917) records the six were brought back to the Tyne.

Alexander Ziolowski (*The Times*, 21 October 1916) escaped on 18 October 1916. His re-capture was reported by the same newspaper three days later.

The Times (6 September 1917) reported that Osterhoff, Fraas, Ehlen & Haussner had escaped. The 17 September edition reported that Osterhoff had been re-captured. Two days later the same newspaper reported the other three were back in custody.

The Times (19 October 1917) reported five unnamed internees had escaped. The same newspaper, dated 24 October, reported they had been recaptured.

The Hawick News (8 November 1918) stated a local man was charged with procuring cigarettes for a PoW.

During the camp's existence thirty-six soldiers died whilst being interned, and were buried in a graveyard near to the railway station.

It is believed the camp was cleared of its internees by November 1919. Letters from the PoW hospital have been recorded up to September 1919.

Forty years on, *The Hawick News* (19 June 1959) reported that the Ministry of Defence had informed the county council that the dismantling of Stobs was nearing completion.

Murray (*Stobs Castle 1903–1959*, 1988) wrote:

> When you visit the camp area today it is difficult to visualise a training camp with all the paraphernalia connected to it. For example, the men, munitions, horses, railway line and equipment have disappeared. Today it is deserted, save for a couple of buildings, and as each year passes the tarmac road surfaces become more and more overgrown and in a state of disrepair.

The POWIB (1919) cites Stobs's code as Stbs (IWM: Facsimile K4655). Its hospital is cited separately. The FPHS (1973) cites Stobs, Hawick.

DKF 15: Nach dem Bericht des Schweizer Delegierten de Stürler vom 6. November 1918, waren bis zu diesem Zeitpunkt im Lager Stobs noch keine Kohlen zur Heizung der Wohnbaracken ausgegeben worden. Während des Aufenthaltes des Kriegsgefangenen Wigger im Lager Stobs, bis Anfang Mai 1918, ereignete sich folgender Vorfall: Nach einem Fluchtversuch dreier Gefangener wurde vom Lagerkommandanten als Strafmaßregel folgender Befehl erlassen:

Der Verkauf von Blutwurst wird gänzlich aufgehoben. Theater und Konzerte Müssen auf 6 Wochen unterbleiben. Das Betreten der neutralen Zone des Gefangenenlagers genügt, um ohne Anruf und dergleichen niedergeschossen zu werden. Wegen dieser Fälle von harter Bestrafung, Mißhandlung durch englische Unteroffiziere, Unterdrückung von Beschwerdebriefen an die Schutzmacht und Verhängung von Sammelstrafen, wurde von der englischen Regierung mit tunlichster Beschleunigung Abstellung dieser Mängel gefordert.

STOCKTON (see Codford St Mary).

STOCKTON (see Rugby).

STOKE EDITH (OS: SO 60- 40-). An agricultural group, its POWIB (1919) code was Shrw (Lmr) (S E) (IWM: Facsimile K4655) making it a satellite of Leominster.

Its address is cited as 42 West Street, Leominster by that organisation. There is also an entry for it made by the FPHS (1973). Its TA was Priswarian: Stoke Edith, Tarrington (ADM 1/8506/265–120667). These entries are the only evidence that this camp existed. However, Stoke Edith Park, built by Paul Foley, *c.*1696, may hold the key to this camp's location.

STOKE GREEN: Stoke House, Wexham (OS: SU 987 824). An agricultural group, it was attached to Denham Lodge AD. Its POWIB (1919) code was Fe (D L) (S G) (IWM: Facsimile K4655). A HO document cites its TA as Priswarian: Wexham (ADM 1/8506/265–120667). The FPHS (1973) cite both Stoke Green and Stoke House in their listings. Stoke House stands at the corner of Grays Park Road and Stoke Green. Built in 1821 of yellow brick, it has tripartite windows and a veranda along the front.

STONE (OS: SJ 903 339). Attached to agricultural depot at Ashbourne, the camp's code was Bro (Ash) (St) (IWM: Facsimile K4655). A HO document cites the camp was in the town's High Street. Its TA was Priswarian: Mill Factory, High Street, Stone (ADM 1/8506/265–120667). It is also cited by the FPHS (1973).

STONELY GRANGE (OS: n/a). The listings of the FPHS (1973) spell it Stoneley Grange. A possible location is Stoneley Green, but no evidence of a camp can be traced there. Stoneley Wood in South Yorkshire is situated 5 miles in either direction from Norton and Eckington, both cited as having camps. Stoneleigh is near to Deddington. The last possible location is Stonely Grange, near to Kimbolton Castle. Stonely Grange an impressive Grade II Listed building that has been converted into ten self-contained flats. It stands in grounds of around 11 acres. There is a Coach House at the approach to the Grange.

STONEY STRATFORD (see Yardley Gobion).

STOPSLEY (OS: TL 10- 23-). Only the name of Private G. Price is recorded on an extract taken from the PoWs employment time sheets of November 1918, for Stopsley. The sheets are held by Bedfordshire County Record Office (WW1/AC/PW/1 & 2). The camp's location is not known.

STORRINGTON (OS: TQ 101 139). Sandgate was a large estate; the house stood north of the main thoroughfare. It became a working camp, its POWIB (1919) code was Pa (San) (IWM: Facsimile K4655). Sandgate was cited by the FPHS (1973). Its TA was Priswarian: Sandgate, Storrington, Pulborough (ADM 1/8506/265–120667).

During WWI, the pine trees on the Sandgate Estate and Heath Common were felled and sent to France to be used as pit and trench props.

The house was demolished after the Second World War and the sand on which it stood is being extracted for the building industry. Quarrying is still done today.

STOULTON (OS: SO 90- 49-). *The Worcester Evening News* (7 November 1998) carried the following headline: Austrian Prisoners Who Were Held Near Norton Barracks. It gave an account of Ted Clissold's childhood. Ted was 96 years young when he stated:

> It [the camp] was on farmland immediately east of today's M5 Whittington junction, and housed scores of Austrian PoWs, who were guarded by soldiers from the nearby Norton Barracks.

Exaggerations of the Austrians being well fed, and living a life of luxury, were dispelled when Clissold witnessed them cooking great chunks of fat, outside, in large boilers, the result to be consumed with dark coloured bread. Their huts were Spartan. Some of the internees worked, under guard, on the farm of Mr Deakin of Stoulton (later to become Smedley's) earning 3d a day. A few PoWs, caught trying to roast a few potatoes, were punished and were banned from his farm, thus depriving them of their 1s.6d (7.5p) per week. He believes sixteen Austrians who died in the flu pandemic were buried at Norton.

Stoulton is cited by the FPHS (1973) and was an agricultural group attached to Pershore. Its POWIB (1919) code was Dor (Per) (Sn) (IWM: Facsimile K4655).

STOW PARK: Marton (OS: SK 886 810). An agricultural group attached to Bracebridge AD was based here. Its POWIB (1919) code was Bro (Bbe) (St P) (IWM: Facsimile K4655). It is recorded as Stow Park, Lincs. by the FPHS (1973). It had the TA, Priswarian: Stow Park, Morton (sic), Bourne, Lincs. (ADM 1/8506/265–120667).

STOWELL (OS: ST 68- 22-). An agricultural group, its POWIB code was Dor (Gil) (Sto). Its TA was Priswarian: Stowell, Templecombe (ADM 1/8506/265–120667). It is also cited by the FPHS (1973). During March and April 1919, Dr A. de Sturler and Monsieur R. de Sturler inspected Stowell. Their findings are at the National Archives at Kew (FO 383/506). Attached to Gillingham, the location of the camp remains a mystery.

STRATFORD ST MARY (OS: TM 04- 34-). Cited by the HO, its TA was Priswarian: Stratford St Mary (ADM 1/8506/265–120667). Stratford St Mary was inspected by Dr A. de Sturler and Monsieur R. de Sturler during April and May 1919. Their findings are held at the National Archives, at Kew (FO 383/507).

STRATFORD UPON AVON (see Shottery).

STRATHORD: nr Luncarty (OS: NO 09- 29-). Cited by the HO, its TA was Priswarian: Strathord (ADM 1/8506/265–120667).

Near Loak stood an elegant house, with a large estate, which belonged to Lord Nairne, whose wife is known for her love of Scottish music. As Jacobean sympathisers, their lands were confiscated and bought by the Duke of Atholl. The house has since been demolished, but its ruins could still be seen in 1945. Perhaps this estate may hold the key to the location of the PoW camp.

STURMINSTER NEWTON (OS: ST 78- 14-). One of the many camps that have disappeared from history, with nothing recorded about it, but it is cited by the FPHS (1973). One possible candidate for the site of this camp may be the town's former mill. There is proof that such places were used at other locations. In 1904, a state-of-the-art water turbine was installed to provide power to grinding machinery. Standing on the south side of the town, today the mill has been transformed into a museum.

SUDBURY (OS: SK 160 320). In contrast to the FPHS (1973), which cites this camp was in Suffolk, there is primary evidence to support the POWIB (1919) claim that this camp was in Derbyshire. The latter cites it as a satellite of Burton upon Trent and gave it the code Bro (Brt) (Sb) (IWM: Facsimile K4655). Also a HO document cites its TA as Priswarian: Sudbury, Derbyshire (ADM 1/8506/265–120667).

Minutes of the Ilkeston District of the Derbyshire WAC state in 1918 there was a shortage of labour to cultivate Sudbury Park. This problem could have been remedied by the introduction of PoWs, as *The Derby Daily Telegraph* (10 July 1918) cites Sudbury as one of places in the county being made ready to accommodate PoWs.

During March 1919, Dr A. de Sturler inspected the camp at Sudbury in Derbyshire. His findings are held at the National Archives at Kew (FO 383/506).

A HO document cites the camp was at the former Nestlé Cheese Factory situated near to The Boar's Head. Today it is the site of a residential home.

SUMMERFIELD (OS: TF 446 385). An obituary to a local solicitor is the only evidence there was a PoW camp at Summerfield. Carried by *The Lynn News* of 16 February 1922, part of it read:

> In the Great War, Mr Beloe was in command of a detachment of the National Reserve Guard, which was quartered in St. James's Hall, Lynn. Subsequently he was transferred to Hunstanton, and during the last two years of the war he was Commandant of the Prisoner-of-war camps at Burnham Market, Houghton, Snettisham, Summerfield, and elsewhere.

SUNDON PARK (OS: TL 054 254). Only the names of the guard that went to Sundon between November 1918 and October 1919 were recorded in an extract taken from the PoWs' employment time sheets employed there, held at the Bedfordshire County Record Office (WW1/AC/PW/1 &2).

SUTTON BONINGTON (see Kegworth).

SUTTON BRIDGE (see Wingland).

SUTTON SCARSDALE (OS: SK 441 689). Listed with others, Sutton Scarsdale was cited as awaiting the arrival of PoWs to work on the land, according to *The Derby Daily Telegraph* (10 July 1918). The most obvious place to hold them would have been at Sutton Scarsdale Hall, which is described as being a two-storey building, standing in some 5,090 acres of land, and was built 1724 by Francis Smith of Warwick for the 4th Earl of Scarsdale, around the core of an earlier house. The Hall then had several owners before, in 1919, it was abandoned. When bought by a speculator, the roof was stripped of its lead, which accelerated the hall's demise. In the 1950s, Sir Osbert Sitwell bought the ruinous Hall, before passing it on to the Department of the Environment, in 1969. The building has undergone a programme of refurbishment, but, while still magnificent, it remains a ruin.

There is no primary evidence to suggest any PoWs were at the Hall, or its grounds, but a minute of the Derbyshire WAC (21 December 1918) expressed concerns about not completing the harvest in proper time, mainly due to the weather and the shortage of skilled men. The minute concluded that thirty German prisoners, in five gangs, were following threshers in the Chesterfield area (D331/1/27).

SUTTON VENY: Longbridge Deverill (OS: ST 898 427). Sutton Veny and Longbridge Deverill are cited separately by the FPHS (1973). The POWIB (1919) cites Dor (Su V) (IWM: Facsimile K4655) as the code for a working camp at Sutton Veny. The camp's TA was Priswarian: Longbridge Deverill (ADM 1/8506/265–120667). A report of the inspections of the working camps at Dunmow and Sutton Veny are held at the National Archives at Kew (FO 383/432).

Crawford (*Wiltshire and The Great War: Training the Empire's Soldiers*, 1999) cites the camp was split into hutments, numbered 1 to 10, that had opened by November 1914. He cites the first to be interned were civilians and they included some from Ireland. They were accommodated in some of the first huts to be built at Sutton Veny, near Cooper's Bottom. A HO document confirms those interned initially were civilians.

The lines that held the PoWs were numbered 11 to 14 and were set out like a typical army camp, with wooden hutments. Sometimes these lines were referred to as Sand Hill and must not be confused with Sandhill Park, Taunton. The internees worked in the nearby farms.

The Sutton Veny site was used briefly to house Australian troopers awaiting repatriation before it was dismantled. The camp closed on 15 September 1918. The hutments on the Sand Hill site were amongst the first to be demolished when the war was over.

DKF 30: In den Lagern von Rosyth, Eastgate, Uppingham, Belton Park, Tern Hill, Bee Craigs, Hadnall, Sutton Veny, Larkhill, Fovant, Withley (sic) *und Radford sind die Kriegsgefangenen in Zelten untergebracht.*

DKF 31: Auch in Loch Doon, auf der Insel Raasay, in Newlandside, Ceal Aston (sic) *Sutton Veney* (sic), *Bowithick, Netheravon, Yatesbury, Rovrah* (sic), *Port Clarence und Hayrmyres* (sic) *werden die Leute zu sehr ausgenutzt.*

DKF 31: In Joice Green (sic), *Dartford, Linton, Sutton Veney* (sic) *Fovant, und Evesham bestehen Keine Kantine. Die Ausführung der Bestellungen der Kriegsgefangenen durch den Profoß Sergeanten, kann nicht als genügender Ersatz betrachtet werden.*

DKF 32: In Sutton Veney (sic) *sind die Gefangenen so in Anspruch genommen, daß ihnen zur Erholung und für eigene Tätigkeit keine Zeit bleibt.*

DKF 32: Gottesdienst: Die Seelsorge der Kreigsgefangenen ist auf vielen Plätzen sehr vernachlässigt. In den Lagern von Joyce Green, Dartford; Hadnall; Peak Dale Quarries bei Buxton; Sutton Veny; Larkhill; Netheravon; Codford; und Fovant hat noch kein Gottesdienst stattgefunden.

DKF 34: In Fovant, Sutton Veney (sic) *und Larkhill sind trotz früheren Protestes keine Verbesserungen erfolgt.*

SWAFFHAM (OS: TF 815 094). The WAC for Norfolk resolved to inform the Local Government Board that accommodation at Swaffham could be provided to carry out drainage work on the River Wensum in a minute of 27 January 1917 (C/C10/15). It is not known if the local workhouse was used to accommodate those interned at Swaffham, or perhaps if Swaffham Priory was the preferred location.

SWANAGE (OS: SZ 02- 78-). A working camp, it had the POWIB (1919) code Dor (Sw) (IWM: Facsimile K4655). The camp's TA was, Priswarian: Swanage (ADM 1/8506/265–120667). The site of the camp remains a mystery.

SWANSEA (OS: SS 656 929). *The Western Morning News* (11 August 1914) cited there were eighty-five internees being held in Swansea, under guard at Lutland (sic) Street School, pending the formation of a proper camp. The school was in Rutland Street and, as part of a new urban regeneration programme, has been demolished. *The Yorkshire Herald* (12 August 1914) confirmed eighty-five internees were being held in Swansea.

SWAVESEY (OS: TL 365 684). Wood (*Childhood recollections from Swavesey 1914–1918*, n.d.) reckoned the war made little impact on him. As a child it was part of his everyday life:

> Everyday, after school we saw a batch of German prisoners of war marching back past the school up High Street. Peter Ding the roadman walked behind them with a rifle carried, most unprofessionally, over his shoulder. It never occurred to us to enquire where they were billeted – they were just part of the everyday Swavesey scene. I can remember they wore grey uniforms. In later years I was told that they were employed to maintain the ditches and drainage channels. Peter Ding said they were a docile lot, but worked well, and were not particularly well supplied with rations. During their midday break they made a fire and brewed up soup from turnips and swedes, many old wurtzels, kohlrabi and rose hips that they scrounged. Had they decided to try and escape it would have been child's play as Peter Ding had never handled a rifle in his life and knew nothing whatsoever about it!

A house at Swavesey belonging to Mr Wells of Newport, Essex was cited as being suitable to accommodate PoWs according to the minutes of the Cambridgeshire WAC (27 May 1918). The electoral register cited James Wells was a local coal merchant, who resided at Church End, Swavesey, in the years leading up to the war.

T

TADCASTER: Workhouse (OS: SE 479 430). Tadcaster agricultural group was attached to Wetherby agricultural depot. Its POWIB (1919) code was Cat (Wet) (Td) (IWM: Facsimile K4655). Its TA was Priswarian: The Workhouse, Tadcaster (ADM 1/8506/265–120667).

The Tadcaster Union workhouse opened in 1872 on a site to the west of Tadcaster, at the south side of Station Road. The PoWs stayed in wooden huts erected for this purpose that were still in evidence in the 1960s, having housed Lithuanian refuges at the end of the Second World War.

In 1930, the workhouse came under the control of West Riding County Council and was known as The Beeches. It did not join the National Health Service in 1948. The buildings were demolished in 1987, and replaced with a modern building that can be entered from Leeds Road belonging to North Yorkshire County Council.

Larder (*Tadcaster (Bramham Moor) Airfield 1916–1919*, Liddle, 1997) cites there was an airfield at Bramham Moor (OS SE 425 434) that opened in 1916, which had the primary function of protecting Sheffield and Leeds from Zeppelin attack. Surplus to requirements, the airfield was closed in 1919. At its height there were five hangars, but today only one remains: erected in 1917, it was manufactured by D. Anderson & Company. The University of Leeds now owns the site. What connection, if any, the PoW camp had to the airfield has not been established.

TALGARTH: Tregunter Park (OS: SO 134 339). The POWIB (1919) cites Fregunter Park (sic) in Talgarth as being a satellite of Brecon and provides Fg (Bre) (Tal) as its code (IWM: Facsimile K4655). There is local knowledge of PoWs working on farms. It is believed that the PoWs were quartered in Tregunter House, which was demolished in the early 1920s. There is a report on his visit of inspection to Talgarth by Dr A. de Sturler and Monsieur R. de Sturler, during March and April

1919 held at the National Archives at Kew (FO 383/506). The FPHS (1973) has an entry for Talgarth. Its TA was Priswarian: Talgarth (ADM 1/8506/265–120667).

TAUNTON: Sandhill Park (see Sandhill Park).

TAUNTON WORKHOUSE (OS: ST 228 250). Lt-Colonel Boles, the Member of Parliament for Somerset West asked the House if PoWs could be sent, for agricultural purposes, to the Taunton area, to replace the officers that had moved out of Sandhill Park as reported in the *Somerset County Gazette*, *Somerset County Herald*, *The Taunton Courier*, and the *Wellington Weekly News* (all 4 May 1918). In his reply on 7 May 1918, James Macpherson, the Under Secretary of State for War stated that the officers had been sent to Margate, Ramsgate, or Southend.

Minutes of the Somerset County Council WAC (20 & 23 August 1918) cite they had received a letter from the Food Production Department stating that it had been decided to re-open Sandhill Park for officers, again. This time the house was used to intern Austrian and Hungarian officers. The Committee's Executive Officer was instructed to see that the Prisoner Ploughman Depot was not closed before suitable alternative premises could be located. This is the first reference to men rather than officers and their servants being at Sandhill Park. A later minute (13 September 1918) cites there were fifty-five PoWs living at Sandhill Park under canvas.

According to Mark (*Prisoners of war in the British Hands During WW1*, 2007) they were eventually transferred to the workhouse in Taunton. The former workhouse stood on Union Street, which has been re-named Trinity Road. All that remains of the 1838-built structure is the entrance hall which now has residential usage. It was built by Sampson Kempthorpe to his hexagonal shape plan.

TEMPLE BRUER (OS: SP 99- 54-). Quoted as Temple Brener (sic) by the POWIB (1919), it is listed as an agricultural group, attached to Grantham. Its code, Bro (Gr) (Tm), reflects this. Its TA was Priswarian: Temple Bruer, Navenby, Lincs. (ADM 1/8506/265–120667).

Situated in a remote area of Lincolnshire, Temple Farm and its smithy stand amongst the ruins of a former settlement that comprised of at least a church and a preceptory. With the passing of the Knights Templar their property passed into the hands of the Hospitallers, under whose charge the preceptory at Bruer seems to have fallen into disrepair. When Henry VIII also disbanded the Hospitallers he sold Temple Bruer to the Duke of Suffolk. In 1541 the Duke entertained Henry at the preceptory even though the site had by this time become quite dilapidated and tents had to be erected to house all of the entourage. In 1540 the valuation mentioned a farm site, and the preceptory, with orchards, gardens and houses, a rabbit warren, 2,000 acres of sheep ground and a windmill. The property remained as a block until 1935 when it was split up and sold by Lord Lonsborough.

PoWs sent to this area would most probably been engaged in agricultural activities. They could however have been utilised at HMS *Daedalus*, built as an airship base for the Royal Naval Air Service. It was taken over by the RAF, on 5 February 1918, as an officer cadet-training centre and its name was altered to RAF Cranwell to reflect this. During the First World War, RAF Cranwell had emergency landing strips at Temple Bruer and at Griffin Farm (www.RAF-Lincolnshire.info).

TEMPLEMORE: Richmond Barracks (IGR: S 115 715). Walsh (*A History of Templemore and its Environs*, 1991) cites the army barracks at Templemore took ten years to build, and were completed in 1810. They were then the third largest barracks in Ireland, comprising of some 1,500 men (around two battalions at peace-time strength), with accommodation for fifty-four officers, plus married quarters. The buildings formed 'two squares'. At the outbreak of war the 'two squares' were made into four compounds with barbed wire fences, guard platforms, searchlights, etc. Shelters were built in the open compounds for the expected prisoners.

The Times (23 September 1914) reported that 400 internees were to be transferred from mainland Britain to 'a military barracks in the centre of Ireland'. The next edition (24 September 1914) expanded on this by saying the internees were moved to Tipperary from Frith Hill. The *Camberley News* reported that a couple of hundred of the Kaiser's soldiers had been removed by a special train bound for Ireland. It was understood they were to be incarcerated separately from civilian internees held there.

A report emanating out of Germany (20 January 1915) cites there was a 'concentration' camp at Templemore. Some of the PoWs had come from Newbury (CAB 37/123/37). O'Mathuna (*German PoW Mail between Templemore and Germany 1914 and 1915*, 1997) believes there could have been up to 2,000 PoWs in the Richmond Barracks by the end of 1914. When it was decided to transfer them to England, there were 1,500 PoWs detained at the Richmond Barracks.

The official reason the camp was closed was the poor state of the sanitation. It failed to meet the standards that were prescribed in the 1907 Second Hague Peace Conference under the Articles for the Welfare of PoWs. They were transferred out, in batches of 360–400 prisoners at a time, via Dublin and Holyhead, to Lilworth Mill, in Leigh. Both *The Leigh Chronicle* and *The Leigh Journal* carried reports of prisoners arriving from Templemore. According to the former, the first batch to arrive at Leigh, on 5 February 1915, comprised of 360 prisoners, under the escort of Captain Alexander, and fifty men seconded from the Leinster Regiment. The last batch to arrive at Leigh from Templemore Barracks was on 19 February 1915. During January and February 1915, 1,855 PoWs were moved in five batches from Templemore to Leigh, Lancs. On 26 February 1915 it was stated that the barracks at Templemore were now entirely free of German prisoners. In John Jackson's report of visits to camps in February 1915, he stated he did not go to the camp at Templemore because he had been officially informed that the camp had closed.

Despite the camp being declared unfit for use as a PoW camp – according to Walsh (1991) – on 6 March 1915, the Royal Munster Fusiliers arrived and the place became a regular training facility.

The Leigh Chronicle (9 April 1915) cited Major George Goulbourn Tarry left Templemore, to take up the position of commandant at Leigh. After the war the Northampton Regiment were stationed at Templemore. They marched out on 13 February 1922, as the Provisional Irish Government took over the premises. The Irish Army then used the barracks until 1929. During the Second World War the barracks became operational again, and today it is a training centre for the Gardai.

The German War Graves Commission (Volksbund Deutsche Kriegsgräberfürsorge) were able to confirm that the remains of M. Anton Gierszewski (d. 20 November 1914) and Ludwig Spellerburg (d. 21 February 1915) were transferred, from different graveyards in Templemore, to the German War Grave Cemetery at Glencree, in the 1960s.

TEMPSFORD. The village was recorded as being Taemesford in 921; the name is believed to have derived from the fact that the village stands on the River Thames.

There are separate work sheets for Tempsford and Tempsford Hall, held by the Bedfordshire Record Office (WW1/AC/PW/1 & 2). Many of the names of the PoWs were the same for both locations, recorded between June 1919 and October 1919. Accounts for monies paid, the most likely reason for the separate sheets, were issued for both locations.

The POWIB (1919) cited one code, for a working camp, Pa (Tpf). It had the TA Priswarian: Tempsford (ADM 1/8506/265–120667). The entry produced for the FPHS (1973) cites Tempsford.

TEMPSFORD (OS: TL 165 535) and TEMPSFORD HALL (OS: TL 165 535). In 1965, the Tempsford Hall was bought as the new corporate headquarters of J.L. Keir and Co. Ltd. Repaired and redecorated with a four-storey extension added, their corporate headquarters opened in 1967. The former hall was completely gutted when it burnt down in 1896. Its replacement took over three years to rebuild.

Between the wars it had become a private nursing home, and in the Second World War the hall was used to accommodate, and brief, members of the Moon Squadron, the men and women of the Special Operations Executive who were dropped clandestinely by parachute behind enemy lines. For a time after the war, the hall had been a health farm.

TENBURY WELLS: Rochford House (OS: SO 629 684). Rochford House is described as a working camp; its POWIB (1919) code was Dor (Rhd) (IWM: Facsimile K4655). The camp's TA was Priswarian: Rochford, Tenbury Wells (ADM 1/8506/265–120667). The FPHS (1973) cited two entries for Rochford: one in Gloucestershire and one in Essex.

According to the *Tenbury Advertiser* (19 January 1918), Rochford House was on the outskirts of Tenbury Wells. It had been prepared to receive fifty PoWs, from Dorchester, in the first weeks of 1918. The PoWs were expected to work for the local farmers at a rate of 4d per hour. They were also to work on an old road, which is still known today as German Way.

Derby Daily Telegraph (17 September 1918) cited Emil Grus had drowned whilst a party of internees were crossing the River Teme, according to his fellow internees, the previous day. Two others in the boat with him survived. The incident happened near to the Peacock public house, and Scotland Yard had been informed. After several days when his body had not been recovered, his description was released to the press, just in case he was attempting to escape. The *Tenbury Advertiser* (28 December 1918) carried a report from the coroner, G.F.S. Brown, stating that Grus 'accidentally drowned by the capsizing of a boat whilst crossing the River Teme'. Grus's body had been recovered a week earlier at the confluence of the Teme and the Severn, at Powick, some 20 miles down river from Tenbury Wells. Another account states a German PoW drowned when he was returning from work on a farm, on Clee Hill, to his sleeping quarters in a barn near Tenbury Wells. He had tried to take a short cut across the River Teme, at Burford. A photo exists, taken *c.*1918, of Grus with eighteen of his fellow internees posing with two members of the guard.

Miller (per. comm., 26 January 2001) suggested deploying internees at Tenbury was difficult, as some of the local farmers were accused of showing too much leniency towards them. As familiarity grew, some farmers were found to be giving the PoWs leased to them extra food, drinks and tobacco. They were informed that any departure from the conditions laid down could result in them being barred from hiring any other PoW labour. It is known at least two internees worked at Church Farm.

On 1 November 1919, the *Tenbury Advertiser* reported on the departure of the internees from Rochford House. Numbering around forty, they sang as they turned into Teme Street on their way to board a train for Dorchester. The paper also commented on how well they looked in their smart uniforms, unlike our men that had returned from the Fatherland. The article concluded:

> So far as we could gather the men have appreciated their generous treatment and comparative liberty extended to them, and the farmers on whose land they have worked, have on the whole, been quite satisfied with them.

The house is still standing today, but has been converted into flats.

TENDRING (OS: TM 14- 24-). A working camp, its POWIB (1919) code was Pa (Ten) (IWM: Facsimile K4655). It is also cited by the FPHS (1973). It had the TA Priswarian: Tendring, Weeley, Essex (ADM 1/8506/265–120667). The location of the camp remains a mystery. Tendring was inspected by Dr A. de Sturler and Monsieur R. de Sturler, during April and May 1919. Their findings are held at the National Archives at Kew (FO 383/507).

TENTERDEN (OS: TQ 906 322). This was a working camp; its POWIB (1919) code was Pa (Tet) (IWM: Facsimile K4655). It had the TA Priswarian: Tenterden (ADM 1/8506/265–120667). It was also cited by the FPHS (1973). The location of the camp remains a mystery, but Kench Hill House, which is thought to have lain empty during the First World War, could perhaps be the key.

TERN HILL (see Wem).

THETFORD (see Warren Wood).

THING HILL HALL (OS: SO 568 449). The entry for the POWIB (1919) describes it as satellite of Leominster, giving its code as Shrw (Lmr) (Tn) (IWM: Facsimile K4655), and its administration address as 42 West Street, Leominster. The FPHS (1973) cites a camp at Thinghill (sic). The TA stated in the HO documents was Priswarian: Thing Hall, Withington, Herefords. (ADM 1/8506/265–120667).

Kelly's Trade Directory (1913) states Thing Hill Hall was the residence of William F. Abbott. It was a large mansion standing in tastefully laid out grounds of about 60 acres, and commanding extensive views of the surrounding country.

THIRSK (OS: SE 435 823). Thirsk agricultural depot had the POWIB (1919) directory code Cat (Th) (IWM: Facsimile K4655). It had the TA Priswarian: Thirsk (ADM 1/8506/265–120667). The camp was also listed by the FPHS (1973).

The camp was located in Thirsk Union Workhouse which had opened in 1839 on Long Street. After 1930, the building was inherited by the North Riding County Council but stayed empty until it was pressed into military and first-aid use during the Second World War (www.imagesofengland.org.uk). The site was later used as a poultry rearing installation. In 1998 the infirmary was demolished and the surviving main block was converted to residential use.

THORNBURY (OS: ST 632 889). A working camp, its POWIB (1919) code was Dor (Thn) (IWM: Facsimile K4655). It had the TA Priswarian: Thornbury, Bristol. It was also listed by the FPHS (1973).

The Durlsey Gazette (Thornbury Edition, 18 May 1918) cites that some of the forty-two German PoWs billeted at Marlwood Grange were unwell. There was one case of scarlet fever reported, and eight of measles, but none were deemed a cause for alarm. A second report (22 June 1918) referred to articles produced in *The Times* and the *Mirror* by Dr L.M. Williams expressing his concerns that the PoWs were being provided better food than the taxpayers who were paying for the war.

It was cited in *The Times* (15 July 1918) that a PoW named Henneck had been re-captured after escaping from the camp at Thornbury.

THORNTON-LE-MOORS (OS: SJ 446 767). The camp had the TA Priswarian: Thornton-le-Moors, Ince, Cheshire (ADM 1/8506/265–120667), and is cited by the FPHS (1973).

According to correspondence between Mrs Park-Yates of Ince House and her land agent, Mr Linaker, it was envisaged by the military that an intended camp was to be put in a field at Lee's Farm. The site chosen was the bottom field on the right hand side of the road going down to Holme House before you pass the little meadow adjoining the bridge. This was not far from Thornton Mill. There was doubt concerning the selection of the field, and the land agent had entered into correspondence with the military about its suitability. Linaker wrote to Mrs Park-Yates on the 16 August 1918 (DD/GR/388):

> ... I do not think they [the authorities] could have chosen a worse site for the men, as after operating on the lower area of the Gowy Drainage District, they will have many miles to tramp night and morning, and where there are no roads.

Reports on visits of inspection to PoW camps exist. They are held at the National Archives at Kew. Thornton le Moor was inspected by Dr A. de Sturler and Monsieur R. de Sturler during June 1919 (FO 383/508).

THORPE SATCHVILLE (OS: SK 73- 11-). The POWIB (1919) cites it as an agricultural group attached to Croxton Park AD. Its code was Bro (Crx) (Tv) (IWM: Facsimile K4655). Identified as agricultural group No. 113, it had the TA Priswarian: Thorpe Satchville (ADM 1/8506/265–120667).

Thorpe Satchville Hall, a possible site for the camp, was owned by John Otho Paget but occupied by John Shields Crawford, according to *Kelly's Trade Directory* (Leicestershire: 1912).

THURLASTON (see Normanton Hall).

THORLOXTON (OS: ST 27- 30-). Minutes of the Somerset WAC show fifty-five PoWs were transferred from Sandhill Park to Dulverton, Bridgwater, Thorloxton, Kingston Seymour and Clavelshay in equal numbers. Five remained at Sandhill Park, and were being billeted in cottages on the estate.

TILSHEAD (OS: SU 067 472). Crawford (*Wiltshire and The Great War: Training the Empire's Soldiers*, 1999) cites the *Andover Advertiser*'s description of an area east of Tilshead as being one of the first sites to be purchased, in 1897, for military usage. There were two camps set up in the area, known as West Down North (OS: SU 063 494) and West Down South (OS: SU 063 481).

In 1916, an outstation of Number One Balloon School at Rollestone was established nearby. Balloons were flown from sites in the area, with equipment being stored close to the last house on the road from Tilshead to West Down camp. Two balloons were normally kept there and were sometimes moved through the village to the flying areas, with men desperately hanging on to the guy ropes. German prisoners are said to have helped with the maintenance.

The site was relatively isolated, and was accessed by a military road that ran from the Bustard Inn, past Greenlands Farm (OS: SU 067 472) and the West Down South camp.

TIMBERLAND (OS: TF 12- 58-). Cited as an agricultural group, and a satellite of the camp at Grantham, its address was recorded by the POWIB as being in The Maltings, and its code was Bro (Gr) (Tb) (IWM: Facsimile K4655).

Ordnance Survey maps for 1956 show the Malthouse standing between the Cottage and the White House, on Martin Road. It is not marked on later maps.

TIVERTON (OS: SS 957 131). This was an agricultural group attached to Dulverton AD; its POWIB (1919) code was Dor (Dlv) (Ti) (IWM: Facsimile K4655). It is also cited by the FPHS (1973). The HO issued the TA Priswarian: Tiverton (ADM 1/8506/265–120667). The same directory stated its postal address was Tiverton, Parkside. Currently, Parkside is the name of a nursing home at 8 Park Road.

The Western Times (17 January 1917) reported approval had been sought for the use of Tiverton's workhouse to billet PoWs, but this was rejected according to a later report.

The Exeter & Plymouth Gazette (14 May 1917) reported the death of Henry Sullivan Thomas FLS of Parkside, and then reported that the property had been sold at auction on 5 April 1917.

A newspaper clipping, dated 23 August 1917, held by the local library service, states the PoWs were working on farms (1262M/0/O/LD/112/80).

The Western Times (27 June 1919) cited Carl Tropgen, a German PoW, was fined £1, at Tiverton, for stealing potatoes.

TOCKWITH (OS: SE 465 526). Tockwith AG had the POWIB (1919) directory code Cat (P B) (Tok) (IWM: Facsimile K4655). It was a satellite of Pateley Bridge. The camp was situated in Brogden Old Brewery; it had the TA Priswarian: Brogden Old Brewery, Tockwith (ADM 1/8506/265–120667).

There was an airfield at Tockwith (Marston Moor), built around the time of the First World War, which may have some bearing on why this camp was set up, as PoW labour was often used in the construction of early airfield infrastructure.

TODDINGTON (OS: SP 03- 32-). The entry for Toddington describes it as a working camp, citing its POWIB (1919) code as Dor (To) (IWM: Facsimile K4655), but it is also described as having an agricultural group, Winchcombe, attached to it. The camp had the TA Priswarian: Toddington, Winchcombe (ADM 1/8506/265–120667).

Parish Burial Records (P335 IN 1/7) show four PoWs were buried at Toddington Church graveyard, in 1918. Although not proven, this camp may have been located at, or near to Toddington Manor. Wherever it was, the internees complained about vermin getting into their meagre food rations. The PoWs admitted they stole fruit and potatoes to augment their diet, despite being punished if they were caught. Many of the internees claimed that they were not fit for the work demanded of them, and requests to see the doctors at Dorchester were continually being refused. Fuel for heating was also in short supply, lasting only three days a week during the winter months. There were also claims that the camp was badly lit.

According to records, twenty-nine PoWs were billeted at Toddington. The camp's commandant was cited as Lieutenant G. Yelf.

DKF 35: Nach Aussagen des in de Scheeg bei Dieren (Holland) internierten Unteroffiziers Hugo Göbel herrschen im Arbeitslager Taddington (sic) *(Gloucester) schwere Mißstände. Es gibt im Lager außerordentlich viel Ratten und Mäuse. Es ist oft vorgekommen, daß in den Lebensmittelvorräten des Lagers, besonders in den Zwiebacksäcken, ganze Nester junger Ratten und Mäuse gefunden wurden. Auf Vorstellung der Gefangenen bei dem Lagerkommandanten erwiderte derselbe, daß dies ein Zeichen dafür sei, daß die Gefangenen genug zu essen bekämen, denn sonst würde für die Ratten und Mäuse nichts übrig bleiben. Dabei leiden die Gefangenen unter sehr knapper Verpflegung. Als sich einige Gefangene genötigt sahen, von ihren landwirtschaftlichen Arbeiten Kartoffeln und Obst mit ins Lager zu nehmen, wurden dieselben von Kommandanten mit drei Tagen bis zu vier Wochen Arrest bestraft. Die Beleuchtung in den Unterkunftsräumen ist sehr minderwertig. Das erforderliche Material wurde in so geringem Umfange geliefert, daß die Gefangenen in den Wintermonaten nur für drei Tage der Woche Licht hatten, während sie an den übrigen Abenden im Dunkeln sitzen mußten. In diesem Lager waren auch einige Gefangenen untergebracht, die keineswegs zu körperlicher Arbeit fähig waren. Die Bitte dieser Leute, den Schweizer Ärzten vorgestellt zu werden, wurde mit dem Hinweis darauf abgelehnt, daß sie aus dem Lager Dorchester als arbeits fähig dem Kommando überwiesen worden seien. In allen diesen Fällen wurde durch Vermittlung der Schweizerischen Gesandtschaft in London auf Abstellung dieser Mißstande hingewirkt und besonders wiederholt nachdrücklichst Verwahrung gegen die dauernde Unterbringung deutscher Gefangener in Zelten eingelegt.*

TONBRIDGE (OS: TQ 593 486). Leeds University's Brotherton Library has a photograph of PoWs billeted at The Priory, Bordyke, Tonbridge. A paperknife made by a PoW billeted there is part of their collection.

Green (*Tonbridge: A Pictorial History*) states The Priory was originally called Chauntlers. It was built in the eighteenth century. Although the building was never a real priory, it has been home to several well-known locals, among them Thomas Weller and Eliza Acton. *Kelly's Trade Directory* (1915) cites Hugh Woods MD as the occupant of 10 Bordyke (The Priory).

Reports on visits of inspection to the PoW camps at Tonbridge, Marshmoor Sidings, and Hatfield in Hertfordshire by Monsieur de Corragioni d'Orelli, during March 1919 are held at the National Archives, London.

Tonbridge is cited by the FPHS (1973). It had the TA Priswarian: The Priory, Bordyke, Tonbridge (ADM 1/8506/265–120667).

TOTNES: Bridgetown Parish Rooms (OS: SX 809 603). Cited as being at the Bridgetown Parish Rooms, its TA was Priswarian: Bridgetown, Totnes (ADM 1/8506/265–120667). Nothing is known of this camp, that would have existed in the second phase of internment camps set up during the First World War.

TOVIL (OS: TQ 755 545). A working camp, its POWIB (1919) code was Pa (Tov) (IWM: Facsimile K4655). Cited as being at Tovil House, its TA was Priswarian: Tovil (ADM 1/8506/265–120667). The entry listed for this camp by the FPHS (1973) reads Tovil Wrotham. Nothing is known of this camp's history.

Tovil House stands near to where Burial Ground Lane meets Church Street.

TRAWSFYNYDD (Llanfrothen) (OS: SH 721 318). At the turn of the twentieth century, a small military base was established at Bryn Golau, on the southern outskirts of Trawsfynydd. In 1906, a larger, more permanent site was established further south, at Rhiw Goch. The new camp continued to grow, eventually being split, and they became known as North and South camps. The soldiers mainly came in the summer months and were accommodated in tents. Rhiw Goch House, a listed building, built *c.*1610, was used as the officers' mess. In 1911, a military railway station, adjacent to the existing one, was built. A new road to the camp was also built to ease the conveyance of guns, trucks, waggons, horses and personnel to the camp.

During the First World War the camp became a busy centre not just for accommodation for soldiers, but also as an artillery range for both the regular and territorial armies.

The German PoWs were billeted in Rhiw Goch House; its POWIB (1919) code was Fg (Trf) (IWM: Facsimile K4655). The camp's TA was Priswarian: Trawsfynydd (ADM 1/8506/265–120667).

When the military had no further use of the camp, *c.*1958, it was used to accommodate over 800 workers building Trawsfynydd power station. Tin Town, as it was known by the locals, closed in 1971 as a result of widening of the A470.

Police records (11 October 1918) show one Defitanske absconded from Llanfrothen, which is approximately 6.5 miles from Trawsfynydd. When apprehended he was taken to Penrhyndeudraeth Police Station early on the Saturday morning, where he was then handed over to a military escort. The same Cell Book recorded the arrest of Johann Slochold on 21 October 1918, on a charge of larceny from a hencoop. He was fined 15s (75p) and handed over to a military escort at 5.00pm the next day (ZH/13/1: 8596).

TRING (OS: SP 924 114). A Hertfordshire County Council WAC minute (20 March 1918) indicates the plans for Aldbury were being abandoned in favour of a gang to be based at Tring's Station Hotel.

Further minutes state forty PoWs were still awaiting suitable accommodation to be found in Tring on 8 May 1918, and another minute of 1 October 1918 states a migratory gang, consisting of ten PoWs based at Tring, had been wound up, as had gangs at Shenley and Ridge, due to the harvest being completed.

TRURO WORKHOUSE (OS: SW 839 456). *The Western Morning News* (21 August 1914) cited around 110 destitute aliens were landed at Falmouth, and were being held in the Truro Workhouse. Eight of them had sufficient money to travel, and left for London. The Jewish Society in London had been contacted to see if they could be of assistance to another eight or nine, as they were of that faith.

The Western Morning News (3 September 1914) reported that Austrians held at Truro Workhouse had been moved to Dorchester.

The Truro Union Workhouse was built in 1851 on what is now Tregolls Road. The building was designed by William Harris. The main accommodation block had a four storey round building in the centre. There was a separate hospital block. During the First World War Truro workhouse was converted for use as the 210 bed Truro Auxiliary Naval Hospital. It opened in November 1915 and closed in March 1919, after treating 4,000 patients. The workhouse later became St Clement's Hospital but has since been redeveloped for residential use (www.heritage-explorer.co.uk).

TUDDENHAM (see Mildenhall).

TURVEY (OS: SP 945 524). A working camp, it had the POWIB (1919) code Pa (Tur) (IWM: Facsimile K4655). The FPHS (1973) cite this camp too. Identified as being at Homelands, its TA was Priswarian: Turvey (ADM 1/8506/265–120667).

The names of thirty-five PoWs that worked at Turvey between March 1918 and March 1919, along with their guard, are recorded in an extract taken from the PoWs employment time sheets that are held by the Bedfordshire Record Office (WW1/AC/PW/1 & 2).

TUTNALL & COBLEY (OS: SO 98- 70-). A working camp with the POWIB (1919) code Dor (Tut) (IWM: Facsimile K4655). Its TA was Priswarian: Bromsgrove (ADM 1/8506/265–120667). The camp's exact location is unknown. There is an entry for Tutnall is cited in the list produced for the FPHS (1973).

TUXFORD (OS: SK 73- 71-). An agricultural group, it was a satellite to the depot at Kelham. Its POWIB (1919) code was Bro (Kel) (Tu) (IWM: Facsimile K4655), and Its TA was Priswarian: Tuxford (ADM 1/8506/265–120667). The FPHS (1973) also cite this camp. Although the location of the camp remains a mystery it was recorded for posterity in the minutes of the Notts County WAC.

TWYFORD: Knowl Hill (OS: SU 82- 79-). A working camp at Knowl Hill, Berkshire, it had the POWIB (1919) code Dor (Tw) (IWM: Facsimile K4655). Both Twyford and Knowl Hill are cited by the FPHS (1973). This camp's location has not been traced.

TYNEMOUTH: Whitley Bay (OS: NZ 35- 72-). The *Deutsche Kriegsgefangene in Feindesland* (1919) refers to a camp at Newkastle (sic). An insight into the camp's location can be gleaned from its entry that implies they worked in a dock area. In the post-1916 phase PoWs were used in labour gangs throughout the country outside of their places of internment. As there were restrictions put on the distance these men could travel to work, the camp must have been near the docks. The German report does not flatter the actual location, as it states that those interned there were often beaten for no apparent reason.

Tynemouth Union Workhouse, which stood in the dockland area, between Newcastle and Whitley Bay, could have been the location of the camp.

An article appeared in *The Times* (2 February 1917) reporting on the proposal, considered by the Newcastle City Council, that PoWs should be put to quarry working rather than working on roads. What the council resolved to do, remains unanswered.

Whitley Bay was inspected by Dr A. de Sturler and Monsieur R. de Sturler during June 1919. Their findings are held at the National Archives at Kew (FO 383/508). Whitley Bay is also cited by the FPHS (1973).

DKF 30: In Newkastle (sic), *wo nach den dem Kriegsministerium zugegangenen Nachrichten die Kriegsgefangenen mit Laden und Löschen von Dampfern beschäftigt wurden, war die Behandlung der Kreigsgefangenen sehr hart. Bei den geringsten Anlässen wurden sie rücksichtslos geschlagen.*

TYTHERINGTON (OS: ST 632 889). *The Gloucester County Gazette* (18 May 1918) cites around fifty 'aliens', mainly Austrians, were 'engaged in work of national importance' at Tytherington Stone Quarries. The same article cited there were forty-two PoWs at Marlwood Grange. It was reported that German PoWs did damage to the property.

In 2011, developers stated they were involved in 'an ambitious project' being undertaken to make this early Georgian listed building carbon neutral.

TYWYN: Neptune Hall (OS: SH 597 000). Today, Neptune Hall is incorporated into a caravan park, owned by B.R. and R.F. Tunnadine. When asked, the proprietors knew nothing of it being used as an internment camp in the First World War, but believed Italian PoWs might have been billeted there in the Second World War.

Stated by the POWIB (1919) as being at Towyn, this camp was an agricultural depot. It had the code Fg (Ty) (IWM: Facsimile K4655), and supported two satellites at Llanbedr and Machynlleth respectively. The camp's TA was Priswarian: Towyn (sic), Merioneth (ADM 1/8506/265–120667).

There is a report of a visit of inspection to the camps in North Wales. Towyn (sic) is cited in a document held at the National Archives at Kew as a place that received a visit by Dr A. de Sturler and Monsieur R. de Sturler during June 1919 (FO 383/508).

U

UCKFIELD: The Grange (OS: TQ 473 212). A working camp, its POWIB (1919) code was Pa (Uck) (IWM: Facsimile K4655). The camp is cited as being at The Grange, and it had the TA Priswarian: Uckfield (ADM 1/8506/265–120667). It was also cited by the FPHS (1973). Contemporary maps of the area do not show a grange at Uckfield, but there is a Grange Road on them.

UPAVON (OS: SU 157 550). Described as a working camp by the POWIB (1919), its code was Dor (Upw) (IWM: Facsimile K4655). It is also cited by the FPHS (1973). The camp's TA was Priswarian: Upavon, Wilts (ADM 1/8506/265–120667).

Crawford (*Wiltshire and The Great War: Training the Empire's Soldiers*, 1999) has indicated that most internment camps in Wiltshire were attached to military bases, and this was certainly true of Upavon. The Central Flying School used a field at Manningford Bohume, 2 miles north of Upavon. The isolated flying school created its own mystery, when a postcard identified as the Royal Flying Corps' Concentration Camp, shows no aircraft, but just distant tents.

The Western Gazette (13 September 1918) reported four internees from Upavon had escaped. *The Cornishman* (18 September 1918) cited one escapee had been caught. *The Times* (13 September 1918) reported that two Germans, Dunker and Oldenbuttel, had been recaptured, after attempting to escape from Upavon. Another, named as Muller, was caught the following day.

The internees recorded complaints about the poor water supply, to what was a tented camp. The kitchens they also cited did not meet with their demands for cleanliness.

DKF 33: In Upavon, Milldown, Corton (Dorset), und Hendon (Middlesex) waren die Gefangenen noch weiterhin in Zelten untergebracht. In Milldown und Upavon war die Wasserzufuhr unzulänglich.

DKF 34: In Milldown und Upavon war die Wasserzufuhr unzulänglich. Die in den Lagern Upavon, Milldown und Corton als Küchen benutzten offenen Schuppen waren durchaus unhygienisch.

UPPINGHAM (OS: SP 86- 99-). Even the smallest county in England, Rutland, had internment camps during the First World War. Uppingham was cited as an agricultural depot, with, according to the POWIB (1919), Normanton its only satellite.

Its code was Bro (Up) (IWM: Facsimile K4655), and it had the TA Priswarian: Uppingham (ADM 1/8506/265–120667). The FPHS (1973) also cite this camp.

The tented camp was criticised by the internees for its lack of washing facilities, and lack of beds. Claims were made that sixty PoWs slept on bare floorboards.

UPTON (OS: SP 715 604). Based at the Vicarage in Upton, this was a working camp that had the POWIB (1919) code Pa (Upt) (IWM: Facsimile K4655). The camp's TA was Priswarian: Upton, Hunts (ADM 1/8506/265–120667). The FPHS (1973) also cite Upton.

UPTON UPON SEVERN: Holdfast Hall (OS: SO 855 378). *Worcestershire Within Living Memory* records this camp as being at Holdfast Hall. The camp's TA was Priswarian: Holdfast Hall, Upton upon Severn. The Upton upon Severn camp is cited as being an agricultural group. It was attached to Leigh Court, hence its POWIB (1919) code of Dor (Lei) (Up S) (IWM: Facsimile K4655). This camp also features in the listings of the FPHS (1973).

UPWARE – WICKEN (OS: TL 535 704). Described as a working camp, its POWIB (1919) code was Pa (Uw) (IWM: Facsimile K4655). It is also cited by the FPHS (1973). The camp's TA was Priswarian: Upware, Wicken (ADM 1/8506/265–120667).

It was the Romans that originally tried to drain the fens of its water, and when they left the water seeped back to reclaim the land. Several projects of varying ambition and success have been recorded, but the state of the fens today can largely be attributed to Dutch engineer Sir Cornelius Wasterdyk Vermuyden (1595–1677) whose reclamation methods made the first important inroads to drain the fens since the Romans left. But the peoples of Wicken, Burwell and Upware were keen to keep their old traditional fen activities, fishing, fowling, and reed and turf cutting, and so kept their area from being drained until 1840. Hydrological problems make the land unworkable for farming and Wicken Fen became a valued resort for scientists. Currently maintained by the National Trust, it is Britain's oldest nature reserve. Unfortunately, neighbouring fens were requisitioned in 1940 and drained for agricultural use.

What tasks PoWs sent to area were set is not known, nor is the camp's location.

USK (OS: SO 375 100). Described as a satellite of Leominster, it was an agricultural group with the POWIB (1919) code, Shrw (Lmr) (Us) (IWM: Facsimile K4655). Its address is cited as 42 West Street, Leominster. The FPHS (1973) also cites Usk.

It is believed locally that a large house, one of four that stand off the market place, was used to house the internees sent to Usk. A HO document cites the camp was at Ponth-y-carne House, and gives its TA as Priswarian: Usk (ADM 1/8506/265–120667).

Usk was inspected by Dr A. de Sturler and Monsieur R. de Sturler, during March and April 1919. Their findings held at the National Archives at Kew (FO 383/507).

USK: HM Prison (OS: SO 379 500). Usk Prison opened in 1844 as a House of Correction, and has a long and varied history as part of the British system. In 1870, after additions, it became the County Gaol for Monmouthshire, a role it maintained until 1922, when it closed. It re-opened in 1939 as a Closed Borstal and continued in that role until 1964, when it became a Detention Centre. In 1983, Usk became a Youth Custody Centre and from 1988 to 1990 a Young Offenders Institution. In May 1990 it became a Category C Establishment for Adult Vulnerable Prisoners, and continues in that role today.

In 1916, Irishmen that were not shot, or hanged, for their parts in the Easter Rising, but were given prison sentences instead, were sent to Stafford, Usk, Lincoln, Lewes, Aylesbury or Dartmoor Prisons. Their sentences ranged from two years to life imprisonment. Those interned without trial were sent to Frongoch.

When, in December 1916, Lloyd George replaced Asquith as the Prime Minister, those being held without trial began to be released. The last of them were released by Christmas. Then, in June 1917, all those that had been convicted, including Eamon de Valera and Constance Markievicz, were released under a general amnesty.

Then, on 24 April 1918, quietly and without notice, the Defence of the Realm Act was altered to allow internment without trial. This new law also permitted deportation to England. The way was being paved for what became known as the 'German Plot'. It was a device used by the British to justify arresting and transporting to jails in mainland Britain virtually the entire republican leadership, claiming they had entered into treasonable communication with the Germans.

On 8 May 1918, Sir Edward Carson issued a statement to the effect that the government had evidence in their possession that *Sinn Féin* had been in alliance with Germany. When trouble flared again, almost immediately a spate of arrests followed. Seventy-three people were taken into custody on 17/18 May 1918; they included Arthur Griffith, Eamon de Valera, Count Plunkett, Countess Constance Markievicz, Mrs. Tom Clarke, Maud Gonne MacBride, William T. Cosgrave, Joe McGrath, Sean McEntee and Denis McCullough. By the evening of 18 May 1916 they were all on board a British warship at Dun Laoghaire. It was then they were informed that under Section 14B of the Defence of the Realm Act, they were being deported and interned on mainland Britain. After a week in a disused army camp near Holyhead (not traced), they were split up and sent to the prisons at Reading, Birmingham, Brixton, Usk and Gloucester. Some of those held in Gloucester, including de Valera, were subsequently transferred to Lincoln jail. Many were eventually moved to Frongoch.

From their arrival at Usk, they refused to be criminalised by wearing prison uniforms. At the direction of the Home Office the prison governor, Mr Young, capitulated. They also won the right to free association, the right to receive and send letters, and to smoke. This victory was to be an important part in their escape plans.

When the new prison doctor, Dr Morton, took up his duties in the prison, on 1 December, he diagnosed one of the Irishmen, Richard Coleman, as having pneumonia and had him transferred to the prison's hospital. Coleman died on 9 December 1918. The local inquest heard Coleman's brother state that Richard was a strong healthy man at the time of his arrest, and three fellow PoWs attested to the unsanitary conditions in the jail and suggested that improper nursing contributed to his death. These statements got good publicity in the Irish press and added to the campaign to get the PoWs released. The authorities decided to transfer the remaining twenty Irishmen held at Usk to Gloucester Jail on 21 January 1919. Coleman's body was taken back to Dublin, where it lay in state for a week in St Andrew's Church. It was estimated over 15,000 people joined his funeral procession, in driving rain. Shots were fired in salute as he was laid to rest in Glasnevin Cemetery.

The men in Usk, who had been planning a mass break out, decided to make their bid for freedom the night before their transfer. The prisoners got permission to have the cells left unlocked all night, so that their packing could be finished. With a rope ladder fashioned from roller towels and firewood and a grappling hook made from iron curtain bars the only four fit enough to make the attempt to scale the perimeter wall made good their escape. They were McGrath, Mellows, Geraghty and Shouldice. The rest had flu. The four went by hackney cab to Newport Station, where they caught the train to Shrewsbury. There they were met by Tom O'Loughlin, who gave them the money to get to Liverpool. Steve Lanigan, who worked in Liverpool's Custom House, arranged safe passage for them to Dublin. On the day of their escape the first Dáil had assembled in the Mansion House in Dublin.

USSELBY HALL (OS: TF 095 935). Lester (The Society for Lincolnshire History and Archaeology, per. comm., 19 April 1998) believes the remains of huts that survive in the grounds of Usselby Hall may be all that remains of a PoW Camp. The society however could not say from which conflict these concrete bases may have come.

UTTOXETER (OS: SK 103 328). Little is known of this camp, cited as being at Uttoxeter Racecourse. It had the TA Priswarian: Racecourse Buildings, Uttoxeter (ADM 1/8506/265–120667). Attached to Ashbourne, the camp's code was Bro (Ash) (Ut) (IWM: Facsimile K4655). The camp closed on 29 January 1919. It is also cited by the FPHS (1973).

UXBRIDGE (OS: TQ 044 864). The PoWs were interned at Denham Lodge, which stands on the outskirts of Uxbridge. According to locals it was nothing significant to look at, and was demolished in the 1960s, to be replaced by blocks of flats. An entry, produced by the POWIB (1919), cites Fe (D L) (IWM: Facsimile K4655), as its code. It had satellites at Eastcote, Langley Park, Northolt and Stoke Green. The camp's TA was Priswarian: Denham Lodge, Uxbridge. Denham Lodge is also cited by the FPHS (1973).

There was an airfield at Denham prior to the beginning of the war, but it is believed that the internees did not work on it or its infrastructure, but did agricultural work instead.

Private Carl Siebenhuhner was an internee at Denham Lodge, Buckinghamshire. Whilst bathing in the River Colne, near the camp, on Saturday 9 August 1919, he got out of his depth. Seeing that he was in difficulties, his comrades immediately went to his assistance, but without success. Dragging operations were at once instituted, and the body was recovered from the water in less than an hour. At the inquest, held at the Lodge on Tuesday evening, Mr A.E. Charsley, the coroner for South Buckinghamshire, recorded a verdict of accidental death. The funeral took place at Denham on Wednesday. The coffin was covered with a flag, and surmounted with a couple of wreaths of holly and evergreens from his comrades. In addition to the two wreaths, one of the German prisoners carried a beautiful wreath of white carnations, subscribed for by all of his comrades. With his coffin placed on a lorry, the cortege moved off from the camp led by a firing party of the Royal Fusiliers. His fellow PoWs, numbering about forty, followed behind. A single man, he had been a PoW since 1916. The accident was particularly unfortunate as he was expected to return to Germany shortly. The coffin bore the inscription: Siebenhuhner, Carl, 133rd Infantry Regiment, died 9 August 1919, aged 27. The first portion of the burial service was conducted by the rector, the Reverend G.C. Battiscombe, in the church and afterwards six of his comrades, specially chosen because of their near residence to him in Germany, bore the coffin to the grave. When the rector concluded the service, soldiers from the Royal Fusiliers fired three volleys, and then the last post was sounded.

W

WADDESDON (OS: SP 744 165). A working camp with the POWIB (1919) code Pa (Wd) (IWM: Facsimile K4655), it was situated at the far end of Queen Street, beyond the Gardens at the Bothy. The FPHS (1973) also cite it. The camp's TA was Priswarian: Waddesdon (ADM 1/8506/265–120667). The PoWs were employed on local farms and engaged in forestry work.

Tom Carr was posted to Waddesdon as a PoW guard and daily marched his charges down the High Street on their way to Sheepcote Hill. Once off the main road at Warmstone, one prisoner would take his pack whilst another would take his rifle, and they would proceed up the hill towards Cat Lane, singing as they went.

A group photograph of the choir was taken shortly before the camp closed. It depicts a plaque, bearing the date 19 September 1919, held by the camp's choristers.

When the time came for the internees to leave the Waddesdon camp on being repatriated, they marched through the town for the last time. When they turned into the High Street, they began to sing a German lullaby, and many of the townsfolk openly wept as they passed them by.

WAINFLEET (OS: TF 49- 58-). Wainfleet agricultural depot had three satellites attached to it, those of Partney, Withern, and Hogsthorpe. The POWIB (1919) code for Wainfleet was Bro (Wai) (IWM: Facsimile K4655). The FPHS (1973) also cites it. The actual location of the camp remains unknown. The camp's TA was Priswarian: Wainfleet (ADM 1/8506/265–120667).

WAKEFIELD. Two camps, for very different reasons, were set up in Wakefield. One was at the theme park and the other in the prison.

HM PRISON, WAKEFIELD (OS: SE 335 205). McConville (*Irish Political Prisoners, 1848–1922: The Theatres of War*, 2005) cites, for their parts in the Easter Rising, 749 men were sent to Wakefield Prison under Section 14b of the Defence of the Realm Act. They arrived in three batches between 6 May and 2 June 1916. Those not transferred to Frongoch, were released.

LOFTHOUSE PARK (OS: SE 334 253). Near the West Yorkshire village of Lofthouse Gate stood a large Georgian house, known locally as The Mansion. The house, built for the Dealtry family in 1801, stood in 60 acres of partially wooded land, approximately 3 miles north of Wakefield. In 1908, the estate was purchased and turned into an amusement park. A booklet issued by the Lofthouse Gate Methodist Church states the amusement park contained such things as: a helter-skelter; a house of mirrors; two aerial flights; and Kelly's Cottage (a ghost train type experience); along with side shows and a maze. In its centre was a white painted wooden pavilion. Initially, the venture was a success, but as the novelty wore off it was forced to close in 1913. The Blackburn brothers then erected a hangar in one corner of the park to build aeroplanes which they tested and flew over the dormant amusement park. When war broke out in 1914 the government requisitioned the park and turned it into an internment camp. At first it was used to intern civilians detained under the powers of the Defence of the Realm Act.

The camp had three distinct sections, which eventually would contain approximately 500 men in each. The mansion house, which was in the South Camp, was where the camp's commandant lived. Huts used to house the construction workers of nearby dams were bought by the War Office and brought to Lofthouse Gate.

Cohen-Portheim (*Time Stood Still: My Internment in England*, 1931), a German artist, was transferred from Knockaloe on the Isle of Man in mid-1915, to the West Camp at Lofthouse. He describes the three sections of the camp thus:

> The South Camp was built around the former concert hall. It was a warren full of beds, chairs, clothes, and men. Some wooden huts were erected around the hall, to house the overspill. The North Camp was a series of wooden huts with a corrugated steel hall, donated by an Anglo-German benefactor. The West Camp was built on the side of a steep slope. The huts were of corrugated steel construction ... It had the least character and was the most colourless and monotonous of the three. Each camp held around 500 prisoners.

He said the canteen at Lofthouse had a much better variety of goods than had been available to him on IoM. He described Lofthouse as a 'Gentlemen's Camp', where men could pay 10 shillings (50p) per week towards a better diet. Those who could afford to pay towards their keep were given better quarters. Wealthy enemy alien businessmen paid the authority for the 'privilege of staying there'.

They were also allowed to draw up to £3 a week from the camp bank, where £1 had been the limit in Knockaloe. The internees built paths, planted shrubs etc., and built a tennis court. Huts were divided into rooms and furnishings acquired or made. By 1917 those who could afford to purchase and erect small private huts were permitted to do so in South Camp. Food rationing came into force when the Germans declared 'unrestricted submarine warfare'; parcels from friends in England were forbidden and parcels from Germany or Austria were scarce as rationing applied there also.

The Times (24 October 1914) cites there were around 1,000 German prisoners interned at Lofthouse Park, near Wakefield. *The Liverpool Daily Post* (24 October 1914) recorded about 150 aliens being sent from Manchester to Lofthouse, as it was all they could take at that time. The figure of 1,000 cited in *The Times* seems excessive in the light of the US Embassy delegation's visit by Mr Jackson on 3 February 1915, which cited there were only 225 prisoners held there at the time of their visit. The observers noted the camp, which opened in October, was on the site of a former 'unsuccessful pleasure park'. New barracks were being built to expand the capacity, and although the kitchens were good there were complaints about the lack of variety in the diet – it was alleged they had beef every day. The delegation also found out most of the internees had lived for some time in England. Those with wives were allowed visits, many of them British by birth. At the time of the visit there were three internees in the hospital.

US Embassy delegations re-visited the camp on 13 February 1915, and again on 14 June 1915. The latter visit noted there were 1,186 internees in the camp. The South Camp had fifteen huts, which billeted 486 internees. It was noted that there was a gym, and a dining hall, and that the tailors had the use of the former winter garden as a workshop. The hospital had fifty beds. The North Camp contained 503 men in twenty-three huts. One of these huts was used as the Post Office and another, a canteen. All paid extra for their food. A recreation hut was being built, meanwhile a YMCA tent was provided. The West Camp had 221 men distributed between fifteen corrugated iron huts. Of these, two huts were kept for recreational purposes. Each compound had its own library.

The Times (13 April 1915) stated there was a proposal by Rothwell Urban District Council to employ civilian internees from Lofthouse to make a burial ground at Stye

Bank. It was estimated the work, for fifty men, would take eight to nine weeks to complete.

Frederich N. Weiner and Alfred Klapproth were cited in *The Times* (2 June 1915) as having escaped from Lofthouse on 28 May. Their escape was also reported in *The Police Gazette* (1 June, 1915). The latter printed a portrait of Weiner; that was repeated again on 18 June. Weiner, aged 35, had previously been at Edinburgh, coming south on 29 April 1915. Klapproth, aged 30, had formerly been at Donington Hall and was an officer of the Hamburg-America Line. He was moved north on 24 April 1915.

From October 1915 until March 1918, the well-educated internees gave lectures, at first to those less academically minded on an irregular basis, but by 1917 a more formal arrangement was in place with Freiburg University, with the intention that courses would be accredited by that institution at the end of the hostilities. But as the principal and around half of the lecturers were repatriated in early 1918, after the war, the university declined to accept their course work. The camp's college officially closed in March 1918, although some courses continued into May. Unofficial courses began again in September 1918 and there were plans to recommence full courses in January 1919, but by then all the civilians had been moved to the Isle of Man.

The Times (23 December 1915) cited a Christmas programme for the PoWs. The YWCA was to provide hospitality for the guards.

Visits were again made by delegations of the US Embassy on 16 March 1916 and 8 June 1916. On the latter visit it was stated that there were 1,447 civilian prisoners in the camp, of whom 1,322 were Germans, 122 Austrians and 3 Turks. Earlier problems with waterlogging in the lower lying areas of the camp had been resolved and promises were made that cinders and slag would be provided to improve pathways etc. The commandant was cited as Major E.T. Lloyd.

When inspected by the Swiss, in February 1918, Lt-Colonel G.S. Haines was cited as the camp's commandant. Haines had previously been in charge at Newbury, Stratford and Jersey. There were 1,430 internees of which 180 had been designated for release because of their ages.

In February 1918, Cohen-Portheim was transferred, to Boston, to await repatriation. He was then sent to the Netherlands in early November 1918, before being eventually permitted to leave for Berlin.

Up until this time all the internees at Lofthouse had been civilian. In June 1918 a report that emanated from Germany alleged the conditions in the camp were bad, and that barbed-wire fencing was being erected to enclose it. In reply it was stated, from a British source, that the camp at Lofthouse would soon be no longer required for the internment of civilian internees and it would be turned over to the military.

A Swiss inspection of the camp lasted two days. They arrived on 12 September 1918 and completed their work the following day. Their report cited Colonel Rouse was in overall charge.

A breakdown of how many internees were in the camp during their visit showed:

Nationals	*North Camp*	*South Camp*	*West Camp*	*Total*
Germans	312	327	278	917
Austrians	26	41	35	102
Turkish	0	4	2	6
Totals	338	372	315	1,025

The civilians interned at Lofthouse were not given much time to prepare when they were told to make themselves ready to move. Promises that they could take treasured possessions with them were broken as the amount each person could take with them was limited. Upon their arrival in the Isle of Man, a lot of their hand luggage was confiscated and was never returned to its rightful owner. Furniture was left behind, as were the vegetables they had been growing. No pets could be taken, yet pets were allowed at Knockaloe, their final destination. Just seven days after the last civilian had gone, Lofthouse became a camp for officers.

The *Sheffield Daily Telegraph* (26 October 1918) reported Heinz Heinrich Ernst Justus escaped from Wakefield. He had been in Wakefield less than a week. Justus had jumped from the train, at South Elmshall, which was taking him from Holyport to Lofthouse. Justus was recaptured within three days. Suffering from flu, and too ill to stay on the run, he surrendered himself to the police at Cardiff docks. He was returned to Lofthouse to receive medical help. Once recovered, he was tried and sentenced to fifty-six days in Chelmsford's Detention Barracks. In an earlier attempt to get away, whilst interned at Colsterdale, Justus had tried to escape, dressed as a woman. This story was also carried by *The Times*. In an earlier attempt to escape, Justus sent his uniform, and Iron Cross, to the commandant at Holyport in a parcel. They were returned to him, after his stay at Chelmsford Detention Barracks.

Dr F. Schwyzer, Dr A.L. Vischer and Dr A. de Sturler compiled reports of their visits of inspection to the officers' PoW camps at Ripon, Skipton, Lofthouse Park, Kegworth and Donnington Hall during February and March 1919. On 22 February 1919, it was cited only two of the three camps were being utilised. The North Camp had 400 officers, supported by 120 orderlies, and the West Camp had 452 officers, supported by 132 orderlies. Graf von Budingan was cited as the senior officer in the North Camp, and a Major Schulze was in charge of the West Camp. At the time of their visit, the South Camp was dormant.

The Times (24 March 1919) reported Lassen and Sternkops had escaped. There is no record of them being recaptured.

In June 1919 some of the naval officers involved in the scuttling of the German ships at Scapa Flow were brought to Lofthouse. Others, along with other ranks, were taken to Oswestry.

The Times (23 July 1919) cited Hans Ferol was caught at Hull.

Newspaper reports of escapes and recaptures are not always accurate. Often to add to the confusion, those arrested would give different names, or because of poor interpretation their details were recorded wrongly. On 21 July 1919, *The Times* reported Leutnant H.M. Leroi had escaped. *The Times* (12 August 1919) reported Leutnants K.E. Schwerin and H. Ruhlurnd had escaped, but H.M. Leroe had been re-captured. *The Times* (1 September 1919) cited Leutnant Karl Heritz had been recaptured. If Heritz and Schwerin could be identified as being the same person, then that would only leave Ruhlurnd to be traced.

In September 1919, except for the officers that came from Scapa Flow, all the officers and their orderlies were then transferred for repatriation. The rest remained in Wakefield until early November 1919.

The Times (13 November 1919) cited that twenty officers involved in a plan to escape by digging a tunnel were thwarted when an alert guard noticed the surface had collapsed just outside the wire. The report was probably at least a week old as all the internees had already left to go to Donington Hall. Karl Nordmann, a potential absconder for the tunnel, had been transferred to Donington Hall between 4 and 8 November 1919. A prolific writer, he is known to have written his last letter from

Hut 24, Lofthouse North Officers' Camp, on 4 November 1919. His next letter was posted from Donington Hall on 8 November 1919.

A sale of the hutments at Wakefield was advertised in *The Times* (8 May 1920), with other lots going in later editions.

In 1921 there was an attempt by businessmen to revive the amusement park but the pavilion was burnt out in April 1922. The large house was demolished, and Lofthouse Park lay derelict for many years. In the 1930s, Roper's Brickyard was established on part of the site, and later an engineering depot for the local council was also established. A company involved in waste management has used part of the site of the camp, as a depot.

The FPHS (1973) cite Lofthouse Park, Yorkshire in their listings. The camp had the TA Priswarian: Wakefield (ADM 1/8506/265–120667). The camp had the POWIB (1919) code Wf (IWM: Facsimile K4655).

WAKERLEY: nr Stamford (OS: SP 95- 99-). A working camp, it had the POWIB (1919) code Pa (Wa) (IWM: Facsimile K4655). Its TA was Priswarian: Wakerley (ADM 1/8506/265–120667). The FPHS (1973) cites the camp.

Internees sent to Wakerley were put to work in a quarry, and many of them complained they were not fit enough to do the work asked of them. There were also complaints of having nowhere to recuperate. Concerns, too, were expressed by those that were Roman Catholic at having no opportunity to attend mass in an appropriate place of worship.

DKF 31: Die Arbeit ist oft zu schwer und übersteigt die Kräfte der schlecht genährten Leute. Dies ist hauptsächlich in Wackerley (sic) *der Fall. Der weitaus größte Teil der dort in den Eisensteinbrüchen beschäftigten Leute ist arbeitsuntauglich.*

DKF 32: In Wackerley (sic), *Sproxton Moor, Port Clarence und Larkhill fehlen Plätze bzw Räume zur Erholung der Kriegsgefangenen.*

DKF 32: Die Katholiken in Wackerley (sic) *und Bowithick haben noch keine Gelegenheit zur Abhaltung Messen.*

WALKERINGHAM (OS: SK 77- 92-). Minute 13 of the Notts County WAC (28 January 1919) cites there was a migratory gang at Walkeringham. The location where the PoWs stayed is not recorded, and it has become invisible to history. The TA of the camp at Gringley on the Hill was Priswarian: Walkeringham (ADM 1/8506/265–120667).

WALLINGTON (see Watlington).

WALSHAM LE WILLOWS (OS: TM 00- 71-). A working camp, its POWIB (1919) code was Pa (Wal) (IWM: Facsimile K4655). It is cited by the FPHS (1973). The camp's TA was Priswarian: Walsham le Willows (ADM 1/8506/265–120667). The location of this camp remains a mystery. Walsham le Willows was inspected by Dr A. de Sturler and Monsieur R. de Sturler, during April and May 1919. Their findings are held at the National Archives, at Kew (FO 383/507).

WANTAGE (OS: SU 40- 87-). Because it was the birthplace of King Alfred (AD 849), Wantage is thought to have been an important town in Saxon times.

Described as a satellite of Compton, Wantage had the POWIB (1919) code Dor (Cmp) (Wg) (IWM: Facsimile K4655). It is also cited by the FPHS (1973). The location of the camp is not known.

WAREHAM (OS: SY 92- 87-). Cited by the FPHS (1973), Wareham had the TA Priswarian: Wareham (ADM 1/8506/265–120667). Similar sounding Wereham is also cited on the list.

Wareham Quay is the highest point of navigation on the River Frome.

WARMSWORTH HALL (see Doncaster).

WARREN WOOD – THETFORD – CROXTON (OS: TA 800 803). The POWIB (1919) cites this camp twice. Once as Warren Wood and the other as Croxton (OS: TA 875 865). Warren Wood is approximately 7 miles south-east of Croxton. Thetford lies between them. The camp may have been in the Thetford army camp. It was cited by the FPHS (1973) as Warren Wood, Thetford and had the TA Priswarian: Warren Wood, Thetford (ADM 1/8506/265–120667). It was a working camp with the POWIB (1919) code, Pa (W W) (IWM: Facsimile K4655). Like Glendon, Ordfordness, and Mundford, it was a tented encampment.

A complaint of lack of a proper laundry service was directed towards this camp, and of the internees not having adequate clean wearable clothes.

DKF 34: Aus den Berichten der Schweizer Delegierten aus dem Ende des Jahres 1917 über die Arbeitslager in England geht hervor, daß die Zustände in einigen dieser Lager sich gebessert hatten und daß in manchen dementsprechend das Leben erträglich war. Immerhin geben noch einige Lager zu berechtigten Klagen Anlaß. Trotz wiederholten Einspruchs der deutschen Regierung sind in der Lagern Wingland (Lincolnshire), Ordfordneß (Suffolk), West Tofts (Norfolk), Warren Woods (Norfolk), Glendon bei Keltering (sic), *Stratford on Avon, Kerry (Nord Wales), und Shirehampton (Gloucestershire) die Gefangenen immer noch in Zelten untergebracht.*

DKF 34: Die Versorgung der Gefangenen mit genügender Kleidung und Wäsche ist verschiedentlich sehr mangelhaft. Hauptsächlich in den Lagern Warren Woods, West Tofts, Orfordneß und Kerry wird hierüber geklagt.

WASDALE HEAD (OS: NY 184 082). In March 1919 it is cited forty PoWs were working on the road at Wasdale Head. On 20 May 1918 an application had been made to the Cumberland WAC to have fifty PoWs billeted at Wasdale Head, for road marking and the reclamation work of making a new bed for the River Irt. A HO document cites the camp was at Down in the Dale, and gives its TA as Priswarian: Wasdale Head, Cumberland. Down in the Dale is approximately 1 kilometre south of Wasdale Head. The camp opened on 1 January 1919.

The *Whitehaven News* (14 August 1919) cited on Tuesday it was reported that four German prisoners had escaped from the camp at Wasdale Head. The same paper (21 August 2008) reported they had been re-captured in Northumberland on the Thursday, two days after they had absconded. In a week where there were several escape attempts, Birkson, Simon and Marien were named as having escaped from Whitehaven on 12 August 1919. The fourth man remained unnamed.

Wasdale Head was inspected by Dr A. de Sturler and Monsieur R. de Sturler during June 1919. Their findings are held at the National Archives at Kew (FO 383/508).

WATERBEACH (OS: TL 494 655). The only reference to this camp's existence comes in the form of a minute produced by the Cambridgeshire WAC on 6 May 1918. It recorded that Mr Bishop, the supervisor of the internment camp at

Waterbeach, had applied to the authorities to be allowed to take possession of a small bungalow near to the farm where the PoWs in his charge were working.

WATLINGTON, Brightwell (OS: SU 68- 94-). Described as an agricultural group by the POWIB (1919), this camp was attached to Cholsey AD; its code was Dor (Cho) (Wt) (IWM: Facsimile K4655). The camp's TA was Priswarian: Brightwell, Watlington (ADM 1/8506/265–120667). The location of the camp is unknown but Watlington Hall may hold the key to where it was.

The FPHS (1973) has no entry for Watlington, but has one for Wallington. To further confuse the issue, a camp was also recorded at Brightwell, near Grove.

During March 1919, Dr A. de Sturler compiled reports of PoW camps he inspected. He visited Watlington. His findings are held at the National Archives at Kew (FO 383/506).

WATTON (OS: TF 914 005). A request, from George Barton at Watton, seeking PoWs, was forwarded to the Home Grown Timber Committee, according to a minute of the Norfolk WAC of 21 September 1917 (C/C10/17).

WAXHAM: Bridge Farm (OS: TG 446 248). An undisclosed number of PoWs were accommodated at Waxham Bridge Farm, according to a minute of the Norfolk WAC of 31 August 1917 (C/C10/17).

WELBURN (OS: SE 67- 84-). Welburn is a site suggested by the FPHS (1973), but there are two locations with this name in the County of Yorkshire, where the camp was located.

As there appear to be links between the placement of some internment camps and the creation of some early airfields during the First World War, the more probable site would have been the one near to Wombleton, and Welburn Hall. Military records show there was such an airfield near Wombleton.

The second location is near Castle Howard, and a possible connection to the camp at Sinnington then cannot be ruled out.

WELLESBOURNE (OS: SP 279 549). An agricultural depot with the POWIB (1919) code Dor (Wel) (IWM: Facsimile K4655); its address is cited as Holly Lodge. The camp's TA was Priswarian: Holly Lodge, Wellesbourne (ADM 1/8506/265–120667). It is also cited by the FPHS (1973).

Holly Lodge served several owners in various guises before being turned into a hunting lodge by Edward Barclay Lacy at the end of the nineteenth century. The lodge, which stood near to Chapel Street, on an extensive estate that incorporated a farm, was within walking distance of the Peacock and Red Horse public houses.

When the First World War began the lodge stood empty, and was eventually requisitioned by the War Office to become an internment camp. The children of the village often gathered to watch the PoWs exercise in the courtyard. The PoWs gratefully received windfall apples collected by local children. After the war the house was occupied again, and in 1976 it was demolished. Around ten new houses adorn the plot instead (Argyle, per. comm., 28 January 2000).

The Scotsman (19 August 1918) cited three PoWs escaped. *The Times* (19 August 1918) gave their names as Albert Gutzehr, Paul Heidrich and Adolf Kurt, and two days later cited their re-capture.

WELSHPOOL: The Corporation Horse Repository (OS: SJ 229 073). In the seventeenth century, horses were not only bought and sold around Welshpool, they were shown and raced there too. To celebrate a visit by Charles I, in 1645, a race meeting was held at nearby Cofnybran for the first time. Races continued annually there until Oliver Cromwell ruled England, when they were terminated. With the resumption of the monarchy, the race meetings returned, but this time back at Welshpool, where they continued until 1803 when they were then transferred to Oswestry.

There was stabling for around fifty horses at the paddock near Welshpool's Smithfield Market. It was known locally as the Horse Repository. During the First World War the Repository was cited as being an internment camp and was listed by the POWIB (1919) as being a satellite of Kerry-Newtown. It had the code Fg (K N) (Wsh) (IWM: Facsimile K4655). The camp also had the TA Priswarian: Welshpool (ADM 1/8506/265–120667). Welshpool was also cited by the FPHS (1973).

Today, that part of Smithfield Road has been transformed into a car park.

WEM (Tern Hill) (OS: SJ 635 322). Local legend suggests the idea for an airfield at Tern Hill was the inspiration of a balloonist who happened to land there during the early part of the First World War. Created for the Royal Flying Corps it was to become a Royal Air Force establishment until 1976, when it was handed over to the Army, and re-named Clive Barracks. The airfield is used today as a satellite of RAF Shawbury, the main helicopter training school for the British Armed Services.

Like many early airfields created at this time, there was an internment camp close to it. Those interned at Tern Hill were accommodated in tents, and they expressed concerns about the slow delivery of letters and packages mailed to the camp.

Border Counties Advertiser (24 April 1918) reported that the Salop WAC had received reports of work done by PoWs at Bromfield, and Wem, and had agreed to requests for another 200 internees. *Border Counties Advertiser* (1 May 1918) confirmed that the 200 additional PoWs had been requested, and it was hoped to have them in small camps of fifteen to twenty men, or in groups of up to three on single farms, if farmers could accommodate them.

Wem was a satellite of Leominster. Its POWIB (1919) code was Shrw (Lmr) (Wem) (IWM: Facsimile K4655). Wem is also cited by the FPHS (1973). The camp's TA was Priswarian: Leominster (ADM 1/8506/265–120667).

DKF 30: In den Lagern von Rosyth, Eastgate, Uppingham, Belton Park, Tern Hill, Bee Craigs, Hadnall, Sutton Veny, Larkhill, Fovant, Withley (sic) *und Radford sind die Kriegsgefangenen in Zelten untergebracht.*

DKF 32: Die Bestellung der eingehenden Briefe und Pakete ist fast überall, hauptsächlich aber in Tern Hill, Newlandside und Rovrah (sic), *sehr langsam.*

WENDOVER: Halton Park (OS: SP 875 104). Situated in the Chiltern Hills above the village of Halton in Buckinghamshire, RAF Halton stands on land once belonging to the Rothschild family. During the First World War, German PoWs helped to create the infrastructure of the airbase. The camp, a working one, had the POWIB (1919) code Pa (Ha P) (IWM: Facsimile K4655). The FPHS (1973) cite it too.

Since the Norman onquest, there has been a manor house at Halton; then it belonged to the Archbishop of Canterbury. The old house was situated west of the village itself. It had a large park, which was later dissected by the Grand Union Canal. In the mid-sixteenth century, Thomas Cranmer sold the manor to Henry Bradshaw.

After being in the Bradshaw family for a considerable period, it was sold to Sir Francis Dashwood, in 1720, and was then held by that family for almost 150 years. The estate, comprising of some 1,500 acres, was sold to Baron Lionel de Rothschild in 1853. The house, emptied of its contents by its previous owner, lay unoccupied and was allowed to become derelict, and finally to be demolished. On his death in 1879, the estate passed to his son Alfred. It was he who commissioned the new house, which was completed, in the French style, in 1883. For over thirty years it housed sparkling weekend house parties for the cream of British society.

In 1913, 3 Squadron of the Royal Flying Corps was deployed to Halton to a makeshift airfield on what was later to become the Maitland Parade Square.

Following a gentleman's agreement in 1914, Lord Kitchener assembled 20,000 of his 'first 100,000' volunteers on the estate. They lived in tents through an increasingly muddy winter, which forced the authorities to start erecting more durable buildings.

When the 10th Battalion Green Howards was formed it moved to Halton Park. They temporarily moved to Aylesbury on 15 November 1914 to allow the Halton Park facilities to be improved.

In 1916 the Royal Flying Corps moved its air mechanics' school from Hampshire to Halton. It was in this period that German PoWs helped create the infrastructure for the new Halton airfield. This caused some confusion in the nearby village of Wendover. Apparently, the 'funny maternity-styled tunics worn by the airmen' was often mistaken for the uniforms worn by the PoWs, who were also present at Halton from around the same time.

Alfred de Rothschild, the then owner of the Halton Estate, was instrumental in a piece of destruction that was his own making. Knowing the government was short of timber, he offered, in a letter dated 28 February 1917, his wood to Lloyd George. Canadian lumberjacks were brought in to cut down the trees. Local people were horrified to see stumps about shoulder high being left as the trees were felled.

The narrow gauge railway, built to take the cut timber to Wendover Station, was later upgraded to standard gauge. PoW labour may also have been used to remove the felled timbers.

On Rothschild's death in 1918, the House was acquired from the family by the fledgling Royal Air Force, and for over ninety years it has served as the officers' mess.

In 1919, Lord Trenchard established the No. 1 School of Technical Training at RAF Halton, which moved to RAF Cosford in the early 1990s.

There was a second camp in Wendover, at Hale Farm.

WENDOVER: Hale Farm (OS: SP 869 072). What the PoWs sent to Hale Farm did is unknown. The camp's TA was Priswarian: Hale Farm (ADM 1/8506/265–120667). It was one of two camps in the Wendover area: the other being at Halton Park. Hale Farm lay to the south-east of RAF Halton, near to Hale Wood.

WENNINGTON (see Rainham).

WEOBLEY: The Workhouse (OS: SO 394 521). A satellite of Leominster, its POWIB (1919) code was Shrw (Lmr) (Weo) (IWM: Facsimile K4655). Cited as being at Weobly (sic), its address is given as 42 West Street, Leominster. The FPHS (1973) entry is for Weobley, Hereford. The camp's TA was Priswarian: Workhouse, Weobley (ADM 1/8506/265–120667).

A workhouse for eighty inmates was built in 1837 to the north of Weobley. The architect, George Wilkinson, followed the popular cruciform plan with an entrance block at the front, behind which lay the four accommodation wings radiating from a central hub, creating yards for the different classes of pauper. The former workhouse buildings have now been converted for residential use (www.herefordshire.gov.uk).

WEREHAM (OS: TF 684 015). The camp's TA was Priswarian: Wereham, Stoke Ferry (ADM 1/8506/265–120667). Wereham appears on the list produced by the FPHS (1973). They also cite a camp with a similar sounding name, at Wareham. Wereham PoW camp was inspected by Dr A. de Sturler and Monsieur R. de Sturler, during April and May 1919. Their findings are held at the National Archives, at Kew (FO 383/507).

WEST MERSEA (OS: TM 01- 12-). It is cited as Mersea West, Essex by the FPHS (1973), it was a working camp on Mersea Island; its POWIB (1919) code was Pa (Ws) (IWM: Facsimile K4655). The camp's TA was Priswarian: West Mersea (ADM 1/8506/265–120667).

Lockwood (per. comm., 2004) cites PC Charles 'Zepp' Smith was awarded a Merit Star for his part in arresting the crew of a Zeppelin in September 1916, and taking them to the military camp on Mersea Island. The German machine had been hit by anti-aircraft fire in London. Above Chelmsford, it was attacked by aircraft from Hainault Farm, and crashed near New Hall Cottages, at Little Wigborough. Kapitan Alois Bocker marched his crew towards Colchester, where Special Constable Edgar Nicholas saw them, and being suspicious, followed them. As they approached Peldon, they were stopped and arrested by Sergeant Ernest Edwards and Special Constable Elijah Taylor. The crewmen were taken to Peldon Post Office, where PC Smith called the authorities. Taking charge of the situation, Smith then marched the German crewmen to Mersea Island, with Special Constables Fairhead, Hyam, King, May, Meade, Beade, with the aforementioned Taylor and Nicholas assisting them.

West Mersea PoW camp was inspected by Dr A. de Sturler and Monsieur R. de Sturler, during April and May 1919. Their findings are held at the National Archives, at Kew (FO 383/507).

WESTON ON THE GREEN (OS: SP 53- 18-). Described as a working camp by the POWIB (1919), its code was Dor (Wn) (IWM: Facsimile K4655). It is also cited by the FPHS (1973). The camp had the TA Priswarian: Weston on the Green, Bletchington (ADM 1/8506/265–120667). The camp closed on 16 January 1919.

WETHERBY (OS: SE 405 481). Wetherby is described as an agricultural depot by the POWIB (1919), its code being Cat (Wet) (IWM: Facsimile K4655). Tadcaster, Pateley Bridge and Otley were its satellites. Wetherby is also cited by the FPHS (1973).

The present shopping precinct in Wetherby stands on the former sites of Wharfedale Brewery and the old bus station. The brewery opened to supply many of the town's fifteen inns with ale. The first mention of a brewer (and presumably a brewery) at this site was the marriage of John Rhodes in 1756. In 1824, Gregory Rhodes is recorded as being the tenant of 'a newly erected dwelling house and Brewery'. In the closing stages of the First World War, at least 250 PoWs were interned in what was a bottling plant, which looked out onto Castle Gate, off Market Place. Part of this building was below the street level. The PoWs worked on the surrounding farms.

It was not until December 1919 that the last of them left Wetherby. The practice of Dr J.A. Hargreaves was adjacent to the brewery, and he acted as the camp's medical practitioner. Although they had lost a son, killed in 1917, he and his wife empathised with the internees, and in appreciation of the warmth given by his family, when the doctor's daughter married, the Germans erected an arch across the road saying, 'Welcome home Mr and Mrs Waller'. After the war, the plant produced mineral water, and then as a result of the American troops being based there, Coca Cola was produced for a time from concentrates sent from America. The old brewery's offices were now being used by the administration of the West Yorkshire Omnibus Company. The site also housed the town's first Labour Exchange (Lodge, per. comm., 13 October 1998).

WEYHILL (OS: SU 315 467). Cited as being at Weyhill Fair Ground, the camp's TA was Priswarian: Weyhill (ADM 1/8506/265–120667). It was also cited by the FPHS (1973).

Traditionally, fairs were for rural communities to come together to sell produce and livestock; hops and sheep being prominent. It was a time to settle accounts, and for friends and families to re-unite and enjoy themselves before going back to their austere lifestyle. Weyhill had one the largest fairs in the country.

WHEATHAMPSTEAD (OS: TL 174 145). The minutes of the Herts County WAC record a migratory gang at Wheathampstead; this is the only citation of this camp. Its location is unknown and it probably consisted of just a few PoWs engaged in agricultural work.

WHITEBURN: nr Grantshouse (OS: NT 760 643). The only reference to this camp is made in the list produced for the FPHS (1973).

A list of early British airfields, compiled by Robertson (*Bases of Air Strategy: Building Airfields for the RAF 1914–1919*, Higham, 1983) cites Grant's House, Whiteburn. As there is a definite link to the creation of airfields and PoW labour in the First World War, Robertson's entry may be significant.

Grantshouse railway station was on the North British Railway Company line, between Edinburgh and Berwick on Tweed. Although the line is still operational the station has closed. None of its buildings survive today, however there are a number of sidings that have survived. Perhaps the camp was in one of these sidings.

Alternatively it may have been on the nearby Renton estates. The house became the marital home of Mary Eleanor Stirling and Charles Lisle Cookson in the 1880s. When Charles died in October 1919 the death duty incurred had the effect of splitting up the estate. Between the wars, the gardens of Renton House were opened to the public. During the Second World War the estate was sold to a Mr Roberts. Since the then there have been several owners of Renton House.

WHITEHAVEN (OS: NY 938 389). *The Cumberland News* (7 November 2003) cited a story printed in *The Whitehaven News* of August 1919 which reported that the military had taken over Glenholm, a large house previously used as a boarding school for girls, from which to despatch German prisoners as ships became available to take them home. In September, the *Carlisle Journal* reported that the repatriation programme was costing £90,000 a day.

The Western Daily Press (12 August 1919) reported that four PoWs had escaped from Whitehaven. Their escape was also reported in the *Exeter and Plymouth Gazette* the same day.

WHITLEY BAY (see Tynemouth).

WHITTINGTON (OS: SJ 32- 31-). The camp was only cited by the FPHS (1973) and may only be another reference to one of the camps at Oswestry. Exhumations of German PoWs from both World Wars took place at Whittington Cemetery. Their bodies were sent for re-burial to the German War Cemetery at Cannock Chase in the 1960s.

WHITWELL STREET (OS: TG 084 206). A camp earmarked for Whitwell was recorded in the Norfolk War Agricultural minutes of 16 August 1918. It reported on those interned at Whitwell Street who were working on clearing the River Bures. The majority of them were housed in the tannery, which stood on Whitwell common. The rest were billeted at Whitwell Street Camp (C/C10/18). Only one code is cited by the POWIB (1919) for Whitwell. It was satellite of Kenninghall with the code, Pa (Ken) (Whi) (IWM: Facsimile K4655). Whitwell PoW camp was inspected by Dr A. de Sturler and Monsieur R. de Sturler, during April and May 1919. Their findings are held at the National Archives, at Kew (FO 383/507). Whitwell is also cited by the FPHS (1973).

The remains of P.B. Rabe (d. 17 November 1918), of the German army, were exhumed from Whitwell Churchyard in 1961 and moved to Cannock Chase Cemetery. Also transferred with him was an unidentified member of the German Air Service (d. 30 October 1918) who had been buried at Weybourne Churchyard. Because his name is not recorded it is unlikely he was a PoW. It is more likely that he was a pilot or crewmember of an aircraft or Zeppelin that crashed or was brought down in the vicinity (DN/FCB 22/2).

WIGMORE (OS: SO 38- 63-). The camp is cited as being at Kingsland, and had the TA Priswarian: Ross on Wye (ADM 1/8506/265–120667). The PoWs may have been engaged in producing timber, as there was a sawmill at Kingsland dating back to that time. It was an agricultural group, attached to Ross on Wye with the POWIB (1919) code Shrw (R W) (Wig) (IWM: Facsimile K4655).

WIGTON (OS: NY 249 491). It was reported in July 1918 that no British soldiers would be available for farm work that year, but German prisoners would be available, in migratory gangs, from about the second week in August. Provision had to be made for accommodating them and it was then reported, in the *Carlisle Journal*, that thirty PoWs and six guards would be housed in the paupers' ward of Wigton Workhouse. The authorities paid 3d per head each day from 15 August 1918. Similar arrangements were proposed at the workhouse at Kirkby Stephen.

A union workhouse was built *c.*1842, on an 11-acre site, to replace the old parish workhouse, on Cross Lane. It could accommodate up to 250 inmates. After the First World War, the workhouse in 1930 became Highfield House Public Assistance Institution; then under the National Health Service it became Wigton Hospital, which still serves the area today as Wigton Cummunity Hospital.

Cameron's schematic (www.railscot.co.uk) shows Wigtown Station standing on the Maryport to Carlisle line.

WILBY (OS: TM 22- 74-). An agricultural group, it was attached to Haughley agricultural depot. Its POWIB (1919) code was Pa (Hgy) (Wil) (IWM: Facsimile K4655). It is cited by the FPHS (1973). Its TA was Priswarian: Wilby, Eye (ADM 1/8506/265–120667).

WILLINGTON (OS: SK 298 282). A report carried in *The Derby Daily Telegraph* (10 July 1918) reported that The Derbyshire WAC had stated that owing to the country's great dependence on the home harvest, the progress of farm crops was now a matter of general interest, particularly those growing on the newly broken-up land. The report also referred to 'the sudden and heavy call upon farm labour for military service' and that the National Service Department was satisfied that Derbyshire had been 'thoroughly exhausted as a source of men for the army, and every effort was being made to provide replacement labour. The main source would, in the future, be German prisoners, and farmers have so far accepted them in a way that is creditable.'

Camps for the accommodation of German prisoners had already been established at Ashbourne, Bretby, Burton, Ilkeston, Sudbury, and Willington, and camps awaiting the arrival of prisoners had been prepared at Ash, Bakewell, Bolsover, Chapel en le Frith, Darley Dale, Duffield, Eckington, Glossop, Hasland, Newbold, Shardlow, Sutton Scarsdale, and Wirksworth. These camps would provide for around 700 PoWs to work on the land.

Food production targets for the year received a favourable report at another meeting of the Derbyshire WAC, but, because of the expected reduction in labour, similar targets could not be foreseen for the coming year. It was urged that there had been no further recruiting, by the army, of farm workers, and that soldier labour should not be disturbed. It was stated seven internment camps containing 280 men were now in operation, arrangements were being made for six others and applications had been made for a further 235 PoWs for the county.

Morrow (*Willington Memories*, 1991) states that pillars at the front of Willington Hall still bear the marks of the barbed wire that was put around them when the hall was used to intern PoWs in the First World War. It was a satellite of Burton upon Trent, and its POWIB (1919) code was Bro (Brt) (Wl) (IWM: Facsimile K4655). The camp's TA was Priswarian: Willington, Derbyshire (ADM 1/8506/265–120667). Wereham PoW camp was inspected by Dr A. de Sturler in March 1919. His findings are held at the National Archives, at Kew (FO 383/506).

WIMBORNE: Little Canford Farmhouse (OS: ST 047 998). A working camp, its POWIB (1919) code was Dor (Wmb) (IWM: Facsimile K4655). It is also cited by the FPHS (1973). The camp's TA was Priswarian: Wimborne (ADM 1/8506/265–120667). Apart from being based at Little Cranford Farm, nothing is known of this camp.

WINCHCOMBE (OS: SP 02- 28-). Described as a satellite of Toddington agricultural depot, its POWIB (1919) code was Dor (To) (Wm) (IWM: Facsimile K4655). It is also cited by the FPHS (1973). Further proof of this camp's existence has not been found.

WINCHESTER. Three locations in Winchester have been known to house PoWs. These were the prison and two army camps.

HM PRISON WINCHESTER (OS: SU 472 295). At the start of the war, fifty-one Germans, taken from two ships in Southampton, were taken to Winchester Prison to be interviewed. Twenty-seven were allowed to depart, but the remaining twenty-four were detained. Their fate went unrecorded, but presumably they would have been dispatched to the newly prepared camps when they came on line.

The Times (15 August 1914) cites thirty-four of them had been on the White Star's *Oceanic*, and seventeen were taken off an un-named German ship.

Miss Julia B.E. Jacobitz, who had been held in Winchester Prison, was bound over, at Bournemouth Quarter Sessions on 11 January 1916, to comply with the Aliens Restriction Order (FO 383/151).

FLOWERDOWN (OS: SU 457 321). Flowerdown is described as a working camp; it had the POWIB (1919) code Dor (Fld) (IWM: Facsimile K4655). It is also cited by the FPHS (1973). The camp's TA was Priswarian: Flowerdown, Winchester (ADM 1/8506/265–120667). Probably, it was attached to the army camp of that name. The internment camp at Flowerdown closed on 14 September 1918.

MORN HILL (OS: SU 532 289). Described as being at Avington Park, Morn Hill, its TA was Priswarian: Morn Hill Camp (ADM 1/8506/265–120667). The camp was originally for civilians, but later changed to having combatants. This change probably happened as a result of the British government deciding to put the interned civilians on the Isle of Man. It is also cited by the FPHS (1973). The camp closed on 15 September 1918.

WINGLAND: Sutton Bridge (OS: TF 51- 22-). Wingland, at Sutton Bridge, was an agricultural depot that oversaw a satellite camp at Holbeach. Its POWIB (1919) code was Bro (Wgl) (IWM: Facsimile K4655). It had the TA Priswarian: Sutton Bridge (ADM 1/8506/265–120667). Sutton Bridge and Holbeach PoW camps were inspected by Dr A. de Sturler and Monsieur R. de Sturler, during April and May 1919. Their findings are held at the National Archives, at Kew (FO 383/507). The FPHS (1973) cites both Sutton Bridge and Wingland in their list of prison camps. It is described as a tented site. There was an airfield at Sutton Bridge (OS: TF 476 196).

DKF 34: Aus den Berichten der Schweizer Delegierten aus dem Ende des Jahres 1917 über die Arbeitslager in England geht hervor, daß die Zustände in einigen dieser Lager sich gebessert hatten und daß in manchen dementsprechend das Leben erträglich war. Immerhin geben noch einige Lager zu berechtigten Klagen Anlaß. Trotz wiederholten Einspruchs der deutschen Regierung sind in der Lagern Wingland (Lincolnshire), Ordfordneß (Suffolk), West Tofts (Norfolk), Warren Woods (Norfolk), Glendon bei Keltering (sic), *Stratford on Avon, Kerry (Nord Wales), und Shirehampton (Gloucestershire) die Gefangenen immer noch in Zelten untergebracht.*

WINWICK (OS: SP 624 734). Winwick was a working camp; it had the POWIB (1919) code Pa (Win) (IWM: Facsimile K4655). The FPHS (1973) also cite Winwick. The camp's TA was Priswarian: Winwick, Northants (ADM 1/8506/265–120667). Winwick Hall may hold the key to this camp's location.

WIRKSWORTH (OS: SK 28- 53-). *The Derby Daily Telegraph* (10 July 1918) states that a camp was being set up and was awaiting the arrival of PoWs at Wirksworth; and at other places in the county. There is no evidence to support the newspaper's claim.

WISBOROUGH GREEN (OS: TQ 045 266). A working camp, its POWIB (1919) code was Pa (Wis) (IWM: Facsimile K4655). It is also cited by the FPHS (1973). The location of this camp was the Workhouse, its TA being Priswarian: Wisborough Green.

The village hall was built as a poorhouse early in the eighteenth century, allegedly on the foundations of a Benedictine monastery. It had been used to house French prisoners during the Napoleonic Wars. In 1834 it became a workhouse as part of the newly formed Petworth Union. The Wisborough workhouse was used to house children. German PoWs were housed there during the First World War. After the war the buildings were converted into four flats, and a variety of function rooms. When the south wing was condemned, most of the buildings were demolished. The original poorhouse was converted into the village hall in 1955 (www.wisboroughgreen.org/historyvillagehall).

WISETON (OS: SK 71- 89-). According to the minutes of the Notts County WAC (28 January 1919) there was a migratory gang operating out of Wiseton. The whereabouts of this camp has not been established. It may be the camp was at or near to Wiseton Hall, which is believed to date back to *c.*1670. The Acklom family acquired it *c.*1750.

WISSINGTON (OS: TL 952 348). Minute 188 of the Norfolk WAC (22 June 1917) states it was resolved to ask for the return of the seventy-five PoWs working at Wissington. The only location of this name to be found in the UK is in Suffolk, where Wissington Grange stands near to Nayland. There are no reports of PoWs being in that area during the First World War.

WITHERN (OS: TF 43- 82-). Other than it being a satellite of Wainfleet with the POWIB (1919) code Bro (Wai) (Wih), nothing is known about this camp. Perhaps Withern Mill may hold the key to its location. Prior to the First World War it had been a flourmill, before being converted into a factory for producing fruit preserve by Thomas George Tickler, *c.*1882. Tickler owned orchards on a 230-acre estate at Bradley village on the outskirts of Grimsby, and at Laceby. Having enjoyed success from selling large amounts of jam to the government for Boer War troops, he had similar success providing jam for First World War soldiers. Tickler's tinned jam was doubly useful: once its contents were consumed, the empty tins were refilled with explosives and made excellent hand grenades known colloquially as 'Tickler's Artillery'. Tickler died in 1938, and his company stopped trading in 1970. Today the millpond is stocked with trout (www.shonamcisaac.com).

WITNEY. There were two camps created in Witney. The FPHS (1973) only cite Witney once. The POWIB (1919) also cites it once, stating it was a working camp, with the code, Dor (Wit) (IWM: Facsimile K4655).

FLEECE HOTEL (OS: SP 357 094) and WITNEY AERODROME (OS: SP 347 100). The HO cites two locations. One is believed to be a former coaching house, the Fleece Hotel at Eynsham, used to accommodate the PoWs sent to Witney to work. Photographs of the PoWs, taken outside the hotel, exist. The camp's TA was Priswarian: Witney. The other was Witney Aerodrome. Its TA was Priswarian: Aerodrome, Witney (ADM 1/8506/265–120667).

WOBURN (OS: SP 944 335). A working camp, it had the POWIB (1919) code Pa (Wo) (IWM: Facsimile K4655). The FPHS (1973) cite it too. It had the TA Priswarian: Woburn (ADM 1/8506/265–120667).

The 125th Company, Canadian Forestry Corps moved to estates owned by the Duke of Bedford on the outskirts of Woburn Sands, 3 miles from the railway station, and, as their name suggests, they were sent there to fell timber. The advance party consisted of four officers and thirty-two of other ranks. They were billeted in the village, arriving on 18 August 1917. When the rest of the company arrived they erected a camp in a field, just off the Bletchley-Bedford main road, owned by the Reverend Percy Allnutt. His house was used as quarters for the officers. The lower ranks slept at first in tents, before huts were constructed. The first task of the new force was to build a light railway to remove the fallen trees to what they called the Canadian Mill from Aspley Heath, situated 0.5 miles from the main railway line. The first trees were felled on 21 August 1917; by then their ranks had swollen to 112.

When the first PoWs arrived is not known, but in June 1917, the Secretary of the Wolverton Methodist Church's quarterly meetings tendered his resignation after being found guilty at Wolverton Magistrates Court for giving bread to the PoWs. The church's committee however declined to accept his offer, stating he had not broken any 'divine law'.

A decision was made to install a second mill, which they named the Scotch Mill. This began production on 30 August 1917. In September the company was further strengthened by the arrival of one officer and eighty other ranks, plus 105 German PoWs.

In January 1918, it was recorded the PoWs refused to work in the heavy snow that fell in the middle of that month. Two privates, A.E. Pierce and A. Tong, were sent to Woburn between March 1918 and March 1919 to assist the foreman of a PoW working party. Their names appeared in an extract taken from the PoWs' employment time sheets, held by Bedfordshire Record Office.

> More realities of the war were brought home to the villagers by the arrival of prisoners of war. In one instance, about 200 Germans were marched up the High Street under armed guard to a camp in the Duke of Bedford's estate. This proved quite a spectacle and locals turned out in force to see them. Once at the camp, they were put to work lumbering, making trench pit props for the front. A photo of the march and a description of the events have survived (BLARS Z887/1–2). The Germans were not the only ones logging in Woburn, Sands, as the 125th Canadian Forestry Corps were also stationed here …

In a 'war diary' kept by the Canadians, it was recorded in March 1918, 'this company has been receiving daily approximately 122 PoWs from the internment camp at Woburn.' It was also recorded that apart from the sawyer, the setter, the saw filer, and the engineer, the re-located Scotch Mill was being operated solely by the German PoWs. The diary does not state when they left, but the Scotch Mill was shipped to Windsor on 1 June 1918.

In August 1918 it was announced the timber felling operations at Woburn were to be wound down, and the Canadians were expected to go to Brockenhurst or Tilsbury. In October 1918, the Canadian Mill was handed over to the Royal Engineers, as the Canadians prepared to move to Tilsbury. It is recorded by the RE that eighty-seven PoWs assisted them. On 25 November 1918, Majors McCuaig and Wilson met with a representative of the Timber Control to make arrangements for the mill to be handed over to them. The mill was handed over on 6 December 1918.

PoWs are also recorded as clearing the millstream at Aspley Hall. The Domesday Book of 1086 records there was a mill at Hulcote. Later documents cite it was a watermill, which stood near to Aspley Hall. The watercourse continued to be used into the twentieth century as in 1917 it was noted that German PoWs were being used to cleanse Hulcote millstream, until a lack of suitable accommodation forced their withdrawal.

WOKING: Inkerman Barrack's Military Prison (OS: SU 974 584). In 1858 the Home Office bought just over 64 acres of land from the London Necropolis Company, in order to build a prison for disabled prisoners, not just for the physically ill, but also for those suffering from mental illnesses. It was to be known as the Woking

Invalid Convict Prison. Designed by Sir Joshua Jebb and Arthur Blomfield, it consisted of two large wings on either side of a large central tower. The west wing was for the chronically sick and insane, and the east wing was for some of the more able-bodied prisoners. A wall 18 feet high surrounded the whole site. The prison officially opened on 22 March 1860, when 300 prisoners were transferred from the already cramped and inadequate Lewes House of Correction and County Gaol.

In 1867 work began on a second phase – this time for female convicts. The more able-bodied men from the male prison were employed as cheap labour. The new prison opened on 5 May 1869 when 100 women were transferred from Parkhurst Prison, on the Isle of Wight. It became well known for its mosaics department. The women could earn 1s.2d (6p) a day breaking up refuse marble to be laid as mosaic flooring. Some designs were created and exhibited for the International Exhibition of Fine Arts and Industry at the Royal Albert Hall in 1872. It is believed that their labours produced parts of the floor of St Paul's Cathedral, the South Kensington Museums and St John's Church.

In 1886 a decision was made to close both prisons over a ten-year period. By 1888 most of the male prisoners had been transferred out. The buildings were then converted into military barracks and taken over by the army. The former prison was renamed the Inkerman Barracks, after the battle in the Crimean War. The War Office purchased another 20 acres of adjoining land from the London Necropolis Company to be used as part of the parade ground. The first infantry battalion to be quartered there, in 1895, was the 2nd Battalion, The Royal West Surrey Regiment.

The female prison continued to be used for its original purpose until October 1895, when it too was closed. The last of the women were transferred to Holloway Prison. During the First World War the female prison was used as a military hospital, whilst the male one housed troops, including those from the empire.

There are several accounts of PoWs being sentenced and incarcerated at Woking for escaping; for example, for attempting to escape from the camp at Leigh in Lancashire, three Germans PoWs were committed to Woking Prison on 13 July 1915.

Woking Detention Barracks was listed by the POWIB (1919) and its code was W D B (IWM: Facsimile K4655).

International law forbade prisons to be deployed to hold internees, but they were used by the British initially as holding centres until other facilities became available.

A delegation from the US Embassy in London visited the former prison on 7 August 1916 to see Leutnant Cahn of the Bavarian Artillery and Fahnrich-zur-See Johl of SMS *Blücher*. Each had been sentenced to six months for attempting to escape from Handforth; they had arrived 7 May 1916. They also interviewed Fahnrich von Schweinichen, a habitual escapee who had also tried to abscond from the camp at Stobs. Schweinichen was later reported to be at Pattishall (FO 383/190).

Clemens Rücker and Johann Biercher were sentenced to imprisonment for one year each at Woking. Rücker had persistently refused to work and openly defied authority. Biercher also persistently refused to work. He had been sentenced to nine months imprisonment on 9 March 1917 at Winchester.

In September 1947 the Royal Military Police took over the barracks as their home. They vacated the site in 1965 when they moved to Chichester. In December 1968, the Secretary of State for Defence was asked what proposals he had for the use or disposal of the land at Inkerman Barracks. His reply was that 22 acres had been sold or were on offer to the Surrey County Council for education purposes. Parts of the site became available for housing for Woking Borough Council and the Guinness Trust. A couple of rows of Victorian houses, that were originally the prison officers' quarters in Wellington Terrace and Raglan Road, were being renovated, and that is all that remains of the original buildings.

WOMENSWOLD (OS: TR 224 494). A working camp, its POWIB (1919) code was Pa (We) (IWM: Facsimile K4655). It is also cited by the FPHS (1973). Cited as being at Denne Hill Farm, its TA was Priswarian: Denne Hill Farm, Womenswold, Barham.

The house at Denne Hill was built in 1871 for Colonel J.D. Dyson. In more recent times the Loder-Symonds family have been living at Denne Hill, and for two generations been directly involved in running the farm.

WOODBOROUGH: Manor Farm (OS: SK 630 477). An agricultural group operating under Plumtree, it also appears in minutes produced by Notts WAC. Its POWIB (1919) code was Bro (Pl) (Wdb) (IWM: Facsimile K4655). The camp's TA was Priswarian: Woodborough, Epperstone (ADM 1/8506/265–120667).

Local knowledge states the PoWs were housed in the west wing of Manor Farm. Their dormitory was on the upper floor and could accommodate some sixty PoWs. Their bunks were lined up on opposite sides of a long room, and in the middle of the room was a stove.

The owner of Manor Farm at the time of the First World War was a Mr Foster. His son, John Mansfield Foster, in his late eighties, recalls that all but one of the PoWs was friendly. He recalls them working on the farm for about three years, as they did not leave immediately after the war finished. The type of work they did was varied: some worked in the carpenter's shop; some with the market gardeners; some did domestic duties; and, others did general work, including painting.

It is known that the internees drew at least two murals, measuring some 3 feet by 2 feet, on the walls. Sadly, they were destroyed when the building was refurbished in 1989, but photographs of them exist. There was also some residual evidence on a wall to suggest the PoWs may have had a dartboard.

High up on an external wall in the inner courtyard, over a laurel wreath, was drawn a large eagle with text written in German. Translated into English it reads:

We were of good spirits, even in the most difficult times
and tried to be brave confronted by the enemy.
But the force was too great and for all
our endeavours we landed PoWs.

During March 1919, Dr A. de Sturler compiled reports on visits of inspection to the PoW camps. He inspected Woodborough. His findings are held at the National Archives at Kew (FO 383/507).

WOODFORD (see Plympton).

WOODHAM FERRERS (OS: TQ 79- 99-). A working camp, its POWIB (1919) code was Pa (Wod Fr) (IWM: Facsimile K4655). It was also cited by the FPHS (1973) but its location is unknown.

The Times (27 August 1918), according to Mark (*Prisoners of war in British Hands during WW1*, 2007) reported a PoW named Meisner had escaped from Greenwood. His re-capture was reported the next day.

WOODSIDE (see Layston Farm, Perthshire).

WOODSTOCK: The Drill Hall (OS: SP 451 168). Described as a working camp, its address was cited as the Drill Hall. Its POWIB (1919) code was Dor (Wds) (IWM: Facsimile K4655). It had the TA Priswarian: Woodstock (ADM 1/8506/265–120667).

The newly refurbished community centre officially opened in 2012 which saw the tired old 1912 army drill hall updated to a bright and modern meeting hall. Honorary Townsman Nigel Clifford, a lifelong resident of the town and former colonel in the Royal Engineers, explained the history of the drill hall as a military training centre, as stores and finally as a community hall (www.oxonrcc.org.uk).

WOOTTON BASSETT: The Corner House (OS: SU 067 824). Described as an agricultural group attached to Devizes, its POWIB (1919) code was Dor (Dvs) (W B) (IWM: Facsimile K4655); its address is quoted as being the Corner House. The camp's TA was Priswarian: Wootton Bassett (ADM 1/8506/265–120667). The FPHS (1973) also cite Wootton Bassett.

Gringell (*History of Wootton Bassett*, 1977) cites the PoWs were housed at the Royal Oak, which stood on Station Road. In 1864, this sixteenth century two-storey inn had been considerably extended to incorporate a new Upper Assembly Room, measuring 52ft × 18ft, which included a substantial stabling facility at its rear. For many years, the inn played an integral part in hosting the town's social activities, including balls, concerts, plays, and sporting functions, but due to financial difficulties, in 1910 it was forced to cease trading.

A builder's merchant took on the site, and when it failed, Hall's bought the site. In 1924, the Midland Bank opened a branch in the corner block, which had been occupied by a grocer and draper, Watts and Parry. Presumably, this corner block had encompassed the Corner House, suggested by the POWIB (1919).

In more recent times, this site has been occupied by a branch of the supermarket chain, Somerfield.

The town has recently had an honour bestowed on it from the queen and is now called Royal Wootton Basset.

WORCESTER: Leigh Court (OS: SO 785 535). This Worcestershire working camp had the POWIB (1919) code, Dor (Lei) (IWM: Facsimile K4655), with Upton upon Severn as its satellite. Its TA was Priswarian, Leigh, nr Worcester (ADM 1/8506/265–120667). The FPHS (1973) also cites Leigh Court. It had no connection to the parent camp at Leigh, in Lancashire. No further evidence has been found to suggest this camp's location. Records show Lieutenant L.G. Marcus was in charge of the camp, and that on 31 December 1917, twenty-five PoWs were interned there.

It is very likely any PoW arriving at Leigh Court did so at the local railway station. The line from Worcester to Leominster via Bromyard, opened on 1 August 1861, passed through Leigh Court. The line was axed less than 100 years later. All that remains at Leigh Court is the abandoned shell of the original railway station building, with its crumbling platforms, testimony to the forces of nature. The site has had several owners since, mainly angling clubs, which ask visitors to keep out.

Close by is Leigh Court Barn, an outstanding example of medieval English carpentry. The timber-framed barn is the largest cruck structure in Britain. Built for Pershore Abbey in 1344, it is 46 metres (150 feet) long, with eighteen cruck blades, each engineered from a single oak tree.

A new house, built *c.*1820 on the site of a house once owned by the Norton family, could hold the key to the location; in 1852 the house was owned by William Miles.

WORTHY DOWN (OS: SU 471 354). A working camp, it had the POWIB (1919) code Dor (W D) (IWM: Facsimile K4655). Worthy Down is also cited by the FPHS (1973).

Traces of an Iron Age settlement can be seen at Worthy Down, near South Wonston, visible at certain times of the year from the air, along with the old airfield and its infrastructure. Association with the military began in 1917 when a Wireless and Observers School was established in October of that year. During the First World War an airfield was created in 1918, and was used by the Royal Air Force over the next 35 years or so. It became HMS *Kestrel* in May 1939 when it transferred to the Admiralty. Infamous then for its uphill landing, in 1942 it was decided to cease using the airfield as it had become unsuitable for modern aircraft. In 1952 it was re-commissioned as HMS *Ariel*, when the Air Engineering School moved in from Warrington. It remained in the hands of the Royal Navy until late 1960, when it transferred to the Army, and the Royal Army Pay Corps Electronic Accounting Development Unit moved from Devizes to its new computer centre. During World War Two, the base did achieve a notoriety of a kind: William Joyce (Lord Haw Haw) claimed the Germany Navy had sunk HMS *Kestrel*!

Not much is left of the old Worthy Down airfield today. The east-west grass runway is now used for agricultural purposes, and the hangars have long gone.

It is very likely the PoWs sent here were involved in creating the infrastructure of the early airfield at Worthy Down.

WOTTON: Barnwood House (OS: SO 861 179). The earliest known asylum in Gloucester was established near Wotton in 1793, when the site of two houses and an inn were converted for that purpose.

The county's second institution was completed to a plan drawn by William Stark of Edinburgh. On his death in 1813, it was finalised by John Wheeler. Work began in 1814, but was hampered by financial constraints and took nine years to complete. Under the National Health Service it became known as Horton Road Hospital. Horton Road provided care for some 165 years and closed on 31 March 1988.

A third institution, which opened in 1883, was established at Barnwood House, which sits at the foot of the Cotswolds. Built around the existing house, it was to become Coney Hill Hospital in 1948, and closed in 1968. Samuel Whitfield Dawkes was an architect for the Birmingham and Gloucester Railway. He designed engine sheds and houses for railway workers. In 1836, he married Caroline Sarah White of Long Newnton, and by 1840 they were living at Barnwood.

Gloucester Record Office (D37/1/147, 21 February 1917) cites concerns were being expressed about the frost devastation at Barnwood House Lunatic Asylum in February 1917, where Austrian-Hungarian PoWs were working on nearby farms. It was also cited that their consumption of bread, meat and sugar was much higher than anticipated.

WROTHAM (OS: TQ 578 622). The POWIB (1919) cited Bayldon House as the address of an internment camp, and gave its code as Pa (Hlg) (Wro) (IWM: Facsimile K4655), denoting it was a satellite of the camp at Halling. The house stands in School Lane, West Kingsdown. The camp's TA is cited as Priswarian: Wrotham in a HO document. A second document from the same source cites its TA as Priswarian:

Kingsdown (ADM 1/8506/265–120667). These may have been different camps or the same camp that moved to a different location. Incorrectly, the FPHS (1973) cite Tovil Wrotham as one entry.

WYMONDHAM (OS: SK 84- 18-). An agricultural group attached to Croxton Park AD. Its POWIB (1919) code was Bro (Cro) (Wy) (IWM: Facsimile K4655). The camp's TA was Priswarian: Wymondham, Oakham (ADM 1/8506/265–120667). There are several large houses, or their grounds, which could have supported a PoW camp in Wymondham; amongst these are Burfield Hall (*c.*1709), Cavick House (*c.*1720) and Gunvil's Hall (*c.*1580). Wymondham House is cited by *Kelly's Trade Directory* of 1912 as being occupied by Charles Stephen Harvey.

Y

YARBURGH (OS: TF 326 878). The camp was located in the workhouse, its TA Priswarian: The Workhouse, Yarburgh, Falstow reflected this. (ADM 1/8506/265–120667)

YARDLEY GOBION (Stoney Stratford) (OS: SP 780 700). A working camp, it had the POWIB (1919) code Pa (Y G). The FPHS (1973) cite it too. Nearby, Stoney Stratford is also cited by the FPHS.

The Potterspury Poor Law Union was established in 1835. In 1896, its guardians had repairs and alterations done to their workhouse, which was in Yardley Gobion. In 1904, it changed its name to the White House, 'to avoid using the word workhouse being on birth certificates'. Deemed to be unfit for purpose, the workhouse closed in January 1917 and its inmates were dispersed to other institutions. The Northamptonshire VAD then began using the buildings as a convalescent home for wounded soldiers.

In May 1918, the War Office took over control, and around fifty German PoWs were then housed there to work on local farms. After the war the local council tried to transform the site into a children's home, but the Ministry of Health rejected their plan. In 1925 the former workhouse was converted into private rentable accommodation, and is still used for this purpose today. ('Potterspury', in *A History of the County of Northampton*: Volume 5, the Hundred of Cleley, ed. Philip Riden and Charles Insley, 2002, pp. 289–345).

YATE (OS: ST 708 820). In both World Wars, Yate hosted a PoW camp. Osgood (*Archaeology Newsletter* No. 7, 7 April 2004) cites the First World War camp was located just off the Westerleigh Road, at its junction with Stanshawes Drive on what was Eggshill Common. Contemporary Ordnance Survey Maps show this to be where Wapley Camp was located in the Second World War.

According to local legend, the earlier camp interned around 1,000 German PoWs. Much of the site was quarried away in the 1930s when the site became a brick works. Today a lake has formed on what is part of Coopers Engineering Works.

Several locals, of the Yate Oral History Project, attest to the presence of the camp. Ashley Dyer recalled being told fascinating stories by his father, Charles, who was born in 1907. He spoke about the many occasions when the German prisoners were marched along roads at Yate. He used to pump water for them to fill up their flasks, for which he was given pennies. Ashley's grandfather had been badly wounded in the Battle of the Somme in 1916 and as the eldest of five, Charles became responsible for much of the family's well-being. He used to go by pony and trap to the officers' mess to collect the leftover scraps of food from the camp to be given to the pigs. As a boy, Ashley explored the site of the camp. He found copies of *The Times* newspaper from the First World War era used to stuff vent holes in the hutments. The PoWs were employed to erect the sheds of the cattle market, and in other building projects in and around Yate.

The Berkshire Mercury (23 March 1917) cited Jano Chylanzi, a Hungarian, and Karl Perus, an Austrian, had escaped from the Yates Labour Internment Camp on Wednesday. They were observed on Saturday evening by Police Sergeant Pierce proceeding along the road at Twyford, who, suspecting they were aliens, detained them. He communicated with Superintendent Goddard and it was subsequently discovered that they were two men who were on the run. Neither offered resistance. The men stated that on escaping they walked to Cirencester, their object being to make their way to London. They continued on their journey thinking they were making good progress towards their destination, travelling a distance which they put at 25 miles, to find, to their astonishment, they were once more in Cirencester. They then took a train to Reading where on their arrival they set off to walk to London, only to be stopped by Pierce. The escapees had purchased their food in shops and slept rough for the three nights whilst they were at large.

A photograph, taken in 1919, shows a sign from the perimeter of the camp, on which can be read 'Stray dogs found in the camp are liable to be destroyed.'

Yate is cited by the FPHS (1973).

YATESBURY (OS: SU 051 713). Described as a working camp, it had the POWIB (1919) code Dor (Yby) (IWM: Facsimile K4655), and its TA was Priswarian: Yatesbury. It was also cited by the FPHS (1973).

Approximately 4 miles east of Calne, the airfield was opened in 1917 as 27 Group Radio School. It was to close in 1919.

According to *Flight* (1935), the Bristol Aeroplane Co. Ltd purchased the 290-acre site, which lay between Jugglers Lane and the main Calne and Marlborough roads, in 1935. The site included all the old aerodrome buildings. New buildings were erected and the infrastructure was greatly improved. During the Second World War, many wireless operators gained their 'flying time' from there. In April 1969, the station was closed. Because Yatesbury then fell into the North Wessex Downs Area of Outstanding Natural Beauty, the Ministry of Defence was persuaded to remove the huts. The land was then sold off in lots. Some First World War Belfast truss hangars still stand, but have been left to the elements. Later buildings also remain standing, but with their roofs missing. Most are also in poor condition. A plan to restore them is being opposed by English Nature.

According to Crawford (*Wiltshire and The Great War: Training the Empire's Soldiers*, 1999) Leutnant Paul Scheumann, a German officer, scrambled through the barbed wire put around the Yatesbury camp, situated next to the airfield, and made his way to Chippenham wearing a suit fashioned from blankets, and a mackintosh bought locally. There he caught a train to London. He went to the theatre before registering as Thomas Hann, High-street 145, Bristol, as a guest at Bellomo's Private Hotel in Jermyn Street. Signor Bellomo, the hotel proprietor, alerted the police and he was arrested the next morning for, apparently, signing-in in the orthodox German fashion, with the number behind the street name. The *Wiltshire Gazette* carried the story.

Crawford (1999) also cites six PoWs from Yatesbury appeared in court, accused of stealing bacon fat from C. & T. Harris & Co. of Calne. Captain Mursell, the camp's commandant, told the court the accused had bread and coffee before leaving the camp, and took with them a light lunch that consisted of coffee, cheese and bread. Each man's daily allowance was thirteen ounces of bread, one and a half ounces of cheese, and four ounces of beef or horseflesh. In Germany, like many countries on the mainland of Europe, horsemeat was then regularly eaten.

It has been recorded that the internees complained of being overworked to the Swiss observers. They are cited as being housed in huts, but with ineffective lighting. There were also complaints about the camp's water supply.

DKF 30: Diese 14 Lager müssen für die bevorstehende kältere und nasse Jahreszeit als durchaus ungeeignet bezeichnet werden. Unzureichend sind auch die Baracken in Port Clarence und Yatesbury, es sei denn, die Wände der Baracken baldmöglicht verstärkt werden.

DKF 31: Unzureichend sind auch die Baracken in Port Clarence und Yatesbury, es sei denn, daß Wände der Baracken baldmöglichst verstärke werden. Die Beleuchtung der Baracken in Newlandside und Yatesbury bedarf dringend der Änderung.

DKF 31: Gesundheitlich Vorsorge. Sehr empfindlich ist der Mangel an gutem und genügendem Wasser außer in Sproxton Moor, hauptsächlich in Peak Deal (sic) *Quarries bei Buxton, Belfon Park* (sic), *und Yatesbury.*

DKF 31 Auch in Loch Doon, auf der Insel Raasay, in Newlandside, Ceal Aston (sic), *Sutton Veney* (sic), *Bowithick, Netheravon, Yatesbury, Rovrah* (sic), *Port Clarence, und Hayrmyres* (sic) *werden die Leute zu sehr ausgenutzt.*

DKF 32: In Yatesbury wurde seit September 1916 erst zweimal protestantischer Gottesdienst gehalten.

YEOVIL (OS: ST 55- 16-). Minute 3239 of the Somerset County Council WAC (21 May 1918) approved depots for ploughman gangs at Keyford, Priston, Queen Camel, Glastonbury, Wookey, Hinton St George and another near Yeovil. Nothing is known of this depot's location.

YORK. There were three locations in York that billeted PoWs and one that provided medical care. The FPHS (1973) cites three. These were York Castle, Leeman Road, and Hull Road. The third location, cited in local newspapers, where PoWs were billeted, was in the Exhibition Building. All were used in the initial stages of the war, and all closed as other locations became available, including the controversial use of ships.

Reports of York Castle being used are misleading. Clifford's Tower was all that remained of the castle, when in 1825 work began enclosing it, with a huge wall, into a new prison that cut it off from the rest of the city. Four prison blocks radiated off a hub. The buildings became a military detention centre at the turn of the century. These were demolished by the City Council in 1934. Today the Castle Museum and a car park stand in its place. (www.historyofyork.org.uk/themes/victorian/the-victorian-prison-building).

DETENTION BARRACKS (OS: SE 590 523), EXHIBITION BUILDING (OS: SE 605 523) and LEEMAN ROAD (OS: SE 604 514). Reports that PoWs were being housed in the castle are disputed by the Castle Museum's Keeper of the Collection. Blueprints exist showing how the castle was laid out during the war years, and these do not suggest that internees were being kept inside the castle at that time. York Castle was the Detention Barracks for the North East of England from 1900 to 1929.

However, the first report of PoWs being put in York Castle clearly states a party of fifty were placed in the Detention Barracks. Three weeks later the same newspaper states PoWs sent to the castle were being housed in tents.

The following extracts cover that three week period:

> *The York Herald* (9 August 1914) cited a party of fifty internees arrived at the station and were marched to York Castle where they were placed in the Detention Barracks. Later it was learned that most of this group came from the Harrogate area.
>
> *The York Herald* (10 August 1914) carried a picture of released Germans crossing Lendal Bridge on their way to York Station. The story says a number of Germans detained at York Castle were released on Saturday and yesterday.
>
> The *York Herald* (11 August 1914) cited a party of twenty internees were moved from Redford Barracks (Edinburgh) to York Castle.
>
> *The York Herald* (12 August 1914) thought there were now about forty internees being held at York Castle.
>
> *The York Gazette* (15 August 1914) cited batches of Germans had been brought to York Castle during the past week. No antipathy had been shown to them.
>
> *The York Gazette* (22 August 1914) cited that there were well over 100 Germans being detained at York Castle. The paper also reported twenty-five internees were brought to York Castle. Six were sailors from Hartlepool, and nineteen others came from Scarborough.
>
> *The York Herald* (29 August 1914) reports that there are now 130 prisoners at York Castle: they live in tents.

Then, in September there was a report of PoWs being sent to the Exhibition Building. Today, the Exhibition Building is known as the City Art Gallery that stands in St Leonard's Place.

The Museums & Art Gallery Committee's annual report for 1914 states the military authorities had commandeered practically the whole of the Exhibition Building for billeting troops from early in August 1914. During the military occupation, Dublin Fusiliers were stationed there, thus preventing the Gallery being opened to the public from 15 September until 22 October. The report also stated aliens were being held there too, from around 11 September:

> *The York Herald* (12 September 1914) cited further parties of Germans and Austrians arrived at York Castle. As the accommodation was insufficient, 100 of their number were moved to the Exhibition Buildings, where straw mattresses had been provided for bedding. Arrangements were being made to move a further 300 to 400 to the centre, dependent on the completion date of a new camp that was being erected in Leeman Road. From 25 September 1914, Leeman Road was ready to house its first internees. The PoWs were housed in the disused works of the York Engineering Company, standing about 700 yards north-west of the railway station.
>
> *The York Herald* (19 September 1914) reported there were still fifty-four German and Austrian prisoners at York Castle. It then stated another 250 internees were expected to arrive next weekend. The Leeman Road camp was expected to take up to 1,500.

The York Herald (24 September 1914) cited 300 Germans from Redford Barracks, Edinburgh, that included seventy sailors, arrived by train, to go to Leeman Road.

The York Gazette (26 September 1914) confirmed their arrival. It cited one was wounded and he was taken to hospital. The report concluded this was the first occasion that prisoners, other than civilian, had arrived in York.

York Herald (26 September 1914) reported that German internees held in the Exhibition Building had been moved to the Detention Camp in Leeman Road. Nearly 100 men were transferred the previous day, under armed escort, proceeding via St Leonard's Place, Museum St, and Lendal Bridge. Prior to the move, more enemy aliens had arrived. Sixteen had come from Burton, three from Newcastle, and two from Sunderland.

The York Gazette (3 October 1914) stated there were daily visits by large crowds to watch PoWs taking exercise at Leeman Road. It was noted that there were now 1,180 in the camp, 'men from all walks of life', with an extraordinary amount of baggage, stored in one of the bigger sheds. There was no apparent lack of money: the canteen sold tobacco and cigarettes. Plans were in place to intern a further 500.

The York Herald (24 October 1914) reported many aliens were being brought to York from the North. They were all taken to Leeman Road except for one party that was taken to the Castle by mistake.

The papers now carried reports that Leeman Road could not take any more PoWs and that the Exhibition Buildings were to be used again, temporarily, before York Castle was to be used again.

The York Herald (27 October 1914) stated Leeman Road was now full. 150 internees were to be moved to the Exhibition Buildings temporarily – to go to York Castle in a few days.

The York Herald (30 October 1914) clarified this more when it cited aliens were still being held in the Exhibition Buildings. It was also stated that tents, housing more internees, occupied the castle square. These tents were eventually to be replaced with huts, but it was not known when this would happen.

The York Herald (3 November 1914) cited the Archbishop visited the internees at Leeman Road. His visit was also reported in the *Gazette* (7 November 1914). No more reports of PoWs being billeted in Leeman Road are printed.

York Gazette (14 November 1914) cited that because the Exhibition Building was still in the hands of the military authorities, and would not be available for the Christmas post, the General Post Office had planned to use the Guildhall instead to sort the mail.

The City of York's Report of the Estates Committee (4 January 1915) states the YMCA was using the Exhibition Buildings. The report (3 May 1915) noted the Exhibition Buildings had been vacated by the YMCA and was now being used by the Army Pay Corps. A letter of thanks was sent from the Northern Command thanking the Lord Mayor and the City Council for the use of the building.

According to Manz (*New Evidence on Stobs Internment Camp (1914–19)*, 2003), due to its unsanitary conditions, Leeman Road closed in 1915. Panayi (*The Enemy In Our Midst: Germans in Britain during the First World War*, 1991) cites the civilians were transferred from York, before March 1915, to HMT *Royal Edward*, which was moored off Southend-on-Sea.

Medical Facilities

Military hospitals in Britain were not designed to cope with the large numbers of wounded that were being brought back from the front during the First World War. The British Red Cross was instrumental in easing the pressure. Their action was the foresight of Sir Alfred Keogh who had been the Director General of the Army Medical Service from 1905 to 1910. Keogh was also responsible for establishing the Territorial Force in 1911. His revolutionary policy in earmarking public buildings for use as hospitals in times of war proved crucial, and having the appropriate staff to man them saved many lives. The buildings commandeered ranged from private and civilian hospitals, sanatoriums, asylums and workhouse infirmaries to town halls, universities, schools, factories, and private houses. Although auxiliary general hospitals had been intended to meet the needs of the Territorial Force, they received patients from the regular British Army as well as PoWs. Each was intended to accommodate 520 patients. The auxiliary hospitals were attached to central military hospitals and their patients remained under military control.

At the front a wounded soldier would get triage treatment before being moved up the line to an Advanced Dressing Station still close to the front line. It would be manned by members of the Field Ambulance, RAMC. In the event he needed further treatment he would be moved to a Casualty Clearing Station, and if required moved to a base hospital. The seriously wounded would be brought back by hospital ship and tagged for the appropriate hospital for further treatment. PoWs would not have been treated differently.

After treatment, patients were then be sent to convalescent hospitals to recuperate.

ABERGELE: KINMEL PARK MILITARY HOSPITAL (OS: SH 984 805). Kinmel Park was a military base, with a hospital that treated wounded PoWs; the POWIB (1919) cite its code as Km H (IWM: Facsimile K4655). There were 890 beds available.

Taylor (per. comm., 12 January 2001) wrote as the peace process was starting, around 19,000 Canadians were stationed at the Kinmel Park camp in North Wales, with very little to do as they awaited news that they would be sent home. Being harangued by the locals, 500 of them eventually went on the rampage, looting the nearby village of Tinwood. Consequently, fifty-one of them were court-martialled. Their repatriation process was then speeded up.

ALDERSHOT. There were three known facilities in Aldershot that gave respite to hospitalised PoWs. These were the Cambridge Military Hospital, the Connaught Military Hospital and the Aldershot Isolation Hospital.

After the battle of Mons on 20 August 1914, the *Aldershot News* (n.d.) reported the first batches of wounded men were arriving at the Cambridge and Connaught hospitals. They had come from Southampton on Sunday. Most had met with their injuries during the battle of Mons and were moved to their respective hospitals with the utmost care and solicitude.

CAMBRIDGE MILITARY HOSPITAL (OS: SU 869 512). Not to be confused with the hospital of the same name in Cambridge, it is cited by the POWIB (1919) and had the code Ca H (IWM: Facsimile K4655). It was also cited by the OSt.

Located at the Stanhope Lines, it was named after Prince George, Duke of Cambridge, who opened it in 1879. The hospital gained some notoriety for the pioneering plastic surgery unit set up by William Arbuthnot-Lane, Captain Harold Delf Gillies, William Kelsey Fry and Henry Tonks. Gillies (later Sir Harold) had watched and learned from Hippolyte Morestin who was reconstructing faces in the Val-de-Grace Hospital in Paris. On his return to Britain he begged the War Office to set up a similar unit.

The clock tower of the Cambridge once housed a large bell and two smaller ones. The larger was one of a pair – known as the Sebastopol Bells – brought back from the Crimea in 1856. The other is in Windsor Castle. In March 1961, the large bell was removed from the clock tower. From its relocated site in Steeles Road, it was moved again to its present site outside Gun Hill House.

Morrison (*English Military Hospitals: An Architectural History*, n.d.) cites that the Cambridge Military Hospital had accepted a wide range of patients. Small wards were set up to treat officers, prisoners, lunatics, ophthalmic cases and those suffering from venereal diseases and itch (scabies).

Sadly the buildings were proving too costly to maintain and the hospital closed on 2 February 1996. Partly blamed for the high cost of renovation was its location at the top of a hill intended to provide a plentiful supply of clean fresh air due to the influence of Florence Nightingale in its design. Today, plans are in progress to rejuvenate the site. Residential homes are planned.

CONNAUGHT MILITARY HOSPITAL (OS: SU 878 529). Built on the pavilion principle, it opened in 1898, and comprised of four pavilion wards flanking an administration cum kitchen complex, with various subsidiary buildings. A venereal disease unit was added in 1908. Only the administration block (disused) and one ward wing survive. By 1992 the ward wing had been partly demolished.

The Aldershot News (11 September 1914) reported the death of Obermaschinemaat Robert Adler, a PoW. He died of pneumonia in Connaught Military Hospital on 2 September 1914. His funeral was at Deepcut Barracks three days later. He had been the petty officer on the minelayer *Königin Luise*, which was sunk on 5 August in the North Sea. Adler was one of about fifty survivors that had been taken on board HMS *Amphion*. As it returned to port the next morning of the next day the *Amphion* also hit a mine, and sank; one officer and 150 from the crew were lost, together with twenty PoWs. In a twist of fate, it is believed the *Amphion* hit one of the mines laid by the stricken *Königin Luise*.

The POWIB (1919) code for this hospital is Con H (IWM: Facsimile K4655). It was also cited by the OSt. The hospital buildings have been replaced by barrack blocks.

ISOLATION HOSPITAL (OS: SU 876 517). The POWIB (1919) gave it the code A I H (IWM: Facsimile K4655). It was also cited by the OSt.

Standing in Redan Road, the Isolation Hospital opened its doors in 1896. In 1948 it was taken over by the National Health Service; to reflect the change it became the Northfield Hospital and was described in their records as being a mental hospital (NA 6098/1).

BEDFORD MILITARY HOSPITAL (OS: SP 976 325). Its POWIB (1919) code was Bed H (IWM: Facsimile K4655). It was also cited in a List of Prisoners of war Camps in England and Wales and Scotland with Postal and Telegraphic Addresses (May 1918) (ADM 1/8506/265–120667).

The hospital is believed to have been in the town's workhouse. Between 1929 and 1948, it was known as St Peter's Hospital, and after the inauguration of the National Health Service, in 1948, it became the north wing of Bedford General Hospital. The site has been revamped as part of the Bedford Hospital Trust expansion programme, which means most of the original buildings were demolished in 2007, leaving only the original 1795 main building, which is now known as Shires House.

1st BIRMINGHAM WAR HOSPITAL: Rubery Hill (OS: SP 993 77). Tonks and Smout (*Rubery Hill Hospital: A Short History*, 1982) cites the hospital opened its doors in 1882 as Rubery Hill Lunatic Asylum to accommodate some 620 patients. In March 1915, it was designated to be the 1st Birmingham War Hospital, a military hospital. The 2nd Birmingham War Hospital was at Hollymoor.

Rubery Hill remained under War Office jurisdiction until 1919, its POWIB (1919) code was Bm H (IWM: Facsimile K4655). It was also cited by the OSt (1917).

Reconstruction of the hospital began immediately after the war at a cost of £60,000 to the city's administrators. The War Office agreed to pay £25,000 in compensation.

In 1948 the hospital became part of the National Health Service.

BRIGHTON: 2nd EASTERN GENERAL HOSPITAL (OS: TQ 330 051). The first workhouse in Brighton was erected *c.*1730 on the site of the former chapel of the Convent of Saint Bartholomew, in Market Street, where almshouses had previously stood. It could accommodate up to thirty-five paupers. In the early 1800s, it was enlarged to accommodate around 150 inmates. In 1818, a 9-acre site was purchased at Church Hill for a new workhouse. Three years later the new workhouse was opened. Its architect was William Mackie. In 1853, the decision was taken build a new workhouse at Elm Grove. The foundation stone of the town's third workhouse was laid on 11 April 1865. It opened on 12 September 1867 to the designs of J.C. & G. Lansdown of Charing Cross in conjunction with George Maynard, a local man. Their impressive main block to the north of the site is T-shaped. The front was four storeys high, with a central clock tower.

In 1914, Elm Grove Workhouse became the 2nd Eastern General Hospital. It occupied the boys' grammar school, elementary schools, the workhouse and several large houses, including the pavilion.

Between 1915 and 1916, Brighton's Royal Pavilion, with a total of 724 beds, was initially used to treat Indian soldiers until April 1916 when it was re-designated the Kitchener Indian Hospital; then as Pavilion General Hospital to treat limbless men. At that time it had around 2,000 beds. It is believed PoWs were treated there too.

Released by the War Office in 1921, the workhouse became a place for elderly care, until 1930, when it became Brighton Municipal Hospital. Then in 1948 it became part of the National Health Servic and was renamed Brighton General Hospital.

BROCTON WAR HOSPITAL (OS: SJ 984 196). Whitehouse and Whitehouse (*A Town For Four Winters*, 1978) state the Brindley Heath Hospital had 1,000 beds in twelve wards, each measuring 208 feet by 20 feet, at 25-foot intervals connected by a long corridor. It was an integral part of the army camp complex at Brocton.

Reinhold Kempt was a patient. He was not impressed by the staff that treated him. He states his wounds were only looked at once in a ten week period.

The POWIB (1919) cited it, its code was B W H (IWM: Facsimile K4655). It was also cited by the OSt, and by the HO, who gave it the TA Priswopal, Brocton (ADM 1/8506/265–120667).

DKF 39. Der ausgetauschte Gardefüsilier Reinhold Kempf gibt an, daß im Hospital Brocton die ärztliche Behandlung sehr schlecht gewesen sei; so haben die englischen Ärzte seine Wunde in zehn Wochen nur einmal angesehen, und so ist alles dem Sanitätspersonal überlassen, welches mit großer Unsauberkeit seine Tätigkeit verrichtete.

CAMBRIDGE MILITARY HOSPITAL: 1st Eastern General Hospital (OS: TL 441 584). Only cited by the POWIB (1919), its code was C M H (IWM: Facsimile K4655).

The Royal Army Medical Corps established the 1st Eastern General Hospital in 1908, which was then in Addenbrooke Hospital. During the First World War the military hospital moved its headquarters to Trinity College. It had beds in Leys School and in the grounds of Trinity College, and later in the year in temporary buildings on the cricket grounds of Clare College and King's College, to the south of Burrell's Walk. By the end of 1915 it had over 1,500 beds.

The Albert, Griffiths and Bowtell Wards of the Addenbrooke were also commandeered, and were regarded as an extension to the hospital. The last soldiers were withdrawn from these wards in March 1919, and according to Addenbrooke's records, 2,885 soldiers were treated there during the hostilities, but there is no mention of any PoWs being treated there.

CARDIFF: 3rd WESTERN GENERAL HOSPITAL (OS: ST 178 784). The POWIB (1919) issued two codes for the 3rd Western General Hospital: 3 W G H (C) and 3 W G H (N) (IWM: Facsimile K4655). The first was for Cardiff, and the other for Newport. However there is evidence to suggest the latter was at Neath.

The Cardiff site was at the King Edward VII Hospital. Originally known as the Cardiff Dispensary, it was established in 1822 on Newport Road. When it moved into a new building in 1837 it also changed its name to the Glamorgan and Monmouthshire Infirmary and Dispensary. When it moved again, in 1883, to a new site near the junction with Glossop Road, the old buildings were leased to University College of South Wales and Monmouthshire. From 1911 until 1923 the hospital was known as the King Edward VII Hospital; but during the First World War, it was known as the 3rd Western General Hospital (Cardiff) (www.agor.org.uk). In 1923 it became the Cardiff Royal Infirmary, and could accommodate up to 500 patients by the time of the establishment of the NHS in 1948. In more recent times the hospital closed and its patients were transferred to the University Hospital of Wales. The west wing of the Royal has been used as a clinic since 2005 (www.arcw.llgc.org.uk).

CATTERICK MILITARY HOSPITAL (OS: SE 180 974). An integral part of the army camp at Catterick, this hospital had the POWIB (1919) code Ck M H (IWM: Facsimile K4655). It was believed to have had 750 beds available during the First World War.

National Archives records state it opened *c.*1910, and partially closed in 1999. It had been re-branded as the Duchess of Kent Military Hospital in 1976.

According to the *Daily Telegraph*'s website (2001) a defence review found there were not enough military acute in-patient psychiatric cases to justify retaining the unit.

CHISELDON MILITARY HOSPITAL (OS: SU 191 775). Near South Farm, this military hospital opened in June 1915 and eventually had 1,360 beds. The POWIB (1919) cited it, and gave it the code Chs H (IWM: Facsimile K4655).

The station's wooden platform, later replaced by a double-sided concrete one, provided easy access to the hospital (Crawford, *Wiltshire and The Great War: Training the Empire's Soldiers*, 1999). There was also a working camp in Chiseldon.

COLCHESTER MILITARY HOSPITAL (OS: TL 996 380). Listed by the POWIB (1919), its code was Col H (IWM: Facsimile K4655). It was also cited by the OSt.

When new barracks were built at Colchester in 1856, they were serviced by a twenty-hutted hospital complex. In 1896 these huts were replaced with a red brick building.

It closed 17 December 1977.

CROWTHORNE WAR HOSPITAL (OS: SU 852 640). Better known today as Broadmoor Hospital, this hospital had the POWIB (1919) code, Cr H (IWM: Facsimile K4655). It was also cited by the OSt. Although cited in a HO document, its TA was not stated (ADM 1/8506/265–120667).

Official records state that Block One of what was then Broadmoor Criminal Lunatic Asylum became Crowthorpe War Hospital and cared for mentally ill German PoWs.

Lizzie Wertheim, when diagnosed as being mentally ill at Aylesbury Prison, was sent to Broadmoor, where she died in 1919. She was convicted of being a spy in 1914, and along with George Breeckow was executed by firing squad in the Tower of London.

CROYDON: ADDINGTON PARK WAR HOSPITAL (OS: TQ 367 638). Cited by the POWIB (1919), its code was A P H (IWM: Facsimile K4655). It was also cited by the OSt.

When owner Sir John Leigh died in 1737 it took nearly four decades of litigation before Anne Spencer his cousin inherited the estate. She then sold it, *c.*1771, to Barlow Trecothick, Alderman of the City of London and Lord Mayor. Trecothick engaged Robert Mylne as the architect to rebuild the house, but died before the house was complete. It then passed on to his nephew, James Ivers. The building, a Palladian-style mansion of two main storeys, was completed in 1778. In 1807, an Act of Parliament purchased the mansion and its estate for the use of the Archbishops of Canterbury. Six archbishops lived at Addington Palace.

In 1898, Frederick Alexander English, a South African diamond merchant, purchased the house and its grounds. English engaged Richard Norman Shaw to restructure the house. After his death, in 1909, there were attempts to sell the estate. In 1911, a massive housing development was proposed for the park, but it never materialised. A substantial part of the estate was sold to Addington Golf Club in 1913.

In the First World War the house became a hospital for enteric fever and malaria, run by the Red Cross. Although the house remained empty for many years the golf course was eventually opened in 1922. The house was converted, in 1928, into a hotel. The southern part of the estate was sold to the Croydon Corporation in the 1930s to be turned into a public park. The Corporation purchased the remainder of the estate, including the house, in 1951, leasing the park back to the golf club.

In 1953 the mansion was leased to the Royal School of Church Music who resided there until 1996. Now privately owned, the estate is run as a conference centre and country club.

DARTFORD WAR HOSPITAL: GORE FARM (OS: TQ 566 723). Gore Farm Convalescent Smallpox Hospital opened in 1884 with some 1,000 beds under canvas. By 1887, the tents disappeared, to be replaced by wooden huts, capable of taking 850 patients. When an annex was created in 1890 the hutted Gore Farm section became known as the Lower Section. The upper section was again extended in 1902. In 1911, Gore Farm Convalescent Smallpox Hospital and was renamed the Southern Hospital.

During the First World War the Lower Section, now the Lower Southern, became the Dartford War Hospital, which had the POWIB (1919) code, L D H (IWM: Facsimile K4655). It was also cited by the OSt.

Miss W. Greenwood was a member of Queen Alexandra's Imperial Military Nursing Service and was stationed there from May 1916 until October 1916. She wrote that she tended sick German prisoners and internees, before joining HMHS *Britannic*.

Later in the war the combatant Germans were moved out so that most of the site could be given over to the Americans, to treat their wounded. The 'upper' Southern was handed over to the US Military and became US Base Hospital No. 37. The civilian internees remained at the hospital until the end of the war.

There were 263 combatants and twenty-one civilian internees buried within the grounds of nearby Darenth Asylum; their bodies were moved to Cannock Chase in the 1960s.

During the Second World War the Southern Hospital became a general hospital and did not return to treating fevers. It remained a general hospital with the inception of the NHS and began to serve the people of Dartford.

The Southern Hospital closed in 1959. The Lower Southern was partly demolished. The section that survived became the Mabledon Polish Hospital until 1985, when the remaining patients were transferred to Stone House.

DARTFORD ISOLATION HOSPITAL (OS: TQ 557 743). It had the TA, Warspital, Dartford (ADM 1/8506/265–120667). It was also cited by the OSt. This may have been the Bow Arrow Infectious Hospital, thought to have opened in 1893. Rees (*Dartford and the Great War*, 1994) makes no mention of this facility.

DARTFORD: JOYCE GREEN FARM (OS: TQ 544 760). In 1894, to facilitate the creation of a complex of isolation hospital units, parts of the Joyce Green Estate and Marsh Street Farm were purchased for £22,000.

Joyce Green Smallpox Hospital was opened on 28 December 1903. Along with the Orchard and Long Reach, they were collectively known as the River Hospitals, and stood apart from the Gore Farm complex.

Before the war an airfield was created adjacent to the Orchard. The PoWs may have been utilised in upgrading it.

Farming was an integral part of the Joyce Green complex, but 'was somewhat neglected' until organised by Dr Cameron during the First World War. It may be that he utilised the PoWs held in Dartford.

Records show those interned at Joyce Green, Hadnall, Peak Dale, Sutton Veny, Larkhill, Netheravon, Codford, and Fovant were not given the opportunity to attend regular Church Services.

In 1918, 1,000 Russian refugees were accommodated at Joyce Green.

During the Second World War part of the hospital became the Netherlands Hospital and treated many patients from Dunkirk. With the inception of the National Health Service in 1948, it became a general hospital and remained so until its closure in September 2000.

The camp had the TA, Priswarian, Joyce Green (ADM 1/8506/265–120667).

DKF 31: In Joice Green (sic), *Dartford, Linton, Sutton Veney* (sic) *Fovant, und Evesham bestehen Keine Kantine. Die Ausführung der Bestellungen der Kriegsgefangenen durch den Profoß Sergeanten, kann nicht als genügender Ersatz betrachtet werden.*

DKF 32: Gottesdienst: Die Seelsorge der Kreigsgefangenen ist auf vielen Plätzen sehr vernachlässigt. In den Lagern von Joyce Green, Dartford; Hadnall; Peak Dale Quarries bei Buxton; Sutton Veny; Larkhill; Netheravon; Codford; und Fovant hat noch kein Gottesdienst stattgefunden.

DEAL: Royal Marine Infirmary Barracks (OS: TR 377 520). Cited by the POWIB (1919), its code was D M I (IWM: Facsimile K4655).

At Deal, the North, East and South (or Cavalry) barracks were all constructed shortly after the outbreak of the French revolution. When crippled by the cost of the war with France in 1815, many locals in Kent turned their hand to smuggling and the South Barracks played an important part in housing troops that manned the blockades along the coast to stamp out this illegal trade. It later became the coastguard station, which lasted until 1840. The Royal Marines, which were formed in 1664, took over the East Barracks in 1861. It was they who formed the School of Music, and they remained there in various guises until 26 March 1996, moving then to their new quarters at Portsmouth. In 1900 a new infirmary was built to the west of Gladstone Road on what was formerly a drill ground. Known as the Infirmary Barracks, it remained in use until 1988. Today, the site has been redeveloped as Marine Mews.

DENBIGH: NORTH WALES COUNTIES LUNATIC ASYLUM (OS: SJ 052 650). The camp at Queen's Ferry had been cleared of most of its internees by 21 May 1915. The majority had gone to London. A US Embassy report cites the first arrivals from Queen's Ferry appeared at Alexandra Palace on 7 May 1915. By 21 May 1915 the camp had been cleared of all its internees, except for six Germans. They had been moved to the North Wales Counties Lunatic Asylum, near Denbigh.

The Asylum was designed by Thomas Fulljames and built on 20 acres of land donated by Joseph Ablett of Llanber Hall. It opened on 14 November 1848 to house up to 200 patients. To relieve over-crowding, a number of extensions occurred throughout its life. The largest extension undertaken was in 1899, which then allowed 1,500 patients to be offered a wide range of treatments (www.thetimechamber.co.uk).

Various interesting and experimental treatments were tested and developed at Denbigh. In 1871, Turkish baths were installed to treat ailments such as melancholia, and in 1916 all epileptic patients were put on a vegetarian diet. In 1941 electro-convulsive shock therapy was also introduced. The hospital finally closed in 1995. In 2004, Prince Charles visited the site and placed all the buildings under the protection of the Phoenix Trust to ensure that the buildings were safe. This sadly has not happened as the Grade II listed buildings are now derelict and prone to arson attacks similar to one that destroyed the theatre building in recent times.

DERBY: Normanton Barracks (OS: SK 353 333). There is no record of PoWs being held at Normanton Barracks, in Derby. However, the Register of Births, Marriages and Deaths Office for Derby shows G. Ostermaier died on 18 November 1918 in the barrack's hospital as a result of contracting pneumonia. He was buried in Derby's Normanton Cemetery, prior to his remains being exhumed and moved to Cannock Chase in 1961 (D 1372 API 65/75). As the Geneva Convention of 1906 requested that all PoWs should receive the best medical help available, and on contracting pneumonia, he may have been transferred to this facility from a nearby camp.

The barracks, home to the Sherwood Foresters, were demolished in 1982. They had opened on 1 December 1877.

DEVONPORT MILITARY HOSPITAL (OS: SX 463 557). Cited by the POWIB (1919), it had the code Dpt H. It was also cited by the OSt (1917).

The Royal Albert Hospital and Eye Infirmary was established in 1815 as the Dock and Stonehouse Public Dispensary, and was situated for nearly fifty years in Chapel Street, Devonport. Following the death of Queen Victoria's Consort, Prince Albert, on 14 December 1861, it was decided to name the hospital, still under construction to the designs of Devonport architect Alfred Norman, The Royal Albert Hospital. In 1912 the hospital could accommodate up to fifty patients in the general wards, eleven in the special and emergency wards and two in what were called the home wards. About 3,500 outpatients were treated every year. During the First World War, the Admiralty took over part of the hospital for its own use and retained it after the war as its War College and Port Library.

The *Western Morning News* (25 September 1914) cited four German soldiers, recovering from wounds, were being moved from the fortress hospital in Devonport to a compound at Bull Point, Mortehoe.

In 1948, it transferred into the National Health Service, and then, in 1963, became the Devonport Section of the Plymouth General Hospital.

When, on 9 June 1981, Derriford Hospital opened, the Royal Albert Hospital closed.

DOUGLAS: Noble's Hospital (OS: SC 388 773). This was the second of three hospitals on the Isle of Man that bore this name. It was built to replace Henry Bloom Noble's first hospital at the top of Crellin's Hill, which had opened on 4 September 1888. The earlier hospital was later to become The Manx Museum in 1922.

The new hospital stood on Westmoreland Road in upper Douglas. Despite concerns that it was too far out of town, it was built on a 3-acre green field site and opened by the Lieutenant Governor, Lord Raglan, on 11 September 1912. There were beds for fifty-seven patients with the latest X-ray equipment and an in-house electricity generator. Money from the estate of Henry Bloom Noble, who had died in 1903, helped support the hospital (*Isle of Man Family History Journal*, Oct 1986).

During World War One the hospital devoted an entire ward to treating PoWs. It frequently contained twenty to eighty patients at any one time, even though all ordinary cases were dealt with within the various camp hospitals.

The hospital, with every modern appliance, was the admiration of all the Embassy and Legation doctors who visited it. When the Home Secretary paid a visit, there were seven PoW patients.

To meet the needs of a growing and changing island, the hospital has recently been replaced with a newer hospital at Strang (Braddan).

DOVER MILITARY HOSPITAL (OS: TR 323 424). Below the Western Heights, on the seafront at Dover, stands Archcliffe Fort. Thought to date back to the fifteenth century the buildings have been remodelled many times throughout their 400 year existence.

During the First World War some small calibre quick firing guns were installed to prevent landing parties taking advantage of the shelter of the cliff face. But with the emphasis put onto aerial attacks the Western Heights defences superseded it. Such then was its importance that in the 1920s the southern half was demolished to make way for a railway line. It was finally decommissioned in 1956. The widening of the A20 has eaten into it. What remains are presently being used to accommodate the homeless.

The military hospital at Archcliffe was built in 1803. It has also functioned as the headquarters for the local garrison of the Royal Engineers. It is believed to have been demolished in 1962 to make way for industrial redevelopment.

The hospital was cited by the POWIB (1919); its code was Dv H (IWM: Facsimile K4655).

DUBLIN: KING GEORGE V HOSPITAL (IGR: O 160 350). George V was crowned in 1911, and the hospital, which opened in 1913, originally bore his name. Today it is St Bricin's Military Hospital. It stands near Arbour Hill.

It was originally constructed by Royal Engineers, but there have been several additions added. Harry B. Measures was the Director of Barrack Construction from 1909–1915, and plans that bear his name survive. Casey (*The Buildings of Ireland, Dublin: the City within the Grand and Royal Canals and the Circular Road with the Phoenix Park*, 2005) describes the two and three storey red brick buildings as being tall and handsome. The day rooms have shallow bows to their fronts.

The interiors of the hospital are today undergoing renovation to meet their new role of serving the wider community. An interesting feature of the site is a tunnel that used to run, via Arbour Hill Prison, to the former Collins Barracks.

Records show the hospital treated wounded soldiers brought back from the front. There are also records to show men were treated for their wounds in the Easter Rising of 1915. There are no records of PoWs receiving treatment although it was cited by the POWIB (1919), and had the code, G V H (IWM: Facsimile K4655). It was also cited by the OSt (1917).

DUBLIN ROYAL HOSPITAL (IGR: O 160 350). With the Easter Rising quelled, the badly wounded James Connolly was taken to the Royal Hospital to have his wounds treated. He was court-martialled for his part in the affair, and when found guilty he was then taken to Kilmainham Gaol to be executed. The rapidity and brutality of the executions was a shock to the Irish public and the circumstances of Connolly's death was the most shocking: he was unable to stand and was shot whilst strapped to a chair.

Fifteen men, shot for their parts in the Rising between 3 May and 12 May 1916, were placed in an unmarked mass grave (www.executedtoday.com).

EDINBURGH CASTLE HOSPITAL (OS: NT 251 735). Accounts of PoWs taken from the SMS *Mainz* on 31 August 1914, in *The Times*, *The Scotsman*, *The Liverpool Daily Post* and *The Edinburgh Evening News* give conflicting numbers landed at Leith. It appears around eighty to ninety internees were put on a train to Redford. Depending on the newspaper you read around ten to sixteen were wounded, some seriously. They were taken to the castle's hospital by motor vehicles. One of the wounded died shortly after being admitted.

Lady Kate Courtney recorded in her diary on 12 September 1915 that she conversed with Mrs Campbell of Dunstaffnage on a train journey to the capital. She learned of a dying German sailor that Mrs Campbell had visited at the castle.

The POWIB (1919) cited Edinburgh Castle twice. The first reference is to the Detention House and the other is to the castle's hospital. The latter has the code E C H (IWM: Facsimile K4655). It was also cited by the OSt.

EDINBURGH: CRAIGLOCKHART WAR HOSPITAL (OS: NT 222 705). The Craiglockhart estates can be traced as far back as the thirteenth century. In 1873 the City of Edinburgh Parochial Board sold the west part of the estate to the Craiglockhart Estate Company for residential development, and in 1877 some 13 acres of this land was leased to the Craiglockhart Hydropathic Company. The original farmhouse, occupying the site, was demolished, and architects Peddie and Kinnear constructed a 'giant Italian villa' in its place.

In 1880, the Hydropathic opened its doors for business. Standing above Colinton Road, on the north side of Wester Craiglockhart Hill, the building was requisitioned by the military in 1916, and turned into a war hospital for the treatment of shell-shocked officers. It was here in 1917 that the poets Wilfred Owen (1893–1918) and Siegfried Sassoon (1886–1967) met for the first time. During his stay as a patient, Owen published *The Hydra: The Journal of the Craiglockhart War Hospital.*

The hospital's records show that during the First World War sixty-five German PoW Officers were treated for gunshot wounds.

Cameron's schematic shows Craiglockhart Station on the Edinburgh Suburban and Southside Junction Railway. The station closed to passengers in 1964.

In 1985, Napier University bought the building as an annexe to its main campus.

FALMOUTH MILITARY HOSPITAL (OS: SW 782 335). Cited by the POWIB (1919), its code was FA H (IWM: Facsimile K4655).

An agreement was reached, in 1904, between Falmouth Town Council and the Port Sanitary Authority for each to provide their own isolation facilities for a joint venture at Kergillack, Hill Head, Penryn. The top part of the site was to be occupied by the Port Sanitary Authority. During the First World War the site was requisitioned by the military authorities for hospital purposes and additional buildings were constructed. At the end of the war the site was divided between the Port Sanitary Authority and Falmouth Corporation for their respective hospitals.

When the National Health Service was introduced in 1946, the Falmouth Corporation's hospital was no longer required. The Port's hospital was taken over by the Regional Hospital Board. The Falmouth Corporation continued to use the disinfection station until 1949, when the work was transferred to the West Cornwall Hospital Management Committee. The Regional Hospital Board still had an interest in the site on the 31 March 1953, which at that time precluded the Falmouth Corporation from disposing of it.

The site now accommodates three bungalows, which are visible from the A39 Penryn bypass, which opened in 1994 (www.falandtruropha.co.uk).

GLASGOW: 3rd & 4th SCOTTISH GENERAL HOSPITALS (OS: NS 612 690). In September 1914, the Royal Army Medical Corps requisitioned Stobhill Hospital. The first batch of wounded servicemen arrived by a specially converted 'ambulance train' to a temporary railway platform built within the grounds. However there is nothing stating to which general hospital they were going.

The HO only issued one TA for Glasgow, that of Priswarian: Wounded, Glasgow (ADM 1/8506/265–120667). However the POWIB (1919) issued two codes (IWM: Facsimile K4655): one for 3rd Scottish General Hospital (3 S G H (G)), and the other for the 4th Scottish General Hospital (4 S G H (G)). Both are believed to have shared the same site: Stobhill Hospital.

When Keogh envisioned auxiliary hospitals, it was for units of 520 beds; at Stobhill there were 1,040 beds available to treat the incoming wounded that arrived by train to specially built platforms. The workhouse hospital had had sidings for the delivery of coal and other essential goods that had been created by the Caledonian Railway Company.

Stobhill Hospital was built as a poor law provision for Glasgow in September 1904. With 1,867 beds, in twenty-eight two-storey red brick built pavilions connected by corridors, it was envisioned to be one of the showpieces of Glasgow. Its primary function was to treat the chronically sick, children and the elderly. The former were often in the last stages of diseases like tuberculosis and other illnesses brought on by poor living and working conditions. Some also suffered from alcoholism or syphilis.

Ten wards were set aside for children taken into care by the Parish Council. They attended a school nearby. Four wards were designated to the 'feeble, helpless and blind' until they passed on. Unmarried pregnant women were catered for, as were their babies. Birth and death certificates that emanated from the hospital cited its address as 133 Balornock Road.

The archivist of the Greater Glasgow Health Board is not aware of PoWs being treated in establishments run by them during the First World War.

HAWICK: Stobs PoW Hospital (OS: NT 500 102). Cited by the POWIB (1919), its code was Ss H (IWM: Facsimile K4655). It was attached to the vast army camp complex which acted as the parent camp for all of Scotland.

When the camp was visited for a second time by the US Embassy's inspection team, led by Boylston A. Beal, on 13 April 1916, it was reported that the camp was divided into four compounds, 'A', 'B', 'C', & 'D'. The hospital, separate from the compounds, was set in grass, with carefully tended flowerbeds and small groups of fir trees. On the day of the inspection there were sixty-five patients being treated. When required, a surgeon came down from Edinburgh. There were four doctors in the hospital, aided by twenty-eight orderlies recruited from the compounds (FO 383/507).

Murray (*Stobs Castle 1903–1959*, 1988) wrote:

> The camp had many amenities. It had a hospital at the south end. This consisted of an examination room, sick rooms, an operating theatre, apothecary's shop, doctor's surgery, a dentist's, a kitchen and dining room for patients.

She also stated there was a British doctor in charge of the hospital, who was assisted by two German doctors who were PoWs. Six barrack huts were sick rooms, each having their own toilet, washroom and small kitchen. Once a week, the camp's band played at the hospital.

Forty-two internees died at Stobs. In August 1962 their remains were exhumed and sent to Cannock Chase for re-burial. The cemetery has since been left to the elements.

HOSPITAL SHIP: HMHS *LANFRANC* (GRT: 6,287). Built by the Caledon Shipbuilding & Engineering Company of Dundee, it was launched on 18 October 1906, for the Booth Steam Ship Company; the RMS *Lanfranc* operated out of Liverpool to Manaus in South America.

In October 1915 she was re-commissioned as HMHS *Lanfranc*, to be a hospital ship bringing the sick and wounded back from the battlefields of Northern France.

On 17 April 1917, at 19.30 hours, whilst bound for Southampton, the *Lanfranc* was torpedoed by the German submarine *UB-40* some 4 miles northeast of Le Havre. There were 387 patients on board, of which 326 were cot patients. Ironically, 167 were German PoWs. 570 survivors were picked up by the destroyers HMS *Badger* and HMS *Jackal*, aided by *P47* and the French patrol boat *Roitelet*. The survivors were taken to Portsmouth. Seventeen British and seventeen German patients died in the tragedy. The *Lanfranc* was not the only hospital ship to be sunk, but is the only one recorded to have had PoWs on board.

IPSWICH MILITARY HOSPITAL (OS: TM 164 446). Geoffrey J. Pizzey was a British soldier who had been reported missing, but he was later found to be a prisoner of war in Germany. He was repatriated on 2 December 1918, still in need of medical help and taken to the 1st Western General Hospital in Liverpool. He was discharged from the army on 7 March 1919. He then attended Ranelagh Road Military Hospital, Ipswich as an out-patient. Presumably this was the same hospital that had the POWIB (1919) code Ip H (IWM: Facsimile K4655).

LARKHILL: Fargo-Rollestone Military Hospital (OS: SU 109 438). Crawford (*Wiltshire and the Great War: Training the Empire's Soldiers*, 1999) cites there have been military campsites at Fargo and Rollestone dating back to 1904.

At the start of the First World War, four hutments were built at Rollestone (OS: SU 098 448) to augment those at the Larkhill camp. These were dismantled at the end of the war.

It was cited by the POWIB (1919) as being a PoW hospital; its code was F R H (IWM: Facsimile K4655). The hospital was also cited by the OSt. The FPHS (1973) have entries for both Fargo and Larkhill.

Work began on the construction of a 1,200 bed military hospital at Fargo in 1915, on what had been the site of an isolation hospital for horses, brought from the camp at Larkhill.

After the war the disused hospital returned to being a camping ground.

EAST LEEDS WAR HOSPITAL (OS: SE 314 346). Cited by the POWIB (1919), its code was L W H (IWM: Facsimile K4655). It was also cited by the OSt.

Prior to 1925 St James's Hospital was known as Leeds Union Hospital. Affectionately known locally as Jimmy's it has been treating patients at its Beckett Street location for over 130 years. It began life as a 'moral and industrial training school' for the children of the poor, in 1848. To cope with the problem of overcrowding in the workhouse on Lady Lane, in 1858 a new institution was created – the Leeds Union Workhouse. This is now the Thackray Medical Museum.

The new workhouse had accommodation for 784 people, its own chapel, infirmary and lunatic wards. It continued to grow, and in 1874 the first proper hospital was opened to care for its 'sick and decrepit'. By 1881 the infirmary was caring for an average of 400 patients every day. As more liberal attitudes to the treatment of the poor emerged around the turn of the century, many of the children were moved out into the suburbs, as part of the 'scattered homes system'. The workhouse buildings were extended and turned into a permanent hospital for the poor of Leeds. During the First World War the workhouse and its infirmary buildings were known as the East Leeds War Hospital, given over to the treatment of sick and wounded servicemen returning from France. The workhouse inmates were transferred to Hunslet.

It is not known how many PoWs were treated there.

After the war the site was never again used as a workhouse and it was renamed St. James's Hospital.

LEICESTER: 5th NORTHERN GENERAL HOSPITAL (OS: SK 596 028). Cited by the POWIB (1919), its code was Les H (IWM: Facsimile K4655). It was also cited by the OSt.

It is cited as having around 2,600 beds, but they were not all housed at one location. The main site was an old county mental asylum that belonged to the County Council. In 1911, the Territorial Force Medical Officers had taken it over, on the understanding it would be handed over to the military in the event of a national emergency.

When it was handed over, a labour force was brought in to demolish existing outhouses, remove trees, etc. Four long, flat-roofed brick huts were erected to house the RAMC officers. The nurses and medical staff were accommodated in the main building. Later on the North Evington War Hospital, which was a former Poor Law institution, became an annex.

On 9 May 1915, the North Evington War Hospital received its first 100 casualties. Leicester Royal Infirmary, Knighton House Hospital and Gilcross Hospital were three of many affiliated hospitals, put under the command of the old County Mental Asylum.

Part of Leicester University now stands on the site of old asylum.

LIVERPOOL. There were two facilities that treated PoWs in the Liverpool area, the Fazakerley and the Seaforth. Both are cited by the OSt (1917).

1st WESTERN GENERAL HOSPITAL: The City Hospital (OS: SJ 379 971). In 1898, the Harbreck Estate, which included a medium sized country house, farms and cottages, was bought by the Liverpool City Council to build a hospital to treat infectious diseases. A temporary building was erected in 1901 with Harbreck House serving as the nurses' quarters and administration block. The City Hospital opened in 1906; there were nine ward pavilions and four isolation blocks for 350 patients with infectious diseases other than smallpox. It also catered for twenty-five suffers of tuberculosis. The Annexe, as the temporary hospital became known, did not close until the 1950s. The site is now part of Altcourse Prison.

During the war years the hospital was renamed 1st Western General Hospital. It had the POWIB (1919) code Lpl H (IWM: Facsimile K4655).

A separate hospital set up prior to the war to treat infectious diseases was commonly called Sparrow Hall Hospital after the farm that had previously occupied the site. This too was used by the military to treat injured soldiers.

In 1947, the City Hospital changed its name to the Fazakerley Infectious Hospital, before passing from the City's ownership to that of the National Health Service a year later. In 1950 the Fazakerley Sanatorium – which had opened in 1920 – changed its name to Aintree Tuberculosis Hospital. When the Fazakerley District General Hospital was created in 1974 it incorporated the Fazakerley and Aintree hospital buildings. Both hospitals had been self-sufficient, and had their own farms.

In 1999, to reflect its links with the University of Liverpool the hospital's name was changed to University Hospital Aintree. The name changed again in 2006 to the Aintree University Hospitals NHS Foundation Trust (www.liverpoolecho.co.uk).

SEAFORTH CAVALRY BARRACKS HOSPITAL (OS: SJ 328 973). Morrison (*English Military Hospitals: An Architectural History*, Earle, 1996) cites the Seaforth Cavalry Barracks Hospital had been built *c.*1884. It had a single-storey circular ward block which was never popular with the military, although the design was adopted in the 1880s and 1890s into civilian hospitals.

LINCOLN: 4th NORTHERN GENERAL HOSPITAL (OS: SK 988 717). When the German doctor at the camp at South Carlton diagnosed an internee in his care as having tuberculosis, he became frustrated at the attitude of his British counterpart because he continually refused to acknowledge his findings. Only when his patient's condition severely deteriorated was he then transferred to Lincoln Hospital, some 5 miles away. The hospital had around 1,100 beds.

The POWIB (1919) cite the hospital's code as Li H (IWM: Facsimile K4655).

DKF 65: Deutsche Kriegsgefangene In Feindesland. Einen Mann mit schwerer Lungentuberkulose schickte ich mehrmals zum Arzt, der ihm immer wieder als arbeitsfähig bestimmte, bis der Betreffende schließlich kaum mehr bis zum fünf Meilen entfernten Hospital in Lincoln transportfähig war.

LONDON. The military had a hierarchy of treatment for the Territorial Force (TF) that saw the introduction of five general hospitals in London each supported by a chain of hospitals attached to them. These were:

1st London General Hospital (TF), St Gabriel's College, Cormont Road, Camberwell.
2nd London General Hospital (TF), St Mark's College, 552 King's Road, Chelsea.
3rd London General Hospital (TF), Royal Victoria Patriotic School, Trinity Road, Wandsworth.
4th London General Hospital (TF), King's College Hospital, Denmark Hill.
5th London General Hospital (TF), St Thomas' Hospital, Lambeth Palace Road.

BETHNAL GREEN MILITARY HOSPITAL (OS: TQ 345 825). The Bethnal Green Poor Law Union was formed on 25 March 1836. In 1842 a workhouse, designed by Mr Bunning, was erected at a site at Bonner's Hall Fields to the west of the Waterloo Road. By the 1860s the complex was capable of housing 1,400 inmates. In a series of articles written for the *The Lancet* in 1866, the workhouses in London, including Bethnal Green, came in for criticism.

With restrictions put on the number of patients that could be accommodated in the sick wards a separate infirmary was sought. In 1896, Giles, Gough and Trollope designed a new infirmary with 750 beds in eleven pavilions, arranged in pairs either side of a central corridor. At its centre were an administrative block and a laundry block. The entrance block was on Cambridge Heath Road. It opened in March 1900. During the First World War, the infirmary became the Bethnal Green Military Hospital.

In 1930, the infirmary passed into the control of London County Council, and then in 1948 became part of the National Health Service as Bethnal Green Hospital. It took on the role of a geriatric hospital before finally closing in 1992. All of the buildings have been demolished, with the exception of the entrance block on Cambridge Heath Road. The site has been redeveloped for residential use.

It was recorded as having the POWIB (1919) code B G H. It was also cited by the OSt.

CHELSEA: 2nd LONDON GENERAL HOSPITAL (OS: TQ 273 780). Stanley House was built to replace the Brickills that had been built *c.*1691. It stood in King's Road, Chelsea and was an excellent example of a Georgian house of two storeys. The first occupant of the new building was Thomas White. After a succession of owners, some of whom added to the property, in 1840 the house and its grounds were sold by Mr Hamilton to the National Society who built a training school for teachers on the site, which became St Mark's College. According to the 1913 Survey of London, Stanley House was occupied by the Reverend Robert Hudson, the principal of St Mark's College. During the First World War it was to become the 2nd London General Hospital.

Cited by the POWIB (1919): its code was Chl H (IWM: Facsimile K4655) and it was housed at St Mark's College. It was also cited by the OSt.

After the First World War, in 1923, St Mark's merged with St Johns College, which had been established by James Kay-Shuttleworth. The College moved to Plymouth in 1973, and in 1991 became affiliated to the University of Exeter. In 2007 the College became the University College Plymouth St Mark & St John.

CITY OF LONDON HOSPITAL: Homerton (OS: TQ 294 794). The City of London Union had been formally formed on 30 March 1837. A new workhouse for up to 800 inmates was built for it on the south side of Bow Road, and opened in 1849. When, in 1869, it amalgamated with the unions of East London and West London Union it retained the name City of London Union. The new union retained the three workhouses with the Bow Road site becoming infirmary.

When an enlarged Homerton Workhouse re-opened in 1909, the infirmary became superfluous and was closed. However, after a period of standing empty, it reopened in 1912 as the City of London Institution to treat the chronically ill. It was later renamed the Bow Institution and mentally ill patients came here for examination and assessment before being sent to other institutions or being discharged. Around this time it re-adopted the name the City of London Institution.

During the First World War it was turned over to the military. It was given the POWIB (1919) code C L H (IWM: Facsimile K4655). It was also cited by the OSt.

When all the boards of guardians were abolished, in 1930, the City Council was left in control of the workhouses in London. In 1935 fire destroyed the west wing and the main building. In 1936 it was renamed St Clement's Hospital. Although the hospital had been badly damaged in 1944 in the air raids on London, it joined the National Health Service in 1948 and was repaired. By 1959 the hospital was exclusively a psychiatric unit.

In 1968 it became the London Hospital (St Clement's). In 2003 the East London and the City Mental Health NHS Trust decided to sell the site for redevelopment. The Hospital closed in 2005, with its services moving to Mile End Hospital (http://ezitis.myzen.co.uk/stclements.html).

DALSTON: GERMAN HOSPITAL (OS: TQ 334 850). Cited by the POWIB (1919), its code was Ger H (IWM: Facsimile K4655). It was also cited by the OSt.

The German Hospital on Graham Road, Dalston was established in 1845, in a former orphanage. Although its main purpose was to look after Germans that became ill whilst living in Britain, in practice it had British patients too. In 1864 new buildings were erected to increase its capacity and replace the older buildings. When war broke out the hospital continued to treat the sick as usual, but also accept wounded internees as patients.

Scotland Yard reported, on 13 March 1918, that there were fourteen sisters on the staff at Dalston, while there had been twenty working there at the beginning of the war. In the past the hospital had always relied on financial support from wealthy German families, particularly the Schröders. With large numbers of Germans being interned the hospital ran up a substantial deficit. This was very largely covered by a generous grant from the (British) National Relief Fund. After the war it took time to re-establish the hospital's pre-war position. It was not until 1920 that the British government allowed new recruitment of staff from Germany.

Records show the number of internees treated dropped as other medical facilities came on line to treat the sick and wounded.

Year	*No. of Internees Treated*	*Year*	*No. of Internees Treated*
1915	375	1917	52
1916	180	1918	24

In the Second World War the attitude of the British government was rather different. On 28 May 1940 the nursing sisters were all arrested, and interned at Port Erin, on the Isle of Man. Staff from London's hospitals replaced the medical staff interned.

DENMARK HILL: 4th LONDON GENERAL HOSPITAL (OS: TQ 325 760). Denmark Hill is only cited by the OSt.

For the first fifty years of its history King's Hospital served the slums that surrounded Lincoln's Inn Fields. When an Act of Parliament was obtained in 1904 to remove the hospital from Portugal Street to Denmark Hill, which was then a green field site on the outskirts of the capital, work started in 1908. William Pite was chosen as the architect for the new hospital with 600 beds, built in the pavilion style. King Edward VII laid the foundation stone on 20 July 1909.

When the First World War broke out, it became the 4th London General Military Hospital. Only four wards and its casualty unit remained for civilian use. As the casualties brought back from France grew, the hospital extended into nearby Ruskin Park with huts, tents and a wooden bridge across the railway line to reach them. It wasn't until 1919 that the hospital was completely handed back for civilian use, when it again treated the under-nourished and the anaemic, surviving on donations.

By the 1930s the high standards were attracting wealthy patients and in 1937 King's opened a private wing, built with a donation from the Stock Exchange Dramatic and Operatic Society. The Guthrie Wing, as it was called, had a separate art deco entrance. Its wards were small and gained the hospital valuable extra revenue. It also enabled the beds in the main wards to be kept free for poorer patients.

FULHAM MILITARY HOSPITAL (OS: TQ 236 780). Situated on St Dunstan's Road, the hospital had the POWIC code Fu H (IWM: Facsimile K4655). It was also cited by the OSt.

In 1837, the parish of Fulham became part of the newly created Kensington Poor Law Union. The paupers were housed in a number of establishments owned by the union: males were housed at a workhouse at Kensington, the women at Chelsea, boys at Hammersmith, and girls in the former Fulham parish workhouse.

In 1845, the Kensington Poor Law Union was dissolved. In 1848–9, a new Fulham workhouse, for up to 450 inmates, was erected at the east side of Fulham Palace Road. Alfred Gilbert designed it. In 1884, a pavilion-plan infirmary was erected at the north of the workhouse site facing onto St Dunstan's road. On the site was a nurses' home, known as Brandeburgh House, which stood opposite the infirmary at the west side of the Fulham Palace Road, and a casual ward for vagrants that was located at the east of the site, on Margravine Road.

The site later became Fulham Hospital and is now the home of the Charing Cross Hospital. All the former workhouse buildings have been demolished.

HAMMERSMITH MILITARY HOSPITAL (OS: TQ 223 812). Cited by the POWIB (1919), its code was H H (IWM: Facsimile K4655). It was also cited by the OSt.

The parish of Hammersmith became part of the Kensington Poor Law Union in 1837. This resulted in males being housed at Kensington, the women at Chelsea, and girls at Fulham. Boys were housed at Shortlands. In 1845, this union was dissolved. The Fulham and Hammersmith parishes then united to form the Fulham Poor Law Union. This arrangement continued until 1899 when they separated and became separate Poor Law parishes.

In 1902, the Hammersmith union decided to erect a new workhouse and infirmary on a 14-acre site at the north side of Du Cane Road, Hammersmith. Land adjacent to Wormwood Scrubs Prison was purchased from the Ecclesiastical Commissioners to provide care for victims of a smallpox epidemic that had taken place in the winter of 1901–2. A temporary corrugated iron building was erected for the purpose. The foundation stone for the new buildings was laid in July 1903.

The buildings were completed in 1905 to designs of the firm of Giles, Gough and Trollope. The workhouse infirmary was built in 1912. In 1916, the patients and inmates were moved to other establishments and the site was taken over by the War Office for use as the Military Orthopaedic Hospital. It was then renamed the Special Surgical Hospital, and in 1919 became the Ministry of Pensions Hospital. Demands by the Hammersmith Guardians for return of their property finally succeeded, and the site then became a general acute hospital in 1926. By 1930, the infirmary could accommodate 300 patients and the workhouse 575 inmates.

Along with all workhouse hospitals in London, it came under the control of London County Council in 1929, and in 1935 was selected to be the new home of the British Postgraduate Medical School.

The site still serves as Hammersmith Hospital, although many of the original buildings have now been replaced or much altered. Only the administrative block of the workhouse survives today.

KING GEORGE'S HOSPITAL: Stamford Street (OS: TQ 315 804). Cited by the POWIB (1919), it had the code Std H (IWM: Facsimile K4655). It was also cited by the OSt.

Cornwall House was built on Cornwall Road for HM Stationery Office. However, completed *c.*1915, it was converted into an army hospital, known as King George's Hospital. It was ideal for conversion because of its revolutionary fireproof iron and concrete construction. With ten large elevators, a central heating system and its position close to Waterloo station, it treated some 71,000 patients between 1915 and 1919.

In the 1920s it reverted back to its intended use. It housed the HMSO and the office of the Government Chemist. King's College acquired the building in the late 1980s, and it was refurbished and reopened in two phases. The main building was opened in September 1999.

LEWISHAM MILITARY HOSPITAL (OS: TQ 378 746). Cited by the POWIB (1919), its code was L H (IWM: Facsimile K4655). It was also cited by the OSt. The HO cited it, but no TA was attached to its entry (ADM 1/8506/265–120667).

Lewisham Military Hospital was established in Lewisham Workhouse at the start of the First World War. The workhouse, which was built in 1817, stood on Lewisham High Street. In 1877 the site expanded, and at various times throughout the rest of the nineteenth century more buildings were added.

MILE END MILITARY HOSPITAL (OS: TQ 364 826). In 1859 a new workhouse and infirmary that could accommodate up to 500 inmates was built to the north of Mile End Road adjacent to the cemetery for the Maiden Lane Synagogue. Bancroft Road was laid to provide access to it. In 1883, a new infirmary replaced its predecessor and in 1892 a Nurses Training School was established. The institution was taken over by the military authorities during the First World War and the facilities of the hospital were considerably improved. In 1930, the hospital passed to the control of the London County Council. In 1948 it was absorbed into the National Health Service. In 1968 the London Hospital took over its management and it became the London Hospital (Mile End). In 1990, when the London Hospital was granted its title, it became the Royal London Hospital (Mile End). The hospital is now a community hospital under the auspices of the Tower Hamlets Primary Care Trust and cares mainly for elderly patients (http://ezitis.myzen.co.uk/mileend.html).

Cited by the POWIB (1919), its code was M E H (IWM: Facsimile K4655).

MILLBANK HOSPITAL (OS: TQ 292 845). Cited by the POWIB (1919), its code was Mil H (IWM: Facsimile K4655).

The Army Medical School moved from the Royal Victoria Military Hospital, Netley to a temporary location in London, in 1902, before moving into Millbank College in 1907.

The Queen Alexandra's Military Hospital, Millbank opened in July 1905. It was situated by the River Thames in London SW1 adjacent to the Tate Gallery. As with other military hospitals built in this era it was constructed to the Nightingale pattern. King Edward VII and Queen Alexandra officially opened it.

Queen Alexandra was the president of the nursing corps that bears her name.

TOOTING MILITARY HOSPITAL (OS: TQ 271 714). In 1973, building began on the new site for St George's Hospital. The former buildings are now the Lanesborough Hotel that stands on the west side of Hyde Park Corner.

The original St George's Hospital was opened in 1733 in what was then Lanesborough House. It had been built for James Lane, the 2nd Viscount Lanesborough, in 1719.

By the 1800s, the hospital was falling into disrepair and was demolished to make way for a new 350 bed facility. Work on William Wilkins's design began in 1827, and was completed in 1844.

During the First World War, the War Office requisitioned The Grove in Tooting for military purposes. It became the Tooting Military Hospital and operated as a 550-bed hospital between November 1916 and September 1919. Special sections of the hospital were earmarked for infectious diseases, tubercle of the lung, skin, scabies, and venereal cases. There is no mention of PoWs being treated there.

Nearby, in Church Lane, stood buildings, dating from 1888, formerly known as St Joseph's Roman Catholic College. In 1901, they became Tooting Home (OS: TQ 282 712). During the First World War, these buildings became Church Lane Military Hospital. In 1930, the site was taken over by the London County Council and became St Benedict's Hospital, providing care for the chronic sick. It closed in 1981, and was demolished to provide housing. The only reminders are its entrance gateway on Church Lane, and the main block's portico and clock tower, which have been preserved in the grounds of the modern development. Apart from their close proximity there is nothing to link these hospitals.

In 1948, when the National Health Service was introduced, plans were eventually agreed for the Grove Hospital and the nearby Fountain Hospital to become part of St George's on a new site. Fountains stood on the opposite side of Tooting Grove to the Grove. It had begun life as an infectious disease hospital in 1893 before becoming a specialized unit for treating mentally ill children. Its role did not change in the war.

The Grove was the last of the fever hospitals erected by the Metropolitan Asylums Board. It dates from around 1895. It was designed by A. Hessell Tiltman, and covered an area of around 23 acres.

Later additions to the buildings included a new two-storey isolation block at the north-west of the existing isolation blocks, and two new blocks linking the existing nurses' accommodation at the south-east of the site, one erected in the 1920s, the other in 1935. Most of the original hospital buildings were demolished to make way for the new St George's Hospital. Two of the original ward blocks survive, together with some of the nurses' accommodation and later extensions at its south-east corner.

Tooting Military Hospital is cited by the POWIB (1919), its code was T H (IWM: Facsimile K4655). It was also cited by the OSt.

WANDSWORTH: 3rd LONDON GENERAL HOSPITAL (OS: TQ 263 753). Cited by the POWIB (1919), its code is Wds H. The hospital was identified as 3rd London General Hospital and could accommodate over 1,000 officers and men. Patients arrived at a specially built railway station close by. The metamorphosis from school to hospital began in August 1914. The day after war was declared twenty men under the command of Major Miller started the conversion work. More wings, known as Bungalow Town, were added later.

The building was paid for by the Royal Victoria Patriotic Fund, which had been established to provide for the widows and orphans of soldiers killed in the Crimean War. Opened on 1 July 1859, in the Scottish Baronial Gothic style, it was designed by Rhode Hawkins and originally intended to be a girl's orphanage school. In 1872 an annexe for boys was created.

After the war it again returned into the sphere of academia. During World War Two it became a reception centre to process non-British aliens entering the country.

Today the building has been converted into residential flats, augmented by studios and workshops.

WOOLWICH HOSPITAL (OS: TQ 455 783). Cited by the POWIB (1919), its code was Wch H (IWM: Facsimile K4655). It was also cited by the OSt.

Between 1838 and 1868, the parish of Woolwich was part of the Greenwich Poor Law Union. On 10 March 1868, the Woolwich Union was created to include three parishes formerly belonging to the Lewisham Union. On 2 April 1870, the foundation stone for the new Woolwich Union workhouse was laid in Tewson Road by the Reverend Francis Cameron, and bore the inscription 'The poor ye have always with you'. The workhouse was situated between Skittles Alley (now Riverdale road) and Cage Lane (now Lakedale Road) at the south side of Plumstead High Street, and was designed by the firm of Church and Rickwood. In 1872, a separate infirmary was erected to the south of the workhouse. The new buildings consisted of three ward blocks with central staff quarters, kitchens, stores, offices and committee rooms. The wards included accommodation for children and maternity patients, and a special sick bay for vagrants from the casual ward at Hull Place at the north of the workhouse.

In the 1920s, the workhouse became known as the Woolwich Institution, and the infirmary as the Plumstead and District Hospital. In 1930, following the formal end of the workhouse system, control of the site passed to the London County Council. It was then renamed St Nicholas Hospital and, at that time, had 320 beds. As part of the changes, many of the walls that formerly separated different classes of workhouse inmates were removed.

MAIDENHEAD: TAPLOW CANADIAN HOSPITAL (OS: SU 914 925). Cited by the POWIB (1919), its code was T C H (IWM: Facsimile K4655).

Constructed in 1914, the Canadian Red Cross Hospital was located in the grounds of Cliveden Estate, Berkshire. It was to become the Duchess of Connaught Red Cross Hospital. During the Second World War the hospital expanded and was renamed the Canadian Red Cross Memorial Hospital. After the war it became part of the NHS and operated as a general hospital until around 1952, when it became mainly a maternity hospital. The hospital operated until 1985 when it was closed. The building lay derelict until 2006 when the landowners, the National Trust, demolished the buildings to make way for private housing.

MANCHESTER: NELL LANE HOSPITAL: West Didsbury (OS: SJ 837 925). The hospital began its life as part of Chorlton Union Workhouse. When the original workhouse, located at the junction of Stretford New Road and Leaf Street, with accommodation for 300 inmates, proved to be inadequate for the demands of the increasing population and the site could not be expanded, the guardians decided that a completely new building was needed. A site for a new workhouse was chosen on a green-field site at Barlow Moor, Withington, at the north side of what is now Nell Lane. It was erected in 1854–5 to the designs of William Hayley and could accommodate up to 1,500 inmates.

This was the first pavilion planned hospital to be built in England (*c.*1866), designed by Thomas Worthington, was erected to the north of the workhouse. It comprised of five well-spaced ward blocks, linked by a covered way, and each ward could accommodate ninety-six patients. More extensions were added later. In the First World War the hospital was re-named Nell Lane Hospital.

The hospital's POWIB (1919) code was Mn H (IWM: Facsimile K4655). Its TA, Priswarian: Nelane (ADM 1/8506/265–120667). It was also cited by the OSt. During March 1919, Dr A. de Sturler inspected the Nell Lane Hospital. His report is held at the National Archives at Kew (FO 383/506).

The buildings have now all been demolished.

An internee alleged that certain members of staff at this Manchester hospital did not act in a professional manner which resulted in at least two patients dying under anaesthesia, and of another losing an eye when the chloroform being administered, combusted. One doctor was reputed to be under the influence of drink, fell whilst operating, and took instruments from his pocket that also had tobacco in it. It was also claimed many of the patients in the wards were left to untrained first-aiders.

DKF 62: Der ausgetauschte landsturmpflichtige Arzt Dr Buch, Infanteriere-Regiment 44, sagt aus: Im Hospital Nell Lane bei Manchester wurden in dem Unterkunftsraum, im welchem ich mit deutschen Offizieren untergebracht war, Wunden nur in Ausnahmefällen vom Arzt angesehen und verbunden. In der Hauptsache legten die Schwestern bzw Orderlies

(San.-Sold.) Verbände an. Ein deutscher Soldat, welcher nicht Sanitätssoldat und unausgebildet war, leistete ebenfalls Hilfe in sehr Problematischer Weise.

DKF 65: Der ausgetauschte Musketier Heinrich Holz, Reserve-Infanterie-Regiment Nr 229, gibt betreffend Hospital Nell Lane an: Bei der Narkose kamen sehr oft Verbrennungen vor; einem auf diese Weise Chloroformierten wurde das Auge so verbrannt, daß das Auge herausgenommen werden mußte. Am 24 Dezember starben zwei Patienten in der Narkose auf dem Tisch. Einer hatte Splitter im Oberarm, der andere im Schultergelenk. Der betreffende Arzt, welcher Chloroformiert hatte, roch meist stark nach Alkohol. Auch ist mehrmals bemerkt worden, daß er vor Trunksucht hinfiel: die Instruments hatte er in seiner Tasche beim Tabak.

MAUDSFORD: COUNTY LUNATIC ASYLUM (OS: SU 600 859). Maudsford Asylum is reported to have received two German PoWs in November 1914. The asylum's General Statement Book testifies to this in an entry made by the Medical Superintendent. In a previous grievance in the same register, dated September 1914, he noted there was a shortage of male staff. The situation had been exacerbated by the requisition by the War Office of two other nearby asylums and their patients being transferred to Maudsford (D/H10/A4/9).

MULLINGAR DISTRICT ASYLUM: County Westmeath (IGR: N 435 530). The records of the Volksbund Deutsche Kriegsgräberfürsorge show Erwin Schartz died in Mullingar on 16 January 1918. He was buried in the town's cemetery, until his remains were exhumed and taken, like others that had died in internment in Ireland, for re-burial to the newly created German War Cemetery, at Glencree, in the 1960s.

The deaths register for Mullingar, held at the County Clinic, cites that an Edwin Bernard Schartz, aged 39, died on 16 January 1918, having been a former internee at Oldcastle. He was described as being a photographer. Thomas Gerety was present at his death, which was registered by J.D. Kelly on 2 March 1918. Schartz was certified dead, suffering from 'general paralysis of the insane', a condition recorded on his medical history that he had had for seven months, along with 'gangrene of the left lung'.

It would appear from the above evidence that Mullingar was not an internment camp, but must be considered as a place where medical treatment was administered to an internee. O'Farrell (*The Book of Mullingar*, 1986) explained the asylum was built in 1850 to treat the lunatic poor of Westmeath, Meath, and Longford. It was commissioned to hold some 300 patients. Its architect also designed the workhouse at Banbury. The first stage, in Gothic style, was completed in 1855 and this was extended in 1890. At the turn of the century, more land was acquired for the hospital when the Pettiswood Estate was purchased. In 1938, another extension was built, as was an admissions unit. An open door policy was adopted in the 1960s, and with this went a change of name, to St Loan's. Today, the Midland Health Board runs the hospital.

Oldcastle and Duncannon are also cited by the Volksbund Deutsche Kriegsgräberfürsorge (per. comm., 19 February 1997).

NAPSBURY WAR HOSPITAL (OS: TL 155 074). Cited by the POWIB (1919), it had the code, Np H (IWM: Facsimile K4655). It was also cited by the OSt. In peacetime the hospital was called the Middlesex County Asylum.

NEWPORT: 3rd WESTERN GENERAL HOSPITAL. The POWIB (1919) issued two codes for the 3rd Western General Hospital, 3 W G H (C), and

3 W G H (N). Whilst the POWIB cite the Cardiff was a site and Newport was the other, there is anecdotal evidence suggesting the Neath was an annexe of Cardiff (www.british-genealogy.com).

The most likely location for the Newport Hospital was in Monmouthshire, but it may have been in Pembrokeshire.

NEATH SECTION (OS: ST 336 187). Neath Union Workhouse stands on Llantwit Road. It was built to accommodate up to 140 inmates and opened in 1838. It was never adequate for treating the sick, and there were constant complaints about the water supply. When the workhouse was not adopted by Glamorgan County Council as a Public Assistance Institution, following the Hospitals Act, it closed in 1924. It then became known as the Old White House and was used as a youth hostel. Parts of it survive today as a mixture of residential and commercial properties. Any PoWs sent for treatment could have been sent there or they may have gone to the Infirmary which was recorded as the New Graded Infirmary on the 1921 Ordnance Survey Map. When the workhouse closed its patients were re-located to it. Unlike the workhouse, in 1948 the infirmary was absorbed into the National Health Service. It has been called Penrhiwtyn Hospital and the West Glamorgan County Hospital before becoming Neath General Hospital in 2002. It has merged with Port Talbot General Hospital and the integrated hospitals have moved to a site on the Baglan Moors, becoming Neath Port Talbot Hospital.

The Neath General Hospital buildings have now been demolished.

NEWPORT: Monmouthshire (OS: ST 336 187). The industrial school in Caerleon may hold the key. In 1859, Newport's Board of Guardians opened an industrial school in Mill Street. The school closed in 1902 and lay empty until the First World War. After the war it again lay dormant until it became Cambria House and was used as offices by Monmouthshire County Council. In the First World War it was used to treat wounded soldiers. The buildings were demolished and housing now occupies the site.

NEWPORT: Pembrokeshire. If any PoWs were sent for treatment to Newport (Trefdraeth), Pembrokeshire then no location has been found to date.

NETLEY: Royal Victoria Hospital (OS: SU 464 076). Cited by the POWIB (1919), its code was Net H (IWM: Facsimile K4655). It was also cited by the OSt.

Built *c.*1863, the hospital once occupied a vast site and was a prominent landmark on Southampton Water until its demolition, following a fire, in 1966. It had around 1,000 beds.

Several Germans were buried in the hospital's cemetery.

Today, only Block D and the chapel remain. Block D is presently the headquarters of Hampshire's police service, having previously been the hospital's psychiatric unit. Fittingly, the camp's TA was Priswarian: Nerves, Netley (ADM 1/8506/265–120667).

NEWCASTLE UPON TYNE: 1st NORTHERN GENERAL HOSPITAL (OS: NZ 255 644). In 1839 the Newcastle Board of Guardians decided to build a Union Workhouse on Westgate Hill to centralise facilities for Newcastle's poor. The first buildings to be completed were the Administration Block, a school for children and the workhouse which was to give accommodation to the able-bodied poor and care for the sick poor, maternity cases and imbeciles. Around 1859 the Board of

Guardians gave the go-ahead for a separate hospital to be built. In September 1868, work started on a new infirmary located at the west of the site, it was designed by the Newcastle architect Septimus Oswald and was officially opened on 7 December 1870.

By 1914, much development had taken place providing about 500 beds in five buildings. It was to become the 1st Northern General Hospital during the First World War, with the POWIB (1919) code, 1 N G H (N) (IWM: Facsimile K4655).

In 1921 a separate hospital administration was set up and it was renamed Wingrove Hospital. In 1930 under the new Local Government Act it was handed over to the City Council and the name changed to the General Hospital and for many years has been the main hospital for the city of Newcastle upon Tyne.

NORFOLK WAR HOSPITAL: Thorpe St Andrew (OS: TG 280 086). Opened in 1814 as the Norfolk Lunatic Asylum, it was a pioneering county pauper institution. During the First World War it was transformed into the Norfolk War Hospital. It acted as a clearing house for convalescent patients, treating the wounded that arrived at Thorpe Railway Station before discharging them to hospitals around the county.

Cited by the POWIB (1919), its code was T W H (IWM: Facsimile K4655).

A plaque on the building, unveiled by Field Marshal Earl Haig on St Andrews Day 1920, recorded that over 45,000 casualties from Great Britain and its Dominions had been treated there.

It became an integral part of the NHS, known as St Andrew's, until its closure in 1998.

OSWESTRY. A Postal Address was cited as Commandant, Military Hospital, Oswestry (ADM 1/8506/265–120667). In March 1919, Dr A. de Sturler and Monsieur R. de Sturler visited the camp on behalf of the Swiss Legation (FO 383/507). There are two hospitals in Oswestry that might have treated PoWs.

PARK HALL HOSPITAL (OS: SJ 31- 31-). This hospital had the POWIB (1919) code, P H H (IWM: Facsimile K4655).

PoW HOSPITAL (OS: SJ 31- 31-). A hospital clearly defined to treat PoWs was set up at Oswestry. It had the POWIB (1919) code, O P H (IWM: Facsimile K4655).

OXFORD: 3rd SOUTHERN GENERAL HOSPITAL (OS: SP 531 058). Although the number of soldiers in Oxford fluctuated during the First World War, the numbers of wounded increased constantly. When the 3rd Southern General Hospital was created it brought together several buildings under one umbrella and it wasn't long before the newly created hospital was full of wounded soldiers, some of which were German.

The Examination Schools had been taken over as its headquarters. New College Gardens were closed to the public and were lent to the wounded for convalescence. High Wall, a large house owned by Miss Katherine Feilden, in Pullens Lane, Headington was used for treating officer casualties.

The War Office took over Somerville College in 1915, and Cowley Road Workhouse in 1916, and turned both into hospitals. The gardens of Wingfield Convalescent Home had forty huts built on them for recuperation. These hutments, capable of housing forty beds each, became known as the Oxford Orthopaedic Centre. When the number of casualties rapidly increased, buildings in Woodstock Road were taken over by the Radcliffe as an officers' hospital. Wingfield Convalescent Home was handed over by its trustees to the War Office in 1917. The hospital overflowed into

University College and the Masonic Hall. The average daily number of beds in Oxford in early 1918 was about 1,100, and 250 more were added in the summer of that year.

In 1920, the former workhouse, completed in 1865, became Cowley Road Hospital and was given to the city's Public Assistance Committee. With the inception of the welfare state in 1948, its administration transferred to the NHS. Cowley Road Hospital closed in 1981 and was demolished soon after to make way for a housing estate, a new health centre and various other planned facilities.

After the war, Wingfield Convalescent Home, which had opened in 1871, came under the supervision of the Ministry of Pensions. It has since been demolished. This hospital was cited by the OSt.

PAISLEY: DYKEBAR WAR HOSPITAL (OS: NS 495 624). The Renfrew District Lunatic Asylum opened in 1909. According to the *Paisley and Renfrewshire Gazette* (26 February 1916), the asylum was acquired by the military two months before being reported in their paper. Becoming the Dykebar War Hospital, its aim was to treat 'wounds of the spirit'. The paper reported:

> The War Office arranged with the County Council of Renfrewshire for the temporary acquisition of the new and extensive buildings and grounds at Dykebar, comprising Renfrew District Asylum, and for its conversion into a war hospital of unique character. The purpose of the War Office was to collect and treat, under a specially skilled administration, such cases of nervous disorder among soldiers as could not be so practically and beneficially dealt with in ordinary military hospitals.

The archive of the Greater Glasgow Health Board states the hospital was the only one of its kind in Scotland, and could accommodate some 400 patients. The paper also carried a report stating the structural changes at Craw Road Hospital were nearly complete, and that the hospital should be operational to treat wounded soldiers within the month.

The Paisley and Renfrewshire Gazette (18 October 1919) stated that the hospital had reverted to its pre-war usage of treating the civilian population. 'Dykebar Asylum, which was converted into a mental war hospital in January 1916, ceased as such on Wednesday.' During this time it was reported to have successfully treated 3,775 service men, and now only twenty-eight remained. The transition back to civilian use was expected to take two months. There is no mention of PoWs being treated at the institution. The report concluded, 'Dykebar is the last of the Paisley War Hospitals to be given up.'

Re-named Dykebar Hospital, in 1948 it was to come under the umbrella of the National Health Service (Ref. GB 812 AC 18).

The POWIB (1919) cites Dykebar War Hospital, giving it the code Dy H (IWM: Facsimile K4655). It was also cited by the OSt.

PERTH WAR HOSPITAL (OS: NO 113 236). The Bereavement Services Administrative Officer at Perth Crematorium was able to trace the graves of five Germans and one Finn who were buried in Jeanfield Cemetery, Perth. All had been in Perth War Hospital when they died. All were victims of the flu that was prevalent at the time. They were: Gustov Leirman (d. 5 March 1919), Michall Dorsch (d. 6 March 1919), Karl Nuderstrasser (d. 7 March 1919), and Josef Brener (d. 9 March 1919). All had worked at Little Frandy Reservoir; they had all been privates in the 1st Prussian Guards. Johan Zelasni (d. 21 June 1918) was also interned at Glendevon. His cause of death was not stated. The Court of Sessions granted authority for the exhumations of these five men. They were exhumed on 16 August 1962 and transferred to Cannock Chase. In Scotland the channel to have the bodies exhumed was through the courts whereas in England it was a Church matter.

McRae (per. comm., 20 August 2007) reveals the records show John Kopenen died at Perth War Hospital on 20 November 1918; he is buried at Jeanfield Cemetery, Perth. He had been interned at Stanley's Finn Labour Camp, which may, or may not, be linked to the PoW camp at Strathord.

Finland was then a semi-autonomous part of the Russian empire. Its response to the onset of the First World War was somewhat apathetic because its populace was split in its support of German or Russian forces. Only a few thousand Finns enlisted in the Russian cause. In the wake of the February Revolution of 1917 the Finnish National Assembly sought more autonomy, but this was rejected by the Russian Provisional government. The Russians dissolved the National Assembly of Finland in July 1917, but the ensuing elections did not produce the result they had hoped for, and in December a full declaration of independence by the Finnish government was accepted by the new Soviet government. A formal treaty was signed between Finland and the Soviet government in October 1920.

Standing in York Place, Perth County and City Infirmary was purpose-built to the design of William Macdonald Mackenzie in 1836, who had for some thirty years left an impressive legacy of public and domestic buildings in and around Perth.

In the 1920s the Infirmary became Perth County Council's headquarters, and in 1991, the former infirmary was successfully converted into the A.K. Bell Library.

PORTSMOUTH: 5th SOUTHERN GENERAL HOSPITAL (OS: SZ 652 999). Cited by the POWIB (1919), its code is P H (IWM: Facsimile K4655).

Priory School, Portsmouth, opened in November 1888 on a temporary site on Commercial Road. The construction of the school took two years; the buildings were completed in May 1892. Later extensions of the school site led it to cover the site of the old priory and Priory Farm.

In 1905, it was decided that the Francis Avenue School for girls should move to a building next to the boy's school. The annexe, which now forms the main building of the current school, was opened on 4 November 1907.

During the First World War both the boys' and girls' schools were converted into the 5th Southern General Hospital to care for soldiers injured during the war. After the war both schools returned to their previous roles.

PLYMOUTH: 4th SOUTHERN GENERAL HOSPITAL (OS: SX 491 549). Cited by the OSt (1917), it was known as the 4th Southern General Hospital during the First World War. It had around 1,200 beds.

An article appeared in the *Queen's Nurses' Magazine* (October 1914) which stated Nurse Tait McKay was the Acting Matron of 4th Southern General Hospital when Salisbury Road Schools and the adjacent Baptist Church was being transformed into a war hospital of 520 beds. The school was equipped with an operating theatre and an X-ray machine and was completed on 20 August 1914. Patients were immediately admitted from the adjacent forts. The staff consisted of a matron, twenty-two sisters, sixty-eight nurses and two masseuses. Seven of the nurses were Queen's Nurses.

Tait McKay wrote that the first batch of 102 'wounded warriors' arrived from the front on 21 August 1914; forty of these were stretcher cases. The second batch numbered 132; it arrived on 25 September 1914 and included fourteen Germans.

PURFLEET MILITARY HOSPITAL (OS: TQ 549 784). Cited by the POWIB (1919), its code is P M H (IWM: Facsimile K4655).

At the beginning of the school year, in September 1914, the then head teacher of Purfleet Primary School wrote:

> The Great European War, which commenced ... on 4 August last, has been brought home to us by the Military Authority requisitioning the school as a hospital, for the Purfleet Camp, where there are now encamped about 12,000 men. Corrugated iron huts 60′ × 20′ to accommodate these are being hurriedly erected in the fields adjoining the school premises, and also in the fields up as far as Watts' Wood.

By October 1914 the school had been emptied of its furniture and apparatus. It was stored in the old school in the Dipping, with some in Mr. Whitbread's laundry. At this point in time there was no provision to temporarily re-house the 190 children. It was in June of the next year that the school was returned to its purpose. There is no mention of PoWs being treated.

A confidential report, held by the National Archives, from June 1918, describes the contribution of Sister Emma Almey when caring for the sick and wounded in glowing terms. She was a member of the Queen Alexandra's Imperial Military Nursing Service employed at the military hospital at Purfleet at the time (WO 399/100).

READING (No. 1) WAR HOSPITAL (OS: SU 698 737). Cited by the POWIB (1919), its code is R W H (IWM: Facsimile K4655).

The hospital was in Oxford Road. It had opened as the town's second workhouse in 1867. It was built near Battle Farm. The new workhouse followed the design of the East Grinstead workhouse, which was built in 1859. It comprised of receiving blocks, an infirmary with 185 beds, and a fever block. On 1 March 1915, the War Office requisitioned the workhouse for use by the military authorities and all the inmates were transferred to other workhouses in the area. The infirmary patients were moved to the nearby Grovelands School. Within six weeks, the workhouse was transformed into the Reading (No. 1) War Hospital, which linked together with more than twenty other auxiliary hospitals in Berkshire, constituting one of the country's biggest war hospitals.

Following the abolition of the workhouse system in 1929, two years later it became Battle hospital, and recently it was demolished. A branch of the supermarket chain, Tesco, plus some starter homes, now grace the site.

In contrast, Reading Prison was used for internment, after the disturbances in Ireland during 1916.

RICHMOND MILITARY HOSPITAL (OS: TQ 189 741). Cited by the POWIB (1919), its code is R H (IWM: Facsimile K4655). It was also cited by the OSt.

The hospital stood on Grove Road. It was formerly the Richmond Parish Workhouse. Opened in April 1787, it was a two-storey building with an H-shaped plan. Richmond Poor Law Union formally came into being on 6 June 1836 and modifications were made to the infrastructure to bring it into line with the requirements of the Poor Law Amendment (1834) Act. When the workhouse at Barnes closed in August 1836 its inmates were transferred to Richmond. In 1901–2, new infirmary buildings designed by E.J. Partridge were erected at the south-west of the workhouse.

The workhouse, later to become Grove Road Hospital, has now been converted for residential use. Only the main building and the former entrance lodge survive.

SKIPTON: KEIGHLEY WAR HOSPITAL (OS: SE 083 423). When the Swiss visited the PoW camp at Skipton on 24 February 1919, it was noted that thirty of its prisoners had been hospitalised in Keighley. This would probably have been to the Keighley War Hospital, at Riddlesden, some 2 miles from Keighley's town centre.

Scatterley's *Recollections of the War Hospital Keighley and its Auxiliaries, 1916–1919* state it was built as the Keighley and Bingley Fever Hospital. It took on the mantle of Keighley War Hospital when it was given over to the military for treating wounded soldiers on 5 April 1916. The one condition was it had to be returned in a similar state to when it was handed over.

Records show 105 German PoWs were admitted to the hospital. Many had come from Colsterdale. Records show forty-two died and sixty-three were discharged to return to their camps. Another five were reported dead, whilst being transferred. Despite the high mortality rate, the prisoners were impressed with the quality of treatment they received.

SHEFFIELD: 3rd NORTHERN GENERAL HOSPITAL (OS: SK 363 906). The 3rd Northern General Hospital was formed in 1913, under the command of Lt-Colonel J. Sinclair White. By 1914 the strength of his unit had grown to three officers and forty-three other ranks.

The hospital was initially at Brook House, in Gell Street, but moved to the Sheffield Teachers' Training College, in Ecclesfield Road, Firvale, at the start of the war and had become a base hospital for dealing with the wounded coming from the front. They began to arrive in August 1914, after the battle of Mons.

The *Nottingham Evening Post* (19 October 1918) reported Carl Braun, Richard Kummeth and Emile Franke were caught stealing potatoes at 2am the day before, by James Marsden. When the three failed to stop he fired his shotgun, once into the air, then at ground level, hitting Franke in the legs. Franke was not present when Braun and Kemmeth were each charged with stealing potatoes valued at 8 shillings. Both were remanded. It was cited Franke would be fit enough to attend court soon. It was then reported in the press that a German PoW who had been shot was taken to the Firvale hospital on 18 October 1918.

Cited by the POWIB (1919), its code was 3 N G H (Sh) (IWM: Facsimile K4655). It was also cited by the OSt.

SHOTLEY: Naval Sick Quarters (OS: TM 250 338). HMS *Ganges* came into service in 1779 when SS *Bengal* was presented to the navy by the Honourable East India Company, and re-named HMS *Ganges*. She was broken up in 1816. Her successor, launched on 10 November 1821, was built in Bombay. She was to be the last sailing ship to be a sea-going flagship. In 1866, HMS *Ganges* became a boys' training ship anchored in Falmouth harbour where she remained until August 1899. In November 1899, she was transferred to Harwich harbour. HMS *Ganges* remained in Harwich harbour as a boys' training ship until, in 1905, the boys were moved ashore. The base closed in 1976.

During the First World War its medical facility was referred to as the Naval Sick Quarters and it had the POWIB (1919) code S S Q (IWM: Facsimile K4655).

Summers (*HMS Ganges: Boys Training for the Royal Navy*, 1966) wrote of casualties being landed at Shotley during the First World War.

SOUTHSEA HOSPITAL (OS: SU 661 008). Cited by the OSt, Southsea Hospital was the former workhouse on St Marys Road.

Portsea Island Union Workhouse was designed by Thomas Ellis Owen, of Portsmouth, and was erected *c.*1845. The end of the nineteenth century saw the beginning of a major expansion programme of the hospital's facilities at the southern end of the workhouse. Later, its name was changed to St Mary's Hospital. The main workhouse building has now been converted for residential usage.

SUTTON: BELMONT PoW HOSPITAL (OS: TQ 255 624). The POWIB (1919) provided this Surrey based hospital with the code Bel H (IWM: Facsimile K4655). The site is also listed by the FPHS (1973), and it had the TA Warspital: Sutton (ADM 1/8506/265–120667).

In 1919 a number of internees that refused to live under canvas, on medical grounds, were sent to Belmont War Hospital until room for them could be found at Islington, to await repatriation.

Allegations were made that the doctors were too quick to decide to amputate at Belmont, and that hygiene was lacking. On two occasions unidentified orderlies were said to have administered substances to patients that subsequently killed them, and no disciplinary actions were taken against them.

DKF 65: Im Belmont-Hospital erhielt Ende Marz 1918 ein Kranker statt eines Abfurmittels durch einen englischen Sanitater ein Messglas halb voll Kresol ein, abends um 8 Uhr. Gegan 1 Uhr trat der Tod ein.

SUTTON VENY MILITARY HOSPITAL (OS: ST 898 427). Given the code S V H by the POWIB (1919), the Anglican Church's parochial register shows the burials of thirty-eight PoWs took place at St John's Churchyard, Sutton Veny, between July 1916 and early 1919. Their bodies were exhumed between 22 April and 8 May of 1963, and re-buried at the purpose-built German War Cemetery on Cannock Chase (IWM: Facsimile K4566).

Crawford (*Wiltshire and The Great War: Training the Empire's Soldiers*, 1999) cites a hospital was opened with beds for 11 officers and 1,261 men. He later states that 200 wounded Germans were disembarked at Southampton and taken by train to Warminster, where they were dispatched, by motor ambulances, to the military hospital at Sutton Veny. Many deaths at the hospital were attributed to the flu pandemic, but rumours of cholera being present should not be dismissed lightly.

The Swiss delegate found it intriguing that fit men were being better accommodated than the wounded at Sutton Veny. This hospital facility was under canvas. It was reported that although the tents were adequately heated and illuminated at night, during the day the lighting was missing (WRO 941/4).

The POWIB (1919) also cite a working camp at Sutton Veny. The hospital is cited in a HO document (ADM 1/8506/265–120667).

DKF 38: Der schweizerische Delegierte de Sturler weist in seinem Bericht vom 11 Januar 1918 über das Kriegslazarett Sutton Veny auf die bemerkenswerte Tatsache hin, daß die deutschen Patienten in einem Zelte untergebracht sind, während völlig gesunde Gefangene in den verschiedenen Arbeitslagern jetzt behagliche Winterquartiere bewohnen. Das Zelt wird zwar durch einen Ofen geheizt und bei Nacht beleuchtet, bei Tage hingegen ist es dunkel. Der Schutzmachtvertreter ist der Ansicht, daß Kriegsgefangene, die wegen ihres Gesundheitszustandes einem Lazarett überwiesen werden, in besserer Weise als in einem Zelt untergebracht werden müssen.

TIDWORTH BARRACKS HOSPITAL (OS: SU 232 485). It was cited by the OSt.

The villages of North and South Tidworth were transformed in 1897 when the War Department purchased the surrounding land, for military training. Tidworth Barracks opened in 1904; before that all the troops lived in tents or huts.

The hospital was built in 1907 and had between 200 to 300 beds. Parts of the hospital remained open, as M.R.S. Tidworth (Medical Reception Station), when the hospital was closed on 31 March 1977.

WINCHESTER: MAGDALEN CAMP MILITARY HOSPITAL (OS: SU 505 295). In recent times, the site of a 'lost' medieval leper hospital has been excavated near to Winchester that was named after St Magdalen where in the late nineteenth century an isolation hospital was built that had taken its name. In the First World War a military hospital was opened there, its POWIB (1919) was M C M H (IWM: Facsimile K4655).

There were army camps at Morn Hill and Flowerdown.

WORCHESTER: NORTON BARRACKS MILITARY HOSPITAL (OS: SO 869 518). Cited as Worcester Military Hospital in a HO document, its TA, if it had one, was omitted. It was cited by the POWIB (1919) as Norton Military Hospital and had the code N M H (IWM: Facsimile K4655).

In 1872, the War Department purchased 20.5 acres of land to erect barracks at Norton. The new barracks consisted of a gatehouse 'keep' with offices on one side and officers' quarters on the other. There were also two large barrack blocks for the accommodation of soldiers, a cookhouse, two married quarters blocks, and a hospital. A 10-foot high wall enclosed the site. In the centre of the barracks was the parade ground. The hospital, which could accommodate twenty-eight patients, was in the south-east corner. It had a surgery, a kitchen and an isolation ward.

In the 1990s the Ministry of Defence sold the site to property developers.

YORK: THE RETREAT (OS: SE 608 495). According to *The Yorkshire Gazette* (26 September 1914), an internee in need of medical attention had been taken to an unnamed facility. Then, *The York Herald* (5 October 1914) reported that those internees that had just arrived and needed hospitalisation were taken to Fulford Road for treatment.

The most likely place they were taken to would be The Friends' Retreat, on Heslington Lane. William Tuke, a Quaker and philanthropist, whose family were tea and coffee importers, established the Retreat over 200 years ago. Appalled at the squalor and the inhumane conditions he witnessed in York Asylum when a fellow Quaker died, he set about revolutionising the treatment of the insane. The Retreat was opened in 1796, and today still provides a service for people experiencing mental ill health.

The FPHS (1973) cited a camp at Hull Road, York.

German War Graves Commission (Volksbund Deutsche Kriegsgräberfürsorge)

(OS : SJ 984 157)

As a result of neglect of graves of German military personnel and German civilian internees of both World Wars, on 16 October 1959 the governments of the United Kingdom and the Federal Republic of Germany made an agreement about their future care. Both nations agreed that the remains of 5,000 German and Austrian dead would be transferred to a single central cemetery that would allow the graves to be maintained in an appropriate manner.

On land with steeply-rising, pine-covered slopes reminiscent of parts of Germany, Cannock Chase was chosen as the site of the Deutscher Soldatenfriedhof. The land belonged to the Earl of Lichfield. Nearby is a small military cemetery containing mostly the graves of ANZAC troops stationed on the Chase that died in the influenza pandemic of 1918. A small separate section for the crews of the four airships (*SL 11*, *L 32*, *L 31*, *L 48*) shot down in the First World War exists. The cemetery contains the graves of 2,143 from the First World War and 2,786 of the Second World War. Five of the dead from 1914–18 and ninety from 1939–1945 are unknown by name.

The dark, roughly-hewn granite gravestones are arranged in rectangular plots, the gravestones themselves standing in long beds of heather, with grass walkways between the rows, so that both sides of the stones can be seen. The stones are well spaced out, about a yard apart, and each one marks four graves, two on each side. The details given for each man (if known) are name, rank, date of birth and date of death.